Welcome to

The Official Guide to the GRE® General Test

The book you're holding is a one-of-a-kind resource: the only *Graduate Record Examinations® (GRE®)* guide created by the ETS team that produces the actual exam. This book is uniquely suited to help you do your best on this challenging test.

Here's what you'll find inside:

- **Two real, full-length GRE practice tests.** Use actual tests to sharpen your skills and build your confidence.

- **Two simulated, computer-delivered GRE practice tests.** Experience test prep that is as close to the actual test as you can get with the *POWERPREP®* practice tests.

- **Authentic GRE questions with answers and explanations.** Practice with real test questions created by the test makers.

- **ETS's own test-taking strategies.** Learn valuable hints and tips that can help you get your best score.

- **Official information on the GRE General Test.** Get the facts about the test content and structure—straight from ETS.

About ETS

At ETS, we advance quality and equity in education for people worldwide by creating assessments based on rigorous research. ETS serves individuals, educational institutions, and government agencies by providing customized solutions for teacher certification, English language learning, and elementary, secondary, and post-secondary education, as well as conducting educational research, analysis, and policy studies. Founded as a nonprofit in 1947, ETS develops, administers, and scores more than 50 million tests annually—including the *TOEFL®* and *TOEIC®* tests, the *GRE®* tests, and *The Praxis Series®* assessments—in more than 180 countries at over 9,000 locations worldwide. For more information, visit www.ets.org.

IMPORTANT

ETS makes available free test preparation materials for individuals planning to take a GRE test. The *POWERPREP®* practice tests are available for individuals planning to take the computer-delivered GRE General Test, and the *Practice Book for the Paper-based GRE revised General Test, Second Edition,* is available for individuals planning to take the paper-delivered test. The information about how to prepare for the General Test, test-taking strategies, question strategies, etc., that is included in the free test preparation is also included in this *Guide*. The *Guide* also provides you with additional sets of practice questions and two additional full-length practice tests with explanatory materials.

For more information about the GRE General Test, free and low-cost GRE test preparation materials, and other GRE products and services, please visit the GRE website at

www.ets.org/gre

Inquiries concerning the practice test questions in this book should be sent to the GRE testing program at

GRETestQuestionInquiries@ets.org

The Official 第3版
Guide to the
GRE®考试
General Test
官方指南

群言出版社
QUNYAN PRESS

· 北 京 ·

薛艺谌
2019.07

图书在版编目(CIP)数据

GRE考试官方指南：第3版/美国教育考试服务中心
编著；王成霞译. -- 北京：群言出版社，2017（2018.9重印）
  书名原文：The Official Guide to the GRE
General Test: 3rd edition
  ISBN 978-7-5193-0278-8

  Ⅰ.①G… Ⅱ.①美… ②王… Ⅲ.①GRE – 自学参考
资料 Ⅳ.①H310.41

中国版本图书馆CIP数据核字（2017）第065690号

版权登记：京版出图字01—2017—5786

责任编辑： 张　茜
封面设计： 大愚设计

出版发行： 群言出版社
地　　址： 北京市东城区东厂胡同北巷1号（100006）
网　　址： www.qypublish.com（官网书城）
电子信箱： dywh@xdf.cn　qunyancbs@126.com
联系电话： 010-62418641　65267783　65263836
经　　销： 全国新华书店

印　　刷： 北京海石通印刷有限公司
版　　次： 2017年10月第1版　2018年9月第3次印刷
开　　本： 889mm×1194mm　1/16
印　　张： 37.5
字　　数： 787千字
书　　号： ISBN 978-7-5193-0278-8
定　　价： 138.00元

Contents

1 About the *GRE*® General Test   1

2 *GRE*® Analytical Writing   11

3 *GRE*® Verbal Reasoning   43

4

GRE Verbal Reasoning Practice Questions   53

5

GRE Quantitative Reasoning   107

6

GRE Quantitative Reasoning Practice Questions   153

7

GRE® Math Review   217

8

GRE® Practice Test 1   327

9 *GRE*® Practice Test 2   **455**

How to Use This Book

This book provides a large amount of important information about the GRE General Test, the types of questions it includes, and the knowledge and skills that it measures. The book will help you:

- Familiarize yourself with the test format and question types
- Learn valuable test-taking strategies for each question type
- Review the math topics you need to know for the test
- Check your progress with Verbal Reasoning and Quantitative Reasoning practice questions
- Practice your test-taking skills using actual GRE tests

The following five-step program has been designed to help you make the best use of this book.

STEP 1 Learn About the GRE General Test Format

Chapter 1 of this book provides official information about the structure of the GRE General Test. Read this chapter to learn about the different test sections, the number of questions in each section, and the section time limits. You'll also find valuable test-taking strategies from ETS and important information about how the test is scored.

STEP 2 Study the Different GRE Question Types

Chapters 2, 3, and 5 of this book describe the types of questions you'll encounter in the three sections of the GRE General Test. Chapter 2 describes the Analytical Writing section, which requires you to write essays in response to prompts that you will be given. Chapter 3 describes the Verbal Reasoning question types. Chapter 5 describes the Quantitative Reasoning question types. In each case, you will learn what the questions are designed to measure, and you will get tips for answering each question type. You will also see samples of each question type, with helpful explanations.

STEP 3 Practice Answering GRE Verbal and Quantitative Reasoning Questions

Chapters 4 and 6 offer sets of practice Verbal Reasoning and Quantitative Reasoning questions in the format of the GRE General Test. The question sets are arranged in order of increasing difficulty, from easy through medium to hard. Answer the questions in each set, then read through the explanations to see which test topics you found most challenging. Look for patterns. Did specific question formats give you trouble? When did you need to guess at the answer? Use your results to identify your weaknesses and to sharpen your test-taking skills.

STEP 4 Review GRE Math Topics

Chapter 7 provides a review of math topics tested in the GRE General Test Quantitative Reasoning sections. You do not necessarily need to tackle every topic in the review or to work through the review in the order in which it is presented. Skip around if you like, but remember to focus on the topics that you know give you trouble. Each section of the review ends with practice problems that you can use to see how well you have mastered the material. If you get a problem wrong, go back into the review section and re-read the corresponding instructional text.

STEP 5 Take the Practice Tests

Once you have completed your review, get ready for the real exam by taking the authentic GRE Practice Tests in Chapters 8 and 9 of this book. When you take each test, try to simulate actual testing conditions. If you are taking one of the tests in Chapters 8 and 9, sit in a quiet space, time yourself, and work through as much of the test as time allows.

Additional Practice with the *POWERPREP*® Practice Tests

After you have completed the practice tests in this book, you can get even more practice with the *POWERPREP*® practice tests. The POWERPREP practice tests provide a Test Preview Tool and two full-length, computer-delivered GRE practice tests that simulate an actual GRE General Test.

Before beginning the timed practice tests, use the Test Preview Tool to familiarize yourself with each of the question types, formatted as they would be on the actual computer-delivered test. Also use the Tool to become familiar with all of the features of the computer-delivered GRE General Test, such as Help screens, the Review screen, word-processing software for the Analytical Writing section, and the on-screen calculator.

Once you have familiarized yourself with the General Test using the Test Preview Tool, prepare by taking the first full-length, computer-delivered GRE practice test. Each test section will be timed, and you'll learn to pace yourself so that you can earn your highest score in the time allowed. When you have completed the practice test, you will receive scores on the Verbal Reasoning and Quantitative Reasoning measures. You will also be given access to scored sample essays with reader commentary for the essay prompts in the practice test to help you evaluate your performance.

Based on your performance on the first practice test, you may decide to review math concepts or perform other activities designed to strengthen your verbal reasoning, quantitative reasoning, critical thinking, or analytical writing skills. When you have completed those activities, it is time to take the second timed practice test. You can use the results to determine if you need additional practice or if you are ready to take the actual computer-delivered GRE General Test.

To access the POWERPREP practice tests, go to **www.ets.org/gre/powerprep**.

About the *GRE*® General Test

▶ Review basic information on the structure of the test, test preparation, and scoring

Introduction

改革后的GRE普通考试（GRE General Test，以下简称"GRE考试"）——全球最广为接受的研究生入学标准考试——旨在测试学生在研究生院和商学院取得成功所必备的文字推理（Verbal Reasoning）、数量推理（Quantitative Reasoning）、论证思辨（Critical Thinking）和分析性写作（Analytical Writing）这四项技能。

研究生院和商学院的申请者都会参加GRE考试。针对来自不同教育背景和文化背景的申请者，GRE考试提供了一个普遍适用的衡量标准。

高校入学委员会和奖学金评定组将GRE分数和本科成绩单、推荐信以及其他进入硕士阶段学习的资格证明综合在一起对候选人作出评定。

GRE考试在全球160多个国家和地区拥有约1,000个考点。目前在大多数地区，全年都可以进行机考。在中国大陆、中国香港和中国台湾，每月有一到三场机考。在无法实现机考的地区，GRE考试则采用纸笔考试的形式，每年有三场考试。

欲了解有关GRE考试的最新信息，请访问GRE官方网站 www.ets.org/gre。

Structure and Content of the Test

Content

GRE考试由Analytical Writing（分析性写作）、Verbal Reasoning（文字推理）和 Quantitative Reasoning（数量推理）三项测试构成。

- Analytical Writing（分析性写作）测试的能力包括：清楚有效地阐明和支持复杂观点；考查其他观点及论证；支撑一个有针对性的、连贯的讨论；把控标准书面英语的各个要素。分析性写作部分要求考生对给出的任务提供有针对性的回答，从而准确地展现出考生在直接回应问题时的技能。

- Verbal Reasoning（文字推理）测试的能力包括：分析和评估书面材料，综合材料信息；理解词、句和文章的内涵；理解不同单词之间、不同概念之间的关系。文字推理部分主要考查考生的阅读理解能力和推理技能。

- Quantitative Reasoning（数量推理）测试的能力包括：基本的数学技能；对算数、代数和几何的基本数学概念的理解；数据分析。数量推理部分衡量考生理解、说明和分析量化信息的能力，以及运用数学模型解题的能力。

The Computer-delivered GRE General Test

Typical Test Structure

Measure	Number of Questions	Allotted Time
Analytical Writing (One section with two separately timed tasks)	One "Analyze an Issue" task and one "Analyze an Argument" task	30 minutes per task
Verbal Reasoning (Two sections)	20 questions per section	30 minutes per section
Quantitative Reasoning (Two sections)	20 questions per section	35 minutes per section
Unscored* (Position varies)	20 questions	Varies
Research** (At the end of the test)	Varies	Varies

* An unidentified, unscored section that does not count toward a score may be included and may appear in any order after the Analytical Writing section. Questions in the unscored section are being tried out either for possible use in future tests or to ensure that scores on new editions of the test are comparable to scores from earlier editions.

** An identified research section may be included in place of the unscored section. The research section will always appear at the end of the test. Questions in this section are included for ETS research purposes and will not count toward your score.

Analytical Writing总是出现在考试开头。Verbal Reasoning，Quantitative Reasoning及不计分部分可能以任何顺序出现在考试中。因此，考生应该把任何一部分都当成是计分题来做。

考试总时长为3小时45分钟，包括不计分部分。对于Verbal Reasoning和Quantitative Reasoning，每部分前面的考试说明会给出这部分的题目数量和考试时长。对于Analytical Writing，在每项任务给出的同时开始显示计时。

Test Design Features

基于计算机的GRE考试中，Verbal Reasoning和Quantitative Reasoning采用基于"部分"水平（section-level）的自适应考试。计算机将根据考生在第一部分测试的答题表现来选择第二部分测试。

先进的适应性设计还能让考生在每个测试部分中自由地前后翻页，可以继续做题，也可以返回查看做过的题目。其他的设计特点包括：

● 每个测试部分内部有预览和回顾功能

● 设有"标记和检查"功能，考生可以标记一些题目，在本部分所给时间有剩余的情况下回顾检查这些题目

● 允许考生在每个测试部分内修改已做出的答案

● Quantitative Reasoning部分有屏幕计算器功能

The Paper-delivered GRE General Test

Typical Test Structure

Measure	Number of Questions	Allotted Time
Analytical Writing (Two sections)	Section One: "Analyze an Issue" task Section Two: "Analyze an Argument" task	30 minutes per section
Verbal Reasoning (Two sections)	25 questions per section	35 minutes per section
Quantitative Reasoning (Two sections)	25 questions per section	40 minutes per section

Analytical Writing总是出现在考试开头，其他四部分可能以任何顺序出现在考试中。

考试总时长大约为3小时30分钟。每部分前面的考试说明会给出这部分的题目数量和考试时长。

Test Design Features

● 答案直接填写在试题册上，而不是写在单独的答题卡上。

● 在Quantitative Reasoning部分，考点会提供计算器；考生不能使用自带的计算器。有关使用计算器的详细信息可参见*Practice Book for the Paper-based GRE revised General Test*，该手册在以下网址提供 www.ets.org/gre/prepare。

Preparing for the Test

如何备考取决于考生有多少时间可用以及考生对备考方式的个人偏好。至少，在考生参加GRE普通考试之前，应该了解这个考试的基本情况，包括考试程序、题目种类和说明、题目的大致数量，以及每个部分的考试时间。

考试程序包括注册和预约考试日程、日期、时间、地点、费用、成绩递送流程以及一些可用的特殊测试安排。考生可以在*GRE® Information Bulletin*中找到相关说明，这部分信息可在以下网址获得 www.ets.org/gre/bulletinandforms。

参加考试之前，熟悉每部分测试的内容是非常重要的。在这本官方指南中，考生会找到针对各部分测试的特定信息。这些信息将有助于考生理解考试材料类型以及每个测试部分的题目类型。

同样重要的是，考生需要花些时间来准备Analytical Writing部分，包括分析性写作所考查的技能、评分指南、评分等级描述、样题、官方范文以及考官的评论等。

Test-taking Strategies for the Computer-delivered Test

Analytical Writing Section

计算机考试中的Analytical Writing测试使用一个由ETS开发的基本文字处理软件，以使那些熟悉一些特定商业文字处理软件的人没有特别的优势或劣势。该软件包含以下功能：插入文字，删除，剪切，粘贴和撤销上一个操作。该软件中没有诸如拼写检查和语法检查等工具，在最大程度上保证了这些考生与进行纸笔考试的考生之间的公平性。

计划好考试时间也非常重要。每项任务30分钟时间，考生需要留出足够的时间去审题，计划如何答题，以及撰写文章。虽然评分人也明白写作时间有限，并会把考生写的东西当做初稿，但考生仍要尽可能将文章写好。

在每项任务快结束时，留出几分钟时间以检查可能出现的明显错误。虽然偶尔出现的输入错误、拼写错误和语法错误并不会影响考生的分数，但严重的和反复出现的错误将有损文章的整体水平，并拉低考生的分数。

Verbal Reasoning and Quantitative Reasoning Sections

Verbal Reasoning和Quantitative Reasoning部分由多种题型构成。有的需要考生选择一个答案，有的需要考生选择一个或多个答案，还有的需要考生输入一个数值。因此，要确保答案符合题目要求。在Quantitative Reasoning部分，考试中心会给考生提供一个屏幕计算器。

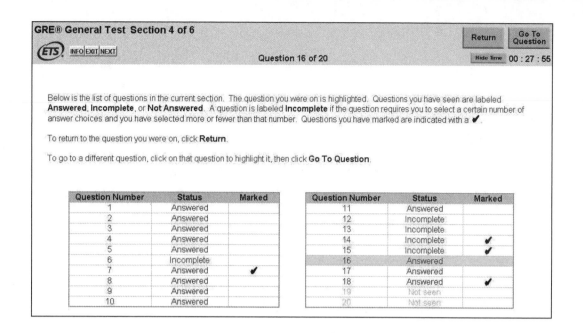

参加GRE计算机考试时，在每一个测试部分内考生都可以跳过那些做起来可能有困难的题目。考试软件有"标记和检查"功能，考生可以标记一些题目，在本部分所给时间内回顾检查这些题目。考试软件还可以让考生查看本部分所有问题的清单，以确认是否解答了所有问题，并标出了考生所标记的问题。在本部分时间有剩余的情况下，考生还可以检查已经解答过的问题并修改答案。

页面顶部会出现一个审查页面小样。这个审查页面旨在帮助考生了解测试进度。不要花太多的时间在审查页面上，因为这会浪费读题和解题的时间。

考生的Verbal Reasoning和Quantitative Reasoning成绩将取决于考生答对题目的数量。注意，答错题并不扣分。因此，为了尽可能多得分，在Verbal Reasoning和Quantitative Reasoning部分，考生最好把所有的题目都答完。

在细心的前提下尽可能快地做题。由于所有问题的权重都是一样的，不要花太多时间去考虑那些觉得有困难或者不熟悉的题目。

在Verbal Reasoning和Quantitative Reasoning部分，如果有时间的话，考生可以先迅速地浏览所有题目，期间只停下来回答有把握的问题，然后再回过头来看那些需要进一步思考的、解决起来有困难的问题。

在正式考试过程中，每部分都只能在规定时间内做一次，一旦完成就不能再返回查看。

Scratch Paper

考生将在考试开始时拿到一份草稿纸。在考试过程中如果需要，也可向监考人员索要更多草稿纸。

Breaks

在第三部分结束后，考生会有10分钟休息时间；在其余各部分之间各有1分钟休息时间。考生可以考虑在规定的休息时间内索取更多的草稿纸。如果在规定休息时间之外的时间进行，考试计时不会暂停，所以一旦测试开始，考生应该不间断作答。

Test-taking Strategies for the Paper-delivered Test

Analytical Writing Sections

在基于纸笔的GRE考试中，Analytical Writing部分的试题将在试题册中给出，要求考生采用手写的方式在提供的空白区域内作答。

计划好考试时间也非常重要。每项任务30分钟，考生需要留出足够的时间去审题，计划如何答题，以及撰写文章。虽然评分人也明白写作时间有限，并会把考生写的东西当作初稿，但是考生仍要尽可能将文章写好。

在每项任务快结束时，留出几分钟时间以检查可能出现的明显错误。虽然偶尔出现的拼写错误和语法错误并不会影响考生的分数，但严重的和反复出现的错误将有损文章的整体水平，并拉低考生的分数。

在纸笔考试的实际考试流程中，考生只能在规定的时间内回答指定部分的作文题目，当监考人员宣布"停止答题"后，考生就不可以再回查已经答过的部分。如果考生这样做，监考人员有权将其逐出考场。

Verbal Reasoning and Quantitative Reasoning Sections

Verbal Reasoning和Quantitative Reasoning部分由多种题型构成。有的需要考生选择一个答案，有的需要考生选择一个或多个答案，还有的需要考生填入一个数值。因此，要确保答案符合题目要求。在Quantitative Reasoning部分，考试中心会给考生提供一个计算器。

在作答Verbal Reasoning和Quantitative Reasoning部分时，考生可以跳过那些觉得可能有困难的题目，在本部分所给时间内回查这些题目。在时间允许的情况下，考生也可以修改该测试部分中任何一道问题的答案（去掉旧答案，填上新答案）。在答题区不要留下任何不必要的痕迹，这有可能被识别为错误答案。但考生可以利用试题册其他空白区域放心地做笔记或演算题目。不提供额外的草稿纸。

考生的Verbal Reasoning和Quantitative Reasoning成绩将取决于答对题目的数量。注意，答错题并不扣分。因此，为了尽可能多得分，在Verbal Reasoning和Quantitative Reasoning部分，考生最好把所有的题目都答完。

在细心的前提下尽可能快地做题。由于所有问题的权重都是一样的，不要花太多时间去考虑那些觉得有困难或者不熟悉的题目。

在Verbal Reasoning和Quantitative Reasoning部分，如果有时间的话，考生可以先迅速地浏览所有题目，期间只回答有把握的问题，然后再回过头来看那些需要进一步思考的、解决起来有困难的问题。

在纸笔考试的实际考试流程中，考生只能在规定的时间内回答指定部分的题目，当监考人员宣布"停止答题"后，考生就不可以再回查已经答过的部分。如果考生这样做了，监考人员有权将其逐出考场。所有的答案都应该写在试题册上。

Breaks

在Analytical Writing第二部分结束后有10分钟的休息时间。

Understanding GRE Scoring

Analytical Writing Measure of the Computer-delivered Test

Analytical Writing部分，每篇文章将由一位经过培训的评分人进行打分，满分为6分。在整个评分过程中，评分人要基于一篇文章的整体质量，看它有没有很好地完成题目所要求的任务。同时，文章还会由电子评分系统（*e-rater*®）进行打分，这个系统由ETS开发，能够识别文章里体现写作水平的一些特征。如果评分人和电子评分系统的两个打分接近，那么这两个分数的平均值就是最后得分；如果两个打分相差较大，那么会请另外一位评分人审核文章并打分，此分数与第一位评分人的分数取平均值，就是最后得分。

两篇文章的得分再取平均值（四舍五入到0~6评分区间内最接近的半分区间）为最终成绩。Analytical Writing部分只给出一个分数。Analytical Writing的考查重点在于考生的批判性思维能力和分析性写作能力。Issue和Argument的评分指南都包含在本书中，同时考生也可以访问如下网址获取这部分信息：www.ets.org/gre/scores/how。

Analytical Writing Measure of the Paper-delivered Test

Analytical Writing部分，每篇文章将由两位评分人分别进行打分，满分为6分。评分人都接受过培训。在整个评分过程中，评分人要基于一篇文章的整体质量，看它有没有很好地完成题目所要求的任务。如果两位评分人所给分数的差异超过1分，将会交由第三位评分人对成绩进行判定；如果差异没有超过1分，则这篇文章的最终成绩为两个分数的平均值。

两篇文章的得分再取平均值（四舍五入到0~6评分区间内最接近的半分区间）为最终成绩。Analytical Writing部分只给出一个分数。Analytical Writing的考查重点在于考生的批判性思维能力和分析性写作能力。Issue和Argument的评分指南都包含在本书中，同时考生也可以访问如下网址获取这部分信息：www.ets.org/gre/scores/how。

Independent Intellectual Activity

在GRE考试评分过程，考生在Analytical Writing部分的文章将由ETS论文相似性检测软件和经验丰富的评分人进行审查。考虑到自主知识产权在研究生院和大学里的重要性，考生的论文应是考生的原作。一篇文章若被证实包含以下情况，ETS将保留取消分数的权利：

- 文字与其他一篇或几篇GRE文章异常相似

- 引用或改写一些出现在公开出版或未出版资源中的文字而不标明出处，包括来自网络的资源及/或由任何第三方提供的资源

- 未经授权使用与他人合作的成果而不标明他人贡献

- 表面看是考生自己写的文章，事实上是从其他地方或其他人那里完全或部分借鉴来的

当出现一个或多个上述情况时，ETS根据专业评分守则就会认为考生的文章不能反映其自主写作能力，而这种能力正是这个考试所考查的。因此，ETS将取消考生Analytical Writing部分的成绩，同时也不能向考生提供GRE考试的分数，因为Analytical Writing是此项考试不可或缺的一部分。

Verbal Reasoning and Quantitative Reasoning Measures of the Computer-delivered Test

在基于计算机的GRE考试中，考生在Verbal Reasoning和Quantitative Reasoning部分的成绩取决于其答对题目的数量。

Verbal Reasoning和Quantitative Reasoning测试采用基于"部分"水平（section-level）的自适应考试。计算机将根据考生在第一部分测试的表现来选择第二部分测试。在每部分中，每个问题对于最终成绩的意义是等同的。对于这两项测试（Verbal Reasoning和Quantitative Reasoning）的任何一项来说，原始分就是考生答对问题的数量。

原始分将通过一个被称之为均衡化的过程转换为标准分。均衡化的过程要考虑不同考试间考题难度的细微差异，以及由于计算机自适应所产生的两部分题目之间的差异。因此，无论第二部分测试什么内容，无论何时参加考试，对一个测试部分给定的标准分反映的是相同的应试水平。

Verbal Reasoning and Quantitative Reasoning Measures of the Paper-delivered Test

对于Verbal Reasoning和Quantitative Reasoning部分的打分分两个步骤。首先，计算出每项测试的原始分。每项测试的原始分都是考生在该项测试两部分题目中答对题目的总数。

然后，原始分将通过一个被称之为均衡化的过程转化为标准分。均衡化的过程要考虑不同考试间考题难度的细微差异。因此，无论考生参加哪次考试，对一个测试部分给定的标准分反映的是相同的应试水平。

Score Reporting

GRE考试将会报告三部分成绩：

- 按照130~170评分区间给出的Verbal Reasoning成绩，最小分数段为1分
- 按照130~170的评分区间给出的Quantitative Reasoning成绩，最小分数段为1分
- 按照0~6评分区间给出的Analytical Writing成绩，最小分数段为0.5分

如果考生在某项测试（Quantitative Reasoning、Verbal Reasoning或者Analytical Writing）中没有回答任何题目，则该项测试会收到没有成绩（No Score, NS）的通知。

关于Analytical Writing各分数等级的具体描述请参见本书41页，也可浏览如下网址获取相关信息：www.ets.org/gre/awscoredescriptions。

The *ScoreSelect*® Option

ScoreSelect®既适用于GRE普通考试，也适用于GRE专项考试，任何有最近五年内有效的GRE考试成绩的考生均可使用。通过该服务，考生可以选择自己满意的成绩寄送给要申请的院校。考生可通过以下两种选择申请四份免费成绩报送：寄送最近的考试成绩或是寄送五年内所有GRE考试成绩。考试过后，考生如果要寄送额外的成绩单，可以通过付费服务选择最近一次的、所有的或者任何一次的考试成绩。需要提醒的是，单次的GRE考试成绩必须给予完整报告。更多信息请访问 www.ets.org/gre/scoreselect。

Score Reporting Time Frames

基于计算机的GRE考试将在考试日期后大约10~15天给出成绩；纸笔考试将在考试后6周内给出成绩。如果考生申请了研究生或商学院项目，需仔细阅读招生截止日期，并及时参加考试，以便成绩能递送到所申请院校。

更多关于成绩报告的信息，请访问：www.ets.org/gre/scores/get。

2 GRE® Analytical Writing

Your goals for this chapter

➤ Recognize the two types of Analytical Writing tasks
➤ Study examples of each type of writing task
➤ Learn strategies for responding to the writing tasks
➤ Review actual student responses and ETS reader commentary

Overview of the Analytical Writing Measure

Analytical Writing（分析性写作）测试考查考生的批判性思维和分析性写作技能、清晰地表达并支持复杂观点的能力、构建和评估论证论据的能力，以及围绕一个主题集中地、有条理地展开讨论的能力。此测试不考查特定的知识内容。

Analytical Writing由两个独立计时的任务构成：

● 一个30分钟的"Analyze an Issue"任务

● 一个30分钟的"Analyze an Argument"任务

Issue任务要求就一个一般性话题提出一个观点，题目中会就如何对该话题进行回应提出明确的写作要求。考生需要评估这个话题，考虑其复杂性，并通过推理和实例展开论证以支持自己的观点。

Argument任务是不同于Issue任务的挑战：它要求考生依据具体的题目要求对已有的论证进行评估。考生需要考虑这个论证是否合乎逻辑，而非简单地赞同或反对其中的观点。

这两项写作任务性质互补：一个要求考生提出观点并提供论据支持其观点，以此来构建考生自己的论证；另一个则要求考生评估别人的论证，包括对其观点及支持证据的评定。

Preparing for the Analytical Writing Measure

每个人——包括那些熟练、自信的写作者——都应该在考前花一些时间来准备Analytical Writing。考生要了解这个题型所考查的技能，并弄清每一部分的评分标准，这一点非常重要。同时，查阅各部分的评分指南、成绩等级描述、作文样题、已被判分的范文以及评分人对每篇范文的评语，这些也是有帮助的。

Analytical Writing的写作题目所涉及的学科领域十分广泛——从艺术、人文学科到社会科学和物理科学，但所有的写作题目都不要求考生具备特定学科的专业知识。事实上，每道试题都会经过实际测评以确保其具备一些重要的特征，其中包括以下几点：

- 无论什么专业或有什么特别兴趣，所有GRE考生都能理解题目并轻松作答。

- 能够诱发考生进行复杂性思考及说服性写作的能力，大学教师认为这种能力在研究生阶段的学习中是至关重要的。

- 考生们的回答能够在文章内容和写作思路上灵活变化。

为了帮助考生准备分析性写作，GRE项目已经公开了整个作文题库，涵盖了考生在考场上可能遇到的所有作文题目。提前熟悉作文题库可能会对考生有所帮助。考生可以通过这个网址查看公开的题库：www.ets.org/gre/awtopics。

General Strategies

- **合理安排时间很重要**。在Issue任务30分钟的时限内，考生要留出足够的时间来思考题目及其具体要求，构思提纲，并最终完成这篇文章。在Argument任务30分钟的时限内，考生也需要留出足够的时间来思考所给论证和具体的题目要求，理清写作思路，并最终完成这篇文章。尽管GRE的评卷人了解考生在写作时受到时间限制，并会把考生的文章当作初稿看待，但考生仍然需要让自己的文章能够在考试条件下达到最佳水平。

- **在每项计时的写作任务结束前留出几分钟时间检查明显的错误**。偶尔的拼写及语法错误并不会影响考生的作文分数，但反复出现的严重错误会影响文章的整体效果，从而拉低考生的分数。

Analyze an Issue Task

Understanding the Issue Task

Issue任务考查考生根据具体的题目要求，就一般性话题进行批判性思考的能力，以及在写作中清晰地表达观点的能力。每一道Issue题目都会提出一个观点，考生可以从不同的角度，将该观点放在不同的情况或条件下对其进行论证。每道Issue题目都会提供具体的写作要求。考生要做的就是依据具体的写作要求展开自己的观点并提供有说服力的案例。在开始写作之前，请仔细阅读作文题目及写作要求，从不同的角度思考问题，并考虑与其相关的论点的复杂性。然后，根据自己准备探讨的观点记录要点，列出用来支持此观点的主要理由和例证。

根据具体的题目要求抓住重点，阐明自己的观点，这非常重要。每项写作任务都会带有以下题目要求中的一种。

- Write a response in which you discuss the extent to which you agree or disagree with the statement and explain your reasoning for the position you take. In developing and supporting your position, you should consider ways in which the statement might or might not hold true and explain how these considerations shape your position.

- Write a response in which you discuss the extent to which you agree or disagree with the recommendation and explain your reasoning for the position you take. In developing and supporting your position, describe specific circumstances in which adopting the recommendation would or would not be advantageous and explain how these examples shape your position.

- Write a response in which you discuss the extent to which you agree or disagree with the claim. In developing and supporting your position, be sure to address the most compelling reasons and/or examples that could be used to challenge your position.

- Write a response in which you discuss which view more closely aligns with your own position and explain your reasoning for the position you take. In developing and supporting your position, you should address both of the views presented.

- Write a response in which you discuss the extent to which you agree or disagree with the claim and the reason on which that claim is based.

- Write a response in which you discuss your views on the policy and explain your reasoning for the position you take. In developing and supporting your position, you should consider the possible consequences of implementing the policy and explain how these consequences shape your position.

GRE评分人在评判考生的文章时并不是要寻找"正确"答案——事实上也没有正确的立场可言。相反，评分人评估的是考生处理特定题目要求的技能，以及考生清晰地表达观点、提出并展开论证以支持其观点的能力。

Understanding the Context for Writing: Purpose and Audience

Issue任务是对批判性思维和说服性写作的锻炼。Issue任务的目的是评判考生能够在何种程度上提供有说服力的论证以支持考生对于题目观点的分析，并且通过写作向学术性读者传递信息。考生的读者是由GRE评分人构成的，他们在如何应用Issue任务评分指南（见第37~38页）中的判分标准方面接受过严格的训练。

为了更好地了解GRE评分人如何把评分标准应用到对具体文章的评分中，考生应该查阅打过分的范文以及评分人的评语。范文样本，尤其是5分和6分水平的范文，能够展示出关于说服性论证的组织、展开以及表达的各种成功策略。评分人的评语会讨论评估和写作的各个具体方面，如实例的使用、对论点的展开和支持、文章的组织、语言的流畅性以及词汇的选择。对于每一篇范文，评分人的评语都会指出文中比较有说服力的内容，也会指出影响文章总体效果的地方。

Preparing for the Issue Task

由于Issue任务旨在考查考生在多年的教育中培养出的说服性写作技巧，因此这项写作任务既不要求考生进行特定的课程学习，也不会偏向那些进行过特殊培训的考生。

很多大学写作教材提供关于说服性写作和论证的建议，或许考生会觉得有所帮助，但这些可能比Issue写作任务所要求的能力更具技术性，也更专业化。考生并不需要知道批判思维和写作的特定术语和策略；相反地，考生只要能在作文中根据具体的题目要求，使用推理、证据和例证来支持自己对某一观点的立场。例如，假设题目要求考生考虑一项要求政府对艺术博物馆提供财政资助的政策以及推行这项政策可能产生的影响。如果你的立场是政府应该资助艺术博物馆，那么你在支持自己的论点时或许应该讨论艺术为什么重要，并解释政府的资助将使每个人都能够参观博物馆。另一方面，如果你的立场是政府不应该资助博物馆，那么你或许应该指出，由于政府资金有限，艺术博物馆不如其他更有社会重要性的机构值得得到政府的资助，这些机构会由于该政策的实施而蒙受损失。或者，如果你认为政府只能在特定的条件下资助博物馆，那么你也许应该把重点放在你认为能够决定艺术博物馆将如何（或者是否）得到政府资助的因素上，如艺术标准、文化意义或政治条件等。在展开立场时所呈现出的批判性思维的技巧远比立场的选择更加重要。

准备Issue任务时，一个很好的方法是通过公开的题库进行写作练习。没有一个适合每一个人的最佳练习方法：有的人喜欢在开始练习时不考虑30分钟的时间限制；另外一些人喜欢开始就进行"计时测验"练习。无论采取哪种方式练习Issue任务，都应该认真阅读题目要求，然后：

- 认真阅读具体的观点和写作要求，并确保自己已理解；如果有不清楚的地方，与朋友或老师一起讨论

- 考虑题目和题目要求与你的观点、经历、曾经阅读过或观察到的事例，以及和认识的人之间的关系；这些是你的知识库，可以用在论证中作为有说服力的理由和例证，从而支持、否定或部分同意题目的观点

- 决定你在该题目上将采用并捍卫的立场

- 决定用来支持你的立场的有说服力的证据（理由和例证）

要记住本项任务测试的是批判性思维和说服性写作的能力。最为切题的文章能够探查题目和题目要求的复杂性。考生在准备Issue任务时，提问自己以下问题或许会有帮助：

- 题目的中心问题具体是什么？

- 题目具体要求我做什么？

- 对于题目中的观点，我全部同意还是部分同意？为什么？

- 题目中的观点是否暗含前提假设？如果有的话，这些前提假设合理吗？

- 题目中的观点是否只在特定条件下成立？如果是的话，是哪些条件？

- 我是否需要解释题目中使用的特定术语或概念？

- 如果我针对题目采取某种立场，有哪些理由可以支持我的立场？

- 有哪些例证——不论是真实的还是虚构的——可以用来阐释这些理由并推进我的观点？哪些例证是最有说服力的？

当考生已经决定要捍卫的立场之后，考虑那些可能与自己立场不同的观点，问自己这样的问题：

- 别人会用什么理由来驳斥或削弱我的观点？

- 在文章中，我应该如何认可或反驳这些观点？

在构思作文时，考生可能会总结自己的立场，并为如何支持这个立场做一些简短的笔记。完成这一步后，仔细查看笔记并决定如何组织文章。然后，在写作中就题目问题展开自己的观点。即使文章没有写完整，考生也应该发现，练习一些题库中的题目并尽可能打出草稿是很有帮助的。练习一些题目之后，可以尝试在30分钟的时限内就一些题目进行写作，以便在实际考试中更好地掌控时间。

考生可以请教授批判性思维和写作的老师对自己文章给出一些反馈，或者就同一题目与其他考生依据评分标准交换评阅，这两种办法都会有所帮助。尽量确定每一篇文章是如何达到或未达到各分数段的评分标准的。把自己的文章与评分标准进行比较，这有助于考生看到需要改进的方面和方法。

The Form of Your Response

考生可以自由选择文章结构和行文方式，只要考生认为这样可以有效地表达自己对于题目和题目要求所持的观点。考生的文章可以——但并非必须——采用从英语作文课或大学写作强化课程中学到的写作策略。GRE评分人并不重视某种特定的行文策略或写作风格；事实上，GRE评分人在接受培训时，要评阅几百份作文，尽管这些作文的内容和形式高度多样化，却表现出同等水平的批判性思维和说服性写作技巧。例如，评分人会看到，一些6分水平的Issue作文以简要介绍作者的立场开头，然后清晰地呈现将要论述的要点。评分人也会看到，另外一些作文会采用不同策略来引入作者的立场，如做出预测、提问一系列问题、描述一个场景或定义题目中的关键术语等。评分人知道，不管是举出多个例证还是提供一个延伸的例证都能取得高分。考生可以查阅Issue范文，尤其是5分和6分水平的范文，来感受其他考生是如何成功地展开和组织他们的论证的。

只要考生认为合适，考生的作文可以包括任意数量的段落——例如，考生很可能需要在阐述每一个新观点时都新起一段。重要的不是例证的数量、段落的数量、抑或论证的形式，而是考生针对题目所持观点的说服力以及向学术性读者传递这些观点时的清晰度和所使用的技能。

Sample Issue Task

As people rely more and more on technology to solve problems, the ability of humans to think for themselves will surely deteriorate.

Discuss the extent to which you agree or disagree with the statement and explain your reasoning for the position you take. In developing and supporting your position, you should consider ways in which the statement might or might not hold true and explain how these considerations shape your position.

Strategies for This Topic

在这个写作任务中，要求考生讨论在何种程度上赞同或者反对题目的观点。因此，考生的立场可以是强烈的赞同或反对，也可以是有保留的赞同或反对。题目还要求考生解释理由并考虑题目观点成立或不成立的情况。优秀的作文无须讨论后面列出的所有或任一要点，通过讨论其他理由和例证同样可以支持其立场。

尽管这个题目适用于各种能力水平的考生，但为了得到高分，紧扣题目并提供清晰、切题的例证和/或理由来支持考生所要表达的观点尤其重要。低水平的作文可能会很长并充满关于现代技术的例子，但这些例子与一个特定的立场的关系可能并不清晰。例如，一个强烈反对题目观点的考生可能会把计算机技术作为思考能力并没有恶化的证据。但仅仅通过计算机技术存在的事实，并不能充分地证明这个观点（或许计算机的容易操作又抑制了我们的思考能力）。要想得到高分，考生应该解释计算机技术以何种方式唤起或需要思考能力。

这个题目可以有各种各样的写法，尤其是考虑到对"the ability of humans to think for themselves"这句话的各种不同的理解。尽管大部分考生会把它当做解决问题的工具，另外一部分考生会把它解释为表达情感和进行社交的手段（例如，与别人沟通交流的工具），这同样是有效的解释。无论怎样理解，考生都可能会谈到计算器、拼写和语法检查等文字处理工具、返税软件、互联网搜索，以及其他常见家用或商用技术的例子。

考生可以同意题目的观点并论证：

● 对技术的依赖导致独立性缺失；我们太依赖于问题解决的技术了，以至于当技术出现故障时，我们会陷入比完全没有技术更糟糕的境地

● 日常的技术，例如计算器和现金出纳机，降低了我们的简单计算能力，这是一种"不用就会失去"的能力，而它是我们思考能力的基础

或者考生可以反对题目的观点，并论证技术提高了我们的思考能力：

● 开发、实现、应用技术需要解决问题的能力

● 技术把我们从繁杂的问题解决（例如计算）中解脱出来，允许我们投入更复杂的思考

● 技术提供了通向我们之前不可能接触到的信息的通道

● 技术把距离遥远的人们联系起来并允许他们进行思想交流

● 技术依赖于人类的思考和选择（技术的每一次应用和进步都是由人类的智慧和决策所推动的）

另一方面，考生也可以开辟中间立场，指出尽管技术会降低某些思考能力，但它也促使了另外一些（或许更重要的）思考能力迅速发展。这样的作文或许会区分复杂问题的解决和简单的"数据维护"（即计算的执行和信息的组织）。其他写作角度可以包括采取历史的、哲学的或社会学的立场；或者使用个人的例证来证明立场，这些都同样有效。考生可以论证说，对技术的依赖，其价值或危害是由使用它的个人或社会决定的；也可以说，只有开发技术的人（技术专家）保持了他们的解决问题的能力，而其他人正在失去这种能力。

再次强调：考生应该避免过于笼统的例证，或者简单地罗列例证而没有发挥。同样重要的是，不要仅仅转述题目观点。请记住，重点是清晰地表达与题目和具体的题目要求有关的观点的能力，以及利用相关理由和/或例证支持这个观点的能力。

Essay Responses and Reader Commentary

Score 6 Response *

The statement linking technology negatively with free thinking plays on recent human experience over the past century. Surely there has been no time in history where the lived lives of people have changed more dramatically. A quick reflection on a typical day reveals how technology has revolutionized the world. Most people commute to work in an automobile that runs on an internal combustion engine. During the workday, chances are high that the employee will interact with a computer that processes information on silicon bridges that are .09 microns wide. Upon leaving home, family members will be reached through wireless networks that utilize satellites orbiting the earth. Each of these common occurences would have been inconceivable at the turn of the 19th century.

The statement attempts to bridge these dramatic changes to a reduction in the ability for humans to think for themselves. The assumption is that an increased reliance on technology negates the need for people to think creatively to solve previous quandaries. Looking back at the introduction, one could argue that without a car, computer, or mobile phone, the hypothetical worker would need to find alternate methods of transport, information processing, and communication. Technology short circuits this thinking by making the problems obsolete.

However, this reliance on technology does not necessarily preclude the creativity that marks the human species. The prior examples reveal that technology allows for convenience. The car, computer, and phone all release additional time for people to live more efficiently. This efficiency does not preclude the need for humans to think for themselves. In fact, technology frees humanity to not only tackle new problems, but may itself create new issues that did not exist without technology. For example, the proliferation of automobiles has introduced a need for fuel conservation on a global scale. With increasing energy demands from emerging markets, global warming becomes a concern inconceivable to the horse-and-buggy generation. Likewise dependence on oil has created nation-states that are not dependent on taxation, allowing ruling parties to oppress minority groups such as women. Solutions to these complex problems require the unfettered imaginations of maverick scientists and politicians.

In contrast to the statement, we can even see how technology frees the human imagination. Consider how the digital revolution and the advent of the internet has allowed for an unprecedented exchange of ideas. WebMD, a popular internet portal for medical information, permits patients to self research symptoms for a more informed doctor visit. This exercise opens pathways of thinking that were previously closed off to the medical layman. With increased interdisciplinary interactions, inspiration can arrive from the most surprising corners. Jeffrey Sachs, one of the architects of the UN Millenium Development Goals, based his ideas on emergency care triage techniques. The unlikely marriage of economics and medicine has healed tense, hyperinflation environments from South America to Eastern Europe.

This last example provides the most hope in how technology actually provides hope to the future of humanity. By increasing our reliance on technology, impossible goals can now be achieved. Consider how the late 20th century witnessed the complete elimination of smallpox. This disease had ravaged the human race since prehistorical days, and yet with the technology of vaccines, free thinking humans dared to imagine a

---

*All responses in this publication are reproduced exactly as written, including errors, misspellings, etc., if any.

world free of smallpox. Using technology, battle plans were drawn out, and smallpox was systematically targeted and eradicated.

Technology will always mark the human experience, from the discovery of fire to the implementation of nanotechnology. Given the history of the human race, there will be no limit to the number of problems, both new and old, for us to tackle. There is no need to retreat to a Luddite attitude to new things, but rather embrace a hopeful posture to the possibilities that technology provides for new avenues of human imagination.

Reader Commentary

The author of this essay stakes out a clear and insightful position on the issue and follows the specific instructions by discussing ways in which the statement might or might not hold true, using specific reasons and examples to support that position. The essay cogently argues that technology does not decrease our ability to think for ourselves. It merely provides "additional time for people to live more efficiently." In fact, the problems that have developed alongside the growth of technology (pollution, political unrest in oil-producing nations) actually call for more creative thinking, not less. In further examples, the essay shows how technology allows for the linking of ideas that may never have been connected in the past (like medicine and economic models), pushing people to think in new ways. Examples are persuasive and fully developed; reasoning is logically sound and well supported.

Ideas in the essay are connected logically, with effective transitions used both between paragraphs ("However," or "In contrast to the statement") and within paragraphs. Sentence structure is varied and complex, and the essay clearly demonstrates facility with the "conventions of standard written English (i.e., grammar, usage, and mechanics)" (see Issue Scoring Guide, pages 37–38), with only minor errors appearing. Thus, this essay meets all the requirements for receiving a top score, a 6.

Score 5 Response

Surely many of us have expressed the following sentiment, or some variation on it, during our daily commutes to work: "People are getting so stupid these days!" Surrounded as we are by striding and strident automatons with cell phones glued to their ears, PDA's gripped in their palms, and omniscient, omnipresent CNN gleaming in their eyeballs, it's tempting to believe that technology has isolated and infantilized us, essentially transforming us into dependent, conformist morons best equipped to sideswip one another in our SUV's.

Furthermore, hanging around with the younger, pre-commute generation, whom tech-savviness seems to have rendered lethal, is even less reassuring. With "Teen People" style trends shooting through the air from tiger-striped PDA to zebra-striped PDA, and with the latest starlet gossip zipping from juicy Blackberry to teeny, turbo-charged cell phone, technology seems to support young people's worst tendencies to follow the crowd. Indeed, they have seemingly evolved into intergalactic conformity police. After all, today's tech-aided teens are, courtesy of authentic, hands-on video games, literally trained to kill; courtesy of chat and instant text messaging, they have their own language; they even have tiny cameras to efficiently photodocument your fashion blunders! Is this adolescence, or paparazzi terrorist training camp?

With all this evidence, it's easy to believe that tech trends and the incorporation of technological wizardry into our everyday lives have served mostly to enforce conformity, promote dependence, heighten comsumerism and materialism, and generally create a culture that values self-absorption and personal entitlement over cooperation and collaboration. However, I argue that we are merely in the inchoate stages of learning to live with technology while still loving one another. After all, even given the examples provided earlier in this essay, it seems clear that technology hasn't impaired our thinking and problem-solving capacities. Certainly it has incapacitated our behavior and manners; certainly our values have taken a severe blow. However, we are inarguably more efficient in our badness these days. We're effective worker bees of ineffectiveness!

If technology has so increased our senses of self-efficacy that we can become veritable agents of the awful, virtual CEO's of selfishness, certainly it can be beneficial. Harnessed correctly, technology can improve our ability to think and act for ourselves. The first challenge is to figure out how to provide technology users with some direly-needed direction.

Reader Commentary

The language of this essay clearly illustrates both its strengths and weaknesses. The flowery and sometimes uncannily keen descriptions are often used to powerful effect, but at other times the writing is awkward and the comparisons somewhat strained. See, for example, the ungainly sequence of independent clauses in the second to last sentence of paragraph 2 ("After all, today's tech-aided teens . . . ").

There is consistent evidence of facility with syntax and complex vocabulary ("Surrounded as we are by striding and strident automatons with cell phones glued to their ears, PDA's gripped in their palms, and omniscient, omnipresent CNN gleaming in their eyeballs, it's tempting to believe . . . "). Such lucid prose, however, is often countered with an over-reliance upon abstractions and tangential reasoning (what does the fact that video games "literally train [teens] to kill" have to do with the use or deterioration of thinking abilities, for example?).

Because this essay takes a complex approach to the issue (arguing, in effect, that technology neither enhances nor reduces our ability to think for ourselves, but can be used to do one or the other depending on the user) and because the author makes use of "appropriate vocabulary and sentence variety" (see Issue Scoring Guide, pages 37–38), a score of 5 is appropriate.

Score 4 Response

In all actuality, I think it is more probable that our bodies will surely deteriorate long before our minds do in any significant amount. Who can't say that technology has made us lazier, but that's the key word, lazy, not stupid. The ever increasing amount of technology that we incorporate into our daily lives makes people think and learn every day, possibly more than ever before. Our abilities to think, learn, philosophize, etc. may even reach limits never dreamed of before by average people. Using technology to solve problems will continue to help us realize our potential as a human race.

If you think about it, using technology to solve more complicating problems gives humans a chance to expand their thinking and learning, opening up whole new worlds for many people. Many of these people are glad for the chance to expand their horizons by learning more, going to new places, and trying new things. If it wasn't for the invention of new technological devices, I wouldn't be sitting at this computer trying to philosophize about technology. It would be extremely hard for children in much poorer countries to learn and think for themselves with out the invention of the internet. Think what an impact the printing press, a technologically superior mackine at the time, had on the ability of the human race to learn and think.

Right now we are seeing a golden age of technology, using it all the time during our every day lives. When we get up there's instant coffee and the microwave and all these great things that help us get ready for our day. But we aren't allowing our minds to deteriorate by using them, we are only making things easier for ourselves and saving time for other important things in our days. Going off to school or work in our cars instead of a horse and buggy. Think of the brain power and genius that was used to come up with that single invention that has changed the way we move across this globe.

Using technology to solve our continually more complicated problems as a human race is definately a good thing. Our ability to think for ourselves isn't deteriorating, it's continuing to grow, moving on to higher though functions and more ingenious ideas. The ability to use what technology we have is an example

Reader Commentary

This essay meets all the criteria of a 4-level essay. The writer develops a clear position ("Using technology to solve problems will continue to help us realize our potential as a human race"). The position is then developed with relevant reasons ("using technology to solve more complicat[ed] problems gives humans a chance to expand their thinking and learning . . ." and "we are seeing a golden age of technology"). Point 1, "Using technology," is supported with the simple, but relevant notions that technology allows us access to information and abilities to which we would not normally have access. Similarly, point 2, "the golden age," is supported by the basic description of our technologically saturated social condition. Though the development and organization of the essay does suffer from an occasional misstep (see paragraph 3's abrupt progression from coffeepots to the benefits of technology to cars), the essay as a whole flows smoothly and logically from one idea to the next.

It is useful to compare this essay to the 3-level essay presented next. Though they both utilize some very superficial discussion and often fail to probe deeply into the issue, this writer does, however, take the analysis a step further. In paragraph 2, the distinction between this essay and the next one (the 3-level response) can most clearly be seen. To support the notion that advances in technology actually help increase thinking ability, the writer draws a clever parallel between the promise of modern, sophisticated technology (computer) and the equally substantial/pervasive technology of the past (printing press).

Like the analysis, the language in this essay clearly meets the requirements for a score of 4. The writer displays sufficient control of language and the conventions of standard written English. The preponderance of mistakes are of a cosmetic nature ("using technology to solve more complicating problems"). There is a sentence fragment ("Going off . . . ") along with a comma splice ("Our ability . . . isn't deteriorating, it's continuing to grow . . . ") in paragraph 4. These errors, though, are minor and do not interfere with the clarity of the ideas being presented.

Score 3 Response

There is no current proof that advancing technology will deteriorate the ability of humans to think. On the contrary, advancements in technology had advanced our vast knowledge in many fields, opening opportunities for further understanding and achievement. For example, the problem of dibilitating illnesses and diseases such as alzheimer's disease is slowing being solved by the technological advancements in stem cell research. The future ability of growing new brain cells and the possibility to reverse the onset of alzheimer's is now becoming a reality. This shows our initiative as humans to better our health demonstrates greater ability of humans to think.

One aspect where the ability of humans may initially be seen as an example of deteriorating minds is the use of internet and cell phones. In the past humans had to seek out information in many different enviroments and aspects of life. Now humans can sit in a chair and type anything into a computer and get an answer. Our reliance on this type of technology can be detrimental if not regulated and regularly substituted for other information sources such as human interactions and hands on learning. I think if humans understand that we should not have such a reliance on computer technology, that we as a species will advance further by utilizing the opportunity of computer technology as well as the other sources of information outside of a computer. Supplementing our knowledge with internet access is surely a way for technology to solve problems while continually advancing the human race.

Reader Commentary

This essay never moves beyond a superficial discussion of the issue. The writer attempts to develop two points: that advancements in technology have progressed our knowledge in many fields and that supplementing rather than relying on technology is "surely a way for technology to solve problems while continually advancing the human race." Each point, then, is developed with relevant but insufficient evidence. In discussing the ability of technology to advance knowledge in many fields (a broad subject rife with possible examples), the writer uses only one limited and very brief example from a specific field (medicine and stem-cell research).

Development of the second point is hindered by a lack of specificity and organization. The writer creates what might most be comparable to an outline. The writer cites a need for regulation/supplementation and warns of the detriment of over-reliance upon technology. However, the explanation of both the problem and the solution is vague and limited ("Our reliance . . . can be detrimental . . . If humans understand that we should not have such a reliance . . . we will advance further"). There is neither explanation of consequences nor clarification of what is meant by "supplementing." This second paragraph is a series of generalizations, which are loosely connected and lack a much-needed grounding.

In the essay, there are some minor language errors and a few more serious flaws (e.g., "The future ability of growing new brain cells" or "One aspect where the ability of humans may initially be seen as an example of deteriorating minds…"). Despite the accumulation of such flaws, though, meaning is generally clear. This essay earns a score of 3, then, primarily for its limited development.

Score 2 Response

In recent centuries, humans have developed the technology very rapidly, and you may accept some merit of it, and you may see a distortion in society occured by it. To be lazy for human in some meaning is one of the fashion issues in thesedays. There are many symptoms and resons of it. However, I can not agree with the statement that the technology make humans to be reluctant to thinkng thoroughly.

Of course, you can see the phenomena of human laziness along with developed technology in some place. However, they would happen in specific condition, not general. What makes human to be laze of thinking is not merely technology, but the the tendency of human that they treat them as a magic stick and a black box. Not understanding the aims and theory of them couses the disapproval problems.

The most important thing to use the thechnology, regardless the new or old, is to comprehend the fundamental idea of them, and to adapt suit tech to tasks in need. Even if you recognize a method as a all-mighty and it is extremely over-spec to your needs, you can not see the result you want. In this procedure, humans have to consider as long as possible to acquire adequate functions. Therefore, humans can not escape from using their brain.

In addition, the technology as it is do not vain automatically, the is created by humans. Thus, the more developed tech and the more you want a convenient life, the more you think and emmit your creativity to breakthrough some banal method sarcastically.

Consequently, if you are not passive to the new tech, but offensive to it, you would not lose your ability to think deeply. Furthermore, you may improve the ability by adopting it.

Reader Commentary

The language of this essay is what most clearly links it to the score point of 2. Amidst sporadic moments of clarity, this essay is marred by serious errors in grammar, usage, and mechanics that often interfere with meaning. It is unclear what the writer means when he/she states, "To be lazy for human in some meaning is one of the fashion issues in thesedays," or " . . . to adapt suit tech to tasks in need." Despite such severe flaws, the writer has made an obvious attempt to respond to the prompt ("I can not agree with the statement that the technology make humans to be reluctant to thinking thoroughly") as well as an unclear attempt to support such an assertion ("Not understanding the aims and theory of them [technology] couses the disapproval problems" and "The most important thing to use the thechnology . . . is to comprehend the fundamental idea of them"). Holistically, the essay displays a seriously flawed but not fundamentally deficient attempt to develop and support its claims.

(Note: In this SPECIFIC case, the analysis is tied directly to the language. As the language falters, so too does the analysis.)

Score 1 Response

Humans have invented machines but they have forgot it and have started everything technically so clearly their thinking process is deterioating.

Reader Commentary

The essay is clearly on topic, as evidenced by the writer's usage of the more significant terms from the prompt: "technically" (technologically), "humans", "thinking" (think) and "deterioating" (deteriorate). Such usage is the only clear evidence of understanding. Meaning aside, the brevity of the essay (one sentence) clearly indicates the writer's inability to develop a response that addresses the specific instructions given ("Discuss the extent to which you agree or disagree with the statement above and explain your reasoning for the position you take").

The language, too, is clearly one-level, as the sentence fails to achieve coherence. The coherent phrases in this one-sentence response are those tied to the prompt: "Humans have invented machines" and "their thinking process is deterioating." Otherwise, the point being made is unclear.

Analyze an Argument Task

Understanding the Argument Task

Argument任务考查考生根据具体的题目要求，理解、分析、评价论证的能力，以及考生在写作中清晰地表达自己的评价的能力。这项任务包含一篇简短的文章，文章的作者提出观点，并用理由和论据来支持这个观点，以此来解释某些行为进程或说明事件。考生的任务是根据题目要求，批判性地检查作者的推理思路，以此讨论作者在文中体现出的逻辑合理性。这就要求考生仔细地阅读该论证和题目要求。考生可以多读几遍题目，对于打算在作答时更全面展开的观点做一些简短的笔记。在阅读这段论证的过程中，应该特别注意以下几点：

● 文中所使用的证据、支撑或证明是什么

● 明确陈述、声明或总结了哪些内容

● 设想或假定的且可能没有证明或证据的内容有哪些

● 哪些内容没有明确提出但可以从已知信息中推断出

此外，考生应该思考该段论证的结构——即把各元素连接起来形成一条推理线的方式；也就是说，考生应该认识到思维过程中那些分离的、有时是隐含的步骤，并考虑每一步到下一步的推导在逻辑上是否合理。沿着这条线，寻找那些作者试图建立逻辑关联所用的过渡词和短语（例如however, thus, therefore, evidently, hence, in conclusion）。

要完成好Argument任务，很重要的一点是要记住考生不需要做的内容。考生不需要去讨论论证中的陈述是否正确或准确，不需要赞同或反对文中的立场，也不需要对该主题表达自己的看法（像在Issue任务中那样）。相反，考生要根据一些具体的要求去评价其他作者的论证的逻辑合理性，以此来体现批判性思维、洞察性阅读和分析性写作，而这些正是大学教师认为在研究生学习中取得成功所必须具备的。

根据题目的具体要求来对论证进行评价是很重要的。每项任务包含以下题目要求中的一种。

● Write a response in which you discuss what specific evidence is needed to evaluate the argument and explain how the evidence would weaken or strengthen the argument.

● Write a response in which you examine the stated and/or unstated assumptions of the argument. Be sure to explain how the argument depends on these assumptions and what the implications are for the argument if the assumptions prove unwarranted.

● Write a response in which you discuss what questions would need to be answered in order to decide whether the recommendation and the argument on which it is based are reasonable. Be sure to explain how the answers to these questions would help to evaluate the recommendation.

- Write a response in which you discuss what questions would need to be answered in order to decide whether the advice and the argument on which it is based are reasonable. Be sure to explain how the answers to these questions would help to evaluate the advice.

- Write a response in which you discuss what questions would need to be answered in order to decide whether the recommendation is likely to have the predicted result. Be sure to explain how the answers to these questions would help to evaluate the recommendation.

- Write a response in which you discuss what questions would need to be answered in order to decide whether the prediction and the argument on which it is based are reasonable. Be sure to explain how the answers to these questions would help to evaluate the prediction.

- Write a response in which you discuss one or more alternative explanations that could rival the proposed explanation and explain how your explanation(s) can plausibly account for the facts presented in the argument.

- Write a response in which you discuss what questions would need to be addressed in order to decide whether the conclusion and the argument on which it is based are reasonable. Be sure to explain how the answers to the questions would help to evaluate the conclusion.

Argument作文首先是一项要求书面作答的批判性思维的任务。因此,考生在评价过程中展现出的分析技巧对其写作成绩有相当大的影响;当然,表达思想时的清晰度对考生的综合成绩也很重要。

Understanding the Context for Writing: Purpose and Audience

这项任务旨在考查考生对他人写的论证过程进行有见地的评价的能力,以及向学术性读者以书面形式有效地表达自己的评价的能力。考生的读者由GRE评分人组成,他们都经过严格的训练并应用Argument作文评分指南上的评分标准(参见第39~40页)进行评分。

如果想要更清楚地了解GRE评分人怎样通过Argument作文评分标准来评估一篇实际的作文,考生需要查阅已评分的Argument范文和评分人的评语。这些范文,特别是5分和6分的范文,将向考生展示如何成功地构思和进行有创意的评论。评分人的评语讨论了分析性写作的一些具体方面,比如观点的说服力、观点的展开和支持、文章的组织、句式的变换以及对语言的驾驭能力。对每篇文章,评分人都会指出其论证有效的和有见地的方面,也会指出削弱其论证有效性的方面。

Preparing for the Argument Task

由于Argument任务旨在评估考生在学习中培养出来的分析性写作和一般推理技能,因而不会要求任何专业课程的学习,接受过专业训练的学生也不会占有优势。很多大学修辞学和写作教科书中有关一般逻辑和批判性思维的章节可能会有所帮助,但这些可能要比这个任务所要求的能力更具体、更专业。GRE考生不需要掌握专业的分析技巧或技术术语。比如有这样一道题：一位小学校长可能得出一个结论，即新的操场设备提高了学生的出勤率，因为自从安装了这些设备以后学生的缺勤率下降了。考生不必知道校长犯了"发生其后，故因其所致"的错误；考生只需要知道，对于出勤率的提高还有其他可能的解释，要举一些常识性的例子，可能还要指出验证这个结论需要具备的内容。比如，缺勤率可能是由于气候变暖而降低的。为使校长的结论有效，这一条解释必须首先排除。

尽管考生不必掌握专业的分析技巧和术语，但还是要熟悉Argument任务的题目要求和一些关键概念，包括以下几种：

- alternative explanation：对于会导致题目事件的其他可能的解释；弱化或限定了最初的解释，因为它也可以成为观察到的事实的原因

- analysis：把某种事物（如一个论证过程）分解成为若干组成部分，以便理解这些部分是如何共同作用从而形成整体的

- argument：充当理由和证据的一个或一系列观点；旨在说明某件事情真假的一系列理由

- assumption：某人为维护某个观点而必须持有的看法，通常是未陈述过的或未检验过的看法；一些被认为理所当然、但若要使得结论成立必须正确的内容

- conclusion：一系列推理的终点，如果推理是合理的，结论就有效；一条最终的论断

- counterexample：一个真实或假想的例子，用来驳斥或反对论证中的一条陈述

- evaluation：对论证中证据和理由的效力和论证总体价值的评判

准备Argument任务的一个很好的方式就是对已公布的Argument任务题目进行书面写作练习。没有一个适合每一个人的最佳练习方法。有的人喜欢在开始练习时不考虑30分钟的时间限制。如果考生采取这种方法，那么就要利用自己所需的时间来分析论证。无论采取哪种方法，考生都应该：

- 仔细阅读论证过程和具体的题目要求——考生可能需要反复阅读

- 尽可能多地找出文中的观点、结论以及隐含的假设，并评估它们的效力

- 想出尽可能多的其他解释和反证

- 想出其他一些能削弱或加强其观点的具体论据

- 问问自己修改哪些论据会让推理更合理

把每一个想法写成简短的笔记。当考生做足分析之后，查看这些笔记，并将它们按照合理的论证顺序排列起来（可以给它们编号）。然后，根据题目的每一项要求，撰写一篇全面而又详尽的评论文章。即便没有写出一篇完整的论文，考生也会发现这对练习分析论证和构思自己的作文非常有帮助。当考生写得更快、更有自信时，就可以开始练习在30分钟内写出一篇文章，以便能在实际考试中更好地掌控速度。例如，考生不能对一个观点进行太过详尽的讨论或提供太多同等效力的例子，这样会导致没有时间阐述别的观点。

考生可以请作文老师、哲学老师或者其他在其课程中强调批判性思维的人对自己的作文给以反馈。与同学交换根据同一题目写出的文章，并根据评分指南互相评论作文，这也能获得很多有用信息。不要过于关注是否给了"正确评分"，而要多看这些文章如何达到或未达到每一个分数的标准，从而了解如何提高。

How to Interpret Numbers, Percentages, and Statistics in Argument Topics

一些Argument任务包含用以支持结论的证据，包括数字、百分比或统计数据。比如，一项Argument任务中可能声称，今年的某一社区活动没有去年流行，因为今年只有100人参加，而去年有150人参加，人数减少了33%。重要的是要记住，题目并不是在让考生做一道含有数字、百分比或统计数据的数学题。相反，考生要做的是对支持结论的这些证据进行评价。在上述的例子中，结论是一项社区活动变得不如以前流行了。考生应该问自己：100人和150人之间的差异能否支持这个结论？注意，这个例子还有其他可能的解释，比如，今年的天气情况可能差得很多，今年的活动举行时间可能不太适宜，今年活动的花费可能增加了，或者今年可能有另外一个受欢迎的活动同时举行。每个原因都可以解释参加人数上的差异，因此就削弱了这个活动"不如以前流行"的结论。同样，依据百分比所代表的实际数字，百分比可能支持也可能削弱一个结论。再比如：学校的戏剧社应该得到更多赞助，因为其会员人数增长了100%。如果以前有100个会员而现在有200个会员，那么这100%的增长可能很重要；然而，如果以前有5个会员而现在有10个会员，那么这个增长或许就没那么重要。记住，在Argument任务中，任何数字、百分比或统计数据都只用来作为支持结论的证据，考生应不断地思考它们是否确实能够支持结论。

The Form of Your Response

考生可以自由选择文章结构和行文方式，只要考生认为这样可以有效地表达自己对论证的评价。考生的文章可以——但并非必须——采用从大学英语作文课或写作强化课程中学到的特定的写作策略。GRE评分人不会重视某种特定的行文策略或写作风格。事实上，

GRE评分人在参加培训时审阅了大量的Argument作文，这些文章尽管在内容和形式上高度多样化，但它们体现出的批判性思维和分析性写作的水平却是类似的。例如，评分人会看到，一些6分水平的文章，行文一开始会对论证进行简要概括，然后清晰地陈述并展开评价要点。评分人知道，考生可以通过展开评价中的几个要点获得高分，也可以通过识别论证中的一个核心要点并深入展开而获得高分。考生可以看一下Argument任务的范文，特别是5分和6分水平的范文，看看其他考生是怎样成功地展开和组织文章的。

考生应该选择自己认为能支持和加强文章整体效果的写作形式和组织结构。这就意味着考生可以使用尽可能多或尽可能少的段落，只要考生认为合适——比如，当讨论转移到一个新的评价观点时，就可以创建一个新的段落。考生可以围绕论证本身的结构来组织自己的评价，逐行地讨论这个论证。或者考生可以先指出一个核心问题，然后进一步讨论与其相关的论证推理过程的缺陷。同样，考生也可以举例子，如果它们有助于阐明重要观点，或者能把讨论进一步推进（但是要记住，就有效地完成Argument任务的能力方面，它考查的是考生的批判性思维和分析性写作的能力，而不是举例子的能力）。对于学术性的评分人来说，在这个任务中，重要的不是作答的形式，而是考生在评估论证中表现出的深刻见解，以及在文章中表现出的清晰表达的能力。

Sample Argument Task

In surveys Mason City residents rank water sports (swimming, boating, and fishing) among their favorite recreational activities. The Mason River flowing through the city is rarely used for these pursuits, however, and the city park department devotes little of its budget to maintaining riverside recreational facilities. For years there have been complaints from residents about the quality of the river's water and the river's smell. In response, the state has recently announced plans to clean up Mason River. Use of the river for water sports is, therefore, sure to increase. The city government should for that reason devote more money in this year's budget to riverside recreational facilities.

Write a response in which you examine the stated and/or unstated assumptions of the argument. Be sure to explain how the argument depends on the assumptions and what the implications are if the assumptions prove unwarranted.

Strategies for This Topic

这个Argument任务引用了一个调查来支持一个预测：对梅森河的使用肯定会增长，因此建议市政府在今年的预算中增加对河边娱乐设施的资金投入。

在展开评价时，考生需要检查这个论证中已列出的和未列出的假设，并讨论如果这些假设被证明是无根据的将意味着什么。一篇成功的作文，就要既讨论论证的假设，又讨论这些假设对于论证所具备的含义。如果一篇作文中没有提到这些方面，那么不管其他方面的质量如何，该作文的得分都不会高于4分。

下面列出了一些论证的假设，和一些基于这些假设进行论证的方式。当然考生的回答完全可以提出下面没有提到的其他要点，也不必提到所有这些要点。这些假设包括：

● 那些把水上运动列为"最喜爱的娱乐活动之一"的人事实上很可能会参加这些活动。（他们也有可能只是喜欢观看。）这个假设支持了以下论点，即在州政府清理了梅森河后，为开展水上运动，对河流的使用肯定会增长，并且市政府应因此而为河边的娱乐设施投入更多的资金。

● 居民在调查中所说的话符合实际。（有可能调查结果夸大了他们对水上运动的兴趣。）这个假设支持了以下论点，即在州政府清理了梅森河后，为开展水上运动，对河流的使用肯定能增长，并且市政府应因此而为河边的娱乐设施投入更多的资金。

● 梅森市居民实际上想在梅森河里进行水上运动。（作为娱乐活动，水上运动有可能被认为是远离城市的度假方式和周末的消遣。）这个假设支持了以下论点，即在州政府清理了梅森河后，为开展水上运动，对河流的使用肯定能增长，并且市政府应因此而向河边的娱乐设施投入更多的资金。

● 公园管理部门投入了很少的预算来维护河边的娱乐设施，意味着这些设施没有被适当地维护。这个假设支持了以下论点，即城市应该在今年的预算中为河边的娱乐设施投入更多资金。如果现有设施得到合理的维护，那么即使对河流在娱乐方面的使用的确会增长，可能也未必需要增加拨款。

● 河边的娱乐设施是为参加水上运动的人们设计的，而并非针对其他一些娱乐消遣。这个假设支持了以下论点，即市政府应该在今年的预算中为河边的娱乐设施投入更多资金。

● 河流的肮脏是它很少被使用的原因，并且对河流的清理将充分地增加对河流在娱乐方面的使用。（居民可能抱怨水质和气味，即使他们并不打算在河中划船、游泳或者钓鱼。）这个假设支持了以下论点，即州政府清理河流的计划会导致因水上运动而对河流的使用增加。

● 对河流的抱怨过多而且不容忽视。这个假设激发了州政府的清理河流的计划，并支持了以下论点，即因水上运动而对河流的使用肯定会增长。（可能这些抱怨只是来自很小的群体，在这种情况下清理河流可能就是对州政府资金的滥用。）

- 州政府会很快着手清理工作，因此要求对今年的预算做出调整。这个假设支持了以下论点，即市政府应该在今年的预算中为河边的娱乐设施投入更多资金。

- 清理工作的进行会使有城市设施可用的河段受益。这个假设支持了以下论点，即市政府应为河边的娱乐设施投入更多资金。

- 如果对娱乐设施的需求增长，市政府就应该在维护娱乐设施方面投入更多的关注。

- 城市应该资助这个新项目，而不是其他一些（公共或私人的）机构或群体。

  如果上述任何一个假设被证明是无根据的，那么这将意味着：

- 论证的逻辑有偏差、无效或不合理。

- 州政府和市政府花钱是没有必要的。

Essay Responses and Reader Commentary

Score 6 Response *

While it may be true that the Mason City government ought to devote more money to riverside recreational facilities, this author's argument does not make a cogent case for increased resources based on river use. It is easy to understand why city residents would want a cleaner river, but this argument is rife with holes and assumptions, and thus, not strong enough to lead to increased funding.

Citing surveys of city residents, the author reports city resident's love of water sports. It is not clear, however, the scope and validity of that survey. For example, the survey could have asked residents if they prefer using the river for water sports or would like to see a hydroelectric dam built, which may have swayed residents toward river sports. The sample may not have been representative of city residents, asking only those residents who live upon the river. The survey may have been 10 pages long, with 2 questions dedicated to river sports. We just do not know. Unless the survey is fully representative, valid, and reliable, it can not be used to effectively back the author's argument.

Additionally, the author implies that residents do not use the river for swimming, boating, and fishing, despite their professed interest, because the water is polluted and smelly. While a polluted, smelly river would likely cut down on river sports, a concrete connection between the resident's lack of river use and the river's current state is not effectively made. Though there have been complaints, we do not know if there have been numerous complaints from a wide range of people, or perhaps from one or two individuals who made numerous complaints. To strengthen his/her argument, the author would benefit from implementing a normed survey asking a wide range of residents why they do not currently use the river.

Building upon the implication that residents do not use the river due to the quality of the river's water and the smell, the author suggests that a river clean up will result in increased river usage. If the river's water quality and smell result from problems which can be cleaned, this may be true. For example, if the decreased water quality

_____

*All responses in this publication are reproduced exactly as written, including errors, misspellings, etc., if any.

and aroma is caused by pollution by factories along the river, this conceivably could be remedied. But if the quality and aroma results from the natural mineral deposits in the water or surrounding rock, this may not be true. There are some bodies of water which emit a strong smell of sulphur due to the geography of the area. This is not something likely to be afffected by a clean-up. Consequently, a river clean up may have no impact upon river usage. Regardless of whether the river's quality is able to be improved or not, the author does not effectively show a connection between water quality and river usage.

A clean, beautiful, safe river often adds to a city's property values, leads to increased tourism and revenue from those who come to take advantage of the river, and a better overall quality of life for residents. For these reasons, city government may decide to invest in improving riverside recreational facilities. However, this author's argument is not likely significantly persuade the city goverment to allocate increased funding.

Reader Commentary

This insightful response identifies important assumptions and thoroughly examines their implications. The proposal to spend more on riverside recreational facilities rests on a number of questionable assumptions, namely that:

- The survey provides a reliable basis for budget planning;
- The river's pollution and odor are the only reasons for its limited recreational use;
- Efforts to clean the water and remove the odor will be successful.

By showing that each assumption is highly suspect, this essay demonstrates the weakness of the entire argument. For example, paragraph 2 points out that the survey might not have used a representative sample, might have offered limited choices, and might have contained very few questions on water sports. Paragraph 3 examines the tenuous connection between complaints and limited use of the river for recreation. Complaints about water quality and odor may be coming from only a few people, and even if such complaints are numerous, other completely different factors may be much more significant in reducing river usage. Finally, paragraph 4 explains that certain geologic features may prevent effective river cleanup. Details such as these provide compelling support.

In addition, careful organization insures that each new point builds upon the previous ones. Note, for example, the clear transitions at the beginning of paragraphs 3 and 4, as well as the logical sequence of sentences within paragraphs (specifically paragraph 4).

Although this essay does contain minor errors, it still conveys ideas fluently. Note the effective word choices (e.g., "rife with...assumptions" and "may have swayed residents"). In addition, sentences are not merely varied; they also display skillful embedding of subordinate elements. Note, for example, the sustained parallelism in the first sentence of the concluding paragraph.

Since this response offers a cogent examination of the argument and also conveys meaning skillfully, it earns a score of 6.

Score 5 Response

The author of this proposal to increase the budget for Mason City riverside recreational facilities offers an interesting argument but to move forward on the proposal would definitely require more information and thought. While the correlations stated are logical and probable, there may be hidden factors that prevent the City from diverting resources to this project.

For example, consider the survey rankings among Mason City residents. The thought is that such high regard for water sports will translate into usage. But, survey responses can hardly be used as indicators of actual behavior. Many surveys conducted after the winter holidays reveal people who list exercise and weight loss as a top priority. Yet every profession does not equal a new gym membership. Even the wording of the survey results remain ambiguous and vague. While water sports may be among the residents' favorite activities, this allows for many other favorites. What remains unknown is the priorities of the general public. Do they favor these water sports above a softball field or soccer field? Are they willing to sacrifice the municipal golf course for better riverside facilities? Indeed the survey hardly provides enough information to discern future use of improved facilities.

Closely linked to the surveys is the bold assumption that a cleaner river will result in increased usage. While it is not illogical to expect some increase, at what level will people begin to use the river? The answer to this question requires a survey to find out the reasons our residents use or do not use the river. Is river water quality the primary limiting factor to usage or the lack of docks and piers? Are people more interested in water sports than the recreational activities that they are already engaged in? These questions will help the city government forecast how much river usage will increase and to assign a proportional increase to the budget.

Likewise, the author is optimistic regarding the state promise to clean the river. We need to hear the source of the voices and consider any ulterior motives. Is this a campaign year and the plans a campaign promise from the state representative? What is the timeline for the clean-up effort? Will the state fully fund this project? We can imagine the misuse of funds in renovating the riverside facilities only to watch the new buildings fall into dilapidation while the state drags the river clean-up.

Last, the author does not consider where these additional funds will be diverted from. The current budget situation must be assessed to determine if this increase can be afforded. In a sense, the City may not be willing to draw money away from other key projects from road improvements to schools and education. The author naively assumes that the money can simply appear without forethought on where it will come from.

Examining all the various angles and factors involved with improving riverside recreational facilities, the argument does not justify increasing the budget. While the proposal does highlight a possibility, more information is required to warrant any action.

Reader Commentary

Each paragraph in the body of this perceptive essay identifies and examines an unstated assumption that is crucial to the argument. The major assumptions discussed are:

● That a survey can accurately predict behavior,
● That cleaning the river will, in itself, increase recreational usage,
● That state plans to clean the river will actually be realized,
● That Mason City can afford to spend more on riverside recreational facilities.

Support within each paragraph is both thoughtful and thorough. Paragraph 2, for example, points out vagueness in the wording of the survey: Even if water sports rank among the favorite recreational activities of Mason City residents, other sports may still be much more popular. Thus, if the first assumption proves unwarranted, the argument to fund riverside facilities—rather than soccer fields or golf courses—becomes much weaker. Paragraph 4 considers several reasons why river cleanup plans may not be successful (the plans may be nothing more than campaign promises, or funding may not be adequate). Thus, the weakness of the third assumption undermines the argument that river recreation will increase and riverside improvements will be needed at all.

Instead of dismissing each assumption in isolation, this response places them in a logical order and considers their connections. Note the appropriate transitions between and within paragraphs, clarifying the links among the assumptions (e.g., "Closely linked to the surveys…" or "The answer to this question requires…").

Along with strong development, this response also displays facility with language. Minor errors in punctuation are present, but word choices are apt and sentences suitably varied in pattern and length. The response uses a number of rhetorical questions, but the implied answers are always clear enough to support the points being made.

Thus, the response satisfies all requirements for a score of 5, but its development is not thorough or compelling enough for a 6.

Score 4 Response

> The problem with the arguement is the assumption that if the Mason River were cleaned up, that people would use it for water sports and recreation. This is not necessarily true, as people may rank water sports among their favorite recreational activities, but that does not mean that those same people have the financial ability, time or equipment to pursue those interests.
>
> However, even if the writer of the arguement is correct in assuming that the Mason River will be used more by the city's residents, the arguement does not say why the recreational facilities need more money. If recreational facilities already exist along the Mason River, why should the city allot more money to fund them? If the recreational facilities already in existence will be used more in the coming years, then they will be making more money for themselves, eliminating the need for the city government to devote more money to them.
>
> According to the arguement, the reason people are not using the Mason River for water sports is because of the smell and the quality of water, not because the recreational facilities are unacceptable.
>
> If the city government alloted more money to the recreational facilities, then the budget is being cut from some other important city project. Also, if the assumptions proved unwarranted, and more people did not use the river for recreation, then much money has been wasted, not only the money for the recreational facilities, but also the money that was used to clean up the river to attract more people in the first place.

Reader Commentary

This competent response identifies some important unstated assumptions:

- That cleaning up the Mason River will lead to increased recreational use,
- That existing facilities along the river need more funding.

Paragraph 1 offers reasons why the first assumption is questionable (e.g., residents may not have the necessary time or money for water sports). Similarly, paragraphs 2 and 3 explain that riverside recreational facilities may already be adequate and may, in fact, produce additional income if usage increases. Thus, the response is adequately developed and satisfactorily organized to show how the argument depends on questionable assumptions.

This essay does not, however, rise to a score of 5 because it fails to consider several other unstated assumptions (e.g., that the survey is reliable or that the efforts to clean the river will be successful). Furthermore, the final paragraph makes some extraneous, unsupported assertions of its own. Mason City may actually have a budget surplus so that cuts to other projects will not be necessary, and cleaning the river may provide other real benefits even if it is not used more for water sports.

This response is generally free of errors in grammar and usage and displays sufficient control of language to support a score of 4.

Score 3 Response

> Surveys are created to speak for the people; however, surveys do not always speak for the whole community. A survey completed by Mason City residents concluded that the residents enjoy water sports as a form of recreation. If that is so evident, why has the river not been used? The blame can not be soley be placed on the city park department. The city park department can only do as much as they observe. The real issue is not the residents use of the river, but their desire for a more pleasant smell and a more pleasant sight. If the city government cleans the river, it might take years for the smell to go away. If the budget is changed to accomodate the clean up of the Mason River, other problems will arise. The residents will then begin to complain about other issues in their city that will be ignored because of the great emphasis being placed on Mason River. If more money is taken out of the budget to clean the river an assumption can be made. This assumption is that the budget for another part of city maintenance or building will be tapped into to. In addition, to the budget being used to clean up Mason River, it will also be allocated in increasing riverside recreational facilites. The government is trying to appease its residents, and one can warrant that the role of the government is to please the people. There are many assumptions being made; however, the government can not make the assumption that people want the river to be cleaned so that they can use it for recreational water activities. The government has to realize the long term effects that their decision will have on the monetary value of their budget.

Reader Commentary

Even though much of this essay is tangential, it offers some relevant examination of the argument's assumptions. The early sentences mention a questionable assumption (that the survey results are reliable) but do not explain how the survey might have been flawed. Then the response drifts to irrelevant matters—a defense of the city park department, a prediction of budget problems, and the problem of pleasing city residents. Some statements even introduce unwarranted assumptions that are not part of the original argument (e.g., "The residents will then begin to complain about other issues," and "This assumption is that the budget for another part of city maintenance or building will be tapped into."). Near the end, the response does correctly note that city government should not assume that residents want to use the river for recreation. Hence, the proposal to increase funding for riverside recreational facilities may not be justified.

In summary, the language in this response is reasonably clear, but its examination of unstated assumptions remains limited, and therefore the essay earns a score of 3.

Score 2 Response

> This statement looks like logical, but there are some wrong sentences in it which is not logical.
>
> First, this statement mentions raking water sports as their favorite recreational activities at the first sentence. However, it seems to have a ralation between the first sentence and the setence which mentions that increase the quality of the river's water and the river's smell. This is a wrong cause and result to solve the problem.
>
> Second, as a reponse to the complaints from residents, the state plan to clean up the river. As a result, the state expects that water sports will increase. When you look at two sentences, the result is not appropriate for the cause.
>
> Third, the last statement is the conclusion. However, even though residents rank water sports, the city government might devote the budget to another issue. This statement is also a wrong cause and result.
>
> In summary, the statement is not logical because there are some errors in it. The supporting setences are not strong enough to support this issue.

Reader Commentary

Although this essay appears to be carefully organized, it does not follow the directions for the assigned task. In his/her vague references to causal fallacies, the writer attempts logical analysis but never refers explicitly or implicitly to any unusual assumptions. Furthermore, several errors in grammar and sentence structure interfere with meaning (e.g., "This statement looks like logical, but there are some wrong sentences in it which is not logical.").

Because this response "does not follow the directions for the assigned task" (see the Argument Scoring Guide, pages 39–40) and contains errors in sentence structure and logical development, it earns a score of 2.

Score 1 Response

> The statement assumes that everyone in Mason City enjoys some sort of recreational activity, which may not be necessarily true. They statement also assumes that if the state cleans up the river, the use of the river for water sports will definitely increase.

Reader Commentary

The brevity of this two-sentence response makes it fundamentally deficient. Sentence one states an assumption that is actually not present in the argument, and sentence two correctly states an assumption but provides no discussion of its implications. Although the response may begin to address the assigned task, it offers no development. As such, it clearly "provides little evidence of the ability to develop an organized response (i.e., is disorganized and/or extremely brief)" (see Argument Scoring Guide, pages 39–40) and should earn a score of 1.

GRE Scoring Guide: Analyze an Issue

Score 6

In addressing the specific task directions, a 6 response presents a cogent, well-articulated analysis of the issue and conveys meaning skillfully.

A typical response in this category
- articulates a clear and insightful position on the issue in accordance with the assigned task
- develops the position fully with compelling reasons and/or persuasive examples
- sustains a well-focused, well-organized analysis, connecting ideas logically
- conveys ideas fluently and precisely, using effective vocabulary and sentence variety
- demonstrates superior facility with the conventions of standard written English (i.e., grammar, usage, and mechanics) but may have minor errors

Score 5

In addressing the specific task directions, a 5 response presents a generally thoughtful, well-developed analysis of the issue and conveys meaning clearly.

A typical response in this category
- presents a clear and well-considered position on the issue in accordance with the assigned task
- develops the position with logically sound reasons and/or well-chosen examples
- is focused and generally well organized, connecting ideas appropriately
- conveys ideas clearly and well, using appropriate vocabulary and sentence variety
- demonstrates facility with the conventions of standard written English but may have minor errors

Score 4

In addressing the specific task directions, a 4 response presents a competent analysis of the issue and conveys meaning with acceptable clarity.

A typical response in this category
- presents a clear position on the issue in accordance with the assigned task
- develops the position with relevant reasons and/or examples
- is adequately focused and organized
- demonstrates sufficient control of language to express ideas with acceptable clarity
- generally demonstrates control of the conventions of standard written English but may have some errors

Score 3

A 3 response demonstrates some competence in addressing the specific task directions, in analyzing the issue, and in conveying meaning but is obviously flawed.

A typical response in this category exhibits ONE OR MORE of the following characteristics:

- is vague or limited in addressing the specific task directions and/or in presenting or developing a position on the issue
- is weak in the use of relevant reasons or examples or relies largely on unsupported claims
- is limited in focus and/or organization
- has problems in language and sentence structure that result in a lack of clarity
- contains occasional major errors or frequent minor errors in grammar, usage, or mechanics that can interfere with meaning

Score 2

A 2 response largely disregards the specific task directions and/or demonstrates serious weaknesses in analytical writing.

A typical response in this category exhibits ONE OR MORE of the following characteristics:

- is unclear or seriously limited in addressing the specific task directions and/or in presenting or developing a position on the issue
- provides few, if any, relevant reasons or examples in support of its claims
- is poorly focused and/or poorly organized
- has serious problems in language and sentence structure that frequently interfere with meaning
- contains serious errors in grammar, usage, or mechanics that frequently obscure meaning

Score 1

A 1 response demonstrates fundamental deficiencies in analytical writing.

A typical response in this category exhibits ONE OR MORE of the following characteristics:

- provides little or no evidence of understanding the issue
- provides little evidence of the ability to develop an organized response (e.g., is disorganized and/or extremely brief)
- has severe problems in language and sentence structure that persistently interfere with meaning
- contains pervasive errors in grammar, usage, or mechanics that result in incoherence

Score 0

Off topic (i.e., provides no evidence of an attempt to respond to the assigned topic), is in a foreign language, merely copies the topic, consists of only keystroke characters, or is illegible or nonverbal.

GRE Scoring Guide: Analyze an Argument

Score 6

In addressing the specific task directions, a 6 response presents a cogent, well-articulated examination of the argument and conveys meaning skillfully.

A typical response in this category
- clearly identifies aspects of the argument relevant to the assigned task and examines them insightfully
- develops ideas cogently, organizes them logically, and connects them with clear transitions
- provides compelling and thorough support for its main points
- conveys ideas fluently and precisely, using effective vocabulary and sentence variety
- demonstrates superior facility with the conventions of standard written English (i.e., grammar, usage, and mechanics) but may have minor errors

Score 5

In addressing the specific task directions, a 5 response presents a generally thoughtful, well-developed examination of the argument and conveys meaning clearly.

A typical response in this category
- clearly identifies aspects of the argument relevant to the assigned task and examines them in a generally perceptive way
- develops ideas clearly, organizes them logically, and connects them with appropriate transitions
- offers generally thoughtful and thorough support for its main points
- conveys ideas clearly and well, using appropriate vocabulary and sentence variety
- demonstrates facility with the conventions of standard written English but may have minor errors

Score 4

In addressing the specific task directions, a 4 response presents a competent examination of the argument and conveys meaning with acceptable clarity.

A typical response in this category
- identifies and examines aspects of the argument relevant to the assigned task but may also discuss some extraneous points
- develops and organizes ideas satisfactorily but may not connect them with transitions
- supports its main points adequately but may be uneven in its support
- demonstrates sufficient control of language to convey ideas with acceptable clarity
- generally demonstrates control of the conventions of standard written English but may have some errors

Score 3

A 3 response demonstrates some competence in addressing the specific task directions, in examining the argument, and in conveying meaning but is obviously flawed.

A typical response in this category exhibits ONE OR MORE of the following characteristics:

- does not identify or examine most of the aspects of the argument relevant to the assigned task, although some relevant examination of the argument is present
- mainly discusses tangential or irrelevant matters, or reasons poorly
- is limited in the logical development and organization of ideas
- offers support of little relevance and value for its main points
- has problems in language and sentence structure that result in a lack of clarity
- contains occasional major errors or frequent minor errors in grammar, usage, or mechanics that can interfere with meaning

Score 2

A 2 response largely disregards the specific task directions and/or demonstrates serious weaknesses in analytical writing.

A typical response in this category exhibits ONE OR MORE of the following characteristics:

- does not present an examination based on logical analysis, but may instead present the writer's own views on the subject
- does not follow the directions for the assigned task
- does not develop ideas, or is poorly organized and illogical
- provides little, if any, relevant or reasonable support for its main points
- has serious problems in language and sentence structure that frequently interfere with meaning
- contains serious errors in grammar, usage, or mechanics that frequently obscure meaning

Score 1

A 1 response demonstrates fundamental deficiencies in analytical writing.

A typical response in this category exhibits ONE OR MORE of the following characteristics:

- provides little or no evidence of understanding the argument
- provides little evidence of the ability to develop an organized response (e.g., is disorganized and/or extremely brief)
- has severe problems in language and sentence structure that persistently interfere with meaning
- contains pervasive errors in grammar, usage, or mechanics that result in incoherence

Score 0

Off topic (i.e., provides no evidence of an attempt to respond to the assigned topic), is in a foreign language, merely copies the topic, consists of only keystroke characters, or is illegible, or nonverbal.

Score Level Descriptions

Although the GRE Analytical Writing measure contains two discrete analytical writing tasks, a single combined score is reported because it is more reliable than is a score for either task alone. The reported score, the average of the scores for the two tasks, ranges from 0 to 6, in half-point increments.

The statements below describe, for each score level, the overall quality of critical thinking and analytical writing demonstrated across both the Issue and Argument tasks. The Analytical Writing section is designed to assess both critical thinking skills and writing ability. Thus, many aspects of analytical writing, including reasoning skills, organization, and degree of control of the conventions of standard written English are taken into consideration in the determination of a final score. For a full description of how these criteria are used to assess essay responses, please refer to the scoring guides for the Issue and Argument tasks, which are available on the GRE website at **www.ets.org/gre/revised/scoreguides**.

Scores 6 and 5.5: Sustains insightful, in-depth analysis of complex ideas; develops and supports main points with logically compelling reasons and/or highly persuasive examples; is well focused and well organized; skillfully uses sentence variety and precise vocabulary to convey meaning effectively; demonstrates superior facility with sentence structure and language usage but may have minor errors that do not interfere with meaning.

Scores 5 and 4.5: Provides generally thoughtful analysis of complex ideas; develops and supports main points with logically sound reasons and/or well-chosen examples; is generally focused and well organized; uses sentence variety and vocabulary to convey meaning clearly; demonstrates good control of sentence structure and language usage but may have minor errors that do not interfere with meaning.

Scores 4 and 3.5: Provides competent analysis of ideas; develops and supports main points with relevant reasons and/or examples; is adequately organized; conveys meaning with reasonable clarity; demonstrates satisfactory control of sentence structure and language usage but may have some errors that affect clarity.

Scores 3 and 2.5: Displays some competence in analytical writing, although the writing is flawed in at least one of the following ways: limited analysis or development; weak organization; weak control of sentence structure or language usage, with errors that often result in vagueness or lack of clarity.

Scores 2 and 1.5: Displays serious weaknesses in analytical writing. The writing is seriously flawed in at least one of the following ways: serious lack of analysis or development; lack of organization; serious and frequent problems in sentence structure or language usage, with errors that obscure meaning.

Scores 1 and 0.5: Displays fundamental deficiencies in analytical writing. The writing is fundamentally flawed in at least one of the following ways: content that is extremely confusing or mostly irrelevant to the assigned tasks; little or no development; severe and pervasive errors that result in incoherence.

Score 0: The examinee's analytical writing skills cannot be evaluated because the responses do not address any part of the assigned tasks, are merely attempts to copy the assignments, are in a foreign language, or display only indecipherable text.

Score NS: The examinee produced no text whatsoever.

3 GRE® Verbal Reasoning

Overview of the Verbal Reasoning Measure

Verbal Reasoning（文字推理）测试考查考生的多方面能力，包括分析和评估文字材料，整合从文字材料中获得的信息，分析句子成分之间的关系，以及识别单词和概念之间的关系。

Verbal Reasoning测试会以几种不同的形式出现，下文将逐一进行详细讲解。大约一半的题目要求考生阅读一段或几段文字，然后回答与所阅读段落相关的问题。另一半题目要求考生阅读、理解并完成给出的句子、句群或段落。很多题目（但并非全部）是标准的单项选择题，要求选出一个正确选项；另有一些题目要求选出多个正确选项；还有一些题目则要求考生从段落中选出一个句子。选项的数量因题型而异。

Verbal Reasoning Question Types

Verbal Reasoning测试包含三种题型：

- Reading Comprehension（阅读理解）

- Text Completion（段落完形填空）

- Sentence Equivalence（同义句填空）

接下来，考生将逐一了解上述题型，并且学习解答这些题型的策略。

Reading Comprehension Questions

Reading Comprehension旨在测试考生多方面的能力，这些能力是他们阅读和理解研究生学习阶段经常会遇到的材料所必需的。这些能力包括：

- 理解单个词语的含义

- 理解单个句子的含义

- 理解段落以及篇幅更长的文本的含义

- 区分主要观点和次要观点

- 概括文章大意

- 从所给信息得出结论

- 根据不完整数据推导未知信息

- 理解文章结构，把握段落之间的联系

- 明确作者的视角

- 明确作者的假设

- 分析文本并得出结论

- 评估优点和缺点

- 得出并评估替代性解释

正如上述列表所示，阅读并理解一个文本远远不只是对其所包含的字与句的消极阅读。还需要积极地深入文本，提出问题，形成并评估假设，思考某特定文本与其他文本和信息间的关系。

阅读理解题目都是基于一篇文章，该文章的长度从一个段落到多个段落不等。每次考试约有10篇文章，大多数文章都只有一个段落，只有1~2篇文章包含多个段落。阅读文章题材广泛，涵盖物理学、生物学、社会科学、艺术和人文等学科以及日常话题，源于各类学术性以及非学术性书籍和期刊。

一般而言，考试中约一半的题目都是基于文章提出的，针对某一篇文章提出的问题的数量从一个到六个不等。问题会涉及上表列出的任何一种类型，从理解特定单词的含义到评估可能会支持或削弱文中观点的证据。很多题目（但并非全部）是标准的单项选择题，要求选出一个正确选项；另有一些题目要求选出多个正确选项；还有一些题目则要求考生从段落中选出一个句子。下文将详细讲解这些题型，考生必须熟悉它们之间的区别。

General Advice

阅读文章选自许多不同学科，来源广泛，考生在考场上可能会遇到极不熟悉的阅读材料。遇到这种情况不要感到沮丧，因为所有问题都围绕着文章所提供的信息，在回答问题时并不需要依靠文章以外的知识。但是如果在考场上遇到特别困难或陌生的文章，考生可以先做别的部分，最后再来处理这篇文章。

- 在回答问题前仔细阅读并分析文章，注意那些能帮助理解文中没有明确表达出来的内容的线索。

  - 注意将主要论点和支持性论点与论据区分开来。
  - 注意区分作者自己提出的观点和复述他人的观点。
  - 与上一条类似，注意区分作者极力提倡的观点和作者只是作为假设和推测而提出的观点。
  - 注意识别观点之间的主要过渡。
  - 注意识别不同观点之间的关系。例如：
    ——它们是相反的还是一致的？
    ——其中一个对另一个起支持作用吗？
    ——其中一个对另一个进行详细的阐释吗？
    ——其中一个是对另一个在具体情境中的应用吗？

- 仔细阅读每一个问题，确保正确理解问题。

- 基于文中信息回答每一个问题，不要借助文章之外的信息。有时候个人观点可能会和文中观点发生冲突；在这种情况下，一定要在文章所营造的上下文语境中回答问题。在考试中，你无需与阅读文章中的任何内容持同样的看法。

Reading Comprehension Multiple-choice Questions: Select One Answer Choice

Description

这是传统的单项选择题，考生需要从五个选项中选择正确的一项。

答题技巧

- 作出选择之前阅读所有选项，即使你已经事先知道了答案。
- 切忌被部分正确或只部分回答了问题的选项所误导。只有最准确并且最完整地回答了问题的选项才是正确选项。还要注意，不要仅仅因为选项本身是一个正确的陈述而选择它。
- 注意上下文。在回答有关单词在文中的含义的问题时，确保选出的一项正确代表了该词在文中的用法。很多单词在不同语境中的意思大相径庭。

Reading Comprehension Multiple-choice Questions: Select One or More Answer Choices

Description

这类问题提供了三个选项，要求考生选出所有正确的选项；可能有一个、两个选项正确，也可能三个选项都正确。只有选出所有正确选项才能得分，部分正确不能得分。这类问题的标志是选项旁边有正方块图形，而不是圆形或椭圆形。

> **答题技巧**
>
> - 单独判断每个选项的正确性。在评估一个选项时，不要考虑其他选项。
> - 确保选出的选项准确并完整地回答了问题。切忌被部分正确或只部分回答了问题的选项所误导。还要注意，不要仅仅因为选项本身是一个正确的陈述而选择它。
> - 当考生认为三个选项都正确时，不要感到困惑。这类问题确实存在三个选项都正确的情况。

Reading Comprehension Questions: Select-in-Passage

Description

这类问题要求考生在文章中选出一个满足题目要求的句子。回答此类问题时，需要在文章中选中一个句子并点击它；被点击的部分呈高亮显示。在篇幅较长的文章中，这类问题通常会出现在特定的一两个段落，目标段落以箭头（→）标示；在这种情况下，点击文中其他位置的句子不会产生高亮显示的效果。

注意： 回答此类问题要求使用计算机，因此GRE笔考中没有此类问题，取而代之的是类似的多项选择题。

> **答题技巧**
>
> - 在作出选择前，仔细地单独判断文中每个相关的句子。不要考虑指定段落之外的任何句子。
> - 不要选择只满足题目部分要求的句子。正确的选项必须完全符合题目的要求。但需要注意的是，题目的描述并不一定是完整的，也就是说，题目不一定充分描述了句子的所有方面。

Sample Question Set

Reviving the practice of using elements of popular music in classical composition, an approach that had been in hibernation in the United States during the 1960s, composer Philip Glass (born 1937) embraced the ethos of popular music in his compositions. Glass based two symphonies on music by rock musicians David Bowie and Brian Eno, but the symphonies' sound is distinctively his. Popular elements do not appear out of place in Glass's classical music, which from its early days has shared certain harmonies and rhythms with rock music. Yet this use of popular elements has not made Glass a composer of popular music. His music is not a version of popular music packaged to attract classical listeners; it is high art for listeners steeped in rock rather than the classics.

Select only one answer choice.

1. The passage addresses which of the following issues related to Glass's use of popular elements in his classical compositions?
   - (A) How it is regarded by listeners who prefer rock to the classics
   - (B) How it has affected the commercial success of Glass's music
   - (C) Whether it has contributed to a revival of interest among other composers in using popular elements in their compositions
   - (D) Whether it has had a detrimental effect on Glass's reputation as a composer of classical music
   - (E) Whether it has caused certain of Glass's works to be derivative in quality

Consider each of the three choices separately and select all that apply.

2. The passage suggests that Glass's work displays which of the following qualities?
   - [A] A return to the use of popular music in classical compositions
   - [B] An attempt to elevate rock music to an artistic status more closely approximating that of classical music
   - [C] A long-standing tendency to incorporate elements from two apparently disparate musical styles

3. Select the sentence that distinguishes two ways of integrating rock and classical music.

Explanation

The passage describes in general terms how Philip Glass uses popular music in his classical compositions and explores how Glass can do this without being imitative. Note that there are no opposing views discussed; the author is simply presenting his or her views.

Question 1: One of the important points that the passage makes is that when Glass uses popular elements in his music, the result is very much his own creation (it is "distinctively his"). In other words, the music is far from being derivative. Thus one issue that the passage addresses is the one referred to in answer **Choice E**—it answers it in the negative. The passage does not discuss the impact of Glass's use of popular elements on listeners, on the commercial success of his music, on other composers, nor on Glass's reputation, so none of Choices A through D is correct.

The correct answer is **Choice E.**

Question 2: To answer this question, it is important to assess each answer choice independently. Since the passage says that Glass revived the use of popular music in classical compositions, answer **Choice A** is clearly correct. On the other hand, the passage also denies that Glass composes popular music or packages it in a way to elevate its status, so answer Choice B is incorrect. Finally, since Glass's style has always mixed elements of rock with classical elements, **Choice C** is correct.

Thus the correct answer is **Choice A** and **Choice C.**

Question 3: Almost every sentence in the passage refers to incorporating rock music in classical compositions, but only the last sentence distinguishes two ways of doing so. It distinguishes between writing rock music in a way that will make it attractive to classical listeners and writing classical music that will be attractive to listeners familiar with rock.

Thus the correct answer is **the last sentence of the passage.**

Text Completion Questions

Description

正如前文所述，出色的考生并不只是吸收字面信息；相反，他们始终保持着阐释和评估的态度，对已阅读的内容展开推理，形成一幅整体画面，并且在阅读过程中根据新获得的信息不断修正这幅画面。Text Completion通过遗漏较短篇章中的关键词来考查考生的这种能力，它要求考生根据篇章中的现有信息选择合适的单词或短语填入空格，从而形成一个连贯的、有意义的整体。

Question Structure

● 由1~5个句子组成的短文

● 1~3个空格

● 每个空格有3个选项（如果只有1个空格，则有5个选项）

● 每个空格的选项是独立发挥作用的；也就是说，一个空格的选项选择不影响另一个空格的选项选择

● 每个空格只有一个正确选项；全部空格选出正确选项才得分，部分正确不得分

答题技巧

不要仅仅考虑选项的各种可能组合；这样做既浪费时间又容易出错。相反，应借助以下方法对文本进行分析：

- 通读短文，整体把握全文。

- 找出特别重要的单词或短语，它们强调了短文的整体结构（类似although或moreover之类的词语），或者它们是理解短文内容的关键。

- 自己思考空格应该填什么词。把自己想出来的认为合适的单词或短语填入空格，然后看看选项中是否有与其类似的单词或短语。

- 没必要一定得先解决第一个空格。或许先解决其他空格更容易一些。先解决更容易解决的空格，然后看看能否完成另一个空格。如果剩余选项填入最后一个空格后都不能构成有意义的整体，那么回过头去重新做题。

- 检查选项的正确性。在完成每个空格后，检查并确保全文在逻辑上、语法上和风格上是连贯统一的。

Sample Questions

> **For each blank select one entry from the corresponding column of choices. Fill all blanks in the way that best completes the text.**

1. It is refreshing to read a book about our planet by an author who does not allow facts to be (i)_____ by politics: well aware of the political disputes about the effects of human activities on climate and biodiversity, this author does not permit them to (ii)_____ his comprehensive description of what we know about our biosphere. He emphasizes the enormous gaps in our knowledge, the sparseness of our observations, and the (iii)_____, calling attention to the many aspects of planetary evolution that must be better understood before we can accurately diagnose the condition of our planet.

Blank (i)	Blank (ii)	Blank (iii)
(A) overshadowed	(D) enhance	(G) plausibility of our hypotheses
(B) invalidated	(E) obscure	(H) certainty of our entitlement
(C) illuminated	(F) underscore	(I) superficiality of our theories

Explanation

The overall tone of the passage is clearly complimentary. To understand what the author of the book is being complimented on, it is useful to focus on the second blank.

Here, we must determine what word would indicate something that the author is praised for not permitting. The only answer choice that fits the case is "obscure," since enhancing and underscoring are generally good things to do, not things one should refrain from doing. Choosing "obscure" clarifies the choice for the first blank; the only choice that fits well with "obscure" is "overshadowed." Notice that trying to fill blank (i) without filling blank (ii) first is very hard—each choice has at least some initial plausibility. Since the third blank requires a phrase that matches "enormous gaps" and "sparseness of our observations," the best choice is "superficiality of our theories."

Thus the correct answer is **overshadowed** (Choice A), **obscure** (Choice E), and **superficiality of our theories** (Choice I).

2. Vain and prone to violence, Caravaggio could not handle success: the more his (i)_____ as an artist increased, the more (ii)_____ his life became.

Blank (i)	Blank (ii)
Ⓐ temperance	Ⓓ tumultuous
Ⓑ notoriety	Ⓔ providential
Ⓒ eminence	Ⓕ dispassionate

Explanation

In this sentence, what follows the colon must explain or spell out what precedes it. So roughly what the second part must say is that as Caravaggio became more successful, his life got more out of control. When one looks for words to fill the blanks, it becomes clear that "tumultuous" is the best fit for blank (ii), since neither of the other choices suggests being out of control. And for blank (i), the best choice is "eminence," since to increase in eminence is a consequence of becoming more successful. It is true that Caravaggio might also increase in notoriety, but an increase in notoriety as an artist is not as clear a sign of success as an increase in eminence.

Thus the correct answer is **eminence** (Choice C) and **tumultuous** (Choice D).

3. In parts of the Arctic, the land grades into the landfast ice so _____ that you can walk off the coast and not know you are over the hidden sea.

Ⓐ permanently
Ⓑ imperceptibly
Ⓒ irregularly
Ⓓ precariously
Ⓔ relentlessly

Explanation

The word that fills the blank has to characterize how the land grades into the ice in a way that explains how you can walk off the coast and over the sea without knowing it. The word that does that is "imperceptibly"; if the land grades imperceptibly into the ice, you might well not know that you had left the land. Describing the shift from land to ice as permanent, irregular, precarious, or relentless would not help to explain how you would fail to know.

Thus the correct answer is **imperceptibly** (Choice B).

Sentence Equivalence Questions

Description

与Text Completion一样，Sentence Equivalence也是考查考生利用现有的不完整信息把句子补充完整的能力，但更注重整句话的意义。此类题目题干为一个只有一个空格的句子，要求考生从六个选项中选出两个选项，这两个选项都能使这句话构成完整的连贯的句子，并且整句话有着一样的含义。

Question Structure

- 组成：
  - 一个句子
  - 一个空格
  - 六个选项
- 要求选出两个选项；全部答对才得分，部分正确不得分。
  这类问题的选项旁标有正方块图形，而不是圆形或椭圆形。

答题技巧

不要单纯地在选项中找同义词，这样很可能会被误导。主要有两个原因：第一，选项中可能含有若干对同义词，其中一些并不能使整句话意义连贯，不能成为正确选项。第二，构成正确选项的词对未必就是同义词，因为在此类问题中，最为关键的是填入两个不同的选项要能使整句话的含义一样。

- 读句子，整体把握句子。
- 找出特别重要的单词或短语，因它们强调了句子的整体结构（类似although或moreover之类的词语），或者它们是理解句子内容的关键。
- 自己思考空格应该填什么词。把自己想出来的认为合适的单词填入空格，然后看看是否有与该词含义相近的两个选项。如果只有一个选项与自己的推测类似，要灵活变通，看看有没有其他选项能填入空格并保证整句话意义连贯。
- 检查选项的正确性。在选出两个单词之后，检查并确保每个单词都能使整句话在逻辑上、语法上和风格上是连贯统一的，并且填入这两个单词，句子的含义完全一样。

Sample Questions

> **Select the <u>two</u> answer choices that, when used to complete the sentence, fit the meaning of the sentence as a whole <u>and</u> produce completed sentences that are alike in meaning.**

1. Although it does contain some pioneering ideas, one would hardly characterize the work as _____.
    - A orthodox
    - B eccentric
    - C original
    - D trifling
    - E conventional
    - F innovative

Explanation

The word "Although" is a crucial signpost here. The work contains some pioneering ideas, but apparently it is not overall a pioneering work. Thus the two words that could fill the blank appropriately are "original" and "innovative." Note that "orthodox" and "conventional" are two words that are very similar in meaning, but neither one completes the sentence sensibly.

Thus the correct answer is **original** (Choice C) and **innovative** (Choice F).

2. It was her view that the country's problems had been _____ by foreign technocrats, so that to ask for such assistance again would be counterproductive.
    - A ameliorated
    - B ascertained
    - C diagnosed
    - D exacerbated
    - E overlooked
    - F worsened

Explanation

The sentence relates a piece of reasoning, as indicated by the presence of "so that": asking for the assistance of foreign technocrats would be counterproductive because of the effects such technocrats have had already. This means that the technocrats must have bad effects; that is, they must have "exacerbated" or "worsened" the country's problems.

Thus the correct answer is **exacerbated** (Choice D) and **worsened** (Choice F).

4 GRE® Verbal Reasoning Practice Questions

Your goals for this chapter

◥ Practice answering *GRE*® Verbal Reasoning questions on your own

◥ Review answers and explanations, particularly for questions you answered incorrectly

本章包含六组GRE Verbal Reasoning（文字推理）练习题。其中三组是关于Text Completion（段落完形填空）以及Sentence Equivalence（同义句填空）的独立题目，另外三组是Reading Comprehension（阅读理解）题目。这些题目按照难度依次递增的顺序排列：前两组为简单题目，中间两组为中等难度题目，最后两组为较难题目。

最后一组练习题后附有参考答案，便于考生快速查阅。本章的最后提供每一道题目的完整解析。每一个解析均与其相对应的问题一同给出，这样，考生可以很清楚地看到问题是什么，以及不同的答案选项是什么。

通过做这些练习，考生可以提高自己的GRE Verbal Reasoning答题技巧。从简单题开始，然后到中等难度题目，最后到较难题目。在答完题后仔细阅读答案解析，尤其要注意那些自己答错的题目。现在，翻过此页，开始练习。

SET 1. Discrete Questions: Easy

> **For Questions 1 to 5, select one entry for each blank from the corresponding column of choices. Fill all blanks in the way that best completes the text.**

1. Dominant interests often benefit most from _____ of governmental interference in business, since they are able to take care of themselves if left alone.

Ⓐ intensification
Ⓑ authorization
Ⓒ centralization
Ⓓ improvisation
Ⓔ elimination

2. Kagan maintains that an infant's reactions to its first stressful experiences are part of a natural process of development, not harbingers of childhood unhappiness or _____ signs of adolescent anxiety.

Ⓐ prophetic
Ⓑ normal
Ⓒ monotonous
Ⓓ virtual
Ⓔ typical

3. An investigation that is _____ can occasionally yield new facts, even notable ones, but typically the appearance of such facts is the result of a search in a definite direction.

Ⓐ timely
Ⓑ unguided
Ⓒ consistent
Ⓓ uncomplicated
Ⓔ subjective

4. It is (i)_____ that so many portrait paintings hang in art museums, since the subject matter seems to dictate a status closer to pictures in the family photograph album than to high art. But perhaps it is the artistic skill with which the portraits are painted that (ii)_____ their presence in art museums.

Blank (i)	Blank (ii)
Ⓐ surprising	Ⓓ challenges
Ⓑ understandable	Ⓔ justifies
Ⓒ irrelevant	Ⓕ changes

5. In stark contrast to his later (i)_____, Simpson was largely (ii)_____ politics during his college years, despite the fact that the campus he attended was rife with political activity.

Blank (i)	Blank (ii)
Ⓐ activism	Ⓓ devoted to
Ⓑ apathy	Ⓔ indifferent to
Ⓒ affability	Ⓕ shaped by

For Questions 6 to 8, select the <u>two</u> answer choices that, when used to complete the sentence, fit the meaning of the sentence as a whole <u>and</u> produce completed sentences that are alike in meaning.

---

6. As my eyesight began to _____, I spent a lot of time writing about it—both poems and "eye journals"—describing what I saw as I looked out through damaged eyes.
    - A deteriorate
    - B sharpen
    - C improve
    - D decline
    - E recover
    - F adjust

7. The judge's standing in the legal community, though shaken by phony allegations of wrongdoing, emerged, at long last, _____ .
    - A unqualified
    - B undiminished
    - C undecided
    - D undamaged
    - E unresolved
    - F unprincipled

8. Modern agricultural practices have been extremely successful in increasing the productivity of major food crops, yet despite heavy use of pesticides, _____ losses to diseases and insect pests are sustained each year.
    - A incongruous
    - B reasonable
    - C significant
    - D considerable
    - E equitable
    - F fortuitous

SET 2. Reading Comprehension Questions: Easy

For each of Questions 1 to 9, select **one** answer choice unless otherwise instructed.

1. A person who agrees to serve as mediator between two warring factions at the request of both abandons by so agreeing the right to take sides later. To take sides at a later point would be to suggest that the earlier presumptive impartiality was a sham.

    The passage above emphasizes which of the following points about mediators?

    (A) They should try to form no opinions of their own about any issue that is related to the dispute.

    (B) They should not agree to serve unless they are committed to maintaining a stance of impartiality.

    (C) They should not agree to serve unless they are equally acceptable to all parties to a dispute.

    (D) They should feel free to take sides in the dispute right from the start, provided that they make their biases publicly known.

    (E) They should reserve the right to abandon their impartiality so as not to be open to the charge of having been deceitful.

Was Felix Mendelssohn (1809–1847) a great composer? On its face, the question seems absurd. One of the most gifted prodigies in the history of music, he produced his first masterpiece at sixteen. From then on, he was recognized as an artist of preternatural abilities, not only as a composer but also as a pianist and conductor. But Mendelssohn's enduring popularity has often been at odds—sometimes quite sharply—with his critical standing. Despite general acknowledgment of his genius, there has been a noticeable reluctance to rank him with, say, Schumann or Brahms. As Haggin put it, Mendelssohn, as a composer, was a "minor master . . . working on a small scale of emotion and texture."

2. Select a sentence in the passage whose function is to indicate the range of Mendelssohn's musical talents.

3. The passage suggests that anyone attempting to evaluate Mendelssohn's career must confront which of the following dichotomies?

    (A) The tension between Mendelssohn's career as a composer and his career as a pianist and conductor

    (B) The contrast between Mendelssohn's popularity and that of Schumann and Brahms

    (C) The discrepancy between Mendelssohn's popularity and his standing among critics

    (D) The inconsistency between Mendelssohn's reputation during his lifetime and his reputation since his death

    (E) The gap between Mendelssohn's prodigious musical beginnings and his decline in later years

4. It can be inferred that the "reluctance" mentioned in the passage is being ascribed to

    (A) most composers since Mendelssohn

    (B) Schumann and Brahms

    (C) the music-listening public

    (D) music critics generally

    (E) Haggin exclusively

5. The author mentions Schumann and Brahms primarily in order to

    (A) provide examples of composers who are often compared with Mendelssohn

    (B) identify certain composers who are more popular than Mendelssohn

    (C) identify composers whom Mendelssohn influenced

    (D) establish the milieu in which Mendelssohn worked

    (E) establish a standard of comparison for Mendelssohn as a composer

Questions 6 and 7 are based on the following reading passage.

While most scholarship on women's employment in the United States recognizes that the Second World War (1939–1945) dramatically changed the role of women in the workforce, these studies also acknowledge that few women remained in manufacturing jobs once men returned from the war. But in agriculture, unlike other industries where women were viewed as temporary workers, women's employment did not end with the war. Instead, the expansion of agriculture and a steady decrease in the number of male farmworkers combined to cause the industry to hire more women in the postwar years. Consequently, the 1950s saw a growing number of women engaged in farm labor, even though rhetoric in the popular media called for the return of women to domestic life.

6. It can be inferred from the passage that the manufacturing and agricultural sectors in the United States following the Second World War differed in which of the following respects?

    Ⓐ The rate of expansion in each sector
    Ⓑ The percentage of employees in each sector who were men
    Ⓒ The trend in the wages of men employed in each sector
    Ⓓ The attitude of the popular media toward the employment of women in each sector
    Ⓔ The extent to which women in each sector were satisfied with their jobs

7. Which of the following statements about women's employment in the United States during and after the Second World War is most clearly supported by the passage?

    Ⓐ Most women who joined the workforce during the Second World War wanted to return to domestic life when the war ended.
    Ⓑ The great majority of women who joined the workforce during the Second World War were employed in manufacturing jobs.
    Ⓒ The end of the Second World War was followed by a large-scale transfer of women workers from manufacturing to agriculture.
    Ⓓ The increase in women's employment that accompanied the Second World War was longer lasting in agriculture than it was in manufacturing.
    Ⓔ The popular media were more forceful in calling for women to join the workforce during the Second World War than in calling for women to return to domestic life after the war.

Since the Hawaiian Islands have never been connected to other land masses, the great variety of plants in Hawaii must be a result of the long-distance dispersal of seeds, a process that requires both a method of transport and an equivalence between the ecology of the source area and that of the recipient area.

There is some dispute about the method of transport involved. Some biologists argue that ocean and air currents are responsible for the transport of plant seeds to Hawaii. Yet the results of flotation experiments and the low temperatures of air currents cast doubt on these hypotheses. More probable is bird transport, either externally, by accidental attachment of the seeds to feathers, or internally, by the swallowing of fruit and subsequent excretion of the seeds. While it is likely that fewer varieties of plant seeds have reached Hawaii externally than internally, more varieties are known to be adapted to external than to internal transport.

8. The author of the passage is primarily concerned with

    (A) discussing different approaches biologists have taken to testing theories about the distribution of plants in Hawaii

    (B) discussing different theories about the transport of plant seeds to Hawaii

    (C) discussing the extent to which air currents are responsible for the dispersal of plant seeds to Hawaii

    (D) resolving a dispute about the adaptability of plant seeds to bird transport

    (E) resolving a dispute about the ability of birds to carry plant seeds long distances

9. The author mentions the results of flotation experiments on plant seeds (lines 7–8) most probably in order to

    (A) support the claim that the distribution of plants in Hawaii is the result of the long-distance dispersal of seeds

    (B) lend credibility to the thesis that air currents provide a method of transport for plant seeds to Hawaii

    (C) suggest that the long-distance dispersal of seeds is a process that requires long periods of time

    (D) challenge the claim that ocean currents are responsible for the transport of plant seeds to Hawaii

    (E) refute the claim that Hawaiian flora evolved independently from flora in other parts of the world

SET 3. Discrete Questions: Medium

> **For Questions 1 to 5, select one entry for each blank from the corresponding column of choices. Fill all blanks in the way that best completes the text.**

1. It comes as no surprise that societies have codes of behavior; the character of the codes, on the other hand, can often be _____ .

(A) predictable
(B) unexpected
(C) admirable
(D) explicit
(E) confusing

2. Like Béla Bartók, Ruth Crawford not only brought a composer's acumen to the notation of folk music, she also had a marked (i)_____ the task. This was clear in her agonizing over how far to try to represent the minute details of a performance in a written text, and this (ii)_____ makes her work a landmark in ethnomusicology.

Blank (i)	Blank (ii)
(A) reverence for	(D) fastidiousness
(B) detachment from	(E) didacticism
(C) curiosity about	(F) iconoclasm

3. Political advertising may well be the most (i)_____ kind of advertising: political candidates are usually quite (ii)_____, yet their campaign advertisements often hide important differences behind smoke screens of smiles and empty slogans.

Blank (i)	Blank (ii)
(A) polemical	(D) interchangeable
(B) effective	(E) dissimilar
(C) deceptive	(F) vocal

4.   Richard M. Russell said 52 percent of the nation's growth since the Second World War had (i)_____ invention. He said, (ii)_____ research, the government's greatest role in assuring continuing innovation is promoting a strong, modern patent office. "Unless we can (iii)_____ original ideas, we will not have invention," Mr. Russell said. Speculating on the state of innovation over the next century, several inventors agreed that the future lay in giving children the tools to think creatively and the motivation to invent.

Blank (i)	Blank (ii)	Blank (iii)
(A) been at the expense of	(D) in addition to restricting	(G) evaluate
(B) no bearing on	(E) aside from supporting	(H) protect
(C) come through	(F) far from exaggerating	(I) disseminate

5.   Statements presented as fact in a patent application are (i)_____ unless a good reason for doubt is found. The invention has only to be deemed "more likely than not" to work in order to receive initial approval. And, although thousands of patents are challenged in court for other reasons, no incentive exists for anyone to expend effort (ii)_____ the science of an erroneous patent. For this reason the endless stream of (iii)_____ devices will continue to yield occasional patents.

Blank (i)	Blank (ii)	Blank (iii)
(A) presumed verifiable	(D) corroborating	(G) novel
(B) carefully scrutinized	(E) advancing	(H) bogus
(C) considered capricious	(F) debunking	(I) obsolete

For Questions 6 to 8, select the <u>two</u> answer choices that, when used to complete the sentence, fit the meaning of the sentence as a whole <u>and</u> produce completed sentences that are alike in meaning.

6. Ever a demanding reader of the fiction of others, the novelist Chase was likewise often the object of _____ analyses by his contemporaries.

   - A exacting
   - B copious
   - C respectful
   - D acerbic
   - E scathing
   - F meticulous

7. Her _____ should not be confused with miserliness; as long as I have known her, she has always been willing to assist those who are in need.

   - A stinginess
   - B diffidence
   - C frugality
   - D illiberality
   - E intolerance
   - F thrift

8. A misconception frequently held by novice writers is that sentence structure mirrors thought: the more convoluted the structure, the more _____ the ideas.

   - A complicated
   - B engaged
   - C essential
   - D fanciful
   - E inconsequential
   - F involved

SET 4. Reading Comprehension Questions: Medium

> For each of Questions 1 to 9, select <u>one</u> answer choice unless otherwise instructed.

Questions 1 and 2 are based on the following reading passage.

I enjoyed *A Dream of Light & Shadow: Portraits of Latin American Women Writers* for the same reasons that, as a child, I avidly consumed women's biographies: the fascination with how the biographical details of another female's life are represented and interpreted.

A Dream offers a rich read, varied in both the lives and texts of the women portrayed, and the perspectives and styles of the sixteen essayists. Yet, as an adult, I have come to demand of any really "great" book a self-consciousness about the tenuous nature of representations of reality, a critical contextualization of florid detail, and a self-awareness of the role of ideology in our lives. In these critical senses, *A Dream* is inadequate.

For the following question, consider each of the choices separately and select all that apply.

1. The author of the passage suggests that *A Dream* falls short in which of the following respects?

   A It does not appear to recognize that representations of reality can be unreliable.

   B It seems to focus on stylistic variety at the expense of accuracy of detail.

   C It offers a wealth of detail without sufficient critical examination of that detail.

2. Which of the following best describes the function of the second sentence ("*A Dream* . . . essayists") in the context of the passage as a whole?

   Ⓐ To give examples of how *A Dream* presents fascinating portraits that display awareness of the tenuous nature of representations of reality

   Ⓑ To elaborate on how *A Dream* fulfills the author's childhood criteria for a pleasurable book

   Ⓒ To suggest that the author enjoyed *A Dream* for reasons more sophisticated than the reasons she enjoyed certain books as a child

   Ⓓ To illustrate ways in which the author finds *A Dream* to be inadequate in certain critical senses

   Ⓔ To imply that *A Dream* is too varied in focus to provide a proper contextualization of the biographical details it offers

3.   During the day in Lake Constance, the zooplankton *D. hyalina* departs for the depths where food is scarce and the water cold. *D. galeata* remains near the warm surface where food is abundant. Even though *D. galeata* grows and reproduces much faster, its population is often outnumbered by *D. hyalina*.

Which of the following, if true, would help resolve the apparent paradox presented above?

(A) The number of species of zooplankton living at the bottom of the lake is twice that of species living at the surface.

(B) Predators of zooplankton, such as whitefish and perch, live and feed near the surface of the lake during the day.

(C) In order to make the most of scarce food resources, *D. hyalina* matures more slowly than *D. galeata*.

(D) *D. galeata* clusters under vegetation during the hottest part of the day to avoid the Sun's rays.

(E) *D. galeata* produces twice as many offspring per individual in any given period of time as does *D. hyalina*.

Tocqueville, apparently, was wrong. Jacksonian America was not a fluid, egalitarian society where individual wealth and poverty were ephemeral conditions. At least so argues E. Pessen in his iconoclastic study of the very rich in the United States between 1825 and 1850.

Pessen does present a quantity of examples, together with some refreshingly intelligible statistics, to establish the existence of an inordinately wealthy class. Though active in commerce or the professions, most of the wealthy were not self-made but had inherited family fortunes. In no sense mercurial, these great fortunes survived the financial panics that destroyed lesser ones. Indeed, in several cities the wealthiest one percent constantly increased its share until by 1850 it owned half of the community's wealth. Although these observations are true, Pessen overestimates their importance by concluding from them that the undoubted progress toward inequality in the late eighteenth century continued in the Jacksonian period and that the United States was a class-ridden, plutocratic society even before industrialization.

4. According to the passage, Pessen indicates that all of the following were true of the very wealthy in the United States between 1825 and 1850 EXCEPT:

    (A) They formed a distinct upper class.

    (B) Many of them were able to increase their holdings.

    (C) Some of them worked as professionals or in business.

    (D) Most of them accumulated their own fortunes.

    (E) Many of them retained their wealth in spite of financial upheavals.

5. Which of the following best states the author's main point?

    (A) Pessen's study has overturned the previously established view of the social and economic structure of early-nineteenth-century America.

    (B) Tocqueville's analysis of the United States in the Jacksonian era remains the definitive account of this period.

    (C) Pessen's study is valuable primarily because it shows the continuity of the social system in the United States throughout the nineteenth century.

    (D) The social patterns and political power of the extremely wealthy in the United States between 1825 and 1850 are well documented.

    (E) Pessen challenges a view of the social and economic systems in the United States from 1825 to 1850, but he draws conclusions that are incorrect.

Questions 6 to 9 are based on the following reading passage.

The evolution of intelligence among early large mammals of the grasslands was due in great measure to the interaction between two ecologically synchronized groups of these animals, the hunting carnivores and the herbivores that they hunted. The interaction resulting from the differences between predator and prey led to a general improvement in brain functions; however, certain components of intelligence were improved far more than others.

The kind of intelligence favored by the interplay of increasingly smarter catchers and increasingly keener escapers is defined by attention—that aspect of mind carrying consciousness forward from one moment to the next. It ranges from a passive, free-floating awareness to a highly focused, active fixation. The range through these states is mediated by the arousal system, a network of tracts converging from sensory systems to integrating centers in the brain stem. From the more relaxed to the more vigorous levels, sensitivity to novelty is increased. The organism is more awake, more vigilant; this increased vigilance results in the apprehension of ever more subtle signals as the organism becomes more sensitive to its surroundings. The processes of arousal and concentration give attention its direction. Arousal is at first general, with a flooding of impulses in the brain stem; then gradually the activation is channeled. Thus begins concentration, the holding of consistent images. One meaning of intelligence is the way in which these images and other alertly searched information are used in the context of previous experience. Consciousness links past attention to the present and permits the integration of details with perceived ends and purposes.

The elements of intelligence and consciousness come together marvelously to produce different styles in predator and prey. Herbivores and carnivores develop different kinds of attention related to escaping or chasing. Although in both kinds of animal, arousal stimulates the production of adrenaline and norepinephrine by the adrenal glands, the effect in herbivores is primarily fear, whereas in carnivores the effect is primarily aggression. For both, arousal attunes the animal to what is ahead. Perhaps it does not experience forethought as we know it, but the animal does experience something like it. The predator is searchingly aggressive, inner-directed, tuned by the nervous system and the adrenal hormones, but aware in a sense closer to human consciousness than, say, a hungry lizard's instinctive snap at a passing beetle. Using past events as a framework, the large mammal predator is working out a relationship between movement and food, sensitive to possibilities in cold trails and distant sounds—and yesterday's unforgotten lessons. The herbivore prey is of a different mind. Its mood of wariness rather than searching and its attitude of general expectancy instead of anticipating are silk-thin veils of tranquillity over an explosive endocrine system.

6. The author refers to a hungry lizard (line 31) primarily in order to
   (A) demonstrate the similarity between the hunting methods of mammals and those of nonmammals
   (B) broaden the application of the argument by including an insectivore as an example
   (C) make a distinction between higher and lower levels of consciousness
   (D) provide an additional illustration of the brutality characteristic of predators
   (E) offer an objection to suggestions that all animals lack consciousness

7. It can be inferred from the passage that in animals less intelligent than the mammals discussed in the passage

   (A) past experience is less helpful in ensuring survival

   (B) attention is more highly focused

   (C) muscular coordination is less highly developed

   (D) there is less need for competition among species

   (E) environment is more important in establishing the proper ratio of prey to predator

8. According to the passage, improvement in brain function among early large mammals resulted primarily from which of the following?

   (A) Interplay of predator and prey

   (B) Persistence of free-floating awareness in animals of the grasslands

   (C) Gradual dominance of warm-blooded mammals over cold-blooded reptiles

   (D) Interaction of early large mammals with less intelligent species

   (E) Improvement of the capacity for memory among herbivores and carnivores

9. According to the passage, as the process of arousal in an organism continues, all of the following may occur EXCEPT

   (A) the production of adrenaline

   (B) the production of norepinephrine

   (C) a heightening of sensitivity to stimuli

   (D) an increase in selectivity with respect to stimuli

   (E) an expansion of the range of states mediated by the brain stem

SET 5. Discrete Questions: Hard

> For Questions 1 to 6, select one entry for each blank from the corresponding column of choices. Fill all blanks in the way that best completes the text.

1. For some time now, _____ has been presumed not to exist: the cynical conviction that everybody has an angle is considered wisdom.

Ⓐ rationality
Ⓑ flexibility
Ⓒ diffidence
Ⓓ disinterestedness
Ⓔ insincerity

2. Human nature and long distances have made exceeding the speed limit a (i)_____ in the state, so the legislators surprised no one when, acceding to public demand, they (ii)_____ increased penalties for speeding.

Blank (i)	Blank (ii)
Ⓐ controversial habit	Ⓓ endorsed
Ⓑ cherished tradition	Ⓔ considered
Ⓒ disquieting ritual	Ⓕ rejected

3. Serling's account of his employer's reckless decision making (i)_____ that company's image as (ii)_____ bureaucracy full of wary managers.

Blank (i)	Blank (ii)
Ⓐ belies	Ⓓ an injudicious
Ⓑ exposes	Ⓔ a disorganized
Ⓒ overshadows	Ⓕ a cautious

4. No other contemporary poet's work has such a well-earned reputation for (i)_____, and there are few whose moral vision is so imperiously unsparing. Of late, however, the almost belligerent demands of his severe and densely forbidding poetry have taken an improbable turn. This new collection is the poet's fourth book in six years—an ample output even for poets of sunny disposition, let alone for one of such (ii)_____ over the previous 50 years. Yet for all his newfound (iii)_____, his poetry is as thorny as ever.

Blank (i)	Blank (ii)	Blank (iii)
Ⓐ patent accessibility	Ⓓ penitential austerity	Ⓖ taciturnity
Ⓑ intrinsic frivolity	Ⓔ intractable prolixity	Ⓗ volubility
Ⓒ near impenetrability	Ⓕ impetuous prodigality	Ⓘ pellucidity

5. Managers who think that strong environmental performance will (i)_____ their company's financial performance often (ii)_____ claims that systems designed to help them manage environmental concerns are valuable tools. By contrast, managers who perceive environmental performance to be (iii)_____ to financial success may view an environmental management system as extraneous. In either situation, and whatever their perceptions, it is a manager's commitment to achieving environmental improvement rather than the mere presence of a system that determines environmental performance.

Blank (i)	Blank (ii)	Blank (iii)
Ⓐ eclipse	Ⓓ uncritically accept	Ⓖ complementary
Ⓑ bolster	Ⓔ appropriately acknowledge	Ⓗ intrinsic
Ⓒ degrade	Ⓕ hotly dispute	Ⓘ peripheral

6. Philosophy, unlike most other subjects, does not try to extend our knowledge by discovering new information about the world. Instead it tries to deepen our understanding through (i)_____ what is already closest to us—the experiences, thoughts, concepts, and activities that make up our lives but that ordinarily escape our notice precisely because they are so familiar. Philosophy begins by finding (ii)_____ the things that are (iii) _____.

Blank (i)	Blank (ii)	Blank (iii)
Ⓐ attainment of	Ⓓ essentially irrelevant	Ⓖ most prosaic
Ⓑ rumination on	Ⓔ utterly mysterious	Ⓗ somewhat hackneyed
Ⓒ detachment from	Ⓕ thoroughly commonplace	Ⓘ refreshingly novel

For Questions 7 to 9, select the <u>two</u> answer choices that, when used to complete the sentence, fit the meaning of the sentence as a whole <u>and</u> produce completed sentences that are alike in meaning.

7. The government's implementation of a new code of ethics appeared intended to shore up the ruling party's standing with an increasingly _____ electorate at a time when the party is besieged by charges that it trades favors for campaign money.

   A aloof
   B placid
   C restive
   D skittish
   E tranquil
   F vociferous

8. Overlarge, uneven, and ultimately disappointing, the retrospective exhibition seems too much like special pleading for a forgotten painter of real but _____ talents.

   A limited
   B partial
   C undiscovered
   D circumscribed
   E prosaic
   F hidden

9. Newspapers report that the former executive has been trying to keep a low profile since his _____ exit from the company.

   A celebrated
   B mysterious
   C long-awaited
   D fortuitous
   E indecorous
   F unseemly

SET 6. Reading Comprehension Questions: Hard

> For each of Questions 1 to 8, select <u>one</u> answer choice unless otherwise instructed.

1. In the United States between 1850 and 1880, the number of farmers continued to increase, but at a rate lower than that of the general population.

    Which of the following statements directly contradicts the information presented above?

    (A) The number of farmers in the general population increased slightly in the 30 years between 1850 and 1880.

    (B) The rate of growth of the United States labor force and the rate of growth of the general population rose simultaneously in the 30 years between 1850 and 1880.

    (C) The proportion of farmers in the United States labor force remained constant in the 30 years between 1850 and 1880.

    (D) The proportion of farmers in the United States labor force decreased from 64 percent in 1850 to 49 percent in 1880.

    (E) The proportion of farmers in the general population increased from 68 percent in 1850 to 72 percent in 1880.

2. A ten-year comparison between the United States and the Soviet Union in terms of crop yields per acre revealed that when only planted acreage is compared, Soviet yields were equal to 68 percent of United States yields. When total agricultural acreage (planted acreage plus fallow acreage) is compared, however, Soviet yield was 114 percent of United States yield.

    From the information above, which of the following can be most reliably inferred about United States and Soviet agriculture during the ten-year period?

    (A) A higher percentage of total agricultural acreage was fallow in the United States than in the Soviet Union.

    (B) The United States had more fallow acreage than planted acreage.

    (C) Fewer total acres of available agricultural land were fallow in the Soviet Union than in the United States.

    (D) The Soviet Union had more planted acreage than fallow acreage.

    (E) The Soviet Union produced a greater volume of crops than the United States produced.

For hot desert locations with access to seawater, a new greenhouse design generates freshwater and cool air. Oriented to the prevailing wind, the front wall of perforated cardboard, moistened by a trickle of seawater pumped in, cools and moistens hot air blowing in. This cool, humidified air accelerates plant growth; little water evaporates from leaves. Though greenhouses normally capture the heat of sunlight, a double-layered roof, the inner layer coated to reflect infrared light outward, allows visible sunlight in but traps solar heat between the two layers. This heated air, drawn down from the roof, then mixes with the greenhouse air as it reaches a second seawater-moistened cardboard wall at the back of the greenhouse. There the air absorbs more moisture before being cooled off again when it meets a seawater-cooled metal wall, which causes moisture in the air to condense. Thus distilled water for irrigating the plants collects.

For the following question, consider each of the choices separately and select all that apply.

3. It can be inferred that the process described in the passage makes use of which of the following?

    A The tendency of hot air to rise
    B The directional movement of wind
    C Variation in the moisture capacity of air

For the following question, consider each of the choices separately and select all that apply.

4. It can be inferred that the greenhouse roof is designed to allow for which of the following?

    A The avoidance of intense solar heat inside the greenhouse
    B The entry of sunlight into the greenhouse to make the plants grow
    C The mixture of heated air with greenhouse air to enhance the collection of moisture

Many critics of Emily Brontë's novel *Wuthering Heights* see its second part as a counterpoint that comments on, if it does not reverse, the first part, where a romantic reading receives more confirmation. Seeing the two parts as a whole is encouraged by the novel's sophisticated structure, revealed in its complex use of narrators and time shifts. Granted that the presence of these elements need not argue for an authorial awareness of novelistic construction comparable to that of Henry James, their presence does encourage attempts to unify the novel's heterogeneous parts. However, any interpretation that seeks to unify all of the novel's diverse elements is bound to be somewhat unconvincing. This is not because such an interpretation necessarily stiffens into a thesis (although rigidity in any interpretation of this or of any novel is always a danger), but because *Wuthering Heights* has recalcitrant elements of undeniable power that, ultimately, resist inclusion in an all-encompassing interpretation. In this respect, *Wuthering Heights* shares a feature of *Hamlet*.

5. According to the passage, which of the following is a true statement about the first and second parts of *Wuthering Heights*?
   Ⓐ The second part has received more attention from critics.
   Ⓑ The second part has little relation to the first part.
   Ⓒ The second part annuls the force of the first part.
   Ⓓ The second part provides less substantiation for a romantic reading.
   Ⓔ The second part is better because it is more realistic.

6. Which of the following inferences about Henry James's awareness of novelistic construction is best supported by the passage?
   Ⓐ James, more than any other novelist, was aware of the difficulties of novelistic construction.
   Ⓑ James was very aware of the details of novelistic construction.
   Ⓒ James's awareness of novelistic construction derived from his reading of Brontë.
   Ⓓ James's awareness of novelistic construction has led most commentators to see unity in his individual novels.
   Ⓔ James's awareness of novelistic construction precluded him from violating the unity of his novels.

7. The author of the passage would be most likely to agree that an interpretation of a novel should
   Ⓐ not try to unite heterogeneous elements in the novel
   Ⓑ not be inflexible in its treatment of the elements in the novel
   Ⓒ not argue that the complex use of narrators or of time shifts indicates a sophisticated structure
   Ⓓ concentrate on those recalcitrant elements of the novel that are outside the novel's main structure
   Ⓔ primarily consider those elements of novelistic construction of which the author of the novel was aware

For the following question, consider each of the choices separately and select all that apply.

8. The author of the passage suggests which of the following about *Hamlet*?

   A *Hamlet* has usually attracted critical interpretations that tend to stiffen into theses.

   B *Hamlet* has elements that are not amenable to an all-encompassing critical interpretation.

   C *Hamlet* is less open to an all-encompassing critical interpretation than is *Wuthering Heights*.

ANSWER KEY

SET 1. Discrete Questions: Easy

1. **Choice E**: elimination
2. **Choice A**: prophetic
3. **Choice B**: unguided
4. **Choice A**: surprising; **Choice E**: justifies
5. **Choice A**: activism; **Choice E**: indifferent to
6. **Choice A**: deteriorate; AND **Choice D**: decline
7. **Choice B**: undiminished; AND **Choice D**: undamaged
8. **Choice C**: significant; AND **Choice D**: considerable

SET 2. Reading Comprehension Questions: Easy

1. **Choice B**: They should not agree to serve unless they are committed to maintaining a stance of impartiality.
2. **Sentence 4**: From then on, he was recognized as an artist of preternatural abilities, not only as a composer but also as a pianist and conductor.
3. **Choice C**: The discrepancy between Mendelssohn's popularity and his standing among critics
4. **Choice D**: music critics generally
5. **Choice E**: establish a standard of comparison for Mendelssohn as a composer
6. **Choice B**: The percentage of employees in each sector who were men
7. **Choice D**: The increase in women's employment that accompanied the Second World War was longer lasting in agriculture than it was in manufacturing.
8. **Choice B**: discussing different theories about the transport of plant seeds to Hawaii
9. **Choice D**: challenge the claim that ocean currents are responsible for the transport of plant seeds to Hawaii

SET 3. Discrete Questions: Medium

1. **Choice B**: unexpected
2. **Choice A**: reverence for; **Choice D**: fastidiousness
3. **Choice C**: deceptive; **Choice E**: dissimilar
4. **Choice C**: come through; **Choice E**: aside from supporting; **Choice H**: protect
5. **Choice A**: presumed verifiable; **Choice F**: debunking; **Choice H**: bogus
6. **Choice A**: exacting; AND **Choice F**: meticulous
7. **Choice C**: frugality; AND **Choice F**: thrift
8. **Choice A**: complicated; AND **Choice F**: involved

SET 4. Reading Comprehension Questions: Medium

1. **Choice A**: It does not appear to recognize that representations of reality can be unreliable; AND **Choice C**: It offers a wealth of detail without sufficient critical examination of that detail.
2. **Choice B**: To elaborate on how *A Dream* fulfills the author's childhood criteria for a pleasurable book
3. **Choice B**: Predators of zooplankton, such as whitefish and perch, live and feed near the surface of the lake during the day.
4. **Choice D**: Most of them accumulated their own fortunes.
5. **Choice E**: Pessen challenges a view of the social and economic systems in the United States from 1825 to 1850, but he draws conclusions that are incorrect.
6. **Choice C**: make a distinction between higher and lower levels of consciousness
7. **Choice A**: past experience is less helpful in ensuring survival
8. **Choice A**: Interplay of predator and prey
9. **Choice E**: an expansion of the range of states mediated by the brain stem

SET 5. Discrete Questions: Hard

1. **Choice D**: disinterestedness
2. **Choice B**: cherished tradition; **Choice F**: rejected
3. **Choice A**: belies; **Choice F**: a cautious
4. **Choice C**: near impenetrability; **Choice D**: penitential austerity; **Choice H**: volubility
5. **Choice B**: bolster; **Choice D**: uncritically accept; **Choice I**: peripheral
6. **Choice B**: rumination on; **Choice E**: utterly mysterious; **Choice G**: most prosaic
7. **Choice C**: restive; AND **Choice D**: skittish
8. **Choice A**: limited; AND **Choice D**: circumscribed
9. **Choice E**: indecorous; AND **Choice F**: unseemly

SET 6. Reading Comprehension Questions: Hard

1. **Choice E**: The proportion of farmers in the general population increased from 68 percent in 1850 to 72 percent in 1880.
2. **Choice A**: A higher percentage of total agricultural acreage was fallow in the United States than in the Soviet Union.
3. **Choice B**: The directional movement of wind; AND **Choice C**: Variation in the moisture capacity of air.
4. **Choice A**: The avoidance of intense solar heat inside the greenhouse; AND **Choice B**: The entry of sunlight into the greenhouse to make the plants grow; AND **Choice C**: The mixture of heated air with greenhouse air to enhance the collection of moisture.
5. **Choice D**: The second part provides less substantiation for a romantic reading.
6. **Choice B**: James was very aware of the details of novelistic construction.
7. **Choice B**: not be inflexible in its treatment of the elements in the novel
8. **Choice B**: *Hamlet* has elements that are not amenable to an all-encompassing critical interpretation.

Answers and Explanations

SET 1. Discrete Questions: Easy

> **For Questions 1 to 5, select one entry for each blank from the corresponding column of choices. Fill all blanks in the way that best completes the text.**

1. Dominant interests often benefit most from _____ of governmental interference in business, since they are able to take care of themselves if left alone.

Ⓐ intensification
Ⓑ authorization
Ⓒ centralization
Ⓓ improvisation
Ⓔ elimination

Explanation

The sentence explains why dominant interests often benefit from a certain condition. Since the explanation is that they are able to take care of themselves if left alone, it follows that the condition is one in which interference is absent. Thus the best answer is "elimination." None of the other answer choices suggests an absence of interference—indeed "intensification," "authorization," and "centralization" suggest quite the opposite.

Thus the correct answer is **elimination** (Choice E).

2. Kagan maintains that an infant's reactions to its first stressful experiences are part of a natural process of development, not harbingers of childhood unhappiness or _____ signs of adolescent anxiety.

Ⓐ prophetic
Ⓑ normal
Ⓒ monotonous
Ⓓ virtual
Ⓔ typical

Explanation

The sentence contrasts the infant's reactions, part of a normal developmental process, with future unhappiness and anxiety. The missing word describes signs of adolescent anxiety as they relate to the infant. Choice A is correct: "prophetic" signs, like harbingers, foretell future occurrences, and for the infant, adolescent anxiety is a future occurrence. Since an infant cannot literally display signs of adolescent anxiety, "normal," "monotonous," and "typical" are all incorrect. And "virtual" is incorrect, because virtual signs are not real signs, and what Kagan is denying is that the infant's reactions are not real signs of later unhappiness.

Thus the correct answer is **prophetic** (Choice A).

3. An investigation that is _____ can occasionally yield new facts, even notable ones, but typically the appearance of such facts is the result of a search in a definite direction.

Ⓐ timely
Ⓑ unguided
Ⓒ consistent
Ⓓ uncomplicated
Ⓔ subjective

Explanation

As the words "can occasionally" and "but typically" indicate, the missing word describes an investigation that contrasts with a "search in a definite direction." Among the answer choices, only "unguided" provides a contrasting description; none of the other choices suggests an appropriate contrast.

Thus the correct answer is **unguided** (Choice B).

4. It is (i)_____ that so many portrait paintings hang in art museums, since the subject matter seems to dictate a status closer to pictures in the family photograph album than to high art. But perhaps it is the artistic skill with which the portraits are painted that (ii)_____ their presence in art museums.

Blank (i)	Blank (ii)
Ⓐ surprising	Ⓓ challenges
Ⓑ understandable	Ⓔ justifies
Ⓒ irrelevant	Ⓕ changes

Explanation

In the part following "since," the first sentence of the paragraph suggests that the subject matter of portraits might not seem to fit with the idea of "high art." So the suggestion is that the presence of portrait paintings in art museums is in that sense odd or unfitting. Of the choices available for Blank (i), "surprising" is the one that expresses this sense. The second sentence, in contrast to the first, offers a point in favor of portraits—"artistic skill." So the second sentence is offering a reason why portraits should be in art museums. Of the choices for Blank (ii), "justifies" is the one that completes that thought.

Thus the correct answer is **surprising** (Choice A) and **justifies** (Choice E).

5. In stark contrast to his later (i)_____, Simpson was largely (ii)_____ politics during his college years, despite the fact that the campus he attended was rife with political activity.

Blank (i)	Blank (ii)
Ⓐ activism	Ⓓ devoted to
Ⓑ apathy	Ⓔ indifferent to
Ⓒ affability	Ⓕ shaped by

Explanation

The sentence tells us that there is a contrast between the way Simpson related to politics in his college years and how he related to politics later in life. So the choices that complete the blanks must contrast with each other. The part of the sentence beginning with "despite" indicates that Simpson's relation to politics in his college years did not involve engagement in the political activity that was "rife." Of the choices for Blank (ii), only "indifferent to" conveys that nonengagement. And of the choices for Blank (i), only "activism" supplies the required contrast with "indifferent to."

Thus the correct answer is **activism** (Choice A) and **indifferent to** (Choice E).

For Questions 6 to 8, select the two answer choices that, when used to complete the sentence, fit the meaning of the sentence as a whole and produce completed sentences that are alike in meaning.

---

6. As my eyesight began to _____, I spent a lot of time writing about it—both poems and "eye journals"—describing what I saw as I looked out through damaged eyes.

    A deteriorate
    B sharpen
    C improve
    D decline
    E recover
    F adjust

Explanation

The author has "damaged" eyes, and any word that fills the blank must reflect that fact. The words that best do so are "deteriorate" and "decline" (Choices A and D), which generate sentences alike in meaning. "Sharpen" and "improve" produce sentences alike in meaning, but neither word makes sense when inserted into the blank. Though "adjust" makes some sense when inserted into the blank, no other option produces a sentence similar in meaning.

Thus the correct answer is **deteriorate** (Choice A) and **decline** (Choice D).

7. The judge's standing in the legal community, though shaken by phony allegations of wrongdoing, emerged, at long last, _____ .

    A unqualified
    B undiminished
    C undecided
    D undamaged
    E unresolved
    F unprincipled

Explanation

The use of the word "though" establishes a contrast between the blank, which requires a description of the judge's standing, and "phony allegations of wrongdoing." Thus the words that best complete the blank must indicate that the judge's reputation was not adversely affected by these allegations. The only words that do so are "undiminished" and "undamaged" (Choices B and D), which produce sentences alike in meaning. "Undecided" and "unresolved" also produce sentences alike in meaning, but neither word makes sense when inserted into the blank.

Thus the correct answer is **undiminished** (Choice B) and **undamaged** (Choice D).

8. Modern agricultural practices have been extremely successful in increasing the productivity of major food crops, yet despite heavy use of pesticides, _____ losses to diseases and insect pests are sustained each year.

   A incongruous
   B reasonable
   C significant
   D considerable
   E equitable
   F fortuitous

Explanation

The word "despite" suggests the level of losses is somehow surprising given the heavy use of pesticides. The only words that describe an appropriate level of losses are "significant" and "considerable" (Choices C and D), which produce sentences alike in meaning. "Reasonable" and "equitable" also produce sentences alike in meaning, but neither word generates the contrast necessary for the sentence to make sense.

Thus the correct answer is **significant** (Choice C) and **considerable** (Choice D).

SET 2. Reading Comprehension Questions: Easy

> **For each of Questions 1 to 9, select <u>one</u> answer choice unless otherwise instructed.**

1. A person who agrees to serve as mediator between two warring factions at the request of both abandons by so agreeing the right to take sides later. To take sides at a later point would be to suggest that the earlier presumptive impartiality was a sham.

   The passage above emphasizes which of the following points about mediators?

   (A) They should try to form no opinions of their own about any issue that is related to the dispute.
   (B) They should not agree to serve unless they are committed to maintaining a stance of impartiality.
   (C) They should not agree to serve unless they are equally acceptable to all parties to a dispute.
   (D) They should feel free to take sides in the dispute right from the start, provided that they make their biases publicly known.
   (E) They should reserve the right to abandon their impartiality so as not to be open to the charge of having been deceitful.

Explanation

By pointing out the consequences of abandoning impartiality, the paragraph points out the importance for mediators of maintaining impartiality at all times. This is the point made in **Choice B**, which is therefore the correct answer. Choice A is incorrect, because it goes further than anything asserted in the passage. The passage does not rule out the possibility that one can have an opinion about issues related to a dispute without taking sides in the actual dispute. Choice C is incorrect because it is a presupposition on which the passage is based rather than the point of the passage; that is, the fact that the mediator is acceptable to both parties is a given, since they both ask the mediator to serve. Choices D and E are both inconsistent with the main point of the passage, the importance of impartiality at all times, so both are incorrect.

Questions 2 to 5 are based on the following reading passage.

Was Felix Mendelssohn (1809–1847) a great composer? On its face, the question seems absurd. One of the most gifted prodigies in the history of music, he produced his first masterpiece at sixteen. From then on, he was recognized as an artist of preternatural abilities, not only as a composer but also as a pianist and conductor. But Mendelssohn's enduring popularity has often been at odds—sometimes quite sharply—with his critical standing. Despite general acknowledgment of his genius, there has been a noticeable reluctance to rank him with, say, Schumann or Brahms. As Haggin put it, Mendelssohn, as a composer, was a "minor master . . . working on a small scale of emotion and texture."

Description

The passage starts by outlining the popular view that Mendelssohn was a great composer and then points out that critics do not generally accord him that status.

2.   Select a sentence in the passage whose function is to indicate the range of Mendelssohn's musical talents.

Explanation

This question asks which sentence in the passage serves to indicate the range of Mendelssohn's musical talents. The correct answer is the **fourth sentence** ("From then . . . conductor"), the only sentence in the passage that mentions Mendelssohn's achievements across three different realms: composing, piano performance, and conducting. All the other sentences can be eliminated because, while they consider the question of Mendelssohn's claim to greatness, they do not specifically discuss the broad range of his musical talents.

3. The passage suggests that anyone attempting to evaluate Mendelssohn's career must confront which of the following dichotomies?

    (A) The tension between Mendelssohn's career as a composer and his career as a pianist and conductor

    (B) The contrast between Mendelssohn's popularity and that of Schumann and Brahms

    (C) The discrepancy between Mendelssohn's popularity and his standing among critics

    (D) The inconsistency between Mendelssohn's reputation during his lifetime and his reputation since his death

    (E) The gap between Mendelssohn's prodigious musical beginnings and his decline in later years

Explanation

The passage clearly presents the discrepancy between Mendelssohn's popularity and his critical standing as an interpretive problem. Therefore, **Choice C** is correct. The other answer choices are incorrect because the passage never indicates that there was any conflict among the different aspects of Mendelssohn's professional life; never discusses Schumann's and Brahms's popularity; does not discuss any differences between Mendelssohn's reputation during his lifetime and after his death; and makes no mention of a decline in Mendelssohn's later life.

4. It can be inferred that the "reluctance" mentioned in the passage is being ascribed to

    (A) most composers since Mendelssohn

    (B) Schumann and Brahms

    (C) the music-listening public

    (D) music critics generally

    (E) Haggin exclusively

Explanation

Choice D is correct. The "reluctance" is mentioned in the context of a discussion about Mendelssohn's critical standing and thus is being ascribed to music critics generally. Choices A and B can be eliminated because the passage does not discuss any composers' views of Mendelssohn. Choice C is incorrect because the word "reluctance" is mentioned only after the passage turns from discussing the popular view of Mendelssohn to the critical view. Choice E is incorrect because the words "As Haggin put it" indicate that Haggin is only one example of critics who have this reluctance.

5. The author mentions Schumann and Brahms primarily in order to

    (A) provide examples of composers who are often compared with Mendelssohn

    (B) identify certain composers who are more popular than Mendelssohn

    (C) identify composers whom Mendelssohn influenced

    (D) establish the milieu in which Mendelssohn worked

    (E) establish a standard of comparison for Mendelssohn as a composer

Explanation

Schumann and Brahms are mentioned as a way of explaining how critics rank Mendelssohn—that is, as less accomplished than some other composers who are widely acknowledged as major. Therefore, **Choice E** is correct. Choice A might look like a correct answer at first glance. However, careful consideration reveals that the point the author is making when Schumann and Brahms are mentioned is not the frequency of that comparison but the results of it. Therefore, Choice A can be eliminated. Choices B, C, and D are incorrect because the passage does not discuss Schumann's and Brahms's popularity, Mendelssohn's influence on other composers, or the milieu in which Mendelssohn worked.

Questions 6 and 7 are based on the following reading passage.

While most scholarship on women's employment in the United States recognizes that the Second World War (1939–1945) dramatically changed the role of women in the workforce, these studies also acknowledge that few women remained in manufacturing jobs once men returned from the war. But in agriculture, unlike other industries where women were viewed as temporary workers, women's employment did not end with the war. Instead, the expansion of agriculture and a steady decrease in the number of male farmworkers combined to cause the industry to hire more women in the postwar years. Consequently, the 1950s saw a growing number of women engaged in farm labor, even though rhetoric in the popular media called for the return of women to domestic life.

Description

The first sentence states that the Second World War led to significant changes in women's employment, but that these changes were largely reversed in manufacturing after the war. The second sentence discusses the fact that unlike in other industries, employment of women in agriculture was more permanent; the third provides more detail regarding the trend in agriculture and the reasons for it; and the fourth summarizes the consequences of the trend.

6. It can be inferred from the passage that the manufacturing and agricultural sectors in the United States following the Second World War differed in which of the following respects?

   (A) The rate of expansion in each sector
   (B) The percentage of employees in each sector who were men
   (C) The trend in the wages of men employed in each sector
   (D) The attitude of the popular media toward the employment of women in each sector
   (E) The extent to which women in each sector were satisfied with their jobs

Explanation

The correct choice for this question is **Choice B**. We are told that few women remained in the manufacturing sector once men returned from the war, while the number of women who worked in agriculture increased after the war as the number of men in agriculture decreased. It is therefore inferable that the percentage of employees working in manufacturing who were men increased while the percentage of employees working in agriculture who were men decreased. Choices A, C, and E are incorrect because the passage provides no information about rates of expansion, wage trends, or women's job satisfaction. Choice D is incorrect because the only mention of the popular media occurs in the final sentence, and no distinction is made between the sectors there.

7. Which of the following statements about women's employment in the United States during and after the Second World War is most clearly supported by the passage?

Ⓐ Most women who joined the workforce during the Second World War wanted to return to domestic life when the war ended.

Ⓑ The great majority of women who joined the workforce during the Second World War were employed in manufacturing jobs.

Ⓒ The end of the Second World War was followed by a large-scale transfer of women workers from manufacturing to agriculture.

Ⓓ The increase in women's employment that accompanied the Second World War was longer lasting in agriculture than it was in manufacturing.

Ⓔ The popular media were more forceful in calling for women to join the workforce during the Second World War than in calling for women to return to domestic life after the war.

Explanation

The correct choice for this question is **Choice D**. We are told in the passage that women's employment in manufacturing fell quickly after men returned from the war. However, not only did women's employment in agriculture not decline after the end of the war, it actually increased. The other choices are incorrect because the passage provides no information about what women who joined the workforce wanted to do; about the distribution of women across industries; about what happened to women who left manufacturing; nor about media appeals for women to join the wartime workforce.

Questions 8 and 9 are based on the following reading passage.

Since the Hawaiian Islands have never been connected to other land masses, the great variety of plants in Hawaii must be a result of the long-distance dispersal of seeds, a process that requires both a method of transport and an equivalence between the ecol-
line ogy of the source area and that of the recipient area.
5   There is some dispute about the method of transport involved. Some biologists argue that ocean and air currents are responsible for the transport of plant seeds to Hawaii. Yet the results of flotation experiments and the low temperatures of air currents cast doubt on these hypotheses. More probable is bird transport, either externally, by accidental attachment of the seeds to feathers, or internally, by the
10   swallowing of fruit and subsequent excretion of the seeds. While it is likely that fewer varieties of plant seeds have reached Hawaii externally than internally, more varieties are known to be adapted to external than to internal transport.

Description

The passage raises the question of how seeds reached the Hawaiian Islands. It introduces one possible method—ocean and air currents—but refers to evidence that casts doubt on that method. It then introduces a second method—bird transport—and discusses two ways in which that might occur.

8.   The author of the passage is primarily concerned with

    Ⓐ discussing different approaches biologists have taken to testing theories about the distribution of plants in Hawaii

    Ⓑ discussing different theories about the transport of plant seeds to Hawaii

    Ⓒ discussing the extent to which air currents are responsible for the dispersal of plant seeds to Hawaii

    Ⓓ resolving a dispute about the adaptability of plant seeds to bird transport

    Ⓔ resolving a dispute about the ability of birds to carry plant seeds long distances

Explanation

Given the description of the passage above, it is clear that **Choice B** is correct: the passage focuses on "different theories about the transport of plant seeds to Hawaii." Choice A can be eliminated: while the passage does refer to flotation experiments, it does not elaborate on experimental methods. Choice C identifies an idea that is part of the passage's main concern, but since this is only one of the competing theories discussed in the passage, not the primary focus, Choice C is incorrect. Choices D and E are incorrect because the passage does not resolve any disputes.

9.   The author mentions the results of flotation experiments on plant seeds (lines 7–8) most probably in order to

    Ⓐ support the claim that the distribution of plants in Hawaii is the result of the long-distance dispersal of seeds

    Ⓑ lend credibility to the thesis that air currents provide a method of transport for plant seeds to Hawaii

    Ⓒ suggest that the long-distance dispersal of seeds is a process that requires long periods of time

    Ⓓ challenge the claim that ocean currents are responsible for the transport of plant seeds to Hawaii

    Ⓔ refute the claim that Hawaiian flora evolved independently from flora in other parts of the world

Explanation

This question asks why the author mentions flotation experiments. Flotation experiments are mentioned in the passage in order to show that some evidence casts doubt on the claim that ocean currents were the means by which seeds were transported to Hawaii. Thus, **Choice D** is correct. Choice A is incorrect since the claim that plant distribution in Hawaii is the result of long-distance dispersal of seeds is a given in the passage, not an idea that the author feels a need to substantiate. Choice B is eliminable since the flotation experiments are introduced at a point where the author is challenging, rather than lending credibility to, the air current hypothesis and because flotation experiments would more likely reflect on ocean currents than air currents. Choice C is eliminable since the passage does not address the length of time required for long-distance seed dispersal. Finally, Choice E is eliminable since it too describes an idea that is not discussed in the passage.

SET 3. Discrete Questions: Medium

> **For Questions 1 to 5, select one entry for each blank from the corresponding column of choices. Fill all blanks in the way that best completes the text.**

1. It comes as no surprise that societies have codes of behavior; the character of the codes, on the other hand, can often be _____ .

Ⓐ	predictable
Ⓑ	unexpected
Ⓒ	admirable
Ⓓ	explicit
Ⓔ	confusing

Explanation

The words "on the other hand" indicate that while the existence of societal codes of behavior is no surprise, their character may be quite surprising. Thus the correct answer is Choice B, **unexpected**, which means the same as surprising. "Predictable" is the very opposite of surprising, and none of the other answer choices means "surprising."

   Thus the correct answer is **unexpected** (Choice B).

2. Like Béla Bartók, Ruth Crawford not only brought a composer's acumen to the notation of folk music, she also had a marked (i)_____ the task. This was clear in her agonizing over how far to try to represent the minute details of a performance in a written text, and this (ii)_____ makes her work a landmark in ethnomusicology.

Blank (i)	Blank (ii)
Ⓐ reverence for	Ⓓ fastidiousness
Ⓑ detachment from	Ⓔ didacticism
Ⓒ curiosity about	Ⓕ iconoclasm

Explanation

In this example, both blanks can be filled by focusing on the statement that Crawford agonized over the details in her representations of folk music performances. The only choice for blank (ii) that matches this description is "fastidiousness"; neither "didacticism" nor "iconoclasm" reflects the notion of agonizing over details. Similarly, only "reverence for" fits in Blank (i), since neither "detachment from" nor "curiosity about" reflects the degree of care Crawford took.

   Thus the correct answer is **reverence for** (Choice A) and **fastidiousness** (Choice D).

3. Political advertising may well be the most (i)_____ kind of advertising: political candidates are usually quite (ii)_____, yet their campaign advertisements often hide important differences behind smoke screens of smiles and empty slogans.

Blank (i)	Blank (ii)
Ⓐ polemical	Ⓓ interchangeable
Ⓑ effective	Ⓔ dissimilar
Ⓒ deceptive	Ⓕ vocal

Explanation

Looking at Blank (i), it is hard to select a correct answer, since all three answer choices fit the immediate context well. Looking to the second part of the sentence, however, we can see such expressions as "hide" and "smoke screens," both of which suggest that the correct answer for Blank (i) is "deceptive." Making that assumption, we can go on to see that the answer for Blank (ii) is "dissimilar," since what is deceptive about political advertisements is that they hide important differences. Reading the sentence again with "deceptive" and "dissimilar" in place confirms those choices.

Thus the correct answer is **deceptive** (Choice C) and **dissimilar** (Choice E).

4. Richard M. Russell said 52 percent of the nation's growth since the Second World War had (i)_____ invention. He said, (ii)_____ research, the government's greatest role in assuring continuing innovation is promoting a strong, modern patent office. "Unless we can (iii)_____ original ideas, we will not have invention," Mr. Russell said. Speculating on the state of innovation over the next century, several inventors agreed that the future lay in giving children the tools to think creatively and the motivation to invent.

Blank (i)	Blank (ii)	Blank (iii)
Ⓐ been at the expense of	Ⓓ in addition to restricting	Ⓖ evaluate
Ⓑ no bearing on	Ⓔ aside from supporting	Ⓗ protect
Ⓒ come through	Ⓕ far from exaggerating	Ⓘ disseminate

Explanation

A quick overview of the paragraph shows that its topic is the encouragement of invention and innovation. This implies that Blank (i) should be filled with "come through," which emphasizes the importance of invention; the other choices suggest that invention is irrelevant or somehow harmed by growth. Again, the only one of the choices for Blank (ii) that continues the theme of encouraging invention is "aside from supporting." Finally, the second sentence emphasizes the importance for innovation of a strong patent office, and this thought is reaffirmed in the following quotation from Mr. Russell, which requires "protect" in Blank (iii).

Thus the correct answer is **come through** (Choice C), **aside from supporting** (Choice E), and **protect** (Choice H).

5. Statements presented as fact in a patent application are (i)_____ unless a good reason for doubt is found. The invention has only to be deemed "more likely than not" to work in order to receive initial approval. And, although thousands of patents are challenged in court for other reasons, no incentive exists for anyone to expend effort (ii)_____ the science of an erroneous patent. For this reason the endless stream of (iii)_____ devices will continue to yield occasional patents.

Blank (i)	Blank (ii)	Blank (iii)
(A) presumed verifiable	(D) corroborating	(G) novel
(B) carefully scrutinized	(E) advancing	(H) bogus
(C) considered capricious	(F) debunking	(I) obsolete

Explanation

The paragraph appears to be explaining some odd or unexpected aspect of the patent process. The third sentence helps to clarify what this aspect is; it discusses challenges to patents. The only choice for Blank (ii) that is concerned with challenging a patent is "debunking," since "corroborating" and "advancing" suggest support instead. This in turn provides the answer for the third blank, since the preceding sentence does explain how "bogus" devices may nonetheless get a patent. And we can also now better understand the first sentence—it too must help explain how bogus devices get patents, which it can do only if the blank is filled with "presumed verifiable," suggesting that patent applications are taken at face value and not dismissed out of hand nor subjected to careful scrutiny.

Thus the correct answer is **presumed verifiable** (Choice A), **debunking** (Choice F), and **bogus** (Choice H).

For Questions 6 to 8, select the <u>two</u> answer choices that, when used to complete the sentence, fit the meaning of the sentence as a whole <u>and</u> produce completed sentences that are alike in meaning.

---

6. Ever a demanding reader of the fiction of others, the novelist Chase was likewise often the object of _____ analyses by his contemporaries.

    A exacting
    B copious
    C respectful
    D acerbic
    E scathing
    F meticulous

Explanation

The use of the word "likewise" indicates that the analyses of Chase's work by contemporaries were like the readings he gave the fiction of others. Since he is described as a "demanding reader," the words that best fit the blank will be similar in meaning to "demanding." The words that meet this requirement are "exacting" (Choice A) and "meticulous" (Choice F), and they produce sentences that are alike in meaning. Although "acerbic analyses" means close to the same thing as "scathing analyses," both "acerbic" and "scathing" have meanings that are quite different from "demanding," so neither fits well in the blank.

Thus the correct answer is **exacting** (Choice A) and **meticulous** (Choice F).

7. Her _____ should not be confused with miserliness; as long as I have known her, she has always been willing to assist those who are in need.

A stinginess
B diffidence
C frugality
D illiberality
E intolerance
F thrift

Explanation

The sentence explains that the person spoken of is not miserly, since she is quite prepared to be generous. So for the sentence to make sense, the word filling the blank has to be something that is consistent with generosity and yet might, by those without a full understanding of her behavior, be mistaken for miserliness. The words "frugality" and "thrift" fulfill this requirement and yield two sentences that are alike in meaning, so that pair forms the correct answer. Neither "stinginess" nor "illiberality" makes sense in the sentence, since they are synonymous with "miserliness" and inconsistent with generosity. Other choices, such as "diffidence," might perhaps make a sensible sentence if placed in the blank but do not form part of the correct answer since they have no companion word that would make a sentence of similar meaning.

Thus the correct answer is **frugality** (Choice C) and **thrift** (Choice F).

8. A misconception frequently held by novice writers is that sentence structure mirrors thought: the more convoluted the structure, the more _____ the ideas.

A complicated
B engaged
C essential
D fanciful
E inconsequential
F involved

Explanation

Because the second half of the sentence illustrates the idea that "structure mirrors thought," any word that fills the blank must be similar in meaning to "convoluted." The two words that are similar to "convoluted" are "complicated" and "involved" (Choices A and F), which produce sentences alike in meaning. "Fanciful," while somewhat similar in meaning to "convoluted," is not as similar to either "complicated" or "involved" as those words are to each other. The other answer choices are not similar in meaning to "convoluted," and thus do not produce coherent sentences.

Thus the correct answer is **complicated** (Choice A) and **involved** (Choice F).

SET 4. Reading Comprehension Questions: Medium

> For each of Questions 1 to 9, select <u>one</u> answer choice unless otherwise instructed.

Questions 1 and 2 are based on the following reading passage.

I enjoyed *A Dream of Light & Shadow: Portraits of Latin American Women Writers* for the same reasons that, as a child, I avidly consumed women's biographies: the fascination with how the biographical details of another female's life are represented and interpreted.

A Dream offers a rich read, varied in both the lives and texts of the women portrayed, and the perspectives and styles of the sixteen essayists. Yet, as an adult, I have come to demand of any really "great" book a self-consciousness about the tenuous nature of representations of reality, a critical contextualization of florid detail, and a self-awareness of the role of ideology in our lives. In these critical senses, *A Dream* is inadequate.

Description

The passage follows the following structure: the first sentence discusses a collection of biographical sketches and what the author found particularly appealing about similar works as a child; the second sentence describes several positive aspects of this particular collection and how it satisfies the author's early interests; the third sentence describes a demanding set of criteria that the author now applies when assessing such work; and in the fourth sentence the author says the collection being discussed does not meet those criteria.

For the following question, consider each of the choices separately and select all that apply.

1. The author of the passage suggests that *A Dream* falls short in which of the following respects?
    - A It does not appear to recognize that representations of reality can be unreliable.
    - B It seems to focus on stylistic variety at the expense of accuracy of detail.
    - C It offers a wealth of detail without sufficient critical examination of that detail.

Explanation

Choices A and C are correct. We know from the final sentence that the collection falls short of several criteria established by the author.

   Choice A is correct: the book does not demonstrate sufficient awareness of the "tenuous nature of representations of reality."

   Choice B is incorrect: there is no mention in the passage of any concern on the part of the author about the accuracy of detail.

   Choice C is correct: the book does not offer an adequate "critical contextualization of florid detail."

2. Which of the following best describes the function of the second sentence ("*A Dream* . . . essayists") in the context of the passage as a whole?

   (A) To give examples of how *A Dream* presents fascinating portraits that display awareness of the tenuous nature of representations of reality

   (B) To elaborate on how *A Dream* fulfills the author's childhood criteria for a pleasurable book

   (C) To suggest that the author enjoyed *A Dream* for reasons more sophisticated than the reasons she enjoyed certain books as a child

   (D) To illustrate ways in which the author finds *A Dream* to be inadequate in certain critical senses

   (E) To imply that *A Dream* is too varied in focus to provide a proper contextualization of the biographical details it offers

Explanation

This question asks about the function of the second sentence. The correct choice is **Choice B**. As discussed in the description of the passage, that sentence describes what is appealing about the collection in the context of the author's childhood tastes. Choice A is incorrect both because the sentence does not provide examples and because the collection does not display an awareness of the tenuous nature of representations of reality. Choice C is not correct: although one might suspect that the author's enjoyment of collections as an adult would be on a more sophisticated level than when she was young, there is no discussion or even suggestion of that in the passage. Choice D is incorrect because the sentence describes the virtues of the collection. The aspects of the collection that the author finds inadequate are not addressed until later. Choice E is incorrect because, according to the passage, the fact that the collection is varied makes it a "rich" read. There is no suggestion that the variety hinders proper contextualization.

3. During the day in Lake Constance, the zooplankton *D. hyalina* departs for the depths where food is scarce and the water cold. *D. galeata* remains near the warm surface where food is abundant. Even though *D. galeata* grows and reproduces much faster, its population is often outnumbered by *D. hyalina*.

   Which of the following, if true, would help resolve the apparent paradox presented above?

   (A) The number of species of zooplankton living at the bottom of the lake is twice that of species living at the surface.

   (B) Predators of zooplankton, such as whitefish and perch, live and feed near the surface of the lake during the day.

   (C) In order to make the most of scarce food resources, *D. hyalina* matures more slowly than *D. galeata*.

   (D) *D. galeata* clusters under vegetation during the hottest part of the day to avoid the Sun's rays.

   (E) *D. galeata* produces twice as many offspring per individual in any given period of time as does *D. hyalina*.

Description

The paragraph presents an apparent paradox: the zooplankton that spends the day in less hospitable conditions often outnumbers the one that stays in more hospitable conditions.

Explanation

The presence of predators of zooplankton feeding near the surface during the day would suggest that *D. galeata* is consumed at a higher rate than *D. hyalina*: this would explain why *D. hyalina* is often more numerous, so **Choice B** is correct. Choices C and E are incorrect because although they help to explain why the two zooplankton reproduce at different rates, they do not help to resolve the apparent paradox. Choices A and D are incorrect because nothing is said in the paragraph to show the relevance of the presence of other species of zooplankton, nor of the habit of clustering under vegetation, to the relative population size of the two species.

Questions 4 and 5 are based on the following reading passage.

Tocqueville, apparently, was wrong. Jacksonian America was not a fluid, egalitarian society where individual wealth and poverty were ephemeral conditions. At least so argues E. Pessen in his iconoclastic study of the very rich in the United States between 1825 and 1850.

Pessen does present a quantity of examples, together with some refreshingly intelligible statistics, to establish the existence of an inordinately wealthy class. Though active in commerce or the professions, most of the wealthy were not self-made but had inherited family fortunes. In no sense mercurial, these great fortunes survived the financial panics that destroyed lesser ones. Indeed, in several cities the wealthiest one percent constantly increased its share until by 1850 it owned half of the community's wealth. Although these observations are true, Pessen overestimates their importance by concluding from them that the undoubted progress toward inequality in the late eighteenth century continued in the Jacksonian period and that the United States was a class-ridden, plutocratic society even before industrialization.

Description

The passage describes Pessen's argument that Jacksonian America was not fluid and egalitarian but class-ridden and plutocratic, and criticizes it for leaping to an unjustified conclusion.

4. According to the passage, Pessen indicates that all of the following were true of the very wealthy in the United States between 1825 and 1850 EXCEPT:
   (A) They formed a distinct upper class.
   (B) Many of them were able to increase their holdings.
   (C) Some of them worked as professionals or in business.
   (D) Most of them accumulated their own fortunes.
   (E) Many of them retained their wealth in spite of financial upheavals.

Explanation

For this question, you are to identify the one statement that CANNOT be correctly attributed to Pessen. Therefore, you must first determine which of the statements given can be attributed to Pessen. According to the passage, Pessen maintains all of the following: there was a class of "inordinately wealthy" Americans (Choice A); in some places that class "constantly increased its share" (Choice B); its members were "active in commerce or the professions" (Choice C); and "these great fortunes survived the financial panics that destroyed lesser ones" (Choice E). However, Pessen also maintains, in contradiction to Choice D, that "most of the wealthy were not self-made but had inherited family fortunes." Therefore, **Choice D** is correct.

5. Which of the following best states the author's main point?

    (A) Pessen's study has overturned the previously established view of the social and economic structure of early-nineteenth-century America.

    (B) Tocqueville's analysis of the United States in the Jacksonian era remains the definitive account of this period.

    (C) Pessen's study is valuable primarily because it shows the continuity of the social system in the United States throughout the nineteenth century.

    (D) The social patterns and political power of the extremely wealthy in the United States between 1825 and 1850 are well documented.

    (E) Pessen challenges a view of the social and economic systems in the United States from 1825 to 1850, but he draws conclusions that are incorrect.

Explanation

It is important to realize that although most of the passage is devoted to describing Pessen's study, the author's main point is to criticize the conclusion Pessen draws. Choices A, C, and D omit any reference to the author's critical evaluation of Pessen's study, and hence are not statements of the author's main point. Choice B is also incorrect. Because Pessen criticizes Tocqueville and the author criticizes Pessen, it might seem that the author's main point is to defend Tocqueville's analysis. However, the passage does not indicate that Tocqueville's analysis is definitive. **Choice E is correct.** According to the first paragraph, Pessen challenges Tocqueville's view, but according to the second paragraph, Pessen's conclusions are incorrect.

Questions 6 to 9 are based on the following reading passage.

The evolution of intelligence among early large mammals of the grasslands was due in great measure to the interaction between two ecologically synchronized groups of these animals, the hunting carnivores and the herbivores that they hunted. The interac-
line   tion resulting from the differences between predator and prey led to a general improve-
5   ment in brain functions; however, certain components of intelligence were improved far more than others.

    The kind of intelligence favored by the interplay of increasingly smarter catchers and increasingly keener escapers is defined by attention—that aspect of mind carrying consciousness forward from one moment to the next. It ranges from a passive,
10   free-floating awareness to a highly focused, active fixation. The range through these states is mediated by the arousal system, a network of tracts converging from sensory systems to integrating centers in the brain stem. From the more relaxed to the more vigorous levels, sensitivity to novelty is increased. The organism is more awake, more vigilant; this increased vigilance results in the apprehension of ever more subtle signals
15   as the organism becomes more sensitive to its surroundings. The processes of arousal and concentration give attention its direction. Arousal is at first general, with a flooding of impulses in the brain stem; then gradually the activation is channeled. Thus begins concentration, the holding of consistent images. One meaning of intelligence is the way in which these images and other alertly searched information are used in the
20   context of previous experience. Consciousness links past attention to the present and permits the integration of details with perceived ends and purposes.

    The elements of intelligence and consciousness come together marvelously to produce different styles in predator and prey. Herbivores and carnivores develop different kinds of attention related to escaping or chasing. Although in both kinds of animal,
25   arousal stimulates the production of adrenaline and norepinephrine by the adrenal

glands, the effect in herbivores is primarily fear, whereas in carnivores the effect is primarily aggression. For both, arousal attunes the animal to what is ahead. Perhaps it does not experience forethought as we know it, but the animal does experience something like it. The predator is searchingly aggressive, inner-directed, tuned by the nervous system and the adrenal hormones, but aware in a sense closer to human consciousness than, say, a hungry lizard's instinctive snap at a passing beetle. Using past events as a framework, the large mammal predator is working out a relationship between movement and food, sensitive to possibilities in cold trails and distant sounds—and yesterday's unforgotten lessons. The herbivore prey is of a different mind. Its mood of wariness rather than searching and its attitude of general expectancy instead of anticipating are silk-thin veils of tranquillity over an explosive endocrine system.

line
30

35

Description

The passage describes improvements in certain components of intelligence among early large mammals of the grasslands. The second paragraph focuses on attention as a primary area of improvement, and the third paragraph outlines how attention differs in predator and prey species.

6. The author refers to a hungry lizard (line 31) primarily in order to
   - (A) demonstrate the similarity between the hunting methods of mammals and those of nonmammals
   - (B) broaden the application of the argument by including an insectivore as an example
   - (C) make a distinction between higher and lower levels of consciousness
   - (D) provide an additional illustration of the brutality characteristic of predators
   - (E) offer an objection to suggestions that all animals lack consciousness

Explanation

Choice C is correct. The "hungry lizard's instinctive snap" is contrasted with the mammal's higher level of awareness. Choices A and B are incorrect. The example of the hungry lizard provides a contrast; it does not demonstrate a similarity or extend the author's argument. Choices D and E are incorrect. Brutality is not mentioned in the passage as a characteristic of predators, and there is no suggestion that all animals lack consciousness.

7. It can be inferred from the passage that in animals less intelligent than the mammals discussed in the passage
   - (A) past experience is less helpful in ensuring survival
   - (B) attention is more highly focused
   - (C) muscular coordination is less highly developed
   - (D) there is less need for competition among species
   - (E) environment is more important in establishing the proper ratio of prey to predator

Explanation

Choice A is correct. In lines 18–20, the author defines intelligence in terms of an animal's use of past experience. In the context of the entire passage, it can be inferred that more intelligent animals, such as the grassland mammals discussed, are better able to use past experience to help them survive than less intelligent animals are. Choice B is incorrect. The second paragraph of the passage indicates that attention is more highly focused in animals of greater, rather than less, intelligence. Choices C, D, and E are incorrect. The author does not discuss muscular coordination as an element in intelligence, gives no indication that in less intelligent species there is less need for competition, and does not discuss how a proper ratio of prey to predator is established.

8. According to the passage, improvement in brain function among early large mammals resulted primarily from which of the following?

    Ⓐ Interplay of predator and prey

    Ⓑ Persistence of free-floating awareness in animals of the grasslands

    Ⓒ Gradual dominance of warm-blooded mammals over cold-blooded reptiles

    Ⓓ Interaction of early large mammals with less intelligent species

    Ⓔ Improvement of the capacity for memory among herbivores and carnivores

Explanation

Choice A is correct. It directly paraphrases the statement in lines 3–5, which describes the author's view of the development of improved brain function in early mammals. Choice B is incorrect. It is likely that the persistence of "free-floating awareness" played a part in the animals' survival, but there is no indication in the passage that brain function improved because of it. Choices C and D are incorrect: the passage does not discuss the relationship between mammals and reptiles or the interaction between large mammals and less intelligent species. Choice E is incorrect. Improved capacity for memory is an improvement in brain function, rather than a reason for improved brain function.

9. According to the passage, as the process of arousal in an organism continues, all of the following may occur EXCEPT

    Ⓐ the production of adrenaline

    Ⓑ the production of norepinephrine

    Ⓒ a heightening of sensitivity to stimuli

    Ⓓ an increase in selectivity with respect to stimuli

    Ⓔ an expansion of the range of states mediated by the brain stem

Explanation

This question asks you what does NOT occur during arousal. To answer the question, you must first determine what does occur. According to the passage, arousal does stimulate the production of adrenaline and norepinephrine (lines 24–26); does increase sensitivity to stimuli (lines 12–13); and does increase concentration on specific stimuli (lines 16–18). Thus Choices A through D all describe consequences of arousal. Only **Choice E** is correct. There is no indication in the passage that the range of states mediated by the brain stem expands during arousal.

SET 5. Discrete Questions: Hard

> **For Questions 1 to 6, select one entry for each blank from the corresponding column of choices. Fill all blanks in the way that best completes the text.**

1. For some time now, _____ has been presumed not to exist: the cynical conviction that everybody has an angle is considered wisdom.

Ⓐ rationality
Ⓑ flexibility
Ⓒ diffidence
Ⓓ disinterestedness
Ⓔ insincerity

Explanation

The colon indicates that the second part of the sentence will explain the first part. The missing word will describe the opposite of the cynical conviction that "everybody has an angle," that is, that each person is concerned primarily with his or her own interests. Since "disinterestedness" means lack of self-interest, Choice D is correct. None of the other answer choices means something that is contrasted with or opposed to being primarily concerned with one's own interests.

   Thus the correct answer is **disinterestedness** (Choice D).

2. Human nature and long distances have made exceeding the speed limit a (i)_____ in the state, so the legislators surprised no one when, acceding to public demand, they (ii)_____ increased penalties for speeding.

Blank (i)	Blank (ii)
Ⓐ controversial habit	Ⓓ endorsed
Ⓑ cherished tradition	Ⓔ considered
Ⓒ disquieting ritual	Ⓕ rejected

Explanation

The reference to human nature and long distances suggest that it is rather routine for drivers to exceed the speed limit in this state. "Cherished tradition" best fits this context for Blank (i), since there is nothing in the sentence to suggest that speeding here is "controversial" or "disquieting." In Blank (ii) we need to consider what the legislature would do that would surprise no one with regard to increased penalties for speeding. Given what we have learned so far, "rejected" is the best answer; it would be surprising if the legislature "endorsed" or even "considered" increased penalties for speeding.

   Thus the correct answer is **cherished tradition** (Choice B) and **rejected** (Choice F).

3. Serling's account of his employer's reckless decision making (i)_____ that company's image as (ii)_____ bureaucracy full of wary managers.

Blank (i)	Blank (ii)
Ⓐ belies	Ⓓ an injudicious
Ⓑ exposes	Ⓔ a disorganized
Ⓒ overshadows	Ⓕ a cautious

Explanation

The correct answer for Blank (i) must support, or at least be consistent with, the contrast between Serling's account, which emphasizes the recklessness of the company's decision making, and the company's image, that of a bureaucracy full of wary managers. For Blank (i), "belies" is the best choice since Serling's account would certainly belie or contradict the company's image. "Exposes" makes little sense since the image presumably is already out in the open, and there is nothing in the sentence that suggests Serling's account "overshadows" the company's image. As for Blank (ii), "a cautious" is the most logical choice. Neither "an injudicious" nor "a disorganized" makes sense in Blank (ii) as they both go against the notion of wariness.

Thus the correct answer is **belies** (Choice A) and **a cautious** (Choice F).

4. No other contemporary poet's work has such a well-earned reputation for (i)_____, and there are few whose moral vision is so imperiously unsparing. Of late, however, the almost belligerent demands of his severe and densely forbidding poetry have taken an improbable turn. This new collection is the poet's fourth book in six years—an ample output even for poets of sunny disposition, let alone for one of such (ii)_____ over the previous 50 years. Yet for all his newfound (iii)_____, his poetry is as thorny as ever.

Blank (i)	Blank (ii)	Blank (iii)
Ⓐ patent accessibility	Ⓓ penitential austerity	Ⓖ taciturnity
Ⓑ intrinsic frivolity	Ⓔ intractable prolixity	Ⓗ volubility
Ⓒ near impenetrability	Ⓕ impetuous prodigality	Ⓘ pellucidity

Explanation

Since the author of the paragraph has described the poet's reputation as "well-earned," the correct completion for Blank (i) must be something that is consistent with what the rest of the passage says about the poet's work. Only "near impenetrability" fulfills this requirement, since the next sentence tells us that the poet's work is "severe" and "densely forbidding," which rule out both accessibility and frivolity. The Blank (ii) completion must contrast with "ample output," and of the available options, only "penitential austerity" does so. Finally, the word in Blank (iii), since it is preceded by "newfound," must refer to the change that has occurred in the poet's work. The change the paragraph has described is an increase in output, so "volubility" is the correct choice.

Thus the correct answer is **near impenetrability** (Choice C), **penitential austerity** (Choice D), and **volubility** (Choice H).

5. Managers who think that strong environmental performance will (i)_____ their company's financial performance often (ii)_____ claims that systems designed to help them manage environmental concerns are valuable tools. By contrast, managers who perceive environmental performance to be (iii)_____ to financial success may view an environmental management system as extraneous. In either situation, and whatever their perceptions, it is a manager's commitment to achieving environmental improvement rather than the mere presence of a system that determines environmental performance.

Blank (i)	Blank (ii)	Blank (iii)
Ⓐ eclipse	Ⓓ uncritically accept	Ⓖ complementary
Ⓑ bolster	Ⓔ appropriately acknowledge	Ⓗ intrinsic
Ⓒ degrade	Ⓕ hotly dispute	Ⓘ peripheral

Explanation

The first two sentences introduce two contrasting sets of managers. The managers identified in the second sentence view systems designed to help manage environmental concerns as "extraneous," suggesting that they would view environmental performance to be "peripheral" (Choice I) to financial performance. The other options for Blank (iii)—"complementary" and "intrinsic"—are not consistent with the idea that environmental management systems are extraneous. With Blank (iii) filled in, we can go back to Blanks (i) and (ii) with greater confidence: "bolster" works best in Blank (i), since the two sets of managers have contrasting views. Blank (ii) is not straightforward—clearly these managers would not "hotly dispute" this claim, but "appropriately acknowledge" is less easily ruled out. "Uncritically accept" makes sense and is confirmed when we look at the final sentence in which the author warns that, in either situation, "the mere presence of a system" is not enough to achieve environmental improvement. In fact, a system is not even necessary. Thus the author of the paragraph does not regard the systems as particularly valuable, ruling out "appropriately acknowledge."

Thus the correct answer is **bolster** (Choice B), **uncritically accept** (Choice D), and **peripheral** (Choice I).

6. Philosophy, unlike most other subjects, does not try to extend our knowledge by discovering new information about the world. Instead it tries to deepen our understanding through (i)_____ what is already closest to us—the experiences, thoughts, concepts, and activities that make up our lives but that ordinarily escape our notice precisely because they are so familiar. Philosophy begins by finding (ii)_____ the things that are (iii) _____.

Blank (i)	Blank (ii)	Blank (iii)
Ⓐ attainment of	Ⓓ essentially irrelevant	Ⓖ most prosaic
Ⓑ rumination on	Ⓔ utterly mysterious	Ⓗ somewhat hackneyed
Ⓒ detachment from	Ⓕ thoroughly commonplace	Ⓘ refreshingly novel

Explanation

The first two sentences present a contrast between extending our knowledge by discovering "new information about the world"—which we are told philosophy does not do—and extending knowledge through some activity involving "things that are closest to us." The first blank asks us to identify that activity, and although "attainment" makes little sense in context, both "rumination on" and "detachment from" have some appeal. However, the clear implication that philosophy attends to things that ordinarily escape our notice eliminates "detachment from" as a correct answer. Blank (ii) requires something that suggests the importance of familiar things as subjects of philosophical rumination, and "utterly mysterious" does just that. "Essentially irrelevant" and "thoroughly commonplace" do not fit logically since they suggest that these "familiar" things are unimportant. Similarly, Blank (iii) needs to be consistent with the description of those things as familiar and close. "Most prosaic" fits that idea while "refreshingly novel" goes in the other direction. "Somewhat hackneyed" has some plausibility but is too negative given the overall tone of the sentence; there is no indication that those things are in any way trite.

Thus the correct answer is **rumination on** (Choice B), **utterly mysterious** (Choice E), and **most prosaic** (Choice G).

> **For Questions 7 to 9, select the two answer choices that, when used to complete the sentence, fit the meaning of the sentence as a whole and produce completed sentences that are alike in meaning.**

7. The government's implementation of a new code of ethics appeared intended to shore up the ruling party's standing with an increasingly _____ electorate at a time when the party is besieged by charges that it trades favors for campaign money.
   A aloof
   B placid
   C restive
   D skittish
   E tranquil
   F vociferous

Explanation

The words filling the blank must be consistent with the idea that the ruling party needs to "shore up" its standing with the electorate. In their own way, Choices A, C, D, and F are consistent with that idea, but only two of these when taken together—"restive" and "skittish"—produce sentences that are alike in meaning. "Aloof" fits the blank reasonably well, but there is no other word offered that is nearly alike in meaning. The same holds for "vociferous." "Placid" and "tranquil" are similar in meaning but do not fit the context of the sentence.

Thus the correct answer is **restive** (Choice C) and **skittish** (Choice D).

8. Overlarge, uneven, and ultimately disappointing, the retrospective exhibition seems too much like special pleading for a forgotten painter of real but _____ talents.

    A limited
    B partial
    C undiscovered
    D circumscribed
    E prosaic
    F hidden

Explanation

The sentence is explaining why the exhibition of the painter's work was unsatisfactory, and since it says that the painter's talents were real, the word in the blank has to indicate why those talents were not, in the opinion of the author of the sentence, good enough. The words "limited" and "circumscribed" do so and also produce sentences that are alike in meaning, so this pair forms the correct answer. Although "undiscovered" and "hidden" are similar in meaning, they do not make sense in the context of the sentence, since they do not indicate why the painter's talents were not adequate. Other choices, such as "partial" and "prosaic" might make sense in context, but none of the other choices that meets that criterion also has a companion choice that would produce another sentence alike in meaning.

Thus the correct answer is **limited** (Choice A) and **circumscribed** (Choice D).

9. Newspapers report that the former executive has been trying to keep a low profile since his _____ exit from the company.

    A celebrated
    B mysterious
    C long-awaited
    D fortuitous
    E indecorous
    F unseemly

Explanation

The sentence needs to be completed with a word that suggests a reason for the executive to wish to keep a low profile. The words "indecorous" and "unseemly" both suggest such a reason, and the sentences completed with those two choices are alike in meaning. Therefore, that pair forms the correct answer. Although one might get a sensible sentence by filling the blank with another choice, such as "long-awaited," none of the other choices that meets that criterion also has a companion choice that would produce another sentence alike in meaning.

Thus the correct answer is **indecorous** (Choice E) and **unseemly** (Choice F).

SET 6. Reading Comprehension Questions: Hard

> **For each of Questions 1 to 8, select <u>one</u> answer choice unless otherwise instructed.**

1. In the United States between 1850 and 1880, the number of farmers continued to increase, but at a rate lower than that of the general population.

    Which of the following statements directly contradicts the information presented above?

    (A) The number of farmers in the general population increased slightly in the 30 years between 1850 and 1880.

    (B) The rate of growth of the United States labor force and the rate of growth of the general population rose simultaneously in the 30 years between 1850 and 1880.

    (C) The proportion of farmers in the United States labor force remained constant in the 30 years between 1850 and 1880.

    (D) The proportion of farmers in the United States labor force decreased from 64 percent in 1850 to 49 percent in 1880.

    (E) The proportion of farmers in the general population increased from 68 percent in 1850 to 72 percent in 1880.

Explanation

The given sentence indicates that the proportion of farmers in the general population decreased from 1850 to 1880. **Choice E** says exactly the opposite—that this proportion increased—and therefore it contradicts the passage and is the correct response. Choice A is incorrect because it agrees with the given sentence, and Choices B, C, and D are all incorrect because they refer to the labor force, about which the given sentence says nothing.

2. A ten-year comparison between the United States and the Soviet Union in terms of crop yields per acre revealed that when only planted acreage is compared, Soviet yields were equal to 68 percent of United States yields. When total agricultural acreage (planted acreage plus fallow acreage) is compared, however, Soviet yield was 114 percent of United States yield.

    From the information above, which of the following can be most reliably inferred about United States and Soviet agriculture during the ten-year period?

    (A) A higher percentage of total agricultural acreage was fallow in the United States than in the Soviet Union.

    (B) The United States had more fallow acreage than planted acreage.

    (C) Fewer total acres of available agricultural land were fallow in the Soviet Union than in the United States.

    (D) The Soviet Union had more planted acreage than fallow acreage.

    (E) The Soviet Union produced a greater volume of crops than the United States produced.

Explanation

If crop yield per planted acre was less in the Soviet Union than it was in the United States, yet crop yield per total (planted plus fallow) agricultural acreage was greater in the Soviet Union than it was in the United States, the percentage of the total acreage that was left fallow must have been lower in the Soviet Union than in the United States. Therefore, **Choice A** is the correct answer. Since the information provided in the paragraph is given in terms of yield per acre, no conclusion can be drawn about actual acreage, so Choices B, C, and D are all incorrect. Similarly, it is impossible to determine the total volume of crops produced in the Soviet Union, so Choice E is incorrect.

Questions 3 and 4 are based on the following reading passage.

For hot desert locations with access to seawater, a new greenhouse design generates freshwater and cool air. Oriented to the prevailing wind, the front wall of perforated cardboard, moistened by a trickle of seawater pumped in, cools and moistens hot air blowing in. This cool, humidified air accelerates plant growth; little water evaporates from leaves. Though greenhouses normally capture the heat of sunlight, a double-layered roof, the inner layer coated to reflect infrared light outward, allows visible sunlight in but traps solar heat between the two layers. This heated air, drawn down from the roof, then mixes with the greenhouse air as it reaches a second seawater-moistened cardboard wall at the back of the greenhouse. There the air absorbs more moisture before being cooled off again when it meets a seawater-cooled metal wall, which causes moisture in the air to condense. Thus distilled water for irrigating the plants collects.

Description

The passage describes a greenhouse design and the process by which the design generates freshwater and cool air in a desert environment lacking in these things.

For the following question, consider each of the choices separately and select all that apply.

3. It can be inferred that the process described in the passage makes use of which of the following?

    A The tendency of hot air to rise

    B The directional movement of wind

    C Variation in the moisture capacity of air

Explanation

Choices B and C are correct. This question asks the reader which of the three phenomena listed in the answer choices is used in the process described in the passage.

Choice A is incorrect: the passage does not indicate that the tendency of hot air to rise is used in the process, and in fact says that heated air is drawn down, not up, as part of the greenhouse design.

Choice B is correct: the second sentence describes the orientation of a perforated cardboard wall toward the prevailing wind so that hot air blows in and is moistened.

Choice C is correct: the process depends on the ability of hot air to contain moisture that is then deposited when the air cools.

For the following question, consider each of the choices separately and select all that apply.

4. It can be inferred that the greenhouse roof is designed to allow for which of the following?

    A The avoidance of intense solar heat inside the greenhouse

    B The entry of sunlight into the greenhouse to make the plants grow

    C The mixture of heated air with greenhouse air to enhance the collection of moisture

Explanation

All three choices are correct. This question asks the reader which of the three effects listed in the answer choices are intended as part of the design of the greenhouse roof.

Choice A is correct: the purpose of the double-layered roof is to trap solar heat before it gets inside the greenhouse proper.

Choice B is correct: the coating on the inner layer of the roof allows visible sunlight into the greenhouse.

Choice C is correct: the last two sentences of the passage describe how heated air from the roof is drawn down to mix with greenhouse air, resulting in the collection of distilled water for irrigation purposes.

Many critics of Emily Brontë's novel *Wuthering Heights* see its second part as a counterpoint that comments on, if it does not reverse, the first part, where a romantic reading receives more confirmation. Seeing the two parts as a whole is encouraged by the novel's sophisticated structure, revealed in its complex use of narrators and time shifts. Granted that the presence of these elements need not argue for an authorial awareness of novelistic construction comparable to that of Henry James, their presence does encourage attempts to unify the novel's heterogeneous parts. However, any interpretation that seeks to unify all of the novel's diverse elements is bound to be somewhat unconvincing. This is not because such an interpretation necessarily stiffens into a thesis (although rigidity in any interpretation of this or of any novel is always a danger), but because *Wuthering Heights* has recalcitrant elements of undeniable power that, ultimately, resist inclusion in an all-encompassing interpretation. In this respect, *Wuthering Heights* shares a feature of *Hamlet*.

Description

The passage discusses a critical view concerning the unity of structure of *Wuthering Heights*, then, following the use of "However," expresses a reservation about that view.

5. According to the passage, which of the following is a true statement about the first and second parts of *Wuthering Heights*?

   (A) The second part has received more attention from critics.
   (B) The second part has little relation to the first part.
   (C) The second part annuls the force of the first part.
   (D) The second part provides less substantiation for a romantic reading.
   (E) The second part is better because it is more realistic.

Explanation

This question requires the reader to identify which of the given relationships between the novel's first and second parts is one that is described in the passage. According to the first sentence, the first part of the novel tends to confirm the "romantic" reading more strongly than the second. Therefore, **Choice D** is correct. Nothing in the passage suggests that critics have paid more attention to the second part, that the two parts have little relation, or that the second part is better. Therefore, Choices A, B, and E are incorrect. Choice C is a more extreme statement than any found in the passage, and therefore it is incorrect.

6. Which of the following inferences about Henry James's awareness of novelistic construction is best supported by the passage?

   (A) James, more than any other novelist, was aware of the difficulties of novelistic construction.
   (B) James was very aware of the details of novelistic construction.
   (C) James's awareness of novelistic construction derived from his reading of Brontë.
   (D) James's awareness of novelistic construction has led most commentators to see unity in his individual novels.
   (E) James's awareness of novelistic construction precluded him from violating the unity of his novels.

Explanation

This question focuses on the passage's mention of Henry James and asks what can be inferred from it. The third sentence implies that James represents a very high degree of authorial awareness of novelistic construction and that no such claim is necessarily being made for Brontë. Thus, **Choice B** is the correct answer. Choice A is incorrect, since the passage does not imply that there are particular difficulties that James understood uniquely among novelists. Choice C is incorrect because the passage does not state or imply that James read Brontë. The passage also does not say anything about commentators' opinions of the unity of James's works; therefore Choice D is incorrect. Choice E is incorrect because the passage itself offers no information about the unity of James's novels.

7. The author of the passage would be most likely to agree that an interpretation of a novel should

    Ⓐ not try to unite heterogeneous elements in the novel

    Ⓑ not be inflexible in its treatment of the elements in the novel

    Ⓒ not argue that the complex use of narrators or of time shifts indicates a sophisticated structure

    Ⓓ concentrate on those recalcitrant elements of the novel that are outside the novel's main structure

    Ⓔ primarily consider those elements of novelistic construction of which the author of the novel was aware

Explanation

This question requires the reader to determine what can be inferred from the passage about its author's view of the interpretation of novels. Choice A may seem attractive because in the passage the author says that *Wuthering Heights* has heterogeneous elements that resist inclusion in a unifying interpretive scheme. Choice A is incorrect, however, because the author does not indicate that the unification of different elements is to be avoided in interpretation generally. By contrast, the author's parenthetical statement about rigidity does present a general warning against inflexibility of interpretation, and it is this that supports **Choice B** as the correct answer. Choice C is incorrect, as the author actually suggests the contrary of this view in the second sentence of the passage. Although the author mentions recalcitrant elements of *Wuthering Heights*, there is no suggestion by the author that such elements deserve a special focus in interpretation. Therefore Choice D is incorrect. The author of the passage does not indicate which elements, if any, of novelistic construction are most worthy of consideration. Therefore Choice E is incorrect.

For the following question, consider each of the choices separately and select all that apply.

8.   The author of the passage suggests which of the following about *Hamlet*?

   A   *Hamlet* has usually attracted critical interpretations that tend to stiffen into theses.

   B   *Hamlet* has elements that are not amenable to an all-encompassing critical interpretation.

   C   *Hamlet* is less open to an all-encompassing critical interpretation than is *Wuthering Heights*.

Explanation

Choice B is correct. This question asks the reader which of the three statements about *Hamlet* listed in the answer choices are suggested by the author of the passage.

   Choice A is incorrect: the passage does not provide information about the characteristics of the usual critical interpretations of *Hamlet*.

   Choice B is correct: *Hamlet* is mentioned only in the final sentence of the passage, which refers to "this respect" in which *Hamlet* and *Wuthering Heights* are similar. The previous sentence reveals the point of similarity referred to: *Wuthering Heights* has elements that resist inclusion in an all-encompassing interpretive framework.

   Choice C is incorrect: the passage mentions only a feature shared between *Hamlet* and *Wuthering Heights*. It does not suggest anything about a difference in their openness to a particular critical interpretation.

5 GRE® Quantitative Reasoning

- ◥ Learn the four types of *GRE*® Quantitative Reasoning questions
- ◥ Learn general problem-solving steps and strategies
- ◥ Get tips for answering each question type
- ◥ Study sample Quantitative Reasoning questions with explanations
- ◥ Learn how to use the on-screen calculator

Overview of the Quantitative Reasoning Measure

GRE考试的Quantitative Reasoning测试考查考生的：

- 基本数学技能

- 对基本数学概念的理解

- 定量推理、建模以及利用定量法解决问题的能力

一些Quantitative Reasoning问题以现实生活为背景提出，其他问题则为纯数学背景。很多问题都是"文字题"，需要翻译成数学语言或建立数学模型。测试包括对以下四个方面的技能、概念和能力的检测。

算术（Arithmetic），包括整数的类型和属性，例如可分性（divisibility）、因式分解（factorization）、质数（prime numbers）、余数（remainders）和奇偶数（odd and even integers）；算术运算（arithmetic operations）、指数（exponents）和根式（radicals）；以及一些概念，如估算（estimation）、百分比（percent）、比率（ratio）、比例（rate）、绝对值（absolute value）、数轴（the number line）、十进制（decimal representation）和数列（sequences of numbers）。

代数（Algebra），包括指数运算（operations with exponents）；因式分解和代数式的化简（factoring and simplifying algebraic expressions）；关系（relations）、函数（functions）、方程（equation）和不等式（inequalities）；求解二次方程和不等式（linear and quadratic equations and inequalities）；求解联立方程和不等式（simultaneous equations and inequalities）；列方程解数学应用题；解析几何（也叫坐标几何，coordinate geometry），包括函数的图像、方程、不等式以及截距和斜率。

几何（Geometry），包括平行线（parallel lines）、垂线（perpendicular lines）、圆（circles）、三角形（triangles）（包括等腰、等边、30°-60°-90°三角形（isosceles, equilateral, and 30°-60°-90° triangles））、四边形（quadrilaterals）、其他多边形（polygons）、全等和相似图形（congruent and similar figures）、三维图形（three-dimensional figures）、面积（area）、周长（perimeter）、体积（volume）、勾股定理（the Pythagorean theorem）和角度计算（angle measurement in degrees）。不考几何证明。

数据分析（Data analysis），包括基本的描述统计学，如平均值（mean）、中位数（median）、众数（mode）、极差（range）、标准差（standard deviation）、四分位差（interquartile range）、四分位数（quartiles）和百分位数（percentiles）；表格和图形中的数据解析，例如线图（line graphs）、柱状图（bar graphs）、饼图（circle graphs）、箱形图（boxplots）、散点图（scatterplots）和频率分布（frequency distributions）；初等概率，如独立事件（independent events）和复合事件（compound events）的概率；随机变量（random variables）和概率分布，包括正态分布（normal distributions）；计算方法，例如组合（combinations）、排列（permutations）和韦恩图（Venn diagrams）。以上这些内容基本上都包含在高中的代数课和初级统计学课程中。不考推断统计学（inferential statistics）的内容。

这部分内容包括高中数学和统计学，考查的水平通常不超过第二册代数（a second course in algebra）；不包括三角学（trigonometry）、微积分（calculus）和其他更高水平的数学内容。关于Quantitative Reasoning测试的内容信息，请参见出版物Math Review for the GRE General Test，或访问以下网址：www.ets.org/gre/prepare，同时这也是本书第七章的内容。

Quantitative Reasoning测试中使用的数学符号、术语和定律与高中阶段的标准用法相同。例如，数轴的正方向为右，距离不能为负，质数大于1。若题目中涉及非标准用法，则会附有详细说明。

除定律外，Quantitative Reasoning部分还运用一些关于上面列出的数量和几何图形的重要假设：

- 所有使用的数字都是实数。
- 除非特殊说明，所有图示都应认为是在同一平面内。
- 几何图形，如线形、圆形、三角形及四边形等，并不一定按比例绘制。也就是说，长度和角度之类的数量与它们在图中显示的也许并不一致。但是，考生应该知道，显示为直线的线条确实是直线，线上的点也都依顺序显示，并且所有的几何对象都处于所显示的相对位置。对于那些与几何图形相关的问题，考生应该基于几何推理得出答案，而不是凭目测估计、比较数量或者通过度量来得出。
- 坐标系，例如平面直角坐标系（xy-plane）和实数线（number line），都是按比例绘制的。因此，考生可以通过目测或度量来对这类图示进行阅读、估算或比较数量。
- 图形数据展示，例如条形图、圆形图和线形图，都是按比例绘制的。因此，考生可以通过目测或度量来对这类图示进行阅读、估算或比较数量。

有关定律和假设的更多信息，请参见出版物*Mathematical Conventions for the GRE General Test*，该出版物可在以下网址找到：www.ets.org/gre/prepare，同时在本章末尾也可以找到相关内容。

General Problem-solving Steps

Quantitative Reasoning 测试部分要求考生利用定量法或数学法去建模、解决问题。通常来讲，解决一道数学题分为以下三个步骤：

Step 1：充分理解问题（Understand the problem）

Step 2：使用策略解题（Carry out a strategy for solving the problem）

Step 3：检查答案 （Check your answer）

以下是关于三个步骤的详细解释以及14个有效的解题策略。

Step 1: Understand the Problem

考生要做的第一步是仔细审题，弄清楚题目所给的信息以及需要解决的问题。

描述数量的信息有些用文字呈现，有些用数学表达式，有些则两者结合。有一些题目中，考生需要读懂并理解表格、几何图、坐标系里的数据。还有一些信息则是以方程、定义以及数量所需满足的前提条件的形式出现。比如说，条件可以是等式、不等式，或者是可以转换成等式、不等式的文字。

除了理解题中所给信息之外，非常重要的一点是，弄清楚还需要知道哪些信息才能解题。比如说，必须找到哪些未知数量才能解题？这些未知数量以什么形式出现？

Step 2: Carry Out a Strategy for Solving the Problem

算出一道数学题不只需要理解问题是什么，包括题目中的数量、数据、题设、未知量以及其他数学方面的信息，更需要决定运用哪些数学信息去解决问题，什么时候运用、如何运用才能找到解题思路，而这是需要策略的。

不同的数学题目可以通过各种不同的策略得到答案，考生也可以用不同的方法解决同一个问题。因此，考生应该建立自己的解题策略资源库，在看到某一题目时就知道该运用哪种解题策略。如果没有恰当的解题策略，考生可能耗时耗力也无法算出正确答案。

确定解题策略之后，就把这个策略付诸实践。如果在解题过程中遇到困难，则需要检查是否在解题过程中有失误。保持开放、灵活的思路对于解题是非常重要的。如果解题过程并没有发现问题，那么可能就是解题策略不对，这时候就需要换一个不同的解题思路。

Step 3: Check Your Answer

解完题之后，需要检查答案是否合理且计算无误。

- 是否回答了题目中的问题？

- 答案是否与题中所给信息冲突？确定答案是否合理只需要回想一个基本的数学事实，并判断答案是否与数学事实相吻合。比如，一个事件的概率必然在0和1之间，且包含0和1；一个几何图形的面积一定是正的。或者，考生也可以利用估算来检查答案是否合理。比如，计算中涉及3个数值相加，每个数值的大小在100到200之间，那么则可以估算出答案的数值一定是在300到600之间。

- 是否在计算时有失误？是否在使用计算器时输入了错误数据？考生可以检查解题的每一个步骤，也可以直接检查答案是否正确。比如，在 $7(3x-2)+4 = 95$ 这个方程式中，如果得到的x值为5，可以把5代入方程中，看 $7(3(5)-2)+4 = 95$ 是否成立。

Strategies

没有一个固定的规则可以帮助考生确定最好的解题策略。选择解题策略的能力是随着考生解题数量的积累而提高的。下面的内容是关于解题策略的简要描述，每个策略都结合本章题目做出示范。这些策略并不代表所有的解题策略，而且除了前四个策略有共性，放在一起先后说明之外，其他解题策略的排列顺序是随机的。

前四项是转化策略，指的是将数学题的呈现方式转换为另外一种形式来表达。

Strategy 1: Translate from Words to an Arithmetic or Algebraic Representation

将文字转化为算术式、代数式。文字题可以通过把冗长复杂的文字转化成简单明晰的数学表达式来解决。比如说，奇数（odd integer）可以用"$2n+1$"来表示（n是整数）。如果题目中说"打车的费用是起步价3美元加上每英里1.25美元"，用数学表达式就是$c=3+1.25m$。通常来说，当考生能够把文字转化成数学表达式，也就能成功解题。

● 详见124页第4题和131页第5题。

Strategy 2: Translate from Words to a Figure or Diagram

将文字转化为图表。如果题目描述了图形但没有配图，考生需要自己画出来，并尽可能地使图形准确，标出所有已知条件和推算出的未知条件。

在几何题以及其他题目中，画图可以帮助考生高效解题。比如，在概率和计数问题中，画图便于考生分析数据，注意到数据之间的关系。

● 详见122页第2题。

Strategy 3: Translate from an Algebraic to a Graphical Representation

将代数转化为图形。很多代数问题可以用坐标表示，可能是只有一个变量的数轴，也可能是有两个变量的平面坐标。通过图形，考生可以更容易看到代数表达式中变量间的关系。

● 详见123页第3题。

Strategy 4: Translate from a Figure to an Arithmetic or Algebraic Representation

将图形转化为算术式、代数式。当题目中给出了图形，把图中的信息用数学表达式呈现出来有利于快速解题。

● 详见116页第4题和130页第3题。

Strategy 5: Simplify an Arithmetic or Algebraic Representation

化简算术式、代数式。算术式、代数式包括了表达式和等式。考生的化简能力有助于迅速解题。化简指百分数转化成小数、不同计量单位之间的转换、合并同类项，以及简化方程等。

● 详见118页第6题和131页第4题。

Strategy 6: Add to a Geometric Figure

补充几何图形。考生可以在解题过程中自行在原几何图形中补充必要的线、点、圆，也可以补充图中尚未标明的已知信息和从题中推测出的新信息。如此，考生可以更清晰地看到图形中的各种关系。比如说，一条线段的长度或是角度的大小。

● 详见123页第3题。

Strategy 7: Find a Pattern

找规律。规律贯穿数学。辨识规律通常是解决复杂题目的第一步，可以帮助考生迅速抓住解题的方向，或者直接得出一个假设，虽然之后还需要用其他的解题策略去证明这个假设。在解题时，如果考生认为题目中有规律可循，但是不确定是什么规律，可以通过具体情况来得出规律。一旦识别出规律，考生便可以用来回答问题。

● 详见128页第4题。

Strategy 8: Search for a Mathematical Relationship

找数量关系。在数学中，数量关系式比数学规律更为常见。题目中可能包含相互联系的数量、逻辑相关的集合，或者几何相关的图形。同样，以文字、代数和图形等呈现的信息之间也可能存在某种关系。要表示数量之间的关系，考生可以引入一个或多个变量来代表数量。一旦数量的关系被确定并表示出来，往往也就找到了解题的关键。

● 详见119页第8题和127页第3题。

Strategy 9: Estimate

估算。有些题目不需要大量计算去得出最后答案，估算便足以解题。考生需要根据具体题目去判断最后的计算结果需要精确到何种程度。需要关注的是，估算的答案和精确的答案之间的差距。同时，估算也可以帮助考生检查答案是否合理。

● 详见116页第3题和124页第4题。

Strategy 10: Trial and Error

Version 1: Make a Reasonable Guess and Then Refine It

合理猜测并完善。有时，最快的解题方法是先对答案做一个合理的猜测，然后去验证它，如果猜测不成立再去改进。这个策略在已规定选项数量的题目中尤为有效。在其他题目中，这个方法也可以帮助考生更好地理解题目。

● 详见126页第1题。

Version 2: Try More Than One Value of a Variable

代入一个以上的变量。在攻克那些含有变量的题目时，代入数值是有效的方法。每个变量最好多代入几个数字。但是，代入几个数字，代入什么数字需依题而定。同时，考生需要判断用数字代替变量这个解题方法是否适用于题目，以及是否能够帮助考生得出一个假设，尽管这个假设需要后续再用其他的解题策略去验证。

- 详见115页第2题和117页第5题。

Strategy 11: Divide into Cases

考虑不同情况。当解决比较复杂的题目时，考生可以把它分解成不同的情况进行解答。这就需要考生考虑到所有的情况。比如，要证明一个结论适用于所有整数，就需要证明其适用于所有正整数、负整数以及零，这样才能确定这个结论是适用于所有整数的，因为整数包括正整数、负整数和零。

- 详见115页第1题和126页第2题。

Strategy 12: Adapt Solutions to Related Problems

根据题目调整解题策略。当遇到与之前做过并且会做的类似题目时，可以尝试用同一个解题策略。

如果新题与做过的题目没有本质上的区别，也就是说新题只是换了数字、表格或者是对象的类别等等这些不足以改变题目架构的信息时，考生就可以用与之前一致的解题思路去做题。

如果新题与做过的题目之间的区别不只是以上那些表面信息，考生则需及时调整解题策略以适应新题中给出的条件。

- 详见127页第3题和128页第4题。

Strategy 13: Determine Whether a Conclusion Follows from the Information Given

判断答案是否由题中信息推断而来。一些问题给出了已知信息并对可能的结论进行了描述，已知信息不一定推断出那个结论。考生需要判断该结论是否由已知信息推出并且具有逻辑性。

如果考生认为结论由题中信息推断而来，需要根据题中所给信息以及所有相关的数学关系，按步骤去证明。此外，也可以通过证明在任何条件下，只要题中已给信息成立，这个结论就成立，来判定结论是由题中信息推断而来。

相反，如果考生认为最终结论不能从题中条件推断出来，也需要进行证明。一种方式是，举出反例证明，也就是当题中所给信息成立，但是最终结论却不成立的情况。如果考生没有找到合适的反例，并不一定意味着结论符合题中的条件，也可能是反例确实存在，只是考生没有成功地找到。

- 详见120页第9题和133页第3题。

Strategy 14: Determine What Additional Information Is Sufficient to Solve a Problem

判断解题需要的附加信息。有时，题中所给信息不足以成功解出题目，需要考生自己去判断还需要什么信息才能解题。此时，考生可以列出所有已知信息以及在分析已知信息时得到的新信息，然后再去判断缺失哪些信息，这对解题是很有帮助的。有时这些信息可以从题设中推导出来，有时则不能。

● 详见133页第3题。

Quantitative Reasoning Question Types

Quantitative Reasoning 测试包含四种题型：

● Quantitative Comparison questions （数量比较题）

● Multiple-choice questions—Select One Answer Choice （单项选择题）

● Multiple-choice questions—Select One or More Answer Choices（多项选择题）

● Numeric Entry questions（数字填空题）

每道题或作为一道单独的题目出现，或作为数据分析题（Data Interpretation set）的其中一问出现。数据分析中所有问题都是基于同一表格、曲线图以及其他形式的数据所提出的。

机考中，在Quantitative Reasoning考试部分，电脑屏幕上方会提供一个具有基本功能的计算器。更多关于使用计算器的信息会在本章后面的内容中作详细阐述。

在纸笔考试中，也会提供手持型计算器。更多关于使用手持型计算器答题的信息可登录网站www.ets.org/gre/prepare参见*Practice Book for the Paper-delivered GRE General Test*（GRE纸笔考试的练习册，是免费提供的）。

Quantitative Comparison Questions

Description

此题型要求考生比较两个数量——数量A和数量B，然后判断哪个叙述符合这两个数量之间的关系。

● Quantity A中的数值较大

● Quantity B 中的数值较大

● 两者相等

● 无法判断哪个数值较大

答题技巧

- **熟悉四个选项**。数量比较题的选项都是一样的，考生有必要熟悉这些选项，尤其是最后一项，"无法判断哪个数值较大"。如果通过计算可以确定这两个数量的大小就绝对不要选择最后一个选项。如果已经确定一个数量大于另外一个，要仔细看清选项，不要把前两个选项混淆。

- **避免不必要的计算**。比较两个数量的大小，有时并不需要费时间计算出具体的数值，只要将题目中给出的一个或两个数量进行简化、转换或估测就可以得到答案。

- **谨记几何图形不一定要按比例画出**。如果几何图中的一项或几项数值不确定，就需要重新画图。画图的时候，保持已知信息对应的图形部分不变，改变未知信息对应的部分。然后检查结果，判断未知部分的可能数值，如线段的长度、角的大小。

- **代入数据**。如果比较题目里的数量是代数表达式，可以通过代入具体数值来比较大小。在给出答案之前，需要全面地考虑可代入数字的可能性，例如，0、正数、负数，大小数，分数、小数。如果在一种情况下Quantity A大于Quantity B，而在另外一种情况下，Quantity B则大于Quantity A，那么就要选择"无法判断哪个数值较大"。

- **先化简再比较**。如果比较的两个数值都是比较复杂的代数或算数表达式，那么就要先进行化简。要一步步地化简，就像计算 $5 = 4x + 3$ 中的 x 值，或是将 $\frac{(3y + 2)}{5} < y$ 这个不等式化简为 $1 < y$ 的过程。开始解题的时候，在 Quantity A 与 Quantity B 之间建立一个比较关系，如下所示：

  Quantity A ⬚ Quantity B

  ⬚表示Quantity A与Quantity B之间的大小关系，可以是大于（＞），小于（＜），等于（＝），或者是无法判断哪个数值较大。考生要一步步去化简，直到可以判断出两个数学式之间的大小，然后最终确定Quantity A和B之间的大小关系。比如，考生在最后一步判断出⬚代表相等（＝）。更多关于此技巧的内容可以参见例题 6~9。

Sample Questions

> Compare Quantity A and Quantity B, using additional information centered above the two quantities if such information is given, and select one of the following four answer choices:
>
> (A)   Quantity A is greater.
>
> (B)   Quantity B is greater.
>
> (C)   The two quantities are equal.
>
> (D)   The relationship cannot be determined from the information given.
>
> A symbol that appears more than once in a question has the same meaning throughout the question.

	Quantity A	Quantity B
1.	The least prime number greater than 24	The greatest prime number less than 28

(A) Quantity A is greater.

(B) Quantity B is greater.

(C) The two quantities are equal.

(D) The relationship cannot be determined from the information given.

Explanation

For the integers greater than 24, note that 25, 26, 27, and 28 are not prime numbers, but 29 is a prime number, as are 31 and many other greater integers. Thus, 29 is the least prime number greater than 24, and Quantity A is 29. For the integers less than 28, note that 27, 26, 25, and 24 are not prime numbers, but 23 is a prime number, as are 19 and several other lesser integers. Thus, 23 is the greatest prime number less than 28, and Quantity B is 23.

The correct answer is Choice A, Quantity A is greater.

This explanation uses the following strategy.

Strategy 11: Divide into Cases

Lionel is younger than Maria.

	Quantity A	Quantity B
2.	Twice Lionel's age	Maria's age

(A) Quantity A is greater.

(B) Quantity B is greater.

(C) The two quantities are equal.

(D) The relationship cannot be determined from the information given.

Explanation

If Lionel's age is 6 years and Maria's age is 10 years, then Quantity A is greater, but if Lionel's age is 4 years and Maria's age is 10 years, then Quantity B is greater. Thus, the relationship cannot be determined.

The correct answer is Choice D, the relationship cannot be determined from the information given.

This explanation uses the following strategies.
Strategy 10: Trial and Error
Strategy 13: Determine Whether a Conclusion Follows from the Information Given

Quantity A	Quantity B
3. 54% of 360	150

Ⓐ Quantity A is greater.
Ⓑ Quantity B is greater.
Ⓒ The two quantities are equal.
Ⓓ The relationship cannot be determined from the information given.

Explanation

Without doing the exact computation, you can see that 54 percent of 360 is greater than $\frac{1}{2}$ of 360, which is 180, and 180 is greater than Quantity B, 150.

Thus, the correct answer is Choice A, Quantity A is greater.

This explanation uses the following strategy.
Strategy 9: Estimate

Figure 1

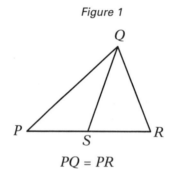

$PQ = PR$

Quantity A	Quantity B
4. PS	SR

Ⓐ Quantity A is greater.
Ⓑ Quantity B is greater.
Ⓒ The two quantities are equal.
Ⓓ The relationship cannot be determined from the information given.

Explanation

From Figure 1, you know that *PQR* is a triangle and that point *S* is between points *P* and *R*, so *PS* < *PR* and *SR* < *PR*. You are also given that *PQ* = *PR*. However, this information is not sufficient to compare *PS* and *SR*. Furthermore, because the figure is not necessarily drawn to scale, you cannot determine the relative sizes of *PS* and *SR* visually from the figure, though they may appear to be equal. The position of *S* can vary along side *PR* anywhere between *P* and *R*. Following are two possible variations of Figure 1, each of which is drawn to be consistent with the information *PQ* = *PR*.

Figure 2

$PQ = PR$

Figure 3

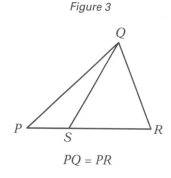

$PQ = PR$

Note that Quantity A is greater in Figure 2 and Quantity B is greater in Figure 3.

Thus, the correct answer is Choice D, the relationship cannot be determined from the information given.

This explanation uses the following strategies.

Strategy 4: Translate from a Figure to an Arithmetic or Algebraic Representation
Strategy 13: Determine Whether a Conclusion Follows from the Information Given

---

$$y = 2x^2 + 7x - 3$$

Quantity A	Quantity B

5. x y

Ⓐ Quantity A is greater.
Ⓑ Quantity B is greater.
Ⓒ The two quantities are equal.
Ⓓ The relationship cannot be determined from the information given.

Explanation

If $x = 0$, then $y = 2(0^2) + 7(0) - 3 = -3$, so in this case, $x > y$; but if $x = 1$, then $y = 2(1^2) + 7(1) - 3 = 6$, so in that case, $y > x$.

Thus, the correct answer is Choice D, the relationship cannot be determined from the information given.

This explanation uses the following strategies.

Strategy 10: Trial and Error
Strategy 13: Determine Whether a Conclusion Follows from the Information Given

Note that plugging numbers into expressions *may not* be conclusive. It *is* conclusive, however, if you get different results after plugging in different numbers: the conclusion is that the relationship cannot be determined from the information given. It is also conclusive if there are only a small number of possible numbers to plug in and all of them yield the same result, say, that Quantity B is greater.

Now suppose that there are an infinite number of possible numbers to plug in. If you plug many of them in and each time the result is, for example, that Quantity A is greater, you still cannot conclude that Quantity A is greater for every possible number that could be plugged in. Further analysis would be necessary and should focus on whether Quantity A is greater for all possible numbers or whether there are numbers for which Quantity A is not greater.

The following sample questions focus on simplifying the comparison.

$$y > 4$$

Quantity A	Quantity B

6. $\dfrac{3y+2}{5}$ y

(A) Quantity A is greater.
(B) Quantity B is greater.
(C) The two quantities are equal.
(D) The relationship cannot be determined from the information given.

Explanation

Set up the initial comparison:

$$\frac{3y+2}{5} \boxed{?}\ y$$

Then simplify:

Step 1: Multiply both sides by 5 to get

$$3y+2 \boxed{?}\ 5y$$

Step 2: Subtract $3y$ from both sides to get

$$2 \boxed{?}\ 2y$$

Step 3: Divide both sides by 2 to get

$$1 \boxed{?}\ y$$

The comparison is now simplified as much as possible. In order to compare 1 and y, note that you are given the information $y > 4$ (above Quantities A and B). It follows from $y > 4$ that $y > 1$, or $1 < y$, so that in the comparison $1 \boxed{?}\ y$, the placeholder $\boxed{?}$ represents *less than* ($<$): $1 < y$.

However, the problem asks for a comparison between Quantity A and Quantity B, not a comparison between 1 and y. To go from the comparison between 1 and y to a comparison between Quantities A and B, start with the last comparison, $1 < y$ and carefully consider each simplification step in reverse order to determine what each comparison implies about the preceding comparison, all the way back to the comparison between Quantities A and B if possible. Since step 3 was "*divide* both sides by 2," *multiplying* both sides of the comparison $1 < y$ by 2 implies the preceding comparison $2 < 2y$, thus reversing step 3. Each simplification step can be reversed as follows:

- Reverse step 3: *multiply* both sides by 2.
- Reverse step 2: *add* $3y$ to both sides.
- Reverse step 1: *divide* both sides by 5.

When each step is reversed, the relationship remains *less than* ($<$), so Quantity A is less than Quantity B.

Thus, the correct answer is Choice B, Quantity B is greater.

This explanation uses the following strategy.

Strategy 5: Simplify an Arithmetic or Algebraic Representation

While some simplification steps like subtracting 3 from both sides or dividing both sides by 10 are always reversible, it is important to note that some steps, like squaring both sides, may not be reversible.

Also, note that when you simplify an *inequality*, the steps of multiplying or dividing both sides by a negative number change the direction of the inequality; for example, if $x < y$, then $-x > -y$. So the relationship in the final, simplified inequality may be the *opposite* of the relationship between Quantities A and B. This is another reason to consider the impact of each step carefully.

	Quantity A	Quantity B
7.	$\dfrac{2^{30} - 2^{29}}{2}$	2^{28}

   Ⓐ Quantity A is greater.
   Ⓑ Quantity B is greater.
   Ⓒ The two quantities are equal.
   Ⓓ The relationship cannot be determined from the information given.

Explanation

Set up the initial comparison:

$$\frac{2^{30} - 2^{29}}{2} \;\boxed{?}\; 2^{28}$$

Then simplify:

Step 1: Multiply both sides by 2 to get

$$2^{30} - 2^{29} \;\boxed{?}\; 2^{29}$$

Step 2: Add 2^{29} to both sides to get

$$2^{30} \;\boxed{?}\; 2^{29} + 2^{29}$$

Step 3: Simplify the right-hand side using the fact that $(2)(2^{29}) = 2^{30}$ to get

$$2^{30} \;\boxed{?}\; 2^{30}$$

The resulting relationship is *equal to* (=). In reverse order, each simplification step implies *equal to* in the preceding comparison. So Quantities A and B are also equal.
   Thus, the correct answer is Choice C, the two quantities are equal.

This explanation uses the following strategy.
Strategy 5: Simplify an Arithmetic or Algebraic Representation

	Quantity A	Quantity B
8.	$x^2 + 1$	$2x - 1$

   Ⓐ Quantity A is greater.
   Ⓑ Quantity B is greater.
   Ⓒ The two quantities are equal.
   Ⓓ The relationship cannot be determined from the information given.

Explanation

Set up the initial comparison:

$$x^2 + 1 \boxed{?} 2x - 1$$

Then simplify by noting that the quadratic polynomial $x^2 - 2x + 1$ can be factored:

Step 1: Subtract $2x$ from both sides to get

$$x^2 - 2x + 1 \boxed{?} -1$$

Step 2: Factor the left-hand side to get

$$(x - 1)^2 \boxed{?} -1$$

The left-hand side of the comparison is the square of a number. Since the square of a number is always greater than or equal to 0, and 0 is greater than -1, the simplified comparison is the inequality $(x - 1)^2 > -1$ and the resulting relationship is *greater than* (>). In reverse order, each simplification step implies the inequality *greater than* (>) in the preceding comparison. Therefore, Quantity A is greater than Quantity B.

The correct answer is Choice A, Quantity A is greater.

This explanation uses the following strategies.
Strategy 5: Simplify an Arithmetic or Algebraic Representation
Strategy 8: Search for a Mathematical Relationship

$$w > 1$$

Quantity A	Quantity B
$7w - 4$	$2w + 5$

9.

(A) Quantity A is greater.
(B) Quantity B is greater.
(C) The two quantities are equal.
(D) The relationship cannot be determined from the information given.

Explanation

Set up the initial comparison:

$$7w - 4 \boxed{?} 2w + 5$$

Then simplify:

Step 1: Subtract $2w$ from both sides and add 4 to both sides to get

$$5w \boxed{?} 9$$

Step 2: Divide both sides by 5 to get

$$w \boxed{?} \frac{9}{5}$$

The comparison cannot be simplified any further. Although you are given that $w > 1$, you still don't know how w compares to $\frac{9}{5}$, or 1.8. For example, if $w = 1.5$, then $w < 1.8$, but if $w = 2$, then $w > 1.8$. In other words, the relationship between w and $\frac{9}{5}$ cannot be determined. Note that each of these simplification steps is reversible, so in reverse order, each simplification step implies that the *relationship cannot be determined* in the preceding comparison. Thus, the relationship between Quantities A and B cannot be determined.

The correct answer is Choice D, the relationship cannot be determined from the information given.

This explanation uses the following strategies.
Strategy 5: Simplify an Arithmetic or Algebraic Representation
Strategy 13: Determine Whether a Conclusion Follows from the Information Given

The strategy of simplifying the comparison works most efficiently when you note that a simplification step is reversible while actually taking the step. Here are some common steps that are always reversible:

- Adding any number or expression to both sides of a comparison
- Subtracting any number or expression from both sides
- Multiplying both sides by any nonzero number or expression
- Dividing both sides by any nonzero number or expression

Remember that if the relationship is an inequality, multiplying or dividing both sides by any *negative* number or expression will yield the opposite inequality. Be aware that some common operations like squaring both sides are generally not reversible and may require further analysis using other information given in the question in order to justify reversing such steps.

Multiple-choice Questions—Select One Answer Choice

Description

此题型是单项选择题。每道题有五个选项，其中只有一个为正确答案。

答题技巧

- **选项中一定有正确答案。** 如果考生得出的答案不包含在所给的五个选项之中，那么可以断定这个答案是不正确的，遇到这种情况可以这样做：

  - 重新仔细审题——考生很可能漏读或误解了重要的细节和信息。

  - 检查计算过程——考生很可能犯计算错误，比如在计算器上输入了错误的数值。

  - 重新评估解题思路——考生很可能在推理过程中出现失误。

- **检查选项。**有些问题考查得详细，问哪个选项有某种特性。考生可能需要单独分析每个选项，或者只有找到选项之间的关系才能更快地确定答案。在另一些题目中，从选项入手更容易解题，比如说把选项直接代入到等式、不等式中，看哪个选项代入后数学式成立。但是也要注意，依次代入选项会比直接推理花费更多时间。

- **对于求近似值的题目，快速浏览选项，判断需要精确到何种程度。**在一些题目中，做题之前浏览一下选项有助于更好地了解问题。如果题目要求精准计算，考生就需要精确地算出每一步，在计算的最后一步根据题目要求取近似值。而在另一些题目中，估算已经足以确定答案，考生就没有必要在计算上浪费时间。

Sample Questions

Select a single answer choice.

1. If $5x + 32 = 4 - 2x$, what is the value of x?

   (A) -4

   (B) -3

   (C) 4

   (D) 7

   (E) 12

Explanation

Solving the equation for x, you get $7x = -28$, and so $x = -4$.

The correct answer is Choice A, -4.

This explanation uses the following strategy.

Strategy 5: Simplify an Arithmetic or Algebraic Representation

2. Which of the following numbers is farthest from the number 1 on the number line?

   (A) -10

   (B) -5

   (C) 0

   (D) 5

   (E) 10

Explanation

Circling each of the answer choices in a sketch of the number line (Figure 4) shows that of the given numbers, −10 is the greatest distance from 1.

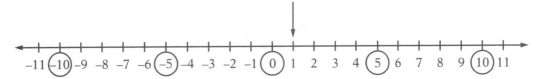

Figure 4

Another way to answer the question is to remember that the distance between two numbers on the number line is equal to the absolute value of the difference of the two numbers. For example, the distance between −10 and 1 is $|-10 - 1| = 11$, and the distance between 10 and 1 is $|10 - 1| = |9| = 9$.
The correct answer is Choice A, −10.

This explanation uses the following strategy.

Strategy 2: Translate from Words to a Figure or Diagram

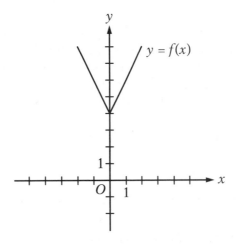

Figure 5

3. The figure above shows the graph of the function f defined by $f(x) = |2x| + 4$ for all numbers x. For which of the following functions g, defined for all numbers x, does the graph of g intersect the graph of f?

    (A) $g(x) = x - 2$

    (B) $g(x) = x + 3$

    (C) $g(x) = 2x - 2$

    (D) $g(x) = 2x + 3$

    (E) $g(x) = 3x - 2$

Explanation

You can see that all five choices are linear functions whose graphs are lines with various slopes and y-intercepts. The graph of Choice A is a line with slope 1 and y-intercept -2, shown in Figure 6.

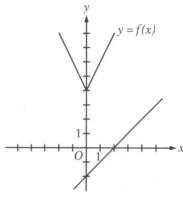

Figure 6

It is clear that this line will not intersect the graph of f to the left of the y-axis. To the right of the y-axis, the graph of f is a line with slope 2, which is greater than slope 1. Consequently, as the value of x increases, the value of y increases faster for f than for g, and therefore the graphs do not intersect to the right of the y-axis. Choice B is similarly ruled out. Note that if the y-intercept of either of the lines in Choices A and B were greater than or equal to 4 instead of less than 4, they would intersect the graph of f.

Choices C and D are lines with slope 2 and y-intercepts less than 4. Hence, they are parallel to the graph of f (to the right of the y-axis) and therefore will not intersect it. Any line with a slope greater than 2 and a y-intercept less than 4, like the line in Choice E, will intersect the graph of f (to the right of the y-axis).

The correct answer is Choice E, $g(x) = 3x - 2$.

This explanation uses the following strategies.

Strategy 3: Translate from an Algebraic to a Graphical Representation
Strategy 6: Add to a Geometric Figure
Strategy 8: Search for a Mathematical Relationship

---

4. A car got 33 miles per gallon using gasoline that cost $2.95 per gallon. Approximately what was the cost, in dollars, of the gasoline used in driving the car 350 miles?

   (A) $10   (B) $20   (C) $30   (D) $40   (E) $50

Explanation

Scanning the answer choices indicates that you can do at least some estimation and still answer confidently. The car used $\frac{350}{33}$ gallons of gasoline, so the cost was $\left(\frac{350}{33}\right)(2.95)$ dollars. You can estimate the product $\left(\frac{350}{33}\right)(2.95)$ by estimating $\frac{350}{33}$ a little low, 10, and estimating 2.95 a little high, 3, to get approximately $(10)(3) = 30$ dollars. You can also use the calculator to compute a more exact answer and then round the answer to the nearest 10 dollars, as suggested by the answer choices. The calculator yields the decimal 31.287... , which rounds to 30 dollars.

Thus, the correct answer is Choice C, $30.

This explanation uses the following strategies.

Strategy 1: Translate from Words to an Arithmetic or Algebraic Representation
Strategy 9: Estimate

5. A certain jar contains 60 jelly beans—22 white, 18 green, 11 yellow, 5 red, and 4 purple. If a jelly bean is to be chosen at random, what is the probability that the jelly bean will be neither red nor purple?

  Ⓐ 0.09
  Ⓑ 0.15
  Ⓒ 0.54
  Ⓓ 0.85
  Ⓔ 0.91

Explanation

Since there are 5 red and 4 purple jelly beans in the jar, there are 51 that are neither red nor purple, and the probability of selecting one of these is $\frac{51}{60}$. Since all of the answer choices are decimals, you must convert the fraction to its decimal equivalent, 0.85.

Thus, the correct answer is Choice D, 0.85.

This explanation uses the following strategies.

Strategy 1: Translate from Words to an Arithmetic or Algebraic Representation
Strategy 5: Simplify an Arithmetic or Algebraic Representation

Multiple-choice Questions—Select One or More Answer Choices

Description

此题型是多项选择题，要求考生选出一个或以上正确答案。题目可能会规定正确选项的数量，也可能让考生自己去判断。此题型的标志是选项旁有正方块图形，不是圆形或椭圆形。

答题技巧

● **注意题目要求选出特定数量的答案还是全部成立的答案。**后者要求考生衡量所有选项之后选出全部正确选项，多选或少选均不得分。记住，多选题也存在只有一个正确选项的情况。

● 有些题设可以帮助考生缩减可选择答案的范围，算出最小或最大可能值。这有助于考生提高解题速度，迅速选出所有正确答案。

● 识别并应用数学规律，避免冗长计算。

Sample Questions

Select one or more answer choices according to the specific question directions.

If the question does not specify how many answer choices to select, select all that apply.

- The correct answer may be just one of the choices or as many as all of the choices, depending on the question.
- No credit is given unless you select all of the correct choices and no others.

If the question specifies how many answer choices to select, select exactly that number of choices.

1. Which two of the following numbers have a product that is between -1 and 0?

   Indicate <u>both</u> of the numbers.

   A -20 C 2^{-4}

   B -10 D 3^{-2}

Explanation

For this question, you must select a pair of answer choices. The product of the pair must be negative, so the possible products are $(-20)(2^{-4})$, $(-20)(3^{-2})$, $(-10)(2^{-4})$, and $(-10)(3^{-2})$. The product must also be greater than -1. The first product is $\frac{-20}{2^4} = -\frac{20}{16} < -1$, the second product is $\frac{-20}{3^2} = -\frac{20}{9} < -1$, and the third product is $\frac{-10}{2^4} = -\frac{10}{16} > -1$, so you can stop there.

   The correct answer consists of Choices B (-10) and C (2^{-4}).

This explanation uses the following strategies.

Strategy 1: Translate from Words to an Arithmetic or Algebraic Representation
Strategy 10: Trial and Error

2. Which of the following integers are multiples of both 2 and 3?

   Indicate <u>all</u> such integers.

   A 8   D 18

   B 9   E 21

   C 12   F 36

Explanation

You can first identify the multiples of 2, which are 8, 12, 18, and 36, and then among the multiples of 2 identify the multiples of 3, which are 12, 18, and 36. Alternatively, if you realize that every number that is a multiple of 2 and 3 is also a multiple of 6, you can identify the choices that are multiples of 6.

   The correct answer consists of Choices C (12), D (18), and F (36).

This explanation uses the following strategies.

Strategy 1: Translate from Words to an Arithmetic or Algebraic Representation
Strategy 11: Divide into Cases

3. Each employee of a certain company is in either Department X or Department Y, and there are more than twice as many employees in Department X as in Department Y. The average (arithmetic mean) salary is $25,000 for the employees in Department X and $35,000 for the employees in Department Y. Which of the following amounts could be the average salary for all of the employees of the company?

Indicate <u>all</u> such amounts.

- [A] $26,000
- [B] $28,000
- [C] $29,000
- [D] $30,000
- [E] $31,000
- [F] $32,000
- [G] $34,000

Explanation

One strategy for answering this kind of question is to find the least and/or greatest possible value. Clearly the average salary is between $25,000 and $35,000, and all of the answer choices are in this interval. Since you are told that there are more employees with the lower average salary, the average salary of all employees must be less than the average of $25,000 and $35,000, which is $30,000. If there were exactly twice as many employees in Department X as in Department Y, then the average salary for all employees would be, to the nearest dollar, the following weighted mean,

$$\frac{(2)(25,000)+(1)(35,000)}{2+1} \approx 28,333 \text{ dollars}$$

where the weight for $25,000 is 2 and the weight for $35,000 is 1. Since there are *more* than twice as many employees in Department X as in Department Y, the actual average salary must be even closer to $25,000 because the weight for $25,000 is greater than 2. This means that $28,333 is the greatest possible average. Among the choices given, the possible values of the average are therefore $26,000 and $28,000.

Thus, the correct answer consists of Choices A ($26,000) and B ($28,000).

Intuitively, you might expect that any amount between $25,000 and $28,333 is a possible value of the average salary. To see that $26,000 is possible, in the weighted mean above, use the respective weights 9 and 1 instead of 2 and 1. To see that $28,000 is possible, use the respective weights 7 and 3.

This explanation uses the following strategies.

Strategy 1: Translate from Words to an Arithmetic or Algebraic Representation
Strategy 8: Search for a Mathematical Relationship
Strategy 12: Adapt Solutions to Related Problems

4. Which of the following could be the units digit of 57^n, where n is a positive integer?

Indicate <u>all</u> such digits.

A	0	F	5
B	1	G	6
C	2	H	7
D	3	I	8
E	4	J	9

Explanation

The units digit of 57^n is the same as the units digit of 7^n for all positive integers n. To see why this is true for $n = 2$, compute 57^2 by hand and observe how its units digit results from the units digit of 7^2. Because this is true for every positive integer n, you need to consider only powers of 7. Beginning with $n = 1$ and proceeding consecutively, the units digits of 7, 7^2, 7^3, 7^4, and 7^5 are 7, 9, 3, 1, and 7, respectively. In this sequence, the first digit, 7, appears again, and the pattern of four digits, 7, 9, 3, 1, repeats without end. Hence, these four digits are the only possible units digits of 7^n and therefore of 57^n.

The correct answer consists of Choices B (1), D (3), H (7), and J (9).

This explanation uses the following strategies.

Strategy 7: Find a Pattern
Strategy 12: Adapt Solutions to Related Problems

Numeric Entry Questions

Description

数字填空题要求考生在问题正下方的一个空格中输入答案，可能是整数或小数；或是要求考生在上下两个空格中填入分数，上面的空格填分子，下面的空格填分母。在机考中，考生需使用键盘和鼠标输入答案。

答题技巧

- **确保答案与题目要求相一致。**因为填空题没有选项来指引答案的形式，考生需要认真读题，确保按照题目要求的形式作答。有些题的答案框前后会有相关标识，提示答案的具体要求。考生要特别注意看清答案的单位是英尺（feet）还是英里（miles），数量级是百万（millions）还是十亿（billions），是填百分数还是小数，等等。

- **按题目要求进行四舍五入。**比如把46.7这个答案进位到整数，考生最后在答题框中输入的数值只能是47。如果某道题的计算过程比较复杂，为了得到准确答案，每一步计算都要十分精确，只在最后一步根据题目要求进行四舍五入。如果题目没有要求对答案进行四舍五入，考生则需输入精确的计算结果。

- **根据题目给出的信息，检查答案是否合理。**考生可以估算或是换一种解题思路去核实自己的答案。

Sample Questions

Enter your answer as an integer or a decimal if there is a single answer box OR as a fraction if there are two separate boxes—one for the numerator and one for the denominator.

To enter an integer or a decimal, either type the number in the answer box using the keyboard or use the Transfer Display button on the calculator.

- First, click on the answer box—a cursor will appear in the box—and then type the number.
- To erase a number, use the Backspace key.
- For a negative sign, type a hyphen. For a decimal point, type a period.
- To remove a negative sign, type the hyphen again and it will disappear; the number will remain.
- The Transfer Display button on the calculator will transfer the calculator display to the answer box.
- Equivalent forms of the correct answer, such as 2.5 and 2.50, are all correct.
- Enter the exact answer unless the question asks you to round your answer.

To enter a fraction, type the numerator and the denominator in the respective boxes using the keyboard.

- For a negative sign, type a hyphen; to remove it, type the hyphen again. A decimal point cannot be used in a fraction.
- The Transfer Display button on the calculator cannot be used for a fraction.
- Fractions do not need to be reduced to lowest terms, though you may need to reduce your fraction to fit in the boxes.

1. One pen costs $0.25 and one marker costs $0.35. At those prices, what is the total cost of 18 pens and 100 markers?

$ [   ]

Explanation

Multiplying $0.25 by 18 yields $4.50, which is the cost of the 18 pens; and multiplying $0.35 by 100 yields $35.00, which is the cost of the 100 markers. The total cost is therefore $4.50 + $35.00 = $39.50. Equivalent decimals, such as $39.5 or $39.500, are considered correct.

Thus, the correct answer is $39.50 (or equivalent).

Note that the dollar symbol is in front of the answer box, so the symbol $ does not need to be entered in the box. In fact, only numbers, a decimal point, and a negative sign can be entered in the answer box.

This explanation uses the following strategy.

Strategy 1: Translate from Words to an Arithmetic or Algebraic Representation

2. Rectangle *R* has length 30 and width 10, and square *S* has length 5. The perimeter of *S* is what fraction of the perimeter of *R*?

Explanation

The perimeter of *R* is 30 + 10 + 30 + 10 = 80, and the perimeter of *S* is (4)(5) = 20. Therefore, the perimeter of *S* is $\frac{20}{80}$ of the perimeter of *R*. To enter the answer $\frac{20}{80}$, you should enter the numerator 20 in the top box and the denominator 80 in the bottom box. Because the fraction does not need to be reduced to lowest terms, any fraction that is equivalent to $\frac{20}{80}$ is also considered correct, as long as it fits in the boxes. For example, both of the fractions $\frac{2}{8}$ and $\frac{1}{4}$ are considered correct.

Thus, the correct answer is $\frac{20}{80}$ (or any equivalent fraction).

This explanation uses the following strategy.

Strategy 1: Translate from Words to an Arithmetic or Algebraic Representation

---

RESULTS OF A USED-CAR AUCTION

	Small Cars	Large Cars
Number of cars offered	32	23
Number of cars sold	16	20
Projected sales total for cars offered (in thousands)	$70	$150
Actual sales total (in thousands)	$41	$120

Figure 7

3. For the large cars sold at an auction that is summarized in the table above, what was the average sale price per car?

$ [   ]

Explanation

From Figure 7, you see that the number of large cars sold was 20 and the sales total for large cars was $120,000 (not $120). Thus the average sale price per car was $\frac{\$120,000}{20} = \$6,000$.

The correct answer is $6,000 (or equivalent).

(Note that the comma in 6,000 will appear automatically in the answer box in the computer-delivered test.)

This explanation uses the following strategy.

Strategy 4: Translate from a Figure to an Arithmetic or Algebraic Representation

4. A merchant made a profit of $5 on the sale of a sweater that cost the merchant $15. What is the profit expressed as a percent of the merchant's cost?

   Give your answer to the <u>nearest whole percent</u>.

   ☐ %

Explanation

The percent profit is $\left(\dfrac{5}{15}\right)(100) = 33.333... = 33.\overline{3}$ percent, which is 33%, to the nearest whole percent.

Thus, the correct answer is 33% (or equivalent).

   If you use the calculator and the Transfer Display button, the number that will be transferred to the answer box is 33.333333, which is incorrect since it is not given to the nearest whole percent. You will need to adjust the number in the answer box by deleting all of the digits to the right of the decimal point (using the Backspace key).

   Also, since you are asked to give the answer as a percent, the decimal equivalent of 33 percent, which is 0.33, is incorrect. The percent symbol next to the answer box indicates that the form of the answer must be a percent. Entering 0.33 in the box would give the erroneous answer 0.33%.

This explanation uses the following strategies.

Strategy 1: Translate from Words to an Arithmetic or Algebraic Representation
Strategy 5: Simplify an Arithmetic or Algebraic Representation

---

5. Working alone at its constant rate, machine A produces k liters of a chemical in 10 minutes. Working alone at its constant rate, machine B produces k liters of the chemical in 15 minutes. How many minutes does it take machines A and B, working simultaneously at their respective constant rates, to produce k liters of the chemical?

   ☐ minutes

Explanation

Machine A produces $\dfrac{k}{10}$ liters per minute, and machine B produces $\dfrac{k}{15}$ liters per minute. So when the machines work simultaneously, the rate at which the chemical is produced is the sum of these two rates, which is $\dfrac{k}{10} + \dfrac{k}{15} = k\left(\dfrac{1}{10} + \dfrac{1}{15}\right) = k\left(\dfrac{25}{150}\right) = \dfrac{k}{6}$ liters per minute. To compute the time required to produce k liters at this rate, divide the amount k by the rate $\dfrac{k}{6}$ to get $\dfrac{k}{\frac{k}{6}} = 6$.

Therefore, the correct answer is 6 minutes (or equivalent).

   One way to check that the answer of 6 minutes is reasonable is to observe that if the slower rate of machine B were the same as machine A's faster rate of k liters in 10 minutes, then the two machines, working simultaneously, would take half the time, or 5 minutes, to produce the k liters. So the answer has to be *greater than 5 minutes*. Similarly, if the faster rate of machine A were the same as machine *B*'s slower rate of *k* liters in 15 minutes, then the two machines would take half the time, or 7.5 minutes, to produce the *k* liters. So the answer has to be *less than 7.5 minutes*. Thus, the answer of 6 minutes is reasonable compared to the lower estimate of 5 minutes and the upper estimate of 7.5 minutes.

This explanation uses the following strategies.
Strategy 1: Translate from Words to an Arithmetic or Algebraic Representation
Strategy 5: Simplify an Arithmetic or Algebraic Representation
Strategy 8: Search for a Mathematical Relationship

Data Interpretation Sets

Description

数据分析题以题组形式出现，所有问题都基于同一个表格、图表或是其他的数据形式。题目要求考生解读或分析已给数据。题型包括单项选择题、多项选择题以及数字填空题。

答题技巧

● 答题前对图表有一个大致了解，但不要花费时间关注图中每个细节。考生只需要关注那些和问题相关的信息。了解坐标轴、标度表示的意义，出现在标题、标注、说明文字中的数量单位或数量级（例如：billions），以及对数据的任何说明。

● 条形图、饼状图以及其他类型的图表都是根据比例绘制的，可以直接读取或估算数据。比如，考生可以根据饼状图中的面积大小或条形图的高低比较所对应的数值大小，但是要注意，标度数据不连续或起点不是从0开始的条形图不能按上述方法直接比较大小。

● 对任何问题的回答必须基于图表所提供的信息、既定事实（例如：一年中的天数），以及数学知识。不能根据从其他来源获得的信息以及背景知识进行主观臆断。

Sample Questions

Questions 1 to 3 are based on the following data.

ANNUAL PERCENT CHANGE IN DOLLAR AMOUNT OF SALES AT FIVE RETAIL STORES FROM 2006 TO 2008

Store	Percent Change from 2006 to 2007	Percent Change from 2007 to 2008
P	10	−10
Q	−20	9
R	5	12
S	−7	−15
T	17	−8

Figure 8

1. If the dollar amount of sales at Store *P* was $800,000 for 2006, what was the dollar amount of sales at that store for 2008?

   (A) $727,200   (D) $880,000

   (B) $792,000   (E) $968,000

   (C) $800,000

Explanation

According to Figure 8, if the dollar amount of sales at Store *P* was $800,000 for 2006, then it was 10 percent greater for 2007, which is 110 percent of that amount, or $880,000. For 2008 the amount was 90 percent of $880,000, which is $792,000.

The correct answer is Choice B, $792,000.

Note that an increase of 10 percent for one year and a decrease of 10 percent for the following year does not result in the same dollar amount as the original dollar amount, because the base that is used in computing the percents is $800,000 for the first change but $880,000 for the second change.

This explanation uses the following strategies.

Strategy 4: Translate from a Figure to an Arithmetic or Algebraic Representation
Strategy 5: Simplify an Arithmetic or Algebraic Representation

2. At Store *T*, the dollar amount of sales for 2007 was what percent of the dollar amount of sales for 2008?

   Give your answer to the <u>nearest 0.1 percent</u>.

   [   ] %

Explanation

If *A* is the dollar amount of sales at Store *T* for 2007, then 8 percent of *A*, or 0.08*A*, is the amount of decrease from 2007 to 2008. Thus $A - 0.08A = 0.92A$ is the dollar amount for 2008. Therefore, the desired percent can be obtained by dividing *A* by 0.92*A*, which equals $\frac{A}{0.92A} = \frac{1}{0.92} = 1.0869565....$ Expressed as a percent and rounded to the nearest 0.1 percent, this number is 108.7%.

Thus, the correct answer is 108.7% (or equivalent).

This explanation uses the following strategies.

Strategy 4: Translate from a Figure to an Arithmetic or Algebraic Representation
Strategy 5: Simplify an Arithmetic or Algebraic Representation

3. Based on the information given, which of the following statements must be true?

   Indicate <u>all</u> such statements.

   [A] For 2008 the dollar amount of sales at Store *R* was greater than that at each of the other four stores.

   [B] The dollar amount of sales at Store *S* for 2008 was 22 percent less than that for 2006.

   [C] The dollar amount of sales at Store *R* for 2008 was more than 17 percent greater than that for 2006.

Explanation

For Choice A, since the only data given in Figure 8 are percent changes from year to year, there is no way to compare the actual dollar amount of sales at the stores for 2008 or for any other year. Even though Store R had the greatest percent increase from 2006 to 2008, its actual dollar amount of sales for 2008 may have been much smaller than that for any of the other four stores, and therefore Choice A is not necessarily true.

For Choice B, even though the sum of the two percent decreases would suggest a 22 percent decrease, the bases of the percents are different. If B is the dollar amount of sales at Store S for 2006, then the dollar amount for 2007 is 93 percent of B, or $0.93B$, and the dollar amount for 2008 is given by $(0.85)(0.93)B$, which is $0.7905B$. Note that this represents a percent decrease of $100 - 79.05$, or 20.95 percent, which is not equal to 22 percent, and so Choice B is not true.

For Choice C, if C is the dollar amount of sales at Store R for 2006, then the dollar amount for 2007 is given by $1.05C$ and the dollar amount for 2008 is given by $(1.12)(1.05)C$, which is $1.176C$. Note that this represents a 17.6 percent increase, which is greater than 17 percent, so Choice C must be true.

Therefore, the correct answer consists of only Choice C (The dollar amount of sales at Store R for 2008 was more than 17 percent greater than that for 2006).

This explanation uses the following strategies.

Strategy 1: Translate from Words to an Arithmetic or Algebraic Representation
Strategy 4: Translate from a Figure to an Arithmetic or Algebraic Representation
Strategy 5: Simplify an Arithmetic or Algebraic Representation
Strategy 13: Determine Whether a Conclusion Follows from the Information Given
Strategy 14: Determine What Additional Information Is Sufficient to Solve a Problem

Using the Calculator

在 Quantitative Reasoning测试中，因为像长除法、平方根这样的计算比较耗时，在机考中考生可用屏幕上方的计算器（如Figure 9 所示）进行计算。

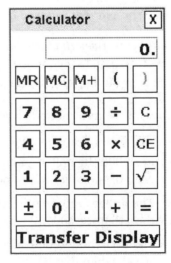

Figure 9

尽管计算器可以节省计算时间，但是请注意，计算器只能作为辅助工具，考生仍需要依靠数学知识去判断计算器给出的结果是否合理，以及如何根据计算结果去解决题目中的问题。关于在Quantitative Reasoning测试中使用计算器的方法，如下所示：

● 有很多问题不涉及复杂的计算，没必要都用计算器。

● 当计算过程比较复杂，比如长除法、平方根、加减法、多位数乘法，考生则需要使用计算器。

● 如果心算比使用计算器更快得出结果，像$10-490$、$(4)(70)$、$\frac{4,300}{10}$、$\sqrt{25}$以及30^2这样的计算，就不需要使用计算器。

● 当题目要求答案为分数形式时，就不要使用计算器，因为计算器只能给出小数。

● 有些题目通过推理和估算会比使用计算器更快得出答案。

● 在使用计算器之前估算一下答案，这样考生就能判断计算器算出的结果是否合理，也可以避免因输入错误导致结果错误的情况。

以下是主要针对机考中屏幕计算器的使用指南：

● 当使用鼠标和键盘输入数据时，注意不要输错数字或指令。

● 注意计算器上所有的按键，包括Transfer Display。

● Transfer Display用在只有一个空的数字填空题中，帮助考生把计算结果直接填入到答案空格中。考生需要核对转入的答案形式是否符合题目要求。比如，如果题目要求考生对答案进行四舍五入或者要求答案是百分比的形式，就要根据题目要求调整答案。

● 请注意，计算器会遵循运算顺序，也就是说，在一个需要一级以上运算的数学表达式中，计算器会根据计算惯例决定先做哪个部分的运算。运算顺序如下：括号、乘方（包括平方根）、乘除法（按从左至右的顺序），加减法（按从左至右的顺序）。例如，根据运算法则，$1+2\times4$的值是9。因为在这个计算中，首先要算2×4，然后再加1。在Quantitative Reasoning机考测试中，屏幕上计算器就是像这样进行计算的。（注意：许多初级计算器遵循不同的运算顺序——按照输入计算器的先后顺序，比如，$1+2\times4$的结果也可能是12。计算器会先运算$1+2$，再算3×4，得到的结果则为12。）

- 机考中的计算器除了有括号键，还有三个记忆储存键，分别是读取储存数据键（memory recall）MR、清除储存数据键（memory clear）MC、相加当前数据和储存数据键（memory sum）M+。这三个按键功能与其他计算器并无区别。

- 某些计算是不能进行的。比如，被零除或给负数开平方根。如果考生输入6÷0=，计算器就会显示ERROR。同样地，如果输入1 ± √ ，计算器也会显示ERROR，此时考生需要按下清除键C。

- 计算器最多能显示8位数字。如果计算结果大于99,999,999，计算器则会显示ERROR。比如，计算10,000,000 × 10 = 会导致计算器显示ERROR，清除错误必须按 C 键。如果计算结果是小于0.0000001的正数，或者是10^{-7}，显示的计算结果则为0。

Below are some examples of computations using the calculator.

1. Compute $4+\dfrac{6.73}{2}$.

Explanation

Enter 4 + 6.73 ÷ 2 = to get 7.365. Alternatively, enter 6.73 ÷ 2 = to get 3.365, and then enter + 4 = to get **7.365**.

2. Compute $-\dfrac{8.4+9.3}{70}$.

Explanation

Since division takes precedence over addition in the order of operations, you need to override that precedence in order to compute this fraction. Here are two ways to do that. You can use the parentheses for the addition in the numerator, entering (8.4 + 9.3) ÷ 70 = ± to get −0.2528571. Or you can use the equals sign after 9.3, entering 8.4 + 9.3 = ÷ 70 = ± to get the same result. In the second way, note that pressing the first = is essential, because without it, 8.4 + 9.3 ÷ 70 = ± would erroneously compute $-\left(8.4+\dfrac{9.3}{70}\right)$ instead.

Incidentally, the exact value of the expression $-\dfrac{8.4+9.3}{70}$ is the repeating decimal $-0.25\overline{285714}$, where the digits 285714 repeat without end, but the calculator rounds the decimal to **−0.2528571**.

3. Find the length, to the nearest 0.01, of the hypotenuse of a right triangle with legs of length 21 and 54; that is, use the Pythagorean theorem and calculate $\sqrt{21^2+54^2}$.

Explanation

Enter 21 × 21 + 54 × 54 = √ to get 57.939624. Again, pressing the = before the √ is essential because 21 × 21 + 54 × 54 √ = would erroneously compute $21^2 + 54\sqrt{54}$. This is because the square root would take precedence over the multiplication in the order of operations. Note that parentheses could be used, as in $\boxed{(}\, 21\, \boxed{\times}\, 21\, \boxed{)}\, \boxed{+}\, \boxed{(}\, 54\, \boxed{\times}\, 54\, \boxed{)}\, \boxed{=}\, \boxed{\sqrt{}}$, but they are not necessary because the multiplications already take precedence over the addition.

Incidentally, the exact answer is a nonterminating, nonrepeating decimal, or an irrational number, but the calculator rounds the decimal to 57.939624. Finally, note that the problem asks for the answer to the nearest 0.01, so the correct answer is **57.94**.

---

4. Compute $(-15)^3$.

Explanation

Enter 15 $\boxed{\pm}$ $\boxed{\times}$ 15 $\boxed{\pm}$ $\boxed{\times}$ 15 $\boxed{\pm}$ $\boxed{=}$ to get **–3,375**.

---

5. Convert 6 miles per hour to feet per second.

Explanation

The solution to this problem uses the conversion factors 1 mile = 5,280 feet and 1 hour = 3,600 seconds as follows:

$$\left(\frac{6 \text{ miles}}{1 \text{ hour}}\right)\left(\frac{5{,}280 \text{ feet}}{1 \text{ mile}}\right)\left(\frac{1 \text{ hour}}{3{,}600 \text{ seconds}}\right) = ?\,\frac{\text{feet}}{\text{second}}$$

Enter 6 $\boxed{\times}$ 5280 $\boxed{\div}$ 3600 $\boxed{=}$ to get 8.8. Alternatively, enter 6 $\boxed{\times}$ 5280 $\boxed{=}$ to get the result 31,680, and then enter $\boxed{\div}$ 3600 $\boxed{=}$ to get **8.8 feet per second**.

---

6. At a fund-raising event, 43 participants donated $60 each, 21 participants donated $80 each, and 16 participants donated $100 each. What was the average (arithmetic mean) donation per participant, in dollars?

Explanation

The solution to this problem is to compute the weighted mean $\dfrac{(43)(60)+(21)(80)+(16)(100)}{43+21+16}$. You can use the memory buttons and parentheses for this computation as follows:

Enter 43 $\boxed{\times}$ 60 $\boxed{=}$ $\boxed{M+}$ 21 $\boxed{\times}$ 80 $\boxed{=}$ $\boxed{M+}$ 16 $\boxed{\times}$ 100 $\boxed{=}$ $\boxed{M+}$ $\boxed{MR}$ $\boxed{\div}$ $\boxed{(}$ 43 $\boxed{+}$ 21 $\boxed{+}$ 16 $\boxed{)}$ $\boxed{=}$ to get 73.25, or **$73.25 per participant**.

When the $\boxed{M+}$ button is first used, the number in the calculator display is stored in memory and an **M** appears to the left of the display to show that the memory function is in use. Each subsequent use of the $\boxed{M+}$ button adds the number in the current display to the number stored in memory and replaces the number stored in memory by the sum. When the $\boxed{MR}$ button is pressed in the computation above, the current value in memory, 5,860, is displayed. To clear the memory, use the $\boxed{MC}$ button, and the **M** next to the display disappears.

Mathematical Conventions for the Quantitative Reasoning Measure of the GRE® General Test

The mathematical symbols and terminology used in the Quantitative Reasoning measure of the test are conventional at the high school level, and most of these appear in the *Math Review*. Whenever nonstandard or special notation or terminology is used in a test question, it is explicitly introduced in the question. However, there are some particular assumptions about numbers and geometric figures that are made throughout the test. These assumptions appear in the test at the beginning of the Quantitative Reasoning sections, and they are elaborated below.

Also, some notation and terminology, while standard at the high school level in many countries, may be different from those used in other countries or from those used at higher or lower levels of mathematics. Such notation and terminology are clarified below. Because it is impossible to ascertain which notation and terminology should be clarified for an individual test taker, more material than necessary may be included.

Finally, there are some guidelines for how certain information given in test questions should be interpreted and used in the context of answering the questions—information such as certain words, phrases, quantities, mathematical expressions, and displays of data. These guidelines appear at the end.

Numbers and Quantities

1. All numbers used in the test questions are real numbers. In particular, integers and both rational and irrational numbers are to be considered, but imaginary numbers are not. This is the main assumption regarding numbers. Also, all quantities are real numbers, although quantities may involve units of measurement.

2. Numbers are expressed in base 10 unless otherwise noted, using the 10 digits 0 through 9 and a period to the right of the ones digit, or units digit, for the decimal point. Also, in numbers that are 1,000 or greater, commas are used to separate groups of three digits to the left of the decimal point.

3. When a positive integer is described by the number of its digits, for example, a two-digit integer, the digits that are counted include the ones digit and all the digits further to the left, where the leftmost digit is not 0. For example, 5,000 is a four-digit integer, whereas 031 is not considered to be a three-digit integer.

4. Some other conventions involving numbers:

    one billion means 1,000,000,000, or 10^9 (not 10^{12}, as in some countries);

    one dozen means 12;

    the Greek letter π represents the ratio of the circumference of a circle to its diameter and is approximately 3.14.

5. When a positive number is to be rounded to a certain decimal place and the number is halfway between the two nearest possibilities, the number should be rounded to the greater possibility.

Example A: 23.5 rounded to the nearest integer is 24.

Example B: 123.985 rounded to the nearest 0.01 is 123.99.

When the number to be rounded is negative, the number should be rounded to the lesser possibility.

Example C: −36.5 rounded to the nearest integer is −37.

6. Repeating decimals are sometimes written with a bar over the digits that repeat, as in $\frac{25}{12} = 2.08\overline{3}$ and $\frac{1}{7} = 0.\overline{142857}$.

7. If r, s, and t are integers and $rs = t$, then r and s are **factors**, or **divisors**, of t; also, t is a **multiple** of r (and of s) and t is **divisible** by r (and by s). The factors of an integer include positive and negative integers.

Example A: −7 is a factor of 35.

Example B: 8 is a factor of −40.

Example C: The integer 4 has six factors: −4, −2, −1, 1, 2, and 4.

The terms **factor**, **divisor**, and **divisible** are used only when r, s, and t are integers. However, the term **multiple** can be used with any real numbers s and t provided that r is an integer.

Example A: 1.2 is a multiple of 0.4.

Example B: -2π is a multiple of π.

8. The **least common multiple** of two nonzero integers a and b is the least positive integer that is a multiple of both a and b. The **greatest common divisor** (or **greatest common factor**) of a and b is the greatest positive integer that is a divisor of both a and b.

9. If an integer n is divided by a nonzero integer d resulting in a quotient q with remainder r, then $n = qd + r$, where $0 \le r < |d|$. Furthermore, $r = 0$ if and only if n is a multiple of d.

Example A: When 20 is divided by 7, the quotient is 2 and the remainder is 6.

Example B: When 21 is divided by 7, the quotient is 3 and the remainder is 0.

Example C: When −17 is divided by 7, the quotient is −3 and the remainder is 4.

10. A **prime number** is an integer greater than 1 that has only two positive divisors: 1 and itself. The first five prime numbers are 2, 3, 5, 7, and 11. A **composite number** is an integer greater than 1 that is not a prime number. The first five composite numbers are 4, 6, 8, 9, and 10.

11. Odd and even integers are not necessarily positive.

Example A: −7 is odd.

Example B: −18 and 0 are even.

12. The integer 0 is neither positive nor negative.

Mathematical Expressions, Symbols, and Variables

1. As is common in algebra, italic letters like x are used to denote numbers, constants, and variables. Letters are also used to label various objects, such as line ℓ, point P, function f, set S, list T, event E, random variable X, Brand X, City Y, and Company Z. The meaning of a letter is determined by the context.

2. When numbers, constants, or variables are given, their possible values are all real numbers unless otherwise restricted. It is common to restrict the possible values in various ways. Here are three examples.

    Example A: n is a nonzero integer.

    Example B: $1 \le x < \pi$

    Example C: T is the tens digits of a two-digit positive integer, so T is an integer from 1 to 9.

3. Standard mathematical symbols at the high school level are used. These include the standard symbols for the arithmetic operations of addition, subtraction, multiplication, and division ($+$, $-$, $\times$, and $\div$), though multiplication is usually denoted by juxtaposition, often with parentheses, for example, $2y$ and $(3)(4.5)$,

    and division is usually denoted with a horizontal fraction bar, for example, $\dfrac{w}{3}$.

    Sometimes mixed numbers, or mixed fractions, are used, like $4\dfrac{3}{8}$ and $-10\dfrac{1}{2}$.

    (The mixed number $4\dfrac{3}{8}$ is equal to the fraction $\dfrac{35}{8}$, and the mixed number

    $-10\dfrac{1}{2}$ is equal to the fraction $-\dfrac{21}{2}$.) Exponents are also used, for example,

    $2^{10} = 1{,}024$, $10^{-2} = \dfrac{1}{100}$, and $x^0 = 1$ for all nonzero numbers x.

4. Mathematical expressions are to be interpreted with respect to **order of operations**, which establishes which operations are performed before others in an expression. The order is as follows: parentheses, exponentiation, negation, multiplication and division (from left to right), addition and subtraction (from left to right).

    Example A: The value of the expression $1 + 2 \times 4$ is 9, because the expression is evaluated by first multiplying 2 and 4 and then adding 1 to the result.

    Example B: -3^2 means "the negative of '3 squared'" because exponentiation takes precedence over negation. Therefore, $-3^2 = -9$, but $(-3)^2 = 9$ because parentheses take precedence over exponentiation.

5.   Here are examples of ten other standard symbols with their meanings.

Symbol	Meaning
$x \leq y$	x is less than or equal to y
$x \neq y$	x is not equal to y
$x \approx y$	x is approximately equal to y
$\lvert x \rvert$	the absolute value of x
$\sqrt{x}$	the nonnegative square root of x, where $x \geq 0$
$-\sqrt{x}$	the negative square root of x, where $x > 0$
$n!$	n factorial, which is the product of all positive integers less than or equal to n, where n is any positive integer and, as a special definition, $0! = 1$.
$k \parallel m$	lines k and m are parallel
$k \perp m$	lines k and m are perpendicular
$\angle B$	angle B

6.   Because all numbers are assumed to be real, some expressions are not defined. Here are three examples.

Example A: For every number x, the expression $\dfrac{x}{0}$ is not defined.

Example B: If $x < 0$, then $\sqrt{x}$ is not defined.

Example C: 0^0 is not defined.

7.   Sometimes special symbols or notation are introduced in a question. Here are two examples.

Example A: The operation $\lozenge$ is defined for all integers r and s by $r \lozenge s = \dfrac{rs}{1+r^2}$.

Example B: The operation $\sim$ is defined for all nonzero numbers x by $\sim x = -\dfrac{1}{x}$.

8.   Sometimes juxtaposition of letters does *not* denote multiplication, as in "consider a three-digit positive integer denoted by BCD, where B, C, and D are digits." Whether or not juxtaposition of letters denotes multiplication depends on the context in which the juxtaposition occurs.

9.   Standard function notation is used in the test, as shown in the following three examples.

Example A: The function g is defined for all $x \neq 2$ by $g(x) = \dfrac{1}{2-x}$.

Example B: If the domain of a function f is not given explicitly, it is assumed to be the set of all real numbers x for which $f(x)$ is a real number.

Example C: If f and g are two functions, then the **composition** of g with f is denoted by $g(f(x))$.

Geometry

1. In questions involving geometry, the conventions of plane (or Euclidean) geometry are followed, including the assumption that the sum of the measures of the interior angles of a triangle is 180 degrees.

2. Lines are assumed to be "straight" lines that extend in both directions without end.

3. Angle measures are in degrees and are assumed to be positive and less than or equal to 360 degrees.

4. When a square, circle, polygon, or other closed geometric figure is described in words but not shown, the figure is assumed to enclose a convex region. It is also assumed that such a closed geometric figure is not just a single point or a line segment. For example, a description of a quadrilateral *cannot* refer to any of the following geometric figures.

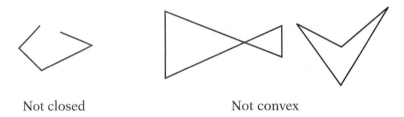

Not closed   Not convex

Mathematical Conventions Figure 1

5. The phrase **area of a rectangle** means the area of the region enclosed by the rectangle. The same terminology applies to circles, triangles, and other closed figures.

6. The **distance between a point and a line** is the length of the perpendicular line segment from the point to the line, which is the shortest distance between the point and the line. Similarly, the **distance between two parallel lines** is the distance between a point on one line and the other line.

7. In a geometric context, the phrase **similar triangles** (or other figures) means that the figures have the same shape. See the Geometry part of the *Math Review* for further explanation of the terms **similar** and **congruent**.

Geometric Figures

1. Geometric figures consist of points, lines, line segments, curves (such as circles), angles, and regions; also included are labels, markings, or shadings that identify these objects or their sizes. A point is indicated by a dot, a label, or the intersection of two or more lines or curves. Points, lines, angles, etc., that are shown as distinct are indeed distinct. All figures are assumed to lie in a plane unless otherwise indicated.

2. If points *A*, *B*, and *C* do not lie on the same line, then line segments *AB* and *BC* form two angles with vertex *B*: one angle with measure less than 180° and the other with measure greater than 180°, as shown in the following figure. Unless otherwise indicated, angle *ABC*, also called angle *B*, refers to the *smaller* of the two angles.

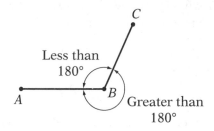

Mathematical Conventions Figure 2

3. The notation *AB* may mean the line segment with endpoints *A* and *B*, or it may mean the length of the line segment. It may also mean the line containing points *A* and *B*. The meaning can be determined from the context.

4. Geometric figures *are not necessarily* drawn to scale. That is, you should *not* assume that quantities such as lengths and angle measures are as they appear in a figure. However, you should assume that lines shown as straight are actually straight, and when curves are shown, you should assume they are not straight. Also, assume that points on a line or a curve are in the order shown, points shown to be on opposite sides of a line or curve are so oriented, and more generally, assume all geometric objects are in the relative positions shown. For questions with geometric figures, you should base your answers on geometric reasoning, not on estimating or comparing quantities by sight or by measurement.

    To illustrate some of the conventions regarding geometric figures, consider the following figure.

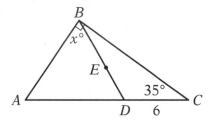

Mathematical Conventions Figure 3

The following seven statements about the preceding figure are consistent with the way the figure is drawn, and you should assume that they are in fact true.

Statement 1: Points *A*, *D*, and *C* are distinct. Point *D* lies between points *A* and *C*, and the line containing them is straight.

Statement 2: The length of line segment *AD* is less than the length of line segment *AC*.

Statement 3: *ABC*, *ABD*, and *DBC* are triangles.

Statement 4: Point *E* lies on line segment *BD*.

Statement 5: Angle *ABC* is a right angle, as indicated by the small square symbol at point *B*.

Statement 6: The length of line segment *DC* is 6, and the measure of angle *C* is 35 degrees.

Statement 7: The measure of angle *ABD* is *x* degrees, and *x* < 90.

The following four statements about the preceding figure are consistent with the way the figure is drawn; however, you should *not* assume that they are in fact true.

Statement 1: The length of line segment *AD* is greater than the length of line segment *DC*.

Statement 2: The measures of angles *BAD* and *BDA* are equal.

Statement 3: The measure of angle *DBC* is less than *x* degrees.

Statement 4: The area of triangle *ABD* is greater than the area of triangle *DBC*.

For another illustration, consider the following figure.

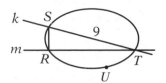

Mathematical Conventions Figure 4

The following five statements about the preceding figure are consistent with the way the figure is drawn, and according to the preceding conventions, you should assume that they are in fact true.

Statement 1: Points *R*, *S*, *T*, and *U* lie on a closed curve.

Statement 2: Line *k* intersects the closed curve at points *S* and *T*.

Statement 3: Points *S* and *U* are on opposite sides of line *m*.

Statement 4: The length of side *ST* is 9.

Statement 5: The area of the region enclosed by the curve is greater than the area of triangle *RST*.

The statement "angle *SRT* is a right angle" is consistent with the way the figure is drawn, but you should *not* assume that angle *SRT* is a right angle.

Coordinate Systems

1. Coordinate systems, such as *xy*-planes and number lines, *are* drawn to scale. Therefore, you can read, estimate, or compare quantities in such figures by sight or by measurement, including geometric figures that appear in coordinate systems.

2. When a number line is drawn horizontally, the positive direction is to the right unless otherwise noted. When a number line is drawn vertically, the positive direction is upward unless otherwise noted.

3. As in geometry, distances in a coordinate system are nonnegative.

4. The *xy*-plane may also be referred to as the rectangular coordinate plane or the rectangular coordinate system.

5. In the *xy*-plane, the *x*-axis is horizontal and the positive direction of the *x*-axis is to the right. The *y*-axis is vertical, and the positive direction is upward. The units

on the *x*-axis have the same length as the units on the *y*-axis unless otherwise noted. The *x*-axis and the *y*-axis intersect at the origin *O*, and they partition the plane into four quadrants, as shown in the following figure.

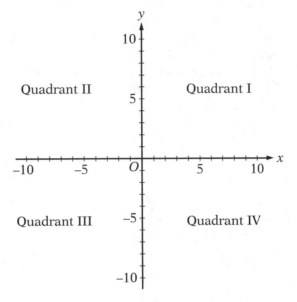

Mathematical Conventions Figure 5

6. Each point in the *xy*-plane has coordinates (x, y) that give its location with respect to the axes; for example, the point $P(2, -8)$ is located 2 units to the right of the *y*-axis and 8 units below the *x*-axis, as shown in the following figure.

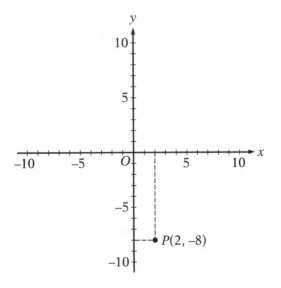

Mathematical Conventions Figure 6

7. Intermediate grid lines or tick marks in a coordinate system are evenly spaced unless otherwise noted.

8. The term *x*-**intercept** refers to the *x*-coordinate of the point at which a graph in the *xy*-plane intersects the *x*-axis. The term *y*-**intercept** is used analogously. Sometimes the terms *x*-**intercept** and *y*-**intercept** refer to the actual intersection points.

Sets, Lists, and Sequences

1. Sets of numbers or other elements appear in some questions. Some sets are infinite, such as the set of integers; other sets are finite and may have all of their elements listed within curly brackets, such as the set {2, 4, 6, 8}. When the elements of a set are given, repetitions are *not* counted as additional elements and the order of the elements is *not* relevant. Elements are also called **members**. A set with one or more members is called **nonempty**; there is a set with no members, called the **empty set** and denoted by ∅. If A and B are sets, then the **intersection** of A and B, denoted by $A \cap B$, is the set of elements that are in both A and B, and the **union** of A and B, denoted by $A \cup B$, is the set of elements that are in A or B, or both. If all of the elements in A are also in B, then A is a **subset** of B. By convention, the empty set is a subset of every set. If A and B have no elements in common, they are called **disjoint** sets or **mutually exclusive** sets.

2. Lists of numbers or other elements are also used in the test. When the elements of a list are given, repetitions *are* counted as additional elements and the order of the elements *is* relevant.

   Example: The list 3, 1, 2, 3, 3 contains five numbers, and the first, fourth, and fifth numbers in the list are each 3.

3. The terms **data set** and **set of data** are not sets in the mathematical sense given above. Rather they refer to a list of data because there may be repetitions in the data, and if there are repetitions, they would be relevant.

4. Sequences are lists that may have a finite or infinite number of elements, or terms. The terms of a sequence can be represented by a fixed letter along with a subscript that indicates the order of a term in the sequence. Ellipsis dots are used to indicate the presence of terms that are not explicitly listed. Ellipsis dots at the end of a list of terms indicate that there is no last term; that is, the sequence is infinite.

   Example: $a_1, a_2, a_3, \ldots, a_n, \ldots$ represents an infinite sequence in which the first term is a_1, the second term is a_2, and more generally, the nth term is a_n for every positive integer n.

   Sometimes the nth term of a sequence is given by a formula, such as $b_n = 2^n + 1$. Sometimes the first few terms of a sequence are given explicitly, as in the following sequence of consecutive even negative integers: −2, −4, −6, −8, −10, ...

5. Sets of consecutive integers are sometimes described by indicating the first and last integer, as in "the integers from 0 to 9, inclusive." This phrase refers to 10 integers, with or without "inclusive" at the end. Thus, the phrase "during the years from 1985 to 2005" refers to 21 years.

Data and Statistics

1. Numerical data are sometimes given in lists and sometimes displayed in other ways, such as in tables, bar graphs, or circle graphs. Various statistics, or measures of data, appear in questions: measures of central tendency—mean, median, and mode; measures of position—quartiles and percentiles; and measures of dispersion—standard deviation, range, and interquartile range.

2. The term **average** is used in two ways, with and without the qualification "(arithmetic mean)." For a list of data, the **average (arithmetic mean)** of the data is the sum of the data divided by the number of data. The term **average** does not refer to either **median** or **mode** in the test. Without the qualification of "arithmetic mean," **average** can refer to a rate or the ratio of one quantity to another, as in "average number of miles per hour" or "average weight per truckload."

3. For a finite set or list of numbers, the **mean** of the numbers refers to the *arithmetic mean* unless otherwise noted.

4. The **median** of an odd number of data is the middle number when the data are listed in increasing order; the **median** of an even number of data is the arithmetic mean of the two middle numbers when the data are listed in increasing order.

5. For a list of data, the **mode** of the data is the most frequently occurring number in the list. Thus, there may be more than one mode for a list of data.

6. For data listed in increasing order, the **first quartile**, **second quartile**, and **third quartile** of the data are three numbers that divide the data into four groups that are roughly equal in size. The first group of numbers is from the least number up to the first quartile. The second group is from the first quartile up to the second quartile, which is also the median of the data. The third group is from the second quartile up to the third quartile, and the fourth group is from the third quartile up to the greatest number. Note that the four groups themselves are sometimes referred to as quartiles—**first quartile**, **second quartile**, **third quartile**, and **fourth quartile**. The latter usage is clarified by the word "in," as in the phrase "the cow's weight is *in* the third quartile of the weights of the herd."

7. For data listed in increasing order, the **percentiles** of the data are 99 numbers that divide the data into 100 groups that are roughly equal in size. The 25th percentile equals the first quartile; the 50th percentile equals the second quartile, or median; and the 75th percentile equals the third quartile.

8. For a list of data, where the arithmetic mean is denoted by m, the **standard deviation** of the data refers to the nonnegative square root of the mean of the squared differences between m and each of the data. The standard deviation is a measure of the spread of the data about the mean. The greater the standard deviation, the greater the spread of the data about the mean. This statistic is also known as the **population standard deviation** (not to be confused with the "sample standard deviation," a closely related statistic).

9. For a list of data, the **range** of the data is the greatest number in the list minus the least number. The **interquartile range** of the data is the third quartile minus the first quartile.

Data Distributions and Probability Distributions

1. Some questions display data in **frequency distributions**, where discrete data values are repeated with various frequencies or where preestablished intervals of possible values have frequencies corresponding to the numbers of values in the intervals.

   Example: The lifetimes, rounded to the nearest hour, of 300 lightbulbs are in the following 10 intervals: 501 to 550 hours, 551 to 600 hours, 601 to 650 hours, and so on, up to 951 to 1,000 hours. Consequently, each of the intervals has a number, or frequency, of lifetimes, and the sum of the 10 frequencies is 300.

2. Questions may involve **relative frequency distributions**, where each frequency of a frequency distribution is divided by the total number of data in the distribution, resulting in a relative frequency. In the example above, the 10 frequencies of the 10 intervals would each be divided by 300, yielding 10 relative frequencies.

3. When a question refers to a random selection or a random sample, all possible samples of equal size have the same probability of being selected unless there is information to the contrary.

4. Some questions describe **probability experiments**, or **random experiments**, that have a finite number of possible **outcomes**. In a random experiment, any particular set of outcomes is called an **event**, and every event E has a **probability**, denoted by $P(E)$, where $0 \le P(E) \le 1$. If each outcome of an experiment is equally likely, then the probability of an event E is defined as the following ratio.

$$P(E) = \frac{\text{the number of outcomes in the event } E}{\text{the number of possible outcomes in the experiment}}$$

5. If E and F are two events in an experiment, then "E and F" is an event, which is the set of outcomes that are in the intersection of events E and F. Another event is "E or F," which is the set of outcomes that are in the union of events E and F.

6. If E and F are two events and E and F are mutually exclusive, then $P(E \text{ and } F) = 0$.

7. If E and F are two events such that the occurrence of either event does not affect the occurrence of the other, then E and F are said to be **independent** events. Events E and F are independent if and only if $P(E \text{ and } F) = P(E) \, P(F)$.

8. A **random variable** is a variable that represents values resulting from a random experiment. The values of the random variable may be the actual outcomes of the experiment if the outcomes are numerical, or the random variable may be related to the outcomes more indirectly. In either case, random variables can be used to describe events in terms of numbers.

9. A random variable from an experiment with only a finite number of possible outcomes also has only a finite number of values and is called a **discrete random variable**. When the values of a random variable form a continuous interval of real numbers, such as all of the numbers between 0 and 2, the random variable is called a **continuous random variable**.

10. Every value of a discrete random variable X, say $X = a$, has a probability denoted by $P(X = a)$, or by just $P(a)$. A histogram (or a table) showing all of the values of X and their probabilities $P(X)$ is called the **probability distribution** of X. The **mean of the random variable** X is the sum of the products $XP(X)$ for all values of X.

11. The mean of a random variable X is also called the **expected value** of X or the **mean of the probability distribution** of X.

12. For a continuous random variable X, every interval of values, say $a \leq X \leq b$, has a probability, which is denoted by $P(a \leq X \leq b)$. The **probability distribution** of X can be represented by a curve in the xy-plane. The curve is the graph of a function f whose values are nonnegative. The curve $y = f(x)$ is related to the probability of each interval $a \leq X \leq b$ in the following way: $P(a \leq X \leq b)$ is equal to the area of the region that is below the curve, above the x-axis, and between the vertical lines $x = a$ and $x = b$. The area of the entire region under the curve is 1.

13. The **mean of a continuous random variable** X is the point m on the x-axis at which the region under the distribution curve would perfectly balance if a fulcrum were placed at $x = m$. The **median** of X is the point M on the x-axis at which the line $x = M$ divides the region under the distribution curve into two regions of equal area.

14. The **standard deviation of a random variable** X is a measure of dispersion, which indicates how spread out the probability distribution of X is from its mean. The greater the standard deviation of a random variable, the greater the spread of its distribution about its mean. This statistic is also known as the **standard deviation of the probability distribution** of X.

15. One of the most important probability distributions is the **normal distribution**, whose distribution curve is shaped like a bell. A random variable X with this distribution is called **normally distributed**. The curve is symmetric about the line $x = m$, where m is the mean as well as the median. The right and left tails of the distribution approach the x-axis but never touch it.

16. The **standard normal distribution** has mean 0 and standard deviation 1. The following figure shows the standard normal distribution, including approximate probabilities corresponding to the six intervals shown.

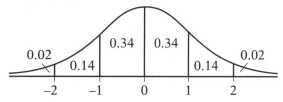

Mathematical Conventions Figure 7

Graphical Representations of Data

1. Graphical data presentations, such as bar graphs, circle graphs, and line graphs, *are* drawn to scale; therefore, you can read, estimate, or compare data values by sight or by measurement.

2. Scales, grid lines, dots, bars, shadings, solid and dashed lines, legends, etc., are used on graphs to indicate the data. Sometimes scales that do not begin at 0 are used, and sometimes broken scales are used.

3. Standard conventions apply to graphs of data unless otherwise indicated. For example, a circle graph represents 100 percent of the data indicated in the graph's title, and the areas of the individual sectors are proportional to the percents they represent.

4. In Venn diagrams, various sets of objects are represented by circular regions and by regions formed by intersections of the circles. In some Venn diagrams, all of the circles are inside a rectangular region that represents a universal set. A number placed in a region is the number of elements in the subset represented by the smallest region containing the number, unless otherwise noted. Sometimes a number is placed above a circular region to indicate the number of elements in the set represented by the circular region.

Miscellaneous Guidelines for Interpreting and Using Information in Test Questions

1. Numbers given in a question are to be used as exact numbers, even though in some real-life settings they are likely to have been rounded.

    Example: If a question states that "30 percent of the company's profit was from health products," then 30 is to be used as an exact number; it is not to be treated as though it were a nearby number, say, 29 or 30.1, that has been rounded up or down.

2. An integer that is given as the number of certain objects, whether in a real-life or pure-math setting, is to be taken as the total number of such objects.

    Example: If a question states that "a bag contains 50 marbles, and 23 of the marbles are red," then 50 is to be taken as the total number of marbles in the bag and 23 is to be taken as the total number of red marbles in the bag, so that the other 27 marbles are not red. Fractions and percents are understood in a similar way, so "one-fifth, or 20 percent, of the 50 marbles in the bag are green" means that 10 marbles in the bag are green and 40 marbles are not green.

3. When a multiple-choice question asks for an approximate quantity without stipulating a degree of approximation, the correct answer is the choice that is closest in value to the quantity that can be computed from the information given.

4. Unless otherwise indicated, the phrase "difference between two quantities" is assumed to mean "positive difference," that is, the greater quantity minus the lesser quantity.

    Example: "For which two consecutive years was the difference in annual rainfall least?" means "for which two consecutive years was the **absolute value of the difference** in annual rainfall least?"

5. When the term **profit** is used in a question, it refers to **gross profit**, which is the sales revenue minus the cost of production or acquisition. The profit does not involve any other amounts unless they are explicitly given.

6. The common meaning of terms such as **months** and **years** and other everyday terms are assumed in questions where the terms appear.

7. In questions involving real-life scenarios in which a variable is given to represent a number of existing objects or a monetary amount, the context implies that the variable is greater than 0 unless otherwise noted.

   Example: "Jane sold x rugs and deposited her profit of y dollars into her savings account" implies that x and y are greater than 0.

8. Some quantities may involve units, such as inches, pounds, and Celsius degrees, while other quantities are pure numbers. Any units of measurement, such as English units or metric units, may be used. However, if an answer to a question requires converting one unit of measurement to another, then the relationship between the units is given in the question, unless the relationship is a common one, such as the relationships between minutes and hours, dollars and cents, and metric units like centimeters and meters.

9. In any question, there may be some information that is not needed for obtaining the correct answer.

10. When reading questions, do not introduce unwarranted assumptions.

    Example A: If a question describes a trip that begins and ends at certain times, the intended answer will assume that the times are unaffected by crossing time zones or by changes to the local time for daylight savings, unless those matters are explicitly mentioned.

    Example B: Do not consider sales taxes on purchases unless explicitly mentioned.

11. The display of data in a Data Interpretation set of questions is the same for each question in the set. Also, the display may contain more than one graph or table. Each question will refer to the data presentation, but it may happen that some part of the data will have no question that refers to it.

12. In a Data Interpretation set of questions, each question should be considered separately from the others. No information except what is given in the display of data should be carried over from one question to another.

13. In many questions, mathematical expressions and words appear together in a phrase. In such a phrase, each mathematical expression should be interpreted *separately* from the words before it is interpreted *along with* the words. For example, if n is an integer, then the phrase "the sum of the first two consecutive integers greater than $n + 6$" means $(n + 7) + (n + 8)$; it does not mean "the sum of the first two consecutive integers greater than n" plus 6, or $(n + 1) + (n + 2) + 6$. That is, the expression $n + 6$ should be interpreted first, separately from the words. However, in a phrase like "the function g is defined for all $x \geq 0$," the phrase "for all $x \geq 0$," is mathematical shorthand for "for all numbers x such that $x \geq 0$."

6

GRE®
Quantitative Reasoning
Practice Questions

Your goals for this chapter

➤ Practice answering *GRE*® Quantitative Reasoning questions on your own
➤ Review answers and explanations, particularly for questions you answered incorrectly

本章共有四组GRE Quantitative Reasoning练习题。前三组题目均包含数量比较题、单项选择题、不定项选择题以及数字填空题，这三组题目按难度依次递增的顺序排列。第一组简单，第二组中等难度，第三组较难。第四组题目为难度不等的数据分析题。

最后一组练习题后附有参考答案，便于考生快速查阅。在本章的最后提供每一道题目的完整解析。每一个解析均与其相对应的问题一同给出，以便考生轻松查阅。

通过做这些练习，考生可以提高自己的GRE Quantitative Reasoning答题技巧。从简单题开始，然后到中等难度题目，最后到较难题目。在答完题后仔细阅读答案及其解析，尤其要注意那些自己答错的题目。

请翻开下一页，参照所给说明，开始本章的练习。

Section Directions

For each question, indicate the best answer, using the directions given.

Notes: All numbers used are real numbers.

All figures are assumed to lie in a plane unless otherwise indicated.

Geometric figures, such as lines, circles, triangles, and quadrilaterals, **are not necessarily** drawn to scale. That is, you should **not** assume that quantities such as lengths and angle measures are as they appear in a figure. You should assume, however, that lines shown as straight are actually straight, points on a line are in the order shown, and more generally, all geometric objects are in the relative positions shown. For questions with geometric figures, you should base your answers on geometric reasoning, not on estimating or comparing quantities by sight or by measurement.

Coordinate systems, such as *xy*-planes and number lines, **are** drawn to scale; therefore, you can read, estimate, or compare quantities in such figures by sight or by measurement.

Graphical data presentations, such as bar graphs, circle graphs, and line graphs, **are** drawn to scale; therefore, you can read, estimate, or compare data values by sight or by measurement.

Directions for Quantitative Comparison questions

> Compare Quantity A and Quantity B, using additional information centered above the two quantities if such information is given. Select one of the following four answer choices and fill in the corresponding oval to the right of the question.
>
> Ⓐ Quantity A is greater.
> Ⓑ Quantity B is greater.
> Ⓒ The two quantities are equal.
> Ⓓ The relationship cannot be determined from the information given.
>
> A symbol that appears more than once in a question has the same meaning throughout the question.

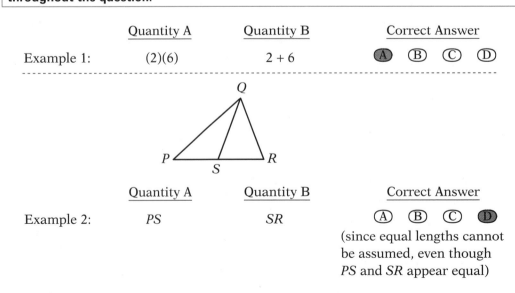

	Quantity A	Quantity B	Correct Answer
Example 1:	(2)(6)	2 + 6	⬤Ⓐ Ⓑ Ⓒ Ⓓ

	Quantity A	Quantity B	Correct Answer
Example 2:	*PS*	*SR*	Ⓐ Ⓑ Ⓒ ⬤Ⓓ

(since equal lengths cannot be assumed, even though *PS* and *SR* appear equal)

Directions for Numeric Entry questions

Enter your answer in the answer box(es) below the question.

- Your answer may be an integer, a decimal, or a fraction, and it may be negative.
- If a question asks for a fraction, there will be two boxes—one for the numerator and one for the denominator.
- Equivalent forms of the correct answer, such as 2.5 and 2.50, are all correct. Fractions do not need to be reduced to lowest terms.
- Enter the exact answer unless the question asks you to round your answer.

SET 1. Discrete Questions: Easy

Quantitative Comparison

For Questions 1 to 6, compare Quantity A and Quantity B, using additional information centered above the two quantities if such information is given. Select one of the following four answer choices and fill in the corresponding oval to the right of the question.

Ⓐ Quantity A is greater.

Ⓑ Quantity B is greater.

Ⓒ The two quantities are equal.

Ⓓ The relationship cannot be determined from the information given.

A symbol that appears more than once in a question has the same meaning throughout the question.

Emma spent $75 buying a used bicycle and $27 repairing it. Then she sold the bicycle for 40 percent more than the total amount she spent buying and repairing it.

	Quantity A	Quantity B	
1.	The price at which Emma sold the bicycle	$140	Ⓐ Ⓑ Ⓒ Ⓓ

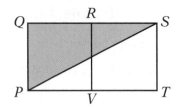

In the figure above, squares *PQRV* and *VRST* have sides of length 6.

Quantity A	Quantity B	
2. The area of the shaded region	36	Ⓐ Ⓑ Ⓒ Ⓓ

In 2009 the property tax on each home in Town *X* was *p* percent of the assessed value of the home, where *p* is a constant. The property tax in 2009 on a home in Town *X* that had an assessed value of $125,000 was $2,500.

Quantity A	Quantity B	
3. The property tax in 2009 on a home in Town *X* that had an assessed value of $160,000	$3,000	Ⓐ Ⓑ Ⓒ Ⓓ

$$x + y = -1$$

Quantity A	Quantity B	
4. x	y	Ⓐ Ⓑ Ⓒ Ⓓ

r, *s*, and *t* are three consecutive odd integers such that $r < s < t$.

Quantity A	Quantity B	
5. $r + s + 1$	$s + t - 1$	Ⓐ Ⓑ Ⓒ Ⓓ

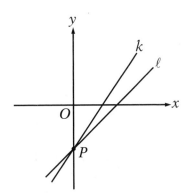

Quantity A	Quantity B

6.   The slope of line k The slope of line ℓ Ⓐ Ⓑ Ⓒ Ⓓ

Multiple-choice Questions—Select One Answer Choice

For Questions 7 to 11, select a single answer choice.

7.   In the figure above, what is the value of $\dfrac{x+y+z}{45}$?

    Ⓐ 2

    Ⓑ 3

    Ⓒ 4

    Ⓓ 5

    Ⓔ 6

8.   A certain store sells two types of pens: one type for $2 per pen and the other type for $3 per pen. If a customer can spend up to $25 to buy pens at the store and there is no sales tax, what is the greatest number of pens the customer can buy?

    Ⓐ 9

    Ⓑ 10

    Ⓒ 11

    Ⓓ 12

    Ⓔ 20

9. If $y = 3x$ and $z = 2y$, what is $x + y + z$ in terms of x?

(A) $10x$
(B) $9x$
(C) $8x$
(D) $6x$
(E) $5x$

10. A certain shipping service charges an insurance fee of $0.75 when shipping any package with contents worth $25.00 or less and an insurance fee of $1.00 when shipping any package with contents worth over $25.00. If Dan uses the shipping company to ship three packages with contents worth $18.25, $25.00, and $127.50, respectively, what is the total insurance fee that the company charges Dan to ship the three packages?

(A) $1.75
(B) $2.25
(C) $2.50
(D) $2.75
(E) $3.00

11. Last year, all purchases of a certain product were made either online or in a store. If 55 percent of the purchases were made online, what was the ratio of the number of purchases made online to the number of purchases made in a store?

(A) 11 to 9
(B) 11 to 5
(C) 10 to 9
(D) 9 to 11
(E) 9 to 10

Numeric Entry

For Questions 12 and 13, enter your answer in the answer box(es) below the question.

- Your answer may be an integer, a decimal, or a fraction, and it may be negative.
- If a question asks for a fraction, there will be two boxes—one for the numerator and one for the denominator.
- Equivalent forms of the correct answer, such as 2.5 and 2.50, are all correct. Fractions do not need to be reduced to lowest terms.
- Enter the exact answer unless the question asks you to round your answer.

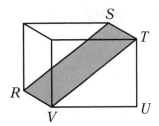

12. In the rectangular solid above, $TU = 3$, $UV = 4$, and $VR = 2$. What is the area of the shaded rectangular region?

    [   ]

13. A list of numbers has a mean of 8 and a standard deviation of 2.5. If x is a number in the list that is 2 standard deviations above the mean, what is the value of x?

    $x =$ [   ]

Multiple-choice Questions—Select One or More Answer Choices

For Question 14, select all the answer choices that apply.

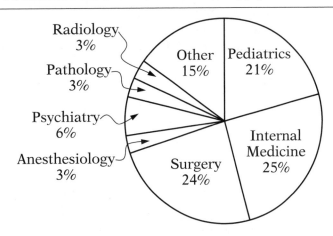

14. The circle graph above shows the distribution of 200,000 physicians by specialty. Which of the following sectors of the circle graph represent more than 40,000 physicians?

    Indicate <u>all</u> such sectors.

    [A] Pediatrics

    [B] Internal Medicine

    [C] Surgery

    [D] Anesthesiology

    [E] Psychiatry

SET 2. Discrete Questions: Medium

Quantitative Comparison

> For Questions 1 to 5, compare Quantity A and Quantity B, using additional information centered above the two quantities if such information is given. Select one of the following four answer choices and fill in the corresponding oval to the right of the question.
>
> (A) Quantity A is greater.
>
> (B) Quantity B is greater.
>
> (C) The two quantities are equal.
>
> (D) The relationship cannot be determined from the information given.
>
> A symbol that appears more than once in a question has the same meaning throughout the question.

Machine R, working alone at a constant rate, produces x units of a product in 30 minutes, and machine S, working alone at a constant rate, produces x units of the product in 48 minutes, where x is a positive integer.

	Quantity A	Quantity B	
1.	The number of units of the product that machine R, working alone at its constant rate, produces in 3 hours	The number of units of the product that machine S, working alone at its constant rate, produces in 4 hours	

Frequency Distribution for List X

Number	1	2	3	5
Frequency	10	20	18	12

Frequency Distribution for List Y

Number	6	7	8	9
Frequency	24	17	10	9

List X and list Y each contain 60 numbers. Frequency distributions for each list are given above. The average (arithmetic mean) of the numbers in list X is 2.7, and the average of the numbers in list Y is 7.1. List Z contains 120 numbers: the 60 numbers in list X and the 60 numbers in list Y.

	Quantity A	Quantity B	
2.	The average of the 120 numbers in list Z	The median of the 120 numbers in list Z	

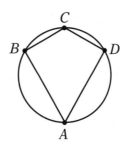

In the figure above, the diameter of the circle is 10.

	Quantity A	Quantity B	
3.	The area of quadrilateral *ABCD*	40	Ⓐ Ⓑ Ⓒ Ⓓ

$$x^2y > 0$$
$$xy^2 < 0$$

	Quantity A	Quantity B	
4.	x	y	Ⓐ Ⓑ Ⓒ Ⓓ

Among the 9,000 people attending a football game at College *C*, there were *x* students from College *C* and *y* students who were <u>not</u> from College *C*.

	Quantity A	Quantity B	
5.	The number of people attending the game who were <u>not</u> students	$9{,}000 - x - y$	Ⓐ Ⓑ Ⓒ Ⓓ

Multiple-choice Questions—Select One Answer Choice

For Questions 6 to 10, select a single answer choice.

6. If $x \neq 0$, which of the following is equivalent to $\dfrac{x(x^2)^3}{x^2}$?

   Ⓐ x^2
   Ⓑ x^3
   Ⓒ x^4
   Ⓓ x^5
   Ⓔ x^6

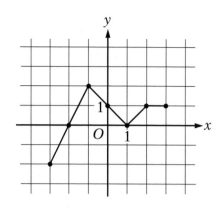

7.   The figure above shows the graph of the function f in the xy-plane. What is the value of $f(f(-1))$?

    (A) -2

    (B) -1

    (C) 0

    (D) 1

    (E) 2

8.   If $\dfrac{d-3n}{7n-d}=1$, which of the following statements describes d in terms of n?

    (A) d is 4 less than n.

    (B) d is 4 more than n.

    (C) d is $\dfrac{3}{7}$ of n.

    (D) d is 2 times n.

    (E) d is 5 times n.

9.   By weight, liquid A makes up 8 percent of solution R and 18 percent of solution S. If 3 grams of solution R are mixed with 7 grams of solution S, then liquid A accounts for what percent of the weight of the resulting solution?

    (A) 10%

    (B) 13%

    (C) 15%

    (D) 19%

    (E) 26%

10.   Of the 700 members of a certain organization, 120 are lawyers. Two members of the organization will be selected at random. Which of the following is closest to the probability that <u>neither</u> of the members selected will be a lawyer?

    (A) 0.5

    (B) 0.6

    (C) 0.7

    (D) 0.8

    (E) 0.9

Numeric Entry

> **For Questions 11 and 12, enter your answer in the answer box(es) below the question.**
>
> - Your answer may be an integer, a decimal, or a fraction, and it may be negative.
> - If a question asks for a fraction, there will be two boxes—one for the numerator and one for the denominator.
> - Equivalent forms of the correct answer, such as 2.5 and 2.50, are all correct. Fractions do not need to be reduced to lowest terms.
> - Enter the exact answer unless the question asks you to round your answer.

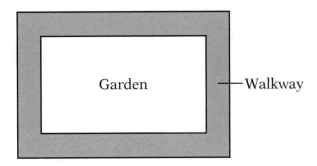

11. The figure above represents a rectangular garden with a walkway around it. The garden is 18 feet long and 12 feet wide. The walkway is uniformly 3 feet wide, and its edges meet at right angles. What is the area of the walkway?

    [   ] square feet

12. Line k lies in the xy-plane. The x-intercept of line k is –4, and line k passes through the midpoint of the line segment whose endpoints are $(2, 9)$ and $(2, 0)$. What is the slope of line k?

    Give your answer as a fraction.

    $$\frac{[\quad]}{[\quad]}$$

Multiple-choice Questions—Select One or More Answer Choices

For Questions 13 and 14, select all the answer choices that apply.

13. If the lengths of two sides of a triangle are 5 and 9, respectively, which of the following could be the length of the third side of the triangle?

    Indicate <u>all</u> such lengths.

    A̲ 3

    B̲ 5

    C̲ 8

    D̲ 15

14. On the number line shown above, the tick marks are equally spaced. Which of the following statements about the numbers x, y, and z must be true?

    Indicate <u>all</u> such statements.

    A̲ $xyz < 0$

    B̲ $x + z = y$

    C̲ $z(y - x) > 0$

SET 3. Discrete Questions: Hard

Quantitative Comparison

> For Questions 1 to 6, compare Quantity A and Quantity B, using additional information centered above the two quantities if such information is given. Select one of the following four answer choices and fill in the corresponding oval to the right of the question.
>
> (A) Quantity A is greater.
>
> (B) Quantity B is greater.
>
> (C) The two quantities are equal.
>
> (D) The relationship cannot be determined from the information given.
>
> A symbol that appears more than once in a question has the same meaning throughout the question.

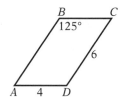

In the figure above, *ABCD* is a parallelogram.

	Quantity A	Quantity B	
1.	The area of the *ABCD*	24	(A) (B) (C) (D)

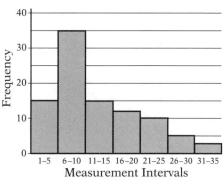

Measurement Intervals

In the course of an experiment, 95 measurements were recorded, and all of the measurements were integers. The 95 measurements were then grouped into 7 measurement intervals. The graph above shows the frequency distribution of the 95 measurements by measurement interval.

	Quantity A	Quantity B	
2.	The average (arithmetic mean) of the 95 measurements	The median of the 95 measurements	(A) (B) (C) (D)

x is an integer greater than 1.

	Quantity A	Quantity B	
3.	3^{x+1}	4^x	Ⓐ Ⓑ Ⓒ Ⓓ

A, B, and C are three rectangles. The length and width of rectangle A are 10 percent greater and 10 percent less, respectively, than the length and width of rectangle C. The length and width of rectangle B are 20 percent greater and 20 percent less, respectively, than the length and width of rectangle C.

	Quantity A	Quantity B	
4.	The area of rectangle A	The area of rectangle B	Ⓐ Ⓑ Ⓒ Ⓓ

The random variable X is normally distributed. The values 650 and 850 are at the 60th and 90th percentiles of the distribution of X, respectively.

	Quantity A	Quantity B	
5.	The value at the 75th percentile of the distribution of X	750	Ⓐ Ⓑ Ⓒ Ⓓ

Set S consists of all positive integers less than 81 that are <u>not</u> equal to the square of an integer.

	Quantity A	Quantity B	
6.	The number of integers in set S	72	Ⓐ Ⓑ Ⓒ Ⓓ

Multiple-choice Questions—Select One Answer Choice

For Questions 7 to 12, select a single answer choice.

7. A manager is forming a 6-person team to work on a certain project. From the 11 candidates available for the team, the manager has already chosen 3 to be on the team. In selecting the other 3 team members, how many different combinations of 3 of the remaining candidates does the manager have to choose from?

   (A) 6
   (B) 24
   (C) 56
   (D) 120
   (E) 462

8. Which of the following could be the graph of all values of x that satisfy the inequality $2 - 5x \leq -\dfrac{6x - 5}{3}$?

   (A)   0

   (B)   0

   (C)   0

   (D)   0

   (E)   0

9. If $1 + x + x^2 + x^3 = 60$, then the average (arithmetic mean) of x, x^2, x^3, and x^4 is equal to which of the following?

   (A) $12x$
   (B) $15x$
   (C) $20x$
   (D) $30x$
   (E) $60x$

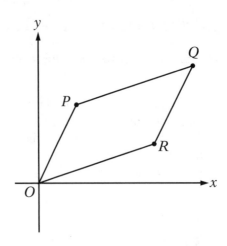

10. Parallelogram $OPQR$ lies in the xy-plane, as shown in the figure above. The coordinates of point P are $(2, 4)$ and the coordinates of point Q are $(8, 6)$. What are the coordinates of point R?

    Ⓐ $(3, 2)$
    Ⓑ $(3, 3)$
    Ⓒ $(4, 4)$
    Ⓓ $(5, 2)$
    Ⓔ $(6, 2)$

11. The relationship between the area A of a circle and its circumference C is given by the formula $A = kC^2$, where k is a constant. What is the value of k?

    Ⓐ $\dfrac{1}{4\pi}$

    Ⓑ $\dfrac{1}{2\pi}$

    Ⓒ $\dfrac{1}{4}$

    Ⓓ 2π

    Ⓔ $4\pi^2$

12. The sequence of numbers $a_1, a_2, a_3, \ldots, a_n, \ldots$ is defined by $a_n = \dfrac{1}{n} - \dfrac{1}{n+2}$ for each integer $n \geq 1$. What is the sum of the first 20 terms of the sequence?

    Ⓐ $\left(1 + \dfrac{1}{2}\right) - \dfrac{1}{20}$

    Ⓑ $\left(1 + \dfrac{1}{2}\right) - \left(\dfrac{1}{21} + \dfrac{1}{22}\right)$

    Ⓒ $1 - \left(\dfrac{1}{20} + \dfrac{1}{22}\right)$

    Ⓓ $1 - \dfrac{1}{22}$

    Ⓔ $\dfrac{1}{20} - \dfrac{1}{22}$

Numeric Entry

> **For Question 13, enter your answer in the answer box(es) below the question.**
>
> - Your answer may be an integer, a decimal, or a fraction, and it may be negative.
> - If a question asks for a fraction, there will be two boxes—one for the numerator and one for the denominator.
> - Equivalent forms of the correct answer, such as 2.5 and 2.50, are all correct. Fractions do not need to be reduced to lowest terms.
> - Enter the exact answer unless the question asks you to round your answer.

Y	Frequency
$\frac{1}{2}$	2
$\frac{3}{4}$	7
$\frac{5}{4}$	8
$\frac{3}{2}$	8
$\frac{7}{4}$	9

13. The table above shows the frequency distribution of the values of a variable Y. What is the mean of the distribution?

    Give your answer to the <u>nearest 0.01</u>.

Multiple-choice Questions—Select One or More Answer Choices

> **For Questions 14 and 15, select all the answer choices that apply.**

14. Let S be the set of all positive integers n such that n^2 is a multiple of both 24 and 108. Which of the following integers are divisors of every integer n in S?

    Indicate <u>all</u> such integers.

    [A] 12

    [B] 24

    [C] 36

    [D] 72

15. The penguins currently living on an island are of two types, Chinstrap penguins and Gentoo penguins. The range of the heights of the Chinstrap penguins on the island is 13.2 centimeters, and the range of the heights of the Gentoo penguins on the island is 15.4 centimeters.

Which of the following statements individually provide(s) sufficient additional information to determine the range of the heights of all the penguins on the island?

Indicate all such statements.

A The tallest Gentoo penguin on the island is 5.8 centimeters taller than the tallest Chinstrap penguin on the island.

B The median height of the Gentoo penguins on the island is 1.1 centimeters greater than the median height of the Chinstrap penguins on the island.

C The average (arithmetic mean) height of the Gentoo penguins on the island is 4.6 centimeters greater than the average height of the Chinstrap penguins on the island.

SET 4. Data Interpretation Sets

For Questions 1 to 7, select a single answer choice unless otherwise directed.

Questions 1 to 3 are based on the following data.

PERCENT OF ADJUNCT FACULTY AND PERCENT OF NON-ADJUNCT
FACULTY AT COLLEGE *X*, BY FIELD
Total adjunct faculty: 200
Total non-adjunct faculty: 250

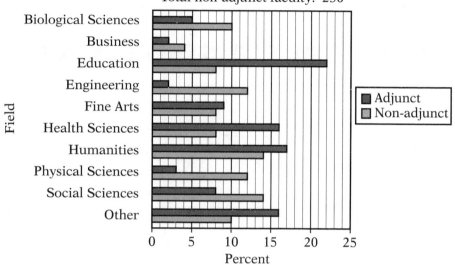

Medium Question

1. There are 275 students in the field of engineering at College *X*.
   Approximately what is the ratio of the number of students in engineering to
   the number of faculty in engineering?

   (A) 8 to 1
   (B) 10 to 1
   (C) 12 to 1
   (D) 14 to 1
   (E) 20 to 1

Medium Question

2. Approximately what percent of the faculty in humanities are non-adjunct
   faculty?

   (A) 35%
   (B) 38%
   (C) 41%
   (D) 45%
   (E) 51%

For Question 3, use the directions for Numeric Entry questions.

Hard Question

3.   For the biological sciences and health sciences faculty combined, $\frac{1}{3}$ of the adjunct and $\frac{2}{9}$ of the non-adjunct faculty are medical doctors. What fraction of all the faculty in those two fields combined are medical doctors?

Questions 4 to 7 are based on the following data.

VALUE OF IMPORTS TO AND EXPORTS FROM COUNTRY *T*, 2000–2009
(in United States dollars)

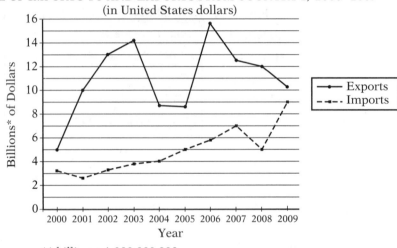

*1 billion = 1,000,000,000

For Question 4, select all the answer choices that apply.

Easy Question

4.   For which of the eight years from 2001 to 2008 did exports exceed imports by more than $5 billion?

Indicate all such years.

- A   2001
- B   2002
- C   2003
- D   2004
- E   2005
- F   2006
- G   2007
- H   2008

Medium Question

5. Which of the following is closest to the average (arithmetic mean) of the 9 changes in the value of imports between consecutive years from 2000 to 2009?

    Ⓐ $260 million

    Ⓑ $320 million

    Ⓒ $400 million

    Ⓓ $480 million

    Ⓔ $640 million

Medium Question

6. In 2008 the value of exports was approximately what percent greater than the value of imports?

    Ⓐ 40%

    Ⓑ 60%

    Ⓒ 70%

    Ⓓ 120%

    Ⓔ 140%

Hard Question

7. If it were discovered that the value of imports shown for 2007 was incorrect and should have been $5 billion instead, then the average (arithmetic mean) value of imports per year for the 10 years shown would have been approximately how much less?

    Ⓐ $200 million

    Ⓑ $50 million

    Ⓒ $20 million

    Ⓓ $7 million

    Ⓔ $5 million

ANSWER KEY

SET 1. Discrete Questions: Easy

1. **Choice A**: Quantity A is greater.
2. **Choice C**: The two quantities are equal.
3. **Choice A**: Quantity A is greater.
4. **Choice D**: The relationship cannot be determined from the information given.
5. **Choice B**: Quantity B is greater.
6. **Choice A**: Quantity A is greater.
7. **Choice C**: 4
8. **Choice D**: 12
9. **Choice A**: $10x$
10. **Choice C**: $2.50
11. **Choice A**: 11 to 9
12. **10**
13. **13**
14. **Choice A**: Pediatrics
    AND
    Choice B: Internal Medicine
    AND
    Choice C: Surgery

SET 2. Discrete Questions: Medium

1. **Choice A**: Quantity A is greater.
2. **Choice B**: Quantity B is greater.
3. **Choice D**: The relationship cannot be determined from the information given.
4. **Choice B**: Quantity B is greater.
5. **Choice C**: The two quantities are equal.
6. **Choice D**: x^5
7. **Choice D**: 1
8. **Choice E**: d is 5 times n.
9. **Choice C**: 15%
10. **Choice C**: 0.7
11. **216**
12. $\dfrac{3}{4}$ (or any equivalent fraction)
13. **Choice B**: 5
    AND
    Choice C: 8
14. **Choice A**: $xyz < 0$
    AND
    Choice B: $x + z = y$
    AND
    Choice C: $z(y - x) > 0$

SET 3. Discrete Questions: Hard

1. **Choice B**: Quantity B is greater.
2. **Choice A**: Quantity A is greater.
3. **Choice D**: The relationship cannot be determined from the information given.
4. **Choice A**: Quantity A is greater.
5. **Choice B**: Quantity B is greater.
6. **Choice C**: The two quantities are equal.
7. **Choice C**: 56
8. **Choice C**:
9. **Choice B**: $15x$ 0
10. **Choice E**: (6, 2)
11. **Choice A**: $\dfrac{1}{4\pi}$
12. **Choice B**: $\left(1+\dfrac{1}{2}\right)-\left(\dfrac{1}{21}+\dfrac{1}{22}\right)$
13. **1.29**
14. **Choice A**: 12
    AND
    Choice C: 36
15. **Choice A**: The tallest Gentoo penguin on the island is 5.8 centimeters taller than the tallest Chinstrap penguin on the island.

SET 4. Data Interpretation Sets

1. **Choice A**: 8 to 1
2. **Choice E**: 51%
3. $\dfrac{24}{87}$ (or any equivalent fraction)
4. **Choice A**: 2001
   AND
   Choice B: 2002
   AND
   Choice C: 2003
   AND
   Choice F: 2006
   AND
   Choice G: 2007
   AND
   Choice H: 2008
5. **Choice E**: $640 million
6. **Choice E**: 140%
7. **Choice A**: $200 million

Answers and Explanations

For the practice questions in this chapter, use the following directions.

Section Directions

For each question, indicate the best answer, using the directions given.

Notes: All numbers used are real numbers.

All figures are assumed to lie in a plane unless otherwise indicated.

Geometric figures, such as lines, circles, triangles, and quadrilaterals, **are not necessarily** drawn to scale. That is, you should **not** assume that quantities such as lengths and angle measures are as they appear in a figure. You should assume, however, that lines shown as straight are actually straight, points on a line are in the order shown, and more generally, all geometric objects are in the relative positions shown. For questions with geometric figures, you should base your answers on geometric reasoning, not on estimating or comparing quantities by sight or by measurement.

Coordinate systems, such as xy-planes and number lines, **are** drawn to scale; therefore, you can read, estimate, or compare quantities in such figures by sight or by measurement.

Graphical data presentations, such as bar graphs, circle graphs, and line graphs, **are** drawn to scale; therefore, you can read, estimate, or compare data values by sight or by measurement.

Directions for Quantitative Comparison questions

Compare Quantity A and Quantity B, using additional information centered above the two quantities if such information is given. Select one of the following four answer choices and fill in the corresponding oval to the right of the question.

Ⓐ Quantity A is greater.

Ⓑ Quantity B is greater.

Ⓒ The two quantities are equal.

Ⓓ The relationship cannot be determined from the information given.

A symbol that appears more than once in a question has the same meaning throughout the question.

Directions for Numeric Entry questions

Enter your answer in the answer box(es) below the question.

- Your answer may be an integer, a decimal, or a fraction, and it may be negative.
- If a question asks for a fraction, there will be two boxes—one for the numerator and one for the denominator.
- Equivalent forms of the correct answer, such as 2.5 and 2.50, are all correct. Fractions do not need to be reduced to lowest terms.
- Enter the exact answer unless the question asks you to round your answer.

SET 1. Discrete Questions: Easy

Quantitative Comparison

For Questions 1 to 6, use the directions for Quantitative Comparison questions.

Emma spent $75 buying a used bicycle and $27 repairing it. Then she sold the bicycle for 40 percent more than the total amount she spent buying and repairing it.

Quantity A	Quantity B	
1. The price at which Emma sold the bicycle	$140	Ⓐ Ⓑ Ⓒ Ⓓ

Explanation

In this question you are asked to compare the price at which Emma sold the bicycle with $140. From the information given, you can conclude that Emma spent a total of $75 + 27 = 102$ dollars buying and repairing the bicycle and that she sold it for 40 percent more than the $102 she spent buying and repairing it. If you notice that 140 is 40 percent more than 100, you can conclude that 40 percent more than 102 is greater than 40 percent more than 100, and therefore, Quantity A is greater than Quantity B. The correct answer is **Choice A**. (If you solve the problem in this way, you do not have to calculate the value of Quantity A.)

Another way to solve the problem is by explicitly calculating the value of Quantity A and comparing the result with $140 directly. Since 40 percent of 102 is $(0.4)(102) = 40.8$, it follows that Quantity A, the price at which Emma sold the bicycle, is $102.00 + 40.80 = 142.80$ dollars. Thus Quantity A, $142.80, is greater than Quantity B, $140, and the correct answer is **Choice A**.

This explanation uses the following strategy.

Strategy 1: Translate from Words to an Arithmetic or Algebraic Representation

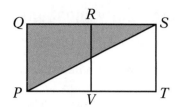

In the figure above, squares *PQRV* and *VRST* have sides of length 6.

Quantity A	Quantity B	
2. The area of the shaded region	36	Ⓐ Ⓑ Ⓒ Ⓓ

Explanation

In this question you are asked to compare the area of the shaded region with 36. You are given that both *PQRV* and *VRST* are squares with sides of length 6. Therefore, you can conclude that the length of *QS* is 12, and the area of the shaded right triangle *PQS* is $\frac{1}{2}(12)(6)$, or 36. Thus Quantity A is equal to Quantity B, and the correct answer is **Choice C**.

This explanation uses the following strategy.

Strategy 4: Translate from a Figure to an Arithmetic or Algebraic Representation

---

In 2009 the property tax on each home in Town *X* was *p* percent of the assessed value of the home, where *p* is a constant. The property tax in 2009 on a home in Town *X* that had an assessed value of $125,000 was $2,500.

Quantity A	Quantity B	
3. The property tax in 2009 on a home in Town *X* that had an assessed value of $160,000	$3,000	Ⓐ Ⓑ Ⓒ Ⓓ

Explanation

Before making the comparison in this problem, you need to analyze the information given to see what it tells you about the value of Quantity A, the property tax in 2009 on a home in Town *X* that had an assessed value of $160,000. One way of doing this is to determine the value of the constant *p* and then use that value to calculate the tax on the home that had an assessed value of $160,000.

Since it is given that a home that had an assessed value of $125,000 had a property tax of $2,500, you can conclude that *p* is equal to $\frac{2,500}{125,000}$, or 2%. Once you know that the property tax is 2% of the assessed value, you can determine that tax on the home that had an assessed value of $160,000 was 2% of 160,000, or 3,200. The correct answer is **Choice A**.

Another way to calculate the property tax on a home with an assessed value of $160,000 is by setting up a proportion. Because the tax rate is the same for each home in Town X, you can let the variable x represent the tax for the home assessed at $160,000 and solve for x as follows.

$$\frac{x}{160,000} = \frac{2,500}{125,000}$$

$$125,000x = (160,000)(2,500)$$

$$x = \frac{(160,000)(2,500)}{125,000}$$

$$x = 3,200$$

The correct answer is **Choice A**.

This explanation uses the following strategies.

Strategy 1: Translate from Words to an Arithmetic or Algebraic Representation
Strategy 8: Search for a Mathematical Relationship

$$x + y = -1$$

	Quantity A		Quantity B	
4.	x		y	Ⓐ Ⓑ Ⓒ Ⓓ

Explanation

One way to approach this question is to plug in values for one of the variables and determine the corresponding value for the other variable.

One way to plug in: Plug in easy values. For example, you can plug in $x = 0$ and find that the corresponding value of y is -1; then you can plug in $y = 0$ and find that the corresponding value of x is -1. Since in the first case x is greater than y and in the second case y is greater than x, the correct answer is **Choice D**, the relationship cannot be determined from the information given.

A second way to plug in: If you prefer to always plug in values of x to determine corresponding values of y, you can begin by writing the equation $x + y = -1$ as $y = -x - 1$. Writing it in this form makes it easier to find the corresponding values of y.

You can start by plugging in the value $x = 0$. For this value of x, the corresponding value of y is $y = -1$, and therefore, x is greater than y. If you continue plugging in a variety of values of x, some negative and some positive, you will see that sometimes x is greater than y and sometimes y is greater than x.

If you inspect the equation $y = -x - 1$, you can conclude that since there is a negative sign in front of the x but not in front of the y, for each value of x that is greater than 0, the corresponding value of y is less than 0; therefore, for each $x > 0$, x is greater than y.

What about negative values of x? A quick inspection of the equation $y = -x - 1$ allows you to conclude that if $x < -1$, then $y > 0$, so y is greater than x.

So for some values of x and y that satisfy the equation, x is greater than y; and for other values, y is greater than x. Therefore, the relationship between the two quantities x and y cannot be determined from the information given, and the correct answer is **Choice D**.

This explanation uses the following strategies.

Strategy 10: Trial and Error
Strategy 13: Determine Whether a Conclusion Follows from the Information Given

---

r, s, and t are three consecutive odd integers such that $r < s < t$.

	Quantity A		Quantity B	
5.	$r + s + 1$		$s + t - 1$	Ⓐ Ⓑ Ⓒ Ⓓ

Explanation

You are given that three numbers, r, s, and t, are consecutive odd integers and that $r < s < t$. This means that if you express the three consecutive odd integers in terms of r, they are r, $r + 2$, and $r + 4$.

One way to approach this problem is to set up a placeholder relationship between the two quantities and simplify it to see what conclusions you can draw.

Simplification 1: Begin simplifying by expressing s and t in terms of r. The steps in this simplification can be done as follows.

$$r+s+1 \;\boxed{?}\; s+t-1$$
$$r+(r+2)+1 \;\boxed{?}\; (r+2)+(r+4)-1$$
$$2r+3 \;\boxed{?}\; 2r+5$$
$$3 \;\boxed{?}\; 5$$

In the last step of the simplification, you can easily see that $3 < 5$. If you follow the simplification steps in reverse, you can see that the placeholder in each step remains unchanged, so you can conclude that Quantity B is greater than Quantity A, and the correct answer is **Choice B**.

Simplification 2: Since the number s appears in both quantities, you can begin the simplification by subtracting s from both sides of the relationship and then express t in terms of r. The steps in this simplification can be done as follows.

$$r+s+1 \;\boxed{?}\; s+t-1$$
$$r+1 \;\boxed{?}\; t-1$$
$$r+1 \;\boxed{?}\; (r+4)-1$$
$$r+1 \;\boxed{?}\; r+3$$
$$1 \;\boxed{?}\; 3$$

In the last step of the simplification, you can easily see that $1 < 3$. If you follow the simplification steps in reverse, you can see that the placeholder in each step remains unchanged, so you can conclude that Quantity B is greater than Quantity A, and the correct answer is **Choice B**.

Note that in this solution, the fact that r is odd is not used; what is used is the fact that the consecutive odd integers differ by 2.

This explanation uses the following strategies.

Strategy 5: Simplify an Arithmetic or Algebraic Representation
Strategy 8: Search for a Mathematical Relationship

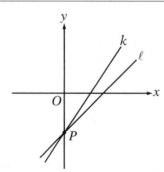

Quantity A	Quantity B
6. The slope of line k	The slope of line ℓ

Explanation

Note that the slope of each of the lines is positive, since each line rises as it goes to the right. Since the slopes of both lines are positive and line k rises faster (or is steeper) than line ℓ, line k has the greater slope, and the correct answer is **Choice A**.

You can also use the definition of the slope to arrive at the correct answer. Slope can be defined as the ratio of "rise" to "run" between any two points on a line, where the rise is the vertical distance between the points and the run is the horizontal distance, and the slope is respectively positive or negative depending on whether the line rises or falls when viewed from left to right. Because both lines pass through point P on the y-axis, they have the same rise from P to the x-axis. However, line ℓ intersects the x-axis at a greater value than line k. Thus, the run of line ℓ from the y-axis to the x-intercept is greater than the run of line k. When the slope is expressed as a ratio, both lines have the same numerator (rise), but line ℓ has a greater denominator (run). The greater denominator results in a lesser fraction and a lesser slope for line ℓ. Therefore, the correct answer is **Choice A**.

This explanation uses the following strategy.

Strategy 4: Translate from a Figure to an Arithmetic or Algebraic Representation

Multiple-choice Questions—Select One Answer Choice

For Questions 7 to 11, select a single answer choice.

7.   In the figure above, what is the value of $\dfrac{x+y+z}{45}$?

   (A) 2

   (B) 3

   (C) 4

   (D) 5

   (E) 6

Explanation

The sum of the measures, in degrees, of the three interior angles of any triangle is 180°. As shown in the figure, the three angles of the triangle have measures of $x°$, $y°$, and $z°$, so $x + y + z = 180$. Therefore, $\dfrac{x+y+z}{45} = \dfrac{180}{45} = 4$, and the correct answer is **Choice C**.

This explanation uses the following strategy.

Strategy 4: Translate from a Figure to an Arithmetic or Algebraic Representation

8. A certain store sells two types of pens: one type for $2 per pen and the other type for $3 per pen. If a customer can spend up to $25 to buy pens at the store and there is no sales tax, what is the greatest number of pens the customer can buy?

    (A) 9

    (B) 10

    (C) 11

    (D) 12

    (E) 20

Explanation

It is fairly clear that the greatest number of pens that can be bought for $25 will consist mostly, if not entirely, of $2 pens. In fact, it is reasonable to begin by looking at how many of the $2 pens the customer can buy if the customer does not buy any $3 pens. It is easy to see that the customer could buy 12 of the $2 pens, with $1 left over.

If the customer bought 11 of the $2 pens, there would be $3 left over with which to buy a $3 pen. In this case, the customer could still buy 12 pens.

If the customer bought 10 of the $2 pens, there would be $5 left over. Only 1 of the $3 pens could be bought with the $5, so in this case, the customer could buy only 11 pens.

As the number of $2 pens decreases, the total number of pens that the customer can buy with $25 decreases as well. Thus the greatest number of pens the customer can buy with $25 is 12. The correct answer is **Choice D**.

This explanation uses the following strategies.

Strategy 1: Translate from Words to an Arithmetic or Algebraic Representation
Strategy 10: Trial and Error

---

9. If $y = 3x$ and $z = 2y$, what is $x + y + z$ in terms of x?

    (A) $10x$

    (B) $9x$

    (C) $8x$

    (D) $6x$

    (E) $5x$

Explanation

It is not necessary to find the individual values of x, y, and z to answer the question. You are asked to rewrite the expression $x + y + z$ as an equivalent expression in terms of x. This means that you need to use the information provided about y and z to express them in terms of the variable x. The variable y is already given in terms of x; that is, $y = 3x$; and because $z = 2y$, it follows that $z = (2)(3x) = 6x$. Using substitution, you can rewrite the expression as follows.

$$x + y + z = x + (3x) + (6x)$$

$$= (1 + 3 + 6)x$$

$$= 10x$$

The correct answer is **Choice A**.

This explanation uses the following strategy.

Strategy 5: Simplify an Arithmetic or Algebraic Representation

10. A certain shipping service charges an insurance fee of $0.75 when shipping any package with contents worth $25.00 or less and an insurance fee of $1.00 when shipping any package with contents worth over $25.00. If Dan uses the shipping company to ship three packages with contents worth $18.25, $25.00, and $127.50, respectively, what is the total insurance fee that the company charges Dan to ship the three packages?

   Ⓐ $1.75
   Ⓑ $2.25
   Ⓒ $2.50
   Ⓓ $2.75
   Ⓔ $3.00

Explanation

Note that two of the packages being shipped have contents that are worth $25.00 or less. Therefore, each of them has an insurance fee of $0.75, for a total of $1.50. The third package has contents worth over $25.00, and it has an insurance fee of $1.00. Therefore, the total insurance fee for the three packages is $1.50 + $1.00 = $2.50, and the correct answer is **Choice C**.

This explanation uses the following strategy.

Strategy 1: Translate from Words to an Arithmetic or Algebraic Representation

---

11. Last year, all purchases of a certain product were made either online or in a store. If 55 percent of the purchases were made online, what was the ratio of the number of purchases made online to the number of purchases made in a store?

   Ⓐ 11 to 9
   Ⓑ 11 to 5
   Ⓒ 10 to 9
   Ⓓ   9 to 11
   Ⓔ   9 to 10

Explanation

Note that because 55 percent of the purchases were made online, it follows that 45 percent of the purchases were made in a store. Therefore, the ratio of the number of purchases made online to the number of purchases made in a store is 55 to 45, or 11 to 9, and the correct answer is **Choice A**.

This explanation uses the following strategy.

Strategy 1: Translate from Words to an Arithmetic or Algebraic Representation

Numeric Entry

For Questions 12 and 13, use the directions for Numeric Entry questions.

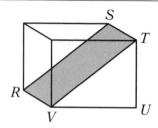

12.   In the rectangular solid above, $TU = 3$, $UV = 4$, and $VR = 2$. What is the area of the shaded rectangular region?

Explanation

To find the area of the shaded rectangular region, you need to multiply the length of the rectangular region by its width. In this question you are given the lengths of three edges: $TU = 3$, $UV = 4$, and $VR = 2$. Note that VR is the length of the shaded rectangle. To find the width of the shaded rectangle, you need to find either RS or VT. Note that VT lies on the front face of the rectangular solid. It is the hypotenuse of right triangle VUT. You know that $UV = 4$ and $TU = 3$, so by the Pythagorean theorem you can conclude that $VT = \sqrt{3^2 + 4^2} = \sqrt{9 + 16} = \sqrt{25} = 5$. Therefore, the area of the shaded rectangular region is $(5)(2) = 10$. The correct answer is **10**.

This explanation uses the following strategies.

Strategy 4: Translate from a Figure to an Arithmetic or Algebraic Representation
Strategy 8: Search for a Mathematical Relationship

13.   A list of numbers has a mean of 8 and a standard deviation of 2.5. If x is a number in the list that is 2 standard deviations above the mean, what is the value of x?

$$x = \boxed{}$$

Explanation

You are given that x is 2 standard deviations above the mean, 8. Because the standard deviation of the numbers in the list is 2.5, it follows that x is $(2)(2.5)$, or 5 units above the mean 8. Therefore, $x = 8 + 5 = 13$, and the correct answer is **13**.

This explanation uses the following strategy.

Strategy 8: Search for a Mathematical Relationship

Multiple-choice Questions—Select One or More Answer Choices

For Question 14, select all the answer choices that apply.

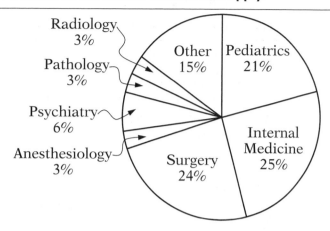

14. The circle graph above shows the distribution of 200,000 physicians by specialty. Which of the following sectors of the circle graph represent more than 40,000 physicians?

    Indicate all such sectors.

    A   Pediatrics

    B   Internal Medicine

    C   Surgery

    D   Anesthesiology

    E   Psychiatry

Explanation

One approach to solve this problem is to find out what percent of 200,000 is 40,000 and then compare this percent with the percents given in the circle graph. Because $\frac{40,000}{200,000} = 0.2$, it follows that 40,000 is 20% of 200,000, and any specialty that has more than 20% of the distribution has more than 40,000 physicians. This is true for the specialties of pediatrics, internal medicine, and surgery. The correct answer consists of **Choices A, B, and C**.

This explanation uses the following strategy.

Strategy 4: Translate from a Figure to an Arithmetic or Algebraic Representation

SET 2. Discrete Questions: Medium

Quantitative Comparison

> **For Questions 1 to 5, use the directions for Quantitative Comparison questions.**

Machine R, working alone at a constant rate, produces x units of a product in 30 minutes, and machine S, working alone at a constant rate, produces x units of the product in 48 minutes, where x is a positive integer.

	Quantity A	Quantity B	
1.	The number of units of the product that machine R, working alone at its constant rate, produces in 3 hours	The number of units of the product that machine S, working alone at its constant rate, produces in 4 hours	

Explanation

In this question you are given that machine R, working alone at its constant rate, produces x units of a product in 30 minutes. Since it is easy to see that 3 hours is 6 times 30 minutes, you can conclude that Quantity A is $6x$.

You can compare $6x$ with Quantity B in two ways.

One: In the additional information centered above the quantities, you are given that machine S, working alone at its constant rate, produces x units of the product in 48 minutes, so you can conclude that machine S can produce $6x$ units of the product in $(6)(48)$ minutes, or 4.8 hours. So in 4 hours, machine S produces less than $6x$ units, and Quantity B is less than $6x$.

Two: First, convert 48 minutes to $\frac{4}{5}$ hour, then find the number of 48-minute periods there are in 4 hours by computing $\frac{4}{\frac{4}{5}} = (4)\left(\frac{5}{4}\right) = 5$. Thus, Quantity B is $5x$.

Either way, Quantity A is greater than Quantity B, and the correct answer is **Choice A**.

This explanation uses the following strategies.

Strategy 1: Translate from Words to an Arithmetic or Algebraic Representation
Strategy 8: Search for a Mathematical Relationship

Frequency Distribution for List X

Number	1	2	3	5
Frequency	10	20	18	12

Frequency Distribution for List Y

Number	6	7	8	9
Frequency	24	17	10	9

List X and list Y each contain 60 numbers. Frequency distributions for each list are given above. The average (arithmetic mean) of the numbers in list X is 2.7, and the average of the numbers in list Y is 7.1. List Z contains 120 numbers: the 60 numbers in list X and the 60 numbers in list Y.

	Quantity A	Quantity B	
2.	The average of the 120 numbers in list Z	The median of the 120 numbers in list Z	

Explanation

In this problem you are asked to compare the average with the median of the 120 numbers in list Z. Since list Z consists of the numbers in lists X and Y combined, it is reasonable to try to use the information about lists X and Y to calculate the average and the median of the numbers in list Z.

To determine the average of the 120 numbers in list Z, you can use the information given about the individual averages of the numbers in lists X and Y. Because lists X and Y each contain 60 numbers, the average of the numbers in list Z is the average of the individual averages of the numbers in lists X and Y. Thus, the average of the numbers in list Z is $\frac{2.7+7.1}{2}$, or 4.9.

To determine the median of the 120 numbers in list Z, first note that list Z contains an even number of numbers, so the median of the numbers in list Z is the average of the middle two numbers when the numbers are listed in increasing order. If you look at the numbers in the two lists, you will see that the 60 numbers in list X are all less than or equal to 5, and the 60 numbers in list Y are all greater than or equal to 6. Thus, the two middle numbers in list Z are 5 and 6, and the average of these numbers is $\frac{5+6}{2}$ or 5.5. Therefore, the median of the numbers in list Z is 5.5, and this is greater than the average of 4.9. The correct answer is **Choice B**.

This explanation uses the following strategies.

Strategy 4: Translate from a Figure to an Arithmetic or Algebraic Representation
Strategy 8: Search for a Mathematical Relationship

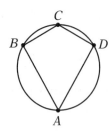

In the figure above, the diameter of the circle is 10.

Quantity A	Quantity B	
3. The area of quadrilateral *ABCD*	40	Ⓐ Ⓑ Ⓒ Ⓓ

Explanation

You are given that the circle has a diameter of 10, and from the figure you can assume that points *A*, *B*, *C*, and *D* lie on the circle in the order shown. However, because figures are not necessarily drawn to scale, you cannot assume anything else about the positions of points *A*, *B*, *C*, and *D* on the circle. Therefore, to get an idea of how various possible positions of these four points could affect the area of quadrilateral *ABCD*, it is a good idea to see how the figure can vary but still have points *A*, *B*, *C*, and *D* in the same order as in the figure above.

One way that you might vary the figure is to evenly space the four points along the circle, as shown below.

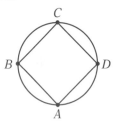

Another way is to draw points *A* and *C* opposite each other, with points *B* and *D* close to point *C*, as shown below.

From these figures you can draw some basic conclusions about the area of *ABCD*.

If points *A* and *C* are opposite each other, with points *B* and *D* very close to point *C*, the area of quadrilateral *ABCD* is very close to 0. Clearly, the area can be less than 40 (Quantity B).

If points *A*, *B*, *C*, and *D* are evenly spaced, the area is not close to 0. How does the area compare with 40? To calculate the area of *ABCD*, draw the diameters *AC* and *BD* in the figure. The two diameters are perpendicular bisectors of each other, so they divide *ABCD* into four right triangles, as shown.

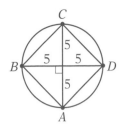

The area of each of the right triangles is $\left(\frac{1}{2}\right)(5)(5)$, or 12.5. Thus, the area of *ABCD* is (4)(12.5), or 50.

Since the area of the quadrilateral in the first figure is less than 40 and the area of the quadrilateral in the second figure is greater than 40, the relationship cannot be determined from the information given. The correct answer is **Choice D**.

This explanation uses the following strategies.

Strategy 4: Translate from a Figure to an Arithmetic or Algebraic Representation
Strategy 6: Add to a Geometric Figure
Strategy 13: Determine Whether a Conclusion Follows from the Information Given

---

$$x^2y > 0$$
$$xy^2 < 0$$

	Quantity A	Quantity B	
4.	x	y	Ⓐ Ⓑ Ⓒ Ⓓ

Explanation

You are given that $x^2y > 0$, which means that the product of the two numbers x^2 and y is positive. Recall that the product of two numbers is positive only if both numbers are positive or both numbers are negative. The square of a number is always greater than or equal to 0. In this case, x^2 cannot equal 0 because the product x^2y is not 0. Thus, x^2 is positive and it follows that y is also positive.

You are also given that $xy^2 < 0$, which means that the product of the two numbers x and y^2 is negative. The product of two numbers is negative only if one of the numbers is negative and the other number is positive. In this case, y^2 cannot be negative because it is the square of a number, and it cannot be 0 because the product x^2y is not 0. Thus, y^2 is positive and so x must be negative.

Because x is negative and y is positive, y must be greater than x, and the correct answer is **Choice B**.

This explanation uses the following strategy.

Strategy 8: Search for a Mathematical Relationship

Among the 9,000 people attending a football game at College *C*, there were x students from College *C* and y students who were <u>not</u> from College *C*.

	Quantity A	Quantity B	
5.	The number of people attending the game who were <u>not</u> students	$9{,}000 - x - y$	Ⓐ Ⓑ Ⓒ Ⓓ

Explanation

In this question you are not told whether all of the 9,000 people attending the game were students. Let z be the number of people attending the game who were not students. The people attending the game can be broken down into three groups: students from College C, students not from College C, and people who were not students. This can be expressed algebraically as $9,000 = x + y + z$, where x represents the number of students from College C attending the game and y represents the number of students attending the game who were not from College C. Therefore, $9,000 - x - y = z$ is the number of people attending the game who were not students. The correct answer is **Choice C**.

This explanation uses the following strategy.

Strategy 1: Translate from Words to an Arithmetic or Algebraic Representation

Multiple-choice Questions—Select One Answer Choice

For Questions 6 to 10, select a single answer choice.

6. If $x \neq 0$, which of the following is equivalent to $\dfrac{x(x^2)^3}{x^2}$?

(A) x^2

(B) x^3

(C) x^4

(D) x^5

(E) x^6

Explanation

To simplify $\dfrac{x(x^2)^3}{x^2}$, it can be helpful to write $(x^2)^3$ as $(x^2)(x^2)(x^2)$ in the given expression; that is, $\dfrac{x(x^2)^3}{x^2} = \dfrac{x(x^2)(x^2)(x^2)}{x^2}$. Because $x \neq 0$, both numerator and denominator can be divided by x^2, and the expression simplifies to $x(x^2)(x^2)$, which, by the rules of exponents, is equal to x^5.

Another way to simplify the expression using the rules of exponents directly is as follows.
$$\frac{x(x^2)^3}{x^2} = \frac{x(x^6)}{x^2} = \frac{x^7}{x^2} = x^5$$

The correct answer is **Choice D**.

This explanation uses the following strategy.

Strategy 5: Simplify an Arithmetic or Algebraic Representation

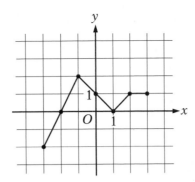

7. The figure above shows the graph of the function f in the xy-plane. What is the value of $f(f(-1))$?

   Ⓐ –2
   Ⓑ –1
   Ⓒ 0

   Ⓓ 1
   Ⓔ 2

Explanation

Note that to find $f(f(-1))$, you must apply the function f twice, first to find the value of $f(-1)$ and then to find the value of $f(f(-1))$. To find the value of $f(-1)$, find the point on the graph of the function f whose x-coordinate is $x = -1$. This point has y-coordinate $y = 2$. Therefore, the value of $f(-1)$ is 2, and $f(f(-1)) = f(2)$. Next you need to find the value of $f(2)$. To find the value of $f(2)$, find the point on the graph whose x-coordinate is $x = 2$. This point has y-coordinate $y = 1$. Therefore, $f(2) = 1$, and because $f(f(-1)) = f(2)$, you can conclude that $f(f(-1)) = 1$. The correct answer is **Choice D**.

This explanation uses the following strategies.

Strategy 4: Translate from a Figure to an Arithmetic or Algebraic Representation
Strategy 12: Adapt Solutions to Related Problems

8. If $\dfrac{d - 3n}{7n - d} = 1$, which of the following statements describes d in terms of n?

   Ⓐ d is 4 less than n.
   Ⓑ d is 4 more than n.
   Ⓒ d is $\dfrac{3}{7}$ of n.

   Ⓓ d is 2 times n.
   Ⓔ d is 5 times n.

Explanation

To describe d in terms of n, you need to solve the equation $\dfrac{d - 3n}{7n - d} = 1$ for d. To simplify the equation, you can begin by multiplying both sides by $7n - d$ and then proceed as follows.

$$(7n - d)\left(\frac{d - 3n}{7n - d}\right) = (7n - d)(1)$$
$$d - 3n = 7n - d$$
$$d = 10n - d$$
$$2d = 10n$$
$$d = 5n$$

The correct answer is **Choice E**.

This explanation uses the following strategy.

Strategy 5: Simplify an Arithmetic or Algebraic Representation

9. By weight, liquid *A* makes up 8 percent of solution *R* and 18 percent of solution *S*. If 3 grams of solution *R* are mixed with 7 grams of solution *S*, then liquid *A* accounts for what percent of the weight of the resulting solution?

   (A) 10%

   (B) 13%

   (C) 15%

   (D) 19%

   (E) 26%

Explanation

Liquid *A* makes up 8 percent of the weight of solution *R* and 18 percent of the weight of solution *S*. Therefore, 3 grams of solution *R* contain (0.08)(3), or 0.24 gram of liquid *A*, and 7 grams of solution *S* contain (0.18)(7), or 1.26 grams of liquid *A*. When the two solutions are mixed, the resulting solution weighs 3 + 7, or 10 grams and contains 0.24 + 1.26, or 1.5 grams of liquid *A*. This means that liquid *A* makes up $\frac{1.5}{10}$, or $\frac{15}{100}$, or 15 percent of the weight of the resulting solution. The correct answer is **Choice C**.

This explanation uses the following strategy.

Strategy 1: Translate from Words to an Arithmetic or Algebraic Representation

---

10. Of the 700 members of a certain organization, 120 are lawyers. Two members of the organization will be selected at random. Which of the following is closest to the probability that <u>neither</u> of the members selected will be a lawyer?

    (A) 0.5

    (B) 0.6

    (C) 0.7

    (D) 0.8

    (E) 0.9

Explanation

The probability that neither of the members selected will be a lawyer is equal to the fraction

$$\frac{\text{the number of ways 2 members who are not lawyers can be selected}}{\text{the number of ways 2 members can be selected}}$$

where the order of selection does not matter.

Since there are 120 members who are lawyers, there must be 700 − 120, or 580 members who are not lawyers. There are 580 ways of selecting a first member who is not a lawyer and 579 ways of selecting a second member who is not a lawyer. Multiplying these two numbers gives the number of ways to select 2 members who are not lawyers. However, in the (580)(579) ways, each group of 2 members who are not lawyers is counted twice. You can see this by considering 2 members, *A* and *B*. The 2 members can be chosen in 2 ways: *A* first, followed by *B*, and *B* first, followed by *A*. To adjust for double counting, you need to divide (580)(579) by 2.

Similarly, the number of ways 2 members can be selected from among the 700 members is (700)(699) divided by 2. Thus, the desired probability is

$$\frac{\frac{(580)(579)}{2}}{\frac{(700)(699)}{2}} = \frac{(580)(579)}{(700)(699)}$$

Since the answer choices are all tenths, you need to approximate the value of this fraction to the nearest tenth. There are several ways to do this approximation. One way is to use your calculator to convert the fraction to a decimal and round the decimal to the nearest tenth.

Another way is to approximate the value of the fraction as follows.

$$\frac{(580)(579)}{(700)(699)} \approx \frac{(600)(600)}{(700)(700)} = \left(\frac{6}{7}\right)^2 = \frac{36}{49} \approx \frac{36}{50} = 0.72$$

Either way, the answer choice that is closest to the value of the fraction is 0.7. The correct answer is **Choice C**.

Another approach to this problem is to consider the random selections as two separate but successive events. The probability of selecting a first member who is not a lawyer is $\frac{580}{700}$, because there are 580 members out of the 700 members who are not lawyers. For the second selection, there are only 699 members left to select from, because one member has already been selected. If the first member selected is not a lawyer, then there are only 579 members left who are not lawyers. So the probability of selecting a second member who is not a lawyer, given the condition that the first member selected was not a lawyer, is $\frac{579}{699}$. The probability that both members selected will not be lawyers is the product of the two probabilities, or $\left(\frac{580}{700}\right)\left(\frac{579}{699}\right)$, which is approximated above as 0.72. The correct answer is **Choice C**.

This explanation uses the following strategies.
Strategy 8: Search for a Mathematical Relationship
Strategy 9: Estimate

Numeric Entry

For Questions 11 and 12, use the directions for Numeric Entry questions.

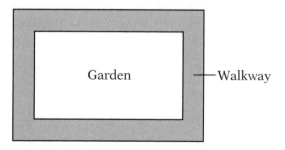

11. The figure above represents a rectangular garden with a walkway around it. The garden is 18 feet long and 12 feet wide. The walkway is uniformly 3 feet wide, and its edges meet at right angles. What is the area of the walkway?

[   ] square feet

Explanation

You can see from the figure that the shaded region is the region between the two rectangles. Looking at the shaded region in this way suggests that the area of the walkway can be calculated as the difference between the area of the larger rectangle and the area of the smaller rectangle.

The region represented by the smaller rectangle is the garden. Since the garden is 18 feet long and 12 feet wide, its area is (18)(12), or 216 square feet.

The region represented by the larger rectangle is the garden and the walkway combined. The length of the region is the length of the garden plus twice the width of the walkway, or 18 + (2)(3) = 24 feet. The width of the region is the width of the garden plus twice the width of the walkway, or 12 + (2)(3) = 18 feet. Therefore, the area of the region represented by the larger rectangle is (24)(18), or 432 square feet, and the area of the walkway is 432 − 216, or 216 square feet.

Another way to approach this problem is to think of the walkway as being composed of four rectangles and four squares, as shown in the figure below.

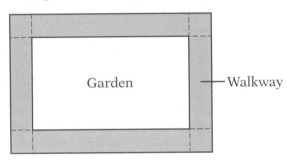

Each of the four squares is 3 feet long and 3 feet wide. The two rectangles running along the length of the garden are 18 feet long and 3 feet wide, and the two rectangles running along the width of the garden are 12 feet long and 3 feet wide. Thus, the area of the walkway is

$$4(3)(3) + 2(18)(3) + 2(12)(3) = 36 + 108 + 72 = 216 \text{ square feet}$$

The correct answer is **216**.

This explanation uses the following strategies.

Strategy 4: Translate from a Figure to an Arithmetic or Algebraic Representation
Strategy 8: Search for a Mathematical Relationship

---

12.   Line k lies in the xy-plane. The x-intercept of line k is −4, and line k passes through the midpoint of the line segment whose endpoints are (2, 9) and (2, 0). What is the slope of line k?

Give your answer as a fraction.

Explanation

You can calculate the slope of a line if you know the coordinates of two points on the line. In this question you are given information about two points on line k, namely,

- the point at which line k crosses the x-axis has x-coordinate −4;
- the midpoint of the line segment with endpoints at (2, 9) and (2, 0) is on line k.

The coordinates of the first point are (–4, 0), since the x-coordinate is –4 and the y-coordinate of every point on the x-axis is 0. For the second point, the midpoint of the line segment is halfway between the endpoints (2, 9) and (2, 0). Thus, the midpoint has x-coordinate 2 and y-coordinate $\frac{9}{2}$, the number halfway between 9 and 0. Based on the coordinates (–4, 0) and $\left(2, \frac{9}{2}\right)$, the slope of line k is

$$\frac{\frac{9}{2}-0}{2-(-4)} = \frac{\frac{9}{2}}{6} = \frac{3}{4}$$

The correct answer is $\frac{3}{4}$ (or any equivalent fraction).

This explanation uses the following strategies.
Strategy 1: Translate from Words into an Arithmetic or Algebraic Representation
Strategy 8: Search for a Mathematical Relationship

Multiple-choice Questions—Select One or More Answer Choices

For Questions 13 and 14, select all the answer choices that apply.

13. If the lengths of two sides of a triangle are 5 and 9, respectively, which of the following could be the length of the third side of the triangle?

    Indicate <u>all</u> such lengths.

    A 3
    B 5
    C 8
    D 15

Explanation
A good way to approach this problem is to think about how much the length of the third side of a triangle with two fixed side lengths can vary. If you think about it a bit, you will see that the smaller the interior angle between the two sides of the triangle is, the smaller the length of the third side is; and the larger the interior angle between the two sides of the triangle is, the larger the length of the third side is. This suggests drawing two triangles, one in which the angle between the two sides is close to 0 degrees and one in which the angle between the two sides is close to 180 degrees, like the triangles below.

   In the triangle in which the angle between the sides of length 5 and 9 is small, you can see that the length of the third side is a bit greater than 9 – 5, or 4. If it were equal to 4, the triangle would degenerate into a line segment.
   In the triangle in which the angle between the sides of length 5 and 9 is large, you can see that the length of the third side is a bit less than 9 + 5, or 14. If it were equal to 14, the triangle would degenerate into a line segment.

Therefore, the length of the third side of the triangle must be greater than 4 and less than 14. Furthermore, it is intuitive that any length between these two numbers can be achieved by some triangle. The correct answer consists of **Choices B and C**.

This explanation uses the following strategies.

Strategy 2: Translate from Words to a Figure or Diagram
Strategy 11: Divide into Cases

---

14.   On the number line shown above, the tick marks are equally spaced. Which of the following statements about the numbers x, y, and z must be true?

Indicate <u>all</u> such statements.

A $xyz < 0$ B $x + z = y$ C $z(y - x) > 0$

Explanation

You can see from their positions on the number line that x is less than 0 and both y and z are greater than 0. Because the tick marks are equally spaced, you can also see that $x = -y$ and $z = 2y$. You need to evaluate each answer choice separately to determine whether it must be true.

Choice A says that the product of the three numbers x, y, and z is less than 0. Recall that the product of three numbers is negative under either of the following two conditions.

- All three numbers are negative.
- One of the numbers is negative and the other two numbers are positive.

Choice A must be true, since x is negative and y and z are positive.

Choice B is the equation $x + z = y$. To see whether the equation must be true, it is a good idea to express two of the variables in terms of the third (that is, to "get rid of" two of the variables). The equations $x = -y$ and $z = 2y$ give x and z in terms of y, so the equation $x + z = y$ can be rewritten, substituting $-y$ for x and $2y$ for z, as $-y + 2y = y$. In this form you can quickly conclude that the equation must be true.

Choice C says that the product of the two numbers z and $y - x$ is greater than 0. Recall that the product of two numbers is positive under either of the following two conditions.

- Both numbers are positive.
- Both numbers are negative.

Since you already know that z is positive, you can conclude that the product $z(y - x)$ will be positive if $y - x$ is positive. By adding x to both sides of the inequality $y - x > 0$, you can see that it is equivalent to the inequality $y > x$, which is clearly true from the number line. Since $y - x$ is positive, the product $z(y - x)$ must be positive.

Therefore, the correct answer consists of **Choices A, B, and C**.

This explanation uses the following strategies.

Strategy 4: Translate from a Figure to an Arithmetic or Algebraic Representation
Strategy 8: Search for a Mathematical Relationship
Strategy 13: Determine Whether a Conclusion Follows from the Information Given

SET 3. Discrete Questions: Hard

Quantitative Comparison

> For Questions 1 to 6, use the directions for Quantitative Comparison questions.

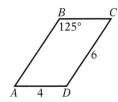

In the figure above, *ABCD* is a parallelogram.

	Quantity A	Quantity B	
1.	The area of the *ABCD*	24	Ⓐ Ⓑ Ⓒ Ⓓ

Explanation

In this question you are asked to compare the area of a parallelogram with an area of 24, given two side lengths and the measure of one interior angle of the parallelogram. Since the measure of the interior angle given is 125°, you can conclude that the parallelogram is not a rectangle.

Recall that the area of a parallelogram is found by multiplying the length of a base by the height corresponding to the base. It is helpful to draw the vertical height from vertex *C* to base *AD* of the parallelogram, as shown in the figure below.

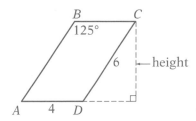

Note that the newly drawn height is a leg in a newly formed right triangle. The hypotenuse of the triangle is a side of the parallelogram and has length 6. Thus, the leg of the triangle, which is the height of the parallelogram, must be less than the hypotenuse 6. The area of the parallelogram is equal to the length of base *AD*, which is 4, times the height, which is less than 6. Since the product of 4 and a number less than 6 must be less than 24, the area of the parallelogram must be less than 24. Quantity B is greater than Quantity A, and the correct answer is **Choice B**.

This explanation uses the following strategies.

Strategy 6: Add to a Geometric Figure
Strategy 8: Search for a Mathematical Relationship

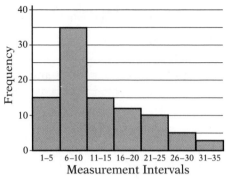

In the course of an experiment, 95 measurements were recorded, and all of the measurements were integers. The 95 measurements were then grouped into 7 measurement intervals. The graph above shows the frequency distribution of the 95 measurements by measurement interval.

Quantity A	Quantity B

2. The average (arithmetic mean) of the 95 measurements   The median of the 95 measurements

Explanation

From the histogram, you can observe that

- all of the measurement intervals are the same size,
- the distribution has a peak at the measurement interval 6–10, and
- more of the measurement intervals are to the right of the peak than are to the left of the peak.

Since in the histogram the 95 measurements have been grouped into intervals, you cannot calculate the exact value of either the average or the median; you must compare them without being able to determine the exact value of either one.

The median of the 95 measurements is the middle measurement when the measurements are listed in increasing order. The middle measurement is the 48th measurement. From the histogram, you can see that the measurement interval 1–5 contains the first 15 measurements, and the measurement interval 6–10 contains the next 35 measurements (that is, measurements 16 through 50). Therefore, the median is in the measurement interval 6–10 and could be 6, 7, 8, 9, or 10.

Estimating the average of the 95 measurements is more complicated.

Since you are asked to compare the average and the median, not necessarily to calculate them, you may ask yourself if you can tell whether the average is greater than or less than the median. Note that visually the measurements in the first three measurement intervals are symmetric around the measurement interval 6–10, so you would expect the average of the measurements in just these three measurement intervals to lie in the 6–10 measurement interval. The 30 measurements in the remaining four measurement intervals are all greater than 10, some significantly greater than 10. Therefore, the average of the 95 measurements is greater than the average of the measurements in the first three measurement intervals, probably greater than 10. At this point it seems likely that the average of the 95 measurements is greater than the median of the 95 measurements. It turns out that this is true.

To actually show that the average must be greater than 10, you can make the average as small as possible and see if the smallest possible average is greater than 10. To make the average as small as possible, assume that all of the measurements in each interval are as small as possible. That is to say, all 15 measurements in the measurement interval 1–5 are equal to 1, all 35 measurements in the measurement interval 6–10 are equal to 6, etc. Under this assumption, the average of the 95 measurements is

$$\frac{(1)(15)+(6)(35)+(11)(15)+(16)(12)+(21)(10)+(26)(5)+(31)(3)}{95}=\frac{1,015}{95}$$

The value of the smallest possible average, $\frac{1,015}{95}$, is greater than 10.

Therefore, since the average of the 95 measurements is greater than 10 and the median is in the measurement interval 6–10, it follows that the average is greater than the median, and the correct answer is **Choice A**.

This explanation uses the following strategies.

Strategy 4: Translate from a Figure to an Arithmetic or Algebraic Representation
Strategy 8: Search for a Mathematical Relationship
Strategy 9: Estimate
Strategy 11: Divide into Cases

---

x is an integer greater than 1.

Quantity A	Quantity B	
3^{x+1}	4^x	Ⓐ Ⓑ Ⓒ Ⓓ

3.

Explanation

One way to approach this question is to plug in numbers for the variables and see what the relationship between the two quantities is for each of the numbers you plug in.

If you plug in $x = 2$, you see that Quantity A is $3^{x+1} = 3^3$, or 27, and Quantity B is $4^x = 4^2$, or 16. In this case, Quantity A is greater than Quantity B.

If you plug in $x = 3$, you see that Quantity A is $3^{x+1} = 3^4$, or 81, and Quantity B is $4^x = 4^3$, or 64. In this case, Quantity A is greater than Quantity B.

If you plug in $x = 4$, you see that Quantity A is $3^{x+1} = 3^5$, or 243, and Quantity B is $4^x = 4^4$, or 256. In this case, Quantity B is greater than Quantity A. Since for $x = 2$ and for $x = 3$, Quantity A is greater than Quantity B, and for $x = 4$, Quantity B is greater than Quantity A, it follows that the relationship between the two quantities cannot be determined. The correct answer is **Choice D**.

Since both quantities are algebraic expressions, another way to approach this problem is to set up a placeholder relationship between the two quantities and simplify it to see what conclusions you can draw.

$$3^{x+1} \boxed{?} 4^x$$

$$3(3^x) \boxed{?} 4^x$$

$$\frac{3(3^x)}{3^x} \boxed{?} \frac{4^x}{3^x}$$

$$3 \boxed{?} \left(\frac{4}{3}\right)^x$$

For any value of x, the value of 3^x is positive, so dividing by 3^x does not change any inequality that could be put in the placeholder. Since each step in this simplification is reversible, this reduces the problem to comparing 3 with $\left(\frac{4}{3}\right)^x$.

You can see that because $\frac{4}{3}$ is greater than 1, the value of $\left(\frac{4}{3}\right)^x$ becomes greater as x becomes larger. In particular, it is greater than 3 for large enough values of x.

For the smallest value of x, $x = 2$, the relationship is $\left(\frac{4}{3}\right)^2 = \frac{16}{9} < 3$.

Since for $x = 2$, Quantity A is greater than Quantity B and for large values of x, Quantity B is greater than Quantity A, it follows that the relationship between the two quantities cannot be determined. The correct answer is **Choice D**.

This explanation uses the following strategies.

Strategy 10: Trial and Error
Strategy 13: Determine Whether a Conclusion Follows from the Information Given

---

A, *B*, and *C* are three rectangles. The length and width of rectangle *A* are 10 percent greater and 10 percent less, respectively, than the length and width of rectangle *C*. The length and width of rectangle *B* are 20 percent greater and 20 percent less, respectively, than the length and width of rectangle *C*.

Quantity A	Quantity B		
4. The area of rectangle *A*	The area of rectangle *B*		

Explanation

In this question you are asked to compare the area of rectangle *A* and the area of rectangle *B*. Since the information given relates the dimensions of both rectangle *A* and rectangle *B* to the corresponding dimensions of rectangle *C*, you can try to use the relationships to make the desired comparison.

If ℓ represents the length of rectangle *C* and *w* represents its width, then the length and width of rectangles *A* and *B* can be translated into algebraic expressions as follows.

- The length of rectangle *A* is 10 percent greater than the length of rectangle *C*, or 1.1ℓ.
- The width of rectangle *A* is 10 percent less than the width of rectangle *C*, or $0.9w$.
- The length of rectangle *B* is 20 percent greater than the length of rectangle *C*, or 1.2ℓ.
- The width of rectangle *B* is 20 percent less than the width of rectangle *C*, or $0.8w$.

In terms of ℓ and *w*, the area of rectangle *A* is $(1.1\ell)(0.9w)$, or $0.99\ell w$.
In terms of ℓ and *w*, the area of rectangle *B* is $(1.2\ell)(0.8w)$, or $0.96\ell w$.
Since $0.99\ell w$ is greater than $0.96\ell w$, Quantity A is greater than Quantity B, and the correct answer is **Choice A**.

This explanation uses the following strategy.

Strategy 1: Translate from Words into an Arithmetic or Algebraic Representation

---

The random variable *X* is normally distributed. The values 650 and 850 are at the 60th and 90th percentiles of the distribution of *X*, respectively.

Quantity A	Quantity B		
5. The value at the 75th percentile of the distribution of *X*	750		

Explanation

You are given that the distribution of random variable *X* is normal and that the values 650 and 850 are at the 60th and 90th percentiles of the distribution, respectively.

Both of the values 650 and 850 are greater than the mean of the distribution. If you draw a rough sketch of the graph of the normal distribution, the sketch could look something like the one below. Note that it is not necessary to know the exact location of 650 and 850, just that both values are above the mean.

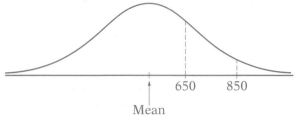

To say that the value 650 is at the 60th percentile of the distribution means, graphically, that 60 percent of the area between the normal curve and the horizontal axis lies to the left of the vertical line segment at 650. To say that 850 is at the 90th percentile of the distribution means that 90 percent of the area between the normal curve and the horizontal axis lies to the left of the vertical line segment at 850.

The value 750 is halfway between 650 and 850. However, because the curve is decreasing in that interval, the area between 650 and 750 is greater than the area between 750 and 850. Since the value at the 75th percentile should divide in half the <u>area</u> between the value at the 60th percentile (650) and the value at the 90th percentile (850), this value is closer to 650 than to 850. Thus you can conclude that Quantity A, the value at the 75th percentile of the distribution of *X*, is less than Quantity B. The correct answer is **Choice B**.

This explanation uses the following strategies.
Strategy 2: Translate from Words to a Figure or Diagram
Strategy 8: Search for a Mathematical Relationship
Strategy 9: Estimate

Set *S* consists of all positive integers less than 81 that are <u>not</u> equal to the square of an integer.

	Quantity A	Quantity B	
6.	The number of integers in set *S*	72	Ⓐ Ⓑ Ⓒ Ⓓ

Explanation

Set *S* consists of all integers from 1 to 80, except those that are equal to the square of an integer. So, Quantity A, the number of integers in set *S*, is equal to the number of positive integers that are less than 81 minus the number of positive integers less than 81 that <u>are</u> equal to the square of an integer.

Clearly, there are 80 positive integers that are less than 81.

One way to determine the number of positive integers less than 81 that are squares of integers is by noticing that 81 is equal to 9^2 and concluding that the squares of the integers from 1 to 8 are all positive integers that are less than 81.

You can also draw this conclusion by squaring each of the positive integers, beginning with 1, until you get to an integer *n* such that n^2 is greater than or equal to 81. Either way, there are 8 positive integers less than 81 that are squares of integers.

Therefore, the number of integers in set S is $80 - 8$, or 72, which is equal to Quantity B. So Quantity A is equal to Quantity B, and the correct answer is **Choice C**.

This explanation uses the following strategy.

Strategy 1: Translate from Words to an Arithmetic or Algebraic Representation

Multiple-choice Questions—Select One Answer Choice

For Questions 7 to 12, select a single answer choice.

7. A manager is forming a 6-person team to work on a certain project. From the 11 candidates available for the team, the manager has already chosen 3 to be on the team. In selecting the other 3 team members, how many different combinations of 3 of the remaining candidates does the manager have to choose from?

   (A) 6
   (B) 24
   (C) 56
   (D) 120
   (E) 462

Explanation

To determine the number of different combinations of 3 of the remaining candidates that the manager has to choose from, you first have to know the number of remaining candidates. Since you know that the manager has already chosen 3 of the 11 candidates to be on the team, it is easy to see that there are 8 remaining candidates. Now you need to count how many different combinations of 3 objects can be chosen from a group of 8 objects.

If you remember the combinations formula, you know that the number of combinations is $\frac{8!}{3!(8-3)!}$ (which is denoted symbolically as $\binom{8}{3}$ or $_8C_3$). You can then calculate the number of different combinations of 3 of the remaining candidates as follows.

$$\frac{8!}{3!(8-3)!} = \frac{(8)(7)(6)(5!)}{(3!)(5!)} = \frac{(8)(7)(6)}{6} = 56$$

The correct answer is **Choice C**.

This explanation uses the following strategy.

Strategy 8: Search for a Mathematical Relationship

8. Which of the following could be the graph of all values of x that satisfy the inequality $2 - 5x \le -\frac{6x-5}{3}$?

   (A)
       0

   (B)
       0

   (C)
       0

   (D)
       0

   (E)
       0

Explanation

To determine which of the graphs is the correct answer, you first need to determine all values of x that satisfy the inequality. To do that you need to simplify the inequality until you isolate x.

You can begin by multiplying both sides of the inequality by 3 to obtain $(3)(2 - 5x) \leq -(6x - 5)$. Note that when you multiply by 3, the right-hand side of the inequality becomes $-(6x - 5)$, not $-6x - 5$.

The rest of the simplification is as follows.

$$(3)(2 - 5x) \leq -6x + 5$$

$$6 - 15x \leq -6x + 5$$

$$-15x \leq -6x - 1$$

$$-9x \leq -1$$

$$x \geq \frac{1}{9}$$

Note that when an inequality is multiplied (or divided) by a negative number, the direction of the inequality reverses.

The graphs in the answer choices are number lines on which only the number 0 is indicated. Therefore, you do not need to locate $\frac{1}{9}$ on the number line; it is enough to know that $\frac{1}{9}$ is a positive number. Choice C is the only choice in which the shaded part of the line is equal to or greater than a positive number. Therefore, the correct answer is **Choice C**.

This explanation uses the following strategy.

Strategy 3: Translate from an Algebraic to a Graphical Representation

---

9. If $1 + x + x^2 + x^3 = 60$, then the average (arithmetic mean) of x, x^2, x^3, and x^4 is equal to which of the following?

    (A) $12x$
    (B) $15x$
    (C) $20x$
    (D) $30x$
    (E) $60x$

Explanation

A quick inspection of the answer choices shows that it is not necessary to solve the equation $1 + x + x^2 + x^3 = 60$ for x to answer this question. You are being asked to express the average of the four quantities x, x^2, x^3, and x^4 in terms of x. To express this average in terms of x, you need to add the 4 quantities and divide the result by 4; that is, $\frac{x + x^2 + x^3 + x^4}{4}$.

The only information given in the question is that the sum of the 4 quantities, $1 + x + x^2 + x^3$, is 60, so you need to think of a way to use this information to simplify the expression $\frac{x + x^2 + x^3 + x^4}{4}$.

Note that the numerator of the fraction is a sum of 4 quantities, each of which has an x term raised to a power. Thus, the expression in the numerator can be factored as $x + x^2 + x^3 + x^4 = x(1 + x + x^2 + x^3)$. By using the information in the question, you can make the following simplification.

$$\frac{x + x^2 + x^3 + x^4}{4} = \frac{x(1 + x + x^2 + x^3)}{4} = \frac{x(60)}{4} = 15x$$

Therefore, the correct answer is **Choice B**.

This explanation uses the following strategy.
Strategy 5: Simplify an Arithmetic or Algebraic Representation

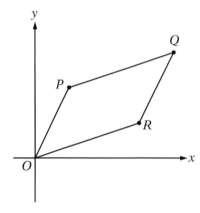

10.   Parallelogram *OPQR* lies in the *xy*-plane, as shown in the figure above. The coordinates of point *P* are (2, 4) and the coordinates of point *Q* are (8, 6). What are the coordinates of point *R*?

Ⓐ (3, 2)
Ⓑ (3, 3)
Ⓒ (4, 4)
Ⓓ (5, 2)
Ⓔ (6, 2)

Explanation

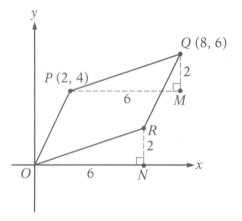

Since *OPQR* is a parallelogram, line segments *PQ* and *OR* have the same length and the same slope. Therefore, in the figure above, *PQM* and *ORN* are congruent right triangles. From the coordinates of *P* and *Q*, the lengths of the legs of triangle

PQM are *PM* = 8 − 2 = 6 and *QM* = 6 − 4 = 2. Thus, the lengths of the legs *ON* and *RN* of triangle *ORN* are also 6 and 2, respectively. So the coordinates of point *R* are (6, 2). The correct answer is **Choice E**.

This explanation uses the following strategies.

Strategy 6: Add to a Geometric Figure
Strategy 8: Search for a Mathematical Relationship

---

11. The relationship between the area *A* of a circle and its circumference *C* is given by the formula $A = kC^2$, where *k* is a constant. What is the value of *k*?

(A) $\dfrac{1}{4\pi}$

(B) $\dfrac{1}{2\pi}$

(C) $\dfrac{1}{4}$

(D) 2π

(E) $4\pi^2$

Explanation

One way to approach this problem is to realize that the value of the constant *k* is the same for all circles. Therefore, you can pick a specific circle and substitute the circumference and the area of that particular circle into the formula and calculate the value of *k*.

Say, for example, that you pick a circle with radius 1. The area of the circle is π and the circumference of the circle is 2π. Inserting these values into the formula gives $\pi = k(2\pi)^2$. Solving this equation for *k* gives $k = \dfrac{1}{4\pi}$, and the correct answer is **Choice A**.

Another way to approach the problem is to express *A* and *C* in terms of a common variable and then solve the resulting equation for *k*. Recall the commonly used formulas for the area and the circumference of a circle: $A = \pi r^2$ and $C = 2\pi r$. Note that in these formulas, both *A* and *C* are expressed in terms of the radius *r*. So, in the formula $A = kC^2$, you can substitute expressions for *A* and *C* in terms of *r*.

Substituting πr^2 for *A* and $2\pi r$ for *C* gives $\pi r^2 = k(2\pi r)^2$.

Now you can determine the value of *k* by solving the equation for *k* as follows.

$$\pi r^2 = k(2\pi r)^2$$
$$\pi r^2 = k(4\pi^2 r^2)$$
$$\pi = k(4\pi^2)$$
$$\frac{1}{4\pi} = k$$

The correct answer is **Choice A**.

This explanation uses the following strategies.

Strategy 5: Simplify an Arithmetic or Algebraic Representation
Strategy 8: Search for a Mathematical Relationship

12. The sequence of numbers $a_1, a_2, a_3, \ldots, a_n, \ldots$ is defined by $a_n = \dfrac{1}{n} - \dfrac{1}{n+2}$ for each integer $n \geq 1$. What is the sum of the first 20 terms of the sequence?

(A) $\left(1 + \dfrac{1}{2}\right) - \dfrac{1}{20}$

(B) $\left(1 + \dfrac{1}{2}\right) - \left(\dfrac{1}{21} + \dfrac{1}{22}\right)$

(C) $1 - \left(\dfrac{1}{20} + \dfrac{1}{22}\right)$

(D) $1 - \dfrac{1}{22}$

(E) $\dfrac{1}{20} - \dfrac{1}{22}$

Explanation

This question asks for the sum of the first 20 terms of the sequence. Obviously, it would be very time-consuming to write out the first 20 terms of the sequence and add them together, so it is reasonable to try to find a more efficient way to calculate the sum. Questions involving sequences can often be answered by looking for a pattern. Scanning the answer choices and noting that they contain fractions with denominators 2, 20, 21, and 22, and nothing in between, seems to confirm that looking for a pattern is a good approach to try.

To look for a pattern, begin by adding the first two terms of the sequence.

$$\left(\frac{1}{1} - \frac{1}{3}\right) + \left(\frac{1}{2} - \frac{1}{4}\right) = \left(\frac{1}{1} + \frac{1}{2}\right) - \left(\frac{1}{3} + \frac{1}{4}\right)$$

Now, if you add the first three terms of the sequence, you get

$$\left(\frac{1}{1} - \frac{1}{3}\right) + \left(\frac{1}{2} - \frac{1}{4}\right) + \left(\frac{1}{3} - \frac{1}{5}\right)$$

Note that you can simplify the sum by canceling the fraction $\frac{1}{3}$; that is, the sum of positive $\frac{1}{3}$ and negative $\frac{1}{3}$ is 0.

$$\left(\frac{1}{1} - \frac{1}{\cancel{3}}\right) + \left(\frac{1}{2} - \frac{1}{4}\right) + \left(\frac{1}{\cancel{3}} - \frac{1}{5}\right) = \left(\frac{1}{1} + \frac{1}{2}\right) - \left(\frac{1}{4} + \frac{1}{5}\right)$$

If you add the first four terms, you get

$$\left(\frac{1}{1} - \frac{1}{3}\right) + \left(\frac{1}{2} - \frac{1}{4}\right) + \left(\frac{1}{3} - \frac{1}{5}\right) + \left(\frac{1}{4} - \frac{1}{6}\right)$$

Again, you can simplify the sum by canceling. This time, you can cancel the fractions $\frac{1}{3}$ and $\frac{1}{4}$.

$$\left(\frac{1}{1} - \frac{1}{\cancel{3}}\right) + \left(\frac{1}{2} - \frac{1}{\cancel{4}}\right) + \left(\frac{1}{\cancel{3}} - \frac{1}{5}\right) + \left(\frac{1}{\cancel{4}} - \frac{1}{6}\right) = \left(\frac{1}{1} + \frac{1}{2}\right) - \left(\frac{1}{5} + \frac{1}{6}\right)$$

If you write out the next two sums and simplify them, you will see that they are

$$\left(\frac{1}{1}+\frac{1}{2}\right)-\left(\frac{1}{6}+\frac{1}{7}\right) \text{ and } \left(\frac{1}{1}+\frac{1}{2}\right)-\left(\frac{1}{7}+\frac{1}{8}\right)$$

Working with the sums makes it clear that this pattern continues to hold as you add more and more terms of the sequence together and that a formula for the sum of the first k terms of the sequence is

$$\left(\frac{1}{1}+\frac{1}{2}\right)-\left(\frac{1}{k+1}+\frac{1}{k+2}\right)$$

Therefore, the sum of the first 20 terms of the sequence is equal to

$$\left(\frac{1}{1}+\frac{1}{2}\right)-\left(\frac{1}{20+1}+\frac{1}{20+2}\right)=\left(1+\frac{1}{2}\right)-\left(\frac{1}{21}+\frac{1}{22}\right)$$

The correct answer is **Choice B**.

This explanation uses the following strategies.
Strategy 5: Simplify an Arithmetic or Algebraic Representation
Strategy 7: Find a Pattern

Numeric Entry

For Question 13, use the directions for Numeric Entry questions.

Y	Frequency
$\frac{1}{2}$	2
$\frac{3}{4}$	7
$\frac{5}{4}$	8
$\frac{3}{2}$	8
$\frac{7}{4}$	9

13. The table above shows the frequency distribution of the values of a variable Y. What is the mean of the distribution?
Give your answer to the <u>nearest 0.01</u>.

$\boxed{}$

Explanation

The mean of the distribution of the variable Y is the sum of all the values of Y divided by the number of values of Y. However, before you begin the summing process, you need to understand how the information is presented in the question. Information about the variable is given in a table, where any repetitions of values have been summarized in the column labeled "Frequency." Reading from the table, you can see that the value $\frac{1}{2}$ occurs twice, the value $\frac{3}{4}$ occurs seven times, and so on. To sum all the values of Y, you could add the value $\frac{1}{2}$ twice, add the value $\frac{3}{4}$ seven times, and continue the addition process in this manner. It is easier, however, to multiply the values by their corresponding frequencies and then sum the individual products, as shown below.

$$(2)\left(\frac{1}{2}\right)+(7)\left(\frac{3}{4}\right)+(8)\left(\frac{5}{4}\right)+(8)\left(\frac{3}{2}\right)+(9)\left(\frac{7}{4}\right)=\frac{4}{4}+\frac{21}{4}+\frac{40}{4}+\frac{48}{4}+\frac{63}{4}$$

$$=\frac{176}{4}$$

$$=44$$

To find the average, you need to divide the sum, 44, by the number of values of Y. The number of values can be found by looking at the column of frequencies in the table. The sum of the numbers in this column, $2 + 7 + 8 + 8 + 9$, or 34, is the number of values of Y. Thus, the mean of the distribution is $\frac{44}{34}$, which, as a decimal, equals 1.2941.... Rounded to the nearest 0.01, the correct answer is **1.29**.

This explanation uses the following strategies.
Strategy 4: Translate from a Figure to an Arithmetic or Algebraic Representation
Strategy 8: Search for a Mathematical Relationship

Multiple-choice Questions—Select One or More Answer Choices

For Questions 14 and 15, select all the answer choices that apply.

14. Let S be the set of all positive integers n such that n^2 is a multiple of both 24 and 108. Which of the following integers are divisors of every integer n in S?
Indicate <u>all</u> such integers.

     A   12

     B   24

     C   36

     D   72

Explanation
To determine which of the integers in the answer choices is a divisor of every positive integer n in S, you must first understand the integers that are in S. Note that in this question you are given information about n^2, not about n itself. Therefore, you must use the information about n^2 to derive information about n.

    The fact that n^2 is a multiple of both 24 and 108 implies that n^2 is a multiple of the least common multiple of 24 and 108. To determine the least common multiple of 24 and 108, factor 24 and 108 into prime factors as $(2^3)(3)$ and $(2^2)(3^3)$, respectively. Because these are prime factorizations, you can conclude that the least common multiple of 24 and 108 is $(2^3)(3^3)$.

Knowing that n^2 must be a multiple of $(2^3)(3^3)$ does not mean that every multiple of $(2^3)(3^3)$ is a possible value of n^2, because n^2 must be the square of an integer. The prime factorization of a square number must contain only even exponents. Thus, the least multiple of $(2^3)(3^3)$ that is a square is $(2^4)(3^4)$. This is the least possible value of n^2, and so the least possible value of n is $(2^2)(3^2)$, or 36. Furthermore, since every value of n^2 is a multiple of $(2^4)(3^4)$, the values of n are the positive multiples of 36; that is, $S = \{36, 72, 108, 144, 180, \ldots\}$.

The question asks for integers that are divisors of every integer n in S, that is, divisors of every positive multiple of 36. Since Choice A, 12, is a divisor of 36, it is also a divisor of every multiple of 36. The same is true for Choice C, 36. Choices B and D, 24 and 72, are not divisors of 36, so they are not divisors of every integer in S. The correct answer consists of **Choices A and C.**

This explanation uses the following strategies.
Strategy 8: Search for a Mathematical Relationship
Strategy 12: Adapt Solutions to Related Problems

---

15. The penguins currently living on an island are of two types, Chinstrap penguins and Gentoo penguins. The range of the heights of the Chinstrap penguins on the island is 13.2 centimeters, and the range of the heights of the Gentoo penguins on the island is 15.4 centimeters.

Which of the following statements <u>individually</u> provide(s) sufficient additional information to determine the range of the heights of all the penguins on the island?

Indicate <u>all</u> such statements.

A The tallest Gentoo penguin on the island is 5.8 centimeters taller than the tallest Chinstrap penguin on the island.

B The median height of the Gentoo penguins on the island is 1.1 centimeters greater than the median height of the Chinstrap penguins on the island.

C The average (arithmetic mean) height of the Gentoo penguins on the island is 4.6 centimeters greater than the average height of the Chinstrap penguins on the island.

Explanation

Choice A tells you that the tallest Gentoo penguin is 5.8 centimeters taller than the tallest Chinstrap penguin. You can combine this information with the given information about the Gentoo and Chinstrap height ranges to place four penguins—the shortest Gentoo, the shortest Chinstrap, the tallest Gentoo, and the tallest Chinstrap—in relative order according to height, as shown in the figure below.

You can see from the figure that the tallest penguin must be a Gentoo and the shortest penguin must be a Chinstrap. You can also see the difference in height between those two penguins, which is the range of the heights of the all the penguins. Therefore, Choice A provides sufficient additional information to determine the range.

Choice B provides information about one of the centers of the data—the median; it does not say anything about how spread out the data are around that center. You are given that the median height of the Gentoos is 1.1 centimeters greater than that of the Chinstraps. First note that it is possible for two different sets of data to have the same median but have very different ranges. Choice B gives the difference between the medians of the Gentoo heights and the Chinstrap heights, without giving the actual medians. However, even if you knew the medians, the fact that the ranges can vary widely indicates that the range of the heights of the all the penguins can also vary widely.

It is possible to construct examples of heights of penguins that satisfy all of the information in the question and in Choice B but have different ranges for the heights of the all the penguins. Here are two such examples, each of which has only three Chinstraps and three Gentoos. Although the examples are small, they illustrate the fact that the range of the heights of the all the penguins can vary. In both examples, the range of Chinstrap heights is 13.2 centimeters, the range of Gentoo heights is 15.4 centimeters, and the difference between the median heights is 1.1 centimeters.

Example 1
Chinstrap heights: 50.0   56.6   63.2   which have a median of 56.6
Gentoo heights: 50.0   57.7   65.4   which have a median of 57.7
Range of heights of all the penguins: 15.4

Example 2
Chinstrap heights: 50.0   56.6   63.2   which have a median of 56.6
Gentoo heights: 51.0   57.7   66.4   which have a median of 57.7
Range of heights of all the penguins: 16.4

Therefore, Choice B does not provide sufficient additional information to determine the range of the heights of the all the penguins.

Choice C provides information about another center of the data—the average. You are given that the average height of the Gentoos is 4.6 centimeters greater than that of the Chinstraps. However, like Choice B, the statement gives no information about how spread out the data are around that center. Again, it is possible for two different sets of data to have the same average but have very different ranges. Examples similar to the two examples above can be constructed that satisfy all of the information in the question and in Choice C but have different ranges for the heights of the all the penguins. Therefore, Choice C does not provide sufficient additional information to determine the range of the heights of the all the penguins.

The correct answer consists of **Choice A**.

This explanation uses the following strategies.
Strategy 2: Translate from Words to a Figure or Diagram
Strategy 11: Divide into Cases
Strategy 14: Determine What Additional Information Is Sufficient to Solve a Problem

SET 4. Data Interpretation Sets

> For Questions 1 to 7, select a single answer choice unless otherwise directed.

Questions 1 to 3 are based on the following data.

PERCENT OF ADJUNCT FACULTY AND PERCENT OF NON-ADJUNCT
FACULTY AT COLLEGE *X*, BY FIELD
Total adjunct faculty: 200
Total non-adjunct faculty: 250

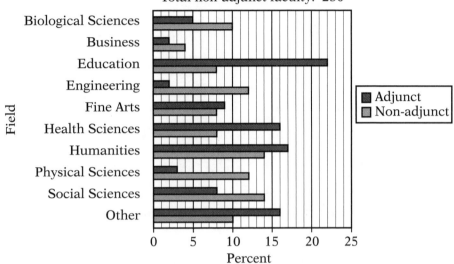

Medium Question

1. There are 275 students in the field of engineering at College *X*. Approximately what is the ratio of the number of students in engineering to the number of faculty in engineering?

   Ⓐ 8 to 1
   Ⓑ 10 to 1
   Ⓒ 12 to 1
   Ⓓ 14 to 1
   Ⓔ 20 to 1

Explanation

According to the graph, 2 percent of the adjunct faculty and 12 percent of the non-adjunct faculty are in the engineering field. To determine the total number of faculty in engineering, you need to add 2 percent of 200, which is 4, to 12 percent of 250, which is 30, to get 34. Thus, the ratio of the numbers of students to faculty in engineering is 275 to 34, which is approximately equal to 280 to 35, or 8 to 1. The correct answer is **Choice A**.

This explanation uses the following strategies.

Strategy 4: Translate from a Figure to an Arithmetic or Algebraic Representation
Strategy 5: Simplify an Arithmetic or Algebraic Representation
Strategy 9: Estimate

Medium Question

2. Approximately what percent of the faculty in humanities are non-adjunct faculty?

   (A) 35%   (D) 45%

   (B) 38%   (E) 51%

   (C) 41%

Explanation

You need to determine the numbers of adjunct and non-adjunct faculty in the humanities field. According to the graph, 17 percent of the 200 adjunct faculty, or 34, and 14 percent of the 250 non-adjunct faculty, or 35, are in humanities. Thus, the fraction of humanities faculty who are non-adjunct faculty is $\frac{35}{34+35} = \frac{35}{69}$, or approximately 0.507. As a percent, the answer choice that is closest to 0.507 is 51 percent. The correct answer is **Choice E**.

This explanation uses the following strategies.

Strategy 4: Translate from a Figure to an Arithmetic or Algebraic Representation
Strategy 5: Simplify an Arithmetic or Algebraic Representation
Strategy 9: Estimate

For Question 3, use the directions for Numeric Entry questions.

Hard Question

3. For the biological sciences and health sciences faculty combined, $\frac{1}{3}$ of the adjunct faculty and $\frac{2}{9}$ of the non-adjunct faculty are medical doctors. What fraction of all the faculty in those two fields combined are medical doctors?

Explanation

You need to determine the number of adjunct faculty and the number of non-adjunct faculty in the combined group. According to the graph, 5 percent of the adjunct faculty, or 10, and 10 percent of the non-adjunct faculty, or 25, are in the biological sciences. Similarly, 16 percent of the adjunct faculty, or 32, and 8 percent of the non-adjunct faculty, or 20, are in the health sciences. When you combine the groups, you get a total of 42 adjunct faculty (10 + 32) and 45 non-adjunct faculty (25 + 20), which is a total of 87 faculty. Medical doctors are $\frac{1}{3}$ of the 42 adjunct faculty, or 14 adjuncts, and $\frac{2}{9}$ of the 45 non-adjunct faculty, or 10 non-adjuncts. Thus, there are 24 medical doctors, and the fraction that are medical doctors is $\frac{24}{87}$. The correct answer is $\frac{\mathbf{24}}{\mathbf{87}}$ (or any equivalent fraction).

This explanation uses the following strategies.

Strategy 4: Translate from a Figure to an Arithmetic or Algebraic Representation
Strategy 5: Simplify an Arithmetic or Algebraic Representation

Questions 4 to 7 are based on the following data.

VALUE OF IMPORTS TO AND EXPORTS FROM COUNTRY *T,* 2000–2009
(in United States dollars)

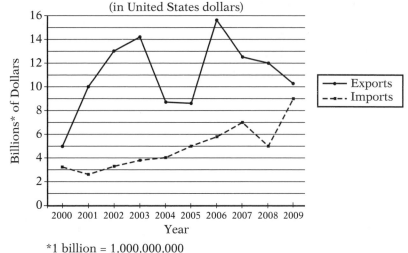

*1 billion = 1,000,000,000

For Question 4, select all the answer choices that apply.

Easy Question

4. For which of the eight years from 2001 to 2008 did exports exceed imports by more than $5 billion?

    Indicate <u>all</u> such years.

    [A] 2001
    [B] 2002
    [C] 2003
    [D] 2004
    [E] 2005
    [F] 2006
    [G] 2007
    [H] 2008

Explanation

Note that for all years shown, the dollar value of exports is greater than the dollar value of imports. For each year, the difference between the dollar value of exports and the dollar value of imports can be read directly from the graph. The difference was more than $5 billion for each of the years 2001, 2002, 2003, 2006, 2007, and 2008. The correct answer consists of **Choices A, B, C, F, G, and H.**

This explanation uses the following strategy.

Strategy 4: Translate from a Figure to an Arithmetic or Algebraic Representation

Medium Question

5. Which of the following is closest to the average (arithmetic mean) of the 9 changes in the value of imports between consecutive years from 2000 to 2009?

    (A) $260 million

    (B) $320 million

    (C) $400 million

    (D) $480 million

    (E) $640 million

Explanation

The average of the 9 changes in the value of imports between consecutive years can be represented as follows, where the function $v(\text{year})$ represents the value of imports for the indicated year.

$$\frac{(v(2001)-v(2000))+(v(2002)-v(2001))+(v(2003) -v(2002))+\cdots+(v(2009)-v(2008))}{9}$$

Note that in the numerator of the fraction, each term, with the exception of $v(2000)$ and $v(2009)$, appears first as positive and then again as negative. The positive and negative pairs sum to 0, and the fraction simplifies to

$$\frac{v(2009)-v(2000)}{9}$$

Reading the values from the graph, you can approximate the value of the simplified fraction as $\frac{9.0-3.2}{9}=\frac{5.8}{9}\approx 0.644$ billion dollars. The answer choice that is closest to $0.644 billion is $640 million. The correct answer is **Choice E**.

This explanation uses the following strategies.

Strategy 4: Translate from a Figure to an Arithmetic or Algebraic Representation
Strategy 5: Simplify an Arithmetic or Algebraic Representation
Strategy 9: Estimate

Medium Question

6. In 2008 the value of exports was approximately what percent greater than the value of imports?

    (A) 40%

    (B) 60%

    (C) 70%

    (D) 120%

    (E) 140%

Explanation

The difference between the value of exports and the value of imports expressed as a percent of the value of imports is

$$\left(\frac{(\text{value of exports})-(\text{value of imports})}{\text{value of imports}}\right)(100\%)$$

In 2008 the value of imports was approximately \$5 billion and the value of exports was approximately \$12 billion, so the value of the fraction is approximately $\dfrac{12-5}{5}$, or $\dfrac{7}{5}$.

Since the fraction is greater than 1, expressing it as a percent will give a percent greater than 100. The fraction is equal to 1.4, or 140 percent. The correct answer is **Choice E**.

This explanation uses the following strategies.
Strategy 4: Translate from a Figure to an Arithmetic or Algebraic Representation
Strategy 5: Simplify an Arithmetic or Algebraic Representation

Hard Question

7. If it were discovered that the value of imports shown for 2007 was incorrect and should have been \$5 billion instead, then the average (arithmetic mean) value of imports per year for the 10 years shown would have been approximately how much less?

Ⓐ \$200 million

Ⓑ   \$50 million

Ⓒ   \$20 million

Ⓓ   \$7 million

Ⓔ   \$5 million

Explanation

To answer this question, you do not need to compute either of the two 10-year averages referred to in the question; you just need to calculate the difference between the two averages.

The average value of imports for the 10 years shown in the graph is found by adding the 10 values and then dividing the sum by 10. The value of imports in 2007 is \$7 billion. If that amount were \$5 billion instead, then the sum of the values would be \$2 billion less. If the sum were \$2 billion less than what it was, then the average would decrease by 2 billion divided by 10, or $\dfrac{2,000,000,000}{10} = 200,000,000$. The average would therefore be \$200 million less, and the correct answer is **Choice A**.

A more algebraic approach to the problem is to let S represent the sum, in billions, of the 10 values of imports in the graph. The average of the 10 values is $\dfrac{S}{10}$. Note that $S - 2$ represents the sum, in billions, of the 10 values adjusted for the \$2 billion correction for 2007. The average of the adjusted sum is $\dfrac{S-2}{10}$. The difference between the two averages is

$$\frac{S}{10} - \frac{S-2}{10} = \frac{S-(S-2)}{10}$$
$$= \frac{S-S+2}{10}$$
$$= \frac{2}{10}$$

The difference is 0.2 billion dollars, or $200 million. The correct answer is **Choice A**.

This explanation uses the following strategies.
Strategy 4: Translate from a Figure to an Arithmetic or Algebraic Representation
Strategy 5: Simplify an Arithmetic or Algebraic Representation

7 GRE® Math Review

本章的数学复习将帮助考生熟悉一些重要的数学技能和概念，涉及算数、代数、几何、数据分析这些方面，对于在GRE数量推理（Quantitative Reasoning）测试中解决问题、进行数量推理非常有用。复习的主要内容包括对很多定义、特征和例子的描述，并且在每个复习部分结束时都提供一组附带答案的练习。然而，需要注意的是，这个复习并不是包罗万象的。考试中可能会出现一些在这个复习中没有进行详细讲解的概念。

如果考生认为哪部分内容不够熟悉或者过于简略，建议去查阅相关的数学教材，以便得到更加详尽的阐述。另外，还可以登录ETS网站上的Khan Academy网页www.ets.org/gre/khan，里面有免费的视频链接，讲解本章的概念。

PART 1. ARITHMETIC

The review of arithmetic begins with integers, fractions, and decimals and progresses to the set of real numbers. The basic arithmetic operations of addition, subtraction, multiplication, and division are discussed, along with exponents and roots. The review of arithmetic ends with the concepts of ratio and percent.

1.1 Integers

The **integers** are the numbers 1, 2, 3, ..., together with their negatives, −1, −2, −3, ..., and 0. Thus, the set of integers is {..., −3, −2, −1, 0, 1, 2, 3, ...}.

The positive integers are greater than 0, the negative integers are less than 0, and 0 is neither positive nor negative. When integers are added, subtracted, or multiplied, the result is always an integer; division of integers is addressed below. The many elementary number facts for these operations, such as $7 + 8 = 15$, $78 − 87 = −9$, $7 − (−18) = 25$, and $(7)(8) = 56$, should be familiar to you; they are not reviewed here. Here are three general facts regarding multiplication of integers.

Fact 1: The product of two positive integers is a positive integer.
Fact 2: The product of two negative integers is a positive integer.
Fact 3: The product of a positive integer and a negative integer is a negative integer.

When integers are multiplied, each of the multiplied integers is called a **factor** or **divisor** of the resulting product. For example, $(2)(3)(10) = 60$, so 2, 3, and 10 are factors of 60. The integers 4, 15, 5, and 12 are also factors of 60, since $(4)(15) = 60$ and $(5)(12) = 60$. The positive factors of 60 are 1, 2, 3, 4, 5, 6, 10, 12, 15, 20, 30, and 60. The negatives of these integers are also factors of 60, since, for example, $(−2)(−30) = 60$. There are no other factors of 60. We say that 60 is a **multiple** of each of its factors and that 60 is **divisible** by each of its divisors. Here are five more examples of factors and multiples.

Example 1.1.1: The positive factors of 100 are 1, 2, 4, 5, 10, 20, 25, 50, and 100.
Example 1.1.2: 25 is a multiple of only six integers: 1, 5, 25, and their negatives.
Example 1.1.3: The list of positive multiples of 25 has no end: 25, 50, 75, 100, ... ; likewise, every nonzero integer has infinitely many multiples.
Example 1.1.4: 1 is a factor of every integer; 1 is not a multiple of any integer except 1 and −1.
Example 1.1.5: 0 is a multiple of every integer; 0 is not a factor of any integer except 0.

The **least common multiple** of two nonzero integers c and d is the least positive integer that is a multiple of both c and d. For example, the least common multiple of 30 and 75 is 150. This is because the positive multiples of 30 are 30, 60, 90, 120, 150, 180, 210, 240, 270, 300, 330, 390, 420, 450, ... , and the positive multiples of 75 are 75, 150, 225, 300, 375, 450, ... Thus, the *common* positive multiples of 30 and 75 are 150, 300, 450, ..., and the least of these is 150.

The **greatest common divisor** (or **greatest common factor**) of two nonzero integers c and d is the greatest positive integer that is a divisor of both c and d. For example, the greatest common divisor of 30 and 75 is 15. This is because the positive divisors of 30 are 1, 2, 3, 5, 6, 10, 15, and 30, and the positive divisors of 75 are 1, 3, 5, 15, 25, and 75. Thus, the *common* positive divisors of 30 and 75 are 1, 3, 5, and 15, and the greatest of these is 15.

When an integer c is divided by an integer d, where d is a divisor of c, the result is always a divisor of c. For example, when 60 is divided by 6 (one of its divisors), the result is 10, which is another divisor of 60. If d is *not* a divisor of c, then the result can be viewed in three different ways. The result can be viewed as a fraction or as a decimal, both of which are discussed later, or the result can be viewed as a **quotient** with a **remainder**, where both are integers. Each view is useful, depending on the context. Fractions and decimals are useful when the result must be viewed as a single number, while quotients with remainders are useful for describing the result in terms of integers only.

Regarding quotients with remainders, consider the integer c and the positive integer d, where d is *not* a divisor of c; for example, the integers 19 and 7. When 19 is divided by 7, the result is greater than 2, since $(2)(7) < 19$, but less than 3, since $19 < (3)(7)$. Because 19 is 5 more than $(2)(7)$, we say that the result of 19 divided by 7 is the quotient 2 with remainder 5, or simply 2 remainder 5. In general, when an integer c is divided by a positive integer d, you first find the greatest multiple of d that is less than or equal to c. That multiple of d can be expressed as the product qd, where q is the quotient. Then the remainder is equal to c minus that multiple of d, or $r = c - qd$, where r is the remainder. The remainder is always greater than or equal to 0 and less than d.

Here are four examples that illustrate a few different cases of division resulting in a quotient and remainder.

Example 1.1.6: 100 divided by 45 is 2 remainder 10, since the greatest multiple of 45 that is less than or equal to 100 is $(2)(45)$, or 90, which is 10 less than 100.

Example 1.1.7: 24 divided by 4 is 6 remainder 0, since the greatest multiple of 4 that is less than or equal to 24 is 24 itself, which is 0 less than 24. In general, the remainder is 0 if and only if c is divisible by d.

Example 1.1.8: 6 divided by 24 is 0 remainder 6, since the greatest multiple of 24 that is less than or equal to 6 is $(0)(24)$, or 0, which is 6 less than 6.

Example 1.1.9: −32 divided by 3 is −11 remainder 1, since the greatest multiple of 3 that is less than or equal to −32 is $(-11)(3)$, or −33, which is 1 less than −32.

Here are five more examples.

Example 1.1.10: 100 divided by 3 is 33 remainder 1, since $100 = (33)(3) + 1$.

Example 1.1.11: 100 divided by 25 is 4 remainder 0, since $100 = (4)(25) + 0$.

Example 1.1.12: 80 divided by 100 is 0 remainder 80, since $80 = (0)(100) + 80$.

Example 1.1.13: −13 divided by 5 is −3 remainder 2, since $-13 = (-3)(5) + 2$.

Example 1.1.14: −73 divided by 10 is −8 remainder 7, since $-73 = (-8)(10) + 7$.

If an integer is divisible by 2, it is called an **even integer**; otherwise, it is an **odd integer**. Note that when an odd integer is divided by 2, the remainder is always 1. The set of even integers is {…, −6, −4, −2, 0, 2, 4, 6, …}, and the set of odd integers is {…, −5, −3, −1, 1, 3, 5, …}. Here are six useful facts regarding the sum and product of even and odd integers.

Fact 1: The sum of two even integers is an even integer.
Fact 2: The sum of two odd integers is an even integer.
Fact 3: The sum of an even integer and an odd integer is an odd integer.
Fact 4: The product of two even integers is an even integer.
Fact 5: The product of two odd integers is an odd integer.
Fact 6: The product of an even integer and an odd integer is an even integer.

A **prime number** is an integer greater than 1 that has only two positive divisors: 1 and itself. The first ten prime numbers are 2, 3, 5, 7, 11, 13, 17, 19, 23, and 29. The integer 14 is not a prime number, since it has four positive divisors: 1, 2, 7, and 14. The integer 1 is not a prime number, and the integer 2 is the only prime number that is even.

Every integer greater than 1 either is a prime number or can be uniquely expressed as a product of factors that are prime numbers, or **prime divisors**. Such an expression is called a **prime factorization**. Here are six examples of prime factorizations.

Example 1.1.15: $12 = (2)(2)(3) = (2^2)(3)$
Example 1.1.16: $14 = (2)(7)$
Example 1.1.17: $81 = (3)(3)(3)(3) = 3^4$
Example 1.1.18: $338 = (2)(13)(13) = (2)(13^2)$
Example 1.1.19: $800 = (2)(2)(2)(2)(2)(5)(5) = (2^5)(5^2)$
Example 1.1.20: $1,155 = (3)(5)(7)(11)$

An integer greater than 1 that is not a prime number is called a **composite number**. The first ten composite numbers are 4, 6, 8, 9, 10, 12, 14, 15, 16, and 18.

1.2 Fractions

A **fraction** is a number of the form $\frac{c}{d}$, where c and d are integers and $d \neq 0$. The integer c is called the **numerator** of the fraction, and d is called the **denominator**. For example, $\frac{-7}{5}$ is a fraction in which -7 is the numerator and 5 is the denominator. Such numbers are also called **rational numbers**. Note that every integer n is a rational number, because n is equal to the fraction $\frac{n}{1}$.

If both the numerator c and the denominator d, where $d \neq 0$, are multiplied by the same nonzero integer, the resulting fraction will be equivalent to $\frac{c}{d}$.

Example 1.2.1: Multiplying the numerator and denominator of the fraction $\frac{-7}{5}$ by 4 gives

$$\frac{-7}{5} = \frac{(-7)(4)}{(5)(4)} = \frac{-28}{20}$$

Multiplying the numerator and denominator of the fraction $\frac{-7}{5}$ by -1 gives

$$\frac{-7}{5} = \frac{(-7)(-1)}{(5)(-1)} = \frac{7}{-5}$$

For all integers c and d, the fractions $\frac{-c}{d}$, $\frac{c}{-d}$, and $-\frac{c}{d}$ are equivalent.

Example 1.2.2: $\frac{-7}{5} = \frac{7}{-5} = -\frac{7}{5}$

If both the numerator and denominator of a fraction have a common factor, then the numerator and denominator can be factored and the fraction can be reduced to an equivalent fraction.

Example 1.2.3: $\frac{40}{72} = \frac{(8)(5)}{(8)(9)} = \frac{5}{9}$

Adding and Subtracting Fractions

To add two fractions with the same denominator, you add the numerators and keep the same denominator.

Example 1.2.4: $-\dfrac{8}{11} + \dfrac{5}{11} = \dfrac{-8+5}{11} = \dfrac{-3}{11} = -\dfrac{3}{11}$

To add two fractions with different denominators, first find a **common denominator**, which is a common multiple of the two denominators. Then convert both fractions to equivalent fractions with the same denominator. Finally, add the numerators and keep the common denominator.

Example 1.2.5: To add the two fractions $\dfrac{1}{3}$ and $-\dfrac{2}{5}$, first note that 15 is a common denominator of the fractions.

Then convert the fractions to equivalent fractions with denominator 15 as follows.

$$\frac{1}{3} = \frac{1(5)}{3(5)} = \frac{5}{15} \text{ and } -\frac{2}{5} = -\frac{2(3)}{5(3)} = -\frac{6}{15}$$

Therefore, the two fractions can be added as follows.

$$\frac{1}{3} + \frac{-2}{5} = \frac{5}{15} + \frac{-6}{15} = \frac{5+(-6)}{15} = -\frac{1}{15}$$

The same method applies to subtraction of fractions.

Multiplying and Dividing Fractions

To multiply two fractions, multiply the two numerators and multiply the two denominators. Here are two examples.

Example 1.2.6: $\left(\dfrac{10}{7}\right)\left(\dfrac{-1}{3}\right) = \dfrac{(10)(-1)}{(7)(3)} = \dfrac{-10}{21} = -\dfrac{10}{21}$

Example 1.2.7: $\left(\dfrac{8}{3}\right)\left(\dfrac{7}{3}\right) = \dfrac{56}{9}$

To divide one fraction by another, first **invert** the second fraction (that is, find its **reciprocal**), then multiply the first fraction by the inverted fraction. Here are two examples.

Example 1.2.8: $\dfrac{17}{8} \div \dfrac{3}{5} = \left(\dfrac{17}{8}\right)\left(\dfrac{5}{3}\right) = \dfrac{85}{24}$

Example 1.2.9: $\dfrac{\frac{3}{10}}{\frac{7}{13}} = \left(\dfrac{3}{10}\right)\left(\dfrac{13}{7}\right) = \dfrac{39}{70}$

Mixed Numbers

An expression such as $4\dfrac{3}{8}$ is called a **mixed number**. It consists of an integer part and a fraction part, where the fraction part has a value between 0 and 1; the mixed number $4\dfrac{3}{8}$ means $4 + \dfrac{3}{8}$.

To convert a mixed number to a fraction, convert the integer part to an equivalent fraction with the same denominator as the fraction, and then add it to the fraction part.

Example 1.2.10: To convert the mixed number $4\frac{3}{8}$ to a fraction, first convert the integer 4 to a fraction with denominator 8, as follows.

$$4 = \frac{4}{1} = \frac{4(8)}{1(8)} = \frac{32}{8}$$

Then add $\frac{3}{8}$ to it to get

$$4\frac{3}{8} = \frac{32}{8} + \frac{3}{8} = \frac{35}{8}$$

Fractional Expressions

Numbers of the form $\frac{c}{d}$, where either c or d is not an integer and $d \neq 0$, are called fractional expressions. Fractional expressions can be manipulated just like fractions. Here are two examples.

Example 1.2.11: Add the numbers $\frac{\pi}{2}$ and $\frac{\pi}{3}$.

Solution: Note that 6 is a common denominator of both numbers. The number $\frac{\pi}{2}$ is equivalent to the number $\frac{3\pi}{6}$, and the number $\frac{\pi}{3}$ is equivalent to the number $\frac{2\pi}{6}$.

Therefore

$$\frac{\pi}{2} + \frac{\pi}{3} = \frac{3\pi}{6} + \frac{2\pi}{6} = \frac{5\pi}{6}$$

Example 1.2.12: Simplify the number $\dfrac{\frac{1}{\sqrt{2}}}{\frac{3}{\sqrt{5}}}$.

Solution: Note that the numerator of the number is $\frac{1}{\sqrt{2}}$ and the denominator of the number is $\frac{3}{\sqrt{5}}$. Note also that the reciprocal of the denominator is $\frac{\sqrt{5}}{3}$.

Therefore,

$$\frac{\frac{1}{\sqrt{2}}}{\frac{3}{\sqrt{5}}} = \left(\frac{1}{\sqrt{2}}\right)\left(\frac{\sqrt{5}}{3}\right)$$

which can be simplified to $\frac{\sqrt{5}}{3\sqrt{2}}$.

Thus, the number $\dfrac{\frac{1}{\sqrt{2}}}{\frac{3}{\sqrt{5}}}$ simplifies to the number $\frac{\sqrt{5}}{3\sqrt{2}}$.

1.3 Exponents and Roots

Exponents

Exponents are used to denote the repeated multiplication of a number by itself; for example, $3^4 = (3)(3)(3)(3) = 81$ and $5^3 = (5)(5)(5) = 125$. In the expression 3^4, 3 is called the **base**, 4 is called the **exponent**, and we read the expression as "3 to the fourth power." Similarly, 5 to the third power is 125.

When the exponent is 2, we call the process **squaring**. Thus, 6 squared is 36; that is, $6^2 = (6)(6) = 36$. Similarly, 7 squared is 49; that is, $7^2 = (7)(7) = 49$.

When negative numbers are raised to powers, the result may be positive or negative; for example, $(-3)^2 = (-3)(-3) = 9$ and $(-3)^5 = (-3)(-3)(-3)(-3)(-3) = -243$. A negative number raised to an even power is always positive, and a negative number raised to an odd power is always negative. Note that $(-3)^2 = (-3)(-3) = 9$, but $-3^2 = -((3)(3)) = -9$. Exponents can also be negative or zero; such exponents are defined as follows.

The exponent zero: For all nonzero numbers a, $a^0 = 1$. The expression 0^0 is undefined.

Negative exponents: For all nonzero numbers a, $a^{-1} = \dfrac{1}{a}$, $a^{-2} = \dfrac{1}{a^2}$, $a^{-3} = \dfrac{1}{a^3}$, and so on.

Note that $(a)(a^{-1}) = (a)\left(\dfrac{1}{a}\right) = 1$.

Roots

A **square root** of a nonnegative number n is a number r such that $r^2 = n$. For example, 4 is a square root of 16 because $4^2 = 16$. Another square root of 16 is -4, since $(-4)^2 = 16$. All positive numbers have two square roots, one positive and one negative. The only square root of 0 is 0. The expression consisting of the square root symbol $\sqrt{\ }$ placed over a nonnegative number denotes the *nonnegative* square root (or the positive square root if the number is greater than 0) of that nonnegative number. Therefore, $\sqrt{100} = 10$, $-\sqrt{100} = -10$, and $\sqrt{0} = 0$. Square roots of negative numbers are not defined in the real number system.

Here are four important rules regarding operations with square roots, where $a > 0$ and $b > 0$.

Rule 1: $(\sqrt{a})^2 = a$
  Example A: $(\sqrt{3})^2 = 3$
  Example B: $(\sqrt{\pi})^2 = \pi$
Rule 2: $\sqrt{a^2} = a$
  Example A: $\sqrt{4} = \sqrt{2^2} = 2$
  Example B: $\sqrt{\pi^2} = \pi$
Rule 3: $\sqrt{a}\sqrt{b} = \sqrt{ab}$
  Example A: $\sqrt{3}\sqrt{10} = \sqrt{30}$
  Example B: $\sqrt{24} = \sqrt{4}\sqrt{6} = 2\sqrt{6}$
Rule 4: $\dfrac{\sqrt{a}}{\sqrt{b}} = \sqrt{\dfrac{a}{b}}$

  Example A: $\dfrac{\sqrt{5}}{\sqrt{15}} = \sqrt{\dfrac{5}{15}} = \sqrt{\dfrac{1}{3}}$

  Example B: $\dfrac{\sqrt{18}}{\sqrt{2}} = \sqrt{\dfrac{18}{2}} = \sqrt{9} = 3$

A square root is a root of order 2. Higher order roots of a positive number n are defined similarly. For orders 3 and 4, the **cube root** of n, written as $\sqrt[3]{n}$, and **fourth root** of n, written as $\sqrt[4]{n}$, represent numbers such that when they are raised to the powers 3 and 4, respectively, the result is n. These roots obey rules similar to those above but with the exponent 2 replaced by 3 or 4 in the first two rules.

There are some notable differences between odd order roots and even order roots (in the real number system):

For odd order roots, there is *exactly one* root for *every* number n, even when n is negative.

For even order roots, there are *exactly two* roots for every *positive* number n and *no* roots for any *negative* number n.

For example, 8 has exactly one cube root, $\sqrt[3]{8} = 2$, but 8 has two fourth roots, $\sqrt[4]{8}$ and $-\sqrt[4]{8}$, whereas -8 has exactly one cube root, $\sqrt[3]{-8} = -2$, but -8 has no fourth root, since it is negative.

1.4 Decimals

The decimal number system is based on representing numbers using powers of 10. The place value of each digit corresponds to a power of 10. For example, the digits of the number 7,532.418 have the following place values.

$$7 \ , \ 5 \ \ 3 \ \ 2 \ \ . \ \ 4 \ \ 1 \ \ 8$$

Thousands, Hundreds, Tens, Ones or Units, Tenths, Hundredths, Thousandths

Arithmetic Figure 1

That is, the number 7,532.418 can be written as

$$7(1{,}000) + 5(100) + 3(10) + 2(1) + 4\left(\frac{1}{10}\right) + 1\left(\frac{1}{100}\right) + 8\left(\frac{1}{1{,}000}\right)$$

Alternatively, it can be written as

$$7\left(10^3\right) + 5\left(10^2\right) + 3\left(10^1\right) + 2\left(10^0\right) + 4\left(10^{-1}\right) + 1\left(10^{-2}\right) + 8\left(10^{-3}\right)$$

If there are a finite number of digits to the right of the decimal point, converting a decimal to an equivalent fraction with integers in the numerator and denominator is a straightforward process. Since each place value is a power of 10, every decimal can be converted to an integer divided by a power of 10. Here are three examples.

Example 1.4.1: $2.3 = 2 + \dfrac{3}{10} = \dfrac{20}{10} + \dfrac{3}{10} = \dfrac{23}{10}$

Example 1.4.2: $90.17 = 90 + \dfrac{17}{100} = \dfrac{9{,}000 + 17}{100} = \dfrac{9{,}017}{100}$

Example 1.4.3: $0.612 = \dfrac{612}{1{,}000}$

Conversely, every fraction with integers in the numerator and denominator can be converted to an equivalent decimal by dividing the numerator by the denominator using long division (which is not in this review). The decimal that results from the long division will either **terminate**, as in $\frac{1}{4} = 0.25$ and $\frac{52}{25} = 2.08$, or **repeat** without end,

as in $\frac{1}{9} = 0.111...$, $\frac{1}{22} = 0.0454545...$, and $\frac{25}{12} = 2.08333...$ One way to indicate the repeating part of a decimal that repeats without end is to use a bar over the digits that repeat. Here are four examples of fractions converted to decimals.

Example 1.4.4: $\frac{3}{8} = 0.375$

Example 1.4.5: $\frac{259}{40} = 6.475$

Example 1.4.6: $-\frac{1}{3} = -0.\overline{3}$

Example 1.4.7: $\frac{15}{14} = 1.0\overline{714285}$

Every fraction with integers in the numerator and denominator is equivalent to a decimal that either terminates or repeats. That is, every rational number can be expressed as a terminating or repeating decimal. The converse is also true; that is, every terminating or repeating decimal represents a rational number.

Not all decimals are terminating or repeating; for instance, the decimal that is equivalent to $\sqrt{2}$ is $1.41421356237...$, and it can be shown that this decimal does not terminate or repeat. Another example is $0.020220222022220222220...$, which has groups of consecutive 2s separated by a 0, where the number of 2s in each successive group increases by one. Since these two decimals do not terminate or repeat, they are not rational numbers. Such numbers are called **irrational numbers**.

1.5 Real Numbers

The set of **real numbers** consists of all rational numbers and all irrational numbers. The real numbers include all integers, fractions, and decimals. The set of real numbers can be represented by a number line called the **real number line**. Arithmetic Figure 2 below is a number line.

Arithmetic Figure 2

Every real number corresponds to a point on the number line, and every point on the number line corresponds to a real number. On the number line, all numbers to the left of 0 are negative and all numbers to the right of 0 are positive. As shown in Arithmetic Figure 2, the negative numbers $-0.4, -1, -\frac{3}{2}, -2, -\sqrt{5}$, and -3 are to the left of 0, and the positive numbers $\frac{1}{2}, 1, \sqrt{2}, 2, 2.6$, and 3 are to the right of 0. Only the number 0 is neither negative nor positive.

A real number x is **less than** a real number y if x is to the left of y on the number line, which is written as $x < y$. A real number y is **greater than** a real number x if y is to the right of x on the number line, which is written as $y > x$. For example, the number line in Arithmetic Figure 2 shows the following three relationships.

Relationship 1: $-\sqrt{5} < -2$

Relationship 2: $\dfrac{1}{2} > 0$

Relationship 3: $1 < \sqrt{2} < 2$

A real number x is **less than or equal to** a real number y if x is to the left of, *or corresponds to the same point as*, y on the number line, which is written as $x \leq y$. A real number y is **greater than or equal to** a real number x if y is to the right of, *or corresponds to the same point as*, x on the number line, which is written as $y \geq x$.

To say that a real number x is between 2 and 3 on the number line means that $x > 2$ and $x < 3$, which can also be written as $2 < x < 3$. The set of all real numbers that are between 2 and 3 is called an **interval**, and $2 < x < 3$ is often used to represent that interval. Note that the endpoints of the interval, 2 and 3, are not included in the interval. Sometimes one or both of the endpoints are to be included in an interval. The following inequalities represent four types of intervals, depending on whether or not the endpoints are included.

Interval type 1: $2 < x < 3$
Interval type 2: $2 \leq x < 3$
Interval type 3: $2 < x \leq 3$
Interval type 4: $2 \leq x \leq 3$

There are also four types of intervals with only one endpoint, each of which consists of all real numbers to the right or to the left of the endpoint and include or do not include the endpoint. The following inequalities represent these types of intervals.

Interval type 1: $x < 4$
Interval type 2: $x \leq 4$
Interval type 3: $x > 4$
Interval type 4: $x \geq 4$

The entire real number line is also considered to be an interval.

Absolute Value

The distance between a number x and 0 on the number line is called the **absolute value** of x, written as $|x|$. Therefore, $|3| = 3$ and $|-3| = 3$ because each of the numbers 3 and -3 is a distance of 3 from 0. Note that if x is positive, then $|x| = x$; if x is negative, then $|x| = -x$; and lastly, $|0| = 0$. It follows that the absolute value of any nonzero number is positive. Here are three examples.

Example 1.5.1: $\left|\sqrt{5}\right| = \sqrt{5}$

Example 1.5.2: $|-23| = -(-23) = 23$

Example 1.5.3: $|-10.2| = 10.2$

Properties of Real Numbers

Here are twelve general properties of real numbers that are used frequently. In each property, r, s, and t are real numbers.

Property 1: $r + s = s + r$ and $rs = sr$.

   Example A: $8 + 2 = 2 + 8 = 10$

   Example B: $(-3)(17) = (17)(-3) = -51$

Property 2: $(r + s) + t = r + (s + t)$ and $(rs)t = r(st)$.

   Example A: $(7 + 3) + 8 = 7 + (3 + 8) = 18$

   Example B: $\left(7\sqrt{2}\right)\sqrt{2} = 7\left(\sqrt{2}\,\sqrt{2}\right) = (7)(2) = 14$

Property 3: $r(s + t) = rs + rt$

   Example: $5(3 + 16) = (5)(3) + (5)(16) = 95$

Property 4: $r + 0 = r$, $(r)(0) = 0$, and $(r)(1) = r$.

Property 5: If $rs = 0$, then either $r = 0$ or $s = 0$ or both.

   Example: If $-2s = 0$, then $s = 0$.

Property 6: Division by 0 is undefined.

   Example A: $5 \div 0$ is undefined.

   Example B: $\dfrac{-7}{0}$ is undefined.

   Example C: $\dfrac{0}{0}$ is undefined.

Property 7: If both r and s are positive, then both $r + s$ and rs are positive.

Property 8: If both r and s are negative, then $r + s$ is negative and rs is positive.

Property 9: If r is positive and s is negative, then rs is negative.

Property 10: $|r + s| \le |r| + |s|$. This is known as the **triangle inequality**.

   Example: If $r = 5$ and $s = -2$, then $|5 + (-2)| = |5 - 2| = |3| = 3$ and

   $|5| + |-2| = 5 + 2 = 7$. Therefore, $|5 + (-2)| \le |5| + |-2|$.

Property 11: $|r||s| = |rs|$

   Example: $|5||-2| = |(5)(-2)| = |-10| = 10$

Property 12: If $r > 1$, then $r^2 > r$. If $0 < s < 1$, then $s^2 < s$.

   Example: $5^2 = 25 > 5$, but $\left(\dfrac{1}{5}\right)^2 = \dfrac{1}{25} < \dfrac{1}{5}$.

1.6 Ratio

The **ratio** of one quantity to another is a way to express their relative sizes, often in the form of a fraction, where the first quantity is the numerator and the second quantity is the denominator. Thus, if s and t are positive quantities, then the ratio of s to t can be written as the fraction $\dfrac{s}{t}$. The notation "s to t" and the notation "$s : t$" are also used to express this ratio. For example, if there are 2 apples and 3 oranges in a basket, we can say that the ratio of the number of apples to the number of oranges is $\dfrac{2}{3}$, or that it is 2 to 3, or that it is 2 : 3. Like fractions, ratios can be reduced to lowest terms.

For example, if there are 8 apples and 12 oranges in a basket, then the ratio of the number of apples to the number of oranges is still 2 to 3. Similarly, the ratio 9 to 12 is equivalent to the ratio 3 to 4.

If three or more positive quantities are being considered, say r, s, and t, then their relative sizes can also be expressed as a ratio with the notation "r to s to t". For example, if there are 5 apples, 30 pears, and 20 oranges in a basket, then the ratio of the number of apples to the number of pears to the number of oranges is 5 to 30 to 20. This ratio can be reduced to 1 to 6 to 4 by dividing each number by the greatest common divisor of 5, 30, and 20, which is 5.

A **proportion** is an equation relating two ratios; for example, $\frac{9}{12} = \frac{3}{4}$. To solve a problem involving ratios, you can often write a proportion and solve it by **cross multiplication**.

Example 1.6.1: To find a number x so that the ratio of x to 49 is the same as the ratio of 3 to 21, you can first write the following equation.

$$\frac{x}{49} = \frac{3}{21}$$

You can then cross multiply to get $21x = (3)(49)$, and finally you can solve for x to get $x = \frac{(3)(49)}{21} = 7$.

1.7 Percent

The term **percent** means *per hundred*, or *hundredths*. Percents are ratios that are often used to represent *parts of a whole*, where the whole is considered as having 100 parts. Percents can be converted to fraction or decimal equivalents. Here are three examples of percents.

Example 1.7.1: 1 percent means 1 part out of 100 parts. The fraction equivalent of 1 percent is $\frac{1}{100}$, and the decimal equivalent is 0.01.

Example 1.7.2: 32 percent means 32 parts out of 100 parts. The fraction equivalent of 32 percent is $\frac{32}{100}$, and the decimal equivalent is 0.32.

Example 1.7.3: 50 percent means 50 parts out of 100 parts. The fraction equivalent of 50 percent is $\frac{50}{100}$, and the decimal equivalent is 0.50.

Note that in the fraction equivalent, the *part* is the numerator of the fraction and the *whole* is the denominator. Percents are often written using the percent symbol, %, instead of the word "percent." Here are five examples of percents written using the % symbol, along with their fraction and decimal equivalents.

Example 1.7.4: $100\% = \frac{100}{100} = 1$

Example 1.7.5: $12\% = \frac{12}{100} = 0.12$

Example 1.7.6: $8\% = \frac{8}{100} = 0.08$

Example 1.7.7: $10\% = \frac{10}{100} = 0.1$

Example 1.7.8: $0.3\% = \frac{0.3}{100} = 0.003$

Be careful not to confuse 0.01 with 0.01%. The percent symbol matters. For example, $0.01 = 1\%$ but $0.01\% = \dfrac{0.01}{100} = 0.0001$.

To compute a *percent*, given the *part* and the *whole*, first divide the part by the whole to get the decimal equivalent, then multiply the result by 100. The percent is that number followed by the word "percent" or the % symbol.

Example 1.7.9: If the whole is 20 and the part is 13, you can find the percent as follows.

$$\frac{part}{whole} = \frac{13}{20} = 0.65 = 65\%$$

Example 1.7.10: What percent of 150 is 12.9 ?

Solution: Here, the whole is 150 and the part is 12.9, so

$$\frac{part}{whole} = \frac{12.9}{150} = 0.086 = 8.6\%$$

To find the *part* that is a certain *percent* of a *whole*, you can either multiply the *whole* by the decimal equivalent of the percent or set up a proportion to find the part.

Example 1.7.11: To find 30% of 350, you can multiply 350 by the decimal equivalent of 30%, or 0.3, as follows.

$$(350)(0.3) = 105$$

Alternatively, to use a proportion to find 30% of 350, you need to find the number of parts of 350 that yields the same ratio as 30 parts out of 100 parts. You want a number x that satisfies the proportion

$$\frac{part}{whole} = \frac{30}{100} \text{ or}$$

$$\frac{x}{350} = \frac{30}{100}$$

Solving for x yields $x = \dfrac{(30)(350)}{100} = 105$, so 30% of 350 is 105.

Given the *percent* and the *part*, you can calculate the *whole*. To do this, either you can use the decimal equivalent of the percent or you can set up a proportion and solve it.

Example 1.7.12: 15 is 60% of what number?

Solution: Use the decimal equivalent of 60%. Because 60% of some number z is 15, multiply z by the decimal equivalent of 60%, or 0.6.

$$0.6z = 15$$

Now solve for z by dividing both sides of the equation by 0.6 as follows.

$$z = \frac{15}{0.6} = 25$$

Using a proportion, look for a number z such that

$$\frac{part}{whole} = \frac{60}{100} \text{ or}$$

$$\frac{15}{z} = \frac{60}{100}$$

Hence, $60z = (15)(100)$, and therefore, $z = \dfrac{(15)(100)}{60} = \dfrac{1,500}{60} = 25$. That is, 15 is 60% of 25.

Percents Greater than 100%

Although the discussion about percent so far assumes a context of a *part* and a *whole*, it is not necessary that the part be less than the whole. In general, the whole is called the **base** of the percent. When the numerator of a percent is greater than the base, the percent is greater than 100%.

Example 1.7.13: 15 is 300% of 5, since

$$\frac{15}{5} = \frac{300}{100}$$

Example 1.7.14: 250% of 16 is 40, since

$$\left(\frac{250}{100}\right)(16) = (2.5)(16) = 40$$

Note that the decimal equivalent of 300% is 3.0 and the decimal equivalent of 250% is 2.5.

Percent Increase, Percent Decrease, and Percent Change

When a quantity changes from an initial positive amount to another positive amount (for example, an employee's salary that is raised), you can compute the amount of change as a percent of the initial amount. This is called **percent change**. If a quantity increases from 600 to 750, then the base of the increase is the initial amount, 600, and the amount of the increase is 750 − 600, or 150. The **percent increase** is found by dividing the amount of increase by the base, as follows.

$$\frac{amount\ of\ increase}{base} = \frac{750 - 600}{600} = \frac{150}{600} = \frac{25}{100} = 25\%$$

We say the percent increase is 25%. Sometimes this computation is written as follows.

$$\left(\frac{750 - 600}{600}\right)(100\%) = \left(\frac{150}{600}\right)(100\%) = 25\%$$

If a quantity doubles in size, then the percent increase is 100%. For example, if a quantity increases from 150 to 300, then the percent increase is calculated as follows.

$$\frac{amount\ of\ increase}{base} = \frac{300 - 150}{150} = \frac{150}{150} = 100\%$$

If a quantity decreases from 500 to 400, calculate the **percent decrease** as follows.

$$\frac{amount\ of\ decrease}{base} = \frac{500 - 400}{500} = \frac{100}{500} = \frac{20}{100} = 20\%$$

The quantity decreased by 20%.

When computing a percent *increase*, the base is the *smaller* number. When computing a percent *decrease*, the base is the *larger* number. In either case, the base is the initial number, before the change.

Example 1.7.15: An investment in a mutual fund increased by 12% in a single day. If the value of the investment before the increase was $1,300, what was the value after the increase?

Solution: The percent increase is 12%. Therefore, the value of the increase is 12% of $1,300, or, using the decimal equivalent, the increase is $(0.12)(\$1,300) = \$156$. Thus, the value of the investment after the change is

$$\$1,300 + \$156 = 1,456$$

Because the final result is the sum of the initial investment (100% of $1,300) and the increase (12% of $1,300), the final result is $100\% + 12\% = 112\%$ of $1,300. Thus, another way to get the final result is to multiply the value of the investment by the decimal equivalent of 112%, which is 1.12:

$$(\$1,300)(1.12) = \$1,456$$

A quantity may have several successive percent changes, where the base of each successive change is the result of the preceding percent change, as is the case in the following example.

Example 1.7.16: On September 1, 2013, the number of children enrolled in a certain preschool was 8% less than the number of children enrolled at the preschool on September 1, 2012. On September 1, 2014, the number of children enrolled in the preschool was 6% greater than the number of children enrolled in the preschool on September 1, 2013. By what percent did the number of students enrolled change from September 1, 2012, to September 1, 2014?

Solution: The *initial* base is the enrollment on September 1, 2012. The first percent change was the 8% decrease in the enrollment from September 1, 2012, to September 1, 2013. As a result of this decrease, the enrollment on September 1, 2013, was $(100 - 8)\%$, or 92%, of the enrollment on September 1, 2012. The decimal equivalent of 92% is 0.92.

So, if n represents the number of children enrolled on September 1, 2012, then the number of children enrolled on September 1, 2013, is equal to $0.92n$.

The *new* base is the enrollment on September 1, 2013, which is $0.92n$. The second percent change was the 6% increase in enrollment from September 1, 2013, to September 1, 2014. As a result of this increase, the enrollment on September 1, 2014, was $(100 + 6)\%$, or 106%, of the enrollment on September 1, 2013. The decimal equivalent of 106% is 1.06.

Thus, the number of children enrolled on September 1, 2014, was $(1.06)(0.92n)$, which is equal to $0.9752n$.

The percent equivalent of 0.9752 is 97.52%, which is 2.48% less than 100%. Thus, the percent change in the enrollment from September 1, 2012, to September 1, 2014, is a 2.48% decrease.

ARITHMETIC EXERCISES

Exercise 1. Evaluate the following.

  (a) $15 - (6 - 4)(-2)$

  (b) $(2 - 17) \div 5$

  (c) $(60 \div 12) - (-7 + 4)$

  (d) $3^4 - (-2)^3$

  (e) $(-5)(-3) - 15$

  (f) $(-2)^4(15 - 18)^4$

  (g) $(20 \div 5)^2(-2 + 6)^3$

  (h) $(-85)(0) - (-17)(3)$

Exercise 2. Evaluate the following.

  (a) $\dfrac{1}{2} - \dfrac{1}{3} + \dfrac{1}{12}$

  (b) $\left(\dfrac{3}{4} + \dfrac{1}{7}\right)\left(\dfrac{-2}{5}\right)$

  (c) $\left(\dfrac{7}{8} - \dfrac{4}{5}\right)^2$

  (d) $\left(\dfrac{3}{-8}\right) \div \left(\dfrac{27}{32}\right)$

Exercise 3. Which of the integers 312, 98, 112, and 144 are divisible by 8 ?

Exercise 4. (a) What is the prime factorization of 372 ?

  (b) What are the positive divisors of 372 ?

Exercise 5. (a) What are the prime divisors of 100 ?

  (b) What are the prime divisors of 144 ?

Exercise 6. Which of the integers 2, 9, 19, 29, 30, 37, 45, 49, 51, 83, 90, and 91 are prime numbers?

Exercise 7. What is the prime factorization of 585 ?

Exercise 8. Which of the following statements are true?

  (a) $-5 < 3.1$

  (b) $\sqrt{16} = 4$

  (c) $7 \div 0 = 0$

  (d) $0 < \left|-\dfrac{1}{7}\right|$

  (e) $0.3 < \dfrac{1}{3}$

  (f) $(-1)^{87} = -1$

  (g) $\sqrt{(-3)^2} < 0$

  (h) $\dfrac{21}{28} = \dfrac{3}{4}$

  (i) $-|-23| = 23$

  (j) $\dfrac{1}{2} > \dfrac{1}{17}$

  (k) $(59^3)(59^2) = 59^6$

  (l) $-\sqrt{25} < -4$

Exercise 9. Find the following.

  (a) 40% of 15

  (b) 150% of 48

  (c) 0.6% of 800

  (d) 15 is 30% of which number?

  (e) 11 is what percent of 55?

Exercise 10. If a person's salary increases from $200 per week to $234 per week, what is the percent increase in the person's salary?

Exercise 11. If an athlete's weight decreases from 160 pounds to 152 pounds, what is the percent decrease in the athlete's weight?

Exercise 12. A particular stock is valued at $40 per share. If the value increases by 20 percent and then decreases by 25 percent, what will be the value of the stock per share after the decrease?

Exercise 13. There are a total of 20 dogs and cats at a kennel. If the ratio of the number of dogs to the number of cats at the kennel is 3 to 2, how many cats are at the kennel?

Exercise 14. The integer c is even, and the integer d is odd. For each of the following integers, indicate whether the integer is even or odd.

(a) $c + 2d$

(b) $2c + d$

(c) cd

(d) c^d

(e) $(c + d)^2$

(f) $c^2 - d^2$

Exercise 15. When the positive integer n is divided by 3, the remainder is 2, and when n is divided by 5, the remainder is 1. What is the least possible value of n ?

ANSWERS TO ARITHMETIC EXERCISES

Exercise 1. (a) 19
　　　　　　　(b) −3
　　　　　　　(c) 8
　　　　　　　(d) 89
　　　　　　　(e) 0
　　　　　　　(f) 1,296
　　　　　　　(g) 1,024
　　　　　　　(h) 51

Exercise 2. (a) $\dfrac{1}{4}$

　　　　　　　(b) $-\dfrac{5}{14}$

　　　　　　　(c) $\dfrac{9}{1,600}$

　　　　　　　(d) $-\dfrac{4}{9}$

Exercise 3. 312, 112, and 144

Exercise 4. (a) $372 = (2^2)(3)(31)$

(b) The positive divisors of 372 are 1, 2, 3, 4, 6, 12, 31, 62, 93, 124, 186, and 372.

Exercise 5. (a) $100 = (2^2)(5^2)$, so the prime divisors are 2 and 5.

(b) $144 = (2^4)(3^2)$, so the prime divisors are 2 and 3.

Exercise 6. 2, 19, 29, 37, and 83

Exercise 7. $585 = (3^2)(5)(13)$

Exercise 8. (a) True
　　　　　　　(b) True
　　　　　　　(c) False; division by 0 is undefined.
　　　　　　　(d) True
　　　　　　　(e) True
　　　　　　　(f) True
　　　　　　　(g) False; $\sqrt{(-3)^2} = \sqrt{9} = 3 > 0$
　　　　　　　(h) True
　　　　　　　(i) False; $-|-23| = -23$
　　　　　　　(j) True
　　　　　　　(k) False; $(59^3)(59^2) = 59^{3+2} = 59^5$
　　　　　　　(l) True

Exercise 9. (a) 6   (d) 50
          (b) 72   (e) 20%
          (c) 4.8

Exercise 10. 17%

Exercise 11. 5%

Exercise 12. $36 per share

Exercise 13. 8 cats

Exercise 14. (a) $c + 2d$ is even.   (d) c^d is even.

          (b) $2c + d$ is odd.   (e) $(c + d)^2$ is odd.

          (c) cd is even.   (f) $c^2 - d^2$ is odd.

Exercise 15. 11

PART 2. ALGEBRA

The review of algebra begins with algebraic expressions, equations, inequalities, and functions and then progresses to several examples of applying them to solve real-life word problems. The review of algebra ends with coordinate geometry and graphs of functions as other important algebraic tools for solving problems.

2.1 Algebraic Expressions

A **variable** is a letter that represents a quantity whose value is unknown. The letters x and y are often used as variables, although any symbol can be used. An **algebraic expression** has one or more variables and can be written as a single **term** or as a sum of terms. Here are four examples of algebraic expressions.

Example 2.1.1: $2x$

Example 2.1.2: $y - \dfrac{1}{4}$

Example 2.1.3: $w^3z + 5z^2 - z^2 + 6$

Example 2.1.4: $\dfrac{8}{n + p}$

In the examples above, $2x$ is a single term, $y - \dfrac{1}{4}$ has two terms, $w^3z + 5z^2 - z^2 + 6$ has four terms, and $\dfrac{8}{n + p}$ has one term.

In the expression $w^3z + 5z^2 - z^2 + 6$, the terms $5z^2$ and $-z^2$ are called **like terms** because they have the same variables, and the corresponding variables have the same exponents. A term that has no variable is called a **constant** term. A number that is multiplied by variables is called the **coefficient** of a term.

A **polynomial** is the sum of a finite number of terms in which each term is either a constant term or a product of a coefficient and one or more variables with positive integer exponents. The **degree** of each term is the sum of the exponents of the variables in the term. A variable that is written without an exponent has degree 1. The degree of a constant term is 0. The **degree of a polynomial** is the greatest degree of its terms.

Polynomials of degrees 2 and 3 are known as quadratic and cubic polynomials, respectively.

Example 2.1.5: The expression $4x^6 + 7x^5 - 3x + 2$ is a polynomial in one variable, x. The polynomial has four terms.

The first term is $4x^6$. The coefficient of this term is 4, and its degree is 6.
The second term is $7x^5$. The coefficient of this term is 7, and its degree is 5.
The third term is $-3x$. The coefficient of this term is -3, and its degree is 1.
The fourth term is 2. This term is a constant, and its degree is 0.

Example 2.1.6: The expression $2x^2 - 7xy^3 - 5$ is a polynomial in two variables, x and y. The polynomial has three terms.

The first term is $2x^2$. The coefficient of this term is 2, and its degree is 2.

The second term is $-7xy^3$. The coefficient of this term is -7; and, since the degree of x is 1 and the degree of y^3 is 3, the degree of the term $-7xy^3$ is 4. The third term is -5, which is a constant term. The degree of this term is 0. In this example, the degrees of the three terms are 2, 4, and 0, so the degree of the polynomial is 4.

Example 2.1.7: The expression $4x^3 - 12x^2 - x + 36$ is a cubic polynomial in one variable.

Operations with Algebraic Expressions

The same rules that govern operations with numbers apply to operations with algebraic expressions.

In an algebraic expression, like terms can be combined by simply adding their coefficients, as the following three examples show.

Example 2.1.8: $2x + 5x = 7x$

Example 2.1.9: $w^3z + 5z^2 - z^2 + 6 = w^3z + 4z^2 + 6$

Example 2.1.10: $3xy + 2x - xy - 3x = 2xy - x$

A number or variable that is a factor of each term in an algebraic expression can be factored out, as the following three examples show.

Example 2.1.11: $4x + 12 = 4(x + 3)$

Example 2.1.12: $15y^2 - 9y = 3y(5y - 3)$

Example 2.1.13: For values of x where it is defined, the algebraic expression

$\dfrac{7x^2 + 14x}{2x + 4}$ can be simplified as follows.

First factor the numerator and the denominator to get $\dfrac{7x(x + 2)}{2(x + 2)}$.

Since $x + 2$ occurs as a factor in both the numerator and the denominator of the expression, canceling it out will give an equivalent fraction for all values of x for which the expression is defined. Thus, for all values of x for which the expression is defined, the expression is equivalent to $\dfrac{7x}{2}$.

(A fraction is not defined when the denominator is equal to 0. The denominator of the original expression was $2(x + 2)$, which is equal to 0 when $x = -2$, so the original expression is defined for all $x \neq -2$.)

To multiply two algebraic expressions, each term of the first expression is multiplied by each term of the second expression and the results are added, as the following example shows.

Example 2.1.14: Multiply $(x + 2)(3x - 7)$ as follows.

First multiply each term of the expression $x + 2$ by each term of the expression $3x - 7$ to get the expression $x(3x) + x(-7) + 2(3x) + 2(-7)$.

Then simplify each term to get $3x^2 - 7x + 6x - 14$.
Finally, combine like terms to get $3x^2 - x - 14$.
So you can conclude that $(x + 2)(3x - 7) = 3x^2 - x - 14$.

A statement of equality between two algebraic expressions that is true for all possible values of the variables involved is called an **identity**. Here are seven examples of identities.

Identity 1: $ca + cb = c(a + b)$
Identity 2: $ca - cb = c(a - b)$
Identity 3: $(a + b)^2 = a^2 + 2ab + b^2$
Identity 4: $(a - b)^2 = a^2 - 2ab + b^2$
Identity 5: $a^2 - b^2 = (a + b)(a - b)$
Identity 6: $(a + b)^3 = a^3 + 3a^2b + 3ab^2 + b^3$
Identity 7: $(a - b)^3 = a^3 - 3a^2b + 3ab^2 - b^3$

Identities can be used to modify and simplify algebraic expressions, as in the following example.

Example 2.1.15: Simplify the algebraic expression $\dfrac{x^2 - 9}{4x - 12}$.

Solution: Use the identity $a^2 - b^2 = (a + b)(a - b)$ to factor the numerator of the expression, and use the identity $ca - cb = c(a - b)$ to factor the denominator of the expression to get

$$\frac{x^2 - 9}{4x - 12} = \frac{(x + 3)(x - 3)}{4(x - 3)}$$

Now, since $x - 3$ occurs as a factor in both the numerator and the denominator, it can be canceled out when $x - 3 \neq 0$, that is, when $x \neq 3$ (since the fraction is not defined when the denominator is 0). Therefore, for all $x \neq 3$, the expression is equivalent to $\dfrac{x + 3}{4}$.

2.2 Rules of Exponents

In the algebraic expression x^a, where x is raised to the power a, x is called the **base** and a is called the **exponent**. For all integers a and b and all positive numbers x, except $x = 1$, the following property holds: If $x^a = x^b$, then $a = b$.

Example: If $2^{3c+1} = 2^{10}$, then $3c + 1 = 10$, and therefore, $c = 3$.

Here are seven basic rules of exponents. In each rule, the bases x and y are nonzero real numbers and the exponents a and b are integers, unless stated otherwise.

Rule 1: $x^{-a} = \dfrac{1}{x^a}$

Example A: $4^{-3} = \dfrac{1}{4^3} = \dfrac{1}{64}$

Example B: $x^{-10} = \dfrac{1}{x^{10}}$

Example C: $\dfrac{1}{2^{-a}} = 2^{a}$

Rule 2: $\left(x^{a}\right)\left(x^{b}\right) = x^{a+b}$

Example A: $\left(3^{2}\right)\left(3^{4}\right) = 3^{2+4} = 3^{6} = 729$

Example B: $\left(y^{3}\right)\left(y^{-1}\right) = y^{2}$

Rule 3: $\dfrac{x^{a}}{x^{b}} = x^{a-b} = \dfrac{1}{x^{b-a}}$

Example A: $\dfrac{5^{7}}{5^{4}} = 5^{7-4} = 5^{3} = 125$

Example B: $\dfrac{t^{3}}{t^{8}} = t^{-5} = \dfrac{1}{t^{5}}$

Rule 4: $x^{0} = 1$

Example A: $7^{0} = 1$

Example B: $(-3)^{0} = 1$

Note that 0^{0} is not defined.

Rule 5: $\left(x^{a}\right)\left(y^{a}\right) = (xy)^{a}$

Example A: $\left(2^{3}\right)\left(3^{3}\right) = 6^{3} = 216$

Example B: $(10z)^{3} = 10^{3}z^{3} = 1{,}000z^{3}$

Rule 6: $\left(\dfrac{x}{y}\right)^{a} = \dfrac{x^{a}}{y^{a}}$

Example A: $\left(\dfrac{3}{4}\right)^{2} = \dfrac{3^{2}}{4^{2}} = \dfrac{9}{16}$

Example B: $\left(\dfrac{r}{4t}\right)^{3} = \dfrac{r^{3}}{64t^{3}}$

Rule 7: $\left(x^{a}\right)^{b} = x^{ab}$

Example A: $\left(2^{5}\right)^{2} = 2^{10} = 1{,}024$

Example B: $\left(3y^{6}\right)^{2} = \left(3^{2}\right)\left(y^{6}\right)^{2} = 9y^{12}$

The rules above are identities that are used to simplify expressions. Sometimes algebraic expressions look like they can be simplified in similar ways, but in fact they cannot. In order to avoid mistakes commonly made when dealing with exponents, keep the following six cases in mind.

Case 1: $(x^{a})(y^{b}) \neq (xy)^{a+b}$

For example, $(2^{4})(3^{2}) \neq (2 \times 3)^{4+2}$, since $(2^{4})(3^{2}) = 144$ and $6^{4+2} = 6^{6} = 46{,}656$.

Case 2: $(x^{a})^{b} \neq x^{a}x^{b}$

Instead, $(x^{a})^{b} = x^{ab}$ and $x^{a}x^{b} = x^{a+b}$; for example, $(4^{2})^{3} = 4^{6}$ and $4^{2}4^{3} = 4^{5}$.

Case 3: $(x + y)^a \neq x^a + y^a$.

In particular, note that $(x + y)^2 = x^2 + 2xy + y^2$; that is, the correct expansion contains the additional term $2xy$.

Case 4: $(-x)^2 \neq -x^2$

Instead, $(-x)^2 = x^2$. Note carefully where each negative sign appears.

Case 5: $\sqrt{x^2 + y^2} \neq x + y$

Case 6: $\dfrac{a}{x + y} \neq \dfrac{a}{x} + \dfrac{a}{y}$

But it *is* true that $\dfrac{x + y}{a} = \dfrac{x}{a} + \dfrac{y}{a}$.

2.3 Solving Linear Equations

An **equation** is a statement of equality between two mathematical expressions. If an equation involves one or more variables, the values of the variables that make the equation true are called the **solutions** of the equation. To **solve an equation** means to find the values of the variables that make the equation true, that is, the values that **satisfy the equation**. Two equations that have the same solutions are called **equivalent equations**. For example, $x + 1 = 2$ and $2x + 2 = 4$ are equivalent equations; both are true when $x = 1$ and are false otherwise. The general method for solving an equation is to find successively simpler equivalent equations so that the simplest equivalent equation makes the solutions obvious.

The following three rules are important for producing equivalent equations.

Rule 1: When the same constant is added to or subtracted from both sides of an equation, the equality is preserved and the new equation is equivalent to the original equation.

Rule 2: When both sides of an equation are multiplied or divided by the same nonzero constant, the equality is preserved and the new equation is equivalent to the original equation.

Rule 3: When an expression that occurs in an equation is replaced by an equivalent expression, the equality is preserved and the new equation is equivalent to the original equation.

Example: Since the expression $2(x + 1)$ is equivalent to the expression $2x + 2$, when the expression $2(x + 1)$ occurs in an equation, it can be replaced by the expression $2x + 2$, and the new equation will be equivalent to the original equation.

A **linear equation** is an equation involving one or more variables in which each term in the equation is either a constant term or a variable multiplied by a coefficient. None of the variables are multiplied together or raised to a power greater than 1. For example, $2x + 1 = 7x$ and $10x - 9y - z = 3$ are linear equations, but $x + y^2 = 0$ and $xz = 3$ are not.

Linear Equations in One Variable

To solve a linear equation in one variable, find successively simpler equivalent equations by combining like terms and applying the rules for producing simpler equivalent equations until the solution is obvious.

Example 2.3.1: Solve the equation $11x - 4 - 8x = 2(x + 4) - 2x$ as follows.

Combine like terms on the left side to get $3x - 4 = 2(x + 4) - 2x$.

Replace $2(x + 4)$ by $2x + 8$ on the right side to get $3x - 4 = 2x + 8 - 2x$.

Combine like terms on the right side to get $3x - 4 = 8$.

Add 4 to both sides to get $3x = 12$.

Divide both sides by 3 to get $\dfrac{3x}{3} = \dfrac{12}{3}$.

Simplify to get $x = 4$.

You can always check your solution by substituting it into the original equation. If the resulting value of the right-hand side of the equation is equal to the resulting value of the left-hand side of the equation, your solution is correct.

Substituting the solution $x = 4$ into the left-hand side of the equation $11x - 4 - 8x = 2(x + 4) - 2x$ gives

$$11x - 4 - 8x = 11(4) - 4 - 8(4) = 44 - 4 - 32 = 8$$

Substituting the solution $x = 4$ into the right-hand side of the equation gives

$$2(x + 4) - 2x = 2(4 + 4) - 2(4) = 2(8) - 8 = 8$$

Since both substitutions give the same result, 8, the solution $x = 4$ is correct.

Note that it is possible for a linear equation to have no solutions. For example, the equation $2x + 3 = 2(7 + x)$ has no solution, since it is equivalent to the equation $3 = 14$, which is false. Also, it is possible that what looks to be a linear equation could turn out to be an identity when you try to solve it. For example, $3x - 6 = -3(2 - x)$ is true for all values of x, so it is an identity.

Linear Equations in Two Variables

A linear equation in two variables, x and y, can be written in the form

$$ax + by = c$$

where a, b, and c are real numbers and neither a nor b is equal to 0. For example, $3x + 2y = 8$ is a linear equation in two variables.

A solution of such an equation is an **ordered pair** of numbers (x, y) that makes the equation true when the values of x and y are substituted into the equation. For example, both the ordered pair $(2, 1)$ and the ordered pair $\left(-\dfrac{2}{3}, 5\right)$ are solutions of the equation $3x + 2y = 8$, but the ordered pair $(1, 2)$ is not a solution. Every linear equation in two variables has infinitely many solutions.

A set of equations in two or more variables is called a **system of equations**, and the equations in the system are called **simultaneous equations**. To solve a system of equations in two variables, x and y, means to find ordered pairs of numbers (x, y) that satisfy all of the equations in the system. Similarly, to solve a system of equations in three variables, x, y, and z, means to find ordered triples of numbers (x, y, z) that satisfy all of the equations in the system. Solutions of systems with more than three variables are defined in a similar way.

Generally, systems of linear equations in two variables consist of two linear equations, each of which contains one or both of the variables. Often, such systems have a unique solution; that is, there is only one ordered pair of numbers that satisfies both equations in the system. However, it is possible that the system will not have any solutions, or that it will have infinitely many solutions.

There are two basic methods for solving systems of linear equations, by **substitution** or by **elimination**. In the substitution method, one equation is manipulated to express one variable in terms of the other. Then the expression is substituted in the other equation.

Example 2.3.2: Use substitution to solve the following system of two equations.

$$4x + 3y = 13$$
$$x + 2y = 2$$

Solution:

Part 1: You can solve for y as follows.

Express x in the second equation in terms of y as $x = 2 - 2y$.

Substitute $2 - 2y$ for x in the first equation to get $4(2 - 2y) + 3y = 13$.

Replace $4(2 - 2y)$ by $8 - 8y$ on the left side to get $8 - 8y + 3y = 13$.

Combine like terms to get $8 - 5y = 13$.

Solving for y gives $y = -1$.

Part 2: Now, you can use the fact that $y = -1$ to solve for x as follows.

Substitute -1 for y in the second equation to get $x + 2(-1) = 2$.

Solving for x gives $x = 4$.

Thus, the solution of the system is $x = 4$ and $y = -1$, or $(x, y) = (4, -1)$.

In the elimination method, the object is to make the coefficients of one variable the same in both equations so that one variable can be eliminated either by adding the equations together or by subtracting one from the other.

Example 2.3.3: Use elimination to solve the following system of two equations.

$$4x + 3y = 13$$
$$x + 2y = 2$$

(Note that this is the same system of equations that was solved by substitution in Example 2.3.2.)

Solution: Multiplying both sides of the second equation by 4 yields $4(x + 2y) = 4(2)$, or $4x + 8y = 8$.

Now you have two equations with the same coefficient of x.

$$4x + 3y = 13$$
$$4x + 8y = 8$$

If you subtract the equation $4x + 8y = 8$ from the equation $4x + 3y = 13$, the result is $-5y = 5$. Thus, $y = -1$, and substituting -1 for y in either of the original equations yields $x = 4$.

Again, the solution of the system is $x = 4$ and $y = -1$, or $(x, y) = (4, -1)$.

2.4 Solving Quadratic Equations

A **quadratic equation** in the variable x is an equation that can be written in the form

$$ax^2 + bx + c = 0$$

where a, b, and c are real numbers and $a \neq 0$. Quadratic equations have zero, one, or two real solutions.

The Quadratic Formula

One way to find solutions of a quadratic equation is to use the **quadratic formula**:

$$x = \frac{-b \pm \sqrt{b^2 - 4ac}}{2a}$$

where the notation $\pm$ is shorthand for indicating two solutions—one that uses the plus sign and the other that uses the minus sign.

Example 2.4.1: In the quadratic equation $2x^2 - x - 6 = 0$, we have $a = 2$, $b = -1$, and $c = -6$. Therefore, the quadratic formula yields

$$x = \frac{-(-1) \pm \sqrt{(-1)^2 - 4(2)(-6)}}{2(2)}$$

When the expression under the square root sign is simplified, we get

$$x = \frac{-(-1) \pm \sqrt{49}}{2(2)}$$

which can be further simplified to

$$x = \frac{1 \pm \sqrt{49}}{4}$$

Finally, since $\sqrt{49} = 7$, we get that

$$x = \frac{1 \pm 7}{4}$$

Hence this quadratic equation has two real solutions: $x = \dfrac{1+7}{4} = 2$ and $x = \dfrac{1-7}{4} = -\dfrac{3}{2}$.

Example 2.4.2: In the quadratic equation $x^2 + 4x + 4 = 0$, we have $a = 1$, $b = 4$, and $c = 4$. Therefore, the quadratic formula yields

$$x = \frac{-4 \pm \sqrt{4^2 - 4(1)(4)}}{2(1)}$$

When the expression under the square root sign is simplified, we get

$$x = \frac{-4 \pm \sqrt{0}}{2(1)}$$

The expression under the square root sign is equal to 0 and $\sqrt{0} = 0$. Therefore, the expression can be simplified to

$$x = \frac{-4}{2(1)} = -2$$

Thus this quadratic equation has only one solution, $x = -2$.

Example 2.4.3: In the quadratic equation $x^2 + x + 5 = 0$, we have $a = 1$, $b = 1$, and $c = 5$. Therefore, the quadratic formula yields

$$x = \frac{-1 \pm \sqrt{(1)^2 - 4(1)(5)}}{2(1)}$$

The expression under the square root sign is equal to -19. Since square roots of negative numbers are not real numbers, x is not a real number, and there is no real solution to this quadratic equation.

Solving Quadratic Equations by Factoring

Some quadratic equations can be solved more quickly by factoring.

Example 2.4.4: The quadratic equation $2x^2 - x - 6 = 0$ in Example 2.4.1 can be factored as $(2x + 3)(x - 2) = 0$. When a product is equal to 0, at least one of the factors must be equal to 0, so either $2x + 3 = 0$ or $x - 2 = 0$.

If $2x + 3 = 0$, then $2x = -3$ and $x = -\frac{3}{2}$.

If $x - 2 = 0$, then $x = 2$.

Thus the solutions are $-\frac{3}{2}$ and 2.

Example 2.4.5: The quadratic equation $5x^2 + 3x - 2 = 0$ can be factored as $(5x - 2)(x + 1) = 0$.

Therefore, either $5x - 2 = 0$ or $x + 1 = 0$.

If $5x - 2 = 0$, then $x = \frac{2}{5}$.

If $x + 1 = 0$, then $x = -1$.

Thus the solutions are $\frac{2}{5}$ and -1.

2.5 Solving Linear Inequalities

A mathematical statement that uses one of the following four inequality signs is called an **inequality**.

$<$ less than
$>$ greater than
$\leq$ less than or equal to
$\geq$ greater than or equal to

Inequalities can involve variables and are similar to equations, except that the two sides are related by one of the inequality signs instead of the equality sign used in equations. For example, the inequality $4x + 1 \leq 7$ is a linear inequality in one variable, which states that $4x + 1$ is less than or equal to 7. To **solve an inequality** means to find the set of all values of the variable that make the inequality true. This set of values is also known as the **solution set** of an inequality. Two inequalities that have the same solution set are called **equivalent inequalities**.

The procedure used to solve a linear inequality is similar to that used to solve a linear equation, which is to simplify the inequality by isolating the variable on one side of the inequality, using the following two rules.

Rule 1: When the same constant is added to or subtracted from both sides of an inequality, the direction of the inequality is preserved and the new inequality is equivalent to the original.

Rule 2: When both sides of the inequality are multiplied or divided by the same nonzero constant, the direction of the inequality is *preserved if the constant is positive* but the direction is *reversed if the constant is negative*. In either case, the new inequality is equivalent to the original.

Example 2.5.1: The inequality $-3x + 5 \le 17$ can be solved as follows.

Subtract 5 from both sides to get $-3x \le 12$.

Divide both sides by -3 and reverse the direction of the inequality to get $\frac{-3x}{-3} \ge \frac{12}{-3}$. That is, $x \ge -4$.

Therefore, the solution set of $-3x + 5 \le 17$ consists of all numbers greater than or equal to -4.

Example 2.5.2: The inequality $\frac{4x + 9}{11} < 5$ can be solved as follows.

Multiply both sides by 11 to get $4x + 9 < 55$.

Subtract 9 from both sides to get $4x < 46$.

Divide both sides by 4 to get $x < \frac{46}{4}$. That is, $x < 11.5$.

Therefore, the solution set of the inequality $\frac{4x + 9}{11} < 5$ consists of all numbers less than 11.5.

2.6 Functions

An algebraic expression in one variable can be used to define a **function** of that variable. Functions are usually denoted by letters such as f, g, and h. For example, the algebraic expression $3x + 5$ can be used to define a function f by

$$f(x) = 3x + 5$$

where $f(x)$ is called the value of f at x and is obtained by substituting the value of x in the expression above. For example, if $x = 1$ is substituted in the expression above, the result is $f(1) = 3(1) + 5 = 8$.

It might be helpful to think of a function f as a machine that takes an input, which is a value of the variable x, and produces the corresponding output, $f(x)$. For any function, each input x gives exactly one output $f(x)$. However, more than one value of x can give the same output $f(x)$. For example, if g is the function defined by $g(x) = x^2 - 2x + 3$, then $g(0) = 3$ and $g(2) = 3$.

The **domain** of a function is the set of all permissible inputs, that is, all permissible values of the variable x. For the functions f and g defined above, the domain is the set of all real numbers. Sometimes the domain of the function is given explicitly and is restricted to a specific set of values of x. For example, we can define the function h by $h(x) = x^2 - 4$ for $-2 \le x \le 2$. Without an explicit restriction, the domain is assumed to be the set of all values of x for which $f(x)$ is a real number.

Example 2.6.1: Let f be the function defined by $f(x) = \dfrac{2x}{x-6}$. In this case, f is not defined at $x = 6$, because $\dfrac{12}{0}$ is not defined. Hence, the domain of f consists of all real numbers except for 6.

Example 2.6.2: Let g be the function defined by $g(x) = x^3 + \sqrt{x+2} - 10$. In this case, $g(x)$ is not a real number if $x < -2$. Hence, the domain of g consists of all real numbers x such that $x \geq -2$.

Example 2.6.3: Let h be the function defined by $h(x) = |x|$, which is the distance between x and 0 on the number line (see Arithmetic, Section 1.5). The domain of h is the set of all real numbers. Also, $h(x) = h(-x)$ for all real numbers x, which reflects the property that on the number line the distance between x and 0 is the same as the distance between $-x$ and 0.

2.7 Applications

Translating verbal descriptions into algebraic expressions is an essential initial step in solving word problems. Three examples of verbal descriptions and their translations are given below.

Example 2.7.1: If the square of the number x is multiplied by 3 and then 10 is added to that product, the result can be represented algebraically by $3x^2 + 10$.

Example 2.7.2: If John's present salary s is increased by 14 percent, then his new salary can be represented algebraically by $1.14s$.

Example 2.7.3: If y gallons of syrup are to be distributed among 5 people so that one particular person gets 1 gallon and the rest of the syrup is divided equally among the remaining 4, then the number of gallons of syrup that each of the 4 people will get can be represented algebraically by $\dfrac{y-1}{4}$.

The remainder of this section gives examples of various applications.

Average, Mixture, Rate, and Work Problems

Example 2.7.4: Ellen has received the following scores on 3 exams: 82, 74, and 90. What score will Ellen need to receive on the next exam so that the average (arithmetic mean) score for the 4 exams will be 85?

Solution: Let x represent the score on Ellen's next exam. This initial step of assigning a variable to the quantity that is sought is an important beginning to solving the problem. Then in terms of x, the average of the 4 exam scores is

$$\frac{82 + 74 + 90 + x}{4}$$

which is supposed to equal 85. Now simplify the expression and set it equal to 85:

$$\frac{82 + 74 + 90 + x}{4} = \frac{246 + x}{4} = 85$$

Solving the resulting linear equation for x, you get $246 + x = 340$, and so $x = 94$.

Therefore, Ellen will need to attain a score of 94 on the next exam.

Example 2.7.5: A mixture of 12 grams of vinegar and oil is 40 percent vinegar, where all of the measurements are by weight. How many grams of oil must be added to the mixture to produce a new mixture that is only 25 percent vinegar?

Solution: Let x represent the number of grams of oil to be added. Then the total number of grams of the new mixture will be $12 + x$, and the total number of grams of vinegar in the new mixture will be $(0.40)(12)$. Since the new mixture must be 25 percent vinegar,

$$\frac{(0.40)(12)}{12 + x} = 0.25$$

Therefore, $(0.40)(12) = (12 + x)(0.25)$.

Simplifying further gives $4.8 = 3 + 0.25x$, so $1.8 = 0.25x$, and $7.2 = x$.

Thus, 7.2 grams of oil must be added to produce a new mixture that is 25 percent vinegar.

Example 2.7.6: In a driving competition, Jeff and Dennis drove the same course at average speeds of 51 miles per hour and 54 miles per hour, respectively. If it took Jeff 40 minutes to drive the course, how long did it take Dennis?

Solution: Let x be the time, in minutes, that it took Dennis to drive the course. The distance d, in miles, is equal to the product of the rate r, in miles per hour, and the time t, in hours; that is,

$$d = rt$$

Note that since the rates are given in miles per *hour*, it is necessary to express the times in hours; for example, 40 minutes equals $\frac{40}{60}$ of an hour. Thus, the distance traveled by Jeff is the product of his speed and his time, $(51)\left(\frac{40}{60}\right)$ miles, and the distance traveled by Dennis is similarly represented by $(54)\left(\frac{x}{60}\right)$ miles.

Since the distances are equal, it follows that $(51)\left(\frac{40}{60}\right) = (54)\left(\frac{x}{60}\right)$.

From this equation it follows that $(51)(40) = 54x$ and $x = \frac{(51)(40)}{54} \approx 37.8$.

Thus, it took Dennis approximately 37.8 minutes to drive the course.

Example 2.7.7: A batch of computer parts consists of n identical parts, where n is a multiple of 60. Working alone at its constant rate, machine A takes 3 hours to produce a batch of computer parts. Working alone at its constant rate, machine B takes 2 hours to produce a batch of computer parts. How long will it take the two machines, working simultaneously at their respective constant rates, to produce a batch of computer parts?

Solution: Since machine A takes 3 hours to produce a batch, machine A can produce $\frac{1}{3}$ of the batch in 1 hour. Similarly, machine B can produce $\frac{1}{2}$ of the batch in 1 hour. If we let x represent the number of hours it takes both machines, working simultaneously, to produce the batch, then the two machines will produce $\frac{1}{x}$ of the batch in 1 hour. When the two machines work together, adding their individual production rates, $\frac{1}{3}$ and $\frac{1}{2}$, gives their combined production rate $\frac{1}{x}$.

Therefore, it follows that $\frac{1}{3} + \frac{1}{2} = \frac{1}{x}$.

This equation is equivalent to $\frac{2}{6} + \frac{3}{6} = \frac{1}{x}$. So $\frac{5}{6} = \frac{1}{x}$ and $\frac{6}{5} = x$.

Thus, working together, the machines will take $\frac{6}{5}$ hours or 1 hour 12 minutes, to produce a batch of computer parts.

Example 2.7.8: At a fruit stand, apples can be purchased for $0.15 each and pears for $0.20 each. At these rates, a bag of apples and pears was purchased for $3.80. If the bag contained 21 pieces of fruit, how many of the pieces were pears?

Solution: If a represents the number of apples purchased and p represents the number of pears purchased, then the total cost of the fruit can be represented by the equation $0.15a + 0.20p = 3.80$, and the total number of pieces of fruit can be represented by the equation $a + p = 21$. Thus to answer the question, you need to solve the following system of equations.

$$0.15a + 0.20p = 3.80$$
$$a + p = 21$$

From the equation for the total number of fruit, $a = 21 - p$.

Substituting $21 - p$ for a in the equation for the total cost gives the equation

$$0.15(21 - p) + 0.20p = 3.80$$

So, $(0.15)(21) - 0.15p + 0.20p = 3.80$, which is equivalent to

$$3.15 - 0.15p + 0.20p = 3.80$$

Therefore $0.05p = 0.65$, and $p = 13$.

Thus, of the 21 pieces of fruit, 13 were pears.

Example 2.7.9: To produce a particular radio model, it costs a manufacturer $30 per radio, and it is assumed that if 500 radios are produced, all of them will be sold. What must be the selling price per radio to ensure that the profit (revenue from the sales minus the total production cost) on the 500 radios is greater than $8,200 ?

Solution: If the selling price per radio is y dollars, then the profit is $500(y - 30)$ dollars.

Therefore, $500(y - 30) > 8,200$.

Simplifying further gives $500y - 15,000 > 8,200$, which simplifies to $500y > 23,200$ and then to $y > 46.4$.

Thus, the selling price must be greater than $46.40 to ensure that the profit is greater than $8,200.

Interest

Some applications involve computing **interest** earned on an investment during a specified time period. The interest can be computed as simple interest or compound interest.

Simple interest is based only on the initial deposit, which serves as the amount on which interest is computed, called the **principal**, for the entire time period. If the amount P is invested at a *simple annual interest rate of r percent*, then the value V of the investment at the end of t years is given by the formula

$$V = P\left(1 + \frac{rt}{100}\right)$$

In the case of **compound interest**, interest is added to the principal at regular time intervals, such as annually, quarterly, and monthly. Each time interest is added to the principal, the interest is said to be compounded. After each compounding, interest is earned on the new principal, which is the sum of the preceding principal and the interest just added. If the amount P is invested at an *annual interest rate of r percent, compounded annually*, then the value V of the investment at the end of t years is given by the formula

$$V = P\left(1 + \frac{r}{100}\right)^t$$

If the amount P is invested at an *annual interest rate of r percent, compounded n times per year*, then the value V of the investment at the end of t years is given by the formula

$$V = P\left(1 + \frac{r}{100n}\right)^{nt}$$

Example 2.7.10: If $10,000 is invested at a simple annual interest rate of 6 percent, what is the value of the investment after half a year?

Solution: According to the formula for simple interest, the value of the investment after $\frac{1}{2}$ year is

$$\$10,000\left(1 + 0.06\left(\frac{1}{2}\right)\right) = \$10,000(1.03) = \$10,300$$

Example 2.7.11: If an amount P is to be invested at an annual interest rate of 3.5 percent, compounded annually, what should be the value of P so that the value of the investment is $1,000 at the end of 3 years? (Give your answer to the nearest dollar.)

Solution: According to the formula for 3.5 percent annual interest, compounded annually, the value of the investment after 3 years is

$$P(1 + 0.035)^3$$

and we set it to be equal to $1,000 as follows.

$$P(1 + 0.035)^3 = \$1,000$$

To find the value of P, we divide both sides of the equation by $(1 + 0.035)^3$.

$$P = \frac{\$1,000}{(1 + 0.035)^3} \approx \$902$$

Thus, to the nearest dollar, $902 should be invested.

Example 2.7.12: A college student expects to earn at least $1,000 in interest on an initial investment of $20,000. If the money is invested for one year at an annual interest rate of r percent, compounded quarterly, what is the least annual interest rate that would achieve the goal? (Give your answer to the nearest 0.1 percent.)

Solution: According to the formula for r percent annual interest, compounded quarterly, the value of the investment after 1 year is

$$\$20,000\left(1+\frac{r}{400}\right)^4$$

By setting this value greater than or equal to $21,000 and solving for r, we get

$$\$20,000\left(1+\frac{r}{400}\right)^4 \geq \$21,000$$

which simplifies to

$$\left(1+\frac{r}{400}\right)^4 \geq 1.05$$

We can use the fact that taking the positive fourth root of each side of an inequality preserves the direction of the inequality. It is also true that taking the positive square root or any other positive root of each side of an inequality preserves the direction of the inequality. Using this fact, take the positive fourth root of both sides of

$$\left(1+\frac{r}{400}\right)^4 \geq 1.05$$

to get

$$1+\frac{r}{400} \geq \sqrt[4]{1.05}$$

which simplifies to

$$r \geq 400(\sqrt[4]{1.05}-1)$$

To compute the positive fourth root of 1.05, we can use the fact that for any number $x \geq 0$, $\sqrt[4]{x} = \sqrt{\sqrt{x}}$.

This allows us to compute the positive fourth root of 1.05 by taking the positive square root of 1.05 and then taking the positive square root of the result.

Therefore we can conclude that

$$400(\sqrt[4]{1.05}-1) = 400\left(\sqrt{\sqrt{1.05}}-1\right) \approx 4.9$$

Since $r \geq 400(\sqrt[4]{1.05}-1)$ and $400(\sqrt[4]{1.05}-1)$, rounded to the nearest 0.1, is 4.9, the least interest rate is approximately 4.9 percent per year, compounded quarterly.

2.8 Coordinate Geometry

Two real number lines that are perpendicular to each other and that intersect at their respective zero points define a **rectangular coordinate system**, often called the **xy-coordinate system** or **xy-plane**. The horizontal number line is called the **x-axis** and the vertical number line is called the **y-axis**. The point where the two axes intersect is called the **origin**, denoted by O. The positive half of the x-axis is to the right of the origin, and the positive half of the y-axis is above the origin. The two axes divide the plane into four regions called **quadrants.** The four quadrants are labeled I, II, III, and IV, as shown in Algebra Figure 1 below.

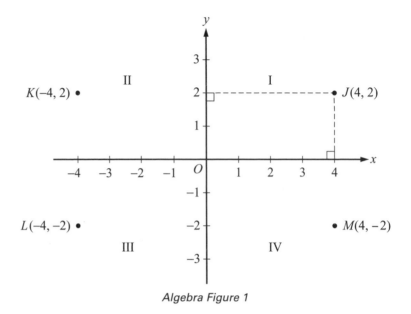

Algebra Figure 1

Each point J in the xy-plane can be identified with an ordered pair (x, y) of real numbers and is denoted by $J(x, y)$. The first number in the ordered pair is called the **x-coordinate**, and the second number is called the **y-coordinate**. A point with coordinates (x, y) is located $|x|$ units to the right of the y-axis if x is positive, or it is located $|x|$ units to the left of the y-axis if x is negative. Also, the point is located $|y|$ units above the x-axis if y is positive, or it is located $|y|$ units below the x-axis if y is negative. If $x = 0$, the point lies on the y-axis, and if $y = 0$, the point lies on the x-axis. The origin has coordinates $(0, 0)$. Unless otherwise noted, the units used on the x-axis and the y-axis are the same.

In Algebra Figure 1 above, the point $J(4, 2)$ is 4 units to the right of the y-axis and 2 units above the x-axis, the point $K(-4, 2)$ is 4 units to the left of the y-axis and 2 units above the x-axis, the point $L(-4, -2)$ is 4 units to the left of the y-axis and 2 units below the x-axis, and the point $M(4, -2)$ is 4 units to the right of the y-axis and 2 units below the x-axis.

Note that the three points $K(-4, 2)$, $L(-4, -2)$, and $M(4, -2)$ have the same coordinates as J except for the signs. These points are geometrically related to J as follows.

- M is the **reflection of J about the x-axis**, or M and J are **symmetric about the x-axis.**

- K is the **reflection of J about the y-axis**, or K and J are **symmetric about the y-axis.**

- L is the **reflection of J about the origin**, or L and J are **symmetric about the origin.**

Calculating the Distance Between Two Points

The distance between two points in the xy-plane can be found by using the Pythagorean theorem. For example, the distance between the two points $Q(-2, -3)$ and $R(4, 1.5)$ in

Algebra Figure 2 below is the length of line segment QR. To find this length, construct a right triangle with hypotenuse QR by drawing a vertical line segment downward from R and a horizontal line segment rightward from Q until these two line segments intersect at the point $S(4, -3)$ forming a right angle, as shown in Algebra Figure 2. Then note that the horizontal side of the triangle has length $4 - (-2) = 6$ and the vertical side of the triangle has length $1.5 - (-3) = 4.5$.

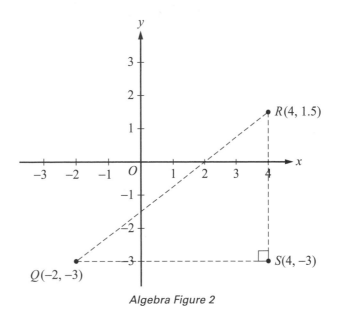

Algebra Figure 2

Since line segment QR is the hypotenuse of the triangle, you can apply the Pythagorean theorem:

$$QR = \sqrt{6^2 + 4.5^2} = \sqrt{56.25} = 7.5$$

(For a discussion of right triangles and the Pythagorean theorem, see Geometry, Section 3.3.)

Graphing Linear Equations and Inequalities

Equations in two variables can be represented as graphs in the coordinate plane. In the xy-plane, the **graph of an equation** in the variables x and y is the set of all points whose ordered pairs (x, y) satisfy the equation.

The graph of a linear equation of the form $y = mx + b$ is a straight line in the xy-plane, where m is called the **slope** of the line and b is called the **y-intercept**.

The **x-intercepts** of a graph are the x-coordinates of the points at which the graph intersects the x-axis. Similarly, the **y-intercepts** of a graph are the y-coordinates of the points at which the graph intersects the y-axis. Sometimes the terms **x-intercept** and **y-intercept** refer to the actual intersection points.

The slope of a line passing through two points $Q(x_1, y_1)$ and $R(x_2, y_2)$, where $x_1 \neq x_2$, is defined as

$$\frac{y_2 - y_1}{x_2 - x_1}$$

This ratio is often called "rise over run," where *rise* is the change in y when moving from Q to R and *run* is the change in x when moving from Q to R. A horizontal line has a slope of 0, since the rise is 0 for any two points on the line. Therefore, the equation of every horizontal line has the form $y = b$, where b is the y-intercept. The slope of a vertical line is not defined, since the run is 0. The equation of every vertical line has the form $x = a$, where a is the x-intercept.

Two lines are **parallel** if their slopes are equal. Two lines are **perpendicular** if their slopes are negative reciprocals of each other. For example, the line with equation $y = 2x + 5$ is perpendicular to the line with equation $y = -\dfrac{1}{2}x + 9$.

Example 2.8.1: Algebra Figure 3 below shows the graph of the line through the points $Q(-2, -3)$ and $R(4, 1.5)$.

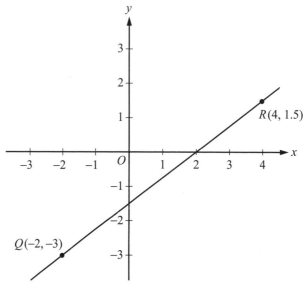

Algebra Figure 3

In Algebra Figure 3 above, the slope of the line passing through the points

$Q(-2, -3)$ and $R(4, 1.5)$ is

$$\frac{1.5 - (-3)}{4 - (-2)} = \frac{4.5}{6} = 0.75$$

Line QR appears to intersect the y-axis close to the point $(0, -1.5)$ so the y-intercept of the line must be close to -1.5. To get the exact value of the y-intercept, substitute the coordinates of any point on the line into the equation $y = 0.75x + b$, and solve it for b.

For example, if you pick the point $Q(-2, -3)$ and substitute its coordinates into the equation, you get $-3 = (0.75)(-2) + b$.

Then adding $(0.75)(2)$ to both sides of the equation yields $b = -3 + (0.75)(2)$, or $b = -1.5$.

Therefore, the equation of line QR is $y = 0.75x - 1.5$.

You can see from the graph in Algebra Figure 3 that the x-intercept of line QR is 2, since QR passes through the point $(2, 0)$. More generally, you can find the x-intercept of a line by setting $y = 0$ in an equation of the line and solving it for x. So you can find the x-intercept of line QR by setting $y = 0$ in the equation $y = 0.75x - 1.5$ and solving it for x as follows.

Setting $y = 0$ in the equation $y = 0.75x - 1.5$ gives the equation $0 = 0.75x - 1.5$. Then adding 1.5 to both sides yields $1.5 = 0.75x$. Finally, dividing both sides by 0.75 yields $x = \dfrac{1.5}{0.75} = 2$.

Graphs of linear equations can be used to illustrate solutions of systems of linear equations and inequalities, as can be seen in Examples 2.8.2 and 2.8.3.

Example 2.8.2: Consider the following system of two linear equations in two variables.

$$4x + 3y = 13$$
$$x + 2y = 2$$

(Note that this system was solved by substitution and by elimination in Section 2.3.) Solving each equation for y in terms of x yields the following equivalent system of equations.

$$y = -\frac{4}{3}x + \frac{13}{3}$$
$$y = -\frac{1}{2}x + 1$$

Algebra Figure 4 below shows the graphs of the two equations in the xy-plane. The solution of the system of equations is the point at which the two graphs intersect, which is $(4, -1)$.

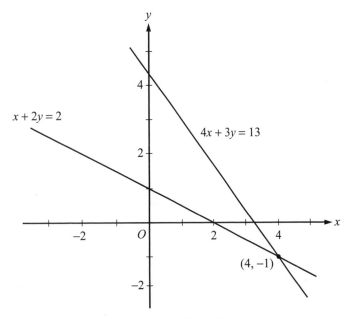

Algebra Figure 4

Example 2.8.3: Consider the following system of two linear inequalities.

$$x - 3y \geq -6$$
$$2x + y \geq -1$$

Solving each inequality for y in terms of x yields the following equivalent system of inequalities.

$$y \le \frac{1}{3}x + 2$$

$$y \ge -2x - 1$$

Each point (x, y) that satisfies the first inequality, $y \le \frac{1}{3}x + 2$, is either on the line $y = \frac{1}{3}x + 2$ or *below* the line because the y-coordinate is either equal to or *less than* $\frac{1}{3}x + 2$. Therefore, the graph of $y \le \frac{1}{3}x + 2$ consists of the line $y = \frac{1}{3}x + 2$ and the entire region below it. Similarly, the graph of $y \ge -2x - 1$ consists of the line $y = -2x - 1$ and the entire region *above* it. Thus, the solution set of the system of inequalities consists of all of the points that lie in the intersection of the two graphs described, which is represented by the shaded region shown in Algebra Figure 5 below, including the two half-lines that form the boundary of the shaded region.

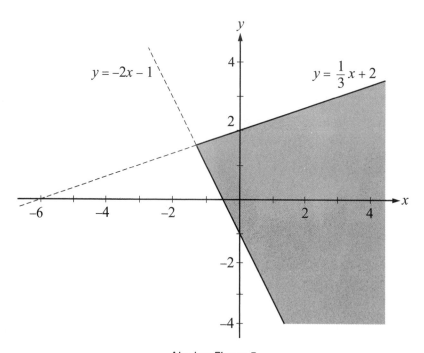

Algebra Figure 5

Symmetry with respect to the x-axis, the y-axis, and the origin is mentioned earlier in this section. Another important symmetry is symmetry with respect to the line with equation $y = x$. The line $y = x$ passes through the origin, has a slope of 1, and makes a 45-degree angle with each axis. For any point with coordinates (a, b), the point with interchanged coordinates (b, a) is the reflection of (a, b) about the line $y = x$; that is, (a, b) and (b, a) are symmetric about the line $y = x$. It follows that interchanging x and y in the equation of any graph yields another graph that is the reflection of the original graph about the line $y = x$.

Example 2.8.4: Consider the line whose equation is $y = 2x + 5$. Interchanging x and y in the equation yields $x = 2y + 5$. Solving this equation for y yields $y = \frac{1}{2}x - \frac{5}{2}$. The line $y = 2x + 5$ and its reflection $y = \frac{1}{2}x - \frac{5}{2}$ are graphed in Algebra Figure 6 that follows.

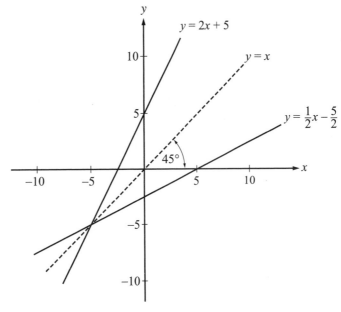

Algebra Figure 6

The line $y = x$ is a **line of symmetry** for the graphs of $y = 2x + 5$ and $y = \dfrac{1}{2}x - \dfrac{5}{2}$.

Graphing Quadratic Equations

The graph of a quadratic equation of the form $y = ax^2 + bx + c$, where a, b, and c are constants and $a \neq 0$, is a **parabola**. The x-intercepts of the parabola are the solutions of the equation $ax^2 + bx + c = 0$. If a is positive, the parabola opens upward and the **vertex** is its lowest point. If a is negative, the parabola opens downward and the vertex is its highest point. Every parabola that is the graph of a quadratic equation of the form $y = ax^2 + bx + c$ is symmetric with itself about the vertical line that passes through its vertex. In particular, the two x-intercepts are equidistant from this line of symmetry.

Example 2.8.5: The quadratic equation $y = x^2 - 2x - 3$ has the graph shown in Algebra Figure 7 below.

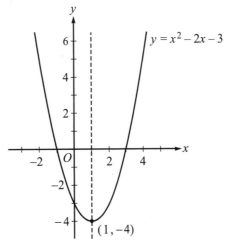

Algebra Figure 7

The graph indicates that the x-intercepts of the parabola are -1 and 3. The values of the x-intercepts can be confirmed by solving the quadratic equation $x^2 - 2x - 3 = 0$ to get $x = -1$ and $x = 3$. The point $(1, -4)$ is the vertex of the parabola, and the line $x = 1$ is its line of symmetry. The y-intercept is the y-coordinate of the point on the parabola at which $x = 0$, which is $y = 0^2 - 2(0) - 3 = -3$.

Graphing Circles

The graph of an equation of the form $(x - a)^2 + (y - b)^2 = r^2$ is a **circle** with its center at the point (a, b) and with radius $r > 0$.

Example 2.8.6: Algebra Figure 8 below shows the graph of two circles in the xy-plane. The larger of the two circles is centered at the origin and has radius 10, so its equation is $x^2 + y^2 = 100$. The smaller of the two circles has center $(6, -5)$ and radius 3, so its equation is $(x - 6)^2 + (y + 5)^2 = 9$.

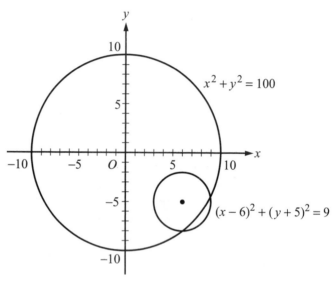

Algebra Figure 8

2.9 Graphs of Functions

The coordinate plane can be used for graphing functions. To graph a function in the xy-plane, you represent each input x and its corresponding output $f(x)$ as a point (x, y), where $y = f(x)$. In other words, you use the x-axis for the input and the y-axis for the output.

Below are several examples of graphs of elementary functions.

Example 2.9.1: Consider the linear function defined by $f(x) = -\frac{1}{2}x + 1$. Its graph in

the xy-plane is the line with the linear equation $y = -\frac{1}{2}x + 1$.

Example 2.9.2: Consider the quadratic function defined by $g(x) = x^2$. The graph of g is the parabola with the quadratic equation $y = x^2$.

The graph of both the linear equation $y = -\dfrac{1}{2}x + 1$ and the quadratic equation $y = x^2$ are shown in Algebra Figure 9 below.

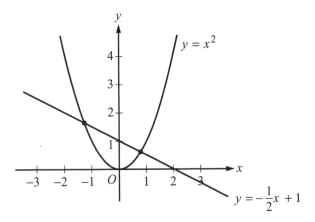

Algebra Figure 9

Note that the graphs of f and g in Algebra Figure 9 above intersect at two points. These are the points at which $g(x) = f(x)$. We can find these points algebraically as follows.

Set $g(x) = f(x)$ and get $x^2 = -\dfrac{1}{2}x + 1$, which is equivalent to $x^2 + \dfrac{1}{2}x - 1 = 0$, or

$2x^2 + x - 2 = 0$.

Then solve the equation $2x^2 + x - 2 = 0$ for x using the quadratic formula and get

$$x = \frac{-1 \pm \sqrt{1+16}}{4}$$

which represents the x-coordinates of the two solutions

$$x = \frac{-1 + \sqrt{17}}{4} \approx 0.78 \quad \text{and} \quad x = \frac{-1 - \sqrt{17}}{4} \approx -1.28.$$

With these input values, the corresponding y-coordinates can be found using either f or g:

$$g\left(\frac{-1+\sqrt{17}}{4}\right) = \left(\frac{-1+\sqrt{17}}{4}\right)^2 \approx 0.61 \quad \text{and} \quad g\left(\frac{-1-\sqrt{17}}{4}\right) = \left(\frac{-1-\sqrt{17}}{4}\right)^2 \approx 1.64.$$

Thus, the two intersection points can be approximated by $(0.78, 0.61)$ and $(-1.28, 1.64)$.

Example 2.9.3: Consider the absolute value function defined by $h(x) = |x|$. By using the definition of absolute value (see Arithmetic, Section 1.5), h can be expressed as a **piecewise-defined** function:

$$h(x) = \begin{cases} x, & x \geq 0 \\ -x, & x < 0 \end{cases}$$

The graph of this function is V-shaped and consists of two linear pieces, $y = x$ and $y = -x$, joined at the origin, as shown in Algebra Figure 10 that follows.

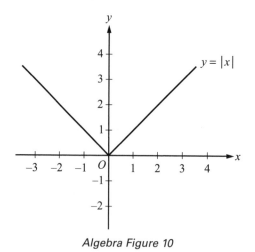

Algebra Figure 10

Example 2.9.4: Consider the positive square root function defined by $j(x) = \sqrt{x}$ for $x \geq 0$. The graph of this function is the upper half of a parabola lying on its side.

Also consider the negative square root function defined by $k(x) = -\sqrt{x}$ for $x \geq 0$. The graph of this function is the lower half of the parabola lying on its side.

The graphs of both of these functions, along with the graph of the parabola $y = x^2$, are shown in Algebra Figure 11 below.

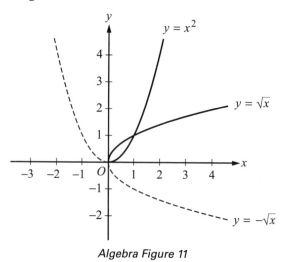

Algebra Figure 11

The graphs of $y = \sqrt{x}$ and $y = -\sqrt{x}$ are halves of a parabola because they are reflections of the right and left halves, respectively, of the parabola $y = x^2$ about the line $y = x$. This follows from squaring both sides of the two square root equations to get $y^2 = x$ and then interchanging x and y to get $y = x^2$.

Also note that $y = -\sqrt{x}$ is the reflection of $y = \sqrt{x}$ about the x-axis. In general, for any function h, the graph of $y = -h(x)$ is the **reflection** of the graph of $y = h(x)$ about the x-axis.

Example 2.9.5: Consider the function defined by $f(x) = |x| + 2$.

The graph of $f(x) = |x| + 2$ is the graph of $y = |x|$ shifted upward by 2 units, as shown in Algebra Figure 12 that follows.

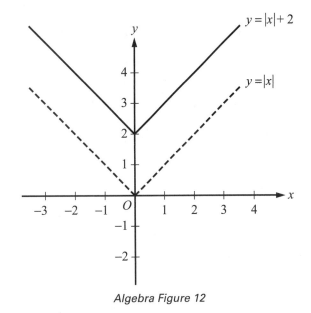

Algebra Figure 12

Similarly, the graph of the function $k(x) = |x| - 5$ is the graph of $y = |x|$ shifted downward by 5 units. (The graph of this function is not shown.)

Example 2.9.6: Consider the function defined by $g(x) = (x + 1)^2$.

The graph of $g(x) = (x + 1)^2$ is the graph of $y = x^2$ shifted to the left by 1 unit, as shown in Algebra Figure 13 below.

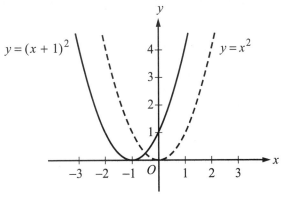

Algebra Figure 13

Similarly, the graph of the function $j(x) = (x - 4)^2$ is the graph of $y = x^2$ shifted to the right by 4 units. (The graph of this function is not shown.)

Note that in Example 2.9.5, the graph of the function $y = |x|$ was shifted upward and downward, and in Example 2.9.6, the graph of the function $y = x^2$ was shifted to the left and to the right. To double-check the direction of a shift, you can plot some corresponding values of the original function and the shifted function.

In general, for any function $h(x)$ and any positive number c, the following are true.

The graph of $h(x) + c$ is the graph of $h(x)$ **shifted upward** by c units.

The graph of $h(x) - c$ is the graph of $h(x)$ **shifted downward** by c units.

The graph of $h(x + c)$ is the graph of $h(x)$ **shifted to the left** by c units.

The graph of $h(x - c)$ is the graph of $h(x)$ **shifted to the right** by c units.

Example 2.9.7: Consider the functions defined by $f(x) = 2|x - 1|$ and $g(x) = -\dfrac{x^2}{4}$.

These functions are related to the absolute value function $|x|$ and the quadratic function x^2, respectively, in more complicated ways than in the preceding two examples.

The graph of $f(x) = 2|x - 1|$ is the graph of $y = |x|$ shifted to the right by 1 unit and then stretched, or dilated, vertically away from the x-axis by a factor of 2, as shown in Algebra Figure 14 below.

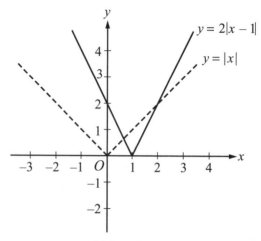

Algebra Figure 14

Similarly, the graph of the function $h(x) = \dfrac{1}{2}|x - 1|$ is the graph of $y = |x|$ shifted to the right by 1 unit and then shrunk, or contracted, vertically toward the x-axis by a factor of $\dfrac{1}{2}$. (The graph of this function is not shown.)

The graph of $g(x) = -\dfrac{x^2}{4}$ is the graph of $y = x^2$ contracted vertically toward the x-axis by a factor of $\dfrac{1}{4}$ and then reflected in the x-axis, as shown in Algebra Figure 15 below.

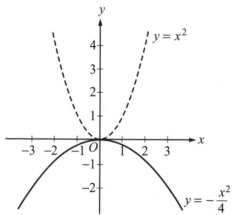

Algebra Figure 15

In general, for any function $h(x)$ and any positive number c, the following are true.
    The graph of $ch(x)$ is the graph of $h(x)$ **stretched vertically** by a factor of c if $c > 1$.
    The graph of $ch(x)$ is the graph of $h(x)$ **shrunk vertically** by a factor of c if $0 < c < 1$.

ALGEBRA EXERCISES

Exercise 1. Find an algebraic expression to represent each of the following.

(a) The square of y is subtracted from 5, and the result is multiplied by 37.

(b) Three times x is squared, and the result is divided by 7.

(c) The product of $x + 4$ and y is added to 18.

Exercise 2. Simplify each of the following algebraic expressions.

(a) $3x^2 - 6 + x + 11 - x^2 + 5x$

(b) $3(5x - 1) - x + 4$

(c) $\dfrac{x^2 - 16}{x - 4}$, where $x \neq 4$

(d) $(2x + 5)(3x - 1)$

Exercise 3. (a) What is the value of $f(x) = 3x^2 - 7x + 23$, when $x = -2$?

(b) What is the value of $h(x) = x^3 - 2x^2 + x - 2$, when $x = 2$?

(c) What is the value of $k(x) = \dfrac{5}{3}x - 7$ when $x = 0$?

Exercise 4. If the function g is defined for all nonzero numbers y by $g(y) = \dfrac{y}{|y|}$, find the value of each of the following.

(a) $g(2)$

(b) $g(-2)$

(c) $g(2) - g(-2)$

Exercise 5. Use the rules of exponents to simplify the following.

(a) $(n^5)(n^{-3})$

(b) $(s^7)(t^7)$

(c) $\dfrac{r^{12}}{r^4}$

(d) $\left(\dfrac{2a}{b}\right)^5$

(e) $\left(w^5\right)^{-3}$

(f) $(5^0)(d^3)$

(g) $\dfrac{\left(x^{10}\right)\left(y^{-1}\right)}{\left(x^{-5}\right)\left(y^5\right)}$

(h) $\left(\dfrac{3x}{y}\right)^2 \div \left(\dfrac{1}{y}\right)^5$

Exercise 6. Solve each of the following equations for x.

(a) $5x - 7 = 28$

(b) $12 - 5x = x + 30$

(c) $5(x + 2) = 1 - 3x$

(d) $(x + 6)(2x - 1) = 0$

(e) $x^2 + 5x - 14 = 0$

(f) $x^2 - x - 1 = 0$

Exercise 7. Solve each of the following systems of equations for x and y.

(a) $x + y = 24$
$x - y = 18$

(b) $3x - y = -5$
$x + 2y = 3$

(c) $15x - 18 - 2y = -3x + y$
$10x + 7y + 20 = 4x + 2$

Exercise 8. Solve each of the following inequalities for x.

    (a) $-3x > 7 + x$

    (b) $25x + 16 \geq 10 - x$

    (c) $16 + x > 8x - 12$

Exercise 9. For a given two-digit positive integer, the tens digit is 5 more than the units digit. The sum of the digits is 11. Find the integer.

Exercise 10. If the ratio of $2x$ to $5y$ is 3 to 4, what is the ratio of x to y ?

Exercise 11. Kathleen's weekly salary was increased by 8 percent to $712.80. What was her weekly salary before the increase?

Exercise 12. A theater sells children's tickets for half the adult ticket price. If 5 adult tickets and 8 children's tickets cost a total of $81, what is the cost of an adult ticket?

Exercise 13. Pat invested a total of $3,000. Part of the money was invested in a money market account that paid 10 percent simple annual interest, and the remainder of the money was invested in a fund that paid 8 percent simple annual interest. If the total interest earned at the end of the first year from these investments was $256, how much did Pat invest at 10 percent and how much at 8 percent?

Exercise 14. Two cars started from the same point and traveled on a straight course in opposite directions for 2 hours, at which time they were 208 miles apart. If one car traveled, on average, 8 miles per hour faster than the other car, what was the average speed of each car for the 2-hour trip?

Exercise 15. A group can charter a particular aircraft at a fixed total cost. If 36 people charter the aircraft rather than 40 people, then the cost per person is greater by $12.

    (a) What is the fixed total cost to charter the aircraft?

    (b) What is the cost per person if 40 people charter the aircraft?

Exercise 16. An antiques dealer bought c antique chairs for a total of x dollars. The dealer sold each chair for y dollars.

    (a) Write an algebraic expression for the profit, P, earned from buying and selling the chairs.

    (b) Write an algebraic expression for the profit per chair.

Exercise 17. Algebra Figure 16 that follows shows right triangle PQR in the xy-plane. Find the following.

    (a) The coordinates of point Q

    (b) The lengths of line segment PQ, line segment QR, and line segment PR

    (c) The perimeter of triangle PQR

    (d) The area of triangle PQR

    (e) The slope, y-intercept, and equation of the line passing through points P and R

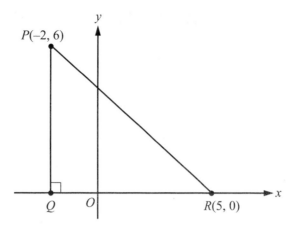

Algebra Figure 16

Exercise 18. In the xy-plane, find the following.

(a) The slope and y-intercept of the line with equation $2y + x = 6$

(b) The equation of the line passing through the point $(3, 2)$ with y-intercept 1

(c) The y-intercept of a line with slope 3 that passes through the point $(-2, 1)$

(d) The x-intercepts of the graphs in parts (a), (b), and (c)

Exercise 19. For the parabola $y = x^2 - 4x - 12$ in the xy-plane, find the following.

(a) The x-intercepts

(b) The y-intercept

(c) The coordinates of the vertex

Exercise 20. For the circle $(x - 1)^2 + (y + 1)^2 = 20$ in the xy-plane, find the following.

(a) The coordinates of the center

(b) The radius

(c) The area

Exercise 21. For each of the following functions, give the domain and a description of the graph $y = f(x)$ in the xy-plane, including its shape, and the x- and y- intercepts.

(a) $f(x) = -4$

(b) $f(x) = 100 - 900x$

(c) $f(x) = 5 - (x + 20)^2$

(d) $f(x) = \sqrt{x + 2}$

(e) $f(x) = x + |x|$

ANSWERS TO ALGEBRA EXERCISES

Exercise 1.　(a)　$37(5 - y^2)$, or $185 - 37y^2$

(b)　$\dfrac{(3x)^2}{7}$, or $\dfrac{9x^2}{7}$

(c)　$18 + (x + 4)(y)$, or $18 + xy + 4y$

Exercise 2.　(a)　$2x^2 + 6x + 5$　　　　　(c)　$x + 4$

(b)　$14x + 1$　　　　　　　　(d)　$6x^2 + 13x - 5$

Exercise 3.　(a)　49

(b)　0

(c)　-7

Exercise 4.　(a)　1

(b)　-1

(c)　2

Exercise 5.　(a)　n^2　　　　　　　　　　(e)　$\dfrac{1}{w^{15}}$

(b)　$(st)^7$　　　　　　　　　(f)　d^3

(c)　r^8　　　　　　　　　　(g)　$\dfrac{x^{15}}{y^6}$

(d)　$\dfrac{32a^5}{b^5}$　　　　　　　　(h)　$9x^2\,y^3$

Exercise 6.　(a)　7

(b)　-3

(c)　$-\dfrac{9}{8}$

(d)　The two solutions are -6 and $\dfrac{1}{2}$.

(e)　The two solutions are -7 and 2.

(f)　The two solutions are $\dfrac{1 + \sqrt{5}}{2}$ and $\dfrac{1 - \sqrt{5}}{2}$.

Exercise 7.　(a)　$x = 21$ and $y = 3$

(b)　$x = -1$ and $y = 2$

(c)　$x = \dfrac{1}{2}$ and $y = -3$

Exercise 8.　(a)　$x < -\dfrac{7}{4}$

(b)　$x \geq -\dfrac{3}{13}$

(c)　$x < 4$

Exercise 9.　83

Exercise 10.　15 to 8

Exercise 11.　$660

Exercise 12.　$9

Exercise 13.　$800 at 10% and $2,200 at 8%

Exercise 14.　48 miles per hour and 56 miles per hour

Exercise 15.　(a) $4,320

　　　　　　　(b) $108

Exercise 16.　(a) $P = cy - x$

　　　　　　　(b) Profit per chair: $\dfrac{P}{c} = \dfrac{cy - x}{c} = y - \dfrac{x}{c}$

Exercise 17.　(a) The coordinates of point Q are $(-2, 0)$.

　　　　　　　(b) The length of PQ is 6, the length of QR is 7, and the length of PR is $\sqrt{85}$.

　　　　　　　(c) $13 + \sqrt{85}$

　　　　　　　(d) 21

　　　　　　　(e) Slope: $-\dfrac{6}{7}$; y-intercept: $\dfrac{30}{7}$

　　　　　　　　　equation of line: $y = -\dfrac{6}{7}x + \dfrac{30}{7}$, or $7y + 6x = 30$

Exercise 18.　(a) Slope: $-\dfrac{1}{2}$; y-intercept: 3

　　　　　　　(b) $y = \dfrac{x}{3} + 1$

　　　　　　　(c) 7

　　　　　　　(d) 6, -3, and $-\dfrac{7}{3}$

Exercise 19.　(a) $x = -2$ and $x = 6$

　　　　　　　(b) $y = -12$

　　　　　　　(c) $(2, -16)$

Exercise 20.　(a) $(1, -1)$

　　　　　　　(b) $\sqrt{20}$

　　　　　　　(c) 20π

Exercise 21.　(a) Domain: the set of all real numbers. The graph is a horizontal line with y-intercept -4 and no x-intercept.

　　　　　　　(b) Domain: the set of all real numbers. The graph is a line with slope -900, y intercept 100, and x-intercept $\dfrac{1}{9}$.

　　　　　　　(c) Domain: the set of all real numbers. The graph is a parabola opening downward with vertex at $(-20, 5)$, line of symmetry $x = -20$, y-intercept -395, and x-intercepts $-20 \pm \sqrt{5}$.

　　　　　　　(d) Domain: the set of numbers greater than or equal to -2. The graph is the upper half of a parabola opening to the right with vertex at $(-2, 0)$, x-intercept -2, and y-intercept $\sqrt{2}$.

　　　　　　　(e) Domain: the set of all real numbers. The graph is two half-lines joined at the origin: one half-line is the negative x-axis and the other is a line starting at the origin with slope 2. Every nonpositive number is an x-intercept, and the y-intercept is 0. The function is equal to the following piecewise-defined function

$$f(x) = \begin{cases} 2x, & x \geq 0 \\ 0, & x < 0 \end{cases}$$

PART 3. GEOMETRY

The review of geometry begins with lines and angles and progresses to other plane figures, such as polygons, triangles, quadrilaterals, and circles. The review of geometry ends with some basic three-dimensional figures. Coordinate geometry is covered in the Algebra part.

3.1 Lines and Angles

A **line** is understood to be a straight line that extends in both directions without ending. Given any two points on a line, a **line segment** is the part of the line that contains the two points and all the points between them. The two points are called **endpoints**. Line segments that have equal lengths are called **congruent line segments**. The point that divides a line segment into two congruent line segments is called the **midpoint** of the line segment.

In Geometry Figure 1 below, A, B, C, and D are points on line m.

Geometry Figure 1

Line segment AB is the part of line m that consists of points A and B and all the points between A and B. According to Geometry Figure 1 above, the lengths of line segments AB, BC, and CD are 8, 6, and 6, respectively. Hence, line segments BC and CD are congruent. Since C is halfway between B and D, point C is the midpoint of line segment BD.

Sometimes the notation AB denotes line segment AB, and sometimes it denotes the **length** of line segment AB. The meaning of the notation can be determined from the context.

When two lines intersect at a point, they form four **angles**. Each angle has a **vertex** at the point of intersection of the two lines. For example, in Geometry Figure 2 below, lines k and m intersect at point P, forming the four angles APC, CPB, BPD, and DPA.

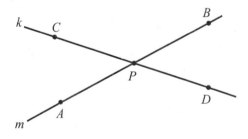

Geometry Figure 2

The first and third of the angles, that is, angles APC and BPD, are called **opposite angles**, also known as **vertical angles**. The second and fourth of the angles, that is, angles CPB and DPA, are also opposite angles. Opposite angles have equal measure, and angles that have equal measure are called **congruent angles**. Hence, opposite angles are congruent. The sum of the measures of the four angles is 360°.

Sometimes the angle symbol $\angle$ is used instead of the word "angle." For example, angle APC can be written as $\angle APC$.

Two lines that intersect to form four congruent angles are called **perpendicular lines**. Each of the four angles has a measure of 90°. An angle with a measure of 90° is called a **right angle**. Geometry Figure 3 below shows two lines, k and m, that are perpendicular, denoted by $k \perp m$.

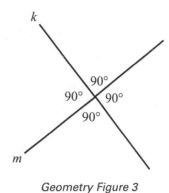

Geometry Figure 3

A common way to indicate that an angle is a right angle is to draw a small square at the vertex of the angle, as shown in Geometry Figure 4 below, where *PON* is a right angle.

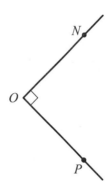

Geometry Figure 4

An angle with measure less than 90° is called an **acute angle**, and an angle with measure between 90° and 180° is called an **obtuse angle**.

Two lines in the same plane that do not intersect are called **parallel lines**. Geometry Figure 5 below shows two lines, k and m, that are parallel, denoted by $k \parallel m$. The two lines are intersected by a third line, p, forming eight angles.

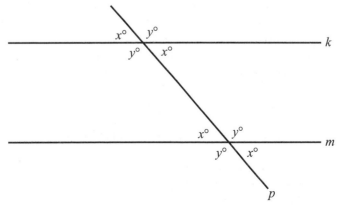

Geometry Figure 5

Note that four of the eight angles in Geometry Figure 5 have the measure $x°$, and the remaining four angles have the measure $y°$, where $x + y = 180$.

3.2 Polygons

A **polygon** is a closed figure formed by three or more line segments, all of which are in the same plane. The line segments are called the **sides** of the polygon. Each side is joined to two other sides at its endpoints, and the endpoints are called **vertices**. In this discussion, the term "polygon" means "convex polygon," that is, a polygon in which the measure of each interior angle is less than 180°. Geometry Figure 6 below contains examples of a triangle, a quadrilateral, and a pentagon, all of which are convex.

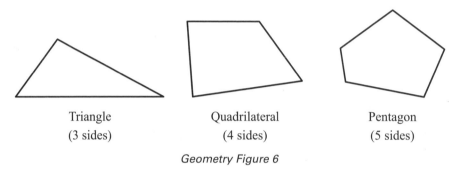

Triangle   Quadrilateral   Pentagon
(3 sides)   (4 sides)   (5 sides)

Geometry Figure 6

The simplest polygon is a **triangle**. Note that a **quadrilateral** can be divided into 2 triangles by drawing a diagonal; and a **pentagon** can be divided into 3 triangles by selecting one of the vertices and drawing 2 line segments connecting the selected vertex to the two nonadjacent vertices, as shown in Geometry Figure 7 below.

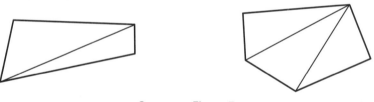

Geometry Figure 7

If a polygon has n sides, it can be divided into $n - 2$ triangles. Since the sum of the measures of the interior angles of a triangle is 180°, it follows that the sum of the measures of the interior angles of an n-sided polygon is $(n - 2)(180°)$. For example, since a quadrilateral has 4 sides, the sum of the measures of the interior angles of a quadrilateral is $(4 - 2)(180°) = 360°$, and since a **hexagon** has 6 sides, the sum of the measures of the interior angles of a hexagon is $(6 - 2)(180°) = 720°$.

A polygon in which all sides are congruent and all interior angles are congruent is called a **regular polygon**. For example, since an **octagon** has 8 sides, the sum of the measures of the interior angles of an octagon is $(8 - 2)(180°) = 1,080°$. Therefore, in a **regular octagon** the measure of each angle is $\frac{1,080°}{8} = 135°$.

The **perimeter** of a polygon is the sum of the lengths of its sides. The **area** of a polygon refers to the area of the region enclosed by the polygon.

In the next two sections, we will look at some basic properties of triangles and quadrilaterals.

3.3 Triangles

Every triangle has three sides and three interior angles. The measures of the interior angles add up to 180°. The length of each side must be less than the sum of the lengths of the other two sides. For example, the sides of a triangle could not have the lengths 4, 7, and 12 because 12 is greater than 4 + 7.

The following are 3 types of special triangles.

Type 1: A triangle with three congruent sides is called an **equilateral triangle**. The measures of the three interior angles of such a triangle are equal, and each measure is 60°.

Type 2: A triangle with at least two congruent sides is called an **isosceles triangle**. If a triangle has two congruent sides, then the angles opposite the two congruent sides are congruent. The converse is also true. For example, in triangle *ABC* in Geometry Figure 8 below, the measure of angle *A* is 50°, the measure of angle *C* is 50°, and the measure of angle *B* is $x°$. Since both angle *A* and angle *C* measure 50°, it follows that the length of *AB* is equal to the length of *BC*. Also, since the sum of the three angles of a triangle is 180°, it follows that $50 + 50 + x = 180$, and the measure of angle *B* is 80°.

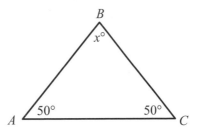

Geometry Figure 8

Type 3: A triangle with an interior right angle is called a **right triangle**. The side opposite the right angle is called the **hypotenuse**; the other two sides are called **legs**. For example, in right triangle *DEF* in Geometry Figure 9 below, side *EF* is the side opposite right angle *D*; therefore *EF* is the hypotenuse and *DE* and *DF* are legs.

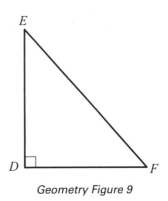

Geometry Figure 9

The Pythagorean Theorem

The **Pythagorean theorem** states that in a right triangle, the square of the length of the hypotenuse is equal to the sum of the squares of the lengths of the legs. Thus, for triangle *DEF* in Geometry Figure 9,

$$(EF)^2 = (DE)^2 + (DF)^2$$

This relationship can be used to find the length of one side of a right triangle if the lengths of the other two sides are known. For example, consider a right triangle with hypotenuse of length 8, a leg of length 5, and another leg of unknown length *x*, as shown in Geometry Figure 10 below.

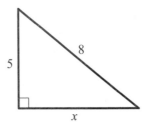

Geometry Figure 10

By the Pythagorean theorem, $8^2 = 5^2 + x^2$. Therefore, $64 = 25 + x^2$ and $39 = x^2$. Since $x^2 = 39$ and *x* must be positive, it follows that $x = \sqrt{39}$, or approximately 6.2.

The Pythagorean theorem can be used to determine the ratios of the lengths of the sides of two special right triangles. One special right triangle is an isosceles right triangle, as shown in Geometry Figure 11 below.

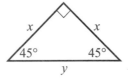

Geometry Figure 11

In Geometry Figure 11, the hypotenuse of the right triangle is of length *y*, both legs are of length *x*, and the angles opposite the legs are both 45-degree angles.

Applying the Pythagorean theorem to the isosceles right triangle in Geometry Figure 11 above shows that the lengths of its sides are in the ratio 1 to 1 to $\sqrt{2}$, as follows.

By the Pythagorean theorem, $y^2 = x^2 + x^2$. Therefore $y^2 = 2x^2$ and $y = \sqrt{2}x$. So the lengths of the sides are in the ratio *x* to *x* to $\sqrt{2}x$, which is the same as the ratio 1 to 1 to $\sqrt{2}$.

The other special right triangle is a 30°-60°-90° right triangle, which is half of an equilateral triangle, as shown in Geometry Figure 12 below.

Geometry Figure 12

Note that the length of the horizontal side, x, is one-half the length of the hypotenuse, $2x$. Applying the Pythagorean theorem to the 30°-60°-90° right triangle shows that the lengths of its sides are in the ratio 1 to $\sqrt{3}$ to 2, as follows.

By the Pythagorean theorem, $x^2 + y^2 = (2x)^2$, which simplifies to $x^2 + y^2 = 4x^2$. Subtracting x^2 from both sides gives $y^2 = 4x^2 - x^2$ or $y^2 = 3x^2$. Therefore, $y = \sqrt{3}x$. Hence, the ratio of the lengths of the three sides of a 30°-60°-90° right triangle is x to $\sqrt{3}x$ to $2x$, which is the same as the ratio 1 to $\sqrt{3}$ to 2.

The Area of a Triangle

The **area** A of a triangle is given by the formula

$$A = \frac{bh}{2}$$

where b is the length of a base, and h is the length of the corresponding height. Geometry Figure 13 below shows a triangle: the length of the horizontal base of the triangle is denoted by b and the length of the corresponding vertical height is denoted by h.

Geometry Figure 13

Any side of a triangle can be used as a base; the height that corresponds to the base is the perpendicular line segment from the opposite vertex to the base (or an extension of the base). Depending on the context, the term "base" can also refer to the *length* of a side of the triangle, and the term "height" can refer to the *length* of the perpendicular line segment from the opposite vertex to that side. The examples in Geometry Figure 14 below show three different configurations of a base and the corresponding height.

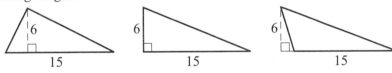

Geometry Figure 14

In all three triangles in Geometry Figure 14 above, the area is $\frac{(15)(6)}{2}$, or 45.

Congruent Triangles and Similar Triangles

Two triangles that have the same shape and size are called **congruent triangles**. More precisely, two triangles are congruent if their vertices can be matched up so that the corresponding angles and the corresponding sides are congruent.

By convention, the statement "triangles PQR and STU are congruent" does not just tell you that the two triangles are congruent, it also tells you what the corresponding parts of the two triangles are. In particular, because the letters in the name of the first triangle are given in the order PQR, and the letters in the name of the second triangle are given in the order STU, the statement tells you that angle P is congruent to angle S, angle Q is congruent to angle T, and angle R is congruent to angle U. It also tells you that sides PQ, QR, and PR in triangle PQR are congruent to sides ST, TU, and SU in triangle STU, respectively.

The following three propositions can be used to determine whether two triangles are congruent by comparing only some of their sides and angles.

Proposition 1: If the three sides of one triangle are congruent to the three sides of another triangle, then the triangles are congruent. This proposition is called Side-Side-Side, or SSS, congruence.

Proposition 2: If two sides and the included angle of one triangle are congruent to two sides and the included angle of another triangle, then the triangles are congruent. This proposition is called Side-Angle-Side, or SAS, congruence.

Proposition 3: If two angles and the included side of one triangle are congruent to two angles and the included side of another triangle, then the triangles are congruent. This proposition is called Angle-Side-Angle, or ASA, congruence. Note that if two angles of one triangle are congruent to two angles of another triangle, then the remaining angles are also congruent to each other, since the sum of the angle measures in any triangle is 180 degrees. Therefore, a similar proposition, called Angle-Angle-Side, or AAS, congruence, follows from ASA congruence.

Two triangles that have the same shape but not necessarily the same size are called **similar triangles**. More precisely, two triangles are similar if their vertices can be matched up so that the corresponding angles are congruent or, equivalently, the lengths of the corresponding sides have the same ratio, called the **scale factor of similarity**. For example, all 30°-60°-90° right triangles are similar triangles, though they may differ in size.

Geometry Figure 15 below shows two similar triangles, triangle ABC and triangle DEF.

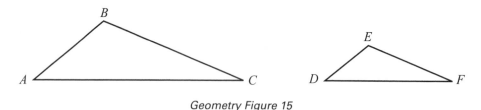

Geometry Figure 15

As with the convention for congruent triangles, the letters in similar triangles ABC and DEF indicate their corresponding parts.

Since triangles ABC and DEF are similar, we have $\dfrac{AB}{DE} = \dfrac{BC}{EF} = \dfrac{AC}{DF}$. By cross multiplication, we can obtain other proportions, such as $\dfrac{AB}{BC} = \dfrac{DE}{EF}$.

3.4 Quadrilaterals

Every quadrilateral has four sides and four interior angles. The measures of the interior angles add up to 360°.

Special Types of Quadrilaterals

The following are four special types of quadrilaterals.

Type 1: A quadrilateral with four right angles is called a **rectangle**. Opposite sides of a rectangle are parallel and congruent, and the two diagonals are also congruent.

Geometry Figure 16 below shows rectangle *ABCD*. In rectangle *ABCD*, opposite sides *AD* and *BC* are parallel and congruent, opposite sides *AB* and *DC* are parallel and congruent, and diagonal *AC* is congruent to diagonal *BD*.

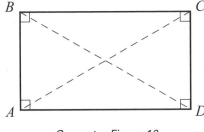

Geometry Figure 16

Type 2: A rectangle with four congruent sides is called a **square**.

Type 3: A quadrilateral in which both pairs of opposite sides are parallel is called a **parallelogram**. In a parallelogram, opposite sides are congruent and opposite angles are congruent.

Note that all rectangles are parallelograms.

Geometry Figure 17 below shows parallelogram *PQRS*. In parallelogram *PQRS*:

Opposite sides *PQ* and *SR* are parallel and congruent.
Opposite sides *QR* and *PS* are parallel and congruent.
Opposite angles *Q* and *S* are congruent.
Opposite angles *P* and *R* are congruent.

In the figure, angles *Q* and *S* are both labeled $x°$, and angles *P* and *R* are both labeled $y°$.

Geometry Figure 17

Type 4: A quadrilateral in which at least one pair of opposite sides is parallel is called a **trapezoid**. Two opposite, parallel sides of the trapezoid are called **bases** of the trapezoid.

Geometry Figure 18 below shows trapezoid *KLMN*. In trapezoid *KLMN*, horizontal side *KN* is parallel to horizontal side *LM*. Sides *KN* and *LM* are the bases of the trapezoid.

Geometry Figure 18

The Areas of the Special Types of Quadrilaterals

For all parallelograms, including rectangles and squares, the **area** A is given by the formula

$$A = bh$$

where b is the length of a base and h is the length of the corresponding height.

Any side of a parallelogram can be used as a base. The height corresponding to the base is the perpendicular line segment from any point on the side opposite the base to the base (or an extension of that base). Depending on the context, the term "base" can also refer to the *length* of a side of the parallelogram, and the term "height" can refer to the *length* of the perpendicular line segment from that side to the opposite side. Examples of finding the areas of a rectangle and a parallelogram are shown in Geometry Figure 19 below.

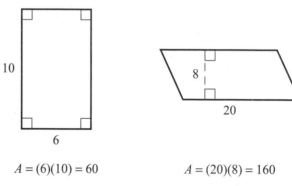

$$A = (6)(10) = 60 \qquad\qquad A = (20)(8) = 160$$

Geometry Figure 19

The **area** A of a trapezoid is given by the formula

$$A = \frac{1}{2}(b_1 + b_2)(h)$$

where b_1 and b_2 are the lengths of the bases of the trapezoid, and h is the corresponding height. For example, for the trapezoid in Geometry Figure 20 below with bases of length 10 and 18 and a height of 7.5, the area is

$$\frac{1}{2}(10 + 18)(7.5) = 105$$

Geometry Figure 20

3.5 Circles

Given a point O in a plane and a positive number r, the set of points in the plane that are a distance of r units from O is called a **circle**. The point O is called the **center** of the circle and the distance r is called the **radius** of the circle. The **diameter** of the circle is twice the radius. Two circles with equal radii are called **congruent circles**.

Any line segment joining two points on the circle is called a **chord**. The terms "radius" and "diameter" can also refer to line segments: A **radius** is any line segment joining a point on the circle and the center of the circle, and a **diameter** is a chord that passes through the center of the circle. In Geometry Figure 21 below, O is the center of the circle, r is length of a radius, PQ is a chord, and ST is a diameter, as well as a chord.

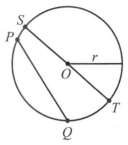

Geometry Figure 21

The distance around a circle is called the **circumference** of the circle, which is analogous to the perimeter of a polygon. The ratio of the circumference C to the diameter d is the same for all circles and is denoted by the Greek letter π; that is,

$$\frac{C}{d} = \pi$$

The value of π is approximately 3.14 and can also be approximated by the fraction $\frac{22}{7}$.

If r is the radius of a circle, then $\frac{C}{d} = \frac{C}{2r} = \pi$, and so the circumference is related to the radius by the equation

$$C = 2\pi r$$

For example, if a circle has a radius of 5.2, then its circumference is

$$(2)(\pi)(5.2) = (10.4)(\pi) \approx (10.4)(3.14)$$

which is approximately 32.7.

Given any two points on a circle, an **arc** is the part of the circle containing the two points and all the points between them. Two points on a circle are always the endpoints of two arcs. An arc is frequently identified by three points to avoid ambiguity. In Geometry Figure 22 below, there are four points on a circle. Going clockwise around the circle, the four points are A, B, C, and D. There are two different arcs between points A and C: arc ABC is the shorter arc between A and C, and arc ADC is the longer arc between A and C.

Geometry Figure 22

A **central angle** of a circle is an angle with its vertex at the center of the circle. The **measure of an arc** is the measure of its central angle, which is the angle formed by two radii that connect the center of the circle to the two endpoints of the arc. An entire circle is considered to be an arc with measure 360°.

In Geometry Figure 23 below, there are four points on a circle: points A, B, C, and D. It is given that the radius of the circle is 5.

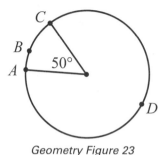

Geometry Figure 23

In Geometry Figure 23, the measure of the shorter arc between points A and C, that is arc ABC, is 50°; and the measure of the longer arc, between points A and C, that is arc ADC, is 310°.

To find the **length of an arc** of a circle, note that the ratio of the length of an arc to the circumference is equal to the ratio of the degree measure of the arc to 360°. For example, since the radius of the circle in Geometry Figure 23 is 5, the circumference of the circle is 10π. Therefore,

$$\frac{\text{length of arc } ABC}{10\pi} = \frac{50}{360}$$

Multiplying both sides by 10π gives

$$\text{length of arc } ABC = \frac{50}{360}(10\pi)$$

Then, since

$$\frac{50}{360}(10\pi) = \frac{25\pi}{18} \approx \frac{(25)(3.14)}{18} \approx 4.4$$

it follows that the length of arc ABC is approximately 4.4.

The **area** of a circle with radius r is equal to πr^2. For example, since the radius of the circle in Geometry Figure 23 above is 5, the area of the circle is $\pi(5^2) = 25\pi$.

A **sector** of a circle is a region bounded by an arc of the circle and two radii. To find the **area of a sector**, note that the ratio of the area of a sector of a circle to the area of the entire circle is equal to the ratio of the degree measure of its arc to 360°. For example, in the circle in Geometry Figure 23 the region bounded by arc ABC and the two radii is a sector with central angle 50°, and the radius of the circle is 5. Therefore, if S represents the area of the sector with central angle 50°, then

$$\frac{S}{25\pi} = \frac{50}{360}$$

Multiplying both sides by 25π gives

$$S = \left(\frac{50}{360}\right)(25\pi)$$

Then, since

$$\left(\frac{50}{360}\right)(25\pi) = \frac{125\pi}{36} \approx \frac{(125)(3.14)}{36} \approx 10.9$$

it follows that the area of the sector with central angle 50° is approximately 10.9.

A **tangent** to a circle is a line that lies in the same plane as the circle and intersects the circle at exactly one point, called the **point of tangency**. If a line is tangent to a circle, then a radius drawn to the point of tangency is perpendicular to the tangent line. The converse is also true; that is, if a radius and a line intersect at a point on the circle and the line is perpendicular to the radius, then the line is a tangent to the circle at the point of intersection. Geometry Figure 24 below shows a circle, a line tangent to the circle at point P, and a radius drawn to point P.

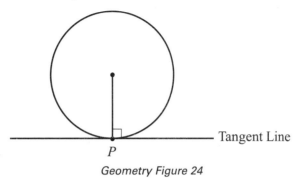

Geometry Figure 24

A polygon is **inscribed** in a circle if all its vertices lie on the circle, or equivalently, the circle is **circumscribed** about the polygon.

Geometry Figure 25 below shows triangle RST inscribed in a circle with center O. The center of the circle is inside the triangle.

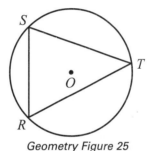

Geometry Figure 25

It is not always the case that if a triangle is inscribed in a circle, the center of the circle is inside the inscribed triangle. It is also possible for the center of the circle to be outside the inscribed triangle, or on one of the sides of the inscribed triangle. Note that if the center of the circle is on one of the sides of the inscribed triangle, that side is a diameter of the circle.

If one side of an inscribed triangle is a diameter of the circle, then the triangle is a right triangle. Conversely, if an inscribed triangle is a right triangle, then one of its sides is a diameter of the circle. Geometry Figure 26 below shows right triangle XYZ inscribed in a circle with center W. In triangle XYZ, side XZ is a diameter of the circle and angle Y is a right angle.

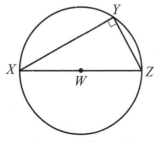

Geometry Figure 26

A polygon is circumscribed about a circle if each side of the polygon is tangent to the circle, or equivalently, the circle is inscribed in the polygon. Geometry Figure 27 below shows quadrilateral *ABCD* circumscribed about a circle with center *O*.

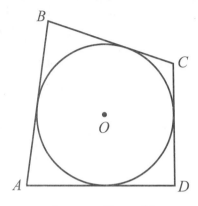

Geometry Figure 27

Two or more circles with the same center are called **concentric circles**, as shown in Geometry Figure 28 below.

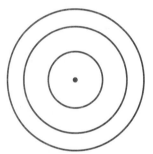

Geometry Figure 28

3.6 Three-Dimensional Figures

Basic three-dimensional figures include rectangular solids, cubes, cylinders, spheres, pyramids, and cones. In this section, we look at some properties of rectangular solids and right circular cylinders.

A **rectangular solid**, or **rectangular prism**, has 6 rectangular surfaces called **faces**, as shown in Geometry Figure 29 below. Adjacent faces are perpendicular to each other. Each line segment that is the intersection of two faces is called an **edge**, and each point at which the edges intersect is called a **vertex**. There are 12 edges and 8 vertices. The dimensions of a rectangular solid are the length *l*, the width *w*, and the height *h*.

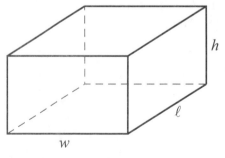

Geometry Figure 29

A rectangular solid with six square faces is called a **cube**, in which case $l = w = h$. The **volume** V of a rectangular solid is the product of its three dimensions, or

$$V = lwh$$

The **surface area** A of a rectangular solid is the sum of the areas of the six faces, or

$$A = 2(lw + lh + wh)$$

For example, if a rectangular solid has length 8.5, width 5, and height 10, then its volume is

$$V = (8.5)(5)(10) = 425$$

and its surface area is

$$A = 2((8.5)(5) + (8.5)(10) + (5)(10)) = 355$$

A **circular cylinder** consists of two bases that are congruent circles lying in parallel planes and a **lateral surface** made of all line segments that join points on the two circles and that are parallel to the line segment joining the centers of the two circles. The latter line segment is called the **axis** of the cylinder.

A **right circular cylinder** is a circular cylinder whose axis is perpendicular to its bases. The **height** of a right circular cylinder is the perpendicular distance between the two bases. Because the axis of a right circular cylinder is perpendicular to both bases, the height of a right circular cylinder is equal to the length of the axis.

The right circular cylinder shown in Geometry Figure 30 below has circular bases with centers P and Q. Line segment PQ is the axis of the cylinder and is perpendicular to both bases. The height of the cylinder is equal to the length of PQ.

Geometry Figure 30

The **volume** V of a right circular cylinder that has height h and a base with radius r is the product of the height and the area of the base, or

$$V = \pi r^2 h$$

The **surface area** A of a right circular cylinder is the sum of the areas of the two bases and the area of its lateral surface, or

$$A = 2(\pi r^2) + 2\pi rh$$

For example, if a right circular cylinder has height 6.5 and a base with radius 3, then its volume is

$$V = \pi(3^2)(6.5) = 58.5\pi$$

and its surface area is

$$A = 2\pi(3^2) + 2\pi(3)(6.5) = 57\pi$$

GEOMETRY EXERCISES

Exercise 1. In Geometry Figure 31 below, the two horizontal lines are parallel. Find the values of x and y.

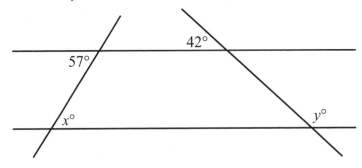

Geometry Figure 31

Exercise 2. In Geometry Figure 32 below, $AC = BC$. Find the values of x and y.

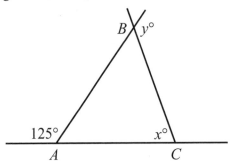

Geometry Figure 32

Exercise 3. In Geometry Figure 33 below, what is the relationship between x, y, and z ?

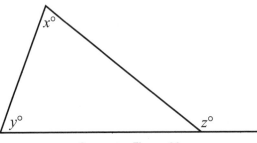

Geometry Figure 33

Exercise 4. What is the sum of the measures of the interior angles of a decagon (10-sided polygon) ?

Exercise 5. If the polygon in exercise 4 is regular, what is the measure of each interior angle?

Exercise 6. The lengths of two sides of an isosceles triangle are 15 and 22. What are the possible values of the perimeter?

Exercise 7. Triangles PQR and XYZ are similar. If $PQ = 6$, $PR = 4$, and $XY = 9$, what is the length of side XZ?

Exercise 8. What are the lengths of sides *NO* and *OP* of triangle *NOP* in Geometry Figure 34 below?

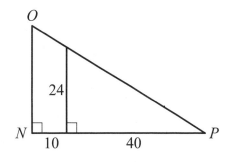

Geometry Figure 34

Exercise 9. In Geometry Figure 35 below, *AB* = *BC* = *CD*. If the area of triangle *CDE* is 42, what is the area of triangle *ADG*?

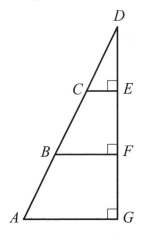

Geometry Figure 35

Exercise 10. In Geometry Figure 36 below, *ABCD* is a rectangle, *AB* = 5, *AF* = 7, and *FD* = 3. Find the following.

    (a) The area of rectangle *ABCD*

    (b) The area of triangle *AEF*

    (c) The length of diagonal *BD*

    (d) The perimeter of rectangle *ABCD*

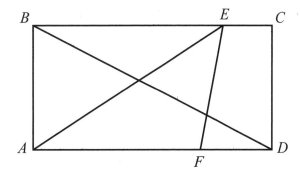

Geometry Figure 36

Exercise 11. In Geometry Figure 37 below, *ABCD* is a parallelogram. Find the following.

    (a) The area of *ABCD*

    (b) The perimeter of *ABCD*

    (c) The length of diagonal *BD*

Geometry Figure 37

Exercise 12. In Geometry Figure 38 below, the circle with center *O* has radius 4. Find the following.

    (a) The circumference of the circle

    (b) The length of arc *ABC*

    (c) The area of the shaded region

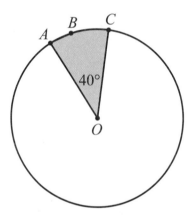

Geometry Figure 38

Exercise 13. Geometry Figure 39 below shows two concentric circles, each with center O.
Given that the larger circle has radius 12 and the smaller circle has radius 7,
find the following.

(a) The circumference of the larger circle

(b) The area of the smaller circle

(c) The area of the shaded region

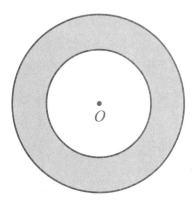

Geometry Figure 39

Exercise 14. For the rectangular solid in Geometry Figure 40 below, find the following.

(a) The surface area of the solid

(b) The length of diagonal AB

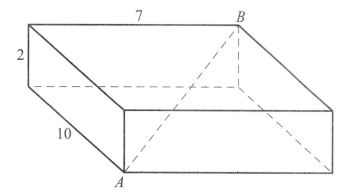

Geometry Figure 40

ANSWERS TO GEOMETRY EXERCISES

Exercise 1. $x = 57$ and $y = 138$

Exercise 2. $x = 70$ and $y = 125$

Exercise 3. $z = x + y$

Exercise 4. $1{,}440°$

Exercise 5. $144°$

Exercise 6. 52 and 59

Exercise 7. 6

Exercise 8. The length of side NO is 30 and the length of side OP is $10\sqrt{34}$.

Exercise 9. 378

Exercise 10. (a) 50

           (b) 17.5

           (c) $5\sqrt{5}$

           (d) 30

Exercise 11. (a) 48

           (b) $24 + 4\sqrt{5}$

           (c) $2\sqrt{29}$

Exercise 12. (a) 8π

           (b) $\dfrac{8\pi}{9}$

           (c) $\dfrac{16\pi}{9}$

Exercise 13. (a) 24π

           (b) 49π

           (c) 95π

Exercise 14. (a) 208

           (b) $3\sqrt{17}$

PART 4. DATA ANALYSIS

The review of data analysis begins with methods for presenting data, followed by counting methods and probability, and then progresses to distributions of data, random variables, and probability distributions. The review of data analysis ends with examples of data interpretation.

4.1 Methods for Presenting Data

Data can be organized and presented using a variety of methods. Tables are commonly used, and there are many graphical and numerical methods as well. In this section, we review tables and some common graphical methods for presenting and summarizing data.

In data analysis, a variable is any characteristic that can vary for a population of individuals or objects. Variables can be **quantitative**, or **numerical**, such as the age of individuals. Variables can also be **categorical**, or **nonnumerical**, such as the eye color of individuals.

Data are collected from a population by observing one or more variables. The **distribution of a variable**, or **distribution of data**, indicates how frequently different categorical or numerical data values are observed in the data.

> **Example 4.1.1:** In a population of students in a sixth-grade classroom, a variable that can be observed is the height of each student. Note that the variable in this example is numerical.

> **Example 4.1.2:** In a population of voters in a city's mayoral election, a variable that can be observed is the candidate that each voter voted for. Note that the variable in this example is nonnumerical.

The **frequency**, or **count**, of a particular category or numerical value is the number of times that the category or numerical value appears in the data. A **frequency distribution** is a table or graph that presents the categories or numerical values along with their corresponding frequencies. The **relative frequency** of a category or a numerical value is the corresponding frequency divided by the total number of data. Relative frequencies may be expressed in terms of percents, fractions, or decimals. A **relative frequency distribution** is a table or graph that presents the relative frequencies of the categories or numerical values.

Tables

Tables are used to present a wide variety of data, including frequency distributions and relative frequency distributions. The rows and columns provide clear associations between categories and data. A frequency distribution is often presented as a 2-column table in which the categories or numerical values of the data are listed in the first column and the corresponding frequencies are listed in the second column. A relative frequency distribution table has the same layout but with relative frequencies instead of frequencies. When data include a large number of categories or numerical values, the categories or values are often grouped together in a smaller number of groups and the corresponding frequencies are given.

Example 4.1.3: A survey was taken to find the number of children in each of 25 families. A list of the 25 values collected in the survey follows.

1   2   0   4   1   3   3   1   2   0   4   5   2   3   2   3   2   4   1   2   3   0   2   3   1

Here are tables that present the resulting frequency distribution and relative frequency distribution of the data.

Frequency Distribution

Number of Children	Frequency
0	3
1	5
2	7
3	6
4	3
5	1
Total	25

Relative Frequency Distribution

Number of Children	Relative Frequency
0	12%
1	20%
2	28%
3	24%
4	12%
5	4%
Total	100%

Note that in the relative frequency distribution table the relative frequencies are expressed as percents and that the total for the relative frequencies is 100%. If the relative frequencies were expressed as decimals or fractions instead of percents, the total would be 1.

Example 4.1.4: Thirty students took a history test. Here is a list of the 30 scores on the test, from least to greatest.

62   63   68   70   72   72   72   75   76   76   76   76   78   78   82
82   85   85   85   85   85   86   87   88   91   91   92   95   97   100

The 30 students achieved 18 different scores on the test. Displaying the frequency distribution of this many different scores would make the frequency distribution table very large, so instead we group the scores into four groups: the scores from 61 to 70, the scores from 71 to 80, the scores from 81 to 90, and the scores from 91 to 100. Here is the frequency distribution of the scores with these groups.

Score	Frequency
61 to 70	4
71 to 80	10
81 to 90	10
91 to 100	6

In addition to being used to present frequency and relative frequency distributions, tables are used to display a wide variety of other data. Here are two examples.

Example 4.1.5: The following table shows the annual per capita income in a certain state, from 1930 to 1980.

Year	Annual Per Capita Income
1930	$656
1940	$680
1950	$1,717
1960	$2,437
1970	$4,198
1980	$10,291

Example 4.1.6: The following table shows the closest and farthest distance of the eight planets from the Sun, in millions of kilometers.

Planet	Closest Distance from the Sun (in millions of kilometers)	Farthest Distance from the Sun (in millions of kilometers)
Mercury	46	70
Venus	107	109
Earth	147	152
Mars	205	249
Jupiter	741	817
Saturn	1,350	1,510
Uranus	2,750	3,000
Neptune	4,450	4,550

Bar Graphs

A frequency distribution or relative frequency distribution of data collected from a population by observing one or more variables can be presented using a **bar graph**, or **bar chart**. In a bar graph, each of the data categories or numerical values is represented by a rectangular bar, and the height of each bar is proportional to the corresponding frequency or relative frequency. All of the bars are drawn with the same width, and the bars can be presented either vertically or horizontally. When data include a large number of different categories of numerical values, the categories or values are often grouped together in several groups and the corresponding frequencies or relative frequencies are given. Bar graphs enable comparisons across several categories more easily than tables do. For example, in a bar graph it is easy to identify the category with the greatest frequency by looking for the bar with the greatest height.

Here are two examples of frequency distributions presented as bar graphs.

Example 4.1.7: Data Analysis Figure 1 is a bar graph with vertical bars. It shows the frequency distribution of one variable, fall 2009 enrollment. The variable is observed for five data categories, Colleges *A*, *B*, *C*, *D*, and *E*.

FALL 2009 ENROLLMENT AT FIVE COLLEGES

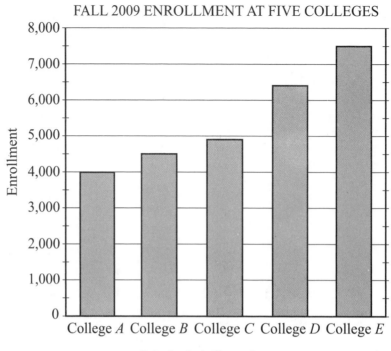

Data Analysis Figure 1

From the graph, we can conclude that the college with the greatest fall 2009 enrollment was College *E* and the college with the least enrollment was College *A*. Also, we can estimate that the enrollment for College *D* was about 6,400.

Example 4.1.8: Data Analysis Figure 2 is a bar graph with vertical bars. It shows the frequency distributions of two variables, fall 2009 enrollment and spring 2010 enrollment. Both variables are observed for three data categories, Colleges *A*, *B*, and *C*.

FALL 2009 AND SPRING 2010 ENROLLMENT AT THREE COLLEGES

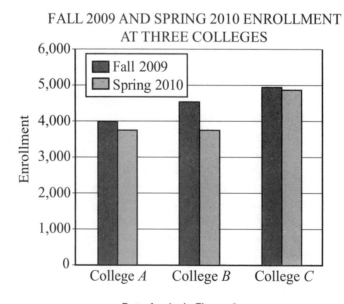

Data Analysis Figure 2

Observe that for all three colleges, the fall 2009 enrollment was greater than the spring 2010 enrollment. Also, the greatest decrease in the enrollment from fall 2009 to spring 2010 occurred at College *B*.

Segmented Bar Graphs

A **segmented bar graph**, or **stacked bar graph**, is similar to a regular bar graph except that in a segmented bar graph, each rectangular bar is divided, or segmented, into smaller rectangles that show how the variable is "separated" into other related variables. For example, rectangular bars representing enrollment can be divided into two smaller rectangles, one representing full-time enrollment and the other representing part-time enrollment, as shown in the following example.

Example 4.1.9: In Data Analysis Figure 3, the fall 2009 enrollment at the five colleges shown in Data Analysis Figure 1 is presented again, but this time each bar has been divided into two segments: one representing full-time enrollment and one representing part-time enrollment.

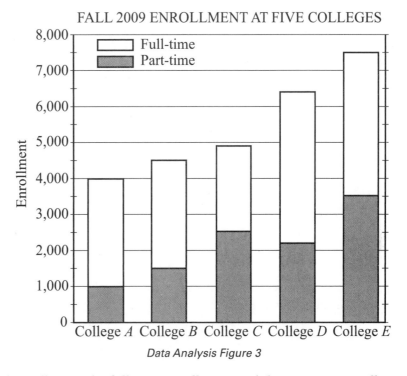

Data Analysis Figure 3

The total enrollment, the full-time enrollment, and the part-time enrollment at the five colleges can be estimated from the segmented bar graph in Data Analysis Figure 3. For example, for College *D*, the total enrollment was a little below 6,500, or approximately 6,400 students; the part-time enrollment was approximately 2,200; and the full-time enrollment was approximately 6,400 – 2,200, or 4,200 students.

Although bar graphs are commonly used to compare frequencies, as in the examples above, they are sometimes used to compare numerical data that could be displayed in a table, such as temperatures, dollar amounts, percents, heights, and weights. Also, the categories sometimes are numerical in nature, such as years or other time intervals.

Histograms

When a list of data is large and contains many different values of a numerical variable, it is useful to organize the data by grouping the values into intervals, often called classes. To do this, divide the entire interval of values into smaller intervals of equal length and then count the values that fall into each interval. In this way, each interval has a frequency and a relative frequency. The intervals and their frequencies (or relative frequencies) are often displayed in a **histogram**. Histograms are graphs of frequency distributions that are similar to bar graphs, but they must have a number line for the horizontal axis, which represents the numerical variable. Also, in a histogram, there are no regular spaces between the bars. Any spaces between bars in a histogram indicate that there are no data in the intervals represented by the spaces.

Example 4.5.1 in Section 4.5 illustrates a histogram with 50 bars.

Numerical variables with just a few values can also be displayed using histograms, where the frequency or relative frequency of each value is represented by a bar centered over the value.

Example 4.1.10: In Example 4.1.3, the relative frequency distribution of the number of children of each of 25 families was presented as a 2-column table. For convenience, the table is repeated below.

Relative Frequency Distribution

Number of Children	Relative Frequency
0	12%
1	20%
2	28%
3	24%
4	12%
5	4%
Total	100%

This relative frequency distribution can also be displayed as a histogram, as shown in the following figure.

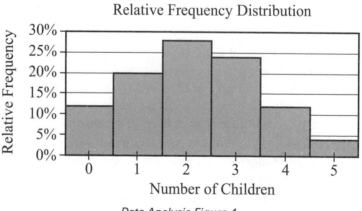

Relative Frequency Distribution

Data Analysis Figure 4

Histograms are useful for identifying the general shape of a distribution of data. Also evident are the "center" and degree of "spread" of the distribution, as well as high-frequency and low-frequency intervals. From the histogram in Data Analysis Figure 4 above, you can see that the distribution is shaped like a mound with one peak; that is, the data are frequent in the middle and sparse at both ends. The central values are 2 and 3, and the distribution is close to being symmetric about those values. Because the bars all have the same width, the area of each bar is proportional to the amount of data that the bar represents. Thus, the areas of the bars indicate where the data are concentrated and where they are not.

Finally, note that because each bar has a width of 1, the sum of the areas of the bars equals the sum of the relative frequencies, which is 100% or 1, depending on whether percents or decimals are used. This fact is central to the discussion of probability distributions in Section 4.5.

Circle Graphs

Circle graphs, often called **pie charts**, are used to represent data that have been separated into a small number of categories. They illustrate how a whole is separated into parts. The data are presented in a circle such that the area of the circle representing each category is proportional to the part of the whole that the category represents.

A circle graph may be used to represent a frequency distribution or a relative frequency distribution. More generally, a circle graph may represent any total amount that is distributed into a small number of categories, as in the following example.

Example 4.1.11:

UNITED STATES PRODUCTION OF PHOTOGRAPHIC
EQUIPMENT AND SUPPLIES IN 1971

Total: $3,980 million

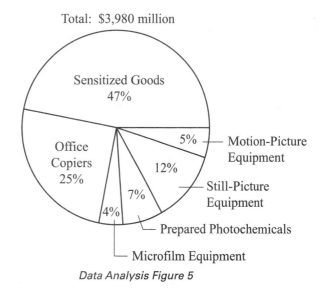

Data Analysis Figure 5

From the graph you can see that Sensitized Goods is the category with the greatest dollar value.

Each part of a circle graph is called a **sector**. Because the area of each sector is proportional to the percent of the whole that the sector represents, the measure of the central angle of a sector is proportional to the percent of 360 degrees that the sector represents. For example, the measure of the central angle of the sector representing the category Prepared Photochemicals is 7 percent of 360 degrees, or 25.2 degrees.

Scatterplots

A **scatterplot** is a type of graph that is useful for showing the relationship between two numerical variables whose values can be observed in a single population of individuals or objects. In a scatterplot, the values of one variable appear on the horizontal axis of a rectangular coordinate system and the values of the other variable appear on the vertical axis. For each individual or object in the data, an ordered pair of numbers is collected, one number for each variable, and the pair is represented by a point in the coordinate system.

A scatterplot makes it possible to observe an overall pattern, or **trend**, in the relationship between the two variables. Also, the strength of the trend as well as striking deviations from the trend are evident. In many cases, a line or a curve that best represents the trend is also displayed in the graph and is used to make predictions about the population.

Example 4.1.12: A bicycle trainer studied 50 bicyclists to examine how the finishing time for a certain bicycle race was related to the amount of physical training each bicyclist did in the three months before the race. To measure the amount of training, the trainer developed a training index, measured in "units" and based on the intensity of each bicyclist's training. The data and the trend of the data, represented by a line, are displayed in the scatterplot in Data Analysis Figure 6 below.

FINISHING TIMES AND TRAINING INDICES
FOR 50 BICYCLISTS IN A RACE

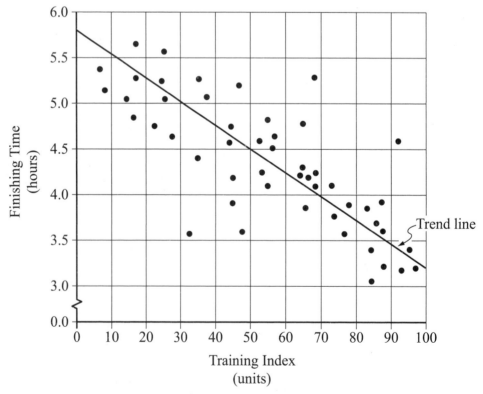

Data Analysis Figure 6

When a trend line is included in the presentation of a scatterplot, you can observe how scattered or close the data are to the trend line, or to put it another way, how well the trend line fits the data. In the scatterplot in Data Analysis Figure 6 above, almost all of the data points are relatively close to the trend line. The scatterplot also shows that the finishing times generally decrease as the training indices increase.

The trend line can be used to make predictions. For example, it can be predicted, based on the trend line, that a bicyclist with a training index of 70 units will finish the race in approximately 4 hours. This value is obtained by noting that the vertical line at the training index of 70 units intersects the trend line very close to 4 hours.

Another prediction that can be made, based on the trend line, is the approximate number of minutes by which a bicyclist will lower his or her finishing time for each increase of 10 training index units. This prediction is derived from the ratio of the change in finishing time to the change in training index, or the slope of the trend line. Note that the slope is negative. To estimate the slope, estimate the coordinates of any two points on the line, for instance, the points at the extreme left and right ends of the line: (0, 5.8) and (100, 3.2). The slope, which is measured in hours per unit, can be computed as follows:

$$\frac{3.2 - 5.8}{100 - 0} = \frac{-2.6}{100} = -0.026$$

The slope can be interpreted as follows: The finishing time is predicted to decrease 0.026 hour for every unit by which the training index increases. Since we want to know how much the finishing time decreases for an increase of *10 units*, we multiply the rate by 10 to get 0.26 hour per 10 units. To compute the decrease in *minutes* per 10 units, we multiply 0.26 by 60 to get approximately 16 minutes. Based on the trend line, it can be predicted that the bicyclist will decrease his or her finishing time by approximately 16 minutes for every increase of 10 training index units.

Line Graphs

A **line graph** is another type of graph that is useful for showing the relationship between two numerical variables, especially if one of the variables is time. A line graph uses a coordinate plane, where each data point represents a pair of values observed for the two numerical variables. There is at most one data point for each value on the horizontal axis, similar to a function. The data points are in order from left to right, and consecutive data points are connected by a line segment.

When one of the variables is time, it is associated with the horizontal axis, which is labeled with regular time intervals. The data points may represent an interval of time, such as an entire day or year, or just an instant of time. Such a line graph is often called a **time series**.

Example 4.1.13:

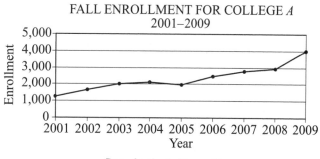

Data Analysis Figure 7

The line graph shows that the greatest increase in fall enrollment between consecutive years was the change from 2008 to 2009. One way to determine this is by noting that the slope of the line segment joining the values for 2008 and 2009 is greater than the slopes of the line segments joining all other consecutive years. Another way to determine this is by noting that the increase in enrollment from 2008 to 2009 was greater than 1,000, but all other increases in enrollment were less than 1,000.

Although line graphs are commonly used to compare frequencies, as in Example 4.1.13 above, they can be used to compare any numerical data as the data change over time, such as temperatures, dollar amounts, percents, heights, and weights.

4.2 Numerical Methods for Describing Data

Data can be described numerically by various **statistics**, or **statistical measures**. These statistical measures are often grouped in three categories: measures of central tendency, measures of position, and measures of dispersion.

Measures of Central Tendency

Measures of **central tendency** indicate the "center" of the data along the number line and are usually reported as values that represent the data. There are three common measures of central tendency:

1. the **arithmetic mean**—usually called the **average** or simply the **mean**
2. the **median**
3. the **mode**

To calculate the **mean** of n numbers, take the sum of the n numbers and divide it by n.

Example 4.2.1: For the five numbers 6, 4, 7, 10, and 4, the mean is
$$\frac{6+4+7+10+4}{5}=\frac{31}{5}=6.2$$

When several values are repeated in a list, it is helpful to think of the mean of the numbers as a **weighted mean** of only those values in the list that are *different*.

Example 4.2.2: Consider the following list of 16 numbers.
$$2, 4, 4, 5, 7, 7, 7, 7, 7, 7, 8, 8, 9, 9, 9, 9$$

There are only 6 different values in the list: 2, 4, 5, 7, 8, and 9. The mean of the numbers in the list can be computed as
$$\frac{1(2)+2(4)+1(5)+6(7)+2(8)+4(9)}{1+2+1+6+2+4}=\frac{109}{16}=6.8125$$

The number of times a value appears in the list, or the frequency, is called the **weight** of that value. So the mean of the 16 numbers is the weighted mean of the values 2, 4, 5, 7, 8, and 9, where the respective weights are 1, 2, 1, 6, 2, and 4. Note that the sum of the weights is the number of numbers in the list, 16.

The mean can be affected by just a few values that lie far above or below the rest of the data, because these values contribute directly to the sum of the data and therefore to the mean. By contrast, the **median** is a measure of central tendency that is fairly unaffected by unusually high or low values relative to the rest of the data.

To calculate the median of n numbers, first order the numbers from least to greatest. If n is odd, then the median is the middle number in the ordered list of numbers. If n is even, then there are *two* middle numbers, and the median is the average of these two numbers.

Example 4.2.3: The five numbers 6, 4, 7, 10, and 4 listed in increasing order are 4, 4, 6, 7, 10, so the median is 6, the middle number. Note that if the number 10 in the list is replaced by the number 24, the mean increases from 6.2 to

$$\frac{4+4+6+7+24}{5} = \frac{45}{5} = 9$$

but the median remains equal to 6. This example shows how the median is relatively unaffected by an unusually large value.

The median, as the "middle value" of an ordered list of numbers, divides the list into roughly two equal parts. However, if the median is equal to one of the data values and it is repeated in the list, then the numbers of data above and below the median may be rather different. For example, the median of the 16 numbers 2, 4, 4, 5, 7, 7, 7, 7, 7, 7, 8, 8, 9, 9, 9, 9 is 7, but four of the data are less than 7 and six of the data are greater than 7.

The **mode** of a list of numbers is the number that occurs most frequently in the list.

Example 4.2.4: The mode of the 6 numbers in the list 1, 3, 6, 4, 3, 5 is 3. A list of numbers may have more than one mode. For example, the list of 11 numbers 1, 2, 3, 3, 3, 5, 7, 10, 10, 10, 20 has two modes, 3 and 10.

Measures of Position

The three most basic **positions**, or locations, in a list of numerical data ordered from least to greatest are the beginning, the end, and the middle. It is useful here to label these as L for the least, G for the greatest, and M for the median. Aside from these, the most common measures of position are **quartiles** and **percentiles**. Like the median M, quartiles and percentiles are numbers that divide the data into roughly equal groups after the data have been ordered from the least value L to the greatest value G. There are three quartile numbers, called the **first quartile,** the **second quartile**, and the **third quartile**, that divide the data into four roughly equal groups; and there are 99 percentile numbers that divide the data into 100 roughly equal groups. As with the mean and median, the quartiles and percentiles may or may not themselves be values in the data.

In the following discussion of quartiles, the symbol Q_1 will be used to denote the first quartile, Q_2 will be used to denote the second quartile, and Q_3 will be used to denote the third quartile.

The numbers Q_1, Q_2, and Q_3 divide the data into 4 roughly equal groups as follows. After the data are listed in increasing order, the first group consists of the data from L to Q_1, the second group is from Q_1 to Q_2, the third group is from Q_2 to Q_3, and the fourth group is from Q_3 to G. Because the number of data may not be divisible by 4, there are various rules to determine the exact values of Q_1 and Q_3, and some statisticians use different rules, but in all cases Q_2 is equal to the median M. We use perhaps the most common rule for determining the values of Q_1 and Q_3. According to this rule, after the data are listed in increasing order, Q_1 is the median of the first half of the data in the ordered list and Q_3 is the median of the second half of the data in the ordered list, as illustrated in the following example.

There are a few variations in the way boxplots are drawn—the position of the ends of the boxes can vary slightly, and some boxplots identify outliers with certain symbols—but all boxplots show the center of the data at the median and illustrate the spread of the data in each of the four quartile groups. As such, boxplots are useful for comparing sets of data side by side.

Example 4.2.7: Two large lists of numerical data, list 1 and list 2, are summarized by the boxplots in the following figure.

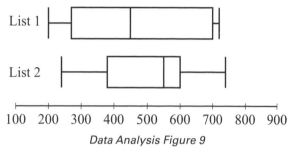

Data Analysis Figure 9

Based on the boxplots, several different comparisons of the two lists can be made. First, the median of list 2, which is approximately 550, is greater than the median of list 1, which is approximately 450. Second, the two measures of spread, range and interquartile range, are greater for list 1 than for list 2. For list 1, these measures are approximately 520 and 430, respectively, and for list 2, they are approximately 500 and 220, respectively.

Unlike the range and the interquartile range, the **standard deviation** is a measure of spread that depends on each number in the list. Using the mean as the center of the data, the standard deviation takes into account how much each value differs from the mean and then takes a type of average of these differences. As a result, the more the data are spread away from the mean, the greater the standard deviation; and the more the data are clustered around the mean, the lesser the standard deviation.

The standard deviation of a group of numerical data is computed by

1. calculating the mean of the values,
2. finding the difference between the mean and each of the values,
3. squaring each of the differences,
4. finding the average of the squared differences, and
5. taking the nonnegative square root of the average of the squared differences.

Example 4.2.8: For the five data 0, 7, 8, 10, and 10, the standard deviation can be computed as follows. First, the mean of the data is 7, and the squared differences from the mean are

$$(7-0)^2, (7-7)^2, (7-8)^2, (7-10)^2, (7-10)^2$$

or 49, 0, 1, 9, 9. The average of the five squared differences is $\frac{68}{5}$, or 13.6, and the positive square root of 13.6 is approximately 3.7.

Note on terminology: The term "standard deviation" defined above is slightly different from another measure of dispersion, the **sample standard deviation**. The latter term is qualified with the word "sample" and is computed by dividing the sum of the squared differences by $n - 1$ instead of n. The sample standard deviation is only slightly different from the standard deviation but is preferred for technical reasons for a sample of data that is taken from a larger population of data. Sometimes the standard deviation is called the **population standard deviation** to help distinguish it from the sample standard deviation.

Example 4.2.9: Six hundred applicants for several post office jobs were rated on a scale from 1 to 50 points. The ratings had a mean of 32.5 points and a standard deviation of 7.1 points. How many standard deviations above or below the mean is a rating of 48 points? A rating of 30 points? A rating of 20 points?

Solution: Let d be the standard deviation, so $d = 7.1$ points. Note that 1 standard deviation above the mean is

$$32.5 + d = 32.5 + 7.1 = 39.6$$

and 2 standard deviations above the mean is

$$32.5 + 2d = 32.5 + 2(7.1) = 46.7$$

Using the same reasoning, if 48 is r standard deviations above the mean, then

$$32.5 + rd = 32.5 + r(7.1) = 48$$

Solving the equation $32.5 + r(7.1) = 48$ for r gives

$$r = \frac{48 - 32.5}{7.1} = \frac{15.5}{7.1} \approx 2.2$$

Similarly, any rating of p points is $\dfrac{p - 32.5}{7.1}$ standard deviations from the mean.

The number of standard deviations that a rating of 30 is away from the mean is

$$\frac{30 - 32.5}{7.1} = \frac{-2.5}{7.1} \approx -0.4$$

where the negative sign indicates that the rating is 0.4 standard deviation *below* the mean.

The number of standard deviations that a rating of 20 is away from the mean is

$$\frac{20 - 32.5}{7.1} = \frac{-12.5}{7.1} \approx -1.8$$

where the negative sign indicates that the rating is 1.8 standard deviations *below* the mean.

To summarize:

1. 48 points is 15.5 points above the mean, or approximately 2.2 standard deviations above the mean.
2. 30 points is 2.5 points below the mean, or approximately 0.4 standard deviation below the mean.
3. 20 points is 12.5 points below the mean, or approximately 1.8 standard deviations below the mean.

One more instance, which may seem trivial, is important to note:

32.5 points is 0 points from the mean, or 0 standard deviations from the mean.

Example 4.2.9 above shows that for a group of data, each value can be located with respect to the mean by using the standard deviation as a ruler. The process of subtracting the mean from each value and then dividing the result by the standard deviation is called **standardization**. Standardization is a useful tool because for each data value, it provides a measure of position relative to the rest of the data independently of the variable for which the data was collected and the units of the variable.

Note that the standardized values 2.2, –0.4, and –1.8 from the last example are all between –3 and 3; that is, the corresponding ratings 48, 30, and 20 are all within 3 standard deviations of the mean. This is not surprising, based on the following fact about the standard deviation.

Fact: In *any group of data*, most of the data are within 3 standard deviations of the mean.

Thus, when *any group of data* are standardized, most of the data are transformed to an interval on the number line centered about 0 and extending from –3 to 3. The mean is always transformed to 0.

4.3 Counting Methods

When a set contains a small number of objects, it is easy to list the objects and count them one by one. When the set is too large to count that way, and when the objects are related in a patterned or systematic way, there are some useful techniques for counting the objects without actually listing them.

Sets and Lists

The term **set** has been used informally in this review to mean a collection of objects that have some property, whether it is the collection of all positive integers, all points in a circular region, or all students in a school that have studied French. The objects of a set are called **members** or **elements**. Some sets are **finite**, which means that their members can be completely counted. Finite sets can, in principle, have all of their members listed, using curly brackets, such as the set of even digits {0, 2, 4, 6, 8}. Sets that are not finite are called **infinite** sets, such as the set of all integers. A set that has no members is called the **empty set** and is denoted by the symbol $\varnothing$. A set with one or more members is called **nonempty**. If A and B are sets and all of the members of A are also members of B, then A is a **subset** of B. For example, {2, 8} is a subset of {0, 2, 4, 6, 8}. Also, by convention, $\varnothing$ is a subset of every set.

A **list** is like a finite set, having members that can all be listed, but with two differences. In a list, the members are ordered—that is, rearranging the members of a list makes it a different list. Thus, the terms "first element," "second element," and so on, make sense in a list. Also, elements can be repeated in a list and the repetitions matter. For example, the list 1, 2, 3, 2 and the list 1, 2, 2, 3 are different lists, each with four elements, and they are both different from the list 1, 2, 3, which has three elements.

In contrast to a list, when the elements of a set are given, repetitions are not counted as additional elements and the order of the elements does not matter. For example, the set {1, 2, 3, 2} and the set {3, 1, 2} are the same set, which has three elements. For any finite set S, the number of elements of S is denoted by $|S|$. Thus, if $S = \{6.2, -9, \pi, 0.01, 0\}$, then $|S| = 5$. Also, $|\varnothing| = 0$.

Sets can be formed from other sets. If S and T are sets, then the **intersection** of S and T is the set of all elements that are in both S and T and is denoted by $S \cap T$. The **union** of S and T is the set of all elements that are in either S or T or both and is denoted by $S \cup T$. If sets S and T have no elements in common, they are called **disjoint** or **mutually exclusive**.

A useful way to represent two or three sets and their possible intersections and unions is a **Venn diagram**. In a Venn diagram, sets are represented by circular regions that overlap if they have elements in common but do not overlap if they are disjoint. Sometimes the circular regions are drawn inside a rectangular region, which represents a **universal set**, of which all other sets involved are subsets.

Example 4.3.1: Data Analysis Figure 10 below is a Venn diagram using circular regions to represent the three sets A, B, and C. In the Venn diagram, the three circular regions are drawn in a rectangular region representing a universal set U.

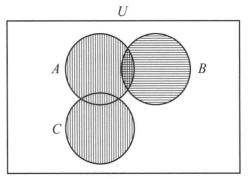

Data Analysis Figure 10

The regions with vertical stripes represent the set $A \cup C$. The regions with horizontal stripes represent the set B. The region with both kinds of stripes represents the set $A \cap B$. The sets B and C are mutually exclusive, often written as $B \cap C = \varnothing$.

The last example can be used to illustrate an elementary counting principle involving intersecting sets, called the **inclusion-exclusion principle**. This principle relates the numbers of elements in the union and intersection of two finite sets. The number of elements in the union of two sets equals the sum of their individual numbers of elements minus the number of elements in their intersection. If the sets in the example are finite, then we have for the union of A and B,

$$|A \cup B| = |A| + |B| - |A \cap B|$$

Because $A \cap B$ is a subset of both A and B, the subtraction is necessary to avoid counting the elements in $A \cap B$ twice. For the union of B and C, we have

$$|B \cup C| = |B| + |C|$$

because $B \cap C = \varnothing$.

Multiplication Principle

Suppose there are two choices to be made sequentially and that the second choice is independent of the first choice. Suppose also that there are k different possibilities for the first choice and m different possibilities for the second choice. The **multiplication principle** states that under those conditions, there are km different possibilities for the pair of choices.

For example, suppose that a meal is to be ordered from a restaurant menu and that the meal consists of one entrée and one dessert. If there are 5 entrées and 3 desserts on the menu, then there are $(5)(3) = 15$ different meals that can be ordered from the menu.

The multiplication principle applies in more complicated situations as well. If there are more than two independent choices to be made, then the number of different possible outcomes of all of the choices is the product of the numbers of possibilities for each choice.

Example 4.3.2: Suppose that a computer password consists of four characters such that the first character is one of the 10 digits from 0 to 9 and each of the next 3 characters is any one of the uppercase letters from the 26 letters of the English alphabet. How many different passwords are possible?

Solution: The description of the password allows repetitions of letters. Thus, there are 10 possible choices for the first character in the password and 26 possible choices for each of the next 3 characters in the password. Therefore, applying the multiplication principle, the number of possible passwords is $(10)(26)(26)(26) = 175,760$.

Note that if repetitions of letters are not allowed in the password, then the choices are not all independent, but a modification of the multiplication principle can still be applied. There are 10 possible choices for the first character in the password, 26 possible choices for the second character, 25 for the third character because the first letter cannot be repeated, and 24 for the fourth character because the first two letters cannot be repeated. Therefore, the number of possible passwords is $(10)(26)(25)(24) = 156,000$.

Example 4.3.3: Each time a coin is tossed, there are 2 possible outcomes—either it lands heads up or it lands tails up. Using this fact and the multiplication principle, you can conclude that if a coin is tossed 8 times, there are $(2)(2)(2)(2)(2)(2)(2)(2) = 2^8 = 256$ possible outcomes.

Permutations and Factorials

Suppose you want to determine the number of different ways the 3 letters A, B, and C can be placed in order from 1st to 3rd. The following is a list of all the possible orders in which the letters can be placed.

$$\text{ABC} \quad \text{ACB} \quad \text{BAC} \quad \text{BCA} \quad \text{CAB} \quad \text{CBA}$$

There are 6 possible orders for the 3 letters.

Now suppose you want to determine the number of different ways the 4 letters A, B, C, and D can be placed in order from 1st to 4th. Listing all of the orders for 4 letters is time-consuming, so it would be useful to be able to count the possible orders without listing them.

To order the 4 letters, one of the 4 letters must be placed first, one of the remaining 3 letters must be placed second, one of the remaining 2 letters must be placed third, and the last remaining letter must be placed fourth. Therefore, applying the multiplication principle, there are $(4)(3)(2)(1)$, or 24, ways to order the 4 letters.

More generally, suppose n objects are to be ordered from 1st to nth, and we want to count the number of ways the objects can be ordered. There are n choices for the first object, $n - 1$ choices for the second object, $n - 2$ choices for the third object, and so on, until there is only 1 choice for the nth object. Thus, applying the multiplication principle, the number of ways to order the n objects is equal to the product

$$n(n-1)(n-2)\cdots(3)(2)(1)$$

Each order is called a **permutation**, and the product above is called the number of permutations of n objects.

Because products of the form $n(n-1)(n-2)\cdots(3)(2)(1)$ occur frequently when counting objects, a special symbol $n!$, called **n-factorial**, is used to denote this product. For example,

$$1! = 1$$
$$2! = (2)(1)$$
$$3! = (3)(2)(1)$$
$$4! = (4)(3)(2)(1)$$

As a special definition, $0! = 1$.

Note that $n! = n(n-1)! = n(n-1)(n-2)! = n(n-1)(n-2)(n-3)!$ and so on.

Example 4.3.4: Suppose that 10 students are going on a bus trip, and each of the students will be assigned to one of the 10 available seats. Then the number of possible different seating arrangements of the students on the bus is

$$10! = (10)(9)(8)(7)(6)(5)(4)(3)(2)(1) = 3,628,800$$

Now suppose you want to determine the number of ways in which you can select 3 of the 5 letters A, B, C, D, and E and place them in order from 1st to 3rd. Reasoning as in the preceding examples, you find that there are $(5)(4)(3)$, or 60, ways to select and order them.

More generally, suppose that k objects will be selected from a set of n objects, where $k \le n$, and the k objects will be placed in order from 1st to kth. Then there are n choices for the first object, $n-1$ choices for the second object, $n-2$ choices for the third object, and so on, until there are $n-k+1$ choices for the kth object. Thus, applying the multiplication principle, the number of ways to select and order k objects from a set of n objects is $n(n-1)(n-2)\ldots(n-k+1)$. It is useful to note that

$$n(n-1)(n-2)\cdots(n-k+1) = n(n-1)(n-2)\cdots(n-k+1)\frac{(n-k)!}{(n-k)!} = \frac{n!}{(n-k)!}$$

This expression represents the number of **permutations of n objects taken k at a time**—that is, the number of ways to select and order k objects out of n objects. This number is commonly denoted by the notation $_nP_k$.

Example 4.3.5: How many different 5-digit positive integers can be formed using the digits 1, 2, 3, 4, 5, 6, and 7 if none of the digits can occur more than once in the integer?

Solution: This example asks how many ways there are to order 5 integers chosen from a set of 7 integers. According to the counting principle above, there are $(7)(6)(5)(4)(3) = 2,520$ ways to do this. Note that this is equal to $\dfrac{7!}{(7-5)!} = \dfrac{(7)(6)(5)(4)(3)(2!)}{2!} = (7)(6)(5)(4)(3)$.

Combinations

Given the 5 letters A, B, C, D, and E, suppose that you want to determine the number of ways in which you can select 3 of the 5 letters, but unlike before, you do not want to count different orders for the 3 letters. The following is a list of all of the ways in which 3 of the 5 letters can be selected without regard to the order of the letters.

$$\text{ABC} \quad \text{ABD} \quad \text{ABE} \quad \text{ACD} \quad \text{ACE}$$
$$\text{ADE} \quad \text{BCD} \quad \text{BCE} \quad \text{BDE} \quad \text{CDE}$$

There are 10 ways of selecting the 3 letters without order. There is a relationship between selecting with order and selecting without order.

The number of ways to select 3 of the 5 letters without order, which is 10, *multiplied by* the number of ways to order the 3 letters, which is 3!, or 6, *is equal to* the number of ways to select 3 of the 5 letters and order them, which is $\dfrac{5!}{2!} = 60$. In short,

$$(\text{number of ways to select without order}) \times (\text{number of ways to order})$$
$$= (\text{number of ways to select with order})$$

This relationship can also be rewritten as follows.

$$(\text{number of ways to select without order}) = \frac{(\text{number of ways to select with order})}{(\text{number of ways to order})}$$

For the example above, the number of ways to select without order is $\dfrac{\frac{5!}{2!}}{3!} = \dfrac{5!}{3!2!} = 10$.

More generally, suppose that k objects will be chosen from a set of n objects, where $k \le n$, but that the k objects will not be put in order. The number of ways in which this can be done is called the number of **combinations of n objects taken k at a time** and is given by the formula $\dfrac{n!}{k!(n-k)!}$.

Another way to refer to the number of combinations of n objects taken k at a time is **n choose k**, and two notations commonly used to denote this number are $_nC_k$ and $\dbinom{n}{k}$.

Example 4.3.6: Suppose you want to select a 3-person committee from a group of 9 students. How many ways are there to do this?

Solution: Since the 3 students on the committee are not ordered, you can use the formula for the combination of 9 objects taken 3 at a time, or "9 choose 3":

$$\frac{9!}{3!(9-3)!} = \frac{9!}{3!6!} = \frac{(9)(8)(7)}{(3)(2)(1)} = 84$$

Using the terminology of sets, given a set S consisting of n elements, n choose k is simply the number of subsets of S that consist of k elements.

The formula for n choose k, which is $\dfrac{n!}{k!(n-k)!}$ also holds when $k = 0$ and $k = n$. Therefore

1. n choose 0 is $\dfrac{n!}{0!n!} = 1$.

   (This reflects the fact that there is only one subset of S with 0 elements, namely the empty set).

2. n choose n is $\dfrac{n!}{n!0!} = 1$.

   (This reflects the fact that there is only one subset of S with n elements, namely the set S itself).

Finally, note that n choose k is always equal to n choose $n - k$, because

$$\frac{n!}{(n-k)!\,(n-(n-k))!} = \frac{n!}{(n-k)!\,k!} = \frac{n!}{k!(n-k)!}$$

4.4 Probability

Probability is a way of describing uncertainty in numerical terms. In this section, we review some of the terminology used in elementary probability theory.

A **probability experiment**, also called a **random experiment**, is an experiment for which the result, or **outcome**, is uncertain. We assume that all of the possible outcomes of an experiment are known before the experiment is performed, but which outcome will actually occur is unknown. The set of all possible outcomes of a random experiment is called the **sample space**, and any particular set of outcomes is called an **event**. For example, consider a cube with faces numbered 1 to 6, called a 6-sided die. Rolling the die once is an experiment in which there are 6 possible outcomes: either 1, 2, 3, 4, 5, or 6 will appear on the top face. The sample space for this experiment is {1, 2, 3, 4, 5, 6}. Here are two examples of events for this experiment.

Event 1: Rolling the number 4. This event has only one outcome.

Event 2: Rolling an odd number. This event has three outcomes.

The **probability** of an event is a number from 0 to 1, inclusive, that indicates the likelihood that the event occurs when the experiment is performed. The greater the number, the more likely the event.

Example 4.4.1: Consider the following experiment. A box contains 15 pieces of paper, each of which has the name of one of the 15 students in a high school class consisting of 7 juniors and 8 seniors, all with different names. The instructor will shake the box for a while and then choose a piece of paper at random and read the name. Here the sample space is the set of 15 names. The assumption of **random selection** means that each of the names is **equally likely** to be selected. If this assumption is made, then the probability that any one particular name will be selected is equal to $\frac{1}{15}$.

For any event E, the probability that E occurs is often written as $P(E)$. For the sample space in this example, $P(E)$, that is, the probability that event E occurs, is equal to

$$\frac{\text{the number of names in the event } E}{15}$$

If J is the event that the student selected is a junior, then $P(J) = \frac{7}{15}$.

In general, for a random experiment with a finite number of possible outcomes, if each outcome is equally likely to occur, then the probability that an event E occurs is defined by

$$P(E) = \frac{\text{the number of outcomes in the event } E}{\text{the number of possible outcomes in the experiment}}$$

In the case of rolling a 6-sided die, if the die is "fair," then the 6 outcomes are equally likely. So the probability of rolling a 4 is $\frac{1}{6}$, and the probability of rolling an odd number (that is, rolling a 1, 3, or 5) can be calculated as $\frac{3}{6} = \frac{1}{2}$.

The following are six general facts about probability.

Fact 1: If an event E is certain to occur, then $P(E) = 1$.

Fact 2: If an event E is certain *not* to occur, then $P(E) = 0$.

Fact 3: If an event E is possible but not certain to occur, then $0 < P(E) < 1$.

Fact 4: The probability that an event E will not occur is equal to $1 - P(E)$.

Fact 5: If E is an event, then the probability of E is the sum of the probabilities of the outcomes in E.

Fact 6: The sum of the probabilities of all possible outcomes of an experiment is 1.

If E and F are two events of an experiment, we consider two other events related to E and F.

Event 1: The event that both E and F occur, that is, outcomes in the set $E \cap F$

Event 2: The event that E or F, or both, occur, that is, outcomes in the set $E \cup F$

Events that cannot occur at the same time are said to be **mutually exclusive**. For example, if a 6-sided die is rolled once, the event of rolling an odd number and the event of rolling an even number are mutually exclusive. But rolling a 4 and rolling an even number are not mutually exclusive, since 4 is an outcome that is common to both events.

For events E and F, we have the following three rules.

Rule 1: P(either E or F, or both, occur) $= P(E) + P(F) - P$(both E and F occur), which is the inclusion-exclusion principle applied to probability.

Rule 2: If E and F are mutually exclusive, then P(both E and F occur) $= 0$, and therefore, P(either E or F, or both, occur) $= P(E) + P(F)$.

Rule 3: E and F are said to be **independent** if the occurrence of either event does not affect the occurrence of the other. If two events E and F are independent, then P(both E and F occur) $= P(E)P(F)$. For example, if a fair 6-sided die is rolled twice, the event E of rolling a 3 on the first roll and the event F of rolling a 3 on the second roll are independent, and the probability of rolling a 3 on both rolls is $P(E)P(F) = \left(\frac{1}{6}\right)\left(\frac{1}{6}\right) = \frac{1}{36}$. In this example, the experiment is actually "rolling the die twice," and each outcome is an ordered pair of results like "4 on the first roll and 1 on the second roll." But event E restricts only the first roll—to a 3—having no effect on the second roll; similarly, event F restricts only the second roll—to a 3—having no effect on the first roll.

Note that if $P(E) \neq 0$ and $P(F) \neq 0$, then events E and F cannot be both mutually exclusive and independent. For if E and F are independent, then P(both E and F occur) $= P(E)P(F) \neq 0$, but if E and F are mutually exclusive, then P(both E and F occur) $= 0$.

It is common to use the shorter notation "E and F" instead of "both E and F occur" and use "E or F" instead of "E or F or both occur." With this notation, we can restate the previous three rules as follows.

Rule 1: $P(E \text{ or } F) = P(E) + P(F) - P(E \text{ and } F)$

Rule 2: $P(E \text{ or } F) = P(E) + P(F)$ if E and F are mutually exclusive.

Rule 3: $P(E \text{ and } F) = P(E)P(F)$ if E and F are independent.

Example 4.4.2: If a fair 6-sided die is rolled once, let E be the event of rolling a 3 and let F be the event of rolling an odd number. These events are *not* independent. This is because rolling a 3 makes certain that the event of rolling an odd number occurs. Note that $P(E \text{ and } F) \neq P(E)P(F)$, since

$$P(E \text{ and } F) = P(E) = \frac{1}{6} \quad \text{and} \quad P(E)P(F) = \left(\frac{1}{6}\right)\left(\frac{1}{2}\right) = \frac{1}{12}$$

Example 4.4.3: A 12-sided die, with faces numbered 1 to 12, is to be rolled once, and each of the 12 possible outcomes is equally likely to occur. The probability of rolling a 4 is $\frac{1}{12}$, so the probability of rolling a number that is *not* a 4 is $1 - \frac{1}{12} = \frac{11}{12}$.

The probability of rolling a number that is either a multiple of 5 (that is, rolling a 5 or a 10) or an odd number (that is, rolling a 1, 3, 5, 7, 9, or 11) is equal to

$$P(\text{multiple of 5}) + P(\text{odd}) - P(\text{multiple of 5 and odd}) = \frac{2}{12} + \frac{6}{12} - \frac{1}{12} = \frac{7}{12}$$

Another way to calculate this probability is to notice that rolling a number that is either a multiple of 5 or an odd number is the same as rolling one of the seven numbers 1, 3, 5, 7, 9, 10, and 11, which are equally likely outcomes. So by using the ratio formula to calculate the probability, the required probability is $\frac{7}{12}$.

Example 4.4.4: Consider an experiment with events A, B, and C for which $P(A) = 0.23$, $P(B) = 0.40$, and $P(C) = 0.85$.

Suppose that events A and B are mutually exclusive and events B and C are independent. What is $P(A \text{ or } B)$ and $P(B \text{ or } C)$?

Solution: Since A and B are mutually exclusive,

$$P(A \text{ or } B) = P(A) + P(B) = 0.23 + 0.40 = 0.63$$

Since B and C are independent, $P(B \text{ and } C) = P(B)P(C)$. So

$$P(B \text{ or } C) = P(B) + P(C) - P(B \text{ and } C) = P(B) + P(C) - P(B) \, P(C)$$

Therefore,

$$P(B \text{ or } C) = 0.40 + 0.85 - (0.40)(0.85) = 1.25 - 0.34 = 0.91$$

Example 4.4.5: Suppose that there is a 6-sided die that is weighted in such a way that each time the die is rolled, the probabilities of rolling any of the numbers from 1 to 5 are all equal, but the probability of rolling a 6 is twice the probability of rolling a 1. When you roll the die once, the 6 outcomes are *not equally likely*. What are the probabilities of the 6 outcomes?

Solution: Let p equal the probability of rolling a 1. Then each of the probabilities of rolling a 2, 3, 4, or 5 is equal to p, and the probability of rolling a 6 is equal to $2p$. Therefore, since the sum of the probabilities of all possible outcomes is 1, it follows that

$$1 = P(1) + P(2) + P(3) + P(4) + P(5) + P(6) = p + p + p + p + p + 2p = 7p$$

So the probability of rolling each of the numbers from 1 to 5 is $\frac{1}{7}$, and the probability of rolling a 6 is $\frac{2}{7}$.

Example 4.4.6: Suppose that you roll the weighted 6-sided die from Example 4.4.5 twice. What is the probability that the first roll will be an odd number and the second roll will be an even number?

Solution: To calculate the probability that the first roll will be odd and the second roll will be even, note that these two events are independent. To calculate the probability that both occur, you must multiply the probabilities of the two independent events. First compute the individual probabilities.

$$P(\text{odd}) = P(1) + P(3) + P(5) = \frac{3}{7}$$

$$P(\text{even}) = P(2) + P(4) + P(6) = \frac{4}{7}$$

Then $P(\text{first roll is odd and second roll is even}) = P(\text{odd})\,P(\text{even}) = \left(\frac{3}{7}\right)\left(\frac{4}{7}\right) = \frac{12}{49}.$

Two events that happen sequentially are not always independent. The occurrence of the first event may affect the occurrence of the second event. In this case, the probability that *both* events happen is equal to the probability that the first event happens multiplied by the probability that, *given that the first event has already happened*, the second event will happen as well.

Example 4.4.7: A box contains 5 orange disks, 4 red disks, and 1 blue disk. You are to select two disks at random and without replacement from the box. What is the probability that the first disk you select will be red and the second disk you select will be orange?

Solution: To solve, you need to calculate the following two probabilities and then multiply them.

1. The probability that the first disk selected from the box will be red
2. The probability that the second disk selected from the box will be orange, given that the first disk selected from the box is red

The probability that the first disk you select will be red is $\frac{4}{10} = \frac{2}{5}$. If the first disk you select is red, there will be 5 orange disks, 3 red disks, and 1 blue disk left in the box, for a total of 9 disks. Therefore, the probability that the second disk you select will be orange, given that the first disk you selected is red, is $\frac{5}{9}$. Multiply the two probabilities to get $\left(\frac{2}{5}\right)\left(\frac{5}{9}\right) = \frac{2}{9}.$

4.5 Distributions of Data, Random Variables, and Probability Distributions

In data analysis, variables whose values depend on chance play an important role in linking distributions of data to probability distributions. Such variables are called random variables. We begin with a review of distributions of data.

Distributions of Data

Recall that relative frequency distributions given in a table or histogram are a common way to show how numerical data are distributed. In a histogram, the areas of the bars indicate where the data are concentrated. The histogram of the relative frequency distribution of the number of children in each of 25 families in Data Analysis Figure 4 below illustrates a small group of data, with only 6 distinct data values and 25 data values altogether. (Note: This is the second occurrence of Data Analysis Figure 4, it was first encountered in Example 4.1.10.)

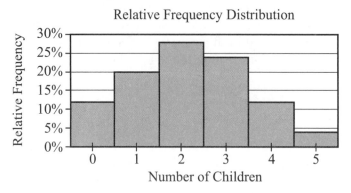

Data Analysis Figure 4 (repeated)

Many groups of data are much larger than 25 and have many more than 6 possible values, which are often measurements of quantities like length, money, or time.

Example 4.5.1: The lifetimes of 800 electric devices were measured. Because the lifetimes had many different values, the measurements were grouped into 50 intervals, or **classes**, of 10 hours each: 601 to 610 hours, 611 to 620 hours, and so on, up to 1,091 to 1,100 hours. The resulting relative frequency distribution, as a histogram, has 50 thin bars and many different bar heights, as shown in Data Analysis Figure 11 below.

Relative Frequency Distribution for Lifetimes of 800 Electric Devices

Data Analysis Figure 11

In the histogram, the median is represented by M, the mean is represented by m, and the standard deviation is represented by d.

According to the graph:

- A data value 1 standard deviation below the mean, represented by $m - d$, is between 660 and 670.
- The median, represented by M, is between 730 and 740.
- The mean, represented by m, is between 750 and 760.

- A data value 1 standard deviation above the mean, represented by $m + d$, is between 840 and 850.
- A data value 2 standard deviations above the mean, represented by $m + 2d$, is approximately 930.
- A data value 3 standard deviations above the mean, represented by $m + 3d$, is between 1,010 and 1,020.

The standard deviation marks show how most of the data are within 3 standard deviations of the mean, that is, between the numbers $m - 3d$ and $m + 3d$. Note that $m + 3d$ is shown in the figure, but $m - 3d$ is not.

The tops of the bars of the relative frequency distribution in the histogram in Data Analysis Figure 11 have a relatively smooth appearance and begin to look like a curve. In general, histograms that represent very large data sets grouped into many classes have a relatively smooth appearance. Consequently, the distribution can be modeled by a smooth curve that is close to the tops of the bars. Such a model retains the shape of the distribution but is independent of classes.

Recall from Example 4.1.10 that the sum of the areas of the bars of a relative frequency histogram is 1. Although the units on the horizontal axis of a histogram vary from one data set to another, the vertical scale can be adjusted (stretched or shrunk) so that the sum of the areas of the bars is 1. With this vertical scale adjustment, the area under the curve that models the distribution is also 1. This model curve is called a **distribution curve**, but it has other names as well, including **density curve** and **frequency curve**.

The purpose of the distribution curve is to give a good illustration of a large distribution of numerical data that does not depend on specific classes. To achieve this, the main property of a distribution curve is that the area under the curve in any vertical slice, just like a histogram bar, represents the proportion of the data that lies in the corresponding interval on the horizontal axis, which is at the base of the slice.

Random Variables

When analyzing data, it is common to choose a value of the data at random and consider that choice as a random experiment, as introduced in Section 4.4. Then, the probabilities of events involving the randomly chosen value may be determined. Given a distribution of data, a variable, say X, may be used to represent a randomly chosen value from the distribution. Such a variable X is an example of a **random variable**, which is a variable whose value is a numerical outcome of a random experiment.

Example 4.5.2: In Example 4.1.3, data consisting of numbers of children in each of 25 families was summarized in a frequency distribution table. For convenience, the frequency distribution table is repeated below.

Frequency Distribution

Number of Children	Frequency
0	3
1	5
2	7
3	6
4	3
5	1
Total	25

Let X be the random variable representing the number of children in a randomly chosen family among the 25 families. What is the probability that $X = 3$? That $X > 3$? That X is less than the mean of the distribution?

Solution: To determine the probability that $X = 3$, realize that this is the same as determining the probability that a family with 3 children will be chosen.

Since there are 6 families with 3 children and each of the 25 families is equally likely to be chosen, the probability that a family with 3 children will be chosen is $\frac{6}{25}$. That is, $X = 3$ is an event, and its probability is $P(X = 3) = \frac{6}{25}$, or 0.24. It is common to use the shorter notation $P(3)$ instead of $P(X = 3)$, so you could write $P(3) = 0.24$.

Note that in the histogram shown in Data Analysis Figure 4 below, the area of the bar corresponding to $X = 3$ as a proportion of the combined areas of all of the bars is equal to this probability. This indicates how probability is related to area in a histogram for a relative frequency distribution. (Note: This is the third occurrence of Data Analysis Figure 4, it was previously encountered in Example 4.1.10 and at the beginning of this section.)

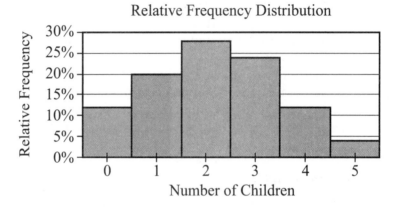

Data Analysis Figure 4 (repeated)

To determine the probability that $X > 3$, notice that the event $X > 3$ is the same as the event "$X = 4$ or $X = 5$". Because $X = 4$ and $X = 5$ are mutually exclusive events, we can use the rules of probability from Section 4.4.

$$P(X > 3) = P(4) + P(5) = \frac{3}{25} + \frac{1}{25} = 0.12 + 0.04 = 0.16$$

To determine the probability that X is less than the mean of the distribution, first compute the mean of the distribution as follows.

$$\frac{0(3) + 1(5) + 2(7) + 3(6) + 4(3) + 5(1)}{25} = \frac{54}{25} = 2.16$$

Then, calculate the probability that X is less than the mean of the distribution (that is, the probability that X is less than 2.16).

$$P(X < 2.16) = P(0) + P(1) + P(2) = \frac{3}{25} + \frac{5}{25} + \frac{7}{25} = \frac{15}{25} = 0.6$$

The following table shows all 6 possible values of X and their probabilities. This table is called the **probability distribution** of the random variable X.

X	P(X)
0	0.12
1	0.20
2	0.28
3	0.24
4	0.12
5	0.04

Note that the probabilities are simply the relative frequencies of the 6 possible values expressed as decimals instead of percents. The following statement indicates a fundamental link between data distributions and probability distributions.

Statement: For a random variable that represents a randomly chosen value from a distribution of data, the probability distribution of the random variable is the same as the relative frequency distribution of the data.

Because the probability distribution and the relative frequency distribution are essentially the same, the probability distribution can be represented by a histogram. Also, all of the descriptive statistics—such as mean, median, and standard deviation—that apply to the distribution of data also apply to the probability distribution. For example, we say that the probability distribution above has a mean of 2.16, a median of 2, and a standard deviation of about 1.3, since the 25 data values have these statistics, as you can check.

These statistics are similarly defined for the random variable X above. Thus, we would say that the **mean of the random variable X** is 2.16. Another name for the mean of a random variable is **expected value**. So we would also say that the expected value of X is 2.16.

Note that the mean of X is equal to

$$\frac{0(3) + 1(5) + 2(7) + 3(6) + 4(3) + 5(1)}{25}$$

which can also be expressed as

$$0\left(\frac{3}{25}\right) + 1\left(\frac{5}{25}\right) + 2\left(\frac{7}{25}\right) + 3\left(\frac{6}{25}\right) + 4\left(\frac{3}{25}\right) + 5\left(\frac{1}{25}\right)$$

which is the same as

$$0P(0) + 1P(1) + 2P(2) + 3P(3) + 4P(4) + 5P(5)$$

Therefore, the mean of the random variable X is the sum of the products $XP(X)$ for all values of X, that is, the sum of each value of X multiplied by its corresponding probability $P(X)$.

The preceding example involves a common type of random variable—one that represents a randomly chosen value from a distribution of data. However, the concept of a random variable is more general. A random variable can be any quantity whose value is the result of a random experiment. The possible values of the random variable are the same as the outcomes of the experiment. So any random experiment with numerical outcomes naturally has a random variable associated with it, as in the following example.

Example 4.5.3: Let Y represent the outcome of the experiment of rolling the weighted 6-sided die in Example 4.4.5. (In that example, the probabilities of rolling any of the numbers from 1 to 5 are all equal, but the probability of rolling a 6 is twice the probability of rolling a 1.) Then Y is a random variable with 6 possible values, the numbers 1 through 6. Each of the six values of Y has a probability. The probability distribution of the random variable Y is shown below, first in a table, then as a histogram.

Table Representing the Probability Distribution of Random Variable Y

Y	$P(Y)$
1	$\dfrac{1}{7}$
2	$\dfrac{1}{7}$
3	$\dfrac{1}{7}$
4	$\dfrac{1}{7}$
5	$\dfrac{1}{7}$
6	$\dfrac{2}{7}$

Histogram Representing the Probability Distribution of Random Variable Y

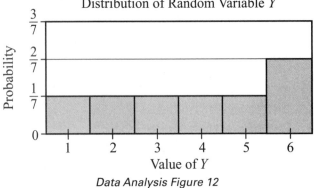

Data Analysis Figure 12

The mean, or expected value, of Y can be computed as

$$P(1) + 2P(2) + 3P(3) + 4P(4) + 5P(5) + 6P(6)$$

which is equal to

$$\left(\frac{1}{7}\right) + 2\left(\frac{1}{7}\right) + 3\left(\frac{1}{7}\right) + 4\left(\frac{1}{7}\right) + 5\left(\frac{1}{7}\right) + 6\left(\frac{2}{7}\right)$$

This sum simplifies to $\dfrac{1}{7} + \dfrac{2}{7} + \dfrac{3}{7} + \dfrac{4}{7} + \dfrac{5}{7} + \dfrac{12}{7}$, or $\dfrac{27}{7}$, which is approximately 3.86.

Both of the random variables X and Y above are examples of **discrete random variables** because their values consist of discrete points on a number line.

A basic fact about probability from Section 4.4 is that the sum of the probabilities of all possible outcomes of an experiment is 1, which can be confirmed by adding all of the probabilities in each of the probability distributions for the random variables X and Y above. Also, the sum of the areas of the bars in a histogram for the probability distribution of a random variable is 1. This fact is related to the following fundamental link between the areas of the bars of a histogram and the probabilities of a discrete random variable.

Fundamental Link: In a histogram representing the probability distribution of a random variable, the area of each bar is proportional to the probability represented by the bar.

If the die in Example 4.4.5 were a fair die instead of weighted, then the probability of each of the outcomes would be $\frac{1}{6}$, and consequently, each of the bars in the histogram of the probability distribution would have the same height. Such a flat histogram indicates a **uniform distribution**, since the probability is distributed uniformly over all possible outcomes.

The Normal Distribution

Many natural processes yield data that have a relative frequency distribution shaped somewhat like a bell, as in the distribution with mean m and standard deviation d in Data Analysis Figure 13 below.

Approximately Normal Relative Frequency Distribution

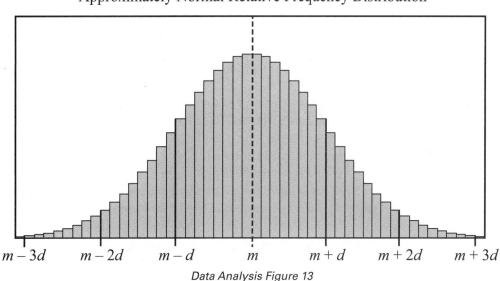

Data Analysis Figure 13

Such data are said to be **approximately normally distributed** and have the following four properties.

Property 1: The mean, median, and mode are all nearly equal.

Property 2: The data are grouped fairly symmetrically about the mean.

Property 3: About two-thirds of the data are within 1 standard deviation of the mean.

Property 4: Almost all of the data are within 2 standard deviations of the mean.

As stated above, you can always associate a random variable X with a distribution of data by letting X be a randomly chosen value from the distribution. If X is such a random variable for the distribution in Data Analysis Figure 13, we say that X is approximately normally distributed.

As described in the example about the lifetimes of 800 electric devices, relative frequency distributions are often approximated using a smooth curve—a distribution curve or density curve—for the tops of the bars in the histogram. The region below such a curve represents a distribution called a **continuous probability distribution**. There are many different continuous probability distributions, but the most important one is the **normal distribution**, which has a bell-shaped curve like the one shown in Data Analysis Figure 14 below.

Normal Distribution

Data Analysis Figure 14

Just as a data distribution has a mean and standard deviation, the normal probability distribution has a mean and standard deviation. Also, the properties listed above for the approximately normal distribution of data hold for the normal distribution, except that the mean, median, and mode are exactly the same and the distribution is perfectly symmetric about the mean.

A normal distribution, though always shaped like a bell, can be centered around any mean and can be spread out to a greater or lesser degree, depending on the standard deviation. The less the standard deviation, the less spread out the curve is; that is to say, at the mean the curve is higher and as you move away from the mean in either direction it drops down toward the horizontal axis faster.

In Data Analysis Figure 15 below there are two normal distributions that have different centers, −10 and 5, respectively, but the spread of the distributions is the same. The two distributions have the same shape, so one can be shifted horizontally onto the other.

Two Normal Distributions with the Same Spread

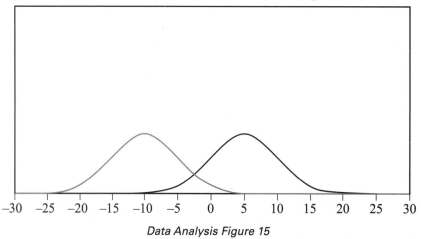

Data Analysis Figure 15

In Data Analysis Figure 16 below there are two normal distributions that have different spreads, but the same center. The mean of both distributions is 0. One of the distributions is high and spread narrowly about the mean; and the other is low and spread widely about the mean. The standard deviation of the high, narrow distribution is less than the standard deviation of the low, wide distribution.

Two Normal Distributions with the Same Center

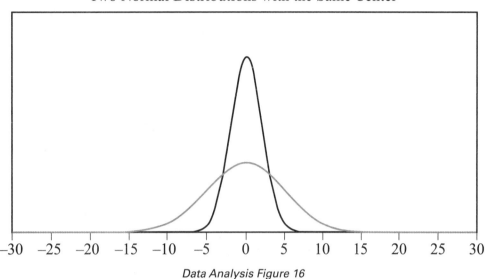

Data Analysis Figure 16

As mentioned earlier, areas of the bars in a histogram for a discrete random variable correspond to probabilities for the values of the random variable; the sum of the areas is 1 and the sum of the probabilities is 1. This is also true for a continuous probability distribution: the area of the region under the curve is 1, and the areas of vertical slices of the region, like the areas of the bars of a histogram, are equal to probabilities of a random variable associated with the distribution. Such a random variable is called a **continuous random variable**, and it plays the same role as a random variable that represents a randomly chosen value from a distribution of data. The main difference is that we seldom consider the event in which a continuous random variable is equal to a single value like $X = 3$; rather, we consider events that are described by intervals of values such as $1 < X < 3$ and $X > 10$. Such events correspond to vertical slices under a continuous probability distribution, and the areas of the vertical slices are the probabilities of the corresponding events. (Consequently, the probability of an event such as $X = 3$ would correspond to the area of a line segment, which is 0.)

Example 4.5.4: If W is a random variable that is normally distributed with a mean of 5 and a standard deviation of 2, what is $P(W > 5)$? Approximately what is $P(3 < W < 7)$? Which of the four numbers 0.5, 0.1, 0.05, or 0.01 is the best estimate of $P(W < -1)$?

Solution: Data Analysis Figure 17 below is a graph of a normal distribution with a mean of 5 and a standard deviation of 2.

The numbers 3 and 7 are 1 standard deviation away from the mean, the numbers 1 and 9 are 2 standard deviations away from the mean, and the numbers −1 and 11 are 3 standard deviations away from the mean.

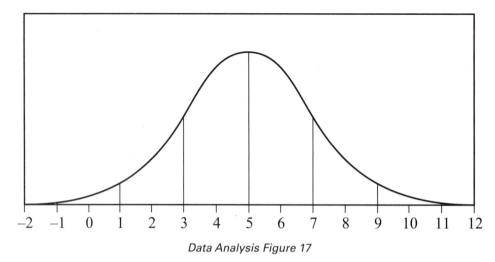

Data Analysis Figure 17

Since the mean of the distribution is 5, and the distribution is symmetric about the mean, the event $W > 5$ corresponds to exactly half of the area under the normal distribution. So $P(W > 5) = \dfrac{1}{2}$.

For the event $3 < W < 7$, note that since the standard deviation of the distribution is 2, the values 3 and 7 are one standard deviation below and above the mean, respectively. Since about two-thirds of the area is within one standard deviation of the mean, $P(3 < W < 7)$ is approximately $\dfrac{2}{3}$.

For the event $W < -1$, note that -1 is 3 standard deviations below the mean. Since the graph makes it fairly clear that the area of the region under the normal curve to the left of -1 is much less than 5 percent of all of the area, the best of the four estimates given for $P(W < -1)$ is 0.01.

The **standard normal distribution** is a normal distribution with a mean of 0 and standard deviation equal to 1. To transform a normal distribution with a mean of m and a standard deviation of d to a standard normal distribution, you standardize the values; that is, you subtract m from any observed value of the normal distribution and then divide the result by d.

Very precise values for probabilities associated with normal distributions can be computed using calculators, computers, or statistical tables for the standard normal distribution. In the preceding example, more precise values for $P(3 < W < 7)$ and $P(W < -1)$ are 0.683 and 0.0013, respectively. Such calculations are beyond the scope of this review.

4.6 Data Interpretation Examples

Example 4.6.1: This example is based on the following table.

DISTRIBUTION OF CUSTOMER COMPLAINTS RECEIVED BY
AIRLINE *P*, 2003 and 2004

Category	2003	2004
Flight problem	20.0%	22.1%
Baggage	18.3	21.8
Customer service	13.1	11.3
Reservation and ticketing	5.8	5.6
Credit	1.0	0.8
Special passenger accommodation	0.9	0.9
Other	40.9	37.5
Total	100.0%	100.0%
Total number of complaints	22,998	13,278

(a) Approximately how many complaints concerning credit were received by Airline *P* in 2003 ?

(b) By approximately what percent did the total number of complaints decrease from 2003 to 2004 ?

(c) Based on the information in the table, which of the following three statements are true?

Statement 1: In each of the years 2003 and 2004, complaints about flight problems, baggage, and customer service together accounted for more than 50 percent of all customer complaints received by Airline *P*.

Statement 2: The number of special passenger accommodation complaints was unchanged from 2003 to 2004.

Statement 3: From 2003 to 2004, the number of flight problem complaints increased by more than 2 percent.

Solutions:

(a) According to the table, in 2003, 1 percent of the total number of complaints concerned credit. Therefore, the number of complaints concerning credit is equal to 1 percent of 22,998. By converting 1 percent to its decimal equivalent, you obtain that the number of complaints in 2003 is equal to (0.01)(22,998), or about 230.

(b) The decrease in the total number of complaints from 2003 to 2004 was 22,998 − 13,278, or 9,720. Therefore, the percent decrease was $\left(\dfrac{9,720}{22,998}\right)(100\%)$, or approximately 42 percent.

(c) Since $20.0 + 18.3 + 13.1$ and $22.1 + 21.8 + 11.3$ are both greater than 50, statement 1 is true. For statement 2, the *percent* of special passenger accommodation complaints *did* remain the same from 2003 to 2004, but the number of such complaints decreased because the total number of complaints decreased. Thus, statement 2 is false. For statement 3, the *percents* shown in the table for flight problems do in fact increase by more than 2 percentage points, but the bases of the percents are different. The total number of complaints in 2004 was much lower than the total number of complaints in 2003, and clearly 20 percent of 22,998 is greater than 22.1 percent of 13,278. So, the number of flight problem complaints actually decreased from 2003 to 2004, and statement 3 is false.

Example 4.6.2: This example is based on the following circle graph.

UNITED STATES PRODUCTION OF PHOTOGRAPHIC EQUIPMENT AND SUPPLIES IN 1971

Total: $3,980 million

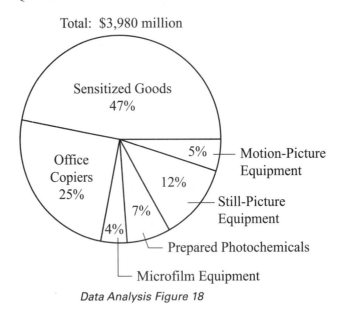

Data Analysis Figure 18

(a) Approximately what was the ratio of the value of sensitized goods to the value of still-picture equipment produced in 1971 in the United States?

(b) If the value of office copiers produced in 1971 was 30 percent greater than the corresponding value in 1970, what was the value of office copiers produced in 1970 ?

Solutions:

(a) The ratio of the value of sensitized goods to the value of still-picture equipment is equal to the ratio of the corresponding percents shown because the percents have the same base, which is the total value. Therefore, the ratio is 47 to 12, or approximately 4 to 1.

(b) The value of office copiers produced in 1971 was 0.25 times $3,980 million, or $995 million. Therefore, if the corresponding value in 1970 was x million dollars, then $1.3x = 995$ million. Solving for x yields $x = \dfrac{995}{1.3} \approx 765$, so the value of office copiers produced in 1970 was approximately $765 million.

Example 4.6.3: In a survey of 250 European travelers, 93 have traveled to Africa, 155 have traveled to Asia, and of these two groups, 70 have traveled to both continents, as illustrated in the Venn diagram below.

TRAVELERS SURVEYED: 250

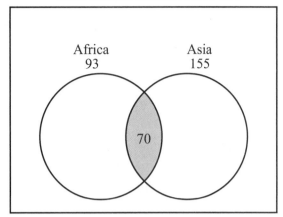

Data Analysis Figure 19

(a) How many of the travelers surveyed have traveled to Africa but *not* to Asia?

(b) How many of the travelers surveyed have traveled to *at least one* of the two continents of Africa and Asia?

(c) How many of the travelers surveyed have traveled *neither* to Africa *nor* to Asia?

Solutions:

In the Venn diagram in Data Analysis Figure 19, the rectangular region represents the set of all travelers surveyed; the two circular regions represent the two sets of travelers to Africa and Asia, respectively; and the shaded region represents the subset of those who have traveled to both continents.

(a) The travelers surveyed who have traveled to Africa but not to Asia are represented in the Venn diagram by *the part of the left circle that is not shaded*. This suggests that the answer can be found by taking the shaded part away from the leftmost circle, in effect, subtracting the 70 from the 93, to get **23** travelers who have traveled to Africa, but not to Asia.

(b) The travelers surveyed who have traveled to at least one of the two continents of Africa and Asia are represented in the Venn diagram by that part of the rectangle that is *in at least one of the two circles*. This suggests adding the two numbers 93 and 155. But the 70 travelers who have traveled to both continents would be counted twice in the sum 93 + 155. To correct the double counting, subtract 70 from the sum so that these 70 travelers are counted only once:

$$93 + 155 - 70 = 178$$

(c) The travelers surveyed who have traveled neither to Africa nor to Asia are represented in the Venn diagram by the part of the rectangle that is not in either circle. Let N be the number of these travelers. Note that the entire rectangular region has two main nonoverlapping parts: the part outside the circles and the part inside the circles. The first part represents N travelers and the second part represents $93 + 155 - 70 = 178$ travelers (from part b). Therefore, $250 = N + 178$, and solving for N yields $N = 250 - 178 = 72$.

DATA ANALYSIS EXERCISES

Exercise 1. The daily temperatures, in degrees Fahrenheit, for 10 days in May were 61, 62, 65, 65, 65, 68, 74, 74, 75, and 77.

    (a) Find the mean, median, mode, and range of the temperatures.

    (b) If each day had been 7 degrees warmer, what would have been the mean, median, mode, and range of those 10 temperatures?

Exercise 2. The numbers of passengers on 9 airline flights were 22, 33, 21, 28, 22, 31, 44, 50, and 19. The standard deviation of these 9 numbers is approximately equal to 10.22.

    (a) Find the mean, median, mode, range, and interquartile range of the 9 numbers.

    (b) If each flight had had 3 times as many passengers, what would have been the mean, median, mode, range, interquartile range, and standard deviation of the 9 numbers?

    (c) If each flight had had 2 fewer passengers, what would have been the interquartile range and standard deviation of the 9 numbers?

Exercise 3. A group of 20 values has a mean of 85 and a median of 80. A different group of 30 values has a mean of 75 and a median of 72.

    (a) What is the mean of the 50 values?

    (b) What is the median of the 50 values?

Exercise 4. Find the mean and median of the values of the random variable X, whose relative frequency distribution is given in the following table.

X	Relative Frequency
0	0.18
1	0.33
2	0.10
3	0.06
4	0.33

Exercise 5. Eight hundred insects were weighed, and the resulting measurements, in milligrams, are summarized in the following boxplot.

Data Analysis Figure 20

    (a) What are the range, the three quartiles, and the interquartile range of the measurements?

    (b) If the 80th percentile of the measurements is 130 milligrams, about how many measurements are between 126 milligrams and 130 milligrams?

Exercise 6. In how many different ways can the letters in the word STUDY be ordered?

Exercise 7.   Martha invited 4 friends to go with her to the movies. There are 120 different ways in which they can sit together in a row of 5 seats, one person per seat. In how many of those ways is Martha sitting in the middle seat?

Exercise 8.   How many 3-digit positive integers are odd and do not contain the digit 5?

Exercise 9.   From a box of 10 lightbulbs, you are to remove 4. How many different sets of 4 lightbulbs could you remove?

Exercise 10.   A talent contest has 8 contestants. Judges must award prizes for first, second, and third places, with no ties.

(a) In how many different ways can the judges award the 3 prizes?

(b) How many different groups of 3 people can get prizes?

Exercise 11.   If an integer is randomly selected from all positive 2-digit integers, what is the probability that the integer chosen has

(a) a 4 in the tens place?

(b) at least one 4 in the tens place or the units place?

(c) no 4 in either place?

Exercise 12.   In a box of 10 electrical parts, 2 are defective.

(a) If you choose one part at random from the box, what is the probability that it is *not* defective?

(b) If you choose two parts at random from the box, without replacement, what is the probability that both are defective?

Exercise 13.   A certain college has 8,978 full-time students, some of whom live on campus and some of whom live off campus.

The following table shows the distribution of the 8,978 full-time students, by class and living arrangement.

	Freshmen	Sophomores	Juniors	Seniors
Live on campus	1,812	1,236	950	542
Live off campus	625	908	1,282	1,623

(a) If one full-time student is selected at random, what is the probability that the student who is chosen will not be a freshman?

(b) If one full-time student who lives off campus is selected at random, what is the probability that the student will be a senior?

(c) If one full-time student who is a freshman or sophomore is selected at random, what is the probability that the student will be a student who lives on campus?

Exercise 14.   Let A, B, C, and D be events for which

$$P(A \text{ or } B) = 0.6, P(A) = 0.2, P(C \text{ or } D) = 0.6, \text{ and } P(C) = 0.5.$$

The events A and B are mutually exclusive, and the events C and D are independent.

(a) Find $P(B)$.

(b) Find $P(D)$.

Exercise 15. Lin and Mark each attempt independently to decode a message. If the probability that Lin will decode the message is 0.80 and the probability that Mark will decode the message is 0.70, find the probability that

(a) both will decode the message

(b) at least one of them will decode the message

(c) neither of them will decode the message

Exercise 16. Data Analysis Figure 21 below shows the graph of a normal distribution with mean m and standard deviation d, including approximate percents of the distribution corresponding to the six regions shown.

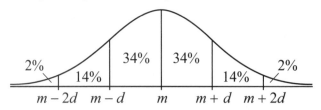

Data Analysis Figure 21

Suppose the heights of a population of 3,000 adult penguins are approximately normally distributed with a mean of 65 centimeters and a standard deviation of 5 centimeters.

(a) Approximately how many of the adult penguins are between 65 centimeters and 75 centimeters tall?

(b) If an adult penguin is chosen at random from the population, approximately what is the probability that the penguin's height will be less than 60 centimeters? Give your answer to the nearest 0.05.

Exercise 17. This exercise is based on the following graph.

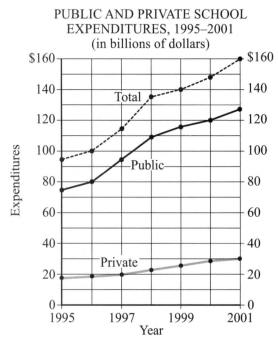

Data Analysis Figure 22

(a) For which year did total expenditures increase the most from the year before?

(b) For 2001, private school expenditures were what percent of total expenditures? Give your answer to the nearest percent.

Exercise 18.   This exercise is based on the following data.

DISTRIBUTION OF WORKFORCE BY OCCUPATIONAL CATEGORY
FOR REGION *Y* IN 2001 AND PROJECTED FOR 2025

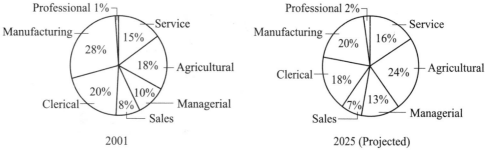

Data Analysis Figure 23

(a) In 2001, how many categories each comprised more than 25 million workers?

(b) What is the ratio of the number of workers in the Agricultural category in 2001 to the projected number of such workers in 2025?

(c) From 2001 to 2025, there is a projected increase in the number of workers in which of the following three categories?

Category 1: Sales

Category 2: Service

Category 3: Clerical

Exercise 19. This exercise is based on the following data.

A FAMILY'S EXPENDITURES AND SAVINGS
AS A PERCENT OF ITS GROSS ANNUAL INCOME*

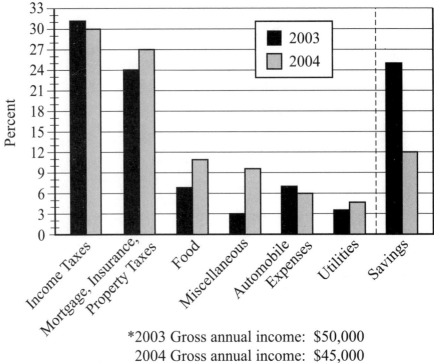

*2003 Gross annual income: $50,000
2004 Gross annual income: $45,000

Data Analysis Figure 24

(a) In 2003 the family used a total of 49 percent of its gross annual income for two of the categories listed. What was the total amount of the family's income used for those same categories in 2004?

(b) Of the seven categories listed, which category of expenditure had the greatest percent increase from 2003 to 2004?

ANSWERS TO DATA ANALYSIS EXERCISES

Exercise 1.   In degrees Fahrenheit, the statistics are

        (a) mean = 68.6, median = 66.5, mode = 65, range = 16

        (b) mean = 75.6, median = 73.5, mode = 72, range = 16

Exercise 2.   (a) mean = 30, median = 28, mode = 22,

            range = 31, interquartile range = 17

        (b) mean = 90, median = 84, mode = 66,

            range = 93, interquartile range = 51,

            standard deviation $\approx 3(10.22) = 30.66$

        (c) interquartile range = 17, standard deviation ≈ 10.22

Exercise 3.   (a) mean = 79

        (b) The median cannot be determined from the information given.

Exercise 4.   mean = 2.03, median = 1

Exercise 5.   (a) range = 41, $Q_1 = 114$, $Q_2 = 118$, $Q_3 = 126$, interquartile range = 12

        (b) 40 measurements

Exercise 6.   5! = 120

Exercise 7.   24

Exercise 8.   288

Exercise 9.   210

Exercise 10.   (a) 336   (b) 56

Exercise 11.   (a) $\dfrac{1}{9}$ (b) $\dfrac{1}{5}$ (c) $\dfrac{4}{5}$

Exercise 12.   (a) $\dfrac{4}{5}$ (b) $\dfrac{1}{45}$

Exercise 13.   (a) $\dfrac{6,541}{8,978}$ (b) $\dfrac{1,623}{4,438}$ (c) $\dfrac{3,048}{4,581}$

Exercise 14.   (a) 0.4   (b) 0.2

Exercise 15.   (a) 0.56   (b) 0.94   (c) 0.06

Exercise 16.   (a) 1,440   (b) 0.15

Exercise 17.   (a) 1998   (b) 19%

Exercise 18.   (a) Three   (b) 9 to 14, or $\dfrac{9}{14}$ (c) Categories 1, 2, and 3

Exercise 19.   (a) $17,550   (b) Miscellaneous

GRE® Practice Test 1

Your goals for this chapter

◢ Take the first full-length authentic *GRE®* General Test under actual test time limits
◢ Check your answers and read explanations for every question
◢ Use your results to identify your strengths and weaknesses

Taking Practice Test 1

现在考生已经熟悉了GRE考试的三大测试内容，可以开始做第一份模拟测试题了，以了解一下自己真正的水平。测试将从下页开始。测试时间为3小时30分钟。每个部分（section）的时间分配出现在该部分的开头。

尝试在真实考试条件下完成模拟测试（一）。找一个安静的地方，留出充足的时间来完成整个测试，不要受到干扰。做完一个section再做另一个section，不要交叉做。用手表或计时器来为每一个section计时。

在本测试的文字推理（Verbal Reasoning）和数量推理（Quantitative Reasoning）部分，考生需要把选项直接标注在书上。但参加真正的GRE机考时，考生要做的是在电脑上点击正确的选项。在本测试的分析性写作（Analytical Writing）部分，作答方式取决于考生计划参加的考试类型。如果考生计划参加机考，在本次测试中就应该使用计算机进行文字录入；如果考生计划参加纸笔考试，就需要准备一些空白纸，把作文手写在纸上。

需要注意的是，本部分的模拟测试在结构上类似于纸笔考试。因此，每部分的题目数量和考试时长与机考不同。测试结果将使考生清楚地知道自己是否已经准备好参加真正的考试，但考生应利用*POWERPREP®*中的模拟试题来更真实地体验机考。

本测试的结尾附带参考答案。考生可以将自己的作答对照参考答案，然后按照说明计算文字推理（Verbal Reasoning）和数量推理（Quantitative Reasoning）部分的得分，评估自己在分析性写作（Analytical Writing）部分的表现。参考答案中还包含对每个问题的解析。仔细阅读解析部分，尤其要注意做错的那些题目。

在完成模拟测试（一）之后，考生就会对自己参加真正的GRE考试的准备情况有更清晰的了解；还能知道自己是否有足够快的速度在规定的时间内完成各个部分，那么相应地是否需要提高做题的速度。考生对自己在这次测试中的表现进行评估后，就可以决定自己需要在哪些方面做更多的准备。如果考生需要更多的考试准备材料和建议，请访问如下网址：www.ets.org/gre/prepare。如果考生感觉自己准备充分，就可以继续做模拟测试（二）（见第九章）。

SECTION 1
Analytical Writing

ANALYZE AN ISSUE

30 minutes

You will be given a brief quotation that states or implies an issue of general interest and specific instructions on how to respond to that issue. You will then have 30 minutes to plan and compose a response according to the specific instructions. A response to any other issue will receive a score of zero.

Make sure that you respond according to the specific instructions and support your position on the issue with reasons and examples drawn from such areas as your reading, experience, observations, and/or academic studies.

Trained GRE readers will evaluate your response for its overall quality, based on how well you:

- Respond to the specific task instructions
- Consider the complexities of the issue
- Organize, develop, and express your ideas
- Support your ideas with relevant reasons and/or examples
- Control the elements of standard written English

Before you begin writing, you may want to think for a few minutes about the issue and the specific task instructions and then plan your response. Be sure to develop your position fully and organize it coherently, but leave time to reread what you have written and make any revisions you think are necessary.

Issue Topic

The best way to teach is to praise positive actions and ignore negative ones.

Write a response in which you discuss the extent to which you agree or disagree with the recommendation and explain your reasoning for the position you take. In developing and supporting your position, describe specific circumstances in which adopting the recommendation would or would not be advantageous and explain how these examples shape your position.

SECTION 2
Analytical Writing

ANALYZE AN ARGUMENT

30 minutes

You will be given a short passage that presents an argument and specific instructions on how to respond to that passage. You will then have 30 minutes to plan and compose a response in which you evaluate the passage according to the specific instructions. A response to any other argument will receive a score of zero.

Note that you are NOT being asked to present your own views on the subject. Make sure that you respond according to the specific instructions and support your evaluation with relevant reasons and/or examples.

Trained GRE readers will evaluate your response for its overall quality, based on how well you:

- Respond to the specific task instructions
- Identify and analyze features of the argument relevant to the assigned task
- Organize, develop, and express your ideas
- Support your analysis with relevant reasons and/or examples
- Control the elements of standard written English

Before you begin writing, you may want to think a few minutes about the argument passage and the specific task instructions and then plan your response. Be sure to develop your response fully and organize it coherently, but leave time to reread what you have written and make any revisions that you think are necessary.

Argument Topic

The following appeared in an article written by Dr. Karp, an anthropologist.

"Twenty years ago, Dr. Field, a noted anthropologist, visited the island of Tertia and concluded from his observations that children in Tertia were reared by an entire village rather than by their own biological parents. However, my recent interviews with children living in the group of islands that includes Tertia show that these children spend much more time talking about their biological parents than about other adults in the village. This research of mine proves that Dr. Field's conclusion about Tertian village culture is invalid and thus that the observation-centered approach to studying cultures is invalid as well. The interview-centered method that my team of graduate students is currently using in Tertia will establish a much more accurate understanding of child-rearing traditions there and in other island cultures."

Write a response in which you discuss what specific evidence is needed to evaluate the argument and explain how the evidence would weaken or strengthen the argument.

NO TEST MATERIAL ON THIS PAGE

SECTION 3
Verbal Reasoning
Time—35 minutes
25 Questions

For each of Questions 1 to 4, select <u>one</u> answer choice unless otherwise instructed.

Questions 1 to 3 are based on the following reading passage.

Whether the languages of the ancient American peoples were used for expressing abstract universal concepts can be clearly answered in the case of Nahuatl. Nahuatl, like Greek and German, is a language that allows the formation of extensive com-
line
pounds. By the combination of radicals or semantic elements, single compound words
5   can express complex conceptual relations, often of an abstract universal character.

    The *tlamatinime* (those who know) were able to use this rich stock of abstract terms to express the nuances of their thought. They also availed themselves of other forms of expression with metaphorical meaning, some probably original, some derived from Toltec coinages. Of these forms, the most characteristic in Nahuatl is the juxtaposition
10   of two words that, because they are synonyms, associated terms, or even contraries, complement each other to evoke one single idea. Used metaphorically, the juxtaposed terms connote specific or essential traits of the being they refer to, introducing a mode of poetry as an almost habitual form of expression.

For the following question, consider each of the choices separately and select all that apply.

1.   Which of the following can be inferred from the passage regarding present-day research relating to Nahuatl?

    A Some record or evidence of the thought of the *tlamatinime* is available.

    B For at least some Nahuatl expressions, researchers are able to trace their derivation from another ancient American language.

    C Researchers believe that in Nahuatl, abstract universal concepts are always expressed metaphorically.

2.   Select the sentence in the passage in which the author introduces a specific Nahuatl mode of expression that is not identified as being shared with certain European languages.

3.   In the context in which it appears, "coinages" (line 9) most nearly means

    (A) adaptations
    (B) creations
    (C) idiosyncrasies
    (D) pronunciations
    (E) currencies

GO ON TO NEXT PAGE ↘

Question 4 is based on the following reading passage.

At a certain period in Earth's history, its atmosphere contained almost no oxygen, although plants were producing vast quantities of oxygen. As a way of reconciling these two facts, scientists have hypothesized that nearly all of the oxygen being produced was taken up by iron on Earth's surface. Clearly, however, **this explanation is inadequate.** New studies show that **the amount of iron on Earth's surface was not sufficient to absorb anywhere near as much oxygen as was being produced.** Therefore, something in addition to the iron on Earth's surface must have absorbed much of the oxygen produced by plant life.

4. In the argument given, the two portions in **boldface** play which of the following roles?

   Ⓐ The first is a claim made by the argument in support of a certain position; the second is that position.

   Ⓑ The first is a judgment made by the argument about a certain explanation; the second is that explanation.

   Ⓒ The first expresses the argument's dismissal of an objection to the position it seeks to establish; the second is that position.

   Ⓓ The first sums up the argument's position with regard to a certain hypothesis; the second provides grounds for that position.

   Ⓔ The first is a concession by the argument that its initial formulation of the position it seeks to establish requires modification; the second presents that position in a modified form.

For Questions 5 to 8, select one entry for each blank from the corresponding column of choices. Fill all blanks in the way that best completes the text.

---

5. In her later years, Bertha Pappenheim was an apostle of noble but already (i)_____ notions, always respected for her integrity, her energy, and her resolve but increasingly out of step and ultimately (ii)_____ even her own organization.

Blank (i)	Blank (ii)
Ⓐ anachronistic	Ⓓ emulated by
Ⓑ accepted	Ⓔ appreciated by
Ⓒ exotic	Ⓕ alienated from

6. The reception given to Kimura's radical theory of molecular evolution shows that when _____ fights orthodoxy to a draw, then novelty has seized a good chunk of space from convention.

Ⓐ imitation
Ⓑ reaction
Ⓒ dogmatism
Ⓓ invention
Ⓔ caution

7. The (i)_____ of Vladimir Nabokov as one of North America's literary giants has thrown the spotlight on his peripheral activities and has thus served to (ii)_____ his efforts as an amateur entomologist.

Blank (i)	Blank (ii)
(A) stigmatization	(D) foreground
(B) lionization	(E) transcend
(C) marginalization	(F) obscure

8. Mathematicians have a distinctive sense of beauty: they strive to present their ideas and results in a clear and compelling fashion, dictated by _____ as well as by logic.

(A) caprice
(B) aesthetics
(C) obligation
(D) methodologies
(E) intellect

GO ON TO NEXT PAGE ↘

For each of Questions 9 to 13, select **one** answer choice unless otherwise instructed.

Questions 9 to 12 are based on the following reading passage.

Animal signals, such as the complex songs of birds, tend to be costly. A bird, by singing, may forfeit time that could otherwise be spent on other important behaviors such as foraging or resting. Singing may also advertise an individual's location to rivals or preda-
line tors and impair the ability to detect their approach. Although these types of cost may
5 be important, discussions of the cost of singing have generally focused on energy costs. Overall the evidence is equivocal: for instance, while Eberhardt found increases in energy consumption during singing for Carolina wrens, Chappell found no effect of crowing on energy consumption in roosters.

To obtain empirical data regarding the energy costs of singing, Thomas examined
10 the relationship between song rate and overnight changes in body mass of male nightingales. Birds store energy as subcutaneous fat deposits or "body reserves"; changes in these reserves can be reliably estimated by measuring changes in body mass. If singing has important energy costs, nightingales should lose more body mass on nights when their song rate is high. Thomas found that nightingales reached a sig-
15 nificantly higher body mass at dusk and lost more mass overnight on nights when their song rate was high.

These results suggest that there may be several costs of singing at night associated with body reserves. The increased metabolic cost of possessing higher body mass contributes to the increased overnight mass loss. The strategic regulation of evening body
20 reserves is also likely to incur additional costs, as nightingales must spend more time foraging in order to build up larger body reserves. The metabolic cost of singing itself may also contribute to increased loss of reserves. This metabolic cost may arise from the muscular and neural activity involved in singing or from behaviors associated with singing. For example, birds may expend more of their reserves on thermoregulation if
25 they spend the night exposed to the wind on a song post than if they are in a sheltered roost site. Thomas's data therefore show that whether or not singing per se has an important metabolic cost, metabolic costs associated with singing can have an important measurable effect on a bird's daily energy budget, at least in birds with high song rates such as nightingales.

9. The primary purpose of the passage is to
   (A) compare the different types of cost involved for certain birds in singing
   (B) question a hypothesis regarding the energy costs of singing for certain birds
   (C) present evidence suggesting that singing has an important energy cost for certain birds
   (D) discuss the benefits provided to an organism by a behavior that is costly in energy
   (E) describe an experiment that supports an alternative model of how birdsong functions

For the following question, consider each of the choices separately and select all that apply.

10. The passage implies that during the day before a night on which a male nightingale's song rate is high, that nightingale probably does which of the following?

    [A] Expends less of its reserves on thermoregulation than on other days
    [B] Stores more energy as body reserves than on other days
    [C] Hides to avoid predators

11. Select the sentence in the first or second paragraph that presents empirical results in support of a hypothesis about the energy costs of singing.

For the following question, consider each of the choices separately and select all that apply.

12. It can be inferred from the passage that compared with other costs of singing, which of the following is true of the energy costs of singing?

    [A] They are the single greatest cost to an individual bird.
    [B] They have generally received more attention from scientists.
    [C] They vary less from one bird species to another.

Question 13 is based on the following reading passage.

In the past ten years, there have been several improvements in mountain-climbing equipment. These improvements have made the sport both safer and more enjoyable for experienced climbers. Despite these improvements, however, the rate of mountain-climbing injuries has doubled in the past ten years.

13. Which of the following, if true, best reconciles the apparent discrepancy presented in the passage?

    (A) Many climbers, lulled into a false sense of security, use the new equipment to attempt climbing feats of which they are not capable.
    (B) Some mountain-climbing injuries are caused by unforeseeable weather conditions.
    (C) Mountain climbing, although a dangerous sport, does not normally result in injury to the experienced climber.
    (D) In the past ten years there have been improvements in mountain-climbing techniques as well as in mountain-climbing equipment.
    (E) Although the rate of mountain-climbing injuries has increased, the rate of mountain-climbing deaths has not changed.

GO ON TO NEXT PAGE ↘

14. Unenlightened authoritarian managers rarely recognize a crucial reason for the low levels of serious conflict among members of democratically run work groups: a modicum of tolerance for dissent often prevents _____.

   (A) demur
   (B) schism
   (C) cooperation
   (D) compliance
   (E) shortsightedness

15. The novelist devotes so much time to avid descriptions of his characters' clothes that the reader soon feels that such _____ concerns, although worthy of attention, have superseded any more directly literary aims.

   (A) didactic
   (B) syntactical
   (C) irrelevant
   (D) sartorial
   (E) frivolous

16. Belanger dances with an (i)_____ that draws one's attention as if by seeking to (ii)_____ it; through finesse and understatement, he manages to seem at once intensely present and curiously detached.

Blank (i)	Blank (ii)
(A) undemonstrative panache	(D) focus
(B) unrestrained enthusiasm	(E) overwhelm
(C) unattractive gawkiness	(F) deflect

17. The most striking thing about the politician is how often his politics have been (i)_____ rather than ideological, as he adapts his political positions at any particular moment to the political realities that constrain him. He does not, however, piously (ii)_____ political principles only to betray them in practice. Rather, he attempts in subtle ways to balance his political self-interest with a (iii)_____, viewing himself as an instrument of some unchanging higher purpose.

Blank (i)	Blank (ii)	Blank (iii)
(A) quixotic	(D) brandish	(G) profound cynicism
(B) self-righteous	(E) flout	(H) deeply felt moral code
(C) strategic	(F) follow	(I) thoroughgoing pragmatism

For each of Questions 18 to 20, select __one__ answer choice unless otherwise instructed.

Questions 18 to 20 are based on the following reading passage.

The condition of scholarship devoted to the history of women in photography is confounding. Recent years have witnessed the posthumous inflation of the role of the hobbyist Alice Austen into that of a pioneering documentarian while dozens of notable

line
5
senior figures—Marion Palfi, whose photographs of civil-rights activities in the South served as early evidence of the need for protective legislation, to name one—received scant attention from scholars. And, while Naomi Rosenblum's synoptic *History of Women Photographers* covers the subject through 1920 in a generally useful fashion, once she reaches the 1920s, when the venues, forms, applications, and movements of the medium expanded exponentially, she resorts to an increasingly terse listing of

10
unfamiliar names, with approaches and careers summarized in a sentence or two.

18. The author of the passage cites Rosenblum's book most likely in order to

(A) suggest that the works documented most thoroughly by historians of women in photography often do not warrant that attention

(B) offer an explanation for the observation that not all aspects of the history of women in photography have received the same level of attention

(C) provide an example of a way in which scholarship on the history of women in photography has been unsatisfactory

(D) suggest that employing a strictly chronological approach when studying the history of women in photography may be unproductive

(E) provide support for the notion that certain personalities in women's photography have attained undue prominence

For the following question, consider each of the choices separately and select all that apply.

19. Which of the following statements about Marion Palfi is supported by the passage?

[A] Marion Palfi's photographs would have received greater recognition from historians had her work been done in an era when most aspects of photography were static rather than in a state of transition.

[B] Alice Austen has achieved greater notoriety than has Marion Palfi primarily because the subjects that Austen photographed were more familiar to her contemporaries.

[C] In addition to providing a record of certain historical events, Marion Palfi's photographs played a role in subsequent events.

20. In the context in which it appears, "inflation" (line 2) most nearly means

(A) exaggeration
(B) acquisition
(C) evaluation
(D) distortion
(E) attenuation

GO ON TO NEXT PAGE ↘

For Questions 21 to 25, select the **two** answer choices that, when used to complete the sentence, fit the meaning of the sentence as a whole **and** produce completed sentences that are alike in meaning.

21. The plan, which the engineers said would save the aquifer by reducing pumping to _____ levels, has passed a governmental environmental review but faces opposition from outdoor and environmental groups.

    A innocuous

    B feasible

    C practicable

    D minimal

    E remedial

    F benign

22. Though feminist in its implications, Yvonne Rainer's 1974 film _____ the filmmaker's active involvement in feminist politics.

    A antedated

    B cloaked

    C portrayed

    D preceded

    E renewed

    F represented

23. Congress is having great difficulty developing a consensus on energy policy, primarily because the policy objectives of various members of Congress rest on such _____ assumptions.

    A commonplace

    B disparate

    C divergent

    D fundamental

    E trite

    F trivial

24. During the opera's most famous aria, the tempo chosen by the orchestra's conductor seemed _____, without necessary relation to what had gone before.

    [A] arbitrary

    [B] capricious

    [C] cautious

    [D] compelling

    [E] exacting

    [F] meticulous

25. Because they had expected the spacecraft Voyager 2 to be able to gather data only about the planets Jupiter and Saturn, scientists were _____ the wealth of information it sent back from Neptune twelve years after leaving Earth.

    [A] anxious for

    [B] confident in

    [C] thrilled about

    [D] keen on

    [E] elated by

    [F] eager for

STOP. This is the end of Section 3.

SECTION 4
Verbal Reasoning
Time—35 minutes
25 Questions

For Questions 1 to 4, select the **two** answer choices that, when used to complete the sentence, fit the meaning of the sentence as a whole and produce completed sentences that are alike in meaning.

1. Only by ignoring decades of mismanagement and inefficiency could investors conclude that a fresh infusion of cash would provide anything other than a _____ solution to the company's financial woes.

   A complete
   B fleeting
   C momentary
   D premature
   E trivial
   F total

2. Some scientists argue that carbon compounds play such a central role in life on Earth because of the possibility of _____ resulting from the carbon atom's ability to form an unending series of different molecules.

   A diversity
   B deviation
   C variety
   D reproduction
   E stability
   F invigoration

3. Given the flood of information presented by the mass media, the only way for someone to keep abreast of the news is to rely on _____ accounts.

   A synoptic
   B abridged
   C sensational
   D copious
   E lurid
   F understated

4. Always circumspect, she was reluctant to make judgments, but once arriving at a conclusion, she was _____ in its defense.

    A deferential

    B intransigent

    C lax

    D negligent

    E obsequious

    F resolute

For each of Questions 5 to 9, select **one** answer choice unless otherwise instructed.

Questions 5 and 6 are based on the following reading passage.

When marine organisms called phytoplankton photosynthesize, they absorb carbon dioxide dissolved in seawater, potentially causing a reduction in the concentration of atmospheric carbon dioxide, a gas that contributes to global warming. However, phytoplankton flourish only in surface waters where iron levels are sufficiently high. Martin therefore hypothesized that adding iron to iron-poor regions of the ocean could help alleviate global warming. While experiments subsequently confirmed that such a procedure increases phytoplankton growth, field tests have shown that such growth does not significantly lower atmospheric carbon dioxide. When phytoplankton utilize carbon dioxide for photosynthesis, the carbon becomes a building block for organic matter, but the carbon leaks back into the atmosphere when predators consume the phytoplankton and respire carbon dioxide.

line

5

10

For the following question, consider each of the choices separately and select all that apply.

5. It can be inferred from the passage that Martin's hypothesis includes which of the following elements?
   - A A correct understanding of how phytoplankton photosynthesis utilizes carbon dioxide
   - B A correct prediction about how the addition of iron to iron-poor waters would affect phytoplankton growth
   - C An incorrect prediction about how phytoplankton growth would affect the concentration of atmospheric carbon dioxide

6. It can be inferred that the author of the passage mentions predators (line 10) primarily in order to
   - Ⓐ help explain why Martin's hypothesis is incorrect
   - Ⓑ identify one effect of adding iron to iron-poor waters
   - Ⓒ indicate how some carbon dioxide is converted to solid organic matter
   - Ⓓ help account for differences in the density of phytoplankton between different regions of the ocean
   - Ⓔ point out a factor that was not anticipated by the scientists who conducted the field tests mentioned in the passage

Question 7 is based on the following reading passage.

Sparva, unlike Treland's other provinces, requires automobile insurers to pay for any medical treatment sought by someone who has been involved in an accident; in the other provinces, insurers pay for nonemergency treatment only if they preapprove the treatment. Clearly, Sparva's less restrictive policy must be the explanation for the fact that altogether insurers there pay for far more treatments after accidents than insurers in other provinces, even though Sparva does not have the largest population.

7.   Which of the following, if true, most strengthens the argument?

(A) Car insurance costs more in Sparva than in any other province.

(B) The cost of medical care in Sparva is higher than the national average.

(C) Different insurance companies have different standards for determining what constitutes emergency treatment.

(D) Fewer insurance companies operate in Sparva than in any other province.

(E) There are fewer traffic accidents annually in Sparva than in any of the provinces of comparable or greater population.

GO ON TO NEXT PAGE ↘

Questions 8 and 9 are based on the following reading passage.

Elements of the Philosophy of Newton, published by Voltaire in 1738, was an early attempt to popularize the scientific ideas of Isaac Newton. In the book's frontispiece, Voltaire is seen writing at his desk, and over him a shaft of light from heaven, the light of truth, passes through Newton to Voltaire's collaborator Madame du Châtelet; she reflects that light onto the inspired Voltaire. Voltaire's book commanded a wide audience, according to Feingold, because "he was neither a mathematician nor a physicist, but a literary giant aloof from the academic disputes over Newtonian ideas." In other words, Voltaire's amateurism in science "was a source of his contemporary appeal, demonstrating for the first time the accessibility of Newton's ideas to nonspecialists."

For the following question, consider each of the choices separately and select all that apply.

8. Which of the following statements about Voltaire's *Elements of the Philosophy of Newton* can be inferred from the passage?
   - A Voltaire's literary stature helped secure a large audience for this attempt to popularize Newton's ideas.
   - B Voltaire's status as a nonscientist was an advantage in this effort to bring Newtonian science to the attention of the general public.
   - C The frontispiece of the book implies that Voltaire's understanding of Newton's ideas was not achieved without assistance.

9. Select the sentence that describes an allegory for Voltaire's acquisition of knowledge concerning Newton's ideas.

For Questions 10 to 13, select one entry for each blank from the corresponding column of choices. Fill all blanks in the way that best completes the text.

10. Ironically, the writer so wary of (i)_____ was (ii)_____ with ink and paper, his novel running to 2,500 shagreen-bound folio pages—a fortune in stationery at the time.

Blank (i)	Blank (ii)
A probity	D acquisitive
B extravagance	E illiberal
C disapprobation	F profligate

11. What readers most commonly remember about John Stuart Mill's classic exploration of the liberty of thought and discussion concerns the danger of (i)_____: in the absence of challenge, one's opinions, even when they are correct, grow weak and flabby. Yet Mill had another reason for encouraging the liberty of thought and discussion: the danger of partiality and incompleteness. Since one's opinions, even under the best circumstances, tend to (ii)_____, and because opinions opposed to one's own rarely turn out to be completely (iii)_____, it is crucial to supplement one's opinions with alternative points of view.

Blank (i)	Blank (ii)	Blank (iii)
Ⓐ tendentiousness	Ⓓ embrace only a portion of the truth	Ⓖ erroneous
Ⓑ complacency	Ⓔ change over time	Ⓗ antithetical
Ⓒ fractiousness	Ⓕ focus on matters close at hand	Ⓘ immutable

12. Just as the authors' book on eels is often a key text for courses in marine vertebrate zoology, their ideas on animal development and phylogeny _____ teaching in this area.

Ⓐ prevent
Ⓑ defy
Ⓒ replicate
Ⓓ inform
Ⓔ use

13. Mechanisms develop whereby every successful species can _____ its innate capacity for population growth with the constraints that arise through its interactions with the natural environment.

Ⓐ enhance
Ⓑ replace
Ⓒ produce
Ⓓ surpass
Ⓔ reconcile

GO ON TO NEXT PAGE ➘

For each of Questions 14 to 16, select <u>one</u> answer choice unless otherwise instructed.

Questions 14 to 16 are based on the following reading passage.

It would be expected that a novel by a figure as prominent as W. E. B. DuBois would attract the attention of literary critics. Additionally, when the novel subtly engages the issue of race, as DuBois' *The Quest of the Silver Fleece* (1911) does, it would be a surprise not to encounter an abundance of scholarly work about that text. But though valuable scholarship has examined DuBois' political and historical thought, his novels have received scant attention. Perhaps DuBois the novelist must wait his turn behind DuBois the philosopher, historian, and editor. But what if the truth lies elsewhere: what if his novels do not speak to current concerns?

14. Which of the following can be inferred from the passage regarding DuBois' *The Quest of the Silver Fleece*?

Ⓐ The lack of attention devoted to *The Quest of the Silver Fleece* can be attributed to the fact that it was DuBois' first novel.

Ⓑ Among DuBois' novels, *The Quest of the Silver Fleece* is unusual in that it has received scant attention from scholars.

Ⓒ *The Quest of the Silver Fleece* has at least one feature that typically would attract the attention of literary scholars.

Ⓓ *The Quest of the Silver Fleece*, given its subtle exploration of race, is probably the best novel written by DuBois.

Ⓔ Much of the scholarly work that has focused on *The Quest of the Silver Fleece* has been surprisingly critical of it.

15. In the fourth sentence ("Perhaps DuBois . . . editor."), the author of the passage is most likely suggesting that

Ⓐ scholars will find that DuBois' novels are more relevant to current concerns than is his work as philosopher, historian, and editor

Ⓑ more scholarly attention will be paid to *The Quest of the Silver Fleece* than to DuBois' other novels

Ⓒ DuBois' novels will come to overshadow his work as philosopher, historian, and editor

Ⓓ DuBois' novels may eventually attract greater scholarly interest than they have to date

Ⓔ it will be shown that DuBois' work as philosopher, historian, and editor had an important influence on his work as novelist

16. Which of the following best describes the central issue with which the passage is concerned?

   Ⓐ The perfunctoriness of much of the critical work devoted to DuBois' novels

   Ⓑ The nature of DuBois' engagement with the issue of race in *The Quest of the Silver Fleece*

   Ⓒ Whether DuBois' novels are of high quality and relevant to current concerns

   Ⓓ The relationship between DuBois the novelist and DuBois the philosopher, historian, and editor

   Ⓔ The degree of consideration that has been given to DuBois' novels, including *The Quest of the Silver Fleece*

For Questions 17 to 20, select one entry for each blank from the corresponding column of choices. Fill all blanks in the way that best completes the text.

---

17. In the midst of so many evasive comments, this forthright statement, whatever its intrinsic merit, plainly stands out as _____.

Ⓐ a paradigm
Ⓑ a misnomer
Ⓒ a profundity
Ⓓ an inaccuracy
Ⓔ an anomaly

18. The activists' energetic work in the service of both woman suffrage and the temperance movement in the late nineteenth century (i)_____ the assertion that the two movements were (ii)_____.

Blank (i)	Blank (ii)
Ⓐ undermines	Ⓓ diffuse
Ⓑ supports	Ⓔ inimical
Ⓒ underscores	Ⓕ predominant

19. There is nothing quite like this movie, and indeed I am not altogether sure there is much more to it than its lovely (i)_____. At a moment when so many films strive to be as (ii)_____ as possible, it is gratifying to find one that is so subtle and puzzling.

Blank (i)	Blank (ii)
Ⓐ peculiarity	Ⓓ indirect
Ⓑ pellucidity	Ⓔ assertive
Ⓒ conventionality	Ⓕ enigmatic

GO ON TO NEXT PAGE ↘

20. Wills argues that certain malarial parasites are especially (i)_____ because they have more recently entered humans than other species and therefore have had (ii)_____ time to evolve toward (iii)_____. Yet there is no reliable evidence that the most harmful *Plasmodium* species has been in humans for a shorter time than less harmful species.

Blank (i)	Blank (ii)	Blank (iii)
Ⓐ populous	Ⓓ ample	Ⓖ virulence
Ⓑ malignant	Ⓔ insufficient	Ⓗ benignity
Ⓒ threatened	Ⓕ adequate	Ⓘ variability

For each of Questions 21 to 25, select <u>one</u> answer choice unless otherwise instructed.

Question 21 is based on the following reading passage.

Saturn's giant moon Titan is the only planetary satellite with a significant atmosphere and the only body in the solar system other than Earth that has a thick atmosphere dominated by molecular nitrogen. For a long time, the big question about Titan's atmosphere was how it could be so thick, given that Jupiter's moons Ganymede and Callisto, which are the same size as Titan, have none. The conditions for acquiring and retaining a thick nitrogen atmosphere are now readily understood. The low temperature of the protosaturnian nebula enabled Titan to acquire the moderately volatile compounds methane and ammonia (later converted to nitrogen) in addition to water. The higher temperatures of Jupiter's moons, which were closer to the Sun, prevented them from acquiring such an atmosphere.

21. According to the passage, Titan differs atmospherically from Ganymede and Callisto because of a difference in
    Ⓐ rate of heat loss
    Ⓑ proximity to the Sun
    Ⓒ availability of methane and ammonia
    Ⓓ distance from its planet
    Ⓔ size

Question 22 is based on the following reading passage.

Observations of the Arctic reveal that the Arctic Ocean is covered by less ice each summer than the previous summer. If this warming trend continues, within 50 years the Arctic Ocean will be ice free during the summer months. This occurrence would in itself have little or no effect on global sea levels, since the melting of ice floating in water does not affect the water level. However, serious consequences to sea levels would eventually result, because _____.

22. Which of the following most logically completes the passage?

    (A) large masses of floating sea ice would continue to form in the wintertime

    (B) significant changes in Arctic sea temperatures would be accompanied by changes in sea temperatures in more temperate parts of the world

    (C) such a warm Arctic Ocean would trigger the melting of massive land-based glaciers in the Arctic

    (D) an ice-free Arctic Ocean would support a very different ecosystem than it does presently

    (E) in the spring, melting sea ice would cause more icebergs to be created and to drift south into shipping routes

GO ON TO NEXT PAGE ↘

Questions 23 to 25 are based on the following reading passage.

In a recent study, David Cressy examines two central questions concerning English immigration to New England in the 1630s: what kinds of people immigrated and why? Using contemporary literary evidence, shipping lists, and customs records, Cressy finds
line that most adult immigrants were skilled in farming or crafts, were literate, and were
5 organized in families. Each of these characteristics sharply distinguishes the 21,000 people who left for New England in the 1630s from most of the approximately 377,000 English people who had immigrated to America by 1700.

With respect to their reasons for immigrating, Cressy does not deny the frequently noted fact that some of the immigrants of the 1630s, most notably the organizers and
10 clergy, advanced religious explanations for departure, but he finds that such explanations usually assumed primacy only in retrospect. When he moves beyond the principal actors, he finds that religious explanations were less frequently offered, and he concludes that most people immigrated because they were recruited by promises of material improvement.

For the following question, consider each of the choices separately and select all that apply.

23. The passage indicates that Cressy would agree with which of the following statements about the organizers among the English immigrants to New England in the 1630s?
    A Some of them offered a religious explanation for their immigration.
    B They did not offer any reasons for their immigration until some time after they had immigrated.
    C They were more likely than the average immigrant to be motivated by material considerations.

24. Select the sentence that provides Cressy's opinion about what motivated English immigrants to go to New England in the 1630s.

25. In the passage, the author is primarily concerned with
    Ⓐ summarizing the findings of an investigation
    Ⓑ analyzing a method of argument
    Ⓒ evaluating a point of view
    Ⓓ hypothesizing about a set of circumstances
    Ⓔ establishing categories

STOP. This is the end of Section 4.

SECTION 5
Quantitative Reasoning
Time—40 minutes
25 Questions

For each question, indicate the best answer, using the directions given.

Notes: All numbers used are real numbers.

All figures are assumed to lie in a plane unless otherwise indicated. Geometric figures, such as lines, circles, triangles, and quadrilaterals, **are not necessarily** drawn to scale. That is, you should **not** assume that quantities such as lengths and angle measures are as they appear in a figure. You should assume, however, that lines shown as straight are actually straight, points on a line are in the order shown, and more generally, all geometric objects are in the relative positions shown. For questions with geometric figures, you should base your answers on geometric reasoning, not on estimating or comparing quantities by sight or by measurement.

Coordinate systems, such as xy-planes and number lines, **are** drawn to scale; therefore, you can read, estimate, or compare quantities in such figures by sight or by measurement.

Graphical data presentations, such as bar graphs, circle graphs, and line graphs, **are** drawn to scale; therefore, you can read, estimate, or compare data values by sight or by measurement.

For each of Questions 1 to 9, compare Quantity A and Quantity B, using additional information centered above the two quantities if such information is given. Select one of the following four answer choices and fill in the corresponding oval to the right of the question.

Ⓐ   **Quantity A is greater.**

Ⓑ   **Quantity B is greater.**

Ⓒ   **The two quantities are equal.**

Ⓓ   **The relationship cannot be determined from the information given.**

A symbol that appears more than once in a question has the same meaning throughout the question.

Quantity A	Quantity B	Correct Answer
Example 1: (2)(6)	2 + 6	⬤Ⓐ Ⓑ Ⓒ Ⓓ

Quantity A	Quantity B	Correct Answer
Example 2: *PS*	*SR*	Ⓐ Ⓑ Ⓒ ⬤Ⓓ

(since equal lengths cannot be assumed, even though *PS* and *SR* appear equal)

Ⓐ	Quantity A is greater.	
Ⓑ	Quantity B is greater.	
Ⓒ	The two quantities are equal.	
Ⓓ	The relationship cannot be determined from the information given.	

O is the center of the circle above.

	Quantity A	Quantity B	
1.	*x*	5	Ⓐ Ⓑ Ⓒ Ⓓ

Runner *A* ran $\dfrac{4}{5}$ kilometer and Runner *B* ran 800 meters.

	Quantity A	Quantity B	
2.	The distance that *A* ran	The distance that *B* ran	Ⓐ Ⓑ Ⓒ Ⓓ

$$x < y < z$$

	Quantity A	Quantity B	
3.	$\dfrac{x+y+z}{3}$	*y*	Ⓐ Ⓑ Ⓒ Ⓓ

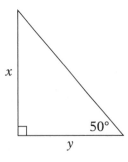

	Quantity A	Quantity B	
4.	$\dfrac{x}{y}$	1	Ⓐ Ⓑ Ⓒ Ⓓ

> (A) Quantity A is greater.
> (B) Quantity B is greater.
> (C) The two quantities are equal.
> (D) The relationship cannot be determined from the information given.

$$0 < x < y < 1$$

	Quantity A	Quantity B	
5.	$1 - y$	$y - x$	(A) (B) (C) (D)

---

p is the probability that event E will occur, and s is the probability that event E will <u>not</u> occur.

	Quantity A	Quantity B	
6.	$p + s$	ps	(A) (B) (C) (D)

X is the set of all integers n that satisfy the inequality $2 \leq |n| \leq 5$.

	Quantity A	Quantity B	
7.	The absolute value of the greatest integer in X	The absolute value of the least integer in X	(A) (B) (C) (D)

---

x and m are positive numbers, and m is a multiple of 3.

	Quantity A	Quantity B	
8.	$\dfrac{x^m}{x^3}$	$x^{m/3}$	(A) (B) (C) (D)

A random variable Y is normally distributed with a mean of 200 and a standard deviation of 10.

	Quantity A	Quantity B	
9.	The probability of the event that the value of Y is greater than 220	$\dfrac{1}{6}$	(A) (B) (C) (D)

GO ON TO NEXT PAGE ↘

Questions 10 to 25 have several different formats. Unless otherwise directed, select a single answer choice. For Numeric Entry questions, follow the instructions below.

Numeric Entry Questions

Enter your answer in the answer box(es) below the question.

- Your answer may be an integer, a decimal, or a fraction, and it may be negative.
- If a question asks for a fraction, there will be two boxes—one for the numerator and one for the denominator.
- Equivalent forms of the correct answer, such as 2.5 and 2.50, are all correct. Fractions do not need to be reduced to lowest terms.
- Enter the exact answer unless the question asks you to round your answer.

10. The ratio of $\frac{1}{3}$ to $\frac{3}{8}$ is equal to the ratio of

   (A) 1 to 8
   (B) 8 to 1
   (C) 8 to 3
   (D) 8 to 9
   (E) 9 to 8

11. A reading list for a humanities course consists of 10 books, of which 4 are biographies and the rest are novels. Each student is required to read a selection of 4 books from the list, including 2 or more biographies. How many selections of 4 books satisfy the requirements?

   (A)   90
   (B) 115
   (C) 130
   (D) 144
   (E) 195

For the following question, enter your answer in the box.

12. In a graduating class of 236 students, 142 took algebra and 121 took chemistry. What is the greatest possible number of students that could have taken both algebra and chemistry?

   [   ] students

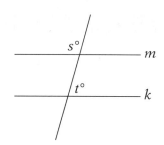

13. In the figure above, if $m \parallel k$ and $s = t + 30$, then $t =$

    Ⓐ 30

    Ⓑ 60

    Ⓒ 75

    Ⓓ 80

    Ⓔ 105

14. If $2x = 3y = 4z = 20$, then $12xyz =$

    Ⓐ 16,000

    Ⓑ 8,000

    Ⓒ 4,000

    Ⓓ 800

    Ⓔ 10

For the following question, select all the answer choices that apply.

15. The total amount that Mary paid for a book was equal to the price of the book plus a sales tax that was 4 percent of the price of the book. Mary paid for the book with a $10 bill and received the correct change, which was less than $3.00. Which of the following statements must be true?

    Indicate <u>all</u> such statements.

    Ⓐ The price of the book was less than $9.50.

    Ⓑ The price of the book was greater than $6.90.

    Ⓒ The sales tax was less than $0.45.

16. If $\dfrac{1}{(2^{11})(5^{17})}$ is expressed as a terminating decimal, how many nonzero digits will the decimal have?

    Ⓐ One

    Ⓑ Two

    Ⓒ Four

    Ⓓ Six

    Ⓔ Eleven

GO ON TO NEXT PAGE ↘

VARIATION IN THE AMOUNT OF CAFFEINE IN COMMON BEVERAGES AND DRUGS*

*Based on 5-ounce cups of coffee, tea, and cocoa; 12-ounce cups of soft drinks; and single doses of drugs.

17. The least amount of caffeine in a 5-ounce cup of drip-brewed coffee exceeds the greatest amount of caffeine in a 5-ounce cup of cocoa by approximately how many milligrams?

  Ⓐ 160
  Ⓑ 80
  Ⓒ 60
  Ⓓ 40
  Ⓔ 20

For the following question, enter your answer in the box.

18. For how many of the 11 categories of beverages and drugs listed in the graph can the amount of caffeine in the given serving size be less than 50 milligrams?

  [   ] categories

19. Approximately what is the minimum amount of caffeine, in milligrams, consumed per day by a person who daily drinks two 10-ounce mugs of percolated coffee and one 12-ounce cup of a caffeinated soft drink?

  Ⓐ 230
  Ⓑ 190
  Ⓒ 140
  Ⓓ 110
  Ⓔ 70

20. Which of the following shows the four types of coffee listed in order according to the range of the amounts of caffeine in a 5-ounce cup, from the least range to the greatest range?

    (A) Decaffeinated, instant, percolated, drip-brewed
    (B) Decaffeinated, instant, drip-brewed, percolated
    (C) Instant, decaffeinated, drip-brewed, percolated
    (D) Instant, drip-brewed, decaffeinated, percolated
    (E) Instant, percolated, drip-brewed, decaffeinated

ENERGY USED PER METER VERSUS SPEED
DURING RUNNING AND WALKING

21. If s is a speed, in miles per hour, at which the energy used per meter during running is twice the energy used per meter during walking, then, according to the graph above, s is between

    (A) 2.5 and 3.0
    (B) 3.0 and 3.5
    (C) 3.5 and 4.0
    (D) 4.0 and 4.5
    (E) 4.5 and 5.0

22. If $n = 2^3$, then $n^n =$

    (A) 2^6
    (B) 2^{11}
    (C) 2^{18}
    (D) 2^{24}
    (E) 2^{27}

GO ON TO NEXT PAGE ↘

For the following question, select all the answer choices that apply.

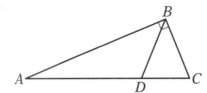

The length of *AB* is $10\sqrt{3}$.

23. Which of the following statements <u>individually</u> provide(s) sufficient additional information to determine the area of triangle *ABC* above?

Indicate <u>all</u> such statements.

[A] *DBC* is an equilateral triangle.

[B] *ABD* is an isosceles triangle.

[C] The length of *BC* is equal to the length of *AD*.

[D] The length of *BC* is 10.

[E] The length of *AD* is 10.

For the following question, enter your answer in the box.

$$a_1, a_2, a_3, \ldots, a_n, \ldots$$

24. In the sequence above, each term after the first term is equal to the preceding term plus the constant *c*. If $a_1 + a_3 + a_5 = 27$, what is the value of $a_2 + a_4$?

$$a_2 + a_4 = \boxed{}$$

25. A desert outpost has a water supply that is sufficient to last 21 days for 15 people. At the same average rate of water consumption per person, how many days would the water supply last for 9 people?

(A) 28.0

(B) 32.5

(C) 35.0

(D) 37.5

(E) 42.0

STOP. This is the end of Section 5.

SECTION 6
Quantitative Reasoning
Time—40 minutes
25 Questions

For each question, indicate the best answer, using the directions given.

Notes: All numbers used are real numbers.

All figures are assumed to lie in a plane unless otherwise indicated.

Geometric figures, such as lines, circles, triangles, and quadrilaterals, **are not necessarily** drawn to scale. That is, you should **not** assume that quantities such as lengths and angle measures are as they appear in a figure. You should assume, however, that lines shown as straight are actually straight, points on a line are in the order shown, and more generally, all geometric objects are in the relative positions shown. For questions with geometric figures, you should base your answers on geometric reasoning, not on estimating or comparing quantities by sight or by measurement.

Coordinate systems, such as xy-planes and number lines, **are** drawn to scale; therefore, you can read, estimate, or compare quantities in such figures by sight or by measurement.

Graphical data presentations, such as bar graphs, circle graphs, and line graphs, **are** drawn to scale; therefore, you can read, estimate, or compare data values by sight or by measurement.

For each of Questions 1 to 9, compare Quantity A and Quantity B, using additional information centered above the two quantities if such information is given. Select one of the following four answer choices and fill in the corresponding oval to the right of the question.

Ⓐ   **Quantity A is greater.**

Ⓑ   **Quantity B is greater.**

Ⓒ   **The two quantities are equal.**

Ⓓ   **The relationship cannot be determined from the information given.**

A symbol that appears more than once in a question has the same meaning throughout the question.

	Quantity A	Quantity B	Correct Answer
Example 1:	(2)(6)	2 + 6	⬤Ⓐ Ⓑ Ⓒ Ⓓ

	Quantity A	Quantity B	Correct Answer
Example 2:	PS	SR	Ⓐ Ⓑ Ⓒ ⬤Ⓓ

(since equal lengths cannot be assumed, even though *PS* and *SR* appear equal)

<table>
<tr><td>Ⓐ</td><td>Quantity A is greater.</td></tr>
<tr><td>Ⓑ</td><td>Quantity B is greater.</td></tr>
<tr><td>Ⓒ</td><td>The two quantities are equal.</td></tr>
<tr><td>Ⓓ</td><td>The relationship cannot be determined from the information given.</td></tr>
</table>

Country	Value of 1 United States Dollar
Argentina	0.93 peso
Kenya	32.08 shillings

	Quantity A	Quantity B	
1.	The dollar value of 1 Argentine peso according to the table above	The dollar value of 1 Kenyan shilling according to the table above	Ⓐ Ⓑ Ⓒ Ⓓ

---

k is a digit in the decimal $1.3k5$, and $1.3k5$ is less than 1.33.

	Quantity A	Quantity B	
2.	k	1	Ⓐ Ⓑ Ⓒ Ⓓ

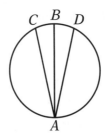

AB is a diameter of the circle above.

	Quantity A	Quantity B	
3.	The length of AB	The average (arithmetic mean) of the lengths of AC and AD	Ⓐ Ⓑ Ⓒ Ⓓ

$$st = \sqrt{10}$$

	Quantity A	Quantity B	
4.	s^2	$\dfrac{10}{t^2}$	Ⓐ Ⓑ Ⓒ Ⓓ

Ⓐ	**Quantity A is greater.**
Ⓑ	**Quantity B is greater.**
Ⓒ	**The two quantities are equal.**
Ⓓ	**The relationship cannot be determined from the information given.**

Three consecutive integers have a sum of –84.

	Quantity A	Quantity B	
5.	The least of the three integers	–28	Ⓐ Ⓑ Ⓒ Ⓓ

In the xy-plane, the equation of line k is $3x - 2y = 0$.

	Quantity A	Quantity B	
6.	The x-intercept of line k	The y-intercept of line k	Ⓐ Ⓑ Ⓒ Ⓓ

---

n is a positive integer that is divisible by 6.

	Quantity A	Quantity B	
7.	The remainder when n is divided by 12	The remainder when n is divided by 18	Ⓐ Ⓑ Ⓒ Ⓓ

$$\frac{1-x}{x-1} = \frac{1}{x}$$

	Quantity A	Quantity B	
8.	x	$-\dfrac{1}{2}$	Ⓐ Ⓑ Ⓒ Ⓓ

In a set of 24 positive integers, 12 of the integers are less than 50. The rest are greater than 50.

	Quantity A	Quantity B	
9.	The median of the 24 integers	50	Ⓐ Ⓑ Ⓒ Ⓓ

GO ON TO NEXT PAGE ↘

10. The fabric needed to make 3 curtains sells for $8.00 per yard and can be purchased only by the full yard. If the length of fabric required for each curtain is 1.6 yards and all of the fabric is purchased as a single length, what is the total cost of the fabric that needs to be purchased for the 3 curtains?

   (A) $40.00
   (B) $38.40
   (C) $24.00
   (D) $16.00
   (E) $12.80

For the following question, select all the answer choices that apply.

11. In the xy-plane, line k is a line that does <u>not</u> pass through the origin.

   Which of the following statements <u>individually</u> provide(s) sufficient additional information to conclude that the slope of line k is negative?

   Indicate <u>all</u> such statements.

   [A] The x-intercept of line k is twice the y-intercept of line k.

   [B] The product of the x-intercept and the y-intercept of line k is positive.

   [C] Line k passes through the points (a, b) and (r, s), where $(a - r)(b - s) < 0$.

	Distance from Centerville (miles)
Freight train	$-10t + 115$
Passenger train	$-20t + 150$

12. The expressions in the table above give the distance from Centerville to each of two trains t hours after 12:00 noon. At what time after 12:00 noon will the trains be equidistant from Centerville?

    (A) 1:30
    (B) 3:30
    (C) 5:10
    (D) 8:50
    (E) 11:30

13. The company at which Mark is employed has 80 employees, each of whom has a different salary. Mark's salary of $43,700 is the second-highest salary in the first quartile of the 80 salaries. If the company were to hire 8 new employees at salaries that are less than the lowest of the 80 salaries, what would Mark's salary be with respect to the quartiles of the 88 salaries at the company, assuming no other changes in the salaries?

    (A) The fourth-highest salary in the first quartile
    (B) The highest salary in the first quartile
    (C) The second-lowest salary in the second quartile
    (D) The third-lowest salary in the second quartile
    (E) The fifth-lowest salary in the second quartile

For the following question, enter your answer in the box.

14. In the xy-plane, the point with coordinates $(-6, -7)$ is the center of circle C. The point with coordinates $(-6, 5)$ lies inside C, and the point with coordinates $(8, -7)$ lies outside C. If m is the radius of C and m is an integer, what is the value of m?

    $m = \boxed{}$

15. If $-\dfrac{m}{19}$ is an even integer, which of the following must be true?
    (A) m is a negative number.
    (B) m is a positive number.
    (C) m is a prime number.
    (D) m is an odd integer.
    (E) m is an even integer.

GO ON TO NEXT PAGE

For the following question, select all the answer choices that apply.

16. The integer v is greater than 1. If v is the square of an integer, which of the following numbers must also be the square of an integer?

    Indicate <u>all</u> such numbers.

    [A] $81v$

    [B] $25v + 10\sqrt{v} + 1$

    [C] $4v^2 + 4\sqrt{v} + 1$

Questions 17 to 20 are based on the following data.

DISTANCE TRAVELED BY A CAR ACCORDING TO THE CAR'S SPEED
WHEN THE DRIVER IS SIGNALED TO STOP

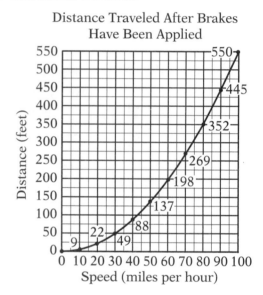

*Reaction time is the time period that begins when the driver is signaled to stop and ends when the driver applies the brakes.

<u>Note</u>: Total stopping distance is the sum of the distance traveled during reaction time and the distance traveled after brakes have been applied.

17. The speed, in miles per hour, at which the car travels a distance of 52 feet during reaction time is closest to which of the following?

    (A)   43

    (B)   47

    (C)   51

    (D)   55

    (E)   59

18. Approximately what is the total stopping distance, in feet, if the car is traveling at a speed of 40 miles per hour when the driver is signaled to stop?

    (A)   130

    (B)   110

    (C)   90

    (D)   70

    (E)   40

19. Of the following, which is the greatest speed, in miles per hour, at which the car can travel and stop with a total stopping distance of less than 200 feet?

    (A)   50

    (B)   55

    (C)   60

    (D)   65

    (E)   70

20. The total stopping distance for the car traveling at 60 miles per hour is approximately what percent greater than the total stopping distance for the car traveling at 50 miles per hour?

    (A)   22%

    (B)   30%

    (C)   38%

    (D)   45%

    (E)   52%

21. What is the least positive integer that is <u>not</u> a factor of 25! and is <u>not</u> a prime number?

    (A)   26

    (B)   28

    (C)   36

    (D)   56

    (E)   58

22. If $0 < a < 1 < b$, which of the following is true about the reciprocals of a and b?

    (A) $1 < \dfrac{1}{a} < \dfrac{1}{b}$

    (B) $\dfrac{1}{a} < 1 < \dfrac{1}{b}$

    (C) $\dfrac{1}{a} < \dfrac{1}{b} < 1$

    (D) $\dfrac{1}{b} < 1 < \dfrac{1}{a}$

    (E) $\dfrac{1}{b} < \dfrac{1}{a} < 1$

GO ON TO NEXT PAGE ↘

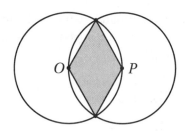

23. In the figure above, *O* and *P* are the centers of the two circles. If each circle has radius *r*, what is the area of the shaded region?

(A) $\dfrac{\sqrt{2}}{2}r^2$

(B) $\dfrac{\sqrt{3}}{2}r^2$

(C) $\sqrt{2}r^2$

(D) $\sqrt{3}r^2$

(E) $2\sqrt{3}r^2$

For the following question, enter your answer in the boxes.

24. Of the 20 lightbulbs in a box, 2 are defective. An inspector will select 2 lightbulbs simultaneously and at random from the box. What is the probability that neither of the lightbulbs selected will be defective?

Give your answer as a fraction.

25. What is the perimeter, in meters, of a rectangular playground 24 meters wide that has the same area as a rectangular playground 64 meters long and 48 meters wide?

(A) 112
(B) 152
(C) 224
(D) 256
(E) 304

STOP. This is the end of Section 6.

Evaluating Your Performance

Now that you have completed Practice Test 1, it is time to evaluate your performance.

Analytical Writing Measure

One way to evaluate your performance on the Issue and Argument topics you answered on this practice test is to compare your essay responses to the scored sample essay responses for these topics and review the rater commentary. Scored sample essay responses and rater commentary are presented starting on page 377 for the one Issue topic and one Argument topic presented in the Analytical Writing sections of Practice Test 1. The Issue and Argument scoring guides start on page 37.

To better understand the analytical writing abilities characteristic of particular score levels, you should review the score level descriptions on page 41.

Verbal Reasoning and Quantitative Reasoning Measures

The tables that follow contain information to help you evaluate your performance on the Verbal Reasoning and Quantitative Reasoning measures of Practice Test 1. An answer key with the correct answers to the questions in the Verbal Reasoning and Quantitative Reasoning sections in this practice test begins on page 371. Compare your answers to the correct answers given in the table, crossing out questions you answered incorrectly or omitted. Partially correct answers should be treated as incorrect. Knowing which questions you answered incorrectly or omitted can help you identify content areas in which you need more practice or review.

The answer key contains additional information to help you evaluate your performance. With each answer, the key provides a number, the P+. The P+ is the percent of a group of actual GRE takers who were administered that same question at a previous test administration and who answered it correctly. P+ is used to gauge the relative difficulty of a test question. The higher the P+, the easier the test question. You can use the P+ to compare your performance on each test question to the performance of other test takers on that same question. For example, if the P+ for a question is 89, that means that 89 percent of GRE test takers who received this question answered it correctly. Alternatively, if the P+ for a question is 14, that means that 14 percent of GRE test takers who received this question answered it correctly. A question with a P+ of 89 may be interpreted as a relatively easy question, and a question with a P+ of 14 may be interpreted as a difficult question.

To calculate your scores on Practice Test 1:

● Add the number of correct answers in Sections 3 and 4 to obtain your raw Verbal Reasoning score.
● Add the number of correct answers in Sections 5 and 6 to obtain your raw Quantitative Reasoning score.
● Once you have calculated your raw scores, refer to the Practice Test 1 score conversion table on pages 375–376. Find the scores on the 130–170 score scales that correspond to your Verbal Reasoning and Quantitative Reasoning raw scores. Note the scaled scores provided.

Once you determine your scaled scores, you will need to evaluate your performance. To get a sense of how test takers are scoring on the Verbal Reasoning and Quantitative Reasoning measures of the actual test, you can review Verbal Reasoning and Quantitative Reasoning percentile ranks on the GRE website at **www.ets.org/gre/percentile** (PDF). A percentile rank for a score indicates the percentage of examinees who took that test and received a lower score. Updated annually in July, this table includes the Verbal Reasoning and Quantitative Reasoning scores on the 130–170 scale in one-point increments and the corresponding percentile ranks. For each score you earned on Practice Test 1, note the percent of GRE test takers who earned lower scores. This is a reasonable indication of your rank among GRE General Test examinees if you took Practice Test 1 under standard timed conditions.

Answer Key

Section 3. Verbal Reasoning

Question Number	P+	Correct Answer
1	39	**Choice A:** Some record or evidence of the thought of the *tlamatinime* is available. AND **Choice B:** For at least some Nahuatl expressions, researchers are able to trace their derivation from another ancient American language.
2	54	**Sentence 6:** Of these forms, the most characteristic in Nahuatl is the juxtaposition of two words that, because they are synonyms, associated terms, or even contraries, complement each other to evoke one single idea.
3	49	**Choice B:** creations
4	48	**Choice D:** The first sums up the argument's position with regard to a certain hypothesis; the second provides grounds for that position.
5	57	**Choice A:** anachronistic; **Choice F:** alienated from
6	63	**Choice D:** invention
7	20	**Choice B:** lionization; **Choice D:** foreground
8	58	**Choice B:** aesthetics
9	69	**Choice C:** present evidence suggesting that singing has an important energy cost for certain birds
10	66	**Choice B:** Stores more energy as body reserves than on other days
11	65	**Sentence 9:** Thomas found that nightingales reached a significantly higher body mass at dusk and lost more mass overnight on nights when their song rate was high.
12	14	**Choice B:** They have generally received more attention from scientists.
13	86	**Choice A:** Many climbers, lulled into a false sense of security, use the new equipment to attempt climbing feats of which they are not capable.
14	46	**Choice B:** schism
15	10	**Choice D:** sartorial
16	36	**Choice A:** undemonstrative panache; **Choice F:** deflect
17	18	**Choice C:** strategic; **Choice D:** brandish; **Choice H:** deeply felt moral code
18	47	**Choice C:** provide an example of a way in which scholarship on the history of women in photography has been unsatisfactory
19	37	**Choice C:** In addition to providing a record of certain historical events, Marion Palfi's photographs played a role in subsequent events.
20	72	**Choice A:** exaggeration
21	24	**Choice A:** innocuous AND **Choice F:** benign
22	39	**Choice A:** antedated AND **Choice D:** preceded
23	61	**Choice B:** disparate AND **Choice C:** divergent
24	67	**Choice A:** arbitrary AND **Choice B:** capricious
25	85	**Choice C:** thrilled about AND **Choice E:** elated by

Answer Key

Section 4. Verbal Reasoning

Question Number	P+	Correct Answer
1	70	**Choice B:** fleeting AND **Choice C:** momentary
2	80	**Choice A:** diversity AND **Choice C:** variety
3	49	**Choice A:** synoptic AND **Choice B:** abridged
4	68	**Choice B:** intransigent AND **Choice F:** resolute
5	26	**Choice A:** A correct understanding of how phytoplankton photosynthesis utilizes carbon dioxide AND **Choice B:** A correct prediction about how the addition of iron to iron-poor waters would affect phytoplankton growth AND **Choice C:** An incorrect prediction about how phytoplankton growth would affect the concentration of atmospheric carbon dioxide
6	26	**Choice A:** help explain why Martin's hypothesis is incorrect
7	31	**Choice E:** There are fewer traffic accidents annually in Sparva than in any of the provinces of comparable or greater population.
8	23	**Choice A:** Voltaire's literary stature helped secure a large audience for this attempt to popularize Newton's ideas. AND **Choice B:** Voltaire's status as a nonscientist was an advantage in this effort to bring Newtonian science to the attention of the general public. AND **Choice C:** The frontispiece of the book implies that Voltaire's understanding of Newton's ideas was not achieved without assistance.
9	82	**Sentence 2:** In the book's frontispiece, Voltaire is seen writing at his desk, and over him a shaft of light from heaven, the light of truth, passes through Newton to Voltaire's collaborator Madame du Châtelet; she reflects that light onto the inspired Voltaire.
10	60	**Choice B:** extravagance; **Choice F:** profligate
11	37	**Choice B:** complacency; **Choice D:** embrace only a portion of the truth; **Choice G:** erroneous
12	35	**Choice D:** inform
13	43	**Choice E:** reconcile
14	54	**Choice C:** *The Quest of the Silver Fleece* has at least one feature that typically would attract the attention of literary scholars.
15	68	**Choice D:** DuBois' novels may eventually attract greater scholarly interest than they have to date
16	49	**Choice E:** The degree of consideration that has been given to DuBois' novels, including *The Quest of the Silver Fleece*
17	50	**Choice E:** an anomaly
18	19	**Choice A:** undermines; **Choice E:** inimical
19	54	**Choice A:** peculiarity; **Choice E:** assertive
20	23	**Choice B:** malignant; **Choice E:** insufficient; **Choice H:** benignity
21	53	**Choice B:** proximity to the Sun
22	59	**Choice C:** such a warm Arctic Ocean would trigger the melting of massive land-based glaciers in the Arctic

Answer Key

Question Number	P+	Correct Answer
23	33	**Choice A:** Some of them offered a religious explanation for their immigration.
24	94	**Sentence 5:** When he moves beyond the principal actors, he finds that religious explanations were less frequently offered, and he concludes that most people immigrated because they were recruited by promises of material improvement.
25	64	**Choice A:** summarizing the findings of an investigation

Section 5. Quantitative Reasoning

Question Number	P+	Correct Answer
1	65	**Choice B:** Quantity B is greater.
2	83	**Choice C:** The two quantities are equal.
3	62	**Choice D:** The relationship cannot be determined from the information given.
4	48	**Choice A:** Quantity A is greater.
5	47	**Choice D:** The relationship cannot be determined from the information given.
6	36	**Choice A:** Quantity A is greater.
7	26	**Choice C:** The two quantities are equal.
8	34	**Choice D:** The relationship cannot be determined from the information given.
9	46	**Choice B:** Quantity B is greater.
10	62	**Choice D:** 8 to 9
11	26	**Choice B:** 115
12	51	**121**
13	52	**Choice C:** 75
14	60	**Choice C:** 4,000
15	18	**Choice C:** The sales tax was less than $0.45.
16	19	**Choice B:** Two
17	69	**Choice D:** 40
18	63	**9**
19	41	**Choice B:** 190
20	60	**Choice B:** Decaffeinated, instant, drip-brewed, percolated
21	70	**Choice A:** 2.5 and 3.0
22	35	**Choice D:** 2^{24}
23	17	**Choice A:** *DBC* is an equilateral triangle. AND **Choice D:** The length of *BC* is 10.
24	51	**18**
25	34	**Choice C:** 35.0

Answer Key

Section 6. Quantitative Reasoning

Question Number	P+	Correct Answer
1	66	**Choice A:** Quantity A is greater.
2	73	**Choice D:** The relationship cannot be determined from the information given.
3	52	**Choice A:** Quantity A is greater.
4	46	**Choice C:** The two quantities are equal.
5	48	**Choice B:** Quantity B is greater.
6	33	**Choice C:** The two quantities are equal.
7	40	**Choice D:** The relationship cannot be determined from the information given.
8	26	**Choice B:** Quantity B is greater.
9	31	**Choice D:** The relationship cannot be determined from the information given.
10	67	**Choice A:** $40.00
11	10	**Choice A:** The x-intercept of line k is twice the y-intercept of line k. AND **Choice B:** The product of the x-intercept and the y-intercept of line k is positive. AND **Choice C:** Line k passes through the points (a, b) and (r, s), where $(a - r)(b - s) < 0$.
12	49	**Choice B:** 3:30
13	27	**Choice E:** The fifth-lowest salary in the second quartile
14	38	**13**
15	40	**Choice E:** m is an even integer.
16	21	**Choice A:** $81v$ AND **Choice B:** $25v + 10\sqrt{v} + 1$
17	79	**Choice B:** 47
18	44	**Choice A:** 130
19	41	**Choice A:** 50
20	30	**Choice C:** 38%
21	11	**Choice E:** 58
22	58	**Choice D:** $\dfrac{1}{b} < 1 < \dfrac{1}{a}$
23	24	**Choice B:** $\dfrac{\sqrt{3}}{2} r^2$
24	15	$\dfrac{153}{190}$ (or any equivalent fraction)
25	30	**Choice E:** 304

Score Conversion Table

Raw Score	Verbal Reasoning Scaled Score	Quantitative Reasoning Scaled Score
50	170	170
49	170	170
48	170	170
47	170	170
46	169	169
45	168	168
44	167	167
43	166	165
42	165	164
41	164	163
40	163	162
39	162	161
38	162	160
37	161	159
36	160	159
35	159	158
34	159	157
33	158	156
32	157	155
31	156	155
30	156	154
29	155	153
28	154	153
27	154	152
26	153	151
25	152	150
24	152	150
23	151	149
22	150	148
21	149	148
20	149	147
19	148	146
18	147	145
17	146	144
16	145	143

Score Conversion Table

Raw Score	Verbal Reasoning Scaled Score	Quantitative Reasoning Scaled Score
15	144	143
14	143	142
13	142	141
12	141	140
11	140	138
10	139	137
9	137	136
8	136	134
7	134	133
6	132	131
5	130	130
4	130	130
3	130	130
2	130	130
1	130	130
0	130	130

Analytical Writing Sample Responses and Reader Commentaries

SECTION 1
Analytical Writing

ANALYZE AN ISSUE

The best way to teach is to praise positive actions and ignore negative ones.

Write a response in which you discuss the extent to which you agree or disagree with the recommendation and explain your reasoning for the position you take. In developing and supporting your position, describe specific circumstances in which adopting the recommendation would or would not be advantageous and explain how these examples shape your position.

Score 6 Response*

The recommendation presents a view that I would agree is successful most of the time, but one that I cannot fully support due to the "all or nothing" impression it gives.

Certainly as an educator I agree fully that the best way to elicit positive response from students is to make use of students' positive energy and then encourage actions that you would like to see repeated. It is human nature that we all want to be accepted and achieve on some level, and when people in authority provide feedback that we have done something well, the drive to repeat the action that was praised is bound to be particularly strong.

This blanket statement would obviously pay dividends in situations in which a teacher desires to have students repeat particular behaviors. For example, if an educator is attempting to teach students proper classroom etiquette, it would be appropriate to openly praise a student who raises his or her hand when wishing to speak or address the class. In such cases, the teacher may also help shape positive behaviors by ignoring a student who is trying to interject without approval from the teacher. In fact, the decision to ignore students who are exhibiting inappropriate behaviors of this type could work very well in this situation, as the stakes are not very high and the intended outcome can likely be achieved by such a method. However, it is important to note here that this tactic would only be effective in such a "low-stakes" situation, as when a student speaks without raising her hand first. As we will discuss below, ignoring a student who hits another student, or engages in more serious misbehaviors, would not be effective or prudent.

To expand on this point, it is important for teachers to be careful when working with the second half of this statement, only ignoring negative actions that are not serious.

---

*NOTE: All responses are reproduced exactly as written, including errors, misspellings, etc., if any.

Take for instance a student who is misbehaving just by chatting with a fellow class-mate. This student might not be presenting much of a problem and may be simply seeking attention. Ignoring the student might, in fact, be the best solution. Now assume the negative action is the improper administering of chemicals in a science experiment or the bullying of a fellow student. To ignore these negative actions would be absurd and negligent. Now you are allowing a problem to persist, one that could potentially lead to much bigger and more dangerous issues. In a more serious situation, addressing the negative actions quickly and properly could stop the problem it in its tracks. It is for reasons like this that I do not advocate the idea that a teacher can be successful by simply ignoring negative actions.

I do, however, greatly support the idea that the central focus of teaching should be to build on and encourage positive actions. However, the author's all-encompasing statement leaves too many negative possibilities for the classroom. Perhaps a better way to phrase this statement would be to say, "The best way to teach is to praise positive actions and ignore negative ones that are not debilitating to class efficiency or the safety of any individual".

Thus, in the original statement, there are indeed some good intentions, and there could be a lot of merit in adopting its basic principles. Data proves that positive support can substantially increase motivation and desire in students and contribute to positive achievements. In fact, most studies of teaching efficacy indicate that praising positive actions and ignoring negative ones can create a more stable and efficient classroom. It needs to be stressed, however, that this tool is only effective at certain levels of misbehavior. As mentioned above, when the behavior is precipitated by feelings of revenge, power or total self-worthlessness, this methodology will likely not work. It is likely to be very successful, however, when the drive behind the misbehavior is simple attention seeking. In many of these instances, if the teacher demonstrates clearly that inappropriate behavior does not result in the gaining of attention, students are more likely to seek attention by behaving properly. Should the student choose this path, then the ignoring has worked and when the positive behavior is exhibited, then the teacher can utilize the first part of the theory and support or praise this behavior. Now it is much more likely to be repeated. If the student does not choose this path and instead elects to raise the actions to a higher level that presents a more serious issue, then ignorance alone cannot work and other methods must be employed.

In conclusion, one can appreciate the credo expressed in this instance, but surely we all can see the potential error of following it through to the extreme.

Reader Commentary

This response receives a 6 for its well-articulated, insightful analysis of the issue. Rather than simply rejecting or accepting the prompt, the writer argues that the recommendation made by the prompt can often be true but is too "all or nothing" to be endorsed without qualification. The writer turns this idea into an insightful position by providing examples and evidence to fully and persuasively support its nuanced argument. The response offers nicely detailed situations that provide compelling support for a claim that the recommendation can, in fact, work. At the same time, it also highlights the recommendation's limits using additional specific, detailed examples. Particularly persuasive is the fourth paragraph, in which the writer compares the impact of ignoring minor behavioral problems like talking in class to the potential costs of ignoring more serious issues like bullying. Thus, the writer recognizes that the prompt's claim, as well as his/her own, is inevitably dependent on the specific context for its success or failure. Throughout the response, the writer demonstrates the ability to convey ideas fluently and precisely, using effective vocabulary and sentence variety. This sentence demonstrates the level of language facility seen throughout the response: "It is human nature that we all want to be accepted and achieve on some level, and when people in authority provide feedback that we have done something well, the drive to repeat the action that was praised is bound to be particularly strong."

Score 5 Response

I partially agree with the statement "The best way to teach is to praise positive actions and ignore negative ones". Children should be rewarded when they perform well; however, they should not be ignored for performing sub-optimally. For purposes of this essay, the term "actions" is defined as behaviors within the classroom.

Utilizing positive reinforcements, such as tangible rewards, can be a good method to teach children. If the teacher praises children for actions that are desirable, then the children are more likely to repeat those actions. For example, a student who completes an assignment on time and does a good job is likely to want to do a good job on the next assignment if he gets positive feedback. Likewise, the children who are not currently engaging in the desirable actions may be more inclined to do so in order to recieve the positive reinforcement.

Conversely, children should not be ignored for negative actions. If a child is not exhibiting appropriate behavior in the classroom, then it is the teacher's responsibility to encourage the child to perform optimally. Ignoring something doesn't make it go away, actions and consequences do. A student who is being disruptive in class will continue to be disruptive unless the teacher does something about it. However, the teacher's actions need be appropriate.

Before the teacher attempts to modify a child's behavior, the teacher needs to try and identify the reason behind the behavior. For instance, children who leave their seat often, stare in to space, or call out of turn may be initially viewed as having poor behavior. However, the teacher may suspect that the child has an attentional problem, and request that the child be tested. If the child does have an attentional problem, then the teacher can work with a related service, such as occupational therapy, to alter the classroom environment in order to cater to the needs of the child. For instance, the teacher could remove some of the stimulating bulliten board displays to make the room more calming to the child. If the child becomes more attentive in class then the teacher was able to assist the child without scorning them or ignoring them. The teacher met the needs of the child and created an enviornment to enable the child to optimally perform in the educational setting.

On the other hand, if the child is tested, and does not have any areas of concern that may be impacting the educational performance in the classroom, then the negative behavior may strictly be due to defiance. In such a case, the teacher still should not ignore the child, because the negative actions may hinder the learning opportunity for the remaining children in the class. As a result, a child who is being disruptive to the learning process of the class should be set apart from the class so that they do not receive the positive reinforcement of peer attention.

The teacher should not ignore the student who is misbehaving, but that does not mean that the teacher just needs to punish. It is better to address the child privately and make sure the child is aware of the negative actions. Once the child is aware, then the teacher should once again try to determine the reason why the child is behaving in a negative manner. Perhaps the child's parents are in the middle of a divorce and the child is outwardly expressing his frustration in the classroom. Or the academic content of the class may not be challenging enough for the child and so he is misbehaving out of boredom. Whatever the reason behind the behavior, the key factor is that the teacher works with the child to try and identify it. Simply punnishing or ignoring the child would not solve the problem, whereas working to create a plan for success in the classroom would. Likewise, rather than punnishing and defeating the child, the teacher is working with and empowering the child; a much more positive outcome to the situation.

Reader Commentary

This strong response presents a thoughtful and well-developed analysis of the issue. In this case the writer argues that teachers need to modify their approach based on context and observation, meaning that a blanket approach cannot be successful. The writer supports this position with relevant reasons and examples that present logically sound support. Note that the task instructions ask writers to discuss circumstances in which adopting the recommendation might or might not prove advantageous, and this response does that quite clearly. In the second paragraph, the writer gives an example of a student who completes an assignment on time and receives positive feedback, showing how the recommendation could prove advantageous. Other examples show circumstances in which adopting the recommendation would not be a good idea, and these various points are brought together to support the writer's position that teachers have to look at the context of the situation and cannot rely on simply ignoring negative actions. This response also demonstrates facility with language, using appropriate vocabulary and sentence variety. Sentences like this one demonstrate the writer's command of the conventions of standard written English: "If the child does have an attentional problem, then the teacher can work with a related service, such as occupational therapy, to alter the classroom environment in order to cater to the needs of the child." There are some minor errors, but overall the response demonstrates strong control of language. Although the response is clearly stronger than a 4, which would simply present a clear position on the issue according to the task instructions, it does not reach the level of a 6 because it does not develop its points in a way that creates a cogent and insightful position. It does, however, present a generally thoughtful and well-developed analysis of the issue, leading to a score of 5.

Score 4 Response

I absolutely agree with the first section of the statement above, but find fault with the latter half.

There is no doubt that praising positive actions is an excellent way to teach, and this method is most clearly exemplified when dealing with much younger children. When a young child is learning basic social behavior, it is imperative that he is encouraged to repeat positive actions. For example, when a child voluntarily shares his toys with another, if a teacher rewards that behavior, the child will understand that this is a good practice, and likely share again in the future.

In contrast, if a child displays negative behavior by stealing a toy away from his playmate, it would be very dangerous for the teacher to ignore this action, for then the child may never recognize that this is unacceptable. In this instance, the child has not learned from the situation at all. So what should a teacher do when faced with such a situation? Punishment is not necessarily the optimal choice, either. Rather than scolding a child for mistreating his playmates and sending him off to a corner, a teacher would be wise to demonstrate the positive alternative: to share his toys instead. In this case, rather than ignoring or punishing negative actions, the teacher could seize the opportunity to reinforce positive behavior, and further extend the child's learning experience.

In summary, positive reinforcement is certainly an excellent method for teaching new methods or behaviors, and encouraging a student to learn more. However to ignore, rather than recognize and correct negative actions, would be a disservice to the student, for he would not know what conclusion to draw from his action.

Reader Commentary

This adequate response follows the task directions and presents a clear position on the issue, supporting its main points with examples that are relevant, if only adequately developed. For instance, the discussion in the second paragraph of a teacher who reinforces the positive behavior of sharing a toy is certainly relevant and on-task (i.e., it describes a situation in which adopting the recommendation would be advantageous). However, the development of this idea does not lead to generally thoughtful or insightful analysis. Instead, it is simply presented as an example. In addition to its adequate development, this response also demonstrates sufficient control of the conventions of standard written English, and its main points are made with reasonable clarity. Some of the sentences demonstrate the syntactical variety normally seen in responses that receive higher scores (e.g., "Rather than scolding a child for mistreating his playmates and sending him off to a corner, a teacher would be wise to demonstrate the positive alternative: to share his toys instead"). However, the overall use of language in this response is merely adequate.

Score 3 Response

Praising postive actions and ignoring negative ones may be a good way to teach but not the best way. Ignoring negative actions could negate all the postive praises given to an individual, having negative actions go unchecked will lead to habits formed that would overwhelm any positive actions that are complementary to an individuals learning process.

For instance, in a classroom full of eight-year old kids; if during a lesson they are making alot of noise, having this ignored would tell the kids that it is okay to be disruptive in class. The individuals in that class would develop the habit of being distruptive hence hindering their learning process. However if the eight-year old kids were immediately told to stop the distruption then it will never become a habit.

Every action needs to have a related consequence follow in a learning environment. In the early years of education, the way they are taught becomes a lifelong habit which is hard to change in later years. If negative actions are not assigned a related consequences then teaching becomes ineffective because the students negative actions soon diminish the ability to do well in school. The way postive actions are dealt with should also be done with negative actions rather than being ignored which in turn enhance the learning environment.

Reader Commentary

Although this response has minor errors in its use of language, it receives a 3 primarily for insufficient overall clarity and for the limited development of its claims. The writer does make an attempt to follow the specific task instructions, and the response has a clear position on the issue, arguing that it is not acceptable practice to ignore negative behaviors. However, the development provided in support of that position is limited. The example of "eight-year old kids" making noise during class can be seen as a situation in which following the recommendation is not advantageous. Instead of developing that point in a logically persuasive way, however, the writer proceeds to make an unsupported assertion about the consequences of following the recommendation ("The individuals in that class would develop the habit of being distruptive hence hindering their learning process"). Another issue that keeps this response at the 3 level is a lack of clarity, particularly in the final paragraph. The final sentence demonstrates this problem with clarity: "The way postive actions are dealt with should also be done with negative actions rather than being ignored which in turn enhance the learning environment." Problems with the structure of this sentence make it difficult to determine the writer's intended meaning.

Score 2 Response

I don't agree with this afirmation, because I think is very important to praise positive actions but also is important to sign the negative ones, in some situations acording to the students level, grade, etc., could be better to put more emphasis in the positive things and if not ignore all the negative ones, do not give so much importance to them, this is particulary important in the lowest levels of education.

But in another situations you must sign the negative things, trying to avoid that the students can repeat them in the future, because I think you can also learn from the negative situations.

For this reason I believe that is important to praise positive actions but is also important no to ignore the negative ones, because in a given situation the student can have troubles recongnising what is right and what is wrong. And finally as a conclusion I think that the best way to teach is combination of praise positive things but also to sign the negative ones.

Reader Commentary

This response clearly fits several characteristics of a 2, as defined by the scoring guide. It is seriously limited in its development, organization, and focus. The response repeats itself rather than developing any of its statements, pointing to an inability to organize a response capable of supporting any specific claims with relevant reasons or examples. Additionally, serious language control problems frequently interfere with meaning. Thus, even though the writer does seem to be making an attempt to respond to the specific task instructions, the response merits a score of 2.

Score 1 Response

> Write a response in which you disuss the extent to which you agree or disagree with the recommendation and explain your reasoning for the position you take. In developing and supporting position, describe specific circumstances in which adopting the recommendation would or would not be advantageous and explain how these examples shape your position.
>
> Author says that The best way to teach is to praise positive actions and ignore negative ones. I agree to this recommendation. Explaining, I strongly believe that the best way to teach is not to praise positive action and ignore negative ones but is making everyone to be a good ones. Specific crimstances lead me which adopting the recommendation as the following:
>
> First, we will lost the good children who have negative maner if we ignore them. Children are future, not all. Praise in negative should not be, teaching to children to best way. I strongly believe adopting this recommeindation would be not advantages.
>
> second, negative ones in today may be a great people in the future. Not only ones behave do worse they are teenage. Teenage in today is not easy for all! Negative ones can not better, if only prainse positive actions, ignore negativeone. Negative ones may not positive be having, but if we praise them only, they not think they should be positive person later.
>
> conclusion, specific circumstances are which adopting the recommendation would not be advantage, I am not agree to the the recommendation. Ignore negative manor when they will not be positive behavrio in futre. But they can, if do not ignore them. we should not ignor negative person but should make them think that they can be a good man future like positive person.

Reader Commentary

This response has severe and pervasive problems in language and sentence structure that, as stated in the scoring guide, consistently interfere with meaning and result in incoherence. The response begins by repeating the prompt, but then the severe problems with language control and organization undermine any evidence of the ability to understand the prompt or to present and develop a clear position. For example, it is not clear what the writer means by the claim that the best way to teach is "making everyone to be a good ones." Severe problems with language control in that sentence and throughout the response prevent it from developing a coherent position on the issue or responding to the specific task instructions. Although the writer makes an attempt at organization, with points marked as first, second, and conclusion, the response actually exhibits little or no evidence of the ability to develop any potential understanding of the prompt into a logical position on the issue.

SECTION 2
Analytical Writing

ANALYZE AN ARGUMENT

The following appeared in an article written by Dr. Karp, an anthropologist.

"Twenty years ago, Dr. Field, a noted anthropologist, visited the island of Tertia and concluded from his observations that children in Tertia were reared by an entire village rather than by their own biological parents. However, my recent interviews with children living in the group of islands that includes Tertia show that these children spend much more time talking about their biological parents than about other adults in the village. This research of mine proves that Dr. Field's conclusion about Tertian village culture is invalid and thus that the observation-centered approach to studying cultures is invalid as well. The interview-centered method that my team of graduate students is currently using in Tertia will establish a much more accurate understanding of child-rearing traditions there and in other island cultures."

Write a response in which you discuss what specific evidence is needed to evaluate the argument and explain how the evidence would weaken or strengthen the argument.

Score 6 Response

It might seem logical, at first glance, to agree with the argument in Dr. Karp's article that children in Tertia actually are raised by their biological parents (and perhaps even, by implication, that an observation-centered approach to anthropological study is not as valid as an interview-centered one). However, in order to fully evaluate this argument, we need to have a significant amount of additional evidence. The argument could end up being much weaker than it seems, or it might actually be quite valid. In order to make that determination, we need to know more then analyze what we learn.

The first piece of evidence that we would need in order to evaluate Dr. Karp's claims is information about whether or not Tertia and the surrounding island group have changed significantly in the past 20 years. Dr. Field conducted his observational study 20 years ago, and it is possible that Tertia has changed significantly since then. For example, if we had evidence that in teh intervening years Westerners had settled on the island and they introduced a more typical Western-style family structure, it would certainly weaken Dr. Karp's argument. In that case, the original study could have been accurate, and Dr. Karp's study could be correct, as well, though his conclusion that Dr. Field's method is ineffective would be seriously weakened.

Another piece of evidence that might help us evaluate this claim involves the exact locations where Dr. Karp's interviews took place. According to this article, Dr. Karp and his graduate students conducted interviews of "children living in the group of islands that includes Tertia." If we were to learn that they never interviewed a single Tertian child, it would significantly weaken the conclusion. It could turn out to be the case, for example, that children on Tertia are raised communally, whereas children on other islands nearby are raised by their biological parents.

In order to fully evaluate this article, we would also need to learn more about the interview questions that Dr. Karp's team used. What exactly did they ask? We don't know, nor do we know what the children's responses actually were. What did they say about their biological parents? The mere fact that they speak more frequently about their biological parents than they do about other adults does not meant hat they are raised by their biological parents. It would significantly undermine Dr. Karp's argument if it turned out that the children said things like how much they missed their parents or how their parents had left them in a communal environment. Without knowing WHAT the children said, it is hard to accept Dr. Karp's conclusion.

It is slightly more difficult to discuss teh evidence we might need in order to evaluate the more interesting claims in Dr. Karp's article, namely his extension of the results of his study to a conclusion that interview-centered methods are inherently more valid than observational-centered approaches. In order to fully evaluate this claim, in fact, we would need to look at many more examples of interview-based and observation-based anthropological studies and we would also need to look into different study designs. Perhaps Dr. Field did not conduct an effective observational study, but other observational approaches could be effective. In order to make such grandiose claims, Dr. Karp really needs a lot of additional evidence (ideally a meta-analysis of hundreds of anthropological studies).

Clearly, then, we need to have additional evidence in order to get a more complete understanding of the strengths and weaknesses of Dr. Karp's article. We need to know about Tertia and the surrounding islands, whether or not they have changed over the past 20 years. We also need to know about study design (Dr. Karp's and Dr. Field's). And we really need a lot more information if we want to extend the results of a study about one island culture to all anthropological fieldwork.

Reader Commentary

This outstanding response clearly addresses the specific task directions and presents a cogent, insightful analysis by specifically detailing the impact that different pieces of evidence would have on the argument. The introductory paragraph sets up the organization of the response, and each body paragraph provides the sort of compelling development typical in responses that receive a score of 6. For example, after the writer discusses possible evidence that Tertian child-rearing practices have changed over the past 20 years, he or she clearly explains the impact information about those changes might have on the argument, saying, "In that case, the original study could have been accurate, and Dr. Karp's study could be correct, as well, though his conclusion that Dr. Field's method is ineffective would be seriously weakened." Not only is this argument compelling, but it also demonstrates sophisticated syntax and facility with language. There is more insightful development in the fifth paragraph, in which the writer examines Dr. Karp's claims about interview-based studies. Although there are a few typos and minor errors here, nothing in the response distracts from the overall fluency of the writing. Sentences like this one demonstrate the fluent and precise diction and varied syntax that are evident throughout the response: "It could turn out to be the case, for example, that children on Tertia are raised communally, whereas children on other islands nearby are raised by their biological parents." Because of its compelling and insightful development and fluent and precise language, this response fits all of the bullet points for a 6.

Score 5 Response

There seems to be an abundance of evidence that, if we were to examine it closely, might make us reconsider Dr. Karp's argument here. If we look first at the evidence that might weaken this argument, we can see a lot of the problems with Dr. Karp's article. It would certainly weaken the argument if we were to discover that Dr. Karp and his students did not actually conduct any of their interviews on the island of Tertia itself. Looking closely at the article, we see that Dr. Karp claims the interviews were conducted with children from the island group that includes Tertia. There is no evidence that they interviewed Tertian children. It would definitely weaken the argument if we were to learn that they interviewed children only on islands close to Tertia. Those islands may or may not have similar child-rearing traditions, and geographic proximity does not guarantee societal similarity.

Another piece of evidence that would weaken the argument could come from transcripts of the interviews themselves. Dr. Karp's article makes the claim that the children "spend much more time talking about their biological parents than about other adults," but he gives no indication of what exactly they say about their biological parents. After all, the children may be talking about how they never see their parents.

One more important piece of evidence that might undermine the argument Dr. Karp is making in this article. He admits that twenty years have passed since Dr. Field's study was conducted, but he does not provide evidence that proves child-rearing techniques have not changed significantly in that time. Any number of factors could have led to a significant shift in how children are raised. Influences from other cultures, significant catastrophic events, or a change in government structures could have led to a change in family dynamics. Any evidence of such changes would clearly undermine Dr. Karp's argument.

If we went looking for evidence that could strengthen the argument, we might also find something interesting. Obviously, some of the evidence above might strengthen the argument if they were NOT as discussed above (e.g., if there were evidence that the Tertian islands have NOT changed since Dr. Field's study or if there were transcripts that showed the children spoke about how much they loved living with their biological parents). However, if we discovered that there are numerous interview-based studies that confirm Dr. Karp's findings, it would go a long way toward bolstering his claim about Tertian child-rearing AND his claim about interview-centered studies being more effective. Another piece of evidence that would strengthen Dr. Karp's argument is undermining Dr. Field's original study. Maybe Dr. Field was sloppy, for example.

Dr. Karp's article, then, ends up looking like something of an empty shell. Depending on the evidence we find to fill it out, we may discover that it is quite convincing, or we could determine that he is full of hot air.

Reader Commentary

This strong response presents a generally thoughtful and well-developed analysis of the argument, and it follows the specific task directions quite clearly. This writer approaches the task by first discussing the evidence that might weaken Dr. Karp's argument and then, in somewhat less depth, considering the evidence that could strengthen it. In both cases the writer analyzes the ways in which the evidence would bear on the argument. For example, the writer notes, "Influences from other cultures, significant catastrophic events, or a change in government structures could have led to a change in family dynamics. Any evidence of such changes would clearly undermine Dr. Karp's argument." Although the development presented here is strong, the response does not present the compelling development required for a 6. For instance, in the first paragraph there is some repetition, and in the third paragraph the reader must fill in the implications of potential "changes" in Tertia, which are not fully fleshed out. How could a catastrophic event or a change in governmental structure have led to changes in child-rearing traditions? The development, then, is strong but not outstanding. Also, the response demonstrates some facility with language, though it does not convey meaning skillfully enough to merit a score of 6. In general, the response demonstrates strong writing skills, in spite of some minor errors like the sentence fragment that begins paragraph three. Sentences like this one demonstrate the quality of the writing seen throughout the response: "Those islands may or may not have similar child-rearing traditions, and geographic proximity does not guarantee societal similarity." In terms of writing skill and analysis, then, this response earns a score of 5.

Score 4 Response

Dr. Karp's arguments that his research proves that obervation-centered research is invalid and that his interview-centered method "will establish a much more accurate understanding of child-rearing traditions there and in other island cultures" need more support. While the findings from Dr. Karp's interviews do challenge Dr. Field's results, one then cannot make the assumption that Dr. Field's research is invalid. This essay will attempt to explain three ways in which Dr. Karp can strengthen his argument.

First, Dr. Karp should provide more information about the content of the interviews. Misinterpretation from observation can be as likely as misinterpretation in interievws. It is possible that while children may spend more time talking about their own biological parents, other people from the village are still assisting in most of the rearing of the child. Perhaps asking the children how much time they spend with their parents, who disciplines them, and other specific questions about rearing would provide a more complete answer about who exactly is raising the children.

Second, Dr. Karp could provide some information about societal changes in the past twenty years. If there have been significant changes on the island of Tertia, it is possible that both anthropologists are correct. Twenty years ago, the entire village raised children, and now, biological parents raise their own children. Recents events could explain the change - such as introduction of Western mass media or changes in government (monarchy to democracy). Perhaps even interviewing adults to get a better understanding on child rearing. Not to mention, interpretting information from children and using that information to generalize about an entire island is not the most effective means.

Thirdly, Dr. Karp needs more proof that the observation-centered approach to studying cultures in invalid. A potential mistake in one article can hardly invalidate an entire method of research. Other anthropologists who employ the interview-centered method need to dispute the work of anthropoligsts who use the observation-centered approach. Only when a significant amount of research can be disproved can an entire method of research be invalidated.

To conclude, Dr. Karp needs to do more research and provide more evidence before his large claims can be fully supported. In fact, it will take more than Dr. Karp alone to prove observation-centered method of research is invalid and further, that the interview-centered method is better. In terms of his own research, Dr. Karp needs to conduct more interviews on the Tertia islands and scientifically prove Dr. Field's research wrong.

Reader Commentary

This adequate response manages to identify some important features of the argument, presenting a competent examination and generally following the task directions. The response does not merit a score of 5 or 6, however, because it does not present compelling or insightful development. The response identifies basic points about the content of the interviews, possible changes in Tertia, and observation-centered studies, but these points are developed only adequately. Development in paragraph four ("Thirdly...") is generic and thin, and the final paragraph just recapitulates the assertions made earlier. The response does follow the specific task instructions, but it does not develop its discussion of specific evidence fully. For example, there is a claim that "specific questions about rearing would provide a more complete answer about who exactly is raising the children," but the response does not explain what sorts of questions would give which answers or how those answers would strengthen or weaken the argument. Also, language control in this response is merely adequate, not strong. There are some typos and other errors (e.g., a sentence fragment in paragraph 3: "Perhaps even interviewing adults to get a better understanding on child rearing"), but the response generally demonstrates control of the conventions of standard written English, and main points are made with reasonable clarity. Because of its adequate control of language and competent analysis, this response earns a score of 4.

Score 3 Response

It will be very inappropriate to condemn Dr. Field's observations and findings. A critical look and analyses of the argument shows that details of Dr. Field's work was not given out. In fact, it is sad on the side of the writer to think that Dr.Fields work is invalid.

First, the fact that the children of Tertia spend much time talking about their biological parents than about other adults in the village can be interpreted in a different way. The writer did not give any clue on what exactly the children were saying about their biological parents. It could be that they were talking about their parents irresponsibility of rearing them by themselves than leaving them in the hands of the whole community to bring them up. In fact, the argument could have been strengthened if the writer gave what exactly the children were talking about.

On the other hand, the writer failed on his or her part as a researcher to look at the time frame from the time Dr. Field did his analyses to the the time writer also conducted His or Her research. This would have given him the insight as what new developments has taken place within the twenty years gap that Dr. Field did His analyses. The writer's argument would have given a lot of meaning if the writer had research into the cultural developments that has taken place since the time Dr. fields last visited and didcompleted His work at Tertia.

Also, as a reader, the tone this writing is not very convincing. It almost seems like Dr. Karp is making Dr. Fields look bad, instead of supporting his own research with information. He really only says one sentence about his own research, the rest of it is about how Fields work is not as good and saying things about Fields work. He needs to have more details about his own work to really sell the reader on it. He needs to write more about what the interview-centered method is, since he does not even say what it is. This will be more convincing if it is less of an attack on Dr. Field and more about the researches.

On the whole the writer's work is incomplete and His or Her criticisms are unfounded. The writer needs to change the qualitative way of His or Her research into a more quatitative approach. If done in this way the impact of His or Her findings will be very strong and convincing.

Reader Commentary

Although this response analyzes some important features of the argument, it is limited in development and often lacks acceptable clarity in expressing its ideas. In particular, this response contains occasional major errors and frequent minor errors that can interfere with meaning. Misused words, subject/verb agreement problems, and other lapses occur throughout the response. In addition to the problems with language control, the response demonstrates limited relevant development. It is true that the response makes an attempt to follow the specific task instructions, identifying the fact that the argument might be strengthened by evidence that the children were talking in a positive manner about their parents. However, the response does not explain exactly *how* this evidence would strengthen the argument. Similarly, there is discussion of the elapsed time between the two studies, but the response does not clarify how information about the "cultural developments" over the past 20 years would strengthen the argument Dr. Karp is making. Additionally, some of the points the response is making are not actually relevant to an analysis of the logic of the argument. The discussion of Dr. Karp's tone in the fourth paragraph, for example, is a rhetorical critique, not a logical one. There is an attempt to talk about evidence ("He needs to have more details…"), but the focus in this paragraph is on "selling" the reader, not creating a persuasive argument. Because of its limited development and language control, this response earns a score of 3.

Score 2 Response

The argument is on the article written by Dr. Karp , an anthropologist and his study and the new plan to study the same in the tertia region.Dr.Karp has written an article on Children in Tertia and about the culture.

The arguement is that they have not mention the type of intreview and the type of questions of the interviwes.They haven't indicate the education level in the children and the background of the children. What are all the things the team is going to observe and study on the child rearing tradition is not clearly mention.

The team is going to study and correlate the tradition with the other island culture but there is a possibility of different environment of other island or differnt biological parents. The resource availability on one island is different than the other is also a possibility . In that situation it is not possible to correlate the culture between to iceland.

There is a possibility , Dr. Field's interview time , lacking of infrastructure in the tartia. There was no developement of schools and other refreshment activity or the parents may not spent enough time with the children due to various reasons and that effect to the children , so they might have spend more time talking about their biological parent.

To support the argument more information about the nature, cultural background and also the type of infrastructure presence in the area is require, the kind of study carring out in the study area is require. Which would help to give more support the argument.

Reader Commentary

This response demonstrates serious weaknesses in analytical writing. There seem to be some attempts at logical analysis, though none that specifically and clearly examine the evidence that might weaken or strengthen the argument. Additionally, there is little or no relevant or reasonable support for the writer's points. In large part, the lack of logical development seems to be due to the serious and frequent problems with language control seen throughout the response. There are basic errors in just about every sentence of the response, and these errors frequently interfere with meaning. This sentence exemplifies the problems seen throughout the response: "There was no developement of schools and other refreshment activity or the parents may not spent enough time with the children due to various reasons and that effect to the children , so they might have spend more time talking about their biological parent." The writer is attempting to discuss some points that are relevant to an analysis of this argument, but meaning is obscured by all of the errors present. However, some meaning can be discerned, and these errors are not severe enough to drop the score to a 1.

Score 1 Response

Twenty years ago Dr field an anthropologist found result after reserch that in small village of tertia children reared by entire village but according to dr karp he talked most of the children that they talk about there boilogical parents. so it conclude that the reserch of dr field is unvalid now and what type of methods dr field used may be not cover all aspects of there culture and also other cultures of other islands. reared the children by entire village is not logical but in some cultures there are some surprizing customs . so may be dr field did not anlysed the culture of that island on various parameters , which we are using now a days.intrveiw with children and observing their behaviour is important because some time the person talk one thing and behave in different way look like either he not telling correct or he is showing his altitude in misguiding way. i think the behaviour of the children shows proper report of reserch and you can observe their altitude to the other adult peoples of the village and to their own biological parents.The expert reserch scholer can easily feel their emotions and behaviour during some time stay with their culture. dr field maybe more research time, maybe, for longer.

Reader Commentary

This fundamentally deficient response mainly consists of a summary of the prompt, and although there is some evidence of understanding, the response provides little evidence of the ability to develop and organize an analysis of the argument. Also, severe problems in language persistently interfere with meaning. In fact, the material that does not come directly from the prompt is more or less incomprehensible.

Answers and Explanations

SECTION 3
Verbal Reasoning
25 Questions with Explanations

For each of Questions 1 to 4, select <u>one</u> answer choice unless otherwise instructed.

Questions 1 to 3 are based on the following reading passage.

Whether the languages of the ancient American peoples were used for expressing abstract universal concepts can be clearly answered in the case of Nahuatl. Nahuatl, like Greek and German, is a language that allows the formation of extensive com-
line pounds. By the combination of radicals or semantic elements, single compound words
5 can express complex conceptual relations, often of an abstract universal character.

The *tlamatinime* (those who know) were able to use this rich stock of abstract terms to express the nuances of their thought. They also availed themselves of other forms of expression with metaphorical meaning, some probably original, some derived from Toltec coinages. Of these forms, the most characteristic in Nahuatl is the juxtaposition
10 of two words that, because they are synonyms, associated terms, or even contraries, complement each other to evoke one single idea. Used metaphorically, the juxtaposed terms connote specific or essential traits of the being they refer to, introducing a mode of poetry as an almost habitual form of expression.

Description

This passage claims that Nahuatl was used to express abstract universal concepts, by combining semantic elements, and goes on to explain that the *tlamatinime* used these terms to express subtle distinctions.

For the following question, consider each of the choices separately and select all that apply.

1. Which of the following can be inferred from the passage regarding present-day research relating to Nahuatl?

   A Some record or evidence of the thought of the *tlamatinime* is available.

   B For at least some Nahuatl expressions, researchers are able to trace their derivation from another ancient American language.

   C Researchers believe that in Nahuatl, abstract universal concepts are always expressed metaphorically.

Explanation

Choices A and B are correct.

Choice A is correct: the *tlamatinime* are mentioned in the first sentence of the second paragraph, where it says they were able to use Nahuatl's stock of abstract terms "to express the nuances of their thought." This suggests that there is some evidence of what those thoughts were, and therefore Choice A can be inferred.

Choice B is correct: according to the next sentence, Nahuatl speakers used "forms of expression with metaphorical meaning," some of which were probably "original" and others "derived from Toltec coinages." That researchers know certain Nahuatl expressions are derived from Toltec suggests that they are able to trace the derivation of some Nahuatl expressions from another language besides Nahuatl, and therefore Choice B may be inferred.

Choice C is incorrect: the passage says that in Nahuatl there are single compound words that can express conceptual relations of an "abstract universal character" and mentions "other forms of expression with metaphorical meaning," but it does not indicate whether metaphorical words or phrases are the only way that abstract universal concepts are expressed in Nahuatl, or whether researchers believe this about Nahuatl. Therefore Choice C cannot be inferred.

2. Select the sentence in the passage in which the author introduces a specific Nahuatl mode of expression that is not identified as being shared with certain European languages.

Explanation

The passage introduces two specific Nahuatl modes of expression. One is the formation of single compound words that are capable of expressing complex conceptual relations (first paragraph); the other is the juxtaposition of two related words to evoke a single idea (second paragraph). In the formation of compounds Nahuatl is described as being "like Greek and German," but the second mode is not identified as being shared with other languages. Therefore the **sixth sentence** ("Of these forms . . . one single idea") is the best choice.

3. In the context in which it appears, "coinages" (line 9) most nearly means
   (A) adaptations
   (B) creations
   (C) idiosyncrasies
   (D) pronunciations
   (E) currencies

Explanation

"Coinage" has two senses that are represented among the answer choices: in one sense it denotes coins and currency, while in the other it denotes things—especially words—that are invented. The fifth sentence draws a contrast between linguistic expressions original to Nahuatl and those derived from Toltec. In this context of original versus derived language, "coinages" means "inventions," not "currencies." Of the answer choices given, "creations" is the nearest equivalent of "coinages" in the sense of "inventions," and therefore **Choice B** is the best answer.

At a certain period in Earth's history, its atmosphere contained almost no oxygen, although plants were producing vast quantities of oxygen. As a way of reconciling these two facts, scientists have hypothesized that nearly all of the oxygen being produced was taken up by iron on Earth's surface. Clearly, however, **this explanation is inadequate.** New studies show that **the amount of iron on Earth's surface was not sufficient to absorb anywhere near as much oxygen as was being produced.** Therefore, something in addition to the iron on Earth's surface must have absorbed much of the oxygen produced by plant life.

4. In the argument given, the two portions in **boldface** play which of the following roles?

    (A) The first is a claim made by the argument in support of a certain position; the second is that position.

    (B) The first is a judgment made by the argument about a certain explanation; the second is that explanation.

    (C) The first expresses the argument's dismissal of an objection to the position it seeks to establish; the second is that position.

    (D) The first sums up the argument's position with regard to a certain hypothesis; the second provides grounds for that position.

    (E) The first is a concession by the argument that its initial formulation of the position it seeks to establish requires modification; the second presents that position in a modified form.

Explanation

The passage presents an argument and the question asks you to identify the role the portions highlighted in boldface play in that argument. The first step in responding is to read through the passage quickly to get an understanding of what is being said. Then it is possible to go back and assess how the parts of the passage fit together into an argument.

In this passage the first sentence presents two pieces of information that seem to be in conflict—the atmosphere contained almost no oxygen even though plants were producing so much of it. The second sentence presents a hypothetical explanation that has been proposed for reconciling the discrepancy—that oxygen was absorbed by iron. The next sentence calls this hypothetical explanation inadequate and the following sentence gives a reason for that judgment—that there was insufficient iron for the proposed explanation to work. Finally, the last sentence draws the conclusion that there must have been something in addition to iron to absorb the oxygen.

Since the highlighted portions in the passage represent the main content of the third and fourth sentences, the task in this question is to find the answer choice whose two parts fit those sentences' roles. It can be seen that answer Choice D fits the requirement: the third sentence does sum up the argument's position about a hypothesis, and the fourth sentence gives grounds for the third. Therefore **Choice D** is the correct answer.

For Questions 5 to 8, select one entry for each blank from the corresponding column of choices. Fill all blanks in the way that best completes the text.

5. In her later years, Bertha Pappenheim was an apostle of noble but already (i)_____ notions, always respected for her integrity, her energy, and her resolve but increasingly out of step and ultimately (ii)_____ even her own organization.

Blank (i)	Blank (ii)
(A) anachronistic	(D) emulated by
(B) accepted	(E) appreciated by
(C) exotic	(F) alienated from

Explanation

The sentence is clearly conveying a contrast since "but" is used twice to indicate something positive and something negative about Pappenheim. The clue to the negative aspect is in the later part of the sentence, where "out of step" leads both to "anachronistic" as the answer for the first blank and "alienated from" as the answer for the second.

Thus, the correct answer is **anachronistic** (Choice A) and **alienated from** (Choice F).

6. The reception given to Kimura's radical theory of molecular evolution shows that when _____ fights orthodoxy to a draw, then novelty has seized a good chunk of space from convention.

(A) imitation
(B) reaction
(C) dogmatism
(D) invention
(E) caution

Explanation

The sentence sets up two parallel, contrasting concepts. The word in the blank must contrast with "orthodoxy," and since "convention" in the second contrasting pair is synonymous with "orthodoxy," the correct answer should be roughly synonymous with "novelty." The word "invention" is the best choice.

Thus, the correct answer is **invention** (Choice D).

7. The (i)_____ of Vladimir Nabokov as one of North America's literary giants has thrown the spotlight on his peripheral activities and has thus served to (ii)_____ his efforts as an amateur entomologist.

Blank (i)	Blank (ii)
(A) stigmatization	(D) foreground
(B) lionization	(E) transcend
(C) marginalization	(F) obscure

Explanation

It is possible to analyze this sentence by starting with either blank. Broadly, it states that something that has happened to Nabokov has called attention to some of his peripheral activities. It would hardly make sense for what had happened to be either stigmatization or marginalization, since both of those activities represent a turning away from him, not a calling attention to him. So the correct answer for the first blank is "lionization," since to lionize means to treat as important. Then, since we are told that Nabokov is a literary giant, entomology must be one of his peripheral activities, so the correct answer for the second blank must be "foreground," which also means "call attention to." Spotlighting something would not result in transcending it or obscuring it, so neither of the other choices is correct.

Thus, the correct answer is **lionization** (Choice B) and **foreground** (Choice D).

8. Mathematicians have a distinctive sense of beauty: they strive to present their ideas and results in a clear and compelling fashion, dictated by _____ as well as by logic.

Ⓐ caprice
Ⓑ aesthetics
Ⓒ obligation
Ⓓ methodologies
Ⓔ intellect

Explanation

The opening statement attributes a "sense of beauty" to mathematicians, and the remainder of the sentence after the colon spells out that observation. Filling in the blank will supply some aspect that balances "logic" and reinforces the view that mathematicians have a sense of beauty; "aesthetics" is the best choice.

Thus, the correct answer is **aesthetics** (Choice B).

For each of Questions 9 to 13, select <u>one</u> answer choice unless otherwise instructed.

Questions 9 to 12 are based on the following reading passage.

Animal signals, such as the complex songs of birds, tend to be costly. A bird, by singing, may forfeit time that could otherwise be spent on other important behaviors such as foraging or resting. Singing may also advertise an individual's location to rivals or predators and impair the ability to detect their approach. Although these types of cost may be important, discussions of the cost of singing have generally focused on energy costs. Overall the evidence is equivocal: for instance, while Eberhardt found increases in energy consumption during singing for Carolina wrens, Chappell found no effect of crowing on energy consumption in roosters.

To obtain empirical data regarding the energy costs of singing, Thomas examined the relationship between song rate and overnight changes in body mass of male nightingales. Birds store energy as subcutaneous fat deposits or "body reserves"; changes in these reserves can be reliably estimated by measuring changes in body mass. If singing has important energy costs, nightingales should lose more body mass

line
15
on nights when their song rate is high. Thomas found that nightingales reached a significantly higher body mass at dusk and lost more mass overnight on nights when their song rate was high.

These results suggest that there may be several costs of singing at night associated with body reserves. The increased metabolic cost of possessing higher body mass contributes to the increased overnight mass loss. The strategic regulation of evening body

20
reserves is also likely to incur additional costs, as nightingales must spend more time foraging in order to build up larger body reserves. The metabolic cost of singing itself may also contribute to increased loss of reserves. This metabolic cost may arise from the muscular and neural activity involved in singing or from behaviors associated with singing. For example, birds may expend more of their reserves on thermoregulation if

25
they spend the night exposed to the wind on a song post than if they are in a sheltered roost site. Thomas's data therefore show that whether or not singing per se has an important metabolic cost, metabolic costs associated with singing can have an important measurable effect on a bird's daily energy budget, at least in birds with high song rates such as nightingales.

Description

The passage mentions various ways in which singing is costly to a bird, but soon focuses on the main topic: the energy costs of singing. The second paragraph then discusses a particular experiment designed to assess the energy costs of singing for nightingales, and the third paragraph identifies a range of different associated costs.

9. The primary purpose of the passage is to
    (A) compare the different types of cost involved for certain birds in singing
    (B) question a hypothesis regarding the energy costs of singing for certain birds
    (C) present evidence suggesting that singing has an important energy cost for certain birds
    (D) discuss the benefits provided to an organism by a behavior that is costly in energy
    (E) describe an experiment that supports an alternative model of how birdsong functions

Explanation

As mentioned above, the first paragraph mentions various costs associated with birdsong, but from that point onward, the focus of the passage is on evidence concerning the energy costs of singing, for nightingales in particular. Thus, the correct answer is **Choice C**. Although the passage mentions other costs, it does not compare them with one another, so Choice A is incorrect. Because the passage does not question any hypotheses, discuss benefits, or advance an alternative model of birdsong, Choices B, D, and E are incorrect.

For the following question, consider each of the choices separately and select all that apply.

10. The passage implies that during the day before a night on which a male nightingale's song rate is high, that nightingale probably does which of the following?

    A Expends less of its reserves on thermoregulation than on other days

    B Stores more energy as body reserves than on other days

    C Hides to avoid predators

Explanation

Choice B is correct.

Choice A is incorrect: the only reference to thermoregulation comes in line 24 and discusses nighttime activity, not daytime activity.

Choice B is correct: the second paragraph explains that birds store energy as fat deposits that can be estimated by measuring body mass, and that body mass at dusk was significantly higher in nightingales on nights when their song rate was higher.

Choice C is incorrect: while the passage does say that singing exposes birds to predators (line 3), it says nothing to suggest that they make special efforts to hide before singing, and in fact it says that nightingales spend extra time foraging (line 20).

11. Select the sentence in the first or second paragraph that presents empirical results in support of a hypothesis about the energy costs of singing.

Explanation

Only two sentences in the relevant portion of the passage contain information that might be considered to be empirical results. The last sentence of the first paragraph contains information about increases in energy consumption but only the last sentence of the second paragraph provides results in support of the only hypothesis in the passage, that nightingales should lose more body mass on nights when their song rate is high. Thus, **sentence 9** ("Thomas found . . . high") is the correct choice.

For the following question, consider each of the choices separately and select all that apply.

12. It can be inferred from the passage that compared with other costs of singing, which of the following is true of the energy costs of singing?

    A They are the single greatest cost to an individual bird.

    B They have generally received more attention from scientists.

    C They vary less from one bird species to another.

Explanation

Choice B is correct.

Choice A is incorrect: you might infer that energy costs of singing are significant but no information is given to suggest that they are greater than other costs.

Choice B is correct: lines 4–5 say that discussions of the costs of singing have generally focused on energy costs.

Choice C is incorrect: the only mention of differences across species occurs in the discussion of the findings of Eberhardt and Chappell. These findings relate to energy costs alone and, if anything, suggest that energy costs vary considerably.

Question 13 is based on the following reading passage.

In the past ten years, there have been several improvements in mountain-climbing equipment. These improvements have made the sport both safer and more enjoyable for experienced climbers. Despite these improvements, however, the rate of mountain-climbing injuries has doubled in the past ten years.

13. Which of the following, if true, best reconciles the apparent discrepancy presented in the passage?

   Ⓐ Many climbers, lulled into a false sense of security, use the new equipment to attempt climbing feats of which they are not capable.

   Ⓑ Some mountain-climbing injuries are caused by unforeseeable weather conditions.

   Ⓒ Mountain climbing, although a dangerous sport, does not normally result in injury to the experienced climber.

   Ⓓ In the past ten years there have been improvements in mountain-climbing techniques as well as in mountain-climbing equipment.

   Ⓔ Although the rate of mountain-climbing injuries has increased, the rate of mountain-climbing deaths has not changed.

Explanation

In this question you are asked to identify the fact that would best reconcile the apparent discrepancy that the passage presents. The discrepancy is that despite improvements in mountain climbing equipment that have made climbing safer, the incidence of mountain-climbing injuries has greatly increased. Choice A explains how this could have happened—the improvements in equipment have led climbers to attempt feats that are beyond their level of skill. Therefore, **Choice A** is the correct answer.

None of the other choices provides information that resolves the discrepancy. Neither Choice B nor Choice C relates to conditions that have changed over the relevant ten-year period. Choices D and E do relate to the relevant period. But if, as Choice D says, techniques as well as equipment have improved, that fact by itself only makes the increase in injuries more puzzling. Choice E provides more data about the consequences of climbing accidents, but doesn't suggest any explanation for the increase in injuries.

For Questions 14 to 17, select one entry for each blank from the corresponding column of choices. Fill all blanks in the way that best completes the text.

---

14. Unenlightened authoritarian managers rarely recognize a crucial reason for the low levels of serious conflict among members of democratically run work groups: a modicum of tolerance for dissent often prevents _____.

Ⓐ demur
Ⓑ schism
Ⓒ cooperation
Ⓓ compliance
Ⓔ shortsightedness

Explanation

The blank must be filled with a word that describes a problem that a work group can suffer, a problem that can be a cause of (or associated with) serious conflict. Of the answer choices, only "schism" fits this description.

   Thus, the correct answer is **schism** (Choice B).

15. The novelist devotes so much time to avid descriptions of his characters' clothes that the reader soon feels that such _____ concerns, although worthy of attention, have superseded any more directly literary aims.

Ⓐ didactic
Ⓑ syntactical
Ⓒ irrelevant
Ⓓ sartorial
Ⓔ frivolous

Explanation

The "concerns" described by the adjective that fills the blank relate to clothing, so "sartorial" fits the blank. Although these concerns could also be described as "irrelevant" or "frivolous," neither of these choices is correct because the sentence identifies the concerns as "worthy of attention."

   Thus, the correct answer is **sartorial** (Choice D).

16. Belanger dances with an (i)_____ that draws one's attention as if by seeking to (ii)_____ it; through finesse and understatement, he manages to seem at once intensely present and curiously detached.

Blank (i)	Blank (ii)
Ⓐ undemonstrative panache	Ⓓ focus
Ⓑ unrestrained enthusiasm	Ⓔ overwhelm
Ⓒ unattractive gawkiness	Ⓕ deflect

Explanation

The point of the sentence is to emphasize contradictory aspects of Belanger's dancing: we are told, for example, that he seems "at once intensely present and curiously detached." Looking at the second blank with this point in mind, we can see that the sentence is saying that Belanger draws attention in some way that would not normally be a means of doing so. The only choice that fits, therefore, is "deflect"; focusing or overwhelming attention would certainly be expected to draw it. And since employing "unrestrained enthusiasm" or "unattractive gawkiness" would not be ways of deflecting attention, the correct choice for the first blank is "undemonstrative panache," another paradoxical term, since "panache" means "dash or flamboyance in style."

Thus, the correct answer is **undemonstrative panache** (Choice A) and **deflect** (Choice F).

17. The most striking thing about the politician is how often his politics have been
(i)_____ rather than ideological, as he adapts his political positions at any particular moment to the political realities that constrain him. He does not, however, piously (ii)_____ political principles only to betray them in practice. Rather, he attempts in subtle ways to balance his political self-interest with a (iii) _____, viewing himself as an instrument of some unchanging higher purpose.

Blank (i)	Blank (ii)	Blank (iii)
(A) quixotic	(D) brandish	(G) profound cynicism
(B) self-righteous	(E) flout	(H) deeply felt moral code
(C) strategic	(F) follow	(I) thoroughgoing pragmatism

Explanation

Since the politician is portrayed as adapting political positions to political realities, blank (i) should be filled with "strategic," which is also the only choice that provides the required contrast with "ideological." The second blank, *brandishing* political principles is what a politician might do piously, while *flouting* is not pious and *following* principles does not make sense when combined with "betray[ing] them in practice." The third blank requires something that would have to be balanced against "political self-interest" and that would be embraced in service of an "unchanging higher purpose," making "deeply felt moral code" the only viable choice.

Thus, the correct answer is **strategic** (Choice C), **brandish** (Choice D), and **deeply felt moral code** (Choice H).

For each of Questions 18 to 20, select **one** answer choice unless otherwise instructed.

Questions 18 to 20 are based on the following reading passage.

The condition of scholarship devoted to the history of women in photography is confounding. Recent years have witnessed the posthumous inflation of the role of the hobbyist Alice Austen into that of a pioneering documentarian while dozens of notable

line
5

senior figures—Marion Palfi, whose photographs of civil-rights activities in the South served as early evidence of the need for protective legislation, to name one—received scant attention from scholars. And, while Naomi Rosenblum's synoptic History of Women Photographers *covers the subject through 1920 in a generally useful fashion, once she reaches the 1920s, when the venues, forms, applications, and movements of the medium expanded exponentially, she resorts to an increasingly terse listing of unfamiliar names, with approaches and careers summarized in a sentence or two.*

10

Description

The passage expresses dismay at the current state of scholarship concerning the history of women in photography: some figures receive disproportionate attention, and past 1920 Rosenblum's book is too sketchy to be useful.

18. The author of the passage cites Rosenblum's book most likely in order to

    (A) suggest that the works documented most thoroughly by historians of women in photography often do not warrant that attention

    (B) offer an explanation for the observation that not all aspects of the history of women in photography have received the same level of attention

    (C) provide an example of a way in which scholarship on the history of women in photography has been unsatisfactory

    (D) suggest that employing a strictly chronological approach when studying the history of women in photography may be unproductive

    (E) provide support for the notion that certain personalities in women's photography have attained undue prominence

Explanation

As mentioned above, the topic of the passage is the unsatisfactory condition of scholarship devoted to the history of women in photography. Since Rosenblum's book is clearly presented as an example of this unsatisfactory scholarship, **Choice C** is the correct answer. Choice D may seem appealing, because a strictly chronological approach might be inadequate to represent the explosive growth of the field in the 1920s. However, the sentence does not develop this idea, and this is not the reason for mentioning Rosenblum.

For the following question, consider each of the choices separately and select all that apply.

19. Which of the following statements about Marion Palfi is supported by the passage?

    A   Marion Palfi's photographs would have received greater recognition from historians had her work been done in an era when most aspects of photography were static rather than in a state of transition.

    B   Alice Austen has achieved greater notoriety than has Marion Palfi primarily because the subjects that Austen photographed were more familiar to her contemporaries.

    C   In addition to providing a record of certain historical events, Marion Palfi's photographs played a role in subsequent events.

Explanation

Choice C is correct.

Choice A is incorrect: the passage does not state whether the period in which Palfi was working was an era when photography was static or in transition.

Choice B is incorrect: the passage does not state the nature of the subjects Austen photographed, nor compare their relative familiarity to those photographed by Palfi.

Choice C is correct: Palfi's photographs played a role in subsequent events because they served as early evidence of the need for protective legislation.

20. In the context in which it appears, "inflation" (line 2) most nearly means
    - Ⓐ exaggeration
    - Ⓑ acquisition
    - Ⓒ evaluation
    - Ⓓ distortion
    - Ⓔ attenuation

Explanation

The term "hobbyist" suggests Austen's relative lack of seriousness as a photographer when compared with "senior figures," yet her role has been elevated to that of a "pioneering documentarian" at the expense of these other figures. Choice D may be appealing in that this elevation could be considered a form of distortion, but Choice A is more specific as well as more in line with the dictionary definition of "inflated" as "expanded to an abnormal or unjustifiable volume or level." Thus, **Choice A**, "exaggeration," is the correct answer.

For Questions 21 to 25, select the two answer choices that, when used to complete the sentence, fit the meaning of the sentence as a whole and produce completed sentences that are alike in meaning.

---

21. The plan, which the engineers said would save the aquifer by reducing pumping to _____ levels, has passed a governmental environmental review but faces opposition from outdoor and environmental groups.
    - A innocuous
    - B feasible
    - C practicable
    - D minimal
    - E remedial
    - F benign

Explanation

If the engineers think that the reduced levels will save the aquifer, they may describe the reduced levels as innocuous, minimal, remedial, or benign. Of these words, only "innocuous" and "benign" produce sentences with the same meaning. The two words "feasible" and "practicable" are similar in meaning, but do not fit the context well, because they imply that the current levels are not feasible or practicable, conflicting with the implication that the current levels, though perhaps undesirable, are nevertheless entirely feasible.

Thus, the correct answer is **innocuous** (Choice A) and **benign** (Choice F).

22. Though feminist in its implications, Yvonne Rainer's 1974 film _____ the filmmaker's active involvement in feminist politics.

- [A] antedated
- [B] cloaked
- [C] portrayed
- [D] preceded
- [E] renewed
- [F] represented

Explanation

The words that fill the blank must fit with the idea that Rainer's film has some feminist implications, but that those are limited compared with her other activities. From the six words offered as answer choices, the pair "antedated" and "preceded" and the pair "portrayed" and "represented" each produce sentences that are similar in meaning. However, only "antedated" and "preceded" make sense in the context of the sentence: Rainer's 1974 film exhibits feminist themes in a limited way because it came before she became active in feminist politics.

Thus, the correct answer is **antedated** (Choice A) and **preceded** (Choice D).

23. Congress is having great difficulty developing a consensus on energy policy, primarily because the policy objectives of various members of Congress rest on such _____ assumptions.

- [A] commonplace
- [B] disparate
- [C] divergent
- [D] fundamental
- [E] trite
- [F] trivial

Explanation

The words that fill the blank must help explain the difficulty of developing a consensus. A lack of agreement on the assumptions that underlie Congress members' policy objectives would contribute to such a difficulty. Accordingly, "disparate" and "divergent" are the best choices because they both indicate disagreement among the members. Although the words "trite" and "trivial" are similar in meaning, triteness and triviality do not help to explain the difficulty in developing a consensus.

Thus, the correct answer is **disparate** (Choice B) and **divergent** (Choice C).

24. During the opera's most famous aria, the tempo chosen by the orchestra's conductor seemed _____, without necessary relation to what had gone before.

- [A] arbitrary
- [B] capricious
- [C] cautious
- [D] compelling
- [E] exacting
- [F] meticulous

Explanation

Any of the offered words could possibly describe a conductor's choice of tempo. However, the phrase "without necessary relation to what had gone before" is presented as an elaboration on the word in the blank. Among the answer choices, only "arbitrary" and "capricious" could be elaborated that way; none of the other choices would be explained by the final phrase.

Thus, the correct answer is **arbitrary** (Choice A) and **capricious** (Choice B).

25. Because they had expected the spacecraft Voyager 2 to be able to gather data only about the planets Jupiter and Saturn, scientists were _____ the wealth of information it sent back from Neptune twelve years after leaving Earth.

    A anxious for
    B confident in
    C thrilled about
    D keen on
    E elated by
    F eager for

Explanation

In the sentence, the words "expected" and "only" imply that the data received from the spacecraft exceeded scientists' expectations. Therefore, the words that fill the blank should describe a reaction to results that are better than hoped for, and the choices "thrilled about" and "elated by" both express such a reaction. The scientists may well also have been eager for, or keen on, the information, but their eagerness is not well explained by the unexpectedness of the information.

Thus, the correct answer is **thrilled about** (Choice C) and **elated by** (Choice E).

SECTION 4
Verbal Reasoning
25 Questions with Explanations

> For Questions 1 to 4, select the <u>two</u> answer choices that, when used to complete the sentence, fit the meaning of the sentence as a whole <u>and</u> produce completed sentences that are alike in meaning.

1. Only by ignoring decades of mismanagement and inefficiency could investors conclude that a fresh infusion of cash would provide anything other than a _____ solution to the company's financial woes.

   [A] complete
   [B] fleeting
   [C] momentary
   [D] premature
   [E] trivial
   [F] total

Explanation

The key phrases that indicate how the blank for this question should be completed are "Only by ignoring decades of mismanagement and inefficiency" and "provide anything other than." Taken together, these phrases indicate that the sentence will not envision a very beneficial or successful resolution of the "financial woes." Among the answer choices, "complete" and "total" are quite close in meaning and would clearly create two sentences very similar in meaning. But those two sentences would be internally contradictory, suggesting that doing something unwise would completely solve a problem. "Fleeting" and "momentary" suggest that the event referred to ("a fresh infusion of cash") might have some beneficial effect, but that it would ultimately not resolve the problem.

Thus, the correct answer is **fleeting** (Choice B) and **momentary** (Choice C).

2. Some scientists argue that carbon compounds play such a central role in life on Earth because of the possibility of _____ resulting from the carbon atom's ability to form an unending series of different molecules.

   [A] diversity
   [B] deviation
   [C] variety
   [D] reproduction
   [E] stability
   [F] invigoration

Explanation

The key phrase that indicates how the blank for this question should be completed is "the ability to form an unending series of different molecules." Among the answer choices, "diversity" and "variety" clearly fit logically with "unending" and "different" and create two very similar sentences. No other pair of choices here would produce two sentences as similar in meaning as those created by placing "diversity" and "variety" in the blank. Thus, the correct answer is **diversity** (Choice A) and **variety** (Choice C).

3. Given the flood of information presented by the mass media, the only way for someone to keep abreast of the news is to rely on _____ accounts.

   A synoptic
   B abridged
   C sensational
   D copious
   E lurid
   F understated

Explanation

The key phrase that indicates how the blank for this question should be completed is "the only way for someone to keep abreast of the news." Among the answer choices, "synoptic" and "abridged," while not synonymous in the strict sense, both fit the logic of this description, "synoptic" because of its emphasis on breadth and generality as opposed to detail, and "abridged" because of its obvious focus on brevity. "Sensational" and "lurid" would create two similar sentences but do not fit the logic for completing the blank, since we would not be relying on sensational or lurid accounts in order to keep abreast of the news.

   Thus, the correct answer is **synoptic** (Choice A) and **abridged** (Choice B).

4. Always circumspect, she was reluctant to make judgments, but once arriving at a conclusion, she was _____ in its defense.

   A deferential
   B intransigent
   C lax
   C negligent
   E obsequious
   F resolute

Explanation

The key phrases that indicate how the blank for this question should be completed are: "circumspect," "reluctant," and "but once." Taken together they point to completing the blank with something that is opposite in some way to the two cited adjectives. Among the answer choices, "intransigent" and "resolute," although not strictly synonymous, both fit the logic of the description given here for completing the blank and create sentences that are similar in meaning. "Lax" and "negligent" are clearly similar in meaning and would create sentences similar in meaning, but they continue the sentiment voiced in the initial clause rather than contrasting with it. "Deferential" and "obsequious" are also similar in meaning, but their emphasis on "politeness," while not strictly synonymous with reluctance and circumspection, like "lax" and "negligent" fail to pick up on the expected contrast.

   Thus, the correct answer is **intransigent** (Choice B) and **resolute** (Choice F).

For each of Questions 5 to 9, select <u>one</u> answer choice unless otherwise instructed.

When marine organisms called phytoplankton photosynthesize, they absorb carbon dioxide dissolved in seawater, potentially causing a reduction in the concentration of atmospheric carbon dioxide, a gas that contributes to global warming. However, phytoplankton flourish only in surface waters where iron levels are sufficiently high.
line
5 Martin therefore hypothesized that adding iron to iron-poor regions of the ocean could help alleviate global warming. While experiments subsequently confirmed that such a procedure increases phytoplankton growth, field tests have shown that such growth does not significantly lower atmospheric carbon dioxide. When phytoplankton utilize carbon dioxide for photosynthesis, the carbon becomes a building block for organic
10 matter, but the carbon leaks back into the atmosphere when predators consume the phytoplankton and respire carbon dioxide.

Description

The paragraph presents a hypotheses about reducing global warming by adding iron to iron-poor areas of the ocean and explains why adding the iron does not have the hoped-for benefit.

For the following question, consider each of the choices separately and select all that apply.

5. It can be inferred from the passage that Martin's hypothesis includes which of the following elements?

   [A] A correct understanding of how phytoplankton photosynthesis utilizes carbon dioxide

   [B] A correct prediction about how the addition of iron to iron-poor waters would affect phytoplankton growth

   [C] An incorrect prediction about how phytoplankton growth would affect the concentration of atmospheric carbon dioxide

Explanation

All three choices are correct. Martin's hypothesis was that adding iron to iron-poor regions of the ocean could help alleviate global warming.

   Choice A is correct: the passage presents Martin as using the standard understanding of how phytoplankton photosynthesize as a basis for the hypothesis.

   Choice B is correct: the passage states that experiments confirmed that adding iron to iron-poor regions increases phytoplankton growth in those regions. Therefore, Martin's prediction about this was correct.

   Choice C is correct: it can be inferred that in Martin's hypothesis the means by which adding iron in certain regions could alleviate global warming is that phytoplankton increase in those regions and absorb atmospheric carbon dioxide. The passage states that predators who consume phytoplankton respire carbon dioxide, so that the carbon dioxide absorbed by phytoplankton reenters the atmosphere. Therefore, Martin's prediction about this was incorrect.

6. It can be inferred that the author of the passage mentions predators (line 10) primarily in order to

  (A) help explain why Martin's hypothesis is incorrect
  (B) identify one effect of adding iron to iron-poor waters
  (C) indicate how some carbon dioxide is converted to solid organic matter
  (D) help account for differences in the density of phytoplankton between different regions of the ocean
  (E) point out a factor that was not anticipated by the scientists who conducted the field tests mentioned in the passage

Explanation

Lines 7–11 of the paragraph present the evidence against Martin's hypothesis. Lines 7–8 present field test results showing that Martin's hypothesis is incorrect, and the last sentence explains these results: the reason the increased phytoplankton resulting from the addition of iron do not reduce atmospheric carbon dioxide is that while the phytoplankton absorb carbon dioxide, the gas reenters the atmosphere when it is respired by phytoplankton predators. Therefore **Choice A** is correct: predators are mentioned to explain why Martin's hypothesis is incorrect. Choice B is not correct because while predators' consumption of phytoplankton and respiration of carbon dioxide might be considered one indirect consequence of adding iron to iron-poor waters, identifying a consequence is not the primary function of the mention of predators. Choice C is incorrect because the reference to predators is used to explain how carbon dioxide reappears as a gas, and Choice D is incorrect because no connection is suggested between predators and the distribution of phytoplankton. Choice E is not correct because it is Martin who did not anticipate this factor, rather than the scientists who conducted the field tests.

Question 7 is based on the following reading passage.

Sparva, unlike Treland's other provinces, requires automobile insurers to pay for any medical treatment sought by someone who has been involved in an accident; in the other provinces, insurers pay for nonemergency treatment only if they preapprove the treatment. Clearly, Sparva's less restrictive policy must be the explanation for the fact that altogether insurers there pay for far more treatments after accidents than insurers in other provinces, even though Sparva does not have the largest population.

Description

The passage tells us that in Sparva automobile insurers pay for far more medical treatments after accidents than they do in Treland's other provinces. The passage concludes that the explanation is to be found in the difference in legal requirements for insurers in Sparva as compared to other provinces.

7. Which of the following, if true, most strengthens the argument?

  (A) Car insurance costs more in Sparva than in any other province.
  (B) The cost of medical care in Sparva is higher than the national average.
  (C) Different insurance companies have different standards for determining what constitutes emergency treatment.
  (D) Fewer insurance companies operate in Sparva than in any other province.
  (E) There are fewer traffic accidents annually in Sparva than in any of the provinces of comparable or greater population.

Explanation

The question asks you to identify among the answer choices a fact that would support the passage's argument. The explanation offered in the passage can be supported by ruling out other explanations that might, given the information presented in the passage, appear likely. One obvious explanation for there being more medical treatments in Sparva is that there are more accidents there. Choice E rules out that explanation. So **Choice E** strengthens the argument in the passage and is the correct answer. Choices A and D each present consequences that are likely results of insurers in Sparva having to pay for more medical treatments. But neither bears on the cause of insurers having to pay for more treatments. Choice B does not strengthen the argument and may weaken it. A higher cost of medical care provides additional motivation for people to seek insurance payments to cover whatever post-accident care they receive. So Choice B might weaken the argument by providing an alternative explanation for insurers paying for more medical treatments in Sparva. According to the passage, whether treatment is emergency treatment is, in other provinces, an important criterion in determining insurers' responsibility. But since this criterion does not apply in Sparva, Choice C is not directly relevant to the point that the passage is trying to establish.

Questions 8 and 9 are based on the following reading passage.

Elements of the Philosophy of Newton, published by Voltaire in 1738, was an early attempt to popularize the scientific ideas of Isaac Newton. In the book's frontispiece, Voltaire is seen writing at his desk, and over him a shaft of light from heaven, the light of truth, passes through Newton to Voltaire's collaborator Madame du Châtelet; she reflects that light onto the inspired Voltaire. Voltaire's book commanded a wide audience, according to Feingold, because "he was neither a mathematician nor a physicist, but a literary giant aloof from the academic disputes over Newtonian ideas." In other words, Voltaire's amateurism in science "was a source of his contemporary appeal, demonstrating for the first time the accessibility of Newton's ideas to nonspecialists."

Description

The paragraph describes Voltaire's book and gives some reasons for its success.

For the following question, consider each of the choices separately and select all that apply.

8. Which of the following statements about Voltaire's *Elements of the Philosophy of Newton* can be inferred from the passage?

   A Voltaire's literary stature helped secure a large audience for this attempt to popularize Newton's ideas.

   B Voltaire's status as a nonscientist was an advantage in this effort to bring Newtonian science to the attention of the general public.

   C The frontispiece of the book implies that Voltaire's understanding of Newton's ideas was not achieved without assistance.

Explanation

All three choices are correct.

   Choice A is correct: the paragraph states that one of the reasons Voltaire's book commanded a wide audience is that he was "a literary giant."

Choice B is correct: the paragraph states that Voltaire's amateurism in science demonstrated that nonspecialists could also understand Newton's ideas.

Choice C is correct: the paragraph refers to Voltaire's collaborator, Madame du Châtelet. In the image described, she serves as the intermediary between Newton and Voltaire, conveying Newton's ideas to Voltaire.

9. Select the sentence that describes an allegory for Voltaire's acquisition of knowledge concerning Newton's ideas.

Explanation

In the image described in the second sentence, Voltaire acquires his knowledge of Newton through Madame du Châtelet, who conveys Newton's ideas—his "light of truth"—to Voltaire. The only other sentence that contains figurative language is the next sentence, in which Voltaire is described as "a literary giant aloof . . . from disputes." However, this image refers not to Voltaire's acquisition of knowledge of Newtonian ideas, but rather to his attitude regarding Newtonian ideas. Therefore **sentence 2** ("In the book's . . . Voltaire") is the correct choice.

For Questions 10 to 13, select one entry for each blank from the corresponding column of choices. Fill all blanks in the way that best completes the text.

---

10. Ironically, the writer so wary of (i)_____ was (ii)_____ with ink and paper, his novel running to 2,500 shagreen-bound folio pages—a fortune in stationery at the time.

Blank (i)	Blank (ii)
(A) probity	(D) acquisitive
(B) extravagance	(E) illiberal
(C) disapprobation	(F) profligate

Explanation

The last part of the sentence provides most of the context needed to fill in the two blanks. The novel was extremely long and required vast amounts of paper. Among the choices for the second blank, only "profligate" matches this lack of restraint. The word "Ironically" indicates that what the writer was "wary of" was something similar to profligacy; of the choices for the first blank, "extravagance" is the closest.

Thus, the correct answer is **extravagance** (Choice B) and **profligate** (Choice F).

11. What readers most commonly remember about John Stuart Mill's classic exploration of the liberty of thought and discussion concerns the danger of (i)_____: in the absence of challenge, one's opinions, even when they are correct, grow weak and flabby. Yet Mill had another reason for encouraging the liberty of thought and discussion: the danger of partiality and incompleteness. Since one's opinions, even under the best circumstances, tend to (ii)_____, and because opinions opposed to one's own rarely turn out to be completely (iii)_____, it is crucial to supplement one's opinions with alternative points of view.

Blank (i)	Blank (ii)	Blank (iii)
Ⓐ tendentiousness	Ⓓ embrace only a portion of the truth	Ⓖ erroneous
Ⓑ complacency	Ⓔ change over time	Ⓗ antithetical
Ⓒ fractiousness	Ⓕ focus on matters close at hand	Ⓘ immutable

Explanation

An overview of the passage suggests that the first sentence is relatively self-contained and that the blank is answerable without the succeeding sentences, where the topic shifts slightly. The colon after the first blank signals that what follows will define the word in the blank and will explain what danger Mill was concerned about. It says that without challenge, one's opinions grow "weak and flabby" and therefore one becomes *complacent*, not tendentious or fractious. A quick reading of the next two sentences suggests that the topic will be another danger that Mill described, "the danger of partiality and incompleteness." Free and open discussion needs to take place because each person's opinion tends to "embrace only a portion of the truth" and others' views are partially right, or never completely "erroneous." The other choices for the second and third blanks deal with change, immediacy, or antithesis, none of which relate to the second danger of "partiality" or "incompleteness."

Thus, the correct answer is **complacency** (Choice B), **embrace only a portion of the truth** (Choice D), and **erroneous** (Choice G).

12. Just as the authors' book on eels is often a key text for courses in marine vertebrate zoology, their ideas on animal development and phylogeny _____ teaching in this area.

Ⓐ prevent
Ⓑ defy
Ⓒ replicate
Ⓓ inform
Ⓔ use

Explanation

The "just as" structure indicates that the second half of the sentence should somehow parallel the idea presented in the first half (i.e., the idea that the authors' book on eels is a "key text" in marine vertebrate zoology). Among the choices given, "inform" is clearly the best choice. "Prevent" and "defy" work in the opposite direction, while "use" and "replicate" would suggest that the authors' ideas are drawing upon the teaching in this area rather than the other way around. "Inform" leads to a meaning that nicely matches the first half of the sentence.

Thus, the correct answer is **inform** (Choice D).

13. Mechanisms develop whereby every successful species can _____ its innate capacity for population growth with the constraints that arise through its interactions with the natural environment.

| Ⓐ enhance |
| Ⓑ replace |
| Ⓒ produce |
| Ⓓ surpass |
| Ⓔ reconcile |

Explanation

A quick overview of the sentence indicates that the blank should be filled with a verb that indicates what a successful species does with its "innate capacity for population growth" in the face of certain constraints on that growth. This analysis suggests that the correct answer will have something to do with adjusting that capacity in the face of these constraints. Of the choices given, "reconcile" is closest to that meaning. None of the other options make for a meaningful, coherent sentence. "Enhance," for example, may fit nicely with "its innate capacity," but it does not make sense with "constraints."

Thus, the correct answer is **reconcile** (Choice E).

For each of Questions 14 to 16, select __one__ answer choice unless otherwise instructed.

Questions 14 to 16 are based on the following reading passage.

It would be expected that a novel by a figure as prominent as W. E. B. DuBois would attract the attention of literary critics. Additionally, when the novel subtly engages the issue of race, as DuBois' *The Quest of the Silver Fleece* (1911) does, it would be a surprise not to encounter an abundance of scholarly work about that text. But though valuable scholarship has examined DuBois' political and historical thought, his novels have received scant attention. Perhaps DuBois the novelist must wait his turn behind DuBois the philosopher, historian, and editor. But what if the truth lies elsewhere: what if his novels do not speak to current concerns?

Description

The paragraph first presents reasons for critical interest in DuBois' novels, but then goes on to explain that there has in fact been very little such interest and speculates as to why that might be.

14. Which of the following can be inferred from the passage regarding DuBois' *The Quest of the Silver Fleece*?

    Ⓐ The lack of attention devoted to *The Quest of the Silver Fleece* can be attributed to the fact that it was DuBois' first novel.

    Ⓑ Among DuBois' novels, *The Quest of the Silver Fleece* is unusual in that it has received scant attention from scholars.

    Ⓒ *The Quest of the Silver Fleece* has at least one feature that typically would attract the attention of literary scholars.

    Ⓓ *The Quest of the Silver Fleece,* given its subtle exploration of race, is probably the best novel written by DuBois.

    Ⓔ Much of the scholarly work that has focused on *The Quest of the Silver Fleece* has been surprisingly critical of it.

Explanation

Choice C is correct. The second sentence states that *The Quest of the Silver Fleece* subtly engages the issue of race and implies that such an issue would attract the attention of literary scholars. The passage provides no information about whether *The Quest of the Silver Fleece* is DuBois' first novel (Choice A), whether it received more or less scholarly attention than his other novels (Choice B), whether it is better than any of his other novels (Choice D), nor about what scholars have said about it (Choice E).

15. In the fourth sentence ("Perhaps DuBois . . . editor."), the author of the passage is most likely suggesting that

    Ⓐ scholars will find that DuBois' novels are more relevant to current concerns than is his work as philosopher, historian, and editor

    Ⓑ more scholarly attention will be paid to *The Quest of the Silver Fleece* than to DuBois' other novels

    Ⓒ DuBois' novels will come to overshadow his work as philosopher, historian, and editor

    Ⓓ DuBois' novels may eventually attract greater scholarly interest than they have to date

    Ⓔ it will be shown that DuBois' work as philosopher, historian, and editor had an important influence on his work as novelist

Explanation

The fourth sentence speculates that once DuBois scholars have exhausted potential avenues of research in the fields of philosophy, history, and editing, they will turn to his novels, so **Choice D** is the correct answer. None of the other choices fits the metaphor in "Perhaps DuBois the novelist must wait his turn."

16. Which of the following best describes the central issue with which the passage is concerned?

    (A) The perfunctoriness of much of the critical work devoted to DuBois' novels

    (B) The nature of DuBois' engagement with the issue of race in *The Quest of the Silver Fleece*

    (C) Whether DuBois' novels are of high quality and relevant to current concerns

    (D) The relationship between DuBois the novelist and DuBois the philosopher, historian, and editor

    (E) The degree of consideration that has been given to DuBois' novels, including *The Quest of the Silver Fleece*

Explanation

The passage focuses on the scant attention given to DuBois' novels, *The Quest of the Silver Fleece* in particular. The first two sentences give reasons to expect greater attention, while the last two offer speculations about the explanation for the scant attention. Thus, **Choice E** is correct. The issues described in the other answer choices are all marginal to the passage, if they are mentioned at all.

> **For Questions 17 to 20, select one entry for each blank from the corresponding column of choices. Fill all blanks in the way that best completes the text.**

17. In the midst of so many evasive comments, this forthright statement, whatever its intrinsic merit, plainly stands out as _____.

(A) a paradigm
(B) a misnomer
(C) a profundity
(D) an inaccuracy
(E) an anomaly

Explanation

The sentence offers a contrast between "many evasive statements" and a single "forthright statement." On that basis alone, one might expect an answer such as "an anomaly." Do any of the other options make for a meaningful, coherent sentence? "A paradigm" is appealing, as is "a profundity," since the forthright statement is clearly presented as something positive. However, we are not in a position to call it paradigmatic or profound, since the sentence withholds judgment on "its intrinsic merit." The same reasoning allows us to eliminate "inaccuracy" and "misnomer." The straightforwardly descriptive "anomaly" is clearly the best choice.

Thus, the correct answer is **an anomaly** (Choice E).

18. The activists' energetic work in the service of both woman suffrage and the temperance movement in the late nineteenth century (i)_____ the assertion that the two movements were (ii)_____.

Blank (i)	Blank (ii)
Ⓐ undermines	Ⓓ diffuse
Ⓑ supports	Ⓔ inimical
Ⓒ underscores	Ⓕ predominant

Explanation

The sentence is about the implications of the activists' energetic work for some assertion about the woman suffrage and temperance movements. The second blank, however, obscures the nature of that assertion. But it is clear that the "energetic work" could either support an assertion that the two movements were similar, or undermine an assertion that the two movements were opposed. "Supports" is offered as a choice for the first blank (as is the somewhat similar "underscores"), but there is no corresponding term in the second blank, nothing along the lines of "similar" or "compatible." "Undermines" and "inimical" make for the only meaningful statement.

Thus, the correct answer is **undermines** (Choice A) and **inimical** (Choice E).

19. There is nothing quite like this movie, and indeed I am not altogether sure there is much more to it than its lovely (i) _____. At a moment when so many films strive to be as (ii)_____ as possible, it is gratifying to find one that is so subtle and puzzling.

Blank (i)	Blank (ii)
Ⓐ peculiarity	Ⓓ indirect
Ⓑ pellucidity	Ⓔ assertive
Ⓒ conventionality	Ⓕ enigmatic

Explanation

The two sentences provide the reader with quite a bit of information about the movie. There is "nothing quite like it" and it is "subtle and puzzling." "Peculiarity" is clearly a solid fit for the first blank, while "conventionality" clearly does not work, given the fact that there is "nothing quite like it." That leaves "pellucidity," which, while it could fit logically in the first sentence in isolation, does not fit the later claim that the movie is "subtle and puzzling." The second blank needs simply to provide a contrast with "subtle and puzzling." Of the choices offered, only "assertive" clearly does that.

Thus, the correct answer is **peculiarity** (Choice A) and **assertive** (Choice E).

20. Wills argues that certain malarial parasites are especially (i)_____ because they have more recently entered humans than other species and therefore have had (ii)_____ time to evolve toward (iii)_____. Yet there is no reliable evidence that the most harmful *Plasmodium* species has been in humans for a shorter time than less harmful species.

Blank (i)	Blank (ii)	Blank (iii)
(A) populous	(D) ample	(G) virulence
(B) malignant	(E) insufficient	(H) benignity
(C) threatened	(F) adequate	(I) variability

Explanation

The "Yet" that begins the second sentence indicates that Wills' position would be supported by evidence that the newer parasites are in humans, the more harmful they are. So Wills' position must be that more recent parasites are especially harmful, implying that "malignant" is the correct choice for the first blank. What follows "therefore" is a potential explanation for the trend that Wills expects, namely an evolution toward harmlessness, implying "benignity" for the third blank, with newer species having had "insufficient" time (second blank) to evolve toward harmlessness.

Thus, the correct answer is **malignant** (Choice B), **insufficient** (Choice E), and **benignity** (Choice H).

For each of questions 21 to 25, select one answer choice unless otherwise instructed.

Question 21 is based on the following reading passage.

Saturn's giant moon Titan is the only planetary satellite with a significant atmosphere and the only body in the solar system other than Earth that has a thick atmosphere dominated by molecular nitrogen. For a long time, the big question about Titan's atmosphere was how it could be so thick, given that Jupiter's moons Ganymede and Callisto, which are the same size as Titan, have none. The conditions for acquiring and retaining a thick nitrogen atmosphere are now readily understood. The low temperature of the protosaturnian nebula enabled Titan to acquire the moderately volatile compounds methane and ammonia (later converted to nitrogen) in addition to water. The higher temperatures of Jupiter's moons, which were closer to the Sun, prevented them from acquiring such an atmosphere.

Description

The paragraph discusses Titan's thick atmosphere and explains the conditions under which a body can have a thick atmosphere.

21. According to the passage, Titan differs atmospherically from Ganymede and Callisto because of a difference in
    (A) rate of heat loss
    (B) proximity to the Sun
    (C) availability of methane and ammonia
    (D) distance from its planet
    (E) size

Explanation

According to the last two sentences of the paragraph, Titan was able to acquire an atmosphere because of a prevailing low temperature, but Ganymede and Callisto could not because they were at a higher temperature. Because the reason for this difference in temperature was their respective distances from the Sun, **Choice B** is correct. The passage says nothing about differences in rate of heat loss, availability of methane and ammonia, or distance from their planets, and it explicitly states that the three moons are the same size.

Question 22 is based on the following reading passage.

Observations of the Arctic reveal that the Arctic Ocean is covered by less ice each summer than the previous summer. If this warming trend continues, within 50 years the Arctic Ocean will be ice free during the summer months. This occurrence would in itself have little or no effect on global sea levels, since the melting of ice floating in water does not affect the water level. However, serious consequences to sea levels would eventually result, because _____.

22. Which of the following most logically completes the passage?
    - (A) large masses of floating sea ice would continue to form in the wintertime
    - (B) significant changes in Arctic sea temperatures would be accompanied by changes in sea temperatures in more temperate parts of the world
    - (C) such a warm Arctic Ocean would trigger the melting of massive land-based glaciers in the Arctic
    - (D) an ice-free Arctic Ocean would support a very different ecosystem than it does presently
    - (E) in the spring, melting sea ice would cause more icebergs to be created and to drift south into shipping routes

Explanation

To logically complete the passage's open-ended "because," something is needed that will explain why the continuation of the warming trend would have serious consequences for sea levels. The passage explains that the melting of the Arctic Ocean ice will not affect sea levels because the contribution that the water contained in that ice makes to sea levels is the same whether the water is frozen or liquid. But Choice C points to a way in which increasing temperatures in the Arctic could add water to the ocean, namely by melting ice on the land. So **Choice C** logically completes the passage and is the correct answer.

Given that the passage has already explained that melting sea ice does not affect sea levels, the formation of sea ice described in Choice A does not explain why there would be consequences for sea levels.

Choices B, D, and E all describe possible consequences of increased temperatures in the Arctic, but none of these consequences suggests a mechanism by which sea levels would change. So none of these options provides a logical completion for the passage.

Questions 23 to 25 are based on the following reading passage.

In a recent study, David Cressy examines two central questions concerning English immigration to New England in the 1630s: what kinds of people immigrated and why? Using contemporary literary evidence, shipping lists, and customs records, Cressy finds that most adult immigrants were skilled in farming or crafts, were literate, and were organized in families. Each of these characteristics sharply distinguishes the 21,000 people who left for New England in the 1630s from most of the approximately 377,000 English people who had immigrated to America by 1700.

With respect to their reasons for immigrating, Cressy does not deny the frequently noted fact that some of the immigrants of the 1630s, most notably the organizers and clergy, advanced religious explanations for departure, but he finds that such explanations usually assumed primacy only in retrospect. When he moves beyond the principal actors, he finds that religious explanations were less frequently offered, and he concludes that most people immigrated because they were recruited by promises of material improvement.

line 5 (margin)
10 (margin)

Description

The passage discusses Cressy's answers to the questions posed in the first sentence. The immigrants were skilled, literate, and in families, and they apparently immigrated to have a better life materially, rather than religiously.

For the following question, consider each of the choices separately and select all that apply.

23. The passage indicates that Cressy would agree with which of the following statements about the organizers among the English immigrants to New England in the 1630s?

 A Some of them offered a religious explanation for their immigration.

 B They did not offer any reasons for their immigration until some time after they had immigrated.

 C They were more likely than the average immigrant to be motivated by material considerations.

Explanation

Choice A is correct.

Choice A is correct: the organizers are mentioned in the second paragraph, where the passage says that Cressy "does not deny" that organizers "advanced religious explanations" for leaving England and immigrating to New England in the 1630s. This suggests that Cressy would agree with the statement in choice A about the organizers.

Choice B is incorrect: in lines 10–11, the passage says that Cressy finds that religious reasons for immigration "assumed primacy" only in retrospect, but this is not the same as Cressy's concluding that no reasons were given at the time of immigration. Therefore it cannot be inferred that Cressy would agree with the statement in Choice B.

Choice C is incorrect: the passage refers in lines 13–14 to "promises of material improvement" as a factor that in Cressy's view motivated most immigrants other than "the principal actors." This suggests that Cressy regards the principal actors, such as organizers, as having been less, not more, motivated by material considerations than average immigrants were. Therefore it cannot be inferred that Cressy would agree with the statement in Choice C.

24. Select the sentence that provides Cressy's opinion about what motivated English immigrants to go to New England in the 1630s.

Explanation

The last sentence says that Cressy "concludes that most people immigrated because they were recruited by promises of material improvement." Because this suggests that Cressy believes immigrants were motivated by these promises to go to New England, **sentence 5** ("When he . . . improvement) is the correct choice. The preceding sentence suggests that Cressy does not believe religion was a primary motive influencing immigrants' decision to immigrate in the 1630s. Thus, although this sentence provides an opinion of Cressy's concerning some immigrants' stated reasons for immigrating, it does not say what motive he believes was actually behind the immigration, and therefore does not answer the question.

25. In the passage, the author is primarily concerned with
    (A) summarizing the findings of an investigation
    (B) analyzing a method of argument
    (C) evaluating a point of view
    (D) hypothesizing about a set of circumstances
    (E) establishing categories

Explanation

The passage is about Cressy's investigation of English immigration to New England in the 1630s, and it summarizes his findings concerning who immigrated and why. **Choice A**, "summarizing the findings of an investigation," is therefore the best description of the author's primary concern in the passage. The passage does not analyze a method of argument, so Choice B is incorrect. Choice C is incorrect because the passage is not primarily concerned with evaluating a point of view: it does not assess the merits or demerits of Cressy's viewpoint. The passage is concerned with reporting Cressy's findings, not with hypothesizing or with establishing categories, so Choices D and E are incorrect.

SECTION 5
Quantitative Reasoning
25 Questions with Explanations

For each of Questions 1 to 9, select one of the following answer choices.
- Ⓐ **Quantity A is greater.**
- Ⓑ **Quantity B is greater.**
- Ⓒ **The two quantities are equal.**
- Ⓓ **The relationship cannot be determined from the information given.**

O is the center of the circle above.

Quantity A	Quantity B	
1. x	5	Ⓐ Ⓑ Ⓒ Ⓓ

Explanation

In this question you are asked to compare x with 5, where x is the length of a line segment from the center of the circle to a point inside the circle. In a circle the easiest line segments to deal with are the radius and the diameter. Looking at the figure in the question, you can see that you can draw two radii, each of which "completes" a right triangle, as shown in the figure below.

Since in one of the triangles the lengths of both legs are known, you can use that triangle to determine the length of the radius of the circle. The triangle has legs of length 3 and 4. If the length of the radius is r, then, using the Pythagorean theorem, you can see that

$$r^2 = 3^2 + 4^2 \text{ or}$$
$$r^2 = 9 + 16 \text{ or}$$
$$r^2 = 25, \text{ and thus, } r = 5$$

Since the length of the radius of the circle is 5 and the line segment of length x is clearly shorter than the radius, you know that $x < 5$, and the correct answer is **Choice B**.

You could also see that the two triangles are congruent, and so $x = 4$, again yielding **Choice B**.

This explanation uses the following strategy.

Strategy 4: Translate from a Figure to an Arithmetic or Algebraic Representation

Runner A ran $\frac{4}{5}$ kilometer and Runner B ran 800 meters.

	Quantity A	Quantity B	
2.	The distance that A ran	The distance that B ran	Ⓐ Ⓑ Ⓒ Ⓓ

Explanation

In this question you are asked to compare two measurements, one given in kilometers and the other in meters. It would be easier to compare these measurements if they were both given in meters or both given in kilometers.

If you choose to convert the distance that Runner B ran from meters to kilometers, you need to use the conversion 1 meter is equal to $\frac{1}{1,000}$ kilometer.

Since B ran 800 meters, it follows that B ran $(800)\left(\frac{1}{1,000}\right)$, or $\frac{4}{5}$ kilometer, which is the same distance that A ran.

If you choose to convert the distance that Runner A ran from kilometers to meters, you need to use the conversion 1 kilometer is equal to 1,000 meters.

Since A ran $\frac{4}{5}$ kilometer, it follows that A ran $\left(\frac{4}{5}\right)(1,000)$, or 800 meters, which is the same distance that B ran. Either way, A and B ran the same distance, and the correct answer is **Choice C**.

This explanation uses the following strategy.

Strategy 1: Translate from Words to an Arithmetic or Algebraic Representation

$$x < y < z$$

	Quantity A	Quantity B	
3.	$\frac{x+y+z}{3}$	y	Ⓐ Ⓑ Ⓒ Ⓓ

Explanation

In this question you are given that $x < y < z$, and you are asked to compare $\frac{x+y+z}{3}$ with y.

Two approaches that you could use to solve this problem are:

    1: Search for a mathematical relationship between the two quantities.
    2: Plug in numbers for the variables.

Approach 1: Note that $\frac{x+y+z}{3}$ is the average of the three numbers x, y, and z and that y is the median. Is the average of 3 numbers always equal to the median? The average could equal the median, but in general they do not have to be equal. Therefore, the correct answer is **Choice D**.

Approach 2: When you plug in numbers for the variables, it is a good idea to consider what kind of numbers are appropriate to plug in and to choose numbers that are easy to work with, if possible.

Since $\frac{x+y+z}{3}$ is the average of the three numbers x, y, and z and you are comparing it to the median, you may want to try plugging in numbers that are evenly spaced and plugging in numbers that are not evenly spaced.

You can plug in numbers that are both evenly spaced and easy to work with. For example, you can plug in $x = 1$, $y = 2$, and $z = 3$. In this case,

$$\frac{x+y+z}{3} = \frac{1+2+3}{3} = \frac{6}{3} = 2, \text{ and so } \frac{x+y+z}{3} = y.$$

You can also plug in numbers that not are not evenly spaced and are easy to work with. For example, you can plug in $x = 3$, $y = 6$, and $z = 12$. In this case,

$$\frac{x+y+z}{3} = \frac{3+6+12}{3} = \frac{21}{3} = 7, \text{ and } \frac{x+y+z}{3} > y. \text{ Since in the first case, } \frac{x+y+z}{3}$$

is equal to y and in the second case, it is greater than y, the relationship between the two quantities $\frac{x+y+z}{3}$ and y cannot be determined from the information given. The correct answer is **Choice D**.

This explanation uses the following strategies.

Strategy 10: Trial and Error
Strategy 11: Divide into Cases
Strategy 12: Adapt Solutions to Related Problems
Strategy 13: Determine Whether a Conclusion Follows from the Information Given

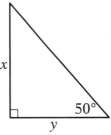

	Quantity A	Quantity B	
4.	$\frac{x}{y}$	1	

Explanation

One way you can solve this problem is by using the following fact:

- If ABC is a triangle and the measure of angle A is greater than the measure of angle B, then the side opposite angle A is longer than the side opposite angle B.

Since the third angle of the triangle measures 40°, you can use the fact above to conclude that the side opposite the 50° angle is longer than the side opposite the 40° angle. So $x > y$, and $\frac{x}{y} > 1$, which yields **Choice A**.

You can also solve this problem without using the fact above. Instead, you can use the strategy of adapting solutions to related problems to determine the relationship between x and y.

Note that the angles in the triangle differ only a little from the angles in a 45°- 45°- 90° triangle. How do the lengths of the legs of a 45°- 45°- 90° triangle compare to the lengths of the legs of the triangle in the question? To make the comparison, add a line segment to the triangle so that the line segment cuts the 50° angle in two parts, making a 45° angle with the horizontal base, as shown in the following figure:

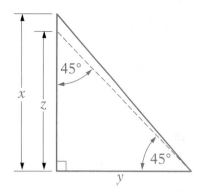

The 45°- 45°- 90° triangle has two 45° angles, so $z = y$, and $\frac{z}{y} = 1$. Since $\frac{z}{y} = 1$ and $x > z$, it follows that $\frac{x}{y} > 1$. The correct answer is **Choice A**.

This explanation uses the following strategies.
Strategy 6: Add to a Geometric Figure
Strategy 8: Search for a Mathematical Relationship
Strategy 12: Adapt Solutions to Related Problems

$$0 < x < y < 1$$

	Quantity A	Quantity B	
5.	$1 - y$	$y - x$	Ⓐ Ⓑ Ⓒ Ⓓ

Explanation

Two approaches that you could use to solve this problem are:

1: Translate from algebra to a number line.
2: Plug in values for the variables.

Approach 1: The following figure represents the information given in the problem on a number line.

On the number line, $1 - y$ is the distance between 1 and y, and $y - x$ is the distance between y and x. If y is exactly halfway between x and 1, then $1 - y$ is equal to $y - x$; and if y is <u>not</u> halfway between x and 1, then $1 - y$ is <u>not</u> equal to $y - x$. But y can be <u>any</u> number between x and 1, so the correct answer is **Choice D**.

Approach 2: Since this problem involves subtraction, it is a good idea to choose values for x and y that are close to each other as well as values that are far apart. For example, if $x = 0.4$ and $y = 0.5$, then $1 - y = 0.5$ and $y - x = 0.1$; and if $x = 0.1$ and $y = 0.9$, then $1 - y = 0.1$ and $y - x = 0.8$. This shows that the relationship cannot be determined, and the correct answer is **Choice D**.

This explanation uses the following strategies.
Strategy 3: Translate from an Algebraic to a Graphical Representation
Strategy 10: Trial and Error
Strategy 11: Divide into Cases
Strategy 13: Determine Whether a Conclusion Follows from the Information Given

p is the probability that event *E* will occur, and *s* is the probability that event *E* will **not** occur.

	Quantity A	Quantity B	
6.	$p + s$	ps	Ⓐ Ⓑ Ⓒ Ⓓ

Explanation

Since event *E* will either occur or not occur, it follows that $p + s = 1$, and the value of Quantity A is always 1. Since Quantity B is the product of the two probabilities *p* and *s*, you need to look at its value for the cases $p = 1$, $p = 0$, and $0 < p < 1$.

If $p = 1$, then $s = 0$; similarly, if $p = 0$, then $s = 1$. In both cases, *ps* is equal to 0.

If $0 < p < 1$, both *p* and *s* are positive and less than 1, so *ps* is positive and less than 1. Since Quantity A is equal to 1 and Quantity B is less than 1, the correct answer is **Choice A**.

This explanation uses the following strategy.

Strategy 11: Divide into Cases

X is the set of all integers *n* that satisfy the inequality $2 \leq |n| \leq 5$.

	Quantity A	Quantity B	
7.	The absolute value of the greatest integer in *X*	The absolute value of the least integer in *X*	Ⓐ Ⓑ Ⓒ Ⓓ

Explanation

When comparing these quantities, it is important to remember that a nonzero number and its negative have the same absolute value. For example, $|-2| = |2| = 2$. Keeping this in mind, you can see that the positive integers 2, 3, 4, and 5 and the negative integers –2, –3, –4, and –5 all satisfy the inequalities $2 \leq |n| \leq 5$, and that these are the only such integers. Thus, the set *X* consists of the integers –5, –4, –3, –2, 2, 3, 4, and 5. The greatest of these integers is 5, and its absolute value is 5. The least of these integers is –5, and its absolute value is also 5. Therefore, Quantity A is equal to Quantity B. The correct answer is **Choice C**.

This explanation uses the following strategy.

Strategy 1: Translate from Words to an Arithmetic or Algebraic Representation

x and *m* are positive numbers, and *m* is a multiple of 3.

	Quantity A	Quantity B	
8.	$\dfrac{x^m}{x^3}$	$x^{m/3}$	Ⓐ Ⓑ Ⓒ Ⓓ

Explanation

Since $\dfrac{x^m}{x^3} = x^{m-3}$, you need to compare x^{m-3} with $x^{m/3}$. Since the base in both expressions is the same, a good strategy to use to solve this problem is to plug in numbers for *m* in both expressions and compare them.

You know that *m* is a multiple of 3, so the least positive integer you can plug in for *m* is 3.

If $m = 3$, then $x^{m-3} = 1$ and $x^{m/3} = x$. Since x can be any positive number, its relationship to 1 cannot be determined from the information given. This example is sufficient to show that the relationship between $\dfrac{x^m}{x^3}$ and $x^{m/3}$ cannot be determined from the information given. The correct answer is **Choice D**.

This explanation uses the following strategies.
Strategy 5: Simplify an Arithmetic or Algebraic Representation
Strategy 10: Trial and Error

> A random variable Y is normally distributed with a mean of 200 and a standard deviation of 10.

	Quantity A	Quantity B	
9.	The probability of the event that the value of Y is greater than 220	$\dfrac{1}{6}$	Ⓐ Ⓑ Ⓒ Ⓓ

Explanation

This problem involves a normal distribution with mean 200 and standard deviation 10. Thus, the value of 210 is 1 standard deviation above the mean, and the value of 220 is 2 standard deviations above the mean. To compare Quantity A with Quantity B, it is not necessary to exactly determine the probability of the event that the value of Y is greater than 220. Remember that in any normal distribution, almost all of the data values, or about 95% of them, fall within 2 standard deviations on either side of the mean. This means that less than 5% of the values in this distribution will be greater than 220. Thus, the probability of the event that the value of Y is greater than 220 must be less than 5%, or $\dfrac{1}{20}$, and this is certainly less than $\dfrac{1}{6}$. The correct answer is **Choice B**.

Another approach to this problem is to draw a normal curve, or "bell-shaped curve," that represents the probability distribution of the random variable Y, as shown in the figure below.

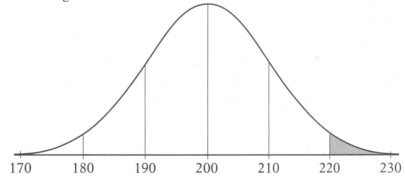

The curve is symmetric about the mean 200. The values of 210, 220, and 230 are equally spaced to the right of 200 and represent 1, 2, and 3 standard deviations, respectively, above the mean. Similarly, the values of 190, 180, and 170 are 1, 2, and 3 standard deviations, respectively, below the mean. Quantity A, the probability of the event that the value of Y is greater than 220, is equal to the area of the shaded region as a fraction of the total area under the curve.

From the figure, you can see that the area under the normal curve has been divided into 6 regions and that these regions are not equal in area. The shaded region is one of the two smallest of the 6 regions, so its area must be less than $\frac{1}{6}$ of the total area under the curve. The correct answer is **Choice B**.

This explanation uses the following strategies.
Strategy 2: Translate from Words to a Figure or Diagram
Strategy 8: Search for a Mathematical Relationship

10.   The ratio of $\frac{1}{3}$ to $\frac{3}{8}$ is equal to the ratio of

    Ⓐ 1 to 8

    Ⓑ 8 to 1

    Ⓒ 8 to 3

    Ⓓ 8 to 9

    Ⓔ 9 to 8

Explanation

Multiplying both parts of a ratio by the same positive number produces an equivalent ratio. While you could multiply both fractions in the ratio by any number, 24 is a good number to choose because it is the least common multiple of 3 and 8. Thus, multiplying both $\frac{1}{3}$ and $\frac{3}{8}$ by 24, you get that the ratio of $\frac{1}{3}$ to $\frac{3}{8}$ is equal to the ratio of 8 to 9. The correct answer is **Choice D**.

An alternate approach to this problem is to express the ratio of $\frac{1}{3}$ to $\frac{3}{8}$ as the fraction $\dfrac{\frac{1}{3}}{\frac{3}{8}}$. This fraction is equivalent to $\left(\frac{1}{3}\right)\left(\frac{8}{3}\right)$, or $\frac{8}{9}$. The correct answer is **Choice D**.

This explanation uses the following strategy.
Strategy 5: Simplify an Arithmetic or Algebraic Representation

11.   A reading list for a humanities course consists of 10 books, of which 4 are biographies and the rest are novels. Each student is required to read a selection of 4 books from the list, including 2 or more biographies. How many selections of 4 books satisfy the requirements?

    Ⓐ   90

    Ⓑ   115

    Ⓒ   130

    Ⓓ   144

    Ⓔ   195

Explanation

The requirement to select 4 books, including 2 or more biographies, means that you have to consider three cases. A student can choose 4 biographies and no novels, or 3 biographies and 1 novel, or 2 biographies and 2 novels.

Case 1: Choose 4 biographies. This case is easy, as there is only 1 way to choose all four biographies and no novels.

In the other two cases, you have to find the number of ways of choosing the biographies and the number of ways of choosing the novels and then multiply these two numbers.

Case 2: Choose 3 biographies and 1 novel. First, you need to find the number of ways of choosing 3 biographies out of 4. If you think of this as <u>not</u> choosing 1 out of the 4, you see that there are 4 choices. The number of ways of choosing 1 novel out of the 6 novels is 6. Therefore, the total number of choices is $(4)(6) = 24$.

Case 3: Choose 2 biographies and 2 novels. First, you need to find the number of ways of choosing 2 biographies out of 4. This number is sometimes called "4 choose 2" or the number of combinations of 4 objects taken 2 at a time. If you remember the combinations formula, you know that the number of combinations is $\dfrac{4!}{2!(4-2)!}$ (which is denoted symbolically as $\binom{4}{2}$ or $_4C_2$). The value of $\dfrac{4!}{2!(4-2)!}$ is $\dfrac{(4)(3)(2!)}{(2)(2!)} = \dfrac{(4)(3)}{2} = 6$. Thus, there are 6 ways to choose 2 biographies out of 4. Similarly, the number of ways to choose 2 novels out of 6 is $\dfrac{6!}{2!4!} = \dfrac{(6)(5)}{2} = 15$. Thus, the total number of ways to choose 2 biographies and 2 novels is $(6)(15) = 90$.

Adding the number of ways to choose the books for each of the three cases, you get a total of $1 + 24 + 90 = 115$. The correct answer is **Choice B**.

This explanation uses the following strategies.

Strategy 1: Translate from Words to an Arithmetic or Algebraic Representation
Strategy 11: Divide into Cases

For the following question, enter your answer in the box.

12. In a graduating class of 236 students, 142 took algebra and 121 took chemistry. What is the greatest possible number of students that could have taken both algebra and chemistry?

[   ] students

Explanation

This is the type of problem for which drawing a Venn diagram is usually helpful. The Venn diagram below is one you could draw to represent the information given in the question.

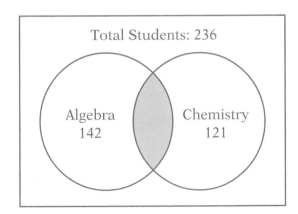

Note that the algebra and chemistry numbers given do not separate out the number of students who took both algebra and chemistry, and that this question asks for the greatest possible number of such students. It is a good idea, therefore, to redraw the Venn diagram with the number of students who took both algebra and chemistry separated out. The revised Venn diagram looks like the one below.

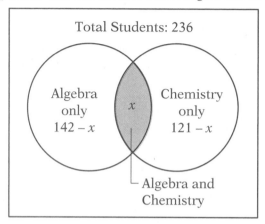

To solve this problem you want the greatest possible value of x. It is clear from the diagram that x cannot be greater than 142 nor greater than 121, otherwise $142 - x$ or $121 - x$ would be negative. Hence, x must be less than or equal to 121. Since there is no information to exclude $x = 121$, the correct answer is **121**.

This explanation uses the following strategy.

Strategy 2: Translate from Words to a Figure or Diagram

13. In the figure above, if $m \parallel k$ and $s = t + 30$, then $t =$

  (A) 30
  (B) 60
  (C) 75
  (D) 80
  (E) 105

Explanation

When trying to solve a geometric problem, it is often helpful to add any known information to the figure. Since corresponding angles have equal measures, you could place two more angle measures on the figure, as shown below.

Now, from the figure, you can see that $s + t = 180$. Therefore, since it is given that $s = t + 30$, you can substitute $t + 30$ for s into the equation $s + t = 180$ and get that $(t + 30) + t = 180$, which can be simplified as follows.

$$(t + 30) + t = 180$$
$$2t = 150$$
$$t = 75$$

The correct answer is **Choice C**.

This explanation uses the following strategy.

Strategy 4: Translate from a Figure to an Arithmetic or Algebraic Representation

14.   If $2x = 3y = 4z = 20$, then $12xyz =$

    Ⓐ 16,000

    Ⓑ   8,000

    Ⓒ   4,000

    Ⓓ   800

    Ⓔ   10

Explanation

One approach you can use to solve this problem is to find the values of all three variables.

$$2x = 20, \quad \text{or} \quad x = 10$$
$$3y = 20, \quad \text{or} \quad y = \frac{20}{3}$$
$$4z = 20, \quad \text{or} \quad z = 5$$

So $12xyz = 12(10)\left(\dfrac{20}{3}\right)(5) = 4{,}000$, and the correct answer is **Choice C**.

Another approach you can use to solve this problem is to notice that $12xyz = \dfrac{(2x)(3y)(4z)}{2} = \dfrac{(20)(20)(20)}{2} = 4{,}000$. Therefore, the correct answer is **Choice C**.

This explanation uses the following strategy.

Strategy 5: Simplify an Arithmetic or Algebraic Representation

For the following question, select all the answer choices that apply.

15.   The total amount that Mary paid for a book was equal to the price of the book plus a sales tax that was 4 percent of the price of the book. Mary paid for the book with a $10 bill and received the correct change, which was less than $3.00. Which of the following statements must be true?

Indicate <u>all</u> such statements.

    $\boxed{\text{A}}$ The price of the book was less than $9.50.

    $\boxed{\text{B}}$ The price of the book was greater than $6.90.

    $\boxed{\text{C}}$ The sales tax was less than $0.45.

Explanation

For this problem you may find it helpful to translate the given information into an algebraic expression. Since the price of the book is unknown, you can call it x dollars, and then the total amount that Mary paid is x dollars plus 4% of x dollars, or $1.04x$ dollars. The problem states that Mary received some change from a $10 bill, so $1.04x$ dollars must be less than $10. Since the change was less than $3.00, the total amount Mary paid for the book must have been greater than $7.00. You can express this information algebraically by the inequality

$$7.00 < 1.04x < 10.00$$

Solving the inequality for x by dividing by 1.04, and rounding, you get

$$6.73 < x < 9.62$$

So you see that x, the price of the book, must be between $6.73 and $9.62, and each price in between is possible. With this information, you can quickly examine the first two statements. Choice A is not necessarily true because the price could be as high as $9.61, and Choice B is not necessarily true because the price could be as low as $6.74.

To examine Choice C, you could compute the tax for the greatest possible price, which would be 4% of 9.61, or $(0.04)(9.61) \approx 0.38$. Since this greatest possible tax is less than $0.45, Choice C must be true.

You can also quickly see that Choice C must be true if you note that 4% of $10.00 would only be $0.40, and since the price must be less than $10.00, the tax must be less than $0.40. The correct answer consists of **Choice C**.

This explanation uses the following strategies.
Strategy 1: Translate from Words to an Arithmetic or Algebraic Representation
Strategy 8: Search for a Mathematical Relationship

16.   If $\dfrac{1}{(2^{11})(5^{17})}$ is expressed as a terminating decimal, how many nonzero digits will the decimal have?

ⓐ One   ⓑ Two   ⓒ Four   ⓓ Six   ⓔ Eleven

Explanation

To convert the fraction to a decimal, it is helpful to first write the fraction in powers of 10. Using the rules of exponents, you can write the following.

$$\frac{1}{(2^{11})(5^{17})} = \frac{1}{(2^{11})(5^{11+6})}$$

$$= \frac{1}{(2^{11})(5^{11})(5^{6})}$$

$$= \frac{1}{(10^{11})(5^{6})}$$

$$= \left(\frac{1}{5}\right)^{6}(10^{-11})$$

$$= (0.2)^{6}(10^{-11})$$

$$= ((2)(10)^{-1})^{6}(10^{-11})$$

$$= (2^{6})(10^{-6})(10^{-11})$$

$$= (2^{6})(10^{-17})$$

$$= (64)(10^{-17})$$

So the decimal has two nonzero digits, 6 and 4. The correct answer is **Choice B**.

This explanation uses the following strategy.
Strategy 5: Simplify an Arithmetic or Algebraic Representation

Questions 17 to 20 are based on the following data.

VARIATION IN THE AMOUNT OF CAFFEINE IN COMMON BEVERAGES AND DRUGS*

Source: Food and Drug Administration

*Based on 5-ounce cups of coffee, tea, and cocoa; 12-ounce cups of soft drinks; and single doses of drugs.

17. The least amount of caffeine in a 5-ounce cup of drip-brewed coffee exceeds the greatest amount of caffeine in a 5-ounce cup of cocoa by approximately how many milligrams?

　Ⓐ 160
　Ⓑ 80
　Ⓒ 60
　Ⓓ 40
　Ⓔ 20

Explanation

Each horizontal bar in the bar graph shows the possible number of milligrams of caffeine in each of the common beverages and drugs. The least possible amount of caffeine in a 5-ounce cup of drip-brewed coffee is about 60 milligrams, and the greatest possible amount of caffeine in a 5-ounce cup of cocoa is about 20 milligrams. So, the difference is approximately 60 – 20, or 40 milligrams. The correct answer is **Choice D**.

　　To check your answer, it is useful to try to solve the problem using another method as well to see if you get the same answer. To solve this problem in another way, note that the distance between each pair of adjacent vertical grid lines represents 25 milligrams of caffeine, and the distance between the high end of the cocoa bar and the low end of the drip-brewed coffee bar is a little more than the distance between a pair of adjacent grid lines. Therefore, the answer is between 25 and 50. Among the choices, only Choice D is between 25 and 50, so the correct answer is **Choice D**.

This explanation uses the following strategies.

Strategy 4: Translate from a Figure to an Arithmetic or Algebraic Representation
Strategy 9: Estimate

For the following question, enter your answer in the box.

18. For how many of the 11 categories of beverages and drugs listed in the graph can the amount of caffeine in the given serving size be less than 50 milligrams?

[   ] categories

Explanation

In the graph, the left edge of each bar tells you what is the least possible amount of caffeine in the corresponding beverage or drug. A beverage or drug can have less than 50 milligrams of caffeine if the left edge of its bar lies to the left of the vertical line corresponding to 50 milligrams of caffeine. From the graph, you see that there are 9 bars for which this is true. There are only 2 bars that lie entirely to the right of the 50-milligram line — the bar for drip-brewed coffee and the bar for weight-loss drugs, diuretics, and stimulants. So there are 9 categories of beverages and drugs that can have less than 50 milligrams of caffeine in the given serving size. The correct answer is **9**.

This explanation uses the following strategy.

Strategy 4: Translate from a Figure to an Arithmetic or Algebraic Representation

19. Approximately what is the minimum amount of caffeine, in milligrams, consumed per day by a person who daily drinks two 10-ounce mugs of percolated coffee and one 12-ounce cup of a caffeinated soft drink?

Ⓐ 230

Ⓑ 190

Ⓒ 140

Ⓓ 110

Ⓔ 70

Explanation

According to the bar graph, the minimum amount of caffeine in a 5-ounce cup of percolated coffee is approximately 40 milligrams. Therefore, the minimum amount of caffeine in two 10-ounce cups of percolated coffee, which is the same as the minimum amount of caffeine in four 5-ounce cups, is approximately (40)(4), or 160 milligrams. The minimum amount of caffeine in a 12-ounce caffeinated soft drink is approximately 30 milligrams. So, the minimum amount of caffeine in two 10-ounce mugs of percolated coffee and one 12-ounce caffeinated soft drink is approximately 160 + 30, or 190 milligrams. The correct answer is **Choice B**.

This explanation uses the following strategies.

Strategy 4: Translate from a Figure to an Arithmetic or Algebraic Representation
Strategy 9: Estimate

20. Which of the following shows the four types of coffee listed in order according to the range of the amounts of caffeine in a 5-ounce cup, from the least range to the greatest range?

Ⓐ Decaffeinated, instant, percolated, drip-brewed

Ⓑ Decaffeinated, instant, drip-brewed, percolated

Ⓒ Instant, decaffeinated, drip-brewed, percolated

Ⓓ Instant, drip-brewed, decaffeinated, percolated

Ⓔ Instant, percolated, drip-brewed, decaffeinated

Explanation

For each of the four types of coffee, the range of the amounts of caffeine is the greatest possible amount minus the least possible amount. In the graph, this difference is represented by the length of the corresponding bar, so you can order the four types of coffee according to the lengths of their corresponding bars, from shortest to longest. From the graph, you can see that the order is decaffeinated coffee, instant coffee, drip-brewed coffee, percolated coffee. The correct answer is **Choice B**.

This explanation uses the following strategy.

Strategy 4: Translate from a Figure to an Arithmetic or Algebraic Representation

ENERGY USED PER METER VERSUS SPEED DURING RUNNING AND WALKING

21. If s is a speed, in miles per hour, at which the energy used per meter during running is twice the energy used per meter during walking, then, according to the graph above, s is between

(A) 2.5 and 3.0
(B) 3.0 and 3.5
(C) 3.5 and 4.0
(D) 4.0 and 4.5
(E) 4.5 and 5.0

Explanation

This question is about the speed at which the energy used per meter during running is twice that used per meter during walking. Graphically, this is the speed for which the running energy is twice as high as the walking energy. Looking at the graph, you can see that for speeds greater than or equal to 3.0 miles per hour, the running energy is less than twice the walking energy, so the desired speed must be less than 3.0. In fact, the desired speed is between 2.0 (the lowest speed on the graph) and 3.0. Looking at the answer choices, you see that there is only one answer choice that is between 2.0 and 3.0; namely, Choice A, which says the desired speed is between 2.5 and 3.0. The correct answer is **Choice A**.

This explanation uses the following strategy.

Strategy 4: Translate from a Figure to an Arithmetic or Algebraic Representation

22. If $n = 2^3$, then $n^n =$

(A) 2^6

(B) 2^{11}

(C) 2^{18}

(D) 2^{24}

(E) 2^{27}

Explanation

When answering a question in which you are asked to calculate the value of an expression, it is often helpful to look at the answer choices first to see what form they are in. In this question the answer choices are all in the form 2 raised to a power, so you should try to achieve that form. It is given that $n = 2^3 = 8$. Therefore, $n^n = (2^3)^8 = 2^{24}$. The correct answer is **Choice D**.

This explanation uses the following strategy.

Strategy 5: Simplify an Arithmetic or Algebraic Representation

For the following question, select all the answer choices that apply.

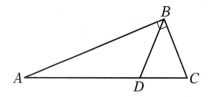

The length of AB is $10\sqrt{3}$.

23. Which of the following statements <u>individually</u> provide(s) sufficient additional information to determine the area of triangle ABC above?

Indicate <u>all</u> such statements.

A DBC is an equilateral triangle.

B ABD is an isosceles triangle.

C The length of BC is equal to the length of AD.

D The length of BC is 10.

E The length of AD is 10.

Explanation

From the figure you know that ABC is a right triangle with its right angle at vertex B. You also know that point D is on the hypotenuse AC. You are given that the length of AB is $10\sqrt{3}$. However, because the figure is not necessarily drawn to scale, you don't know the lengths of AD, DC, and BC. In particular, you don't know where D is on AC.

The area of a triangle is $\frac{1}{2}$(base)(height). Thus, the area of right triangle ABC is equal to $\frac{1}{2}$ of the length of AB times the length of BC. You already know that the length of AB is $10\sqrt{3}$. Any additional information that would allow you to calculate the length of BC would be sufficient to find the area of triangle ABC. You need to consider each of the five statements individually, as follows.

Statement A: DBC is an equilateral triangle. This statement implies that angle *DCB* is a 60° angle; and therefore, triangle *ABC* is a 30°- 60°- 90° triangle. Thus the length of *BC* can be determined, and this statement provides sufficient additional information to determine the area of triangle *ABC*.

Statement B: *ABD* is an isosceles triangle. There is more than one way in which triangle *ABD* can be isosceles. Below are two redrawn figures showing triangle *ABD* as isosceles. In the figure on the left, the length of *AD* is equal to the length of *DB*; and in the figure on the right, the length of *AB* is equal to the length of *AD*.

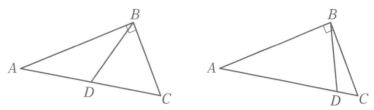

Either of the figures could have been drawn with the length of *BC* even longer. So, statement B does not provide sufficient additional information to determine the area of triangle *ABC*.

Statement C: The length of *BC* is equal to the length of *AD*. You have no way of finding the length of *AD* without making other assumptions, so statement C does not provide sufficient additional information to determine the area of triangle *ABC*.

Statement D: The length of *BC* is 10. The length of *BC* is known, so the area of triangle *ABC* can be found. Statement D provides sufficient additional information to determine the area of triangle *ABC*.

Statement E: The length of *AD* is 10. The relationship between *AD* and *BC* is not known, so statement E does not provide sufficient additional information to determine the area of triangle *ABC*.

Statements A and D individually provide sufficient additional information to determine the area of triangle *ABC*. Therefore, the correct answer consists of **Choices A and D**.

This explanation uses the following strategies.
Strategy 8: Search for a Mathematical Relationship
Strategy 14: Determine What Additional Information Is Sufficient to Solve a Problem

For the following question, enter your answer in the box.

$$a_1, a_2, a_3, \ldots, a_n, \ldots$$

24. In the sequence above, each term after the first term is equal to the preceding term plus the constant c. If $a_1 + a_3 + a_5 = 27$, what is the value of $a_2 + a_4$?

$$a_2 + a_4 = \boxed{}$$

Explanation

Note that answering this question requires information only about the first five terms of the sequence. So it is a good idea to work with the relationships among these five terms to see what is happening.

Since you are given that in this sequence each term after a_1 is c greater than the previous term, you can rewrite the first five terms of the sequence in terms of a_1 and c as follows.

$$a_2 = a_1 + c$$
$$a_3 = a_2 + c = a_1 + 2c$$
$$a_4 = a_1 + 3c$$
$$a_5 = a_1 + 4c$$

From the question, you know that $a_1 + a_3 + a_5 = 27$, and from the equations above, $a_1 + a_3 + a_5 = a_1 + (a_1 + 2c) + (a_1 + 4c) = 3a_1 + 6c$. So you can conclude that $3a_1 + 6c = 27$, or $a_1 + 2c = 9$.

To find $a_2 + a_4$, you can express a_2 and a_4 in terms of a_1 and c and simplify as follows.

$$a_2 + a_4 = (a_1 + c) + (a_1 + 3c)$$
$$= 2a_1 + 4c$$
$$= 2(a_1 + 2c)$$

But $a_1 + 2c = 9$, so $a_2 + a_4 = 2(9) = 18$. The correct answer is **18**.

This explanation uses the following strategies.
Strategy 5: Simplify an Arithmetic or Algebraic Representation
Strategy 7: Find a Pattern

25. A desert outpost has a water supply that is sufficient to last 21 days for 15 people. At the same average rate of water consumption per person, how many days would the water supply last for 9 people?

(A) 28.0
(B) 32.5
(C) 35.0
(D) 37.5
(E) 42.0

Explanation
The water supply is enough for 15 people to survive 21 days. Assuming the same average rate of water consumption per person, 1 person would have enough water to last for $(15)(21) = 315$ days. Therefore, 9 people would have enough water for $\frac{1}{9}$ of the 315 days, or 35 days. The correct answer is **Choice C**.

Another approach to solving this problem is to recognize that the water supply would last $\frac{15}{9}$ as many days for 9 people as it would for 15 people. Therefore, since the water supply would last 21 days for 15 people, it would last $\left(\frac{15}{9}\right)(21)$, or 35 days for 9 people. The correct answer is **Choice C**.

This explanation uses the following strategy.
Strategy 1: Translate from Words to an Arithmetic or Algebraic Representation

SECTION 6
Quantitative Reasoning
25 Questions with Explanations

For each of Questions 1 to 9, select one of the following answer choices.
Ⓐ   **Quantity A is greater.**
Ⓑ   **Quantity B is greater.**
Ⓒ   **The two quantities are equal.**
Ⓓ   **The relationship cannot be determined from the information given.**

Country	Value of 1 United States Dollar
Argentina	0.93 peso
Kenya	32.08 shillings

Quantity A	Quantity B

1. The dollar value of 1 Argentine peso according to the table above | The dollar value of 1 Kenyan shilling according to the table above   Ⓐ Ⓑ Ⓒ Ⓓ

Explanation

When you are answering Quantitative Comparison questions, it is a good time-saving idea to see whether you can determine the relative sizes of the two quantities being compared without doing any calculations.

In the table accompanying this question, both the value of the Argentine peso and the value of the Kenyan shilling are compared to the United States dollar.

Without doing any calculations, you can see from the information given that 1 United States dollar is worth a little less than 1 Argentine peso, so 1 peso is worth more than 1 United States dollar. On the other hand, 1 United States dollar is worth 32.08 Kenyan shillings, so 1 Kenyan shilling is worth only a <u>small fraction</u> of 1 United States dollar. The correct answer is **Choice A**.

This explanation uses the following strategy.
Strategy 9: Estimate

k is a digit in the decimal $1.3k5$, and $1.3k5$ is less than 1.33.

Quantity A	Quantity B

2. k 1   Ⓐ Ⓑ Ⓒ Ⓓ

Explanation

In this question, you are given that k is a digit in the decimal $1.3k5$ and that $1.3k5$ is less than 1.33. So you can see that $1.30 < 1.3k5 < 1.33$. Therefore, $1.3k5$ must equal 1.305 or 1.315 or 1.325, and the digit k must be 0, 1, or 2. The correct answer is **Choice D**.

This explanation uses the following strategies.
Strategy 5: Simplify an Arithmetic or Algebraic Representation
Strategy 13: Determine Whether a Conclusion Follows from the Information Given

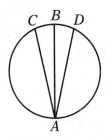

AB is a diameter of the circle above.

Quantity A	Quantity B
3. The length of *AB*	The average (arithmetic mean) of the lengths of *AC* and *AD*

Ⓐ Ⓑ Ⓒ Ⓓ

Explanation

Recall that in a circle, any diameter is longer than any other chord that is not a diameter. You are given that *AB* is a diameter of the circle. It follows that *AC* and *AD* are chords that are not diameters, since there is only one diameter with endpoint *A*. Hence, *AB* is longer than both *AC* and *AD*. Note that the average of two numbers is always less than or equal to the greater of the two numbers. Therefore, the average of the lengths of *AC* and *AD*, which is Quantity B, must be less than the length of *AB*, which is Quantity A. The correct answer is **Choice A**.

This explanation uses the following strategies.

Strategy 4: Translate from a Figure to an Arithmetic or Algebraic Representation
Strategy 8: Search for a Mathematical Relationship

$$st = \sqrt{10}$$

Quantity A	Quantity B
4. s^2	$\dfrac{10}{t^2}$

Ⓐ Ⓑ Ⓒ Ⓓ

Explanation

In this question you are asked to compare s^2 with $\dfrac{10}{t^2}$. Since it is given that $st = \sqrt{10}$, it follows that $(st)^2 = \left(\sqrt{10}\right)^2$, and $s^2 t^2 = 10$. Dividing both sides of the equation $s^2 t^2 = 10$ by t^2, you get $s^2 = \dfrac{10}{t^2}$. The correct answer is **Choice C**.

You can look at this problem in another way. You can use the fact that $st = \sqrt{10}$ to express Quantity A in terms of t. Since $st = \sqrt{10}$, it follows that $s = \dfrac{\sqrt{10}}{t}$, and Quantity A is equal to $\left(\dfrac{\sqrt{10}}{t}\right)^2 = \dfrac{10}{t^2}$, which is the same as Quantity B. The correct answer is **Choice C**.

This explanation uses the following strategy.

Strategy 5: Simplify an Arithmetic or Algebraic Representation

Three consecutive integers have a sum of –84.

Quantity A	Quantity B
5. The least of the three integers	–28

Ⓐ Ⓑ Ⓒ Ⓓ

Explanation

Two approaches you could use to solve this problem are:

1: Translate from words to algebra.
2: Determine a mathematical relationship between the two quantities.

Approach 1: You can represent the least of the three consecutive integers by x, and then the three integers would be represented by x, $x + 1$, and $x + 2$. It is given that the sum of the three integers is –84, so $x + (x + 1) + (x + 2) = -84$. You can solve this equation for x as follows.

$$x + (x + 1) + (x + 2) = -84$$
$$3x + 3 = -84$$
$$3x = -87$$
$$x = -29$$

Since the least of the three integers, –29, is less than –28, the correct answer is **Choice B**.

Approach 2: You could ask yourself what would happen if the least of the three consecutive integers was –28. The three consecutive integers would then be –28, –27, and –26, and their sum would be –81. But you were given that the sum of the three consecutive integers is –84, which is less than –81. Therefore, –28 is greater than the least of the three consecutive integers, and the correct answer is **Choice B**.

This explanation uses the following strategies.

Strategy 1: Translate from Words to an Arithmetic or Algebraic Representation
Strategy 8: Search for a Mathematical Relationship

In the xy-plane, the equation of line k is $3x - 2y = 0$.

Quantity A	Quantity B
6. The x-intercept of line k	The y-intercept of line k

Explanation

Two approaches you could use to solve this problem are:

1: Reason algebraically.
2: Reason geometrically.

Approach 1: To solve this problem algebraically, note that given the equation of a line in the xy-plane, the x-intercept of the line is the value of x when y equals 0, and the y-intercept of the line is the value of y when x equals 0. The equation of line k is $3x - 2y = 0$. If $y = 0$, then $x = 0$; and if $x = 0$, then $y = 0$. Therefore, both the x-intercept and y-intercept of the line are equal to 0, which means that the line passes through the origin. The correct answer is **Choice C**.

Approach 2: To solve this problem geometrically, graph the line with equation $3x - 2y = 0$ in the xy-plane. Since two points determine a straight line, you can do this by plotting two points on the line and drawing the line they determine. The points (0,0) and (2,3) lie on the line, and the graph of the line in the xy-plane is shown in the following figure.

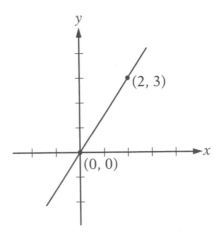

As you can see, the line passes through the origin, and so it crosses both the x-axis and the y-axis at (0,0). The correct answer is **Choice C**.

This explanation uses the following strategies.

Strategy 3: Translate from an Algebraic to a Graphical Representation
Strategy 8: Search for a Mathematical Relationship

n is a positive integer that is divisible by 6.

	Quantity A	Quantity B	
7.	The remainder when n is divided by 12	The remainder when n is divided by 18	Ⓐ Ⓑ Ⓒ Ⓓ

Explanation

One way to compare the two quantities is to plug in a few values of n. If you plug in $n = 36$, you find that both the remainder when n is divided by 12 and the remainder when n is divided by 18 are equal to 0, so Quantity A is equal to Quantity B. However, if you plug in $n = 18$, you find that the remainder when n is divided by 12 is 6 and the remainder when n is divided by 18 is 0, so Quantity B is greater than Quantity A. Therefore, the correct answer is **Choice D**.

Another way to compare the two quantities is to find all of the possible values of Quantity A and Quantity B. The positive integers that are divisible by 6 are 6, 12, 18, 24, 30, 36, etc. When dividing each of these integers by 12, you get a remainder of either 0 or 6, so Quantity A is either 0 or 6. When dividing each of these integers by 18, you get a remainder of either 0 or 6 or 12, so Quantity B is either 0 or 6 or 12. Note that when the value of Quantity B is 12, the value of Quantity A, 0 or 6, is less than the value of Quantity B; but when the value of Quantity B is 0, the value of Quantity A is greater than or equal to the value of Quantity B. Thus, the correct answer is **Choice D**.

This explanation uses the following strategies.

Strategy 10: Trial and Error
Strategy 13: Determine Whether a Conclusion Follows from the Information Given

$$\frac{1-x}{x-1} = \frac{1}{x}$$

	Quantity A	Quantity B	
8.	x	$-\dfrac{1}{2}$	Ⓐ Ⓑ Ⓒ Ⓓ

Explanation

One approach you could use to solve this problem is to solve the equation $\frac{1-x}{x-1} = \frac{1}{x}$ for x. Since fractions are defined only when the denominator is not equal to 0, the denominators of both of the fractions in the equation are nonzero. Therefore, $x \neq 0$ and $x \neq 1$.

To solve the equation for x, begin by multiplying both sides of the equation by the common denominator $x(x+1)$ to get $x(1-x) = (x-1)(1)$. Then proceed as follows.

$$x(1-x) = (x-1)(1)$$
$$x - x^2 = x - 1$$
$$x^2 = 1$$

Since $x^2 = 1$ and $x \neq 1$, it follows that $x = -1$.

Quantity A is equal to -1 and Quantity B is equal to $-\frac{1}{2}$. Therefore, Quantity B is greater, and the correct answer is **Choice B**.

Another approach is to notice that for all values of $x \neq 1$, the value of $\frac{1-x}{x-1}$ is equal to -1. You can try plugging in a few numbers for x to see that this is true. For example, if you plug in $x = 7$, you get $\frac{7-1}{1-7} = \frac{6}{-6} = -1$.

You can also show that for all values of $x \neq 1$, the value of $\frac{1-x}{x-1}$ is equal to -1 algebraically by rewriting $1-x$ as $-(x-1)$. Thus, $\frac{1-x}{x-1} = \frac{-(x-1)}{(x-1)} = -1$. Because the left side of the equation $\frac{1-x}{x-1} = \frac{1}{x}$ is equal to -1, it follows that $-1 = \frac{1}{x}$, and so $x = -1$. Therefore, Quantity A is equal to -1, which is less than Quantity B, $-\frac{1}{2}$, and the correct answer is **Choice B**.

This explanation uses the following strategy.

Strategy 5: Simplify an Arithmetic or Algebraic Representation

> In a set of 24 positive integers, 12 of the integers are less than 50. The rest are greater than 50.

	Quantity A	Quantity B	
9.	The median of the 24 integers	50	Ⓐ Ⓑ Ⓒ Ⓓ

Explanation

In general, the median of a set of n positive integers, where n is even, is obtained by ordering the integers from least to greatest and then calculating the average (arithmetic mean) of the two middle integers. For this set of 24 integers, you do not know the values of the two middle integers; you know only that half of the integers are less than 50 and the other half are greater than 50. If the two middle integers in the list are 49 and 51, the median is 50; and if the two middle integers are 49 and 53, the median is 51. Thus the relationship cannot be determined from the information given, and the correct answer is **Choice D**.

This explanation uses the following strategies.
Strategy 11: Divide into Cases
Strategy 13: Determine Whether a Conclusion Follows from the Information Given

10. The fabric needed to make 3 curtains sells for $8.00 per yard and can be purchased only by the full yard. If the length of fabric required for each curtain is 1.6 yards and all of the fabric is purchased as a single length, what is the total cost of the fabric that needs to be purchased for the 3 curtains?

(A) $40.00

(B) $38.40

(C) $24.00

(D) $16.00

(E) $12.80

Explanation

Since 1.6 yards of fabric are required for each curtain, it follows that (3)(1.6), or 4.8, yards of fabric are required to make the 3 curtains. The fabric can be purchased only by the full yard, so 5 yards of fabric would need to be purchased. Since the fabric sells for $8.00 per yard, the total cost of the fabric is $40.00. The correct answer is **Choice A**.

This explanation uses the following strategy.
Strategy 1: Translate from Words to an Arithmetic or Algebraic Representation

For the following question, select all the answer choices that apply.

11. In the xy-plane, line k is a line that does <u>not</u> pass through the origin. Which of the following statements <u>individually</u> provide(s) sufficient additional information to conclude that the slope of line k is negative?

Indicate <u>all</u> such statements.

A The x-intercept of line k is twice the y-intercept of line k.

B The product of the x-intercept and the y-intercept of line k is positive.

C Line k passes through the points (a, b) and (r, s), where $(a - r)(b - s) < 0$.

Explanation

For questions involving a coordinate system, it is often helpful to draw a figure to visualize the problem situation. If you draw some lines with negative slopes in the xy-plane, such as those in the figure below, you see that for each line that does not pass through the origin, the x- and y-intercepts are either both positive or both negative. Conversely, you can see that if the x- and y-intercepts of a line have the same sign then the slope of the line is negative.

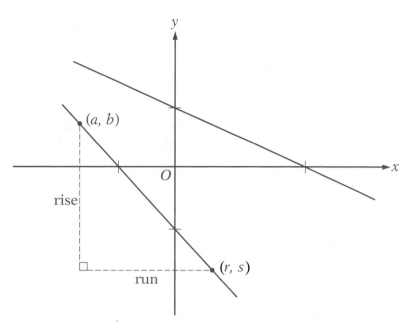

You can use this fact to examine the information given in the first two statements. Remember that you need to evaluate each statement by itself.

Choice A states that the x-intercept is twice the y-intercept, so you can conclude that both intercepts have the same sign, and thus the slope of line k is negative. So the information in Choice A is sufficient to determine that the slope of line k is negative.

Choice B states that the product of the x-intercept and the y-intercept is positive. You know that the product of two numbers is positive if both factors have the same sign. So this information is also sufficient to determine that the slope of line k is negative.

To evaluate Choice C, it is helpful to recall the definition of the slope of a line passing through two given points. You may remember it as "rise over run." If the two points are (a, b) and (r, s), then the slope is $\frac{b-s}{a-r}$.

Choice C states that the product of the quantities $(a - r)$ and $(b - s)$ is negative. Note that these are the denominator and the numerator, respectively, of $\frac{b-s}{a-r}$, the slope of line k. So you can conclude that $(a - r)$ and $(b - s)$ have opposite signs and the slope of line k is negative. The information in Choice C is sufficient to determine that the slope of line k is negative.

So each of the three statements individually provides sufficient information to conclude that the slope of line k is negative. The correct answer consists of **Choices A, B, and C**.

This explanation uses the following strategies.
Strategy 3: Translate from an Algebraic to a Graphical Representation
Strategy 14: Determine What Additional Information Is Sufficient to Solve a Problem

	Distance from Centerville (miles)
Freight train	$-10t + 115$
Passenger train	$-20t + 150$

12. The expressions in the table above give the distance from Centerville to each of two trains t hours after 12:00 noon. At what time after 12:00 noon will the trains be equidistant from Centerville?

    (A) 1:30
    (B) 3:30
    (C) 5:10
    (D) 8:50
    (E) 11:30

Explanation

The distance between the freight train and Centerville at t hours past noon is $-10t + 115$. The distance between the passenger train and Centerville at t hours past noon is $-20t + 150$. To find out at what time the distances will be the same you need to equate the two expressions and solve for t as follows.

$$-10t + 115 = -20t + 150$$
$$10t + 115 = 150$$
$$10t = 35$$
$$t = 3.5$$

Therefore, the two trains will be the same distance from Centerville at 3.5 hours past noon, or at 3:30. The correct answer is **Choice B**.

This explanation uses the following strategies.
Strategy 1: Translate from Words to an Arithmetic or Algebraic Representation
Strategy 5: Simplify an Arithmetic or Algebraic Representation

13. The company at which Mark is employed has 80 employees, each of whom has a different salary. Mark's salary of $43,700 is the second-highest salary in the first quartile of the 80 salaries. If the company were to hire 8 new employees at salaries that are less than the lowest of the 80 salaries, what would Mark's salary be with respect to the quartiles of the 88 salaries at the company, assuming no other changes in the salaries?

    (A) The fourth-highest salary in the first quartile
    (B) The highest salary in the first quartile
    (C) The second-lowest salary in the second quartile
    (D) The third-lowest salary in the second quartile
    (E) The fifth-lowest salary in the second quartile

Explanation

In this question you are told that Mark's salary is the second-highest in the first quartile. From this you can conclude that the word *quartile* refers to one of the four groups that are created by listing the data in increasing order and then dividing the data into four groups of equal size. When the salaries of the 80 employees are listed in order, the 20 lowest salaries (that is, the salaries in the first quartile) are the first

20 salaries in the list. Since Mark's salary is the second-highest in the first quartile, 18 salaries in that quartile are lower than his, and one salary in that quartile is higher than his. After the salaries of the 8 new employees are added, there are 26 salaries that are lower than Mark's. The lowest 22 of those would be in the first quartile of the 88 salaries, and the remaining 4 (salaries 23 to 26) would be in the second quartile, followed by Mark's salary. This puts Mark at the fifth-lowest salary in the second quartile. The correct answer is **Choice E.**

Another way to approach this problem is to think of all 80 salaries numbered in order from least to greatest, the lowest salary at the number 1 position and the greatest salary at the number 80 position. There are 20 positions in each quartile, and Mark's salary is at position 19. The diagram below shows the salary positions and the quartile into which each position falls. Note that position 19, where Mark's salary appears, is second-highest in the first quartile.

First quartile	Second quartile	Third quartile	Fourth quartile
1	21	41	61
2	22	42	62
3	23	43	63
⋮	⋮	⋮	⋮
18	38	58	78
19 ◄—— Mark's	39	59	79
20 salary	40	60	80

To see what Mark's position is with respect to the quartiles of the 88 salaries, you need add the 8 new salaries to the list, renumber the list from 1 to 88, and put 22 salaries in each quartile. Because the 8 new salaries are less than the original 80 salaries, they must be listed in positions 1 through 8, and all salaries in the original list must move up by 8 positions in the renumbered list. In particular, Mark's salary moves from position 19 to position 27. The diagram below shows the renumbered list. Note that Mark's salary is in position 27, the fifth position in the second quartile.

First quartile	Second quartile	Third quartile	Fourth quartile
1 ⎫	23	45	67
2 ⎬ New	24	46	68
⋮ ⎪ salaries	25	47	69
8 ⎭	26	48	70
9 ◄— Salary at	27 ◄— Mark's	49	71
⋮ position 1 of	⋮ salary	⋮	⋮
20 original list	42	64	86
21	43	65	87
22	44	66	88

Since Mark's salary is in the fifth position in the second quartile and the salaries are listed in order from least to greatest, Mark's salary would be the fifth-lowest in the second quartile. The correct answer is **Choice E.**

This explanation uses the following strategies.
Strategy 2: Translate from Words to a Figure or Diagram
Strategy 8: Search for a Mathematical Relationship

For the following question, enter your answer in the box.

14. In the *xy*-plane, the point with coordinates (–6, –7) is the center of circle *C*. The point with coordinates (–6, 5) lies inside *C*, and the point with coordinates (8, –7) lies outside *C*. If *m* is the radius of *C* and *m* is an integer, what is the value of *m*?

$$m = \boxed{}$$

Explanation

A strategy that is often helpful in working with geometry problems is drawing a figure that represents the given information as accurately as possible.

   In this question you are given that the point with coordinates (–6, –7) is the center of circle *C*, the point with coordinates (–6, 5) lies inside circle *C*, and the point with coordinates (8, –7) lies outside circle *C*, so you could draw the following figure.

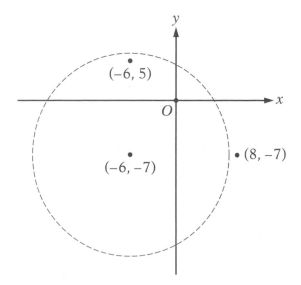

   From the figure, you can see that the distance between (–6, –7) and (–6, 5) is 7 + 5, or 12, and the radius of *C* must be greater than 12. You can also see that the distance between (–6, –7) and (8, –7) is 6 + 8, or 14, and the radius of *C* must be less than 14. Therefore, since the radius is an integer greater than 12 and less than 14, it must be 13. The correct answer is **13**.

This explanation uses the following strategy.

Strategy 2: Translate from Words to a Figure or Diagram

15. If $-\dfrac{m}{19}$ is an even integer, which of the following must be true?

   Ⓐ *m* is a negative number.

   Ⓑ *m* is a positive number.

   Ⓒ *m* is a prime number.

   Ⓓ *m* is an odd integer.

   Ⓔ *m* is an even integer.

Explanation

An even integer is a multiple of 2. If $-\dfrac{m}{19}$ is an even integer, it must equal 2 times some integer k. This means that $-\dfrac{m}{19} = 2k$, or $m = -19(2k) = 2(-19k)$, which is a multiple of 2. Thus m must be an even integer, and the correct answer is **Choice E**. You can see that none of the other choices can be the correct answer by evaluating them as follows.

(A) m does not have to be a negative number for $-\dfrac{m}{19}$ to be even. For example, if $m = 38$, then $-\dfrac{m}{19} = -2$, which is an even number.

(B) m does not have to be a positive number for $-\dfrac{m}{19}$ to be even. For example, if $m = -38$, then $-\dfrac{m}{19} = 2$, which is an even number.

(C) The number used in (A), $m = 38$, shows that m does not have to be a prime number. In fact, because m is the product of at least two prime numbers (2 and 19), m cannot be a prime number.

(D) Since m must be an even integer, m cannot be an odd integer.

This explanation uses the following strategies.

Strategy 8: Search for a Mathematical Relationship
Strategy 13: Determine Whether a Conclusion Follows from the Information Given

For the following question, select all the answer choices that apply.

16. The integer v is greater than 1. If v is the square of an integer, which of the following numbers must also be the square of an integer?

Indicate <u>all</u> such numbers.

A. $81v$ B. $25v + 10\sqrt{v} + 1$ C. $4v^2 + 4\sqrt{v} + 1$

Explanation

If v is the square of an integer, then $\sqrt{v}$ is an integer. You can use this fact, together with the fact that the product and the sum of integers are also integers, to examine the first two choices.

Choice A: The positive square root of $81v$ is $9\sqrt{v}$, which is an integer. So $81v$ is the square of an integer.

Choice B: $25v + 10\sqrt{v} + 1 = (5\sqrt{v} + 1)^2$ and $5\sqrt{v} + 1$ is an integer. So $25v + 10\sqrt{v} + 1$ is the square of an integer.

Choice C: Since there is no obvious way to factor the given expression, you may suspect that it is not the square of an integer. To show that a given statement is not true, it is sufficient to find one counterexample. In this case, you need to find one value of v such that v is the square of an integer but $4v^2 + 4\sqrt{v} + 1$ is not the square of an integer. If $v = 4$, then $4v^2 + 4\sqrt{v} + 1 = 64 + 8 + 1 = 73$, which is not the square of an integer. This proves that $4v^2 + 4\sqrt{v} + 1$ does not have to be the square of an integer.

The correct answer consists of **Choices A and B**.

This explanation uses the following strategies.

Strategy 5: Simplify an Arithmetic or Algebraic Representation
Strategy 13: Determine Whether a Conclusion Follows from the Information Given

DISTANCE TRAVELED BY A CAR ACCORDING TO THE CAR'S SPEED WHEN THE DRIVER IS SIGNALED TO STOP

Distance Traveled During Reaction Time*

Distance Traveled After Brakes Have Been Applied

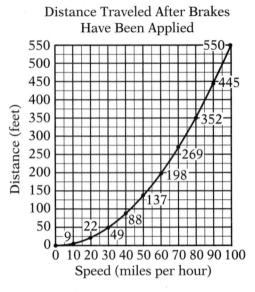

*Reaction time is the time period that begins when the driver is signaled to stop and ends when the driver applies the brakes.

Note: Total stopping distance is the sum of the distance traveled during reaction time and the distance traveled after brakes have been applied.

17. The speed, in miles per hour, at which the car travels a distance of 52 feet during reaction time is closest to which of the following?

(A) 43
(B) 47
(C) 51
(D) 55
(E) 59

Explanation

The data accompanying questions 17 to 20 consists of two graphs. It is a good idea to look at the graphs before you try to answer the questions, so you can become familiar with the information contained in the graphs. Then, as you read each question, you should think about which of the graphs contains the information you need to solve the problem. It could be that all the information you need to solve the problem is contained in one of the graphs, or it could be that you need to get information from both of the graphs.

The graph on the left shows the relationship between the speed of the automobile and the distance it traveled during the reaction time. Therefore, the answer to this question is found using this graph by reading the speed, in miles per hour, corresponding to a distance of 52 feet. A distance of 52 feet is a little above the distance of 50 feet on the vertical axis of the graph. On the graph, the speed corresponding to a distance of 52 feet is a little less than 50 miles per hour. The correct answer is **Choice B**.

This explanation uses the following strategies.

Strategy 4: Translate from a Figure to an Arithmetic or Algebraic Representation
Strategy 9: Estimate

18. Approximately what is the total stopping distance, in feet, if the car is traveling at a speed of 40 miles per hour when the driver is signaled to stop?

(A) 130
(B) 110
(C) 90
(D) 70
(E) 40

Explanation

Since the total stopping distance is the sum of the distance traveled during reaction time and the distance traveled after the brakes have been applied, you need information from both graphs to answer this question. At a speed of 40 miles per hour, the distance traveled during reaction time is a little less than 45 feet, and the distance traveled after the brakes have been applied is 88 feet. Since 45 + 88 = 133, the correct answer is **Choice A**.

This explanation uses the following strategies.

Strategy 4: Translate from a Figure to an Arithmetic or Algebraic Representation
Strategy 9: Estimate

19. Of the following, which is the greatest speed, in miles per hour, at which the car can travel and stop with a total stopping distance of less than 200 feet?

(A) 50
(B) 55
(C) 60
(D) 65
(E) 70

Explanation

Since the total stopping distance is the sum of the distance traveled during reaction time and the distance traveled after the brakes have been applied, you need information from both graphs to answer this question. A good strategy for solving this problem is to calculate the total stopping distance for the speeds given in the options. For a speed of 50 miles per hour, the distance traveled during reaction time is about 55 feet, and the distance traveled after the brakes have been applied is 137 feet; therefore, the total stopping distance is about 55 + 137, or 192 feet. For a speed of 55 miles per hour, the distance traveled during reaction time is about 60 feet, and the distance traveled after the brakes have been applied is about 170 feet; therefore, the total stopping distance is about 60 + 170, or 230 feet. Since the speeds in the remaining choices are greater than 55 miles per hour and both types of stopping distances increase as the speed increases, it follows that the total stopping distances for all the remaining choices are greater than 200 feet. The correct answer is **Choice A**.

This explanation uses the following strategies.

Strategy 4: Translate from a Figure to an Arithmetic or Algebraic Representation
Strategy 9: Estimate

20. The total stopping distance for the car traveling at 60 miles per hour is approximately what percent greater than the total stopping distance for the car traveling at 50 miles per hour?

    (A) 22%   (B) 30%   (C) 38%   (D) 45%   (E) 52%

Explanation

To solve this problem you need to find the total stopping distance at 50 miles per hour and at 60 miles per hour, find their difference, and then express the difference as a percent of the shorter total stopping distance. You need to use both graphs to find the total stopping distances. At 50 miles per hour, the total stopping distance is approximately 55 + 137 = 192 feet; and at 60 miles per hour it is approximately 66 + 198 = 264 feet. The difference of 72 feet as a percent of 192 feet is $\frac{72}{192} = 0.375$, or approximately 38%. The correct answer is **Choice C**.

This explanation uses the following strategies.

Strategy 4: Translate from a Figure to an Arithmetic or Algebraic Representation
Strategy 9: Estimate

21. What is the least positive integer that is <u>not</u> a factor of 25! and is <u>not</u> a prime number?

    (A) 26   (B) 28   (C) 36   (D) 56   (E) 58

Explanation

Note that 25! is equal to the product of all positive integers from 1 to 25, inclusive. Thus, every positive integer less than or equal to 25 is a factor of 25!. Also, any integer greater than 25 that can be expressed as the product of different positive integers less than 25 is a factor of 25!. In view of this, it's reasonable to consider the next few integers greater than 25, including answer choices A and B.

　　Choice A, 26, is equal to (2)(13). Both 2 and 13 are factors of 25!, so 26 is also a factor of 25!. The same is true for 27, or (3)(9), and for Choice B, 28, or (4)(7). However, the next integer, 29, is a prime number greater than 25, and as such, it has no positive factors (other than 1) that are less than or equal to 25. Therefore, 29 is the least positive integer that is <u>not</u> a factor of 25!. However, the question asks for an integer that is <u>not</u> a prime number, so 29 is not the answer.

　　At this point, you could consider 30, 31, 32, etc., but it is quicker to look at the rest of the choices. Choice C, 36, is equal to (4)(9). Both 4 and 9 are factors of 25!, so 36 is also a factor of 25!. Choice D, 56, is equal to (4)(14). Both 4 and 14 are factors of 25!, so 56 is also a factor of 25!. Choice E, 58, is equal to (2)(29). Although 2 is a factor of 25!, the prime number 29, as noted earlier, is not a factor of 25!, and therefore 58 is not a factor of 25!. The correct answer must be **Choice E**.

　　The explanation above uses a process of elimination to arrive at Choice E, which is sometimes the most efficient way to find the correct answer. However, one can also show directly that the correct answer is 58. For if a positive integer n is <u>not</u> a factor of 25!, then one of the following must be true:

    (i) n is a prime number greater than 25, like 29 or 31, or a multiple of such a prime number, like 58 or 62;

    (ii) n is so great a multiple of some prime number less than 25, that it must be greater than 58.

To see that (i) or (ii) is true, recall that every integer greater than 1 has a unique prime factorization, and consider the prime factorization of 25!. The prime factors of 25! are 2, 3, 5, 7, 11, 13, 17, 19, and 23, some of which occur more than once in the product 25!. For example, there are 8 positive multiples of 3 less than 25, namely 3, 6, 9, 12, 15, 18, 21, and 24. The prime number 3 occurs once in each of these multiples, except for 9 and 18, in which it occurs twice. Thus, the factor 3 occurs 10 times in the prime factorization of 25!. The same reasoning can be used to find the number of times that each of the prime factors occur, yielding the prime factorization $25! = (2^{22})(3^{10})(5^6)(7^3)(11^2)(13)(17)(19)(23)$. Any integer whose prime factorization is a combination of one or more of the factors in the prime factorization of 25!, perhaps with lesser exponents, is a factor of 25!. Equivalently, if the positive integer n is not a factor of 25!, then, restating (i) and (ii) above, the prime factorization of n must

    (i) include a prime number greater than 25; or

    (ii) have a greater exponent for one of the prime numbers in the prime factorization of 25!.

For (ii), the least possibilities are 2^{23}, 3^{11}, 5^7, 7^4, 11^3, 13^2, 17^2, 19^2, and 23^2. Clearly, all of these are greater than 58. The least possibility for (i) that is not a prime number is 58, and the least possibility for (ii) is greater than 58, so **Choice E** is the correct answer.

This explanation uses the following strategies.
Strategy 8: Search for a Mathematical Relationship
Strategy 10: Trial and Error

22.   If $0 < a < 1 < b$, which of the following is true about the reciprocals of a and b?

    (A) $1 < \dfrac{1}{a} < \dfrac{1}{b}$

    (B) $\dfrac{1}{a} < 1 < \dfrac{1}{b}$

    (C) $\dfrac{1}{a} < \dfrac{1}{b} < 1$

    (D) $\dfrac{1}{b} < 1 < \dfrac{1}{a}$

    (E) $\dfrac{1}{b} < \dfrac{1}{a} < 1$

Explanation
To answer this question, you must first look at the answer choices. Note that all of the choices are possible orderings of the quantities $\dfrac{1}{a}, \dfrac{1}{b},$ and 1 from least to greatest. So to answer the question, you must put the three quantities in order

from least to greatest. The inequality $0 < a < 1 < b$ tells you that $0 < a < 1$ and that $b > 1$. Since a is a value between 0 and 1, the value of $\frac{1}{a}$ must be greater than 1. Since b is greater than 1, the value of $\frac{1}{b}$ must be less than 1. So you know that $\frac{1}{a} > 1$ and that $\frac{1}{b} < 1$, or combined in one expression, $\frac{1}{b} < 1 < \frac{1}{a}$, and the correct answer is **Choice D**.

This explanation uses the following strategy.
Strategy 5: Simplify an Arithmetic or Algebraic Representation

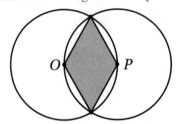

23. In the figure above, O and P are the centers of the two circles. If each circle has radius r, what is the area of the shaded region?

Ⓐ $\frac{\sqrt{2}}{2}r^2$

Ⓑ $\frac{\sqrt{3}}{2}r^2$

Ⓒ $\sqrt{2}r^2$

Ⓓ $\sqrt{3}r^2$

Ⓔ $2\sqrt{3}r^2$

Explanation

If a geometric problem contains a figure, it can be helpful to draw additional lines and add information given in the text of the problem to the figure. For circles, the helpful additional lines are often radii or diameters. In this case, drawing radius OP will divide the shaded region into two triangles, as shown in the figure below.

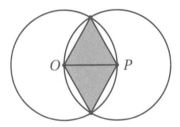

The two circles have the same radius, r. Therefore, in each of the triangles, all three sides have length r, and each of the triangles is equilateral. If you remember from geometry that the height of an equilateral triangle with sides of length r is $\frac{\sqrt{3}}{2}r$, you could use that fact in solving the problem. However, if you do not remember what the height is, you can use the following figure to help you find the height.

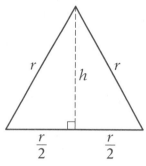

Using the Pythagorean theorem, you get

$$\left(\frac{r}{2}\right)^2 + h^2 = r^2$$

$$\frac{r^2}{4} + h^2 = r^2$$

$$h^2 = \frac{3}{4}r^2$$

$$h = \frac{\sqrt{3}}{2}r$$

So the area of the equilateral triangle is $\frac{1}{2}$(base)(height) $= \frac{1}{2}(r)\left(\frac{\sqrt{3}}{2}r\right) = \frac{\sqrt{3}}{4}r^2$.

Since the shaded region consists of 2 equilateral triangles with sides of length r, the area of the shaded region is $(2)\left(\frac{\sqrt{3}}{4}r^2\right) = \frac{\sqrt{3}}{2}r^2$, and the correct answer is **Choice B.**

This explanation uses the following strategies.
Strategy 6: Add to a Geometric Figure
Strategy 8: Search for a Mathematical Relationship

For the following question, enter your answer in the boxes.

24. Of the 20 lightbulbs in a box, 2 are defective. An inspector will select 2 lightbulbs simultaneously and at random from the box. What is the probability that neither of the lightbulbs selected will be defective?

Give your answer as a fraction.

Explanation
The desired probability corresponds to the fraction

$$\frac{\text{the number of ways that 2 lightbulbs, both of which are not defective, can be chosen}}{\text{the number of ways that 2 lightbulbs can be chosen}}$$

In order to calculate the desired probability, you need to calculate the values of the numerator and the denominator of this fraction.

In the box there are 20 lightbulbs, 18 of which are not defective. The numerator of the fraction is the number of ways that 2 lightbulbs can be chosen from the 18 that are not defective, also known as the number of combinations of 18 objects taken 2 at a time.

If you remember the combinations formula, you know that the number of combinations is $\dfrac{18!}{2!(18-2)!}$ (which is denoted symbolically as $\binom{18}{2}$ or $_{18}C_2$). Simplifying, you get

$$\frac{18!}{2!16!} = \frac{(18)(17)(16!)}{(2)(16!)} = \frac{(18)(17)}{2} = 153$$

Similarly, the denominator of the fraction is the number of ways that 2 lightbulbs can be chosen from the 20 in the box, which is $\binom{20}{2} = \dfrac{20!}{2!18!} = \dfrac{(20)(19)(18!)}{(2)(18!)} = \dfrac{(20)(19)}{2} = 190$. Therefore, the probability that neither of the lightbulbs selected will be defective is $\dfrac{153}{190}$. The correct answer is $\dfrac{153}{190}$ (or any equivalent fraction).

Another approach is to look at the selection of the two lightbulbs separately. The problem states that lightbulbs are selected simultaneously. However, the timing of the selection only ensures that the same lightbulb is not chosen twice. This is equivalent to choosing one lightbulb first and then choosing a second lightbulb without replacing the first. The probability that the first lightbulb selected will not be defective is $\dfrac{18}{20}$. If the first lightbulb selected is not defective, there will be 19 lightbulbs left to choose from, 17 of which are not defective. Thus, the probability that the second lightbulb selected will not be defective is $\dfrac{17}{19}$. The probability that both lightbulbs selected will not be defective is the product of these two probabilities. Thus, the desired probability is $\left(\dfrac{18}{20}\right)\left(\dfrac{17}{19}\right) = \dfrac{153}{190}$. The correct answer is $\dfrac{153}{190}$ (or any equivalent fraction).

This explanation uses the following strategies.
Strategy 1: Translate from Words to an Arithmetic or Algebraic Representation
Strategy 5: Simplify an Arithmetic or Algebraic Representation

25. What is the perimeter, in meters, of a rectangular playground 24 meters wide that has the same area as a rectangular playground 64 meters long and 48 meters wide?

Ⓐ 112   Ⓑ 152   Ⓒ 224   Ⓓ 256   Ⓔ 304

Explanation
The area of the rectangular playground that is 64 meters long and 48 meters wide is $(64)(48) = 3{,}072$ square meters. The second playground, which has the same area, is 24 meters wide and $\dfrac{3{,}072}{24} = 128$ meters long. Therefore, the perimeter of the second playground is $(2)(24) + (2)(128) = 304$ meters. The correct answer is **Choice E.**

This explanation uses the following strategy.
Strategy 1: Translate from Words to an Arithmetic or Algebraic Representation

9 GRE® Practice Test 2

Your goals for this chapter

◥ Take the second full-length authentic *GRE®* General Test under actual test time limits
◥ Check your answers and read explanations for every question
◥ Use your results to identify your strengths and weaknesses

Taking Practice Test 2

考生在做完模拟测试（一）并评估自己的表现后，可以利用模拟测试（二）再次衡量自己参加真正考试的准备情况。测试（二）将从下页开始。测试时间为3小时30分钟。每个部分（section）的时间分配出现在该部分的开头。

尝试在真实考试条件下完成模拟测试（二）。找一个安静的地方，留出充足的时间来完成整个测试，不要受到干扰。做完一个section再做另一个section，不要交叉做。用手表或计时器来为每一个section计时。

在本测试的文字推理（Verbal Reasoning）和数量推理（Quantitative Reasoning）部分，考生需要把选项直接标注在书上。但参加真正的GRE机考时，考生要做的是在电脑上点击正确的选项。在本测试的分析性写作（Analytical Writing）部分，作答方式取决于考生计划参加的考试类型。如果考生计划参加机考，在本次测试中就应该使用计算机进行文字录入；如果考生计划参加纸笔考试，就需要准备一些空白纸，把作文手写在纸上。

需要注意的是，本部分的模拟测试在结构上类似于纸笔考试。因此，每部分的题目数量和考试时长与机考不同。测试结果将使考生清楚地知道自己是否已经准备好参加真正的考试，但考生应利用*POWERPREP®*中的模拟试题来更真实地体验机考。

本测试的结尾附带参考答案。考生可以将自己的作答对照参考答案，然后按照说明计算文字推理（Verbal Reasoning）和数量推理（Quantitative Reasoning）部分的得分，评估自己在分析性写作（Analytical Writing）部分的表现。参考答案中还包含对每个问题的解析。仔细阅读解析部分，尤其要注意做错的那些题目。

在完成模拟测试（二）之后，考生就会对自己参加真正的GRE考试的准备情况有清晰的了解；还能知道自己在哪些地方仍需改进，是否需要提高做题的速度和掌控时间的技能。如果考生需要更多的考试准备材料和建议，请访问如下网址：www.ets.org/gre/prepare。

SECTION 1
Analytical Writing

ANALYZE AN ISSUE

30 minutes

You will be given a brief quotation that states or implies an issue of general interest and specific instructions on how to respond to that issue. You will then have 30 minutes to plan and compose a response according to the specific instructions. A response to any other issue will receive a score of zero.

Make sure that you respond according to the specific instructions and support your position on the issue with reasons and examples drawn from such areas as your reading, experience, observations, and/or academic studies.

Trained GRE readers will evaluate your response for its overall quality, based on how well you:

- Respond to the specific task instructions
- Consider the complexities of the issue
- Organize, develop, and express your ideas
- Support your ideas with relevant reasons and/or examples
- Control the elements of standard written English

Before you begin writing, you may want to think for a few minutes about the issue and the specific task instructions and then plan your response. Be sure to develop your position fully and organize it coherently, but leave time to reread what you have written and make any revisions you think are necessary.

Issue Topic

Some people believe that corporations have a responsibility to promote the well-being of the societies and environments in which they operate. Others believe that the only responsibility of corporations, provided they operate within the law, is to make as much money as possible.

Write a response in which you discuss which view more closely aligns with your own position and explain your reasoning for the position you take. In developing and supporting your position, you should address both of the views presented.

SECTION 2
Analytical Writing

ANALYZE AN ARGUMENT

30 minutes

You will be given a short passage that presents an argument and specific instructions on how to respond to that passage. You will have 30 minutes to plan and compose a response in which you evaluate the passage according to the specific instructions. A response to any other argument will receive a score of zero.

Note that you are NOT being asked to present your own views on the subject. Make sure that you respond according to the specific instructions and support your evaluation with relevant reasons and/or examples.

Trained GRE readers will evaluate your response for its overall quality, based on how well you:

- Respond to the specific task instructions
- Identify and analyze features of the argument relevant to the assigned task
- Organize, develop, and express your ideas
- Support your analysis with relevant reasons and/or examples
- Control the elements of standard written English

Before you begin writing, you may want to think for a few minutes about the argument passage and the specific task instructions and then plan your response. Be sure to develop your response fully and organize it coherently, but leave time to reread what you have written and make any revisions you think are necessary.

Argument Topic

The following appeared in a memorandum from the owner of Movies Galore, a chain of video rental stores.

"In order to reverse the recent decline in our profits, we must reduce operating expenses at Movies Galore's ten video rental stores. Since we are famous for our special bargains, raising our rental prices is not a viable way to improve profits. Last month our store in downtown Marston significantly decreased its operating expenses by closing at 6:00 P.M. rather than 9:00 P.M. and by reducing its stock by eliminating all movies released more than five years ago. Therefore, in order to increase profits without jeopardizing our reputation for offering great movies at low prices, we recommend implementing similar changes in our other nine Movies Galore stores."

Write a response in which you discuss what questions would need to be answered in order to decide whether the recommendation is likely to have the predicted result. Be sure to explain how the answers to these questions would help to evaluate the recommendation.

NO TEST MATERIAL ON THIS PAGE

SECTION 3
Verbal Reasoning
Time—35 minutes
25 Questions

For questions 1 to 8, select <u>one</u> entry for each blank from the corresponding column of choices. Fill all blanks in the way that best completes the text.

1. Although plant and animal species that become established in ecosystems where they did not originate are sometimes referred to by the alarming term "invasive species," many such species are _____ in their new environments.

Ⓐ innocuous
Ⓑ conspicuous
Ⓒ robust
Ⓓ menacing
Ⓔ distinctive

2. Far from being _____ the corporate world because of cutbacks, serious researchers are playing a growing role in innovation at many firms.

Ⓐ lured to
Ⓑ enchanted with
Ⓒ banished from
Ⓓ protected by
Ⓔ immured in

3. The brief survey, published under the title *The Work of Nature: How the Diversity of Life Sustains Us*, is surprisingly (i)_____. Indeed it makes several longer treatments of the effects of lost biodiversity seem (ii)_____.

Blank (i)	Blank (ii)
Ⓐ distorted	Ⓓ redundant
Ⓑ objective	Ⓔ pithy
Ⓒ comprehensive	Ⓕ premature

4. The government has no choice but to (i)_____ the incessant demands for land reform, and yet any governmental action that initiated land reform without requisite attention to agrarian reform would (ii)_____ the overall goal of economic modernization.

Blank (i)	Blank (ii)
Ⓐ anticipate	Ⓓ delineate
Ⓑ heed	Ⓔ condone
Ⓒ silence	Ⓕ compromise

GO ON TO NEXT PAGE ↘

5. Certain music lovers yearn for (i)_____, but when it is achieved, there is something missing; perhaps they feel uncomfortable in a world where nothing discernible is (ii)_____.

Blank (i)	Blank (ii)
(A) novelty	(D) wrong
(B) beauty	(E) visionary
(C) flawlessness	(F) changed

6. Putting a cash value on the ecological services provided by nature—such as the water filtration "service" provided by a forested watershed—has, historically, been a (i)_____ process. Early attempts at such valuation resulted in impressive but (ii)_____ figures that were seized on by environmental advocates and then, when these figures were later (iii)_____, they were used by opponents to tar the whole idea.

Blank (i)	Blank (ii)	Blank (iii)
(A) dispassionate	(D) redundant	(G) ignored
(B) problematic	(E) unsound	(H) discredited
(C) straightforward	(F) understated	(I) confirmed

7. Only with the discovery of an ozone hole over Antarctica in 1985 did chemical companies finally relinquish their opposition to a ban on chlorofluorocarbons (CFCs), which destroy ozone. The discovery suggested that strong political action to halt production of CFCs might be (i)_____, and fortunately, the chemical industry no longer felt compelled to oppose such action: although companies had recently (ii)_____ their research into CFC substitutes, studies they had initiated years earlier had produced (iii)_____ results.

Blank (i)	Blank (ii)	Blank (iii)
(A) imminent	(D) corroborated	(G) encouraging
(B) imprudent	(E) publicized	(H) inconclusive
(C) premature	(F) curtailed	(I) unsurprising

8. The incipient (i)_____ regarding taxes could affect trade between the two countries much more than the (ii)_____ banana imports, which has been going on for years. Unfortunately, the trade regulators seem to be ignoring both disagreements.

Blank (i)	Blank (ii)
(A) row	(D) profitable dealing in
(B) accord	(E) predicament regarding
(C) investigation	(F) festering dispute over

For each of questions 9 to 14, select <u>one</u> answer choice unless otherwise instructed.

Fossil bones of the huge herbivorous dinosaurs known as sauropods were first discovered and studied between 1840 and 1880, providing evidence for the gargantuan dimensions of the adults. The shape of sauropod teeth suggested what they ate. But aside from trackways, or series of fossilized footprints—which established that sauropods at least occasionally lived in herds — fossils incorporating direct evidence of other behavior, such as reproductive behavior, have been almost nonexistent. Because no modern land animals even approach sauropod size, scientists have also lacked a living analogue to use as a guide to possible sauropod behavior. Until the recent discovery of fossilized sauropod nesting grounds, scientists were thus uncertain whether sauropods laid eggs or gave birth to live young.

line

5

10

For the following question, consider each of the choices separately and select all that apply.

9. Which of the following can be inferred from the passage regarding the evidence provided by sauropod teeth?

    A The teeth allow inferences to be made about sauropod social behavior.

    B The shape of the teeth indicates that sauropods were herbivorous.

    C The teeth have no resemblance to those of any modern land animal.

For the following question, consider each of the choices separately and select all that apply.

10. Which of the following can be inferred from the passage regarding the recently discovered fossilized sauropod nesting grounds?

    A They are among the few fossils incorporating direct evidence of sauropod behavior.

    B They confirm the evidence provided by trackways about sauropod behavior.

    C They have forced a reevaluation of theories regarding the nature of sauropod herd behavior.

GO ON TO NEXT PAGE ↘

Some researchers contend that sleep plays no role in the consolidation of declarative memory (i.e., memory involving factual information). These researchers note that people with impairments in rapid eye movement (REM) sleep continue to lead normal
line lives, and they argue that if sleep were crucial for memory, then these individuals
5 would have apparent memory deficits. Yet the same researchers acknowledge that the cognitive capacities of these individuals have never been systematically examined, nor have they been the subject of studies of tasks on which performance reportedly depends on sleep. Even if such studies were done, they could only clarify our understanding of the role of REM sleep, not sleep in general.
10   These researchers also claim that improvements of memory overnight can be explained by the mere passage of time, rather than attributed to sleep. But recent studies of memory performance after sleep—including one demonstrating that sleep stabilizes declarative memories from future interference caused by mental activity during wakefulness—make this claim unsustainable. Certainly there are memory-
15 consolidation processes that occur across periods of wakefulness, some of which neither depend on nor are enhanced by sleep. But when sleep is compared with wakefulness, and performance is better after sleep, then some benefit of sleep for memory must be acknowledged.

11. The primary purpose of the passage is to

  (A) present the evidence that supports a particular claim regarding REM sleep and memory

  (B) describe how various factors contribute to the effect of sleep on memory

  (C) argue against a particular position regarding sleep's role in memory

  (D) summarize the most prevalent theory regarding sleep and memory

  (E) defend the importance of the consolidation of declarative memory

12. According to the author of the passage, which of the following generalizations about memory and sleep is true?

  (A) There are some memory-consolidation processes that have nothing to do with sleep.

  (B) Sleep is more important to the consolidation of declarative memory than to the consolidation of other types of memory.

  (C) REM sleep is more important to memory consolidation than is non-REM sleep.

  (D) There are significant variations in the amount of sleep that people require for the successful consolidation of memory.

  (E) It is likely that memory is more thoroughly consolidated during wakefulness than during sleep.

13. Which of the following best describes the function of the sentence in lines 14–16 ("Certainly…sleep")?

  (A) It provides the reasoning behind a claim about the role of sleep in memory consolidation.

  (B) It explains why a previous claim about sleep and memory is unsustainable.

     Ⓒ It demonstrates why wakefulness is central to the process of declarative memory consolidation.

     Ⓓ It emphasizes the limited role sleep plays in the process of declarative memory consolidation.

     Ⓔ It concedes that the consolidation of declarative memory does not depend entirely on one factor.

14. The importance of the study mentioned in lines 12–14 is that it

     Ⓐ reveals the mechanism by which declarative memory is stabilized during sleep

     Ⓑ identifies a specific function that sleep plays in the memory-consolidation process

     Ⓒ demonstrates that some kinds of mental activity can interfere with memory consolidation

     Ⓓ suggests that sleep and wakefulness are both important to memory consolidation

     Ⓔ explains how the passage of time contributes to memory consolidation

---

For questions 15 to 19, select the <u>two</u> answer choices that, when used to complete the sentence, fit the meaning of the sentence as a whole <u>and</u> produce completed sentences that are alike in meaning.

---

15. In American Indian art, the supposed distinction between modern and traditional was fabricated by critics, and when artists have control over interpretation of their own work, the distinction appears, happily, to have been _____.

     A eliminated
     B reinforced
     C put to rest
     D intensified
     E recognized
     F established

16. Notwithstanding their _____ regarding other issues, township residents have consistently passed the board of education's annual budget.

     A accord
     B indecision
     C consensus
     D disagreement
     E divergence
     F enthusiasm

17. Some of the company's supporters charged that the negative report had been motivated by a broader political assault on the company that was designed to help market rivals who would like to see the company _____.

    A reined in
    B bolstered
    C indemnified
    D propped up
    E manacled
    F lionized

18. Skeptics contend that any scheme for charging visitors to Web sites that rewards the vendor adequately would require steep prices, _____ the kind of frequent, casual use of Web sites that surfers now take for granted.

    A bridling
    B exciting
    C forbidding
    D inhibiting
    E provoking
    F reversing

19. It seems obvious that Miles Davis' _____ the Juilliard School, which resulted in his decision to drop out, was based on the school's training of musicians for a kind of music that he did not want to play.

    A disaffection with
    B dislocation of
    C disentanglement from
    D subversion of
    E displacement of
    F estrangement from

> **For each of questions 20 to 25, select <u>one</u> answer choice unless otherwise instructed.**

Question 20 is based on the following reading passage.

Astronomers found a large body orbiting close to the star Upsilon Andromedae. The standard theory of planet formation holds that no planet that large could be formed so close to a star, leading to the suggestion that the body is a companion star. A subsequent discovery puts that suggestion in doubt: two other large bodies were found orbiting close to Upsilon Andromedae, and the standard theory of companion stars allows for at most one companion star.

20. Which of the following, if true, most helps to resolve the status of the orbiting body without casting doubt on the two standard theories mentioned?

Ⓐ The smaller a planet orbiting a star is, and the farther away it is from the star, the less likely it is to be discovered.

Ⓑ If a planet's orbit is disturbed, the planet can be drawn by gravity toward the star it is orbiting.

Ⓒ The largest of the bodies orbiting Upsilon Andromedae is the farthest away from the star, and the smallest is the nearest.

Ⓓ It is likely that there are many stars, in addition to Upsilon Andromedae and the Sun, that are orbited by more than one smaller body.

Ⓔ In most cases of companion stars, the smaller companion is much fainter than the larger star.

Question 21 is based on the following reading passage.

In Gilavia, the number of reported workplace injuries has declined 16 percent in the last five years. However, perhaps part of the decline results from injuries going unreported: many employers have introduced safety-incentive programs, such as prize drawings for which only employees who have a perfect work-safety record are eligible. Since a workplace injury would disqualify an employee from such programs, some employees might be concealing injury, when it is feasible to do so.

21. Which of the following, if true in Gilavia, most strongly supports the proposed explanation?

Ⓐ In the last five years, there has been no decline in the number of workplace injuries leading to immediate admission to a hospital emergency room.

Ⓑ Employers generally have to pay financial compensation to employees who suffer work-related injuries.

Ⓒ Many injuries that happen on the job are injuries that would be impossible to conceal and yet would not be severe enough to require any change to either the employee's work schedule or the employee's job responsibilities.

Ⓓ A continuing shift in employment patterns has led to a decline in the percentage of the workforce that is employed in the dangerous occupations in which workplace injuries are likely.

Ⓔ Employers who have instituted safety-incentive programs do not in general have a lower proportion of reported workplace injuries among their employees than do employers without such programs.

GO ON TO NEXT PAGE ↘

The attribution of early-nineteenth-century English fiction is notoriously problematic. Fewer than half of new novels published in Britain between 1800 and 1829 had the author's true name printed on the title page. Most of these titles have subsequently
line
5   been attributed, either through the author's own acknowledgment of a previously anonymous or pseudonymous work, or through bibliographical research. One important tool available to researchers is the list of earlier works "by the author" often found on title pages. But such lists are as likely to create new confusion as they are to solve old problems. Title pages were generally prepared last in the publication process, often without full authorial assent, and in the last-minute rush to press, mistakes were fre-
10 quently made.

For the following question, consider each of the choices separately and select all that apply.

22. The passage suggests that which of the following factors contributes to the "notoriously problematic" (line 1) nature of authorial attribution in early-nineteenth-century English fiction?

    A   The unwillingness of any writers to acknowledge their authorship of works that were originally published anonymously or pseudonymously

    B   The possibility that the title page of a work may attribute works written by other authors to the author of that work

    C   The possibility that the author's name printed on a title page is fictitious

For the following question, consider each of the choices separately and select all that apply.

23. The passage suggests that which of the following is frequently true of the title pages of early-nineteenth-century English novels?

    A   The title page was prepared for printing in a hurried manner.

    B   Material on the title page was included without the author's knowledge or approval.

    C   Information on the title page was deliberately falsified to make the novel more marketable.

Questions 24 and 25 are based on the following reading passage.

The more definitions a given noun has, the more valuable is each one. Multiple definitions, each subtly different from all the others, convey multiple shades of meaning. They expand the uses of the word; language is enriched, thought is widened, and interpretations increase or dilate to fill the potentialities of association. The very impossibility of absoluteness in the definition of certain nouns adds to the levels of connotation they may reach. The inner life of a writer often says more than most readers can know; the mind of a reader can discover truths that go beyond the intent or perhaps even the comprehension of the writer. And all of it finds expression because a word can mean many things.

line

5

24. In the context in which it appears, "shades" (line 2) most nearly means

(A) reminders

(B) nuances

(C) obscurities

(D) coverings

(E) degrees

25. The passage suggests that a writer's use of nouns that have multiple definitions can have which of the following effects on the relationship between writer and reader?

(A) It can encourage the reader to consider how the writer's life might have influenced the work.

(B) It can cause the reader to become frustrated with the writer's failure to distinguish between subtle shades of meaning.

(C) It can allow the reader to discern in a work certain meanings that the writer did not foresee.

(D) It allows the writer to provide the reader with clues beyond the word itself in order to avoid ambiguity.

(E) It allows the writer to present unfamiliar ideas to the reader more efficiently.

STOP. This is the end of Section 3.

SECTION 4
Verbal Reasoning
Time—35 minutes
25 Questions

For questions 1 to 8, select <u>one</u> entry for each blank from the corresponding column of choices. Fill all blanks in the way that best completes the text.

---

1. The unexplained digressions into the finer points of quantum electrodynamics are so _____ that even readers with a physics degree would be wise to keep a textbook handy to make sense of them.

Ⓐ uninteresting
Ⓑ controversial
Ⓒ unsophisticated
Ⓓ frustrating
Ⓔ humorless

2. The belief that politicians might become _____ after their election to office led to the appointment of ethics officers at various levels of government.

Ⓐ scrupulous
Ⓑ entrenched
Ⓒ venal
Ⓓ puzzled
Ⓔ artificial

3. Even the charisma and technical prowess of two fine actors are not _____ the task of fully invigorating a gray domestic drama with a tired tale to tell.

Ⓐ required for
Ⓑ interested in
Ⓒ preferred for
Ⓓ adequate to
Ⓔ inferior to

4. There may be a threshold below which blood pressure reductions become _____ given that a long-running study showed no decreased heart risk for drops in blood pressure below a certain point.

Ⓐ worthwhile
Ⓑ indiscernible
Ⓒ arduous
Ⓓ significant
Ⓔ superfluous

5. Unlike the problems in recent financial scandals, issues raised by the regulators in this case appear largely to pertain to unwieldy accounting rules that are open to widely divergent interpretations—not to (i)_____ transactions designed to (ii)_____ corporate malfeasance.

Blank (i)	Blank (ii)
Ⓐ sham	Ⓓ cloak
Ⓑ unpremeditated	Ⓔ ameliorate
Ⓒ justifiable	Ⓕ illuminate

6. Everyone has routines that govern their work. The myth is that artists are somehow different, that they reject (i)_____, but of course that's not true: most artists work as the rest of us do, (ii)_____, day by day, according to their own customs.

Blank (i)	Blank (ii)
Ⓐ latitude	Ⓓ impetuously
Ⓑ habit	Ⓔ ploddingly
Ⓒ materialism	Ⓕ sporadically

7. Repression of painful memories is sometimes called "willed forgetting." Yet true forgetting is (i)_____ than the phenomenon of repressed memory. In spite of the effort that it (ii)_____, repressing unwanted memories is less (iii)_____ than truly forgetting them, for repressed memories are prone to come back.

Blank (i)	Blank (ii)	Blank (iii)
Ⓐ less controlled	Ⓓ eases	Ⓖ permanent
Ⓑ different in its effect	Ⓔ conveys	Ⓗ arduous
Ⓒ far more common	Ⓕ entails	Ⓘ immediate

8. Rather than viewing the Massachusetts Bay Colony's antinomian controversy as the inevitable (i)_____ of the intransigent opposing forces of radical and (ii)_____ beliefs, male and female piety, (iii)_____ and secular power, and the like, as other critics have, Winship argues that the crisis was not "fixed and structural."

Blank (i)	Blank (ii)	Blank (iii)
Ⓐ dissolution	Ⓓ revolutionary	Ⓖ clerical
Ⓑ melding	Ⓔ orthodox	Ⓗ civil
Ⓒ collision	Ⓕ questionable	Ⓘ cerebral

GO ON TO NEXT PAGE ↘

Questions 9 to 12 are based on the following reading passage.

Until recently, many anthropologists assumed that the environment of what is now the southwestern United States shaped the social history and culture of the region's indigenous peoples. Building on this assumption, archaeologists asserted that adverse environmental conditions and droughts were responsible for the disappearances and migrations of southwestern populations from many sites they once inhabited.

However, such deterministic arguments fail to acknowledge that local environmental variability in the Southwest makes generalizing about that environment difficult. To examine the relationship between environmental variation and sociocultural change in the Western Pueblo region of central Arizona, which indigenous tribes have occupied continuously for at least 800 years, a research team recently reconstructed the climatic, vegetational, and erosional cycles of past centuries. The researchers found it impossible to provide a single, generally applicable characterization of environmental conditions for the region. Rather, they found that local areas experienced different patterns of rainfall, wind, and erosion, and that such conditions had prevailed in the Southwest for the last 1,400 years. Rainfall, for example, varied within and between local valley systems, so that even adjacent agricultural fields can produce significantly different yields.

The researchers characterized episodes of variation in southwestern environments by frequency: low-frequency environmental processes occur in cycles longer than one human generation, which generally is considered to last about 25 years, and high-frequency processes have shorter cycles. The researchers pointed out that low-frequency processes, such as fluctuations in stream flow and groundwater levels, would not usually be apparent to human populations. In contrast, high-frequency fluctuations such as seasonal temperature variations are observable and somewhat predictable, so that groups could have adapted their behaviors accordingly. When the researchers compared sequences of sociocultural change in the Western Pueblo region with episodes of low- and high-frequency environmental variation, however, they found no simple correlation between environmental process and sociocultural change or persistence.

Although early Pueblo peoples did protect themselves against environmental risk and uncertainty, they responded variously on different occasions to similar patterns of high-frequency climatic and environmental change. The researchers identified seven major adaptive responses, including increased mobility, relocation of permanent settlements, changes in subsistence foods, and reliance on trade with other groups. These findings suggest that groups' adaptive choices depended on cultural and social as well as environmental factors and were flexible strategies rather than uncomplicated reactions to environmental change. Environmental conditions mattered, but they were rarely, if ever, sufficient to account for sociocultural persistence and change. Group size and composition, culture, contact with other groups, and individual choices and actions were—barring catastrophes such as floods or earthquakes—more significant for a population's survival than were climate and environment.

9. The passage is primarily concerned with
    (A) explaining why certain research findings have created controversy
    (B) pointing out the flaws in a research methodology and suggesting a different approach
    (C) presenting evidence to challenge an explanation and offering an alternative explanation
    (D) elucidating the means by which certain groups have adapted to their environment
    (E) defending a long-held interpretation by presenting new research findings

10. Which of the following findings would most strongly support the assertion made by the archaeologists mentioned in line 3?
    (A) A population remained in a certain region at least a century after erosion wore away much of the topsoil that sustained grass for their grazing animals.
    (B) The range of a certain group's agricultural activity increased over a century of gradual decrease in annual rainfall.
    (C) As winters grew increasingly mild in a certain region, the nomadic residents of the region continued to move between their summer and winter encampments.
    (D) An agricultural population began to trade for supplies of a grain instead of producing the grain in its own fields as it had in the past.
    (E) A half century of drought and falling groundwater levels caused a certain population to abandon their settlements along a riverbank.

11. The fact that "adjacent agricultural fields can produce significantly different yields" (lines 16–17) is offered as evidence of the
    (A) unpredictability of the climate and environment of the southwestern United States
    (B) difficulty of producing a consistent food supply for a large population in the Western Pueblo region
    (C) lack of water and land suitable for cultivation in central Arizona
    (D) local climatic variation in the environment of the southwestern United States
    (E) high-frequency environmental processes at work in the southwestern United States

12. It can be inferred from the passage that which of the following activities is NOT an example of a population responding to high-frequency environmental processes?

    (A) Developing watertight jars in which to collect and store water during the rainy season

    (B) Building multistory dwellings in low-lying areas to avoid the flash flooding that occurs each summer

    (C) Moving a village because groundwater levels have changed over the last generation

    (D) Trading with other groups for furs from which to make winter clothes

    (E) Moving one's herds of grazing animals each year between summer and winter pastures

---

Questions 13 and 14 are based on the following reading passage.

Arctic sea ice comes in two varieties. Seasonal ice forms in winter and then melts in summer, while perennial ice persists year-round. To the untrained eye, all sea ice looks similar, but by licking it, one can estimate how long a particular piece has been float-
line   ing around. When ice begins to form in seawater, it forces out salt, which has no place
  5   in the crystal structure. As the ice gets thicker, the rejected salt collects in tiny pockets of brine too highly concentrated to freeze. A piece of first-year ice will taste salty. Even-tually, if the ice survives, these pockets of brine drain out through fine, veinlike chan-nels, and the ice becomes fresher; multiyear ice can even be melted and drunk.

For the following question, consider each of the choices separately and select all that apply.

13. The passage mentions which of the following as being a characteristic of seasonal ice?

    [A] It is similar in appearance to perennial ice.

    [B] It is typically filled with fine, veinlike channels.

    [C] It tastes saltier than perennial ice.

14. In the context in which it appears, "fine" (line 7) most nearly means

    (A) acceptable

    (B) elegant

    (C) precise

    (D) pure

    (E) small

> **For questions 15 to 18, select the <u>two</u> answer choices that, when used to complete the sentence, fit the meaning of the sentence as a whole <u>and</u> produce completed sentences that are alike in meaning.**

15. It would have been disingenuous of the candidate to appear _____ when her opponent won the election, but she congratulated the victor nonetheless.
    - A gracious
    - B ecstatic
    - C crestfallen
    - D indifferent
    - E euphoric
    - F disgruntled

16. As market forces penetrate firms and bid up the value of attributes of labor that are more measurable than is the knowledge born of experience, it can be expected that trends in wages will not _____ those whose main value lies in such experiential knowledge.
    - A favor
    - B aid
    - C affect
    - D forsake
    - E betray
    - F differentiate

17. The point we might still take from the First World War is the old one that wars are always, as one historian aptly put it, _____: they produce unforeseeable results.
    - A unsurprising
    - B astounding
    - C conventional
    - D ruinous
    - E stunning
    - F devastating

18. This is the kind of movie—stuffed with intimations of faraway strife and people in suits talking frantically on cell phones and walkie-talkies—that is conventionally described as a political thriller, but the film is as apolitical as it is _____.
    - A intense
    - B unprecedented
    - C subtle
    - D humdrum
    - E refined
    - F dull

GO ON TO NEXT PAGE ↘

For each of questions 19 to 25, select <u>one</u> answer choice unless otherwise instructed.

Questions 19 and 20 are based on the following reading passage.

Historians credit repeated locust invasions in the nineteenth century with reshaping United States agriculture west of the Mississippi River. Admonished by government entomologists, farmers began to diversify. Wheat had come to nearly monopolize the

line   region, but it was particularly vulnerable to the locusts. In 1873, just before the locusts'

5   most withering offensive, nearly two-thirds of Minnesota farmland was producing wheat; by the invasions' last year, that fraction had dropped to less than one-sixth. Farmers learned that peas and beans were far less vulnerable to the insects, and corn was a more robust grain than wheat. In addition to planting alternative crops, many farmers turned to dairy and beef production. Although pastures were often damaged

10   by the locusts, these lands were almost always left in better shape than the crops were.

For the following question, consider each of the choices separately and select all that apply.

19. According to the passage, before the recommendations by the government entomologists, which of the following was true about farming west of the Mississippi River?

    [A] Farmers focused primarily on growing wheat.

    [B] Peas and beans had not yet been planted in the region.

    [C] A relatively small portion of farmland was devoted to crops other than wheat.

20. In the context in which it appears, "robust" (line 8) most nearly means

    (A) crude

    (B) demanding

    (C) productive

    (D) vigorous

    (E) rich

In 1998 the United States Department of Transportation received nearly 10,000 consumer complaints about airlines; in 1999 it received over 20,000. Moreover, the number of complaints per 100,000 passengers also more than doubled. In both years the vast majority of complaints concerned flight delays, cancellations, mishandled baggage, and customer service. Clearly, therefore, despite the United States airline industry's serious efforts to improve performance in these areas, passenger dissatisfaction with airline service increased significantly in 1999.

21. Which of the following, if true, most seriously weakens the argument?

(A) Although the percentage of flights that arrived on time dropped slightly overall, from 77 percent in 1998 to 76 percent in 1999, some United States airlines' 1999 on-time rate was actually better than their 1998 on-time rate.

(B) The number of passengers flying on United States airlines was significantly higher in 1999 than in 1998.

(C) Fewer bags per 1,000 passengers flying on United States airlines were lost or delayed in 1999 than in 1998.

(D) The appearance in 1999 of many new Internet sites that relay complaints directly to the Department of Transportation has made filing a complaint about airlines much easier for consumers than ever before.

(E) Although the number of consumer complaints increased for every major United States airline in 1999, for some airlines the extent of the increase was substantial, whereas for others it was extremely small.

Nineteenth-century architect Eugène-Emmanuel Viollet-le-Duc contended that Paris's Notre-Dame cathedral, built primarily in the late twelfth century, was supported from the very beginning by a system of flying buttresses—a series of exterior arches (flyers) and their supports (buttresses)—which permitted the construction of taller vaulted buildings with slimmer walls and interior supports than had been possible previously. Other commentators insist, however, that Notre-Dame did not have flying buttresses until the thirteenth or fourteenth century, when they were added to update the building aesthetically and correct its structural flaws. Although post-twelfth-century modifications and renovations complicate efforts to resolve this controversy—all pre-fifteenth-century flyers have been replaced, and the buttresses have been rebuilt and/or resurfaced—it is nevertheless possible to tell that both the nave and the choir, the church's two major parts, have always had flying buttresses. It is clear, now that nineteenth-century paint and plaster have been removed, that the nave's lower buttresses date from the twelfth century. Moreover, the choir's lower flyers have chevron (zigzag) decoration. Chevron decoration, which was characteristic of the second half of the twelfth century and was out of favor by the fourteenth century, is entirely absent from modifications to the building that can be dated with confidence to the thirteenth century.

22. The passage is primarily concerned with
    (A) tracing the development of a controversy
    (B) discussing obstacles to resolving a controversy
    (C) arguing in support of one side in a controversy
    (D) analyzing the assumptions underlying the claims made in a controversy
    (E) explaining why evidence relevant to a controversy has been overlooked

23. The claim of the "other commentators" (line 6) suggests that they believe which of the following about Notre-Dame?
    (A) It was the inspiration for many vaulted cathedrals built in the thirteenth and fourteenth centuries.
    (B) Its design flaws were not apparent until flying buttresses were added in the thirteenth or fourteenth century.
    (C) Its flying buttresses are embellished with decoration characteristic of the thirteenth and fourteenth centuries.
    (D) It had been modified in some respects before flying buttresses were added in the thirteenth or fourteenth century.
    (E) It was originally constructed in an architectural style that was considered outmoded by the thirteenth or fourteenth century.

24. The author's argument concerning Notre-Dame's flying buttresses depends on which of the following assumptions about the choir's lower flyers?

  Ⓐ They accurately reproduce the decoration on the choir's original lower flyers.

  Ⓑ They have a type of decoration used exclusively for exterior surfaces.

  Ⓒ They were the models for the choir's original upper flyers.

  Ⓓ They were the models for the nave's original lower flyers.

  Ⓔ They were constructed after the nave's flyers were constructed.

Question 25 is based on the following reading passage.

The average temperature of the lobster-rich waters off the coast of Foerkland has been increasing for some years. In warmer water, lobsters grow faster. In particular, lobster larvae take less time to reach the size at which they are no longer vulnerable to predation by young cod, the chief threat to their survival. Consequently, the survival rate of lobster larvae must be going up, and the lobster population in Foerkland's coastal waters is bound to increase.

25. Which of the following, if true, most seriously weakens the argument?

  Ⓐ There are indications that in recent years the fishing fleet operating off the coast of Foerkland has been taking cod at an unsustainably high rate.

  Ⓑ The increase in water temperatures off Foerkland has not been as pronounced as the increase in average soil temperatures in Foerkland.

  Ⓒ Because of their speeded-up growth, lobsters now get large enough to be legal catch before they reach reproductive maturity.

  Ⓓ Even though lobsters grow faster in warmer waters, warmer waters have no effect on the maximum size to which a lobster can eventually grow.

  Ⓔ Cod are a cold-water species, and the increasing water temperatures have caused a northward shift in Foerkland's cod population.

STOP. This is the end of Section 4.

SECTION 5
Quantitative Reasoning
Time—40 minutes
25 Questions

For each question, indicate the best answer, using the directions given.

Notes: All numbers used are real numbers.

All figures are assumed to lie in a plane unless otherwise indicated.

Geometric figures, such as lines, circles, triangles, and quadrilaterals, **are not necessarily** drawn to scale. That is, you should **not** assume that quantities such as lengths and angle measures are as they appear in a figure. You should assume, however, that lines shown as straight are actually straight, points on a line are in the order shown, and more generally, all geometric objects are in the relative positions shown. For questions with geometric figures, you should base your answers on geometric reasoning, not on estimating or comparing quantities by sight or by measurement.

Coordinate systems, such as xy-planes and number lines, **are** drawn to scale; therefore, you can read, estimate, or compare quantities in such figures by sight or by measurement.

Graphical data presentations, such as bar graphs, circle graphs, and line graphs, **are** drawn to scale; therefore, you can read, estimate, or compare data values by sight or by measurement.

For each of Questions 1 to 9, compare Quantity A and Quantity B, using additional information centered above the two quantities if such information is given. Select one of the following four answer choices and fill in the corresponding oval to the right of the question.

Ⓐ   **Quantity A is greater.**
Ⓑ   **Quantity B is greater.**
Ⓒ   **The two quantities are equal.**
Ⓓ   **The relationship cannot be determined from the information given.**

A symbol that appears more than once in a question has the same meaning throughout the question.

	Quantity A	Quantity B	Correct Answer
Example 1:	(2)(6)	2 + 6	● Ⓑ Ⓒ Ⓓ

	Quantity A	Quantity B	Correct Answer
Example 2:	PS	SR	Ⓐ Ⓑ Ⓒ ●

(since equal lengths cannot be assumed, even though PS and SR appear equal)

Ⓐ	**Quantity A is greater.**
Ⓑ	**Quantity B is greater.**
Ⓒ	**The two quantities are equal.**
Ⓓ	**The relationship cannot be determined from the information given.**

	Quantity A	Quantity B	
1.	$\dfrac{3^{-1}}{4^{-1}}$	$\dfrac{4}{3}$	Ⓐ Ⓑ Ⓒ Ⓓ

$$x < 1 \text{ and } x \neq 0$$

	Quantity A	Quantity B	
2.	$x^2 + 1$	$x^3 + 1$	Ⓐ Ⓑ Ⓒ Ⓓ

$$x > 0$$

	Quantity A	Quantity B	
3.	0.5% of x	$\dfrac{1}{2}x$	Ⓐ Ⓑ Ⓒ Ⓓ

The median income of a group of College C graduates six months after graduation was \$3,000 higher than the median income of a group of College D graduates six months after graduation.

	Quantity A	Quantity B	
4.	The 75th percentile of the incomes of the group of College C graduates six months after graduation	The 75th percentile of the incomes of the group of College D graduates six months after graduation	Ⓐ Ⓑ Ⓒ Ⓓ

GO ON TO NEXT PAGE ➘

(A) **Quantity A is greater.**
(B) **Quantity B is greater.**
(C) **The two quantities are equal.**
(D) **The relationship cannot be determined from the information given.**

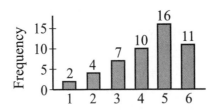

The graph above shows the frequency distribution of 50 integer values varying from 1 to 6.

Quantity A	Quantity B

5. The average (arithmetic mean) of the 50 values   The median of the 50 values   (A) (B) (C) (D)

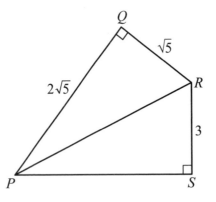

Quantity A	Quantity B

6. The area of triangle *PQR*   The area of triangle *PSR*   (A) (B) (C) (D)

Quantity A	Quantity B

7. The sum of the odd integers from 1 to 199   The sum of the even integers from 2 to 198   (A) (B) (C) (D)

---

s and *t* are positive integers, and $32^s = 2^t$.

Quantity A	Quantity B

8. $\dfrac{s}{t}$ $\dfrac{1}{5}$ (A) (B) (C) (D)

Ⓐ Quantity A is greater.
Ⓑ Quantity B is greater.
Ⓒ The two quantities are equal.
Ⓓ The relationship cannot be determined from the information given.

In a quality-control test, 50 boxes—each containing 30 machine parts—were examined for defective parts. The number of defective parts was recorded for each box, and the average (arithmetic mean) of the 50 recorded numbers of defective parts per box was 1.12. Only one error was made in recording the 50 numbers: "1" defective part in a certain box was incorrectly recorded as "10".

Quantity A	Quantity B	
9. The actual average number of defective parts per box	0.94	Ⓐ Ⓑ Ⓒ Ⓓ

Questions 10 to 25 have several different formats. Unless otherwise directed, select a single answer choice. For Numeric Entry questions, follow the instructions below.

Numeric Entry Questions
Enter your answer in the answer box(es) below the question.

- Your answer may be an integer, a decimal, or a fraction, and it may be negative.
- If a question asks for a fraction, there will be two boxes—one for the numerator and one for the denominator.
- Equivalent forms of the correct answer, such as 2.5 and 2.50, are all correct. Fractions do not need to be reduced to lowest terms.
- Enter the exact answer unless the question asks you to round your answer.

10. In year Y, the population of Colorado was approximately half that of New Jersey, and the land area of Colorado was approximately 14 times that of New Jersey. The population density (number of persons per unit of land area) of Colorado in year Y was approximately how many times the population density of New Jersey?

Ⓐ $\frac{1}{28}$

Ⓑ $\frac{1}{14}$

Ⓒ $\frac{1}{7}$

Ⓓ $\frac{1}{4}$

Ⓔ $\frac{1}{2}$

GO ON TO NEXT PAGE

For the following question, enter your answer in the box.

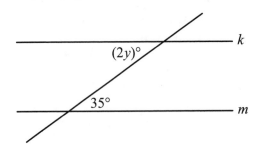

11. In the figure above, line k is parallel to line m. What is the value of y?

$$y = \boxed{}$$

12. The numbers in data set S have a standard deviation of 5. If a new data set is formed by adding 3 to each number in S, what is the standard deviation of the numbers in the new data set?

   Ⓐ 2

   Ⓑ 3

   Ⓒ 5

   Ⓓ 8

   Ⓔ 15

13. If $\dfrac{2y-3}{y} = \dfrac{3-y}{2}$, which of the following could be the value of y?

   Ⓐ 4

   Ⓑ 1

   Ⓒ −1

   Ⓓ −3

   Ⓔ −5

For the following question, select all the answer choices that apply.

14. List K consists of the numbers −10, −5, 0, 5, and 10. Which of the following lists of numbers have the same range as the numbers in list K?

Indicate <u>all</u> such lists.

   A −15, −1, 0, 1, 15

   B −7, −4, −2, 1, 13

   C 0, 1, 2, 5, 8, 10

   D 2, 3, 5, 15, 19, 22

   E 4, 5, 6, 24

15. Aisha's income in 2004 was 20 percent greater than her income in 2003. What is the ratio of Aisha's income in 2004 to her income in 2003?

    (A) 1 to 5
    (B) 5 to 6
    (C) 6 to 5
    (D) 5 to 1
    (E) 20 to 1

16. Jacob's weekly take-home pay is n dollars. Each week he uses $\dfrac{4n}{5}$ dollars for expenses and saves the rest. At those rates, how many weeks will it take Jacob to save $500, in terms of n?

    (A) $\dfrac{500}{n}$

    (B) $\dfrac{2{,}500}{n}$

    (C) $\dfrac{n}{625}$

    (D) $\dfrac{n}{2{,}500}$

    (E) $625n$

Questions 17 to 20 are based on the following data.

LENGTH OF UNEMPLOYMENT FOR WORKERS IN REGION *X* FOR TWO INDUSTRIES, 2003

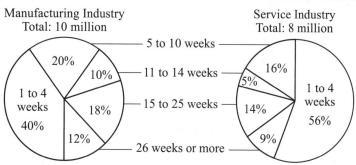

Note: The circle graphs show the distributions of workers who were unemployed for at least 1 week in 2003, by length of unemployment, rounded to the nearest week.

17. In the circle graphs, the degree measure of the central angle of the sector representing the number of workers unemployed for 11 to 14 weeks is how much greater in the manufacturing industry graph than in the service industry graph?

    (A) 5°
    (B) 10°
    (C) 15°
    (D) 18°
    (E) 20°

GO ON TO NEXT PAGE

18. Which of the following could be the median length of unemployment, in weeks, for manufacturing industry workers who were unemployed for at least 1 week?

    Ⓐ   4
    Ⓑ   8
    Ⓒ   12
    Ⓓ   16
    Ⓔ   20

19. If one of the workers in the manufacturing and service industries who were unemployed for at least 1 week will be randomly selected, what is the probability that the person selected will be a service industry worker who was unemployed for 26 weeks or more?

    Ⓐ   0.04
    Ⓑ   0.09
    Ⓒ   0.21
    Ⓓ   0.40
    Ⓔ   0.90

20. The ratio of the number of manufacturing industry workers who were unemployed for 5 to 10 weeks to the number of service industry workers who were unemployed for 5 to 10 weeks is closest to which of the following?

    Ⓐ   5 to 4
    Ⓑ   6 to 5
    Ⓒ   3 to 2
    Ⓓ   5 to 2
    Ⓔ   7 to 6

For the following question, select all the answer choices that apply.

21. If $|t + 3| > 5$, which of the following could be the value of t?

Indicate <u>all</u> such values.

    ☐ A   −9
    ☐ B   −6
    ☐ C   −2
    ☐ D   0
    ☐ E   2
    ☐ F   3

22. The operation $\otimes$ is defined for all integers x and y as $x \otimes y = xy - y$. If x and y are positive integers, which of the following CANNOT be zero?

    (A) $x \otimes y$
    (B) $y \otimes x$
    (C) $(x - 1) \otimes y$
    (D) $(x + 1) \otimes y$
    (E) $x \otimes (y - 1)$

23. P, Q, and R are three points in a plane, and R does not lie on line PQ. Which of the following is true about the set of all points in the plane that are the same distance from all three points?

    (A) It contains no points.
    (B) It contains one point.
    (C) It contains two points.
    (D) It is a line.
    (E) It is a circle.

24. If $x < y < 0$, which of the following inequalities must be true?

    (A) $y + 1 < x$
    (B) $y - 1 < x$
    (C) $xy^2 < x$
    (D) $xy < y^2$
    (E) $xy < x^2$

For the following question, enter your answer in the box.

25. What is the length of a diagonal of a rectangle that has width 5 and perimeter 34?

    [   ]

STOP. This is the end of Section 5.

SECTION 6
Quantitative Reasoning
Time—40 minutes
25 Questions

For each question, indicate the best answer, using the directions given.

Notes: All numbers used are real numbers.

All figures are assumed to lie in a plane unless otherwise indicated. Geometric figures, such as lines, circles, triangles, and quadrilaterals, **are not necessarily** drawn to scale. That is, you should **not** assume that quantities such as lengths and angle measures are as they appear in a figure. You should assume, however, that lines shown as straight are actually straight, points on a line are in the order shown, and more generally, all geometric objects are in the relative positions shown. For questions with geometric figures, you should base your answers on geometric reasoning, not on estimating or comparing quantities by sight or by measurement.

Coordinate systems, such as *xy*-planes and number lines, **are** drawn to scale; therefore, you can read, estimate, or compare quantities in such figures by sight or by measurement.

Graphical data presentations, such as bar graphs, circle graphs, and line graphs, **are** drawn to scale; therefore, you can read, estimate, or compare data values by sight or by measurement.

For each of Questions 1 to 9, compare Quantity A and Quantity B, using additional information centered above the two quantities if such information is given. Select one of the following four answer choices and fill in the corresponding oval to the right of the question.

(A) Quantity A is greater.
(B) Quantity B is greater.
(C) The two quantities are equal.
(D) The relationship cannot be determined from the information given.

A symbol that appears more than once in a question has the same meaning throughout the question.

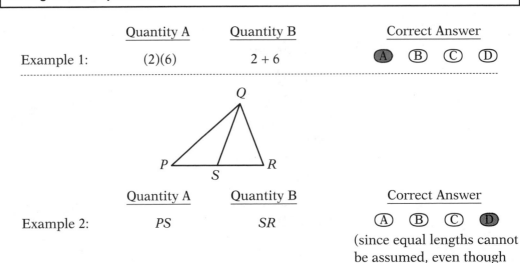

	Quantity A	Quantity B	Correct Answer
Example 1:	(2)(6)	2 + 6	(A) ⬤ (B) (C) (D)

	Quantity A	Quantity B	Correct Answer
Example 2:	*PS*	*SR*	(A) (B) (C) (D) ⬤

(since equal lengths cannot be assumed, even though *PS* and *SR* appear equal)

(A) **Quantity A is greater.**
(B) **Quantity B is greater.**
(C) **The two quantities are equal.**
(D) **The relationship cannot be determined from the information given.**

A circle is inscribed in a square with sides of length 5.

	Quantity A	Quantity B	
1.	The circumference of the circle	15	(A) (B) (C) (D)

$$2u + v = 14$$
$$uv = 0$$

	Quantity A	Quantity B	
2.	u	v	(A) (B) (C) (D)

	Quantity A	Quantity B	
3.	$950^{2,000}$	$10^{6,000}$	(A) (B) (C) (D)

Set A consists of 40 integers, and set B consists of 150 integers. The number of integers that are in both set A and set B is 20.

	Quantity A	Quantity B	
4.	The total number of integers that are in set A or set B, or both	170	(A) (B) (C) (D)

GO ON TO NEXT PAGE ↘

(A)	**Quantity A is greater.**
(B)	**Quantity B is greater.**
(C)	**The two quantities are equal.**
(D)	**The relationship cannot be determined from the information given.**

x is a negative integer.

       Quantity A   Quantity B

5. 2^x 3^{x+1} (A) (B) (C) (D)

$$(x + 3)(y - 4) = 0$$

       Quantity A   Quantity B

6. xy -12 (A) (B) (C) (D)

Geoff used $630 to buy a new guitar. This amount was 15 percent of his earnings last summer.

       Quantity A   Quantity B

7. The amount of Geoff's $3,570   (A) (B) (C) (D)
earnings last summer <u>not</u>
used to buy the new guitar

Set S consists of 5 objects.

       Quantity A   Quantity B

8. The number of subsets   The number of subsets   (A) (B) (C) (D)
of set S that consist of   of set S that consist of
1 object   4 objects

(A) Quantity A is greater.
(B) Quantity B is greater.
(C) The two quantities are equal.
(D) The relationship cannot be determined from the information given.

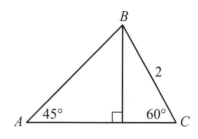

Quantity A	Quantity B

9. The length of line segment AC   3   (A)   (B)   (C)   (D)

Questions 10 to 25 have several different formats. Unless otherwise directed, select a single answer choice. For Numeric Entry questions, follow the instructions below.

Numeric Entry Questions
Enter your answer in the answer box(es) below the question.

- Your answer may be an integer, a decimal, or a fraction, and it may be negative.
- If a question asks for a fraction, there will be two boxes—one for the numerator and one for the denominator.
- Equivalent forms of the correct answer, such as 2.5 and 2.50, are all correct. Fractions do not need to be reduced to lowest terms.
- Enter the exact answer unless the question asks you to round your answer.

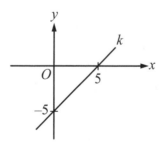

10. What is the slope of line k in the xy-plane above?

(A) −5
(B) −1
(C) 0
(D) 1
(E) 5

GO ON TO NEXT PAGE ↘

$$b - 3, b - 1, b + 2, b + 3, b + 4$$

11. The median of the five terms listed above is 5, where b is a constant. What is the average (arithmetic mean) of the five terms?

    (A) 3

    (B) 4

    (C) 5

    (D) 6

    (E) 7

For the following question, enter your answer in the box.

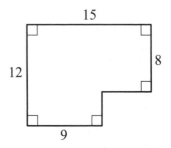

12. What is the area of the region shown above?

    [   ]

13. During a one-year study, biologists observed the number of fish in a certain pond as well as the percent of the fish that were catfish. At the beginning of the year, there were 300 fish in the pond, of which 15 percent were catfish; and at the end of the year, there were 400 fish in the pond, of which 10 percent were catfish. From the beginning of the year to the end of the year, the number of catfish in the pond

    (A) decreased by more than 5%

    (B) decreased by 5%

    (C) did not change

    (D) increased by 5%

    (E) increased by more than 5%

For the following question, enter your answer in the box.

14. On a radio tower, a red light flashes every 6 seconds and a blue light flashes every 10 seconds. If both lights flash together at a certain time, how many seconds later will both lights flash together the next time?

    [   ] seconds

For the following question, select all the answer choices that apply.

15.   If $a < b < 0$, which of the following numbers must be positive?

Indicate <u>all</u> such numbers.

- [A] $a - b$
- [B] $a^2 - b^2$
- [C] ab
- [D] $a^2 b$
- [E] $a^2 b + ab^2$

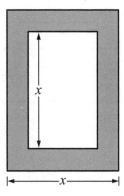

16.   A flat rectangular picture, represented by the unshaded region in the figure above, is mounted in a flat rectangular frame, represented by the shaded region. The frame is 1 inch wide on all sides. For what value of x, in inches, is the area of the frame equal to the area of the picture?

- (A) 4
- (B) 5
- (C) 6
- (D) 7
- (E) 8

GO ON TO NEXT PAGE ↘

PERCENT OF THE 300 PEOPLE IN GROUP 1 AND THE 400 PEOPLE
IN GROUP 2 WHO HAVE SELECTED AILMENTS

Respiratory Ailment	Percent of People in Group 1 Who Have Ailment	Percent of People in Group 2 Who Have Ailment
Allergic sensitivity to endotoxins	14%	21%
Asthma (allergic)	3%	4%
Asthma (nonallergic)	2%	3%
Hay fever	4%	10%
Sneezing and itchy eyes	8%	11%
Wheezing (allergic)	5%	6%
Wheezing (nonallergic)	2%	5%

17. The number of people in group 2 who have hay fever is how much greater than the number of people in group 1 who have hay fever?

 (A) 37
 (B) 35
 (C) 32
 (D) 28
 (E) 24

18. For the seven ailments, what is the median of the numbers of people in group 2 who have the ailments?

 (A) 20
 (B) 22
 (C) 24
 (D) 26
 (E) 28

19. The number of people in group 1 who have the ailment wheezing (allergic) is what percent greater than the number of people in group 1 who have the ailment wheezing (nonallergic)?

 (A) 50%
 (B) 75%
 (C) 150%
 (D) 200%
 (E) 300%

For the following question, enter your answer in the boxes.

20. What is the ratio of the number of people in group 2 with the ailment sneezing and itchy eyes to the total number of people in both groups with the ailment sneezing and itchy eyes?

    Give your answer as a fraction.

21. Of the people in a certain survey, 58 percent were at most 40 years old and 70 percent were at most 60 years old. If 252 of the people in the survey were more than 40 years old and at most 60 years old, what was the total number of people in the survey?

    Ⓐ 1,900
    Ⓑ 2,100
    Ⓒ 2,400
    Ⓓ 2,700
    Ⓔ 3,000

22. If $x > 0$, which of the following is equal to 1.25 percent of x?

    Ⓐ $\dfrac{x}{80}$

    Ⓑ $\dfrac{x}{8}$

    Ⓒ $\dfrac{x}{4}$

    Ⓓ $\dfrac{5x}{8}$

    Ⓔ $\dfrac{3x}{4}$

23. Alice earns d dollars and has t percent of what she earns deducted for taxes. How much of what she earns does Alice have left after taxes?

    Ⓐ $d(1 - 100t)$ dollars
    Ⓑ $d(1 - 10t)$ dollars
    Ⓒ $d(1 - t)$ dollars
    Ⓓ $d(1 - 0.1t)$ dollars
    Ⓔ $d(1 - 0.01t)$ dollars

GO ON TO NEXT PAGE ↘

For the following question, select all the answer choices that apply.

24. A student made a conjecture that for any integer n, the integer $4n + 3$ is a prime number. Which of the following values of n could be used to disprove the student's conjecture?

    Indicate all such values.

    [A] 1
    [B] 3
    [C] 4
    [D] 6
    [E] 7

25. Eight points are equally spaced on a circle. If 4 of the 8 points are to be chosen at random, what is the probability that a quadrilateral having the 4 points chosen as vertices will be a square?

    (A) $\dfrac{1}{70}$

    (B) $\dfrac{1}{35}$

    (C) $\dfrac{1}{7}$

    (D) $\dfrac{1}{4}$

    (E) $\dfrac{1}{2}$

STOP. This is the end of Section 6.

Evaluating Your Performance

Now that you have completed Practice Test 2, it is time to evaluate your performance.

Analytical Writing Measure

One way to evaluate your performance on the Issue and Argument topics you answered on this practice test is to compare your essay responses with the scored sample essay responses for these topics and review the rater commentary. Scored sample essay responses and rater commentary are presented starting on page 481 for the one Issue topic and one Argument topic presented in the Analytical Writing sections of Practice Test 2. The Issue and Argument scoring guides start on page 37.

To better understand the analytical writing abilities characteristic of particular score levels, you should review the score level descriptions on page 41.

Verbal Reasoning and Quantitative Reasoning Measures

The tables that follow contain information to help you evaluate your performance on the Verbal Reasoning and Quantitative Reasoning measures of Practice Test 2. An answer key with the correct answers to the questions in the Verbal Reasoning and Quantitative Reasoning sections in this practice test begins on page 475. Compare your answers with the correct answers given in the table, crossing out questions you answered incorrectly or omitted. Partially correct answers should be treated as incorrect. Knowing which questions you answered incorrectly or omitted can help you identify content areas in which you need more practice or review.

The answer key contains additional information to help you evaluate your performance. With each answer, the key provides a number, the P+. The P+ is the percent of a group of actual GRE takers who were administered that same question at a previous test administration and who answered it correctly. P+ is used to gauge the relative difficulty of a test question. The higher the P+, the easier the test question. You can use the P+ to compare your performance on each test question to the performance of other test takers on that same question. For example, if the P+ for a question is 89, that means that 89 percent of GRE test takers who received this question answered it correctly. Alternatively, if the P+ for a question is 14, that means that 14 percent of GRE test takers who received this question answered it correctly. A question with a P+ of 89 may be interpreted as a relatively easy question, and a question with a P+ of 14 may be interpreted as a difficult question.

To calculate your scores on Practice Test 2:

- Add the number of correct answers in Sections 3 and 4 to obtain your raw Verbal Reasoning score.
- Add the number of correct answers in Sections 5 and 6 to obtain your raw Quantitative Reasoning score.
- Once you have calculated your raw scores, refer to the Practice Test 2 score conversion table on pages 479–480. Find the scores on the 130–170 score scales that correspond to your Verbal Reasoning and Quantitative Reasoning raw scores. Note the scaled scores provided.

Once you determine your scaled scores, you will need to evaluate your performance. To get a sense of how test takers are scoring on the Verbal Reasoning and Quantitative Reasoning measures of the actual test, you can review Verbal Reasoning and Quantitative Reasoning percentile ranks on the GRE website at **www.ets.org/gre/percentile** (PDF). A percentile rank for a score indicates the percentage of examinees who took that test and received a lower score. Updated annually in July, this table includes the Verbal Reasoning and Quantitative Reasoning scores on the 130–170 scale in one-point increments and the corresponding percentile ranks. For each score you earned on Practice Test 2, note the percent of GRE test takers who earned lower scores. This is a reasonable indication of your rank among GRE General Test examinees if you took Practice Test 2 under standard timed conditions.

Answer Key

Section 3. Verbal Reasoning

Question Number	P+	Correct Answer
1	71	**Choice A:** innocuous
2	68	**Choice C:** banished from
3	41	**Choice C:** comprehensive; **Choice D:** redundant
4	74	**Choice B:** heed; **Choice F:** compromise
5	71	**Choice C:** flawlessness; **Choice D:** wrong
6	55	**Choice B:** problematic; **Choice E:** unsound; **Choice H:** discredited
7	28	**Choice A:** imminent; **Choice F:** curtailed; **Choice G:** encouraging
8	38	**Choice A:** row; **Choice F:** festering dispute over
9	74	**Choice B:** The shape of the teeth indicates that sauropods were herbivorous.
10	54	**Choice A:** They are among the few fossils incorporating direct evidence of sauropod behavior.
11	66	**Choice C:** argue against a particular position regarding sleep's role in memory
12	60	**Choice A:** There are some memory-consolidation processes that have nothing to do with sleep.
13	73	**Choice E:** It concedes that the consolidation of declarative memory does not depend entirely on one factor.
14	60	**Choice B:** identifies a specific function that sleep plays in the memory-consolidation process
15	74	**Choice A:** eliminated AND **Choice C:** put to rest
16	41	**Choice D:** disagreement AND **Choice E:** divergence
17	27	**Choice A:** reined in AND **Choice E:** manacled
18	45	**Choice A:** bridling AND **Choice D:** inhibiting
19	56	**Choice A:** disaffection with AND **Choice F:** estrangement from
20	42	**Choice B:** If a planet's orbit is disturbed, the planet can be drawn by gravity toward the star it is orbiting.
21	35	**Choice A:** In the last five years, there has been no decline in the number of workplace injuries leading to immediate admission to a hospital emergency room.
22	51	**Choice B:** The possibility that the title page of a work may attribute works written by other authors to the author of that work AND **Choice C:** The possibility that the author's name printed on a title page is fictitious
23	83	**Choice A:** The title page was prepared for printing in a hurried manner. AND **Choice B:** Material on the title page was included without the author's knowledge or approval.
24	37	**Choice B:** nuances
25	78	**Choice C:** It can allow the reader to discern in a work certain meanings that the writer did not foresee.

Answer Key

Section 4. Verbal Reasoning

Question Number	P+	Correct Answer
1	72	**Choice D:** frustrating
2	50	**Choice C:** venal
3	80	**Choice D:** adequate to
4	59	**Choice E:** superfluous
5	48	**Choice A:** sham; **Choice D:** cloak
6	61	**Choice B:** habit; **Choice E:** ploddingly
7	41	**Choice B:** different in its effect; **Choice F:** entails; **Choice G:** permanent
8	40	**Choice C:** collision; **Choice E:** orthodox; **Choice G:** clerical
9	74	**Choice C:** presenting evidence to challenge an explanation and offering an alternative explanation
10	84	**Choice E:** A half century of drought and falling groundwater levels caused a certain population to abandon their settlements along a riverbank.
11	68	**Choice D:** local climatic variation in the environment of the southwestern United States
12	48	**Choice C:** Moving a village because groundwater levels have changed over the last generation
13	69	**Choice A:** It is similar in appearance to perennial ice. AND **Choice C:** It tastes saltier than perennial ice.
14	93	**Choice E:** small
15	56	**Choice B:** ecstatic AND **Choice E:** euphoric
16	75	**Choice A:** favor AND **Choice B:** aid
17	53	**Choice B:** astounding AND **Choice E:** stunning
18	59	**Choice D:** humdrum AND **Choice F:** dull
19	66	**Choice A:** Farmers focused primarily on growing wheat. AND **Choice C:** A relatively small portion of farmland was devoted to crops other than wheat.
20	44	**Choice D:** vigorous
21	55	**Choice D:** The appearance in 1999 of many new Internet sites that relay complaints directly to the Department of Transportation has made filing a complaint about airlines much easier for consumers than ever before.
22	46	**Choice C:** arguing in support of one side in a controversy
23	42	**Choice E:** It was originally constructed in an architectural style that was considered outmoded by the thirteenth or fourteenth century.
24	40	**Choice A:** They accurately reproduce the decoration on the choir's original lower flyers.
25	57	**Choice C:** Because of their speeded-up growth, lobsters now get large enough to be legal catch before they reach reproductive maturity.

Answer Key

Section 5. Quantitative Reasoning

Question Number	P+	Correct Answer
1	63	**Choice C:** The two quantities are equal.
2	80	**Choice A:** Quantity A is greater.
3	63	**Choice B:** Quantity B is greater.
4	45	**Choice D:** The relationship cannot be determined from the information given.
5	67	**Choice B:** Quantity B is greater.
6	73	**Choice B:** Quantity B is greater.
7	48	**Choice A:** Quantity A is greater.
8	59	**Choice C:** The two quantities are equal.
9	35	**Choice C:** The two quantities are equal.
10	60	**Choice A:** $\frac{1}{28}$
11	84	**17.5**
12	54	**Choice C:** 5
13	76	**Choice D:** -3
14	65	**Choice B:** $-7, -4, -2, 1, 13$ AND **Choice D:** 2, 3, 5, 15, 19, 22 AND **Choice E:** 4, 5, 6, 24
15	66	**Choice C:** 6 to 5
16	51	**Choice B:** $\frac{2,500}{n}$
17	51	**Choice D:** 18°
18	49	**Choice B:** 8
19	51	**Choice A:** 0.04
20	45	**Choice C:** 3 to 2
21	69	**Choice A:** -9 AND **Choice F:** 3
22	42	**Choice D:** $(x + 1) \otimes y$
23	41	**Choice B:** It contains one point.
24	40	**Choice E:** $xy < x^2$
25	62	**13**

Answer Key

Section 6. Quantitative Reasoning

Question Number	P+	Correct Answer
1	73	**Choice A:** Quantity A is greater.
2	69	**Choice D:** The relationship cannot be determined from the information given.
3	64	**Choice B:** Quantity B is greater.
4	41	**Choice C:** The two quantities are equal.
5	36	**Choice D:** The relationship cannot be determined from the information given.
6	42	**Choice D:** The relationship cannot be determined from the information given.
7	72	**Choice C:** The two quantities are equal.
8	28	**Choice C:** The two quantities are equal.
9	36	**Choice B:** Quantity B is greater.
10	69	**Choice D:** 1
11	69	**Choice B:** 4
12	78	**156**
13	66	**Choice A:** decreased by more than 5%
14	72	**30**
15	58	**Choice B:** $a^2 - b^2$ AND **Choice C:** ab
16	46	**Choice C:** 6
17	90	**Choice D:** 28
18	82	**Choice C:** 24
19	56	**Choice C:** 150%
20	66	$\frac{44}{68}$ (or any equivalent fraction)
21	58	**Choice B:** 2,100
22	45	**Choice A:** $\frac{x}{80}$
23	37	**Choice E:** $d(1 - 0.01t)$ dollars
24	53	**Choice B:** 3 AND **Choice D:** 6
25	32	**Choice B:** $\frac{1}{35}$

Score Conversion Table

Raw Score	Verbal Reasoning Scaled Score	Quantitative Reasoning Scaled Score
50	170	170
49	170	169
48	169	167
47	168	165
46	167	164
45	166	163
44	165	162
43	164	161
42	163	160
41	162	159
40	161	158
39	160	157
38	160	157
37	159	156
36	158	155
35	158	155
34	157	154
33	156	153
32	156	153
31	155	152
30	154	152
29	154	151
28	153	150
27	152	150
26	152	149
25	151	149
24	150	148
23	149	148
22	149	147
21	148	146
20	147	146
19	147	145
18	146	145
17	145	144

Raw Score	Verbal Reasoning Scaled Score	Quantitative Reasoning Scaled Score
16	144	143
15	143	143
14	142	142
13	141	141
12	140	140
11	139	139
10	138	138
9	137	137
8	135	136
7	134	135
6	132	134
5	130	132
4	130	130
3	130	130
2	130	130
1	130	130
0	130	130

Analytical Writing Sample Responses and Reader Commentaries

SECTION 1
Analytical Writing

ANALYZE AN ISSUE

Some people believe that corporations have a responsibility to promote the well-being of the societies and environments in which they operate. Others believe that the only responsibility of corporations, provided they operate within the law, is to make as much money as possible.

Write a response in which you discuss which view more closely aligns with your own position and explain your reasoning for the position you take. In developing and supporting your position, you should address both of the views presented.

*Score 6 Response**

It is not uncommon for some to argue that, in the world in which we live, corporations have a responsibility to society and to the environment in which they operate. Proponents of this view would argue that major environmental catastrophes (e.g., the oil spill in the Gulf) are key examples of the damage that can be wrought when corporations are allowed to operate unchecked. Yet within that very statement lies a contradiction that undermines this kind of thinking—it is necessary for outside forces to check the behavior of corporations, because we do not expect corporations to behave in such a manner. In fact, the expectation is simply that corporations will follow the law, and in the course of doing so, engage in every possible tactic to their advantage in the pursuit of more and greater profit. To expect otherwise from corporations is to fail to understand their puropose and their very structure.

The corporation arose as a model of business in which capital could be raised through the contributions of stockholders; investors purchases shares in a company, and their money is then used as the operating capital for the company. Shareholders buy stock not because they are hoping to better make the world a better place or because they have a desire to improve the quality of life but because they expect to see a return in their investment in this company. The company may itself have generally altruistic goals (perhaps it is a think tank that advises the government on how to improve relations with the Middle East, or perhaps it is a company built around finding alternative forms of energy), but the immediate expectation of the investor is that he himself will see dividends, or profits, from the investment he has made. This is even more true in the case of companies that are purely profit driven and which do not have

---

*NOTE: All responses are reproduced exactly as written, including errors, misspellings, etc., if any.

goals that are particularly directed toward social improvement—a description that applies to the vast majority of corporations.

Is it a bad thing to have a corporation negatively affect the environment (and by extentsion, its inhabitants)? To pump noxious fumes into the atmosphere as a by-product of its manufacturing processes? Of course, and this is why agencies such as the EPA were established and why governments—federal, state, and local—are expected to monitor such companies to ensure that such practices fall within the boundaries of legal expectations. Any and all corporations should be expected to temper their pursuit of profit with the necessity of following those safeguards that have been legislated as protections. But the assumption that corporations have an inherent obligation or responsibility to go above and beyond that to actively PROMOTE the environment and the well-being of society is absurd.

Engaging in practices to adhere to legal expectations to protect society and the environment is costly to corporations. If the very purpose of a corporation is to generate profits, and the obligation to adhere to safety expectations established by law cuts into those profits, then to expect corporations to embrace such practices beyond what is required is to presume that they willingly engage in an inherently self-destructive process: the unnecessary lowering of profits. This is antithetical to the very concept of the corporation. Treehuggers everywhere should be pleased that environmental protections exist, but to expect corporations to "make the world a better place" is to embrace altruism to the point that it becomes delusion.

This is not to say that we should reject efforts to hold corporations accountable. In fact, the opposite is true—we should be vigilant with the business world and maintain our expectations that corporations do not make their profits at the EXPENSE of the well-being of society. But that role must be fulfilled by a watchdog, not the corporation itself, and those expectations must be imposed UPON the corporations, not expected FROM them.

Reader Commentary

This response receives a 6 for developing an insightful position on the issue in accordance with the assigned task, skillfully weaving a position that takes into consideration both of the statements in the prompt. Beginning in the first paragraph, the writer rejects the idea that corporations themselves "have a responsibility to promote the well-being of the societies and environments in which they operate." In the second paragraph, the writer offers compelling reasons for this rejection by discussing the purpose and structure of corporations. The writer then considers the role of government in promoting corporations' social and environmental responsibility, developing the position fully. A cogent statement of the writer's position appears at the conclusion of the response: "we should be vigilant with the business world and maintain our expectations that corporations do not make their profits at the EXPENSE of the well-being of society. But that role must be fulfilled by a watchdog, not the corporation itself." The response as a whole is logically organized, with each paragraph serving as a stepping stone in the development of the writer's position. It also demonstrates the writer's ability to convey ideas fluently and precisely, using effective vocabulary and sentence variety. This sentence demonstrates the level of language facility seen throughout the response: "If the very purpose of a corporation is to generate profits, and the obligation to adhere to safety expectations established by law cuts into those profits, then to expect corporations to embrace such practices beyond what is required is to presume that they willingly engage in an inherently self-destructive process: the unnecessary lowering of profits." Here the writer has skillfully maintained control of complex syntax and diction while making a logically compelling point. The sentence demonstrates the outstanding nature of this response.

Score 5 Response

In order to survive, corporations must make money. Successful corporations try and make as much money as possible. Yet this incentive to make money does not mean that a corporation can be a detriment to the society in which it operates. Corporations have a duty and a responsability to ensure the well being of the society in which they are a part.

Contributing to the well being of a society is actually benefical to a corporation in many cases. One of these is making sure that workers are well taken care of. Absenteeism and neglect while on duty are a big problem for corporations, as is attracting the best workers, who hopefully will lower the risks caused by absenteeism and neglect. One way that corporations can attract these workers is by offering them generous benefits. If, for example, an employer includes with employment a good health care plan, they will be able to attract better workers than one that does not, and that will aid the corporation greatly. Health care plans provided by employers mean that these people have at their disposal health coverage, which means that they have the care they need if they get sick. This also might encourage preventive care, something that has been shown to reduce the cost and risk of developing other major ailments.

Another area where corporations providing support for themselves and society is in the creation of human capital. Globalization and increased education means that employers need a better educated workforce more than ever. One way that employers can contribute to this is by sponsoring worker training programs, or paying for their employees to return to school. This creates a more educated workforce for employers, as well as may increase the loyalty of employees to an employer. An employee who received an education sponsored by an employer may be thankful for receiving that education, and may work harder for that employer. This creates a benefit for employers and employees.

The main reason that corporations have a duty to contribute to the well being of society is that they are a part of the society. Even though they have an economic desire to make a profit, corporations also should think long term about actions they take which could hurt their company. A good example of this is BP, after the recent oil spill in the gulf. Their desire to make a profit meant that they did not keep up on all of their safety regulations and standards, and the result of the then faulty equipment caused a massive spill. This cost them huge amounts of money to clean up, as well as the fines they had to pay for causing this. The biggest loss for BP however is that there brand name will be associated in the US and abroad as the company that caused this giant oil spill. As the spill was happening, many people boycotted the company, resulting in lost potential revenue. They may realize that as they lose business to people upset by the spill, that making sure a spill didn't happen in the first place was cheaper.

Another reason corporations have to ensure the well-being of a society is that by makign a society better off, a company may have more consumers. This is especially true for corporations that sell goods for middle and upper class consumers. If a corporation tries to bring people up and increase the overall economic well being of society, they may find that more and more people have to ability to afford their goods.

This could generate huge new profits for this corporation, since their pool of potential consumers has gone up considerably. Concentrating on the long term here means that corporations can increase their pool of potential consumers.

By denying responsabilty to a society, a corporation is only looking at the possible short term profits, not the potential long term ones. While in the short term it may work for a corporation to ignore their societal responsability, it is advantageous in the long term for the entire corporation to make sure society is getting better. The potential for new markets, products, production processes and other beneficial factors that come from promoting well being is quite large. This is something that corportions should be ready and willing to take advantage of, and something that society should hold them accountable for.

Reader Commentary

This strong response receives a 5 for its thoughtful, well-developed analysis of the issue. In this case, the writer argues that corporations do indeed have a responsibility to promote the well-being of the societies and environments in which they operate, offering several reasons and well-chosen examples to explain why it is in the interests of corporations to fulfill these responsibilities. The writer clearly follows the task directions by addressing the two views provided by the prompt, both explicitly in the opening paragraph and more subtly throughout the response. While the writer clearly signals at the beginning his or her alignment with the first position ("Corporations have a duty and a responsability to ensure the well being of the society of which they are a part"), the paragraphs that follow in fact acknowledge the writer's opening statement ("In order to survive, corporations must make money"). In areas such as employee health care and education, as well as in relation to broader issues such as the environment and the general level of prosperity in society, the writer argues that corporations should strive to meet their social obligations because in the long term, it is economically advantageous to do so. The various reasons and examples offered are brought together to support a thoughtful position that implicitly suggests that the two views are not as mutually exclusive as they might first appear. The response also demonstrates considerable facility with language. There are some minor errors, but overall the writer's control of language is strong, demonstrating sentence variety and appropriate use of vocabulary. The response lacks the superior fluency and precision of a 6 but nevertheless conveys meaning clearly and well. Discernibly stronger than the adequate level of analysis in a 4, the response has thoughtful, nuanced analysis of the issue that earns it a score of 5.

Score 4 Response

While some people may believe that corporations have a responsibility to protect society, others believe that the only purpose of a corporation is to make money. I agree that making profits is important. In the grand scheme of things, though, all companies have a responsibility to watch out for their customers. Their customers are how they make their money. If they're not watching out for their customers, they obviously will see a drop in their profits.

Consider light bulbs. This is an invention that has all kinds of potential for serious accidents. It is basically just a glass globe with electricity running through it! If a bulb gets too hot, it could potentially start a fire. Similarly, if someone removed the glass from around the tungsten wire, you'd basically have an exposed electrical wire that could hurt anyone who touched it. Makers of light bulbs know and understand all these dangers. They want consumers to purchase their products, so the first and smartest way to make that happen is to ensure that the products are safe and thus more attractive to the customer base. If everyone who used light bulbs was afraid of getting zapped profits would obviously go down and light bulbs would not be a very profitable enterprise.

This same thinking applies to all major products. The automobile is one of the most dangerous tools man uses. Tens of thousands of automobile drivers die every year in accidents. Insuring that the vehicles contain designs and parts that promote customer safety is a main focus of car manufacturers. Certain parts of of cars were built with promoting driver's well-being in mind. For instance, air bags, anti-lock braking systems, online crash reporting. These features are considered standard now, and they were all developed to increase the safety of consumers. These features were not cheap to develop, but car manufacturers improved their profits anyway because they developed products with public safety in mind, which is what customers expect. If this symbiosis relationship wasn't true, then we would still have cars without airbags or even seatbelts. Worrying about the safety and actually improving it for customers is not just a basic responsibility of corporations, but it drives their profits, too.

In conclusion, its pretty clear that a corporation's desire to make more profits is in line with a corporation's responsibility to consumers. Increasing the focus on consumers, worrying about taking care of them and the environment, can only lead to bigger profits and success for corporations in the long run.

Reader Commentary

This adequate response follows the task directions and presents a clear position on the issue. It supports and develops its position competently, using relevant examples. In accordance with the assigned task, the response addresses both of the competing positions. Specifically, its position and the examples it develops argue that businesses can care about both profits and ethical responsibility through the ways they develop products. The development of examples and ideas, while adequate, is not as thoughtful or compelling as would be needed to earn higher scores. For instance, both of the examples the response uses are about product safety; the discussion of automobile design does not advance the position much more than the prior discussion of lightbulb production. Language control in the response is also competent. It demonstrates sufficient control of the conventions of standard written English, and its main points are made with acceptable clarity. The response features a few grammatical and mechanical errors (e.g., "Certain parts of of cars..." and "symbiosis relationship") and some awkward sentences. However, for the 4 range, GRE raters allow for minor errors in responses like this one that holistically demonstrate sufficient clarity and control. Overall, then, this response demonstrates adequate development and control of language, making the score of 4 appropriate.

Score 3 Response

Corporations can be viewed as both beneficial and bad. This statement addresses both views that many people have about corporations. Views come from personal experiences and is the reason why some people like corporations and why some people do not.

Half of this argument deals with people that like the idea of corporations. Some people believe that corporations help stmiulate societies and promote the well being of society. These people are ones that have never encountered a corupt corporation. Just like in any other aspects of life, people can get images of something as being good if they only brush the outside. It isn't until they are being faced with a problem within a particular corporation where they either work for them or have just dealt with them. Also, people that are benefited from corporations are obviously going to like the idea of an corporation.

The other side of this argument is that many people believe corporations are just money hungry. This can be seen in many corporations throughout America. Many small business owners will side with this argument. The problem lies that this is corporate America and the little businesses are being taking over by larger corporations. As Mark Twain once said, "The vast amount of money is only in a couple of hands". This statement still lies true today. In addition, corporations are large and with that being said they lead to more lines of coruption. In small buisnesses, the owners can oversee their store entirely. Can these corporation owners really oversee everything that is going on? Ask any employee at a corporate office if they believe their workplace is being ran how they think the corporation would want it. One is likely to find the answer that it is not.

Just like any other issue there are two sides to the story. The problem with this issue is that most will agree that corporations are only there to make money. They don't care about the people that are helping them make money. They only care at the end of the day how much money they made.

Reader Commentary

This response receives a score of 3 primarily because it is limited in focus. Rather than addressing the conflicting views of corporate responsibility given in the prompt, the response instead incorrectly casts the two positions as "people that like the idea of corporations" and people who "believe corporations are just money hungry." The writer proceeds to develop an explanation of these two positions, citing the various qualities that lead each group of people to their beliefs, but the response concludes by declaring that "there are two sides to the story" without adopting any position of its own. This highlights another limitation of the response, the fact that it does not completely address the specific task directions. Although the response does discuss the two opposing positions, it never discusses which view more closely aligns with the writer's own. The response does contain adequate organization, and the writing demonstrates a sufficient control of language. Sentences such as "Just like in any other aspects of life, people can get images of something as being good if they only brush the outside" are typical of the writing in this response and, despite the presence of some errors, demonstrate a sufficient control of the conventions of standard written English. However, even though the response demonstrates some qualities of a 4, its problems with focus and its failure to develop a clear position on the issue in accordance with the assigned task mean that it merits a score of 3.

Score 2 Response

> I think corporations have a responsibility to not only follow the law but also work with the societies and enviroments they are in. Our societies and environments in this age are affected by corporations' operations. An example of this is BP's accident in the Gulf of Mexico—they might have been following the law and regulations, but once an accident happens, our societies and environments are affected. Many fishermen and businesses around the area have been affected by the accident. Now BP faces so many liabilities and needs to pay money. As a result, they are loosing more than they made in the past.
>
> It is also important that corporations makes as much as money possible. If they do well, there might be more employment opportunities for people and more taxes for the city, states and federal which help our country's economy better.
>
> However, there are always choices that corporations can take and they can make money by promoting the well-being of the societies and environments. It might cost them more but it will also help to save thier expenses.

Reader Commentary

This seriously flawed response attempts to address the task directions by considering both of the views presented in the prompt. The first paragraph seems to embrace the first view given in the prompt when it asserts that "corporations have a responsibility to…work with the societies and environments they are in." The writer uses the example of the BP oil spill in the Gulf of Mexico to demonstrate that "our societies and environments in this age are affected by corporations' operations," but, apart from restating these same claims, the paragraph provides no real support for this position. Instead, the writer moves on to a discussion of the financial implications of the oil spill for BP. The second paragraph then makes an abrupt transition to a discussion of the prompt's second view and again seems to embrace this position when it claims that "it is also important that corporations makes as much as money possible." This position is supported with a single relevant but undeveloped reason. Although the writer attempts to reconcile the two positions in the last paragraph by arguing that "there are always choices that corporations can take and they can make money by promoting the well-being of the societies and environments," the response provides no support for this position beyond its unsupported and contradictory claim that "it might cost them more but it will also help to save their expenses." Overall, then, this response provides few examples in support of its claims. The response's poor focus and its very limited support, then, warrant a score of 2.

Score 1 Response

It is certainly true that some people believe that corporations have a responsibility to promote the well being of societies and environments. On the other hand, some other people argue that the only responsibility of corporations, provided they operate within the law, is to make as much money as possible. It is easy to see why it would be difficult for some people to decide between these two positions.

The responsibility of all citizens of a society, including corporate citizens, is ultimately to further the well being of the society as a whole. It takes little more than examining the recent United States financial crisis to see the ill effects suffered by society at large when corporations focus on maximizing profits.

Reader Commentary

This response earns a score of 1 because it provides little evidence of the ability to develop an organized response. The first paragraph begins with a nearly word-for-word restatement of the prompt, which increases the length of the response but does not demonstrate the ability to develop a position on the issue in relation to the specific task instructions. The final sentence in the first paragraph is analytically empty in that it could be applied to any prompt that asks writers to discuss two competing positions. The writer does nothing to relate that sentence to this specific prompt. The second paragraph, then, is all that the writer has provided in terms of original analysis of the issue. Although it does demonstrate understanding of the issue, it fits the "extremely brief" description from the scoring guide description of a 1. Because of the extreme brevity of its analysis, then, this response merits a score of 1.

SECTION 2
Analytical Writing

ANALYZE AN ARGUMENT

The following appeared in a memorandum from the owner of Movies Galore, a chain of video rental stores.

"In order to reverse the recent decline in our profits, we must reduce operating expenses at Movies Galore's ten video rental stores. Since we are famous for our special bargains, raising our rental prices is not a viable way to improve profits. Last month our store in downtown Marston significantly decreased its operating expenses by closing at 6:00 P.M. rather than 9:00 P.M. and by reducing its stock by eliminating all movies released more than five years ago. Therefore, in order to increase profits without jeopardizing our reputation for offering great movies at low prices, we recommend implementing similar changes in our other nine Movies Galore stores."

Write a response in which you discuss what questions would need to be addressed in order to decide whether implementing the recommendation is likely to have the predicted result and explain how the answers to those questions would help to evaluate the recommendation.

Score 6 Response

One question which needs to be addressed before implementing the recommendation is whether there are not other ways to improve profits besides cutting operating expenses. Without proof, the author decides, first, that there are only two viable options for increasing the profits of Movies Galore: raising rental prices, and cutting costs. He rules out the first course, and hence claims the second option must be chosen. But it seems there may be alternative methods of increasing profits, such as initiating advertising campaigns or closing unprofitable Movies Galore locations.

Even if it is granted that there are only two options for increasing profitability—cutting costs, and raising rental prices—one might wonder why raising rental prices is so unthinkable. The author implies that because Movies Galore is famous for special bargains, raising the rental prices would eliminate this competitive advantage and decrease profitability. However, in making this conclusion, he makes several assumptions without considering questions that need to be addressed. First, he assumes that there is no room to raise current prices and yet maintain lower prices than competitors. One would need to ask if prices could be increased slightly, while keeping them cheap. Even if there is no room for such a strategy, the author assumes that Movies Galore's reputation for bargain pricing would evaporate if they increased their prices slightly. Perhaps such a reputation would be widespread enough to persist despite a slight increase in prices. And thirdly, even if the reputation for bargains would be eliminated by an increase in prices, the author assumes that Movies Galore cannot change course and be successful in some other way. Perhaps it could instead become known as the store with the friendliest employees. Perhaps it already is, and the author is wrong to believe that a causal relationship between bargain prices and success exists, when the real cause of Movies Galore's good reputation is entirely independent of its prices. The author needs to answer these questions to convince us that profits are caused by bargains, and not by the other factors that may be involved.

Another question that needs to be raised is whether or not the downtown Marston store is truly analogous to the other nine Movies Galore stores. The author seems to assume that because the cost-cutting measures worked at the Marston location, it will work at the others, but this is far from clear. Perhaps the patrons of the other Movies Galore locations would resent such changes in the hours and stock of their local stores.

Perhaps the most important question that needs to be asked is whether the Marston location's changes truly increased profitability. The author writes that the Marston store decreased operating expenses by closing earlier and cutting its stock, but he makes no mention of increased profitability. It is quite possible that the Marston location's profits decreased as a result of their cost cutting, and this is a question that needs to be addressed. The author then jumps to the conclusion that taking similar measures would increase profitability at other locations, though such a connection has not even been established at the Marston store.

Even if the cost-cutting measures increased profitability at the Marston store last month (and a causal relationship, though presumably assumed, is still far from evident), there is no guarantee that such measures would continue to increase profitability over time. One would need to ask: Why not observe how the Marston location's action affect profitability over several months, before implementing such sweeping changes at every store? A single month is a very short time span, and the habits of customers may change slowly. As word gets around that the Marston store has cut their hours and their selection, they may in fact jeopardize their reputation for offering "great movies at low prices." After all, the name of the franchise is Movies Galore, and by drastically reducing the available selection, they may alienate their customer base. If, as mentioned above, Movies Galore is famous for more than its great bargains—if customers prefer Movies Galore because of its selections, as well—then such a move may drastically reduce profits over time. It seems extremely rash to implement such a new and relatively untried strategy at every Movies Galore location, before the effects can be fully observed and interpreted.

Reader Commentary

This outstanding response clearly addresses the specific task directions and presents a cogent, insightful analysis by discussing specific questions that need to be addressed in order to analyze the argument presented. It is worth noting that although the directions ask for questions, it is not necessary that these be phrased in question form. The response articulately discusses the information needed to evaluate whether the recommendation is likely to have the predicted result and demonstrates how this information would help to evaluate the recommendation. There are many examples of ways in which the writer addresses questions without putting them in question form (e.g., "he assumes that there is no room to raise current prices and yet maintain lower prices than competitors. One would need to ask..." or "it seems there may be alternative methods of increasing profits"). Throughout this response, the writer provides the cogent development typical of a 6 response. For example, the discussion of Movies Galore's reputation gets at a number of flaws in the argument's reasoning, making nuanced points (e.g., "Perhaps it could instead become known as the store with the friendliest employees. Perhaps it already is…") that create a compelling case for the writer's objections. Transitions are natural, and the paragraphs build on one another, succinctly and completely developing the writer's points. Because of its compelling and insightful development and fluent and precise language, this response fits all of the bullet points for a score of 6.

Score 5 Response

Management's prediction that declining profits could be reversed by reducing operating hours and reducing stock seems to be rash since there is little evidence that proper research has been conducted. It may be true that profits could be restored by cutting operating costs, but management needs to ask whether making these changes would have a negative impact on its best sources of revenue.

The management states that the downtown Marston store "significantly decreased its operating expenses by closing at 6:00pm rather than 9:00pm." It is reasonable to think that closing at 6:00pm rather than 9:00pm would decrease operating expenses, but the business is concerned with renting movies and these may be the busiest and most profitable hours of operation. Could it be that most people renting movies have normal working hours and have leisure time at night and to fill that time they turn to renting movies? If management researches its daily rental history, it may discover that its peak rental hours are between 6:00pm and 9:00pm. If this is the case, the store could lose significant income or even go out of business altogether. If management wants to reverse a decline in profits by cutting hours of operation and thereby reducing expenses, it would be advantageous to determine through research which block of time during the day is the least profitable and then cut those hours of operation. For instance, if it is found that profits are lowest during the morning hours or around noon, it would be better to close the store during those hours rather than during the hours that bring in the greatest profits.

The management then states that operating expenses will also be cut "by eliminating all movies released ore than five years ago." Again, more research is needed in order to determine if this would indeed help reverse the decline in profits that Movies Galore is experiencing. Is it possible that the success of a movie rental business is based on its ability to provide customers with a wide array of movie selections, both new and old? It could be dangerous for this business to eliminate its stock of older movies without first determining the percentages of income that come from each product. Management should research its history of movie rentals in order to determine if a significant percentage of its profits come from the rental of older movies. Even if little profit does come from older movies, it may still be unwise to eliminate the stock of older movies. If Movies Galore maintains a variety of movies, a person searching for a current movie may decide to rent an older movie as well. This may be especially relevent in the case of a new movie that is a sequel to an older movie or part of a trilogy. Reducing movie variety may also damage the reputation of the stores. The management states that Movie Galore already has a "reputation for offering great movies." If movie variety is suddenly reduced, the stores may gain a negative reputation.

Overall, the management makes a prediction that is untrustworthy and potentially damaging. More research should be conducted to see if indeed such changes to cut operation costs will be effective, and if not, what should be done instead. If the proper investigation is implemented by the management, Movies Galore stores may reverse the recent decline of profits.

Reader Commentary

This strong response presents a generally thoughtful and well-developed analysis of the argument, and it follows the specific task directions clearly. The response approaches the task by asking questions that seek to understand whether the management of Movies Galore truly understands where its greatest profits are generated. It first questions whether closing the stores between 6:00 and 9:00 pm would be optimal since that is when people with "normal working hours" might have the leisure to rent movies, and, then, it questions whether eliminating movies released more than five years ago would be prudent since it is possible that profits rely on carrying "a wide array of movie selections, both new and old." In both cases, the writer indicates the specific kinds of information that management would need to gather (e.g., "If management researches its daily rental history, it may discover that its peak rental hours are between 6:00pm and 9:00pm") in order to determine whether its prediction is valid. Likewise, in both cases, the writer also analyzes the ways that this specific information would impact the predicted result (e.g., "If this is the case, the store could lose significant income or even go out of business altogether"). In general, then, development of the points the writer makes is thorough, but it is not as compelling as that required for a 6. Also, the response, on the whole, demonstrates facility with written English; however, it lacks the fluency necessary to merit a score of 6. In general, writing skills, in spite of a few spelling errors and some repetitious sentence structuring (several sentences in both the second and third paragraphs depend upon an "if…then" construction) are strong, as evidenced by the following characteristic sentence: "It is reasonable to think that closing at 6:00pm rather than 9:00pm would decrease operating expenses, but the business is concerned with renting movies and these may be the busiest and most profitable hours of operation." In terms of writing skill and analysis, then, this response earns a score of 5.

Score 4 Response

The owner of Movies Galore is proposing a reduction in operating expenses in all of its chain stores. This reduction would consist of closing the stores 3 hours early and reducing its stock to include movies released only within the last 5 years. To determine if this proposition would be effective in increasing profits across the chain, several pieces of additional information would be needed.

First, it is necessary to ask if the Marston store is similar to the other Movies Galore stores. If this is not the case, the proposition might have quite the opposite of the intended effect. The performance of the other stores would be a critical piece to this proposition since what works for one store, may not work for another.

Second, what effect did the reduction in operating expenses had on store profits in Marston? Because the declines in profit are termed to be "recent" and that the reduction of operating expenses happened within the last month, this is unclear. It is possible that only a brief period of low profits, consistent with variablity in the market, spurred the reduction and this actually caused a greater decrease in profits. It is also possible that no improvements have been seen in profits since the reduction, rendering it ineffective. Data regarding profits from several months before and several months after the reduction in operating expenses would be necessary to determine if this reduction was at all helpful.

Finally, to what degree did each of the two changes made, closing early and getting rid of older movies, affect profits? To determine if such a change would be helpful, it is important to understand how each variable contributed to the end result, assuming that it was effective. Perhaps closing early resulted in such a decline in the operating costs as employees did not have to be paid, that the reduction in their stock was unnecessary. It could be the the stock reduction actually decreased profits but this was masked by the increased profits caused by closing early. A more in depth analysis of the variables involved is necessary.

To accept such an extreme change in the practices of these stores, the preceeding recommendations should be followed. Specifically, the necessity of the reduction in other stores shoudl be determined, data regarding the effectiveness of the reduction in operating expenses in the Marston store should be analyzed, and an analysis of the components of this reduction should be completed.

Reader Commentary

This adequate response presents a competent examination of the argument and conveys meaning with acceptable clarity. In accordance with the task directions, the response raises appropriate questions that could help to evaluate the recommendation and its predicted result. Unlike the thoughtful development of a 5-level response, however, this response develops its ideas (i.e., answers to the questions it raises) unevenly, sometimes underdeveloping key claims. For example, the relatively brief second paragraph supports the assertion that the downtown Marston store may not be comparable to the chain's other stores, but it does so with minimal reasoning. Other body paragraphs more satisfactorily develop questions about the timing of the recommendation and the profits that have actually been generated, while the conclusion merely recapitulates the assertions made earlier. A basic organizational structure, aided by the use of simple transitions between paragraphs and sufficient sentence variety within paragraphs, are other qualities of this response that underscore its adequacy. The language control is also adequate, demonstrating control, but not facility, with the conventions of standard written English. There are some minor grammatical errors and typos (e.g., there is a tense error in paragraph 3: "what effect did the reduction in operating expenses had on store profits in Marston?"; there is also vague diction in the same paragraph: "Because the declines in profit are termed to be 'recent' and that the reduction of operating expenses happened within the last month, this is unclear"), but the response manages to convey ideas with acceptable clarity overall. Because of its adequate analytical development and language control, this response earns a score of 4.

Score 3 Response

It is imperative that "Movies Galore" must find a way to reduce operating expenses without jepardizing its popularity with the customer. The option of reducing operating hours and reducing its stock of avalible movies is a good start, however these two ideas need some revising in order for them to be successful in turning the company's profits around.

The reduction of hours needs to be reversed. Instead of closing earlier they should open later. People go to the video store to rent movies more frequently in the evening hours than in the morning. In the morning is when most customers return movies. The adjustment in hours can be structured so that the store opens later in the morning, and costomers can simply return the movies in a drop box, allowing the store to remain open later in the evening for people who want to rent movies.

Reducing the stock by "eliminating all movies released more than five years ago" is a good way to reduce costs, but again it may hurt buisness. Unlike food moves don't go bad after a certain amount of time. In some cases it is quite the opposite, they become classics. It would be bad business to assume that people will not want to rent movies over five years old, and "Movies Galore" might actually lose customers if they do so. Instead of eliminating an entire group of movies of a certain age, spread the reduction of stock throughout the entire store, making it a more subtle reduction to the consumer, but an effective cost-saver to the store.

The basic ideas of cutting stock and reducing operating hours do indicate saving money, however only if it is done correctly with both the business and the consumer in mind. It is obvious that "Movies Galore" has the consumer in mind because of its refusal to jeopardize their reputation "for offering great movies at a low price." So they need to consider exactly how their proposals are going to impact the consumer and whether or not they will actually lose business by putting these policies in place.

If teh management at "Movies Galore" uses good business sense then there is no reason that their declining profits cannot be turned around, with little to no affect on the consumer.

Reader Commentary

While this response conveys ideas with acceptable clarity, despite an occasional error, it earns a score in the lower half because it mainly discusses tangential matters. The introductory paragraph, for example, suggests that instead of presenting an examination of the prompt's logic, the response will offer business advice to turn "the company's profits around." And that is what paragraphs 2 and 4 do: they avoid relevant analysis and instead engage in analyzing tangential matters and generally agreeing with the prompt. Paragraph 2, for example, implicitly agrees with the reduction in hours but suggests that a better business tactic would be to switch the early closing for a later closing and later opening. Paragraph 4 agrees with the overall recommendation and concludes that Movies Galore is generally going in the right business direction. What relevant analysis is present occurs in paragraph 3, which questions the wisdom of reducing the stock of older movies since this might hurt rather than help profitability. So, although the response exhibits competent control of the conventions of standard written English, it does not manage to exhibit adequate development of relevant analysis. The fact that its relevant analysis is greatly outweighed by tangential material and business advice indicates that the response is limited in addressing the specific task directions. Thus, it merits a score of 3.

Score 2 Response

In order to reverse the decrease or decline in the profits it is very necessary to take some steps which are benefical to both the customer and the seller. Thus to increase the profits, offering movies at low prices can be one of the ways. This will not only increase the purchasing ability of the customers but also bring about an increase in the sales and the profits made by the company. Raising the rental prices of the videos would not be a better option because this will not lead to an increase in the profits made by the company. If the customers will get videos in lower price in comparsion to the rent, they will prefer to purchase more videos then taking them on the rent.

The increase in the profits can also be brought about by giving various exciting offers at different occassions, for example- buy three and get one free video at the time of Christmas , New Year etc can attract more and more customers towards the stores and also bring about an increase in the profits earned by the stores.

Increase in the video sales can also be brought about by offering several discount schemes when the hit and great movies are being released.Thus, in order to increase the profits without jeopardizing the reputation of the stores , it is recommended to implement the similar changes as mentioned above in all the other nine Movies Galore stores.

Reader Commentary

This response clearly fits the second bulleted description of a 2 in the scoring guide. It does not follow the directions of the assigned task. Instead of discussing questions that need to be addressed in order to determine if the recommendation is likely to have the predicted result, the writer merely posits potential strategies to increase profits. The response also develops ideas poorly and contains serious errors in grammar, usage, and mechanics, such as in this sentence: "If the customers will get videos in lower price in comparsion to the rent, they will prefer to purchase more videos then taking them on the rent." However, it is the response's overall disregard of the specific task directions that earns it a score of 2.

Score 1 Response

Yes reducing the price of the movies would attract more coustmers.No one will be ready to purchase a movie for a high price rather than that they could see the movie in a theater.Watching a movie in the theater would be lesser than renting the movie.

It is stated that making special bargains and increasing the rental prices will not result in yeilding any profits.

They had to shut down their store at 6:00pm instead of 9:00pm

Reader Commentary

This response is fundamentally deficient. Although the response arguably offers some evidence that the writer understands the basic subject matter, it provides little evidence of understanding the argument made in the prompt. The "Yes" that begins the first sentence makes it seem as if the writer is responding to a claim made in the prompt, but the fact that the remainder of the sentence makes a claim that never appears in the prompt (i.e., "reducing the price of the movies would attract more coustmers") suggests, at best, a very limited understanding of the argument. Although the brief opening paragraph is somewhat relevant to the argument's assertion that "raising our rental prices is not a viable way to improve profits," it is not sufficient to demonstrate either that the writer understands the argument or that the writer is able to develop an organized response. The second paragraph consists almost entirely of verbatim or poorly paraphrased material from the prompt and, as such, provides no additional evidence either that the writer understands the argument or that the writer has the ability to develop an organized response. Thus, despite its relatively clear use of language, this response demonstrates fundamental deficiencies in analytical writing that warrant a score of 1.

Answers and Explanations

SECTION 3
Verbal Reasoning
25 Questions with Explanations

> **For questions 1 to 8, select <u>one</u> entry for each blank from the corresponding column of choices. Fill all blanks in the way that best completes the text.**

1. Although plant and animal species that become established in ecosystems where they did not originate are sometimes referred to by the alarming term "invasive species," many such species are _____ in their new environments.

(A) innocuous
(B) conspicuous
(C) robust
(D) menacing
(E) distinctive

Explanation

The sentence begins with "Although," indicating that the correct answer will contrast in tone with the "alarming term 'invasive species.'" The only answer choice that provides the necessary contrast is "innocuous." All the other choices are consistent with being alarming.

   Thus, the correct answer is **innocuous** (Choice A).

2. Far from being _____ the corporate world because of cutbacks, serious researchers are playing a growing role in innovation at many firms.

(A) lured to
(B) enchanted with
(C) banished from
(D) protected by
(E) immured in

Explanation

The words "Far from being" and the mention of "cutbacks" imply that the correct answer will create a contrast with the idea that "serious researchers are playing a growing role in innovation." Being "banished from" the corporate world and playing a growing role in it are strongly contrasted. Choices A, B, D, and E do not create any such contrast.

   Thus, the correct answer is **banished from** (Choice C).

3. The brief survey, published under the title *The Work of Nature: How the Diversity of Life Sustains Us*, is surprisingly (i)_____. Indeed it makes several longer treatments of the effects of lost biodiversity seem (ii)_____.

Blank (i)	Blank (ii)
(A) distorted	(D) redundant
(B) objective	(E) pithy
(C) comprehensive	(F) premature

Explanation

In this question, it is hard to select an answer for either blank in isolation. The "brief survey," like any survey, could in fact be surprisingly "distorted," "objective," or "comprehensive." The contrast in the following sentence with "longer treatments" suggests that the brevity of the survey is important. Of the three choices, only "comprehensive" is particularly unexpected of a *brief* survey.

Provisionally accepting "comprehensive" makes it easier to analyze the second blank. If the short survey is surprisingly comprehensive, then longer treatments may not convey any useful additional information, making them "redundant." Longer works are unlikely to seem "pithy" in comparison to shorter ones, and "premature" makes little sense in this context.

Reading the sentence again with "comprehensive" and "redundant" filling the blanks confirms that these two choices result in a coherent whole.

Thus, the correct answer is **comprehensive** (Choice C) and **redundant** (Choice D).

4. The government has no choice but to (i)_____ the incessant demands for land reform, and yet any governmental action that initiated land reform without requisite attention to agrarian reform would (ii)_____ the overall goal of economic modernization.

Blank (i)	Blank (ii)
(A) anticipate	(D) delineate
(B) heed	(E) condone
(C) silence	(F) compromise

Explanation

The sentence informs us that the government has an "overall goal," and the use of "and yet" indicates that initiating land reform without attending to agrarian reform would have some negative consequence for that goal. Thus, the only answer choice that fits the second blank is "compromise." The use of "and yet" also implies that the government's response to the demands for land reform must be in line with initiating such reform, so Choice C, "silence," is incorrect. The description of the demands as "incessant" implies that the demands already exist, so "anticipate" is incorrect. Only "heed" describes an appropriate response.

Thus, the correct answer is **heed** (Choice B) and **compromise** (Choice F).

5. Certain music lovers yearn for (i)_____, but when it is achieved, there is something missing; perhaps they feel uncomfortable in a world where nothing discernible is (ii)_____.

Blank (i)	Blank (ii)
(A) novelty	(D) wrong
(B) beauty	(E) visionary
(C) flawlessness	(F) changed

Explanation

The structure of the sentence alerts us that it will describe a kind of contradiction or paradox: music lovers want something, but when they get what they want, they discover some cause for dissatisfaction. Among the answer choices, the only two words that produce such a paradox are "flawlessness" and "wrong"—the music lovers long for flawlessness but are unsatisfied with a world in which nothing is wrong.

Thus, the correct answer is **flawlessness** (Choice C) and **wrong** (Choice D).

6. Putting a cash value on the ecological services provided by nature—such as the water filtration "service" provided by a forested watershed—has, historically, been a (i)_____ process. Early attempts at such valuation resulted in impressive but (ii)_____ figures that were seized on by environmental advocates, and then, when these figures were later (iii)_____, they were used by opponents to tar the whole idea.

Blank (i)	Blank (ii)	Blank (iii)
(A) dispassionate	(D) redundant	(G) ignored
(B) problematic	(E) unsound	(H) discredited
(C) straightforward	(F) understated	(I) confirmed

Explanation

The correct response for the first blank cannot be determined without considering the second sentence. The correct choice for the second blank, however, can be determined more readily. Neither Choice D, "redundant," nor Choice F, "understated," makes sense when coupled with the preceding "impressive but." Since the figures were "used by opponents to tar the whole idea," Choice E, "unsound," is the word that makes the most sense in this context.

Once "unsound" is selected for the second blank, it follows that "confirmed" cannot be correct for the third blank. And if the figures were "used by opponents," then they cannot have been "ignored." Since the figures were unsound, it is natural that they would later be "discredited."

Now that the figures have been characterized as unsound and discredited, it is possible to identify the correct response for the first blank. From the second sentence it is clear that the process of putting a cash value on the ecological services provided by nature is neither "dispassionate" nor "straightforward." It is instead "problematic."

Thus, the correct answer is **problematic** (Choice B); **unsound** (Choice E); and **discredited** (Choice H).

7. Only with the discovery of an ozone hole over Antarctica in 1985 did chemical companies finally relinquish their opposition to a ban on chlorofluorocarbons (CFCs), which destroy ozone. The discovery suggested that strong political action to halt production of CFCs might be (i)_____, and fortunately, the chemical industry no longer felt compelled to oppose such action: although companies had recently (ii)_____ their research into CFC substitutes, studies they had initiated years earlier had produced (iii)_____ results.

Blank (i)	Blank (ii)	Blank (iii)
(A) imminent	(D) corroborated	(G) encouraging
(B) imprudent	(E) publicized	(H) inconclusive
(C) premature	(F) curtailed	(I) unsurprising

Explanation

According to the first sentence, chemical companies opposed a ban on CFCs and then changed their stance in 1985 with the discovery of an ozone hole.

In the first blank, only "imminent" is compatible with the discovery of an ozone hole linked to CFCs: such a discovery would suggest that "strong political action" is required, not that it is "imprudent" or "premature."

What follows the colon in the second sentence explains why the chemical industry "no longer felt compelled to oppose" a ban on CFCs. In order for the industry to drop its opposition, the outcome of the studies into CFC substitutes must have been positive. Among the choices for the third blank, only "encouraging" has a sufficiently positive connotation.

Finally, the word "although" after the colon indicates that the second blank should contrast with the third blank in some way. Since the completed third blank now indicates that studies of CFC substitutes have been successful, "curtailed" makes the most sense in the second blank. "Corroborated" and "publicized" do not contrast appropriately with the success of the studies.

Thus, the correct answer is **imminent** (Choice A); **curtailed** (Choice F); and **encouraging** (Choice G).

8. The incipient (i)_____ regarding taxes could affect trade between the two countries much more than the (ii)_____ banana imports, which has been going on for years. Unfortunately, the trade regulators seem to be ignoring both disagreements.

Blank (i)	Blank (ii)
(A) row	(D) profitable dealing in
(B) accord	(E) predicament regarding
(C) investigation	(F) festering dispute over

Explanation

The words "both disagreements" at the end of the second sentence indicate that both blanks should be filled with words or phrases that are synonyms for "disagreement." "Row" and "festering dispute over" are the only choices that describe kinds of disagreement. (Note that the word "row" has many meanings, one of which is "a quarrel.")

Thus, the correct answer is **row** (Choice A) and **festering dispute over** (Choice F).

For each of questions 9 to 14, select <u>one</u> answer choice unless otherwise instructed.

Questions 9 and 10 are based on the following reading passage.

Fossil bones of the huge herbivorous dinosaurs known as sauropods were first discovered and studied between 1840 and 1880, providing evidence for the gargantuan dimensions of the adults. The shape of sauropod teeth suggested what they ate. But
line
5 aside from trackways, or series of fossilized footprints—which established that sauropods at least occasionally lived in herds—fossils incorporating direct evidence of other behavior, such as reproductive behavior, have been almost nonexistent. Because no modern land animals even approach sauropod size, scientists have also lacked a living analogue to use as a guide to possible sauropod behavior. Until the recent discovery of fossilized sauropod nesting grounds, scientists were thus uncertain whether sauropods
10 laid eggs or gave birth to live young.

Description

The passage outlines what was learned about sauropods after the discovery of their fossilized bones in the nineteenth century, including what has been inferred about their behavior from the fossil record.

For the following question, consider each of the choices separately and select all that apply.

9. Which of the following can be inferred from the passage regarding the evidence provided by sauropod teeth?
    - A The teeth allow inferences to be made about sauropod social behavior.
    - B The shape of the teeth indicates that sauropods were herbivorous.
    - C The teeth have no resemblance to those of any modern land animal.

Explanation

Choice B is the only correct answer.

Choice A is incorrect: the passage mentions that fossilized footprints permit the inference that sauropods exhibited herd behavior, but there is no indication that this or any other social behavior can be inferred from sauropod teeth.

Choice B is correct: the passage states that sauropods were herbivorous (feeding on plants) and that "the shape of sauropod teeth suggested what they ate."

Choice C is incorrect: the passage says that there are no modern land animals similar in size to sauropods, not that there are no such animals with similar teeth.

For the following question, consider each of the choices separately and select all that apply.

10. Which of the following can be inferred from the passage regarding the recently discovered fossilized sauropod nesting grounds?

    A   They are among the few fossils incorporating direct evidence of sauropod behavior.

    B   They confirm the evidence provided by trackways about sauropod behavior.

    C   They have forced a reevaluation of theories regarding the nature of sauropod herd behavior.

Explanation

Choice A is the only correct answer.

Choice A is correct: the last sentence of the passage implies that the discovery of fossilized sauropod nesting grounds resolved the question of whether sauropods laid eggs or gave birth to live young and therefore provided evidence of sauropods' reproductive behavior. Until this discovery, except for the trackways that showed herd behavior, "fossils incorporating direct evidence" of sauropod behavior were "almost nonexistent" (lines 5–6).

Choice B is incorrect: according to the passage, trackways provided evidence of herd behavior, whereas fossilized nesting grounds provided evidence concerning reproductive behavior. There is no information in the passage to suggest that the nesting grounds confirmed evidence provided by the trackways, or even that the trackway evidence needed confirming.

Choice C is incorrect: the passage presents fossilized nesting grounds as providing evidence about reproductive behavior, not herd behavior. Nothing in the passage suggests that there are theories of the nature of sauropod herd behavior that have been reevaluated.

Some researchers contend that sleep plays no role in the consolidation of declarative memory (i.e., memory involving factual information). These researchers note that people with impairments in rapid eye movement (REM) sleep continue to lead normal lives, and they argue that if sleep were crucial for memory, then these individuals would have apparent memory deficits. Yet the same researchers acknowledge that the cognitive capacities of these individuals have never been systematically examined, nor have they been the subject of studies of tasks on which performance reportedly depends on sleep. Even if such studies were done, they could only clarify our understanding of the role of REM sleep, not sleep in general.

These researchers also claim that improvements of memory overnight can be explained by the mere passage of time, rather than attributed to sleep. But recent studies of memory performance after sleep—including one demonstrating that sleep stabilizes declarative memories from future interference caused by mental activity during wakefulness—make this claim unsustainable. Certainly there are memory consolidation processes that occur across periods of wakefulness, some of which neither depend on nor are enhanced by sleep. But when sleep is compared with wakefulness, and performance is better after sleep, then some benefit of sleep for memory must be acknowledged.

Description

The passage presents and then rebuts two arguments made by researchers who question the contribution of sleep to the consolidation of declarative memory (memory involving factual information). The first argument is that people with impairments to REM sleep continue to lead normal lives. In response, the passage says that these researchers themselves acknowledge the absence of systematic study of such individuals' cognitive abilities, study that would be necessary in order to fully support the researchers' claim. The passage also points out that the researchers' claim applies only to REM sleep rather than to sleep in general. The second claim is that improvements of memory that occur overnight might be explained merely by the passage of time. In response, the passage cites research findings that demonstrate the role of sleep in stabilizing declarative memory.

11. The primary purpose of the passage is to

    (A) present the evidence that supports a particular claim regarding REM sleep and memory

    (B) describe how various factors contribute to the effect of sleep on memory

    (C) argue against a particular position regarding sleep's role in memory

    (D) summarize the most prevalent theory regarding sleep and memory

    (E) defend the importance of the consolidation of declarative memory

Explanation

As described above, the purpose of the passage as a whole is to argue against the view held by some researchers that sleep plays no role in the consolidation of declarative memory. Therefore, **Choice C** is correct. Choice A is incorrect: the passage does mention REM sleep twice in the first paragraph, but its primary purpose is not to examine REM sleep in particular, and it does not present evidence related to REM sleep. Choice B is incorrect: the passage is concerned with the effect of sleep on memory, but not with any factors that contribute to that effect. Choice D is incorrect: the passage does not summarize a theory. Instead, it cites a claim and then assesses and rejects that claim. Choice E is incorrect: although the passage is about the consolidation of declarative memory, it does nothing to defend its importance.

12. According to the author of the passage, which of the following generalizations about memory and sleep is true?

(A) There are some memory-consolidation processes that have nothing to do with sleep.

(B) Sleep is more important to the consolidation of declarative memory than to the consolidation of other types of memory.

(C) REM sleep is more important to memory consolidation than is non-REM sleep.

(D) There are significant variations in the amount of sleep that people require for the successful consolidation of memory.

(E) It is likely that memory is more thoroughly consolidated during wakefulness than during sleep.

Explanation

The passage states that "there are memory-consolidation processes that occur across periods of wakefulness." Accordingly, **Choice A** is correct. Choices B, C, and D are incorrect: the passage does not discuss types of memory other than consolidative memory, the relative importance to consolidative memory of REM and non-REM sleep, or differences among individuals in the amount of sleep they require. Choice E is also incorrect: the passage suggests that the truth is the opposite of what this answer choice states. The last sentence of the passage indicates that performance on memory tasks has been found to be better after sleep than after periods of wakefulness.

13. Which of the following best describes the function of the sentence in lines 14–16 ("Certainly...sleep")?

(A) It provides the reasoning behind a claim about the role of sleep in memory consolidation.

(B) It explains why a previous claim about sleep and memory is unsustainable.

(C) It demonstrates why wakefulness is central to the process of declarative memory consolidation.

(D) It emphasizes the limited role sleep plays in the process of declarative memory consolidation.

(E) It concedes that the consolidation of declarative memory does not depend entirely on one factor.

Explanation

The cited sentence begins with the word "Certainly," a clue that the sentence will concede that the researchers are not entirely wrong: in this instance, they are not wrong about memory consolidation occurring during periods of wakefulness. Thus, **Choice E** is correct. Choice A is incorrect: the sentence deals with memory consolidation during wakefulness, not with the role of sleep in memory consolidation. Choice B is incorrect: the sentence does follow an assertion that the researchers' claim is unsustainable, but it does not explain why it is unsustainable. Choice C is incorrect: the sentence does not demonstrate anything. It acknowledges that memory consolidation occurs during wakeful periods but does not identify wakefulness as central to the process. Choice D is incorrect: while the sentence does acknowledge that some memory-consolidation processes are not dependent on sleep, it does not go so far as to claim that sleep plays a limited role in memory consolidation generally.

14. The importance of the study mentioned in lines 12–14 is that it
   (A) reveals the mechanism by which declarative memory is stabilized during sleep
   (B) identifies a specific function that sleep plays in the memory-consolidation process
   (C) demonstrates that some kinds of mental activity can interfere with memory consolidation
   (D) suggests that sleep and wakefulness are both important to memory consolidation
   (E) explains how the passage of time contributes to memory consolidation

Explanation

The question asks what "the importance of the study mentioned in lines 12–14" is. The study is described as having shown that sleep stabilizes declarative memory from future interference caused by mental activity during wakefulness. This protection of memory from interference is the "specific function" played by sleep mentioned in Choice B. Therefore, **Choice B** is correct. Choice A is incorrect: there is no description of any mechanism, or specific process, by which declarative memory is stabilized. Although Choices C, D, and E each involve issues connected with the study, those connections are all tangential.

> For questions 15 to 19, select the **two** answer choices that, when used to complete the sentence, fit the meaning of the sentence as a whole **and** produce completed sentences that are alike in meaning.

15. In American Indian art, the supposed distinction between modern and traditional was fabricated by critics, and when artists have control over interpretation of their own work, the distinction appears, happily, to have been _____.
   A eliminated
   B reinforced
   C put to rest
   D intensified
   E recognized
   F established

Explanation

By characterizing the distinction as "supposed" and "fabricated," the sentence indicates that the distinction has no basis in reality. Accordingly, when the sentence reports a happy outcome, this must mean that the distinction has been abandoned or rejected. Only "eliminated" and "put to rest" convey that sense; all the other answer choices suggest that the distinction is maintained, or even strengthened.

   Thus, the correct answer is **eliminated** (Choice A) and **put to rest** (Choice C).

16. Notwithstanding their _____ regarding other issues, township residents have consistently passed the board of education's annual budget.

   A accord
   B indecision
   C consensus
   D disagreement
   E divergence
   F enthusiasm

Explanation

By using the word "Notwithstanding," the sentence sets up a contrast between the township residents' behavior regarding the "other issues" and their behavior regarding the board's annual budget, which they have "consistently passed." "Accord" and "consensus" are similar in meaning but do not provide the required contrast. Only "disagreement" and "divergence" provide the necessary contrast and lead to two sentences nearly alike in meaning. "Indecision" fits the context, but there is no other word among the possible choices that matches it closely.

   Thus, the correct answer is **disagreement** (Choice D) and **divergence** (Choice E).

17. Some of the company's supporters charged that the negative report had been motivated by a broader political assault on the company that was designed to help market rivals who would like to see the company _____.

   A reined in
   B bolstered
   C indemnified
   D propped up
   E manacled
   F lionized

Explanation

The "market rivals" would clearly like to see the company experience some negative outcome. Only "reined in" and "manacled" describe such an outcome; the other choices all describe positive results for the company.

   Thus, the correct answer is **reined in** (Choice A) and **manacled** (Choice E).

18. Skeptics contend that any scheme for charging visitors to Web sites that rewards the vendor adequately would require steep prices, _____ the kind of frequent, casual use of Web sites that surfers now take for granted.

    A bridling
    B exciting
    C forbidding
    D inhibiting
    E provoking
    F reversing

Explanation

The sentence concerns skeptics' reaction to a plan to generate revenue by charging visitors to Web sites. To justify the skeptics' reaction, the "steep prices" must be associated with a decrease in visitor volume. Only "bridling" and "inhibiting" are consistent with this logic and result in sentences nearly alike in meaning. "Forbidding" is too strong: steep prices might dissuade a casual visitor, but they would not forbid one. Although "exciting" and "provoking" can be similar in meaning, they do not fit the logic of the sentence.

Thus, the correct answer is **bridling** (Choice A) and **inhibiting** (Choice D).

19. It seems obvious that Miles Davis' _____ the Juilliard School, which resulted in his decision to drop out, was based on the school's training of musicians for a kind of music that he did not want to play.

    A disaffection with
    B dislocation of
    C disentanglement from
    D subversion of
    E displacement of
    F estrangement from

Explanation

The sentence asserts a logical relationship between Davis' attitude toward the school (as indicated in the blank) and his "decision to drop out." Only "disaffection with" and "estrangement from" are consistent with a decision to drop out and result in sentences nearly alike in meaning.

Thus, the correct answer is **disaffection with** (Choice A) and **estrangement from** (Choice F).

For each of questions 20 to 25, select <u>one</u> answer choice unless otherwise instructed.

Astronomers found a large body orbiting close to the star Upsilon Andromedae. The standard theory of planet formation holds that no planet that large could be formed so close to a star, leading to the suggestion that the body is a companion star. A subsequent discovery puts that suggestion in doubt: two other large bodies were found orbiting close to Upsilon Andromedae, and the standard theory of companion stars allows for at most one companion star.

20. Which of the following, if true, most helps to resolve the status of the orbiting body without casting doubt on the two standard theories mentioned?

Ⓐ The smaller a planet orbiting a star is, and the farther away it is from the star, the less likely it is to be discovered.

Ⓑ If a planet's orbit is disturbed, the planet can be drawn by gravity toward the star it is orbiting.

Ⓒ The largest of the bodies orbiting Upsilon Andromedae is the farthest away from the star, and the smallest is the nearest.

Ⓓ It is likely that there are many stars, in addition to Upsilon Andromedae and the Sun, that are orbited by more than one smaller body.

Ⓔ In most cases of companion stars, the smaller companion is much fainter than the larger star.

Explanation

The passage outlines a conflict between two standard theories—one of planet formation, the other of companion stars—and observations of one large body, and later two others, orbiting close to a star. The question asks what would resolve this conflict without casting doubt on either one of the theories.

Choice B is correct: if, as it asserts, it is possible for a planet to be formed relatively far from a star and later move closer to it, then the observed large bodies found close to Upsilon Andromedae can be planets without casting doubt on the standard theory of planet formation. This explanation also leaves the standard theory of companion stars intact.

Choice A is incorrect because it describes difficulties with discovering a small planet far from a star, not anything pertaining to a large body near a star. Choice C is incorrect as well, since whatever the relative size and position of the three bodies may be, all three appear to be too close according to the standard theories. Choice D is incorrect because the pervasiveness of stars with multiple orbiting bodies has nothing to do with the status of the large bodies discussed in the passage. Choice E is similarly irrelevant and thus incorrect: information about the brightness of a star relative to its companion star does not help clarify the status of the large bodies discussed in the passage.

In Gilavia, the number of reported workplace injuries has declined 16 percent in the last five years. However, perhaps part of the decline results from injuries going unreported: many employers have introduced safety-incentive programs, such as prize drawings for which only employees who have a perfect work-safety record are eligible. Since a workplace injury would disqualify an employee from such programs, some employees might be concealing injury, when it is feasible to do so.

21. Which of the following, if true in Gilavia, most strongly supports the proposed explanation?

    (A) In the last five years, there has been no decline in the number of workplace injuries leading to immediate admission to a hospital emergency room.

    (B) Employers generally have to pay financial compensation to employees who suffer work-related injuries.

    (C) Many injuries that happen on the job are injuries that would be impossible to conceal and yet would not be severe enough to require any change to either the employee's work schedule or the employee's job responsibilities.

    (D) A continuing shift in employment patterns has led to a decline in the percentage of the workforce that is employed in the dangerous occupations in which workplace injuries are likely.

    (E) Employers who have instituted safety-incentive programs do not in general have a lower proportion of reported workplace injuries among their employees than do employers without such programs.

Explanation

The question asks what would support the claim that the decline in reported workplace injuries in Gilavia may be the result of incentives for workers to not report those injuries that they can conceal. If the number of injuries that cannot be concealed—such as injuries requiring immediate emergency care—has not declined in the same period, that could help bolster the claim that the decline in overall reported injuries may be a result of concealable injuries going unreported rather than an actual decline in workplace injuries in general, so **Choice A** is correct.

If employers have to provide financial compensation to employees injured on the job, employees would have an incentive to report injuries. More reported injuries would not support the author's argument, making Choice B incorrect. Choice C is incorrect because the fact that some injuries that cannot be concealed do not result in lost time or changed responsibilities has nothing to do with whether concealable injuries are going unreported. While a decline in dangerous occupations could well result in a decrease in workplace injuries, this fact would challenge the author's argument, not support it, so Choice D is incorrect. Similarly, if employers with safety-incentive programs do not see any drop in reported injuries compared to employers without such programs, the author's argument would be weakened, not supported, making Choice E incorrect.

The attribution of early-nineteenth-century English fiction is notoriously problematic. Fewer than half of new novels published in Britain between 1800 and 1829 had the author's true name printed on the title page. Most of these titles have subsequently been attributed, either through the author's own acknowledgment of a previously *line* anonymous or pseudonymous work or through bibliographical research. One impor- 5 tant tool available to researchers is the list of earlier works "by the author" often found on title pages. But such lists are as likely to create new confusion as they are to solve old problems. Title pages were generally prepared last in the publication process, often without full authorial assent, and in the last-minute rush to press, mistakes were fre- 10 quently made.

Description

The passage discusses the reasons why identifying the authors of early-nineteenth-century British fiction poses significant challenges. The passage explains that few authors during this period used their real names and goes on to describe how title pages can facilitate—but also hamper—efforts to attribute these works.

For the following question, consider each of the choices separately and select all that apply.

22. The passage suggests that which of the following factors contributes to the "notoriously problematic" (line 1) nature of authorial attribution in early-nineteenth-century English fiction?

    A The unwillingness of any writers to acknowledge their authorship of works that were originally published anonymously or pseudonymously

    B The possibility that the title page of a work may attribute works written by other authors to the author of that work

    C The possibility that the author's name printed on a title page is fictitious

Explanation

Choices B and C are correct.

Choice A is incorrect: the passage mentions that the attribution of early-nineteenth-century fiction was sometimes achieved when the author came forward to acknowledge a previously anonymous work (lines 4–5), so Choice A can be eliminated.

Choice B is correct: in lines 5–7, the passage mentions that "one important tool available to researchers is the list of earlier works 'by the author' often found on title pages," but goes on to say that these title pages were prepared hastily and "frequently" contained mistakes (lines 8–10). Since the mistake most likely to "create new confusion" would be the inclusion of works not written by the author, Choice B may be inferred.

Choice C is correct: in lines 2–3, the passage states, "Fewer than half of the new novels published in Britain...had the author's true name printed on the title page." Line 5 suggests that pseudonyms—fictitious names—were commonly used. Hence, Choice C may be inferred.

For the following question, consider each of the choices separately and select all that apply.

23. The passage suggests that which of the following is frequently true of the title pages of early-nineteenth-century English novels?

    A The title page was prepared for printing in a hurried manner.

    B Material on the title page was included without the author's knowledge or approval.

    C Information on the title page was deliberately falsified to make the novel more marketable.

Explanation

Choices A and B are correct.

    Choice A is correct: the passage mentions that title pages were prepared last and that mistakes often occurred "in the last-minute rush to press" (line 9). This indicates that title pages were often prepared for printing in a hurried manner; hence, Choice A can be inferred.

    Choice B is correct: the passage includes the detail that title pages were often prepared for printing "without full authorial assent" (line 9); hence, Choice B can be inferred.

    Choice C is incorrect: nowhere does the passage speculate about commercial motives for falsifying information on title pages. Choice C, therefore, cannot be inferred.

Questions 24 and 25 are based on the following reading passage.

The more definitions a given noun has, the more valuable is each one. Multiple definitions, each subtly different from all the others, convey multiple shades of meaning. They expand the uses of the word; language is enriched, thought is widened, and interpretations increase or dilate to fill the potentialities of association. The very impossibility of absoluteness in the definition of certain nouns adds to the levels of connotation they may reach. The inner life of a writer often says more than most readers can know; the mind of a reader can discover truths that go beyond the intent or perhaps even the comprehension of the writer. And all of it finds expression because a word can mean many things.

line
5

Description

The passage claims that the capacity of words to have multiple meanings can greatly enhance the resources of a language. The passage describes how this increases possibilities for interpretation and the expression of ideas, thus enriching the relationship between readers and writers.

24. In the context in which it appears, "shades" (line 2) most nearly means

    Ⓐ reminders

    Ⓑ nuances

    Ⓒ obscurities

    Ⓓ coverings

    Ⓔ degrees

Explanation

In the context in which it appears, "shades" is used to refer to the subtle distinctions in meaning that are made possible by "multiple definitions, each subtly different from all the others." Since the sentence deals with multiple definitions conveying meaning, Choice C ("obscurities") and the more literal Choice D ("coverings") may be eliminated. In deciding between Choice B and Choice E, one should bear in mind that the sentence focuses on subtle differences in meaning as opposed to different degrees of emphasis for the same meaning. **Choice B**, "nuances," best captures this sense of slight variations in meaning and is therefore the correct answer.

25. The passage suggests that a writer's use of nouns that have multiple definitions can have which of the following effects on the relationship between writer and reader?

    (A) It can encourage the reader to consider how the writer's life might have influenced the work.
    (B) It can cause the reader to become frustrated with the writer's failure to distinguish between subtle shades of meaning.
    (C) It can allow the reader to discern in a work certain meanings that the writer did not foresee.
    (D) It allows the writer to provide the reader with clues beyond the word itself in order to avoid ambiguity.
    (E) It allows the writer to present unfamiliar ideas to the reader more efficiently.

Explanation

Lines 7–8 clearly indicate that multiple meanings of words enable readers to "discover truths that go beyond the intent or perhaps even the comprehension of the writer"; hence, **Choice C** is the correct answer. Choices A, B, D, and E all deal with topics that are not mentioned in the passage: the writer's life, the reader's frustration, the avoidance of ambiguity, and the question of how efficiently multiple definitions can aid in the presentation of unfamiliar ideas.

SECTION 4
Verbal Reasoning
25 Questions with Explanations

> **For questions 1 to 8, select <u>one</u> entry for each blank from the corresponding column of choices. Fill all blanks in the way that best completes the text.**

1. The unexplained digressions into the finer points of quantum electrodynamics are so _____ that even readers with a physics degree would be wise to keep a textbook handy to make sense of them.

Ⓐ	uninteresting
Ⓑ	controversial
Ⓒ	unsophisticated
Ⓓ	frustrating
Ⓔ	humorless

Explanation

An initial reading of this sentence might suggest that the blank should be filled with a word like "complex" that indicates how hard it is to "make sense of" the digressions. However, there is no such word among the answer choices. Focusing on the second half of the sentence suggests a different interpretation. According to the sentence, it would be "wise to" make sense of the digressions, and a textbook would help the reader to do so. If the digressions are "uninteresting," "unsophisticated," or "humorless," the sentence provides no reason to think it would be wise to make sense of them, and if they are "controversial," it provides no reason to think that a textbook would help. Only if the digressions are "frustrating" does the sentence make a coherent whole.

Thus, the correct answer is **frustrating** (Choice D).

2. The belief that politicians might become _____ after their election to office led to the appointment of ethics officers at various levels of government.

Ⓐ	scrupulous
Ⓑ	entrenched
Ⓒ	venal
Ⓓ	puzzled
Ⓔ	artificial

Explanation

If a certain belief led to the appointment of ethics officers, that belief must concern some ethical issue. Of the choices provided, only "venal" fits that context. Although several of the other choices are not necessarily positive characteristics, none of them involves ethics.

Thus, the correct answer is **venal** (Choice C).

3. Even the charisma and technical prowess of two fine actors are not _____ the task of fully invigorating a gray domestic drama with a tired tale to tell.

Ⓐ required for
Ⓑ interested in
Ⓒ preferred for
Ⓓ adequate to
Ⓔ inferior to

Explanation

The "task" described in the second half of the sentence clearly presents the actors with a challenge. The "even the" followed by positive characteristics indicates that the actors did not meet that challenge; "adequate to" is the only answer choice that conveys this sense.

Thus, the correct answer is **adequate to** (Choice D).

4. There may be a threshold below which blood pressure reductions become _____ given that a long-running study showed no decreased heart risk for drops in blood pressure below a certain point.

Ⓐ worthwhile
Ⓑ indiscernible
Ⓒ arduous
Ⓓ significant
Ⓔ superfluous

Explanation

The portion of the sentence that begins with "given that" provides a reason for a conclusion reached in the first part of the sentence. Since the study "showed no decreased heart risk for drops in blood pressure below a certain point," that point may be a threshold below which reductions in blood pressure provide no benefit; that is, they may be "superfluous."

Thus, the correct answer is **superfluous** (Choice E).

5. Unlike the problems in recent financial scandals, issues raised by the regulators in this case appear largely to pertain to unwieldy accounting rules that are open to widely divergent interpretations—not to (i)_____ transactions designed to (ii)_____ corporate malfeasance.

Blank (i)	Blank (ii)
(A) sham	(D) cloak
(B) unpremeditated	(E) ameliorate
(C) justifiable	(F) illuminate

Explanation

The "Unlike" at the beginning of the sentence and the "not to" that follows the dash set up a contrast between the relatively innocent problems in the current case and the issues involved in the "recent financial scandals." Clearly, these latter issues must have involved wrongdoing. Looking at the second blank, only transactions designed to "cloak" corporate malfeasance would qualify: both ameliorating and illuminating malfeasance are positive actions. For the first blank, only "sham" fits; "unpremeditated" or "justifiable" transactions could not be designed to cloak malfeasance.

Thus, the correct answer is **sham** (Choice A) and **cloak** (Choice D).

6. Everyone has routines that govern their work. The myth is that artists are somehow different, that they reject (i)_____, but of course that's not true: most artists work as the rest of us do, (ii)_____, day by day, according to their own customs.

Blank (i)	Blank (ii)
(A) latitude	(D) impetuously
(B) habit	(E) ploddingly
(C) materialism	(F) sporadically

Explanation

The passage conveys the sense that artists are like everyone else in that they have "routines that govern their work." This view is contrasted with a myth that artists are "somehow different." In the first blank, only "habit" is something whose rejection presents a contrast with being governed by work routines. Rejecting "latitude" might well match being governed by work routines, and though "materialism" is sometimes rejected by artists, it is not relevant to having work routines. The second blank describes how artists "work as the rest of us do"; only "ploddingly" is consistent with the emphasis on routines and "day by day" work.

Thus, the correct answer is **habit** (Choice B) and **ploddingly** (Choice E).

7. Repression of painful memories is sometimes called "willed forgetting." Yet true forgetting is (i)_____ than the phenomenon of repressed memory. In spite of the effort that it (ii)_____, repressing unwanted memories is less (iii)_____ than truly forgetting them, for repressed memories are prone to come back.

Blank (i)	Blank (ii)	Blank (iii)
Ⓐ less controlled	Ⓓ eases	Ⓖ permanent
Ⓑ different in its effect	Ⓔ conveys	Ⓗ arduous
Ⓒ far more common	Ⓕ entails	Ⓘ immediate

Explanation

This question is best answered by first completing the third blank.

The third sentence sets up a comparison between repressing memories and forgetting them. The word "for" indicates that the last part of the sentence—"repressed memories are prone to come back"—presents the basis of that comparison. Choice G, "permanent," is the only choice that is related to the tendency to come back.

Working backward, the sentence begins with "In spite of," suggesting that the correct choice for the second blank is contrary to what one might expect. One would ordinarily expect that something entailing effort would be more rather than less permanent. Neither "eases" nor "conveys" sets up such an expectation.

Filling the second and third blanks makes it possible to fill the first blank. Nothing in the completed text suggests that true forgetting is "more common" or "less controlled" than the repression of painful memories, but it does suggest that true forgetting is different in its effect—it is more permanent. Thus, Choice B, "different in its effect," is correct.

Thus, the correct answer is **different in its effect** (Choice B), **entails** (Choice F), and **permanent** (Choice G).

8. Rather than viewing the Massachusetts Bay Colony's antinomian controversy as the inevitable (i)_____ of the intransigent opposing forces of radical and (ii)_____ beliefs, male and female piety, (iii)_____ and secular power, and the like, as other critics have, Winship argues that the crisis was not "fixed and structural."

Blank (i)	Blank (ii)	Blank (iii)
Ⓐ dissolution	Ⓓ revolutionary	Ⓖ clerical
Ⓑ melding	Ⓔ orthodox	Ⓗ civil
Ⓒ collision	Ⓕ questionable	Ⓘ cerebral

Explanation

The words "Rather than" indicate that the other critics, unlike Winship, think of the controversy as "fixed and structural." Since both "dissolution" and "melding" of "intransigent opposing forces" would tend to lessen the controversy, only "collision" (Choice C) fits the first blank. The second and third blanks appear in a series of examples of such opposing forces; only "orthodox" contrasts with "radical" in the second blank and only "clerical" contrasts with "secular" in the third blank.

Thus, the correct answer is **collision** (Choice C), **orthodox** (Choice E), and **clerical** (Choice G).

Questions 9 to 12 are based on the following reading passage.

Until recently, many anthropologists assumed that the environment of what is now the southwestern United States shaped the social history and culture of the region's indigenous peoples. Building on this assumption, archaeologists asserted that adverse envi-
ronmental conditions and droughts were responsible for the disappearances and
migrations of southwestern populations from many sites they once inhabited.

However, such deterministic arguments fail to acknowledge that local environmental variability in the Southwest makes generalizing about that environment difficult. To
examine the relationship between environmental variation and sociocultural change in
the Western Pueblo region of central Arizona, which indigenous tribes have occupied
continuously for at least 800 years, a research team recently reconstructed the climatic,
vegetational, and erosional cycles of past centuries. The researchers found it impossible to provide a single, generally applicable characterization of environmental conditions for the region. Rather, they found that local areas experienced different patterns
of rainfall, wind, and erosion, and that such conditions had prevailed in the Southwest
for the last 1,400 years. Rainfall, for example, varied within and between local valley
systems, so that even adjacent agricultural fields can produce significantly different
yields.

The researchers characterized episodes of variation in southwestern environments
by frequency: low-frequency environmental processes occur in cycles longer than one
human generation, which generally is considered to last about 25 years, and high-
frequency processes have shorter cycles. The researchers pointed out that low-frequency
processes, such as fluctuations in stream flow and groundwater levels, would not usually be apparent to human populations. In contrast, high-frequency fluctuations such
as seasonal temperature variations are observable and somewhat predictable, so that
groups could have adapted their behaviors accordingly. When the researchers compared sequences of sociocultural change in the Western Pueblo region with episodes of
low- and high-frequency environmental variation, however, they found no simple correlation between environmental process and sociocultural change or persistence.

Although early Pueblo peoples did protect themselves against environmental risk and
uncertainty, they responded variously on different occasions to similar patterns of high-
frequency climatic and environmental change. The researchers identified seven major
adaptive responses, including increased mobility, relocation of permanent settlements,
changes in subsistence foods, and reliance on trade with other groups. These findings
suggest that groups' adaptive choices depended on cultural and social as well as environmental factors and were flexible strategies rather than uncomplicated reactions to
environmental change. Environmental conditions mattered, but they were rarely, if ever,
sufficient to account for sociocultural persistence and change. Group size and composition, culture, contact with other groups, and individual choices and actions were—
barring catastrophes such as floods or earthquakes—more significant for a population's
survival than were climate and environment.

Description

The passage describes research that bears on a presumed historical relationship
between environmental variation and sociocultural change among indigenous people
of the southwestern United States. The author mentions in the first paragraph that
many anthropologists believed until recently that environmental variations explain

changes in the human populations of the region. The passage then goes on to point out studies that show problems with this explanation, including the lack of generally applicable characterizations of the environment in the region and lack of correlation between environmental changes and sociocultural changes. In the final paragraph the author mentions an alternative explanation in researchers' findings suggesting that responses to environmental changes varied according to differing factors such as group size and composition, culture, contact with other groups, and individual choices.

9. The passage is primarily concerned with
    (A) explaining why certain research findings have created controversy
    (B) pointing out the flaws in a research methodology and suggesting a different approach
    (C) presenting evidence to challenge an explanation and offering an alternative explanation
    (D) elucidating the means by which certain groups have adapted to their environment
    (E) defending a long-held interpretation by presenting new research findings

Explanation

As the description above indicates, **Choice C** is the best answer: the passage introduces an explanation, presents evidence that challenges it, and offers an alternative explanation. The passage does not mention the creation of controversy or discuss flaws in research methodology; therefore, Choices A and B are incorrect. Although the passage reports findings that different groups used different adaptive responses to environmental conditions, there is no focus on the adaptations used by particular groups, so Choice D is incorrect. The passage presents recent research findings but not in defense of a long-held interpretation; therefore, Choice E is incorrect.

10. Which of the following findings would most strongly support the assertion made by the archaeologists mentioned in line 3?
    (A) A population remained in a certain region at least a century after erosion wore away much of the topsoil that sustained grass for their grazing animals.
    (B) The range of a certain group's agricultural activity increased over a century of gradual decrease in annual rainfall.
    (C) As winters grew increasingly mild in a certain region, the nomadic residents of the region continued to move between their summer and winter encampments.
    (D) An agricultural population began to trade for supplies of a grain instead of producing the grain in its own fields as it had in the past.
    (E) A half century of drought and falling groundwater levels caused a certain population to abandon their settlements along a riverbank.

Explanation

The archaeologists mentioned in line 3 asserted that adverse environmental conditions caused southwestern populations to move or disappear. The question asks which finding would support this assertion.

Choices A, B, and C all describe populations that did *not* move away or disappear in the face of environmental changes, and hence are all incorrect. Choice D is incorrect because it does not mention a change in environmental conditions and therefore cannot support an assertion about the effects of changing environmental conditions. **Choice E** is the best answer: it mentions an adverse environmental change (a long drought) that caused a population to leave the site it had inhabited, which would support the archaeologists' assertion that such environmental changes caused such population changes.

11. The fact that "adjacent agricultural fields can produce significantly different yields" (lines 16–17) is offered as evidence of the
    (A) unpredictability of the climate and environment of the southwestern United States
    (B) difficulty of producing a consistent food supply for a large population in the Western Pueblo region
    (C) lack of water and land suitable for cultivation in central Arizona
    (D) local climatic variation in the environment of the southwestern United States
    (E) high-frequency environmental processes at work in the southwestern United States

Explanation

Choice D is the correct answer: the second paragraph says rainfall variations between local valleys cause different agricultural yields between adjacent fields and gives this as an example of how climate is not uniform within the Southwest but rather can vary significantly from place to place. Choice A is incorrect: while such variability might give rise to unpredictability, that is not how the difference in agricultural yields is being used as evidence in the passage. Choices B and C are incorrect: the passage does not make or report a claim about feeding large populations, nor does it assert that central Arizona lacks land suitable for cultivation. Choice E is incorrect: a discussion of high- and low-frequency processes occurs in the third paragraph, but the author does not present geographic differences in rainfall and agricultural yield as either a high- or a low-frequency environmental process.

12. It can be inferred from the passage that which of the following activities is NOT an example of a population responding to high-frequency environmental processes?
    (A) Developing watertight jars in which to collect and store water during the rainy season
    (B) Building multistory dwellings in low-lying areas to avoid the flash flooding that occurs each summer
    (C) Moving a village because groundwater levels have changed over the last generation
    (D) Trading with other groups for furs from which to make winter clothes.
    (E) Moving one's herds of grazing animals each year between summer and winter pastures

Explanation

The phrasing of the question indicates that all but one of the answer choices are examples of a population responding to a high-frequency environmental process. You are asked to choose the one answer choice that does not provide such an example. Choices

A, B, D, and E are incorrect because they all present responses to high-frequency environmental processes: developing water-storage jars to adapt to seasonal rainfall variations, adapting dwellings in response to seasonal flooding, trading to acquire clothing in adaptation to seasonal temperature variations, and moving grazing herds seasonally. **Choice C** is the best answer: the passage mentions fluctuations in ground water levels as a *low*-frequency process (lines 21–22); moving a village because of a change that takes place over the course of a generation is *not* a response to a high-frequency process.

Questions 13 and 14 are based on the following reading passage.

Arctic sea ice comes in two varieties. Seasonal ice forms in winter and then melts in summer, while perennial ice persists year-round. To the untrained eye, all sea ice looks similar, but by licking it, one can estimate how long a particular piece has been float-
line
5   ing around. When ice begins to form in seawater, it forces out salt, which has no place in the crystal structure. As the ice gets thicker, the rejected salt collects in tiny pockets of brine too highly concentrated to freeze. A piece of first-year ice will taste salty. Eventually, if the ice survives, these pockets of brine drain out through fine, veinlike channels, and the ice becomes fresher; multiyear ice can even be melted and drunk.

Description

The passage describes two varieties of Arctic sea ice and explains how the freezing process causes seasonal ice to taste much saltier than perennial ice.

For the following question, consider each of the choices separately and select all that apply.

13. The passage mentions which of the following as being a characteristic of seasonal ice?
   A. It is similar in appearance to perennial ice.
   B. It is typically filled with fine, veinlike channels.
   C. It tastes saltier than perennial ice.

Explanation

Choices A and C are correct.

   Choice A is correct: the passage states that "to the untrained eye, all sea ice looks similar" (lines 2–3).

   Choice B is incorrect: it is clear that perennial ice contains fine, veinlike channels, but the passage does not mention whether seasonal ice contains them.

   Choice C is correct: in lines 6–8, the passage establishes that first-year ice tastes salty but eventually gets fresher if the ice survives.

14. In the context in which it appears, "fine" (line 7) most nearly means
    (A) acceptable
    (B) elegant
    (C) precise
    (D) pure
    (E) small

Explanation

"Fine" appears in the context of an explanation of how the brine drains out; in such a context, it must be being used to describe a physical characteristic of the channels. In addition, the word "Eventually" implies that the draining is a slow process. Only **Choice E**, "small," helps to explain why the process is slow and is therefore the best choice. None of the other choices contributes to the explanation.

For questions 15 to 18, select the <u>two</u> answer choices that, when used to complete the sentence, fit the meaning of the sentence as a whole <u>and</u> produce completed sentences that are alike in meaning.

---

15. It would have been disingenuous of the candidate to appear _____ when her opponent won the election, but she congratulated the victor nonetheless.
    [A] gracious
    [B] ecstatic
    [C] crestfallen
    [D] indifferent
    [E] euphoric
    [F] disgruntled

Explanation

To answer the question, one must understand what sort of reaction on the part of a losing candidate would appear "disingenuous." Certainly "ecstatic" and "euphoric" reactions would be highly disingenuous or insincere. "Gracious" also fits the blank, but there is no other word offered that is nearly alike in meaning.

Thus, the correct answer is **ecstatic** (Choice B) and **euphoric** (Choice E).

16. As market forces penetrate firms and bid up the value of attributes of labor that are more measurable than is the knowledge born of experience, it can be expected that trends in wages will not _____ those whose main value lies in such experiential knowledge.
    [A] favor
    [B] aid
    [C] affect
    [D] forsake
    [E] betray
    [F] differentiate

Explanation

The sentence states that market forces are bidding up the value of certain attributes of labor that are "more measurable than is the knowledge born of experience." The blank has to do with trends in wages for those whose main value in the labor force lies in "experiential knowledge." Since experiential knowledge appears to be losing value in the bidding war for labor, the blank needs to be filled in a way that leads to something negative. Given the "not" that precedes the blank, "favor" and "aid" make for such an outcome and result in sentences alike in meaning.

   Thus, the correct answer is **favor** (Choice A) and **aid** (Choice B).

17. The point we might still take from the First World War is the old one that wars are always, as one historian aptly put it, _____: they produce unforeseeable results.
   A unsurprising
   B astounding
   C conventional
   D ruinous
   E stunning
   F devastating

Explanation

The colon after the blank indicates a definitional relationship between the blanked word and the phrase that follows the colon. The two answer choices for which "they produce unforeseeable results" would most clearly serve as a definition are "astounding" and "stunning." While "ruinous" and "devastating" might be adjectives describing the effects of war, they clearly do not fit the logical structure of this sentence, since they are not by definition "unforeseeable."

   Thus, the correct answer is **astounding** (Choice B) and **stunning** (Choice E).

18. This is the kind of movie—stuffed with intimations of faraway strife and people in suits talking frantically on cell phones and walkie-talkies—that is conventionally described as a political thriller, but the film is as apolitical as it is _____.
   A intense
   B unprecedented
   C subtle
   D humdrum
   E refined
   F dull

Explanation

The sentence suggests that the film is not well described by the conventional term "political thriller." The film is not political but rather apolitical, and the phrase "as apolitical as it is…" sets up a parallel between "apolitical" and the blanked word; therefore, the blanked word should go against the term "political thriller" in the same way that "apolitical" does. "Humdrum" and "dull" are the opposite of "thrilling" and are therefore the best choices.

   Thus, the correct answer is **humdrum** (Choice D) and **dull** (Choice F).

For each of questions 19 to 25, select <u>one</u> answer choice unless otherwise instructed.

Questions 19 and 20 are based on the following reading passage.

Historians credit repeated locust invasions in the nineteenth century with reshaping United States agriculture west of the Mississippi River. Admonished by government entomologists, farmers began to diversify. Wheat had come to nearly monopolize the
line region, but it was particularly vulnerable to the locusts. In 1873, just before the locusts'
5   most withering offensive, nearly two-thirds of Minnesota farmland was producing wheat; by the invasions' last year, that fraction had dropped to less than one-sixth. Farmers learned that peas and beans were far less vulnerable to the insects, and corn was a more robust grain than wheat. In addition to planting alternative crops, many farmers turned to dairy and beef production. Although pastures were often damaged
10   by the locusts, these lands were almost always left in better shape than the crops were.

Description

The passage explains how the damage caused by repeated invasions of locusts in the nineteenth century caused farmers west of the Mississippi River to diversify. Since wheat, the dominant crop in the region, was especially susceptible to damage from locusts, it made sense for farmers to lower their wheat production and raise their production of other crops and animals less vulnerable to locust invasions.

For the following question, consider each of the choices separately and select all that apply.

19. According to the passage, before the recommendations by the government entomologists, which of the following was true about farming west of the Mississippi River?

   A   Farmers focused primarily on growing wheat.
   B   Peas and beans had not yet been planted in the region.
   C   A relatively small portion of farmland was devoted to crops other than wheat.

Explanation

Choices A and C are correct.

   Choice A is correct: according to the passage, "wheat had come to nearly monopolize the region" prior to the recommendations of government entomologists.

   Choice B is incorrect: although wheat was the dominant crop, there is no indication that peas and beans had not been planted in the region prior to the admonishments of government entomologists.

   Choice C is correct: given that wheat was the dominant crop, only a relatively small portion of farmland could have been devoted to other crops.

20. In the context in which it appears, "robust" (line 8) most nearly means

    Ⓐ crude

    Ⓑ demanding

    Ⓒ productive

    Ⓓ vigorous

    Ⓔ rich

Explanation

In discussing the advantages of less vulnerable crops, the author describes corn as "robust." Of the choices presented, "vigorous" is most similar in meaning to "robust." Neither "crude" nor "demanding" is an advantage, and although being "productive" or "rich" might be desirable, neither matches the meaning of "robust" in this context. Therefore, **Choice D** is the correct answer.

Question 21 is based on the following reading passage.

In 1998 the United States Department of Transportation received nearly 10,000 consumer complaints about airlines; in 1999 it received over 20,000. Moreover, the number of complaints per 100,000 passengers also more than doubled. In both years the vast majority of complaints concerned flight delays, cancellations, mishandled baggage, and customer service. Clearly, therefore, despite the United States airline industry's serious efforts to improve performance in these areas, passenger dissatisfaction with airline service increased significantly in 1999.

21. Which of the following, if true, most seriously weakens the argument?

    Ⓐ Although the percentage of flights that arrived on time dropped slightly overall, from 77 percent in 1998 to 76 percent in 1999, some United States airlines' 1999 on-time rate was actually better than their 1998 on-time rate.

    Ⓑ The number of passengers flying on United States airlines was significantly higher in 1999 than in 1998.

    Ⓒ Fewer bags per 1,000 passengers flying on United States airlines were lost or delayed in 1999 than in 1998.

    Ⓓ The appearance in 1999 of many new Internet sites that relay complaints directly to the Department of Transportation has made filing a complaint about airlines much easier for consumers than ever before.

    Ⓔ Although the number of consumer complaints increased for every major United States airline in 1999, for some airlines the extent of the increase was substantial, whereas for others it was extremely small.

Explanation

The passage describes two different year-over-year increases in airline passenger complaints: both the absolute number of complaints and the rate of complaints more than doubled from 1998 to 1999. From these facts, the author of the passage concludes that passenger dissatisfaction with airline service significantly increased in the same period.

Choice D is the correct answer: it weakens the argument because it presents a scenario in which the increase in complaints and in the rate of complaints could merely be the result of an easier means of filing complaints, not an actual increase in passenger dissatisfaction.

Choice A and Choice C are incorrect because neither presents a scenario that bears directly on the claim that passenger dissatisfaction increased from 1998 to 1999. Choice E is incorrect: the fact that some airlines experienced a smaller increase than others does not change the fact that all airlines experienced an increase and thus cannot weaken the argument. Choice B could be correct if the passage discussed only the change in the absolute number of complaints, since more passengers could account for more complaints without entailing an increase in dissatisfaction. But the passage also says that the rate of complaints increased, making Choice B incorrect.

Questions 22 to 24 are based on the following reading passage.

Nineteenth-century architect Eugène-Emmanuel Viollet-le-Duc contended that Paris's Notre-Dame cathedral, built primarily in the late twelfth century, was supported from the very beginning by a system of flying buttresses—a series of exterior arches (flyers)
line
5   and their supports (buttresses)—which permitted the construction of taller vaulted buildings with slimmer walls and interior supports than had been possible previously. Other commentators insist, however, that Notre-Dame did not have flying buttresses until the thirteenth or fourteenth century, when they were added to update the building aesthetically and correct its structural flaws. Although post-twelfth-century modifications and renovations complicate efforts to resolve this controversy—all pre-
10   fifteenth-century flyers have been replaced, and the buttresses have been rebuilt and/or resurfaced—it is nevertheless possible to tell that both the nave and the choir, the church's two major parts, have always had flying buttresses. It is clear, now that nineteenth-century paint and plaster have been removed, that the nave's lower buttresses date from the twelfth century. Moreover, the choir's lower flyers have chevron
15   (zigzag) decoration. Chevron decoration, which was characteristic of the second half of the twelfth century and was out of favor by the fourteenth century, is entirely absent from modifications to the building that can be dated with confidence to the thirteenth century.

Description

The passage describes a disagreement about when Notre-Dame cathedral was supported by flying buttresses, with Viollet-le-Duc arguing that buttresses were present from the cathedral's construction in the late twelfth century and others claiming the buttresses were built later. The author of the passage goes on to present evidence that suggests that Viollet-le-Duc's argument is correct.

22. The passage is primarily concerned with
    (A) tracing the development of a controversy
    (B) discussing obstacles to resolving a controversy
    (C) arguing in support of one side in a controversy
    (D) analyzing the assumptions underlying the claims made in a controversy
    (E) explaining why evidence relevant to a controversy has been overlooked

Explanation

As the description above indicates, **Choice C** is correct: the passage supports one side in a controversy. Choice A is incorrect because while the passage describes a controversy, it makes no mention of how that controversy developed. The passage also does not discuss any obstacles to resolving the controversy, any assumptions underlying the claims in the controversy, or any reasons why pertinent evidence may have been over-looked, so Choice B, Choice D, and Choice E are all incorrect.

23. The claim of the "other commentators" (line 6) suggests that they believe which of the following about Notre-Dame?

    (A) It was the inspiration for many vaulted cathedrals built in the thirteenth and fourteenth centuries.

    (B) Its design flaws were not apparent until flying buttresses were added in the thirteenth or fourteenth century.

    (C) Its flying buttresses are embellished with decoration characteristic of the thirteenth and fourteenth centuries.

    (D) It had been modified in some respects before flying buttresses were added in the thirteenth or fourteenth century.

    (E) It was originally constructed in an architectural style that was considered outmoded by the thirteenth or fourteenth century.

Explanation

The passage states that the "other commentators" claim that Notre-Dame first received flying buttresses when it was updated for aesthetic and structural reasons in the thirteenth or fourteenth century. This claim thus suggests that the aesthetics of Notre-Dame were then seen as out of date, making **Choice E** correct. Choice A is incorrect because the passage does not include any information about other cathedrals, let alone attribute a view of them to the other commentators. While the other commentators do suggest that the design of Notre-Dame was seen as flawed in the thirteenth or fourteenth century, they say that flying buttresses were added to correct these flaws, not that the flaws became apparent after the addition of the flying buttresses, which makes Choice B incorrect. Choice C is incorrect because the passage does not attribute any views of the embellishments on the flying buttresses to the other commentators; similarly, Choice D is incorrect because the passage does not describe the other commentators as discussing any modifications prior to the thirteenth or fourteenth century.

24. The author's argument concerning Notre-Dame's flying buttresses depends on which of the following assumptions about the choir's lower flyers?

    (A) They accurately reproduce the decoration on the choir's original lower flyers.

    (B) They have a type of decoration used exclusively for exterior surfaces.

    (C) They were the models for the choir's original upper flyers.

    (D) They were the models for the nave's original lower flyers.

    (E) They were constructed after the nave's flyers were constructed.

Explanation

The author supports the claim that flying buttresses were present on Notre-Dame from the twelfth century by noting that the choir's lower flyers feature a chevron decoration that was characteristic of the twelfth century. But since all flyers constructed prior to the fifteenth century have been replaced, the chevron decorations can indicate only that flyers were present in the twelfth century if those decorations accurately reproduce the decorations that existed on the original flyers. Thus, **Choice A** is the correct answer.

Choice B is incorrect: whether chevron decorations are used only on the exterior is not a point of dispute in the passage. Choices C, D, and E are all incorrect: no part of the argument turns on any claim about the choir's upper flyers, the nave's lower flyers, or the sequence in which the choir's and the nave's flyers were constructed.

Question 25 is based on the following reading passage.

The average temperature of the lobster-rich waters off the coast of Foerkland has been increasing for some years. In warmer water, lobsters grow faster. In particular, lobster larvae take less time to reach the size at which they are no longer vulnerable to predation by young cod, the chief threat to their survival. Consequently, the survival rate of lobster larvae must be going up, and the lobster population in Foerkland's coastal waters is bound to increase.

25. Which of the following, if true, most seriously weakens the argument?
    (A) There are indications that in recent years the fishing fleet operating off the coast of Foerkland has been taking cod at an unsustainably high rate.
    (B) The increase in water temperatures off Foerkland has not been as pronounced as the increase in average soil temperatures in Foerkland.
    (C) Because of their speeded-up growth, lobsters now get large enough to be legal catch before they reach reproductive maturity.
    (D) Even though lobsters grow faster in warmer waters, warmer waters have no effect on the maximum size to which a lobster can eventually grow.
    (E) Cod are a cold-water species, and the increasing water temperatures have caused a northward shift in Foerkland's cod population.

Explanation

The argument in the passage concludes that the survival rate of lobster larvae is increasing and that the lobster population will increase. The basis for the conclusion is that the change in the water temperature, by speeding the growth of lobster larvae, has made them less vulnerable to predation by cod. However, Choice C points to a way that the faster growth of individual lobsters could create a threat to the population: lobsters that have not yet reproduced might be large enough to be legally caught. Thus, **Choice C** weakens the argument and is the correct answer.

Among the other choices, Choice A tends, if anything, to support the passage's conclusion, by suggesting further reduction in the risks of predation by cod. The other choices have no clear bearing on the argument.

SECTION 5
Quantitative Reasoning
25 Questions with Explanations

For each of Questions 1 to 9, select one of the following answer choices.
Ⓐ Quantity A is greater.
Ⓑ Quantity B is greater.
Ⓒ The two quantities are equal.
Ⓓ The relationship cannot be determined from the information given.

Quantity A	Quantity B	
$\dfrac{3^{-1}}{4^{-1}}$	$\dfrac{4}{3}$	Ⓐ Ⓑ Ⓒ Ⓓ

1.

Explanation

In this question, you are asked to compare $\dfrac{3^{-1}}{4^{-1}}$ with $\dfrac{4}{3}$. Recall that if a is a

nonzero number, then $a^{-1} = \dfrac{1}{a}$ and $\dfrac{1}{a^{-1}} = a$. Using these rules of exponents, you can see that

$$\frac{3^{-1}}{4^{-1}} = (3^{-1})\left(\frac{1}{4^{-1}}\right) = \left(\frac{1}{3}\right)(4) = \frac{4}{3}$$

Thus, $\dfrac{3^{-1}}{4^{-1}} = \dfrac{4}{3}$, and the correct answer is **Choice C**.

This explanation uses the following strategy.
Strategy 5: Simplify an Arithmetic or Algebraic Representation

$$x < 1 \text{ and } x \neq 0$$

Quantity A	Quantity B	
$x^2 + 1$	$x^3 + 1$	Ⓐ Ⓑ Ⓒ Ⓓ

2.

Explanation

In this question, you are given that $x < 1$ and $x \neq 0$, and you are asked to compare $x^2 + 1$ with $x^3 + 1$. One way to approach this problem is to set up a comparison between the two quantities using a placeholder symbol to represent the relationship between them as follows.

$$x^2 + 1 \boxed{?} x^3 + 1$$

Then simplify the comparison.
   Step 1: Subtract 1 from both sides to get

$$x^2 \boxed{?} x^3$$

   Step 2: Since $x \neq 0$, you can divide both sides by the positive quantity x^2 to get

$$1 \boxed{?} x$$

Since you are given that $x < 1$, or $1 > x$, you can conclude that the placeholder $?$ in the simplified comparison 1 $?$ x represents *greater than* ($>$). Note that the strategy of simplifying the comparison requires you to consider whether the steps in the simplification are reversible. This is because you must arrive at a conclusion about the initial comparison, not the simplified comparison. If you follow the simplification steps in reverse, you can see that the placeholder in each step remains unchanged: $1 > x$ implies $x^2 > x^3$ because multiplying by the positive number x^2 retains the inequality *greater than* ($>$). Also, $x^2 > x^3$ implies $x^2 + 1 > x^3 + 1$. Therefore, Quantity A is greater than Quantity B, and the correct answer is **Choice A**.

This explanation uses the following strategy.
Strategy 5: Simplify an Arithmetic or Algebraic Representation

$$x > 0$$

Quantity A	Quantity B	
3. 0.5% of x	$\frac{1}{2}x$	Ⓐ Ⓑ Ⓒ Ⓓ

Explanation

In this question, you are given that $x > 0$, and you are asked to compare 0.5% of x with $\frac{1}{2}x$. Recall that $\frac{1}{2}$ of a number is the same as 50% of the number.

Therefore, $\frac{1}{2}x$ is equal to 50% of x. Since $x > 0$, it follows that 50% of x is greater than 0.5% of x. The correct answer is **Choice B**.

You could also make the comparison by rewriting 0.5% of x as a fraction of x and then comparing the result with $\frac{1}{2}x$. Rewrite 0.5% of x as a fraction of x as follows.

$$\frac{0.5}{100}x = \frac{5}{1,000}x$$

Since $x > 0$, it follows that $\frac{5}{1,000}x$ is less than $\frac{1}{2}x$, and Quantity B is greater than Quantity A. The correct answer is **Choice B**.

This explanation uses the following strategy.
Strategy 5: Simplify an Arithmetic or Algebraic Representation

The median income of a group of College C graduates six months after graduation was $3,000 higher than the median income of a group of College D graduates six months after graduation.

Quantity A	Quantity B	
4. The 75th percentile of the incomes of the group of College C graduates six months after graduation	The 75th percentile of the incomes of the group of College D graduates six months after graduation	Ⓐ Ⓑ Ⓒ Ⓓ

Explanation

In this question, you are asked to compare the 75th percentiles of the incomes of two groups of college graduates six months after graduation. The only information you are given is that the median income of the group in Quantity A is $3,000 greater than the median income of the group in Quantity B.

Recall that the median of a group of numbers is the middle number (or the average of the two middle numbers) when the numbers are listed from least to greatest. The median is also equal to the 50th percentile. The median does not indicate anything about the spread of the numbers in the group. In particular, for each group of incomes, you do not know how much greater than the median the 75th percentile of the group of incomes is, nor do you know the relationship between the 75th percentiles of the two groups. Since the relationship between Quantity A and Quantity B cannot be determined, the correct answer is **Choice D**.

This explanation uses the following strategies.
Strategy 8: Search for a Mathematical Relationship
Strategy 13: Determine Whether a Conclusion Follows from the Information Given

The graph above shows the frequency distribution of 50 integer values varying from 1 to 6.

Quantity A	Quantity B	
5. The average (arithmetic mean) of the 50 values	The median of the 50 values	

Explanation

In this question, you are given a graph of the frequency distribution of 50 integer values and are asked to compare the average (arithmetic mean) with the median of the distribution.

In general, the median of a group of n values, where n is even, is obtained by ordering the values from least to greatest and then calculating the average (arithmetic mean) of the two middle values. So, for the 50 values shown in the graph, the median is the average of the 25th and 26th values, both of which are equal to 5. Therefore, the median of the 50 values is 5.

Once you know that the median of the 50 values is 5, the comparison simplifies to comparing the average of the 50 values with 5. You can make this comparison without actually calculating the average by noting from the graph that of the 50 values,

11 values are 1 unit above 5,
16 values are equal to 5,
10 values are 1 unit below 5, and
13 values are more than 1 unit below 5.

Since the part of the distribution that is below 5 contains 23 values—13 of which are more than 1 unit below 5—and the part of the distribution that is above 5 contains 11 values—none of which is more than 1 unit above 5—the average (arithmetic mean) of the 50 values must be less than 5. The correct answer is **Choice B**.

Alternatively, you can calculate the average of the 50 values as follows.

$$\frac{(1)(2)+(2)(4)+(3)(7)+(4)(10)+(5)(16)+(6)(11)}{50} = \frac{217}{50}$$

Thus the average of the 50 values, $\frac{217}{50}$, or 4.34, is less than the median of the 50 values, 5. The correct answer is **Choice B**.

This explanation uses the following strategies.

Strategy 4: Translate from a Figure to an Arithmetic or Algebraic Representation
Strategy 8: Search for a Mathematical Relationship

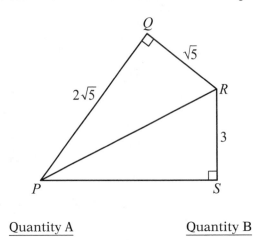

Quantity A	Quantity B	
6. The area of triangle *PQR*	The area of triangle *PSR*	

Explanation

In this question, you are asked to compare the area of triangle *PQR* with the area of triangle *PSR*. Note that both triangles are right triangles and that line segment *PR* is the hypotenuse of both triangles. Recall that the area of a triangle is equal to one-half the product of a base and the height corresponding to the base. Also, for any right triangle, the lengths of the two legs of the triangle are a base and the corresponding height.

   The area of triangle PQR: In the figure, it is given that the length of leg *PQ* is $2\sqrt{5}$ and the length of leg *QR* is $\sqrt{5}$. Therefore, you can conclude that the area of triangle *PQR* is $\frac{1}{2}(2\sqrt{5})(\sqrt{5})$, or 5.

   The area of triangle PSR: To calculate the area of triangle *PSR*, you need to know the lengths of the legs *PS* and *RS*. From the figure, you know that the length of *RS* is 3, but you do not know the length of *PS*. How can you determine the length of *PS*? If, in addition to the length of *RS*, you knew the length of hypotenuse *PR*, you could use the Pythagorean theorem to determine the length of *PS*. So, to find the length of *PS*, you first need to find the length of hypotenuse *PR*.

   Recall that *PR* is also the hypotenuse of triangle *PQR*. The lengths of legs *PQ* and *QR* of triangle *PQR* are $2\sqrt{5}$ and $\sqrt{5}$, respectively. By the Pythagorean theorem,

$$(PR)^2 = (PQ)^2 + (QR)^2$$
$$= \left(2\sqrt{5}\right)^2 + \left(\sqrt{5}\right)^2$$
$$= 20 + 5$$
$$= 25$$

Thus, the length of *PR* is $\sqrt{25}$, or 5.

Returning to triangle *PSR*, you now know that the length of hypotenuse *PR* is 5 and the length of leg *RS* is 3. Therefore, by the Pythagorean theorem,

$$3^2 + (PS)^2 = 5^2$$
$$9 + (PS)^2 = 25$$
$$(PS)^2 = 25 - 9$$
$$(PS)^2 = 16$$

and the length of *PS* is 4.

Since legs *PS* and *RS* have lengths 4 and 3, respectively, the area of triangle *PSR* is $\frac{1}{2}(4)(3)$, or 6. Recall that you have already determined that the area of triangle *PQR* is 5. So Quantity B, the area of triangle *PSR*, is greater than Quantity A, the area of triangle *PQR*, and the correct answer is **Choice B**.

This explanation uses the following strategies.

Strategy 4: Translate from a Figure to an Arithmetic or Algebraic Representation
Strategy 8: Search for a Mathematical Relationship

Quantity A	Quantity B	
7. The sum of the odd integers from 1 to 199	The sum of the even integers from 2 to 198	

Explanation

In this question, you are asked to compare the sum of the odd integers from 1 to 199 with the sum of the even integers from 2 to 198. Both of these sums involve many integers. How many integers are in each sum? Note that there are 200 integers from 1 to 200, where 100 of them are even and 100 of them are odd. The 100 odd integers are precisely the odd integers in Quantity A, whereas the 100 even integers include one more integer, 200, than the even integers in Quantity B. So Quantity A is the sum of 100 integers and Quantity B is the sum of 99 integers.

It would be very time-consuming to write out all the terms in each sum and add them together. Therefore, it is reasonable to find a more efficient way to calculate the sums or to find a way to compare the sums without actually calculating them. To find a more efficient way to calculate the two sums, it is often useful to look for ways to rearrange the terms in the sum so that they can be added more easily. You can begin by writing a few terms from the beginning and the end of the sum.

For the sum of the 100 odd integers from 1 to 199, you could write

$$1 + 3 + 5 + \ldots + 195 + 197 + 199$$

You can pair the odd integers in the sum and add the two integers in each pair as follows.

$$1 + 3 + 5 + \ldots + 195 + 197 + 199$$

200
200
200

Note that the sum of the integers in each of the three pairs shown is 200. You can continue pairing terms in the sum in this way until all 100 terms have been rearranged in 50 pairs, where the sum of each pair is 200. It follows that

$$1 + 3 + 5 + \ldots + 195 + 197 + 199 = (1 + 199) + (3 + 197) + (5 + 195) + \ldots + (99 + 101)$$
$$= 50(200)$$
$$= 10,000$$

Now consider the sum of the 99 even integers from 2 to 198. For this sum, you could write

$$2 + 4 + 6 + \ldots + 194 + 196 + 198$$

In this sum, note that

the sum of the 1st and 99th terms is $2 + 198 = 200$
the sum of the 2nd and 98th terms is $4 + 196 = 200$

You can continue pairing terms in this way until 98 of the 99 terms in the sum have been rearranged into 49 pairs and the 50th term is unpaired. Note that the unpaired term is 100 (the 50th positive even integer). It follows that

$$2 + 4 + \ldots + 98 + 100 + 102 + \ldots + 196 + 198 = (2 + 198) + (4 + 196) + \ldots + (98 + 102) + 100$$
$$= 49(200) + 100$$
$$= 9{,}900$$

Therefore, Quantity A, 10,000, is greater than Quantity B, 9,900, and the correct answer is **Choice A**.

Alternatively, you can try to compare the two sums without actually calculating them. Recall that Quantity A is the sum of the 100 odd integers from 1 to 199, and Quantity B is the sum of the 99 even integers from 2 to 198. Write each sum with the terms in increasing order, as follows, pairing the nth term in Quantity B with the nth term in Quantity A and noting that there is no term in Quantity B that is paired with the 100th term, 199, in Quantity A.

Quantity A: $1 + 3 + 5 + \ldots + 193 + 195 + 197 + 199$
Quantity B: $2 + 4 + 6 + \ldots + 194 + 196 + 198$

Note that each of the 99 terms in Quantity B is 1 more than its paired term in Quantity A, so Quantity B is 99 more than the sum of all the terms in Quantity A excluding the last term, 199. Consequently, Quantity A is $199 - 99$ more than Quantity B—that is, 100 more than Quantity B—and the correct answer is **Choice A**.

This explanation uses the following strategy.
Strategy 7: Find a Pattern

s and t are positive integers, and $32^s = 2^t$.

Quantity A	Quantity B	
8. $\dfrac{s}{t}$	$\dfrac{1}{5}$	Ⓐ Ⓑ Ⓒ Ⓓ

Explanation

In this question, you are given that s and t are positive integers and that $32^s = 2^t$, and you are asked to compare $\dfrac{s}{t}$ with $\dfrac{1}{5}$. Since the expression $\dfrac{s}{t}$ involves the variables s and t, you need to look for a relationship between s and t using the equation $32^s = 2^t$.

If the two bases in this equation were equal, then the exponents would be equal. However, one of the bases is 32 and the other is 2. This suggests making the two bases equal by rewriting 32 as a power of 2 if it is possible to do so. In fact, $32 = 2^5$. Therefore, $32^s = (2^5)^s = 2^{5s}$, and the equation $32^s = 2^t$ can be rewritten as $2^{5s} = 2^t$. In the rewritten equation, the bases are equal, so you can conclude that $5s = t$.

Since $5s = t$, it follows that $\frac{s}{t} = \frac{1}{5}$. Quantity A is equal to Quantity B, and the correct answer is **Choice C**.

This explanation uses the following strategy.

Strategy 5: Simplify an Arithmetic or Algebraic Representation

> In a quality-control test, 50 boxes—each containing 30 machine parts—were examined for defective parts. The number of defective parts was recorded for each box, and the average (arithmetic mean) of the 50 recorded numbers of defective parts per box was 1.12. Only one error was made in recording the 50 numbers: "1" defective part in a certain box was incorrectly recorded as "10".

	Quantity A	Quantity B	
9.	The actual average number of defective parts per box	0.94	Ⓐ Ⓑ Ⓒ Ⓓ

Explanation

In this question, you are given that the number of defective parts in each of 50 boxes was recorded and that the average of the 50 recorded numbers was 1.12. You are also given that an error was made in recording one of the 50 numbers—the number 10 was recorded instead of the number 1—so the actual number of defective parts in this box is 9 less than the recorded number. Then you are asked to compare the actual average number of defective parts per box with 0.94.

To determine the actual average number of defective parts per box, first note that the sum of the 50 recorded numbers equals the average of the 50 recorded numbers times 50—that is, (1.12)(50), or 56.

Now you know that for 49 of the 50 boxes, the actual number of defective parts is equal to the recorded number; and for one box, the actual number is 9 less than the recorded number. From this you can conclude that the sum of the 50 actual numbers is equal to the sum of the 50 recorded numbers minus 9. So the sum of the actual numbers of defective parts is 56 – 9, or 47.

Therefore, the actual average number of defective parts per box is $\frac{47}{50}$, or 0.94. Quantity A is equal to Quantity B, and the correct answer is **Choice C**.

This explanation uses the following strategy.

Strategy 1: Translate from Words to an Arithmetic or Algebraic Representation

10. In year Y, the population of Colorado was approximately half that of New Jersey, and the land area of Colorado was approximately 14 times that of New Jersey. The population density (number of persons per unit of land area) of Colorado in year Y was approximately how many times the population density of New Jersey?

    Ⓐ $\frac{1}{28}$ Ⓑ $\frac{1}{14}$ Ⓒ $\frac{1}{7}$ Ⓓ $\frac{1}{4}$ Ⓔ $\frac{1}{2}$

Explanation

The information given in the question can be rewritten algebraically as follows.

$$\text{population of Colorado} \approx \left(\frac{1}{2}\right) \times (\text{population of New Jersey})$$

$$\text{land area of Colorado} \approx (14) \times (\text{land area of New Jersey})$$

Using the information given and the fact that population density is the number of persons per unit of land area, you can express the population density of Colorado in terms of the population density of New Jersey as follows.

$$\text{population density of Colorado} = \frac{\text{population of Colorado}}{\text{land area of Colorado}}$$

$$\approx \frac{\left(\frac{1}{2}\right) \times (\text{population of New Jersey})}{(14) \times (\text{land area of New Jersey})}$$

$$\approx \left(\frac{1}{2}\right) \times \frac{1}{14} \times \frac{\text{population of New Jersey}}{\text{land area of New Jersey}}$$

$$\approx \left(\frac{1}{28}\right) \times (\text{population density of New Jersey})$$

Thus, the population density of Colorado was approximately $\frac{1}{28}$ times the population density of New Jersey. The correct answer is **Choice A**.

This explanation uses the following strategy.

Strategy 1: Translate from Words to an Arithmetic or Algebraic Representation

For the following question, enter your answer in the box.

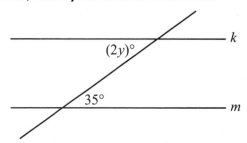

11. In the figure above, line k is parallel to line m. What is the value of y?

$$y = \boxed{}$$

Explanation

In the figure, the angles with measures $(2y)°$ and $35°$ are between parallel lines k and m, and they are on opposite sides of the line that crosses k and m. Therefore, you can conclude that these two angles are congruent. So $2y = 35$, and $y = \frac{35}{2} = 17.5$. The correct answer is **17.5**.

This explanation uses the following strategy.

Strategy 4: Translate from a Figure to an Arithmetic or Algebraic Representation

12. The numbers in data set S have a standard deviation of 5. If a new data set is formed by adding 3 to each number in S, what is the standard deviation of the numbers in the new data set?

    (A) 2

    (B) 3

    (C) 5

    (D) 8

    (E) 15

Explanation

Recall that the standard deviation of the numbers in a data set is a measure of the spread of the numbers about the mean of the numbers. The new data set is formed by adding the <u>same</u> number, 3, to <u>each</u> number in data set S. Thus, the mean of the numbers in the new data set is 3 more than the mean of the numbers in S, but the spread of the numbers in the new data set about the mean of the numbers in the new data set is the same as the spread of the numbers in S about the mean of the numbers in S. Because the standard deviation of the numbers in S is 5, the standard deviation of the numbers in the new data set is also 5. The correct answer is **Choice C**.

This explanation uses the following strategy.

Strategy 8: Search for a Mathematical Relationship

13. If $\dfrac{2y-3}{y} = \dfrac{3-y}{2}$, which of the following could be the value of y?

    (A) 4

    (B) 1

    (C) −1

    (D) −3

    (E) −5

Explanation

One approach to answer the question is to solve the equation for y as follows.

$$2(2y-3) = y(3-y)$$
$$4y-6 = 3y-y^2$$
$$y^2 + y - 6 = 0$$
$$(y+3)(y-2) = 0$$

Since a product equals 0 only if at least one of the factors equals 0,

$$y + 3 = 0 \quad \text{or} \quad y - 2 = 0$$
$$y = -3 \quad \text{or} \quad y = 2$$

Thus, there are two values of y that satisfy the equation, −3 and 2. The value −3 is Choice D, and the value 2 is not among the answer choices. The correct answer is **Choice D**.

Another approach is to determine, for each answer choice, whether the equation holds. To do this, you can substitute the answer choice for y in the equation $\dfrac{2y-3}{y} = \dfrac{3-y}{2}$, replace the equals sign in the equation by the placeholder symbol $\overset{?}{=}$, and then simplify to see whether the two expressions are in fact equal.

For Choice A, substituting $y = 4$ in the equation $\dfrac{2y-3}{y} = \dfrac{3-y}{2}$ and replacing the equals sign = with the placeholder symbol $\overset{?}{=}$ yields the relationship $\dfrac{2(4)-3}{4} \overset{?}{=} \dfrac{3-4}{2}$, which can be simplified as follows.

$$\frac{2(4)-3}{4} \overset{?}{=} \frac{3-4}{2}$$
$$\frac{8-3}{4} \overset{?}{=} \frac{-1}{2}$$
$$\frac{5}{4} \overset{?}{=} -\frac{1}{2}$$

Since $\dfrac{5}{4} \neq -\dfrac{1}{2}$, you can conclude that the placeholder symbol does not represent equality, and therefore the equation does not hold for $y = 4$.

If you continue evaluating the answer choices, you will find that the correct answer is **Choice D**, –3. To see that the equation $\dfrac{2y-3}{y} = \dfrac{3-y}{2}$ is true when $y = -3$, substitute $y = -3$ in the equation and replace the equals sign = with the placeholder symbol $\overset{?}{=}$. This yields the relationship $\dfrac{2(-3)-3}{-3} \overset{?}{=} \dfrac{3-(-3)}{2}$. This relationship can be simplified as follows.

$$\frac{2(-3)-3}{-3} \overset{?}{=} \frac{3-(-3)}{2}$$
$$\frac{-6-3}{-3} \overset{?}{=} \frac{3+3}{2}$$
$$\frac{-9}{-3} \overset{?}{=} \frac{6}{2}$$
$$3 \overset{?}{=} 3$$

Since $3 = 3$, you can conclude that the placeholder symbol represents equality, and therefore the equation holds for $y = -3$. The correct answer is **Choice D**.

This explanation uses the following strategy.

Strategy 5: Simplify an Arithmetic or Algebraic Representation

For the following question, select all the answer choices that apply.

14. List K consists of the numbers –10, –5, 0, 5, and 10. Which of the following lists of numbers have the same range as the numbers in list K?

    Indicate <u>all</u> such lists.

    A   –15, –1, 0, 1, 15   D   2, 3, 5, 15, 19, 22

    B   –7, –4, –2, 1, 13   E   4, 5, 6, 24

    C   0, 1, 2, 5, 8, 10

Explanation

Recall that the range of a list of numbers is defined as the difference between the greatest number and the least number in the list. The greatest number in list K is 10 and the least number is -10. Therefore, the range of the numbers in list K is $10 - (-10) = 10 + 10 = 20$. So, to answer the question, you need to consider each list of numbers given in the choices and determine whether that list of numbers has a range of 20.

Note that in each of the choices, the numbers are listed in order from least to greatest. Therefore, you need to look only at the first number and last number in each list to determine which lists have a range of 20. The ranges can be calculated quickly as follows.

Choice A: The greatest number is 15 and the least number is -15; therefore, the range is $15 - (-15) = 15 + 15 = 30$.

Choice B: The greatest number is 13 and the least number is -7; therefore, the range is $13 - (-7) = 13 + 7 = 20$.

Choice C: The greatest number is 10 and the least number is 0; therefore, the range is $10 - 0 = 10$.

Choice D: The greatest number is 22 and the least number is 2; therefore, the range is $22 - 2 = 20$.

Choice E: The greatest number is 24 and the least number is 4; therefore, the range is $24 - 4 = 20$.

In each of Choices B, D, and E, the range is 20. The correct answer consists of **Choices B, D, and E**.

This explanation uses the following strategy.

Strategy 8: Search for a Mathematical Relationship

15. Aisha's income in 2004 was 20 percent greater than her income in 2003. What is the ratio of Aisha's income in 2004 to her income in 2003?

Ⓐ 1 to 5   Ⓓ 5 to 1

Ⓑ 5 to 6   Ⓔ 20 to 1

Ⓒ 6 to 5

Explanation

Because Aisha's income in 2004 was 20% greater than her income in 2003, her income in 2004 was equal to

(100% of her income in 2003) + (20% of her income in 2003)

which is 120% of her income in 2003. Therefore, the ratio of her income in 2004 to her income in 2003 is 120 to 100, which is equivalent to 6 to 5. The correct answer is **Choice C**.

Alternatively, to say that Aisha's income in 2004 was 20% greater than her income in 2003 is the same as saying that her income increased by $\frac{1}{5}$. Therefore, her income in 2004 was $\frac{6}{5}$ of her income in 2003, and the ratio of her income in 2004 to her income in 2003 is 6 to 5. The correct answer is **Choice C**.

This explanation uses the following strategy.

Strategy 1: Translate from Words to an Arithmetic or Algebraic Representation

16. Jacob's weekly take-home pay is n dollars. Each week he uses $\frac{4n}{5}$ dollars for expenses and saves the rest. At those rates, how many weeks will it take Jacob to save $500, in terms of n?

(A) $\dfrac{500}{n}$

(B) $\dfrac{2,500}{n}$

(C) $\dfrac{n}{625}$

(D) $\dfrac{n}{2,500}$

(E) $625n$

Explanation

It may be helpful to consider how you would determine the number of weeks it would take Jacob to save $500 if you knew how much he saved each week. For example, suppose Jacob saved $25 each week. At that rate, it is easy to see that it would take him $500 \div 25$, or 20, weeks to save $500. Using this example, you can see that the number of weeks it will take Jacob to save $500 is equal to 500 divided by the amount he saves each week.

Now use the information given in the question to determine an algebraic expression representing the amount Jacob saved each week. In the question, you are given that Jacob's weekly expenses are $\frac{4n}{5}$ dollars. Therefore, the amount he saves each week is equal to his weekly take-home pay minus his weekly expenses, or $n - \frac{4n}{5} = \frac{5n}{5} - \frac{4n}{5} = \frac{5n-4n}{5} = \frac{n}{5}$ dollars.

Recall that you had already concluded that the number of weeks it will take Jacob to save $500 is equal to 500 divided by the amount he saves each week. So the number of weeks it will take Jacob to save $500 is

$500 \div \frac{n}{5} = 500 \times \frac{5}{n} = \frac{2,500}{n}$. The correct answer is **Choice B**.

This explanation uses the following strategy.

Strategy 1: Translate from Words to an Arithmetic or Algebraic Representation

Questions 17 to 20 are based on the following data.

LENGTH OF UNEMPLOYMENT FOR WORKERS IN REGION X FOR TWO INDUSTRIES, 2003

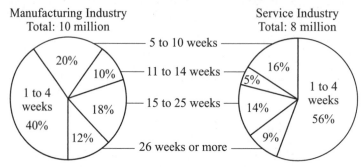

Note: The circle graphs show the distributions of workers who were unemployed for at least 1 week in 2003, by length of unemployment, rounded to the nearest week.

17. In the circle graphs, the degree measure of the central angle of the sector representing the number of workers unemployed for 11 to 14 weeks is how much greater in the manufacturing industry graph than in the service industry graph?

    (A) 5°   (D) 18°
    (B) 10°   (E) 20°
    (C) 15°

Explanation

Recall that in a circle graph, the degree measure of the central angle of a sector representing n percent of the data is equal to n percent of 360°.

  The degree measure of the sector representing the number of workers unemployed for 11 to 14 weeks is 10% of 360°, or 36°, for the manufacturing industry graph and is 5% of 360°, or 18°, for the service industry graph. Since $36° - 18° = 18°$, the measure of the central angle of that sector in the manufacturing industry graph is 18° greater than the measure of the central angle of the corresponding sector in the service industry graph. The correct answer is **Choice D**.

This explanation uses the following strategy.

Strategy 4: Translate from a Figure to an Arithmetic or Algebraic Representation

18. Which of the following could be the median length of unemployment, in weeks, for manufacturing industry workers who were unemployed for at least 1 week?

    (A) 4   (D) 16
    (B) 8   (E) 20
    (C) 12

Explanation

Note that the sectors in the manufacturing industry circle graph separate the unemployed manufacturing industry workers into five groups by length of unemployment; also, the percent of workers within each of the five groups is given. Also note that there are 10 million lengths of unemployment, one length for each of the 10 million workers. Since the lengths are rounded to whole numbers of weeks, most of the 10 million lengths must be repetitions. The median length of unemployment is the average of the two middle lengths when the lengths are listed in order from least to greatest; that is, the median is the number at which 50% of the lengths have been listed.

  To find the median length, first note that the group with the shortest unemployment lengths, 1 to 4 weeks, accounts for the first 40% of the lengths in the ordered list. Then, because the group with the next longer lengths, 5 to 10 weeks, accounts for the next 20% of the lengths in the list, the number at which 50% of the lengths have been listed is in this group. So the median length is in the 5-to-10 week interval. Among the answer choices, the only choice that is in the 5-to-10 week interval is Choice B, 8. The correct answer is **Choice B**.

This explanation uses the following strategies.

Strategy 4: Translate from a Figure to an Arithmetic or Algebraic Representation
Strategy 8: Search for a Mathematical Relationship

19. If one of the workers in the manufacturing and service industries who were unemployed for at least 1 week will be randomly selected, what is the probability that the person selected will be a service industry worker who was unemployed for 26 weeks or more?

    (A) 0.04
    (B) 0.09
    (C) 0.21
    (D) 0.40
    (E) 0.90

Explanation

The probability that the person selected will be a service industry worker who was unemployed for 26 weeks or more is equal to the following fraction.

$$\frac{\text{the number of service industry workers who were unemployed 26 weeks or more}}{\text{the number of workers in the two industries who were unemployed at least 1 week}}$$

The number of workers in the two industries who were unemployed for at least 1 week is the sum of the total numbers of workers represented by the two graphs, or 10 million + 8 million = 18 million.

According to the graph for the service industry, the number of workers who were unemployed for 26 weeks or more is 9% of 8 million, or 0.72 million. Therefore, the desired probability is $\frac{0.72\text{ million}}{18\text{ million}} = \frac{72}{1,800} = 0.04$. The correct answer is **Choice A**.

This explanation uses the following strategies.

Strategy 4: Translate from a Figure to an Arithmetic or Algebraic Representation
Strategy 8: Search for a Mathematical Relationship

20. The ratio of the number of manufacturing industry workers who were unemployed for 5 to 10 weeks to the number of service industry workers who were unemployed for 5 to 10 weeks is closest to which of the following?

    (A) 5 to 4
    (B) 6 to 5
    (C) 3 to 2
    (D) 5 to 2
    (E) 7 to 6

Explanation

According to the graphs, the number of manufacturing industry workers who were unemployed for 5 to 10 weeks is 20% of 10 million, or 2 million; and the number of service industry workers who were unemployed for 5 to 10 weeks is 16% of 8 million, or 1.28 million. Thus, the ratio of the two numbers is 2 to 1.28.

To answer the question, you must now determine which of the answer choices is closest to the ratio 2 to 1.28. A good way to compare ratios is to express each ratio as a fraction and then as a decimal, and then to compare the decimals. The ratio 2 to 1.28 can be expressed as the fraction $\frac{2}{1.28}$, which is equal to the decimal 1.5625.

Now look at the answer choices. As you go through the answer choices, keep in mind that you are trying to determine which is closest to 1.5625.

Choice A: 5 to 4 can be expressed as $\frac{5}{4}$, which is equal to 1.25.

Choice B: 6 to 5 can be expressed as $\frac{6}{5}$, which is equal to 1.2.

Choice C: 3 to 2 can be expressed as $\frac{3}{2}$, which is equal to 1.5. Note that this ratio is close to 1.5625.

Choice D: 5 to 2 can be expressed as $\frac{5}{2}$, which is equal to 2.5.

Choice E: 7 to 6 can be expressed as $\frac{7}{6}$, which is approximately equal to 1.17.

Of the five choices, the ratio in Choice C is closest to 1.5625. The correct answer is **Choice C**.

This explanation uses the following strategies.
Strategy 4: Translate from a Figure to an Arithmetic or Algebraic Representation
Strategy 5: Simplify an Arithmetic or Algebraic Representation

For the following question, select all the answer choices that apply.

21. If $|t + 3| > 5$, which of the following could be the value of t?

    Indicate <u>all</u> such values.

    A   −9

    B   −6

    C   −2

    D   0

    E   2

    F   3

Explanation

One way to approach this question is to substitute each of the answer choices into the inequality and determine which ones satisfy the inequality. If you do this, you will see that Choice A, −9, and Choice F, 3, satisfy the inequality, but the other answer choices do not. The correct answer consists of **Choices A and F**.

An algebraic approach to the question is to note that the inequality $|t + 3| > 5$ is satisfied whenever $t + 3 > 5$ or $t + 3 < -5$, that is, whenever $t > 2$ or $t < -8$. Therefore, all values of t greater than 2 or less than −8 satisfy the inequality $|t + 3| > 5$. The only answer choices that meet those conditions are −9, Choice A, and 3, Choice F. The correct answer consists of **Choices A and F**.

This explanation uses the following strategy.
Strategy 5: Simplify an Arithmetic or Algebraic Representation

22. The operation $\otimes$ is defined for all integers x and y as $x \otimes y = xy - y$. If x and y are positive integers, which of the following CANNOT be zero?

(A) $x \otimes y$

(B) $y \otimes x$

(C) $(x - 1) \otimes y$

(D) $(x + 1) \otimes y$

(E) $x \otimes (y - 1)$

Explanation

In the formula $x \otimes y = xy - y$, the variables x and y are placeholders that can be replaced by integers or by expressions representing integers. Here are two examples.

If x is replaced by 3 and y is replaced by 4, then the formula gives

$$3 \otimes 4 = (3)(4) - 4 = 12 - 4 = 8$$

If x is replaced by $x - 1$ and y is replaced by 2, then the formula gives

$$(x - 1) \otimes 2 = ((x - 1)(2)) - 2 = 2x - 2 - 2 = 2x - 4$$

Scanning the answer choices, you can see that all of them are of the form

"first expression" $\otimes$ "second expression"

For each answer choice, you must determine whether the answer choice can be equal to 0 for some positive integers x and y. Are there positive integers x and y for which the answer choice is equal to 0? If not, then that answer choice is the correct answer.

Choice A: $x \otimes y$. Using the formula, try to find positive integers x and y for which $x \otimes y = 0$, that is, for which $xy - y = 0$. To solve this equation, note that factoring y out of the left-hand side of the equation $xy - y = 0$ gives the equation $(x - 1)y = 0$. So now you must find positive integers x and y such that the product of the two numbers $x - 1$ and y is 0. Since the product of two numbers is 0 only if at least one of the numbers is 0, it follows that the product of $x - 1$ and y will be 0 if $x = 1$, no matter what the value of y is. For example, if $x = 1$ and $y = 2$, then $x \otimes y = 1 \otimes 2 = (1)(2) - 2 = 0$, and both x and y are positive integers. Therefore, Choice A is not correct, since there are positive integers x and y for which $x \otimes y = 0$.

Choice B: $y \otimes x$. This is similar to Choice A, except the x and y are interchanged. Therefore, you might try the example in Choice A but with the values of x and y interchanged: $y = 1$ and $x = 2$. Using the formula, $y \otimes x = yx - x = (1)(2) - 2 = 0$. Therefore, Choice B is not correct, since there are positive integers x and y for which $y \otimes x = 0$.

Choice C: $(x - 1) \otimes y$. Using the formula, try to find positive integers x and y for which $(x - 1) \otimes y = 0$, that is, for which $(x - 1)y - y = 0$. Factoring y out of the left-hand side of the equation $(x - 1)y - y = 0$ yields $(x - 1 - 1)y = (x - 2)y = 0$. Here the product of the two numbers $x - 2$ and y is 0. So the product will be 0 if $x = 2$, no matter what the value of y is. For example, if $x = 2$ and $y = 10$, then $(x - 1) \otimes y = (2 - 1) \otimes 10 = 1 \otimes 10 = (1)(10) - 10 = 0$, and both x and y are positive integers. Therefore, Choice C is not correct, since there are positive integers x and y for which $(x - 1) \otimes y = 0$.

Choice D: $(x + 1) \otimes y$. Using the formula, try to find positive integers x and y for which $(x + 1) \otimes y = 0$, that is, for which $(x + 1)y - y = 0$. Factoring y out of the left-hand side of the equation $(x + 1)y - y = 0$ yields $(x + 1 - 1)y = xy = 0$. Here the product of x and y is 0, so $x = 0$ or $y = 0$. Since both x and y must be positive but 0 is not positive, it follows that there are no positive integers x and y for which $(x + 1) \otimes y = 0$. The correct answer is **Choice D**.

Choice E: $x \otimes (y - 1)$ cannot be correct, since Choice D is correct, but Choice E is considered here for completeness. Using the formula, try to find positive integers x and y for which $x \otimes (y - 1) = 0$, that is, for which $x(y - 1) - (y - 1) = 0$. Factoring $y - 1$ out of the left-hand side of the equation $x(y - 1) - (y - 1) = 0$ yields $(x - 1)(y - 1) = 0$. Here the product of the two numbers $x - 1$ and $y - 1$ is 0. So the product will be 0 if $x = 1$ or $y = 1$, no matter what the value of the other variable is. For example, if $x = 20$ and $y = 1$, then $x \otimes (y - 1) = 20 \otimes (1 - 1) = 20 \otimes 0 = (20)(0) - 0 = 0$, and both x and y are positive integers. Therefore, Choice E is not correct, since there are positive integers x and y for which $x \otimes (y - 1) = 0$.

This explanation uses the following strategies.

Strategy 5: Simplify an Arithmetic or Algebraic Representation
Strategy 10: Trial and Error
Strategy 11: Divide into Cases
Strategy 13: Determine Whether a Conclusion Follows from the Information Given

23. *P, Q,* and *R* are three points in a plane, and *R* does not lie on line *PQ*. Which of the following is true about the set of all points in the plane that are the same distance from all three points?

   (A) It contains no points.
   (B) It contains one point.
   (C) It contains two points.
   (D) It is a line.
   (E) It is a circle.

Explanation

First consider just two of the three points, say *P* and *Q*, and the set of points in the plane that are the same distance from them. Clearly the midpoint of line segment *PQ* is such a point. Are there others? You may recall from geometry that the points on the line that bisects *PQ* and is perpendicular to *PQ* are all the points that are equidistant from *P* and *Q*. Similarly, the points in the plane that lie on the perpendicular bisector of line segment *PR* are all the points that are equidistant from points *P* and *R*.

Because *R* does not lie on line *PQ*, line segments *PQ* and *PR* do not lie on the same line, and so their respective perpendicular bisectors are not parallel. Therefore, you can conclude that the two perpendicular bisectors intersect at a point. The point of intersection is on both perpendicular bisectors, so it is equidistant from *P* and *Q* as well as from *P* and *R*. Therefore, the point of intersection is equidistant from all three points. Are there any other points that are equidistant from *P, Q,* and *R*? If there were, they would be on both perpendicular bisectors, but in fact only one point lies on both lines. The correct answer is **Choice B**.

This explanation uses the following strategy.

Strategy 8: Search for a Mathematical Relationship

24. If $x < y < 0$, which of the following inequalities must be true?

   (A) $y + 1 < x$
   (B) $y - 1 < x$
   (C) $xy^2 < x$
   (D) $xy < y^2$
   (E) $xy < x^2$

Explanation

The conditions stated in the question, $x < y < 0$, tell you that x and y are negative numbers and that y is greater than x. Keep this in mind as you evaluate each of the inequalities in the answer choices, to see whether the inequality must be true.

   Choice A: $y + 1 < x$. According to the conditions given in the question, y is greater than x. Since y is greater than x and $y + 1$ is greater than y, it follows that $y + 1$ is greater than x. So it cannot be true that $y + 1 < x$. Therefore, Choice A is not the correct answer.

   Choice B: $y - 1 < x$. While it is true that both x and $y - 1$ are less than y, it may not be true that $y - 1 < x$. Consider what happens if $y = -2$ and $x = -7$. In this case, the inequality $y - 1 < x$ becomes $-3 < -7$, which is false. Therefore, Choice B is not the correct answer.

   Choice C: $xy^2 < x$. Note that y^2 is positive and x is negative, so xy^2 is negative. Is the negative number xy^2 less than the negative number x? It depends on whether $y^2 > 1$ or $y^2 < 1$. Consider what happens if $x = -4$ and $y = -\dfrac{1}{2}$, where $y^2 < 1$. In this case, the inequality $xy^2 < x$ becomes $-1 < -4$, which is false. Therefore, Choice C is not the correct answer.

   Choice D: $xy < y^2$. Since y is a negative number, multiplying both sides of the inequality $x < y$ by y reverses the inequality, resulting in the inequality $xy > y^2$. So it cannot be true that $xy < y^2$. Therefore, Choice D is not the correct answer.

   Since Choices A through D have been eliminated, the correct answer is Choice E.

   Choice E: You can show that the inequality in Choice E, $xy < x^2$, must be true as follows: Multiply both sides of the given inequality $x < y$ by x to obtain the inequality $x^2 > xy$, reversing the direction of the inequality because x is negative. Therefore, the inequality $xy < x^2$ must be true, and the correct answer is **Choice E**.

This explanation uses the following strategies.

Strategy 5: Simplify an Arithmetic or Algebraic Representation
Strategy 10: Trial and Error
Strategy 11: Divide into Cases
Strategy 13: Determine Whether a Conclusion Follows from the Information Given

For the following question, enter your answer in the box.

25. What is the length of a diagonal of a rectangle that has width 5 and perimeter 34?

Explanation

In this question, you are given that a rectangle has width 5 and perimeter 34, and you are asked to find the length of a diagonal of the rectangle. Let L and W represent the length and width of the rectangle, respectively, and let D represent the length of a diagonal. Note that you are not given L but you are given that $W = 5$ and that the perimeter is 34. Because the perimeter is equal to $L + L + W + W$, or $2(L + W)$, you can determine L as follows.

$$2(L + 5) = 34$$
$$L + 5 = 17$$
$$L = 12$$

The following figure shows a rectangle of length 12, width 5, and diagonal of length D.

From the figure, you can see that the diagonal is the hypotenuse of a right triangle with legs of length 5 and 12. Therefore, by the Pythagorean theorem,

$$5^2 + 12^2 = D^2$$
$$25 + 144 = D^2$$
$$169 = D^2$$
$$13 = D$$

The length of the diagonal is 13, so the correct answer is **13**.

This explanation uses the following strategies.

Strategy 2: Translate from Words to a Figure or Diagram
Strategy 8: Search for a Mathematical Relationship

SECTION 6
Quantitative Reasoning
25 Questions with Explanations

For each of Questions 1 to 9, select one of the following answer choices.

Ⓐ   Quantity A is greater.
Ⓑ   Quantity B is greater.
Ⓒ   The two quantities are equal.
Ⓓ   The relationship cannot be determined from the information given.

A circle is inscribed in a square with sides of length 5.

Quantity A	Quantity B	
1. The circumference of the circle	15	Ⓐ Ⓑ Ⓒ Ⓓ

Explanation

In this question, you are given that a circle is inscribed in a square with sides of length 5 and are asked to compare the circumference of the circle with 15. Since the circle is inscribed in the square, the diameter of the circle is equal to the length of a side of the square, or 5. Thus, the circumference of the circle is 5π. Because π is greater than 3, it follows that 5π is greater than 15. Therefore, Quantity A is greater than Quantity B, and the correct answer is **Choice A**.

This explanation uses the following strategy.

Strategy 1: Translate from Words to an Arithmetic or Algebraic Representation

$$2u + v = 14$$
$$uv = 0$$

Quantity A	Quantity B	
2. u	v	Ⓐ Ⓑ Ⓒ Ⓓ

Explanation

In this question, you are asked to compare u with v, given that $2u + v = 14$ and $uv = 0$.

Consider the equation $uv = 0$. Since a product can equal 0 only if at least one of the factors in the product equals 0, you know that $u = 0$ or $v = 0$, or both. But since you are also given that $2u + v = 14$, it follows that u and v cannot both equal 0.

Knowing that either $u = 0$ or $v = 0$, you can substitute 0 into the equation $2u + v = 14$ for either u or v in order to determine the relationship between u and v if it is possible to do so from the information given. If $u = 0$, then $2u + v = 14$ simplifies to $v = 14$. In this case, u is less than v. However, if $v = 0$, then $2u + v = 14$ simplifies to $2u = 14$, or $u = 7$. And in this case, u is greater than v.

In the first case, $u < v$, and in the second case, $u > v$. Therefore, the relationship between the two quantities u and v cannot be determined from the information given, and the correct answer is **Choice D**.

This explanation uses the following strategies.

Strategy 5: Simplify an Arithmetic or Algebraic Representation
Strategy 13: Determine Whether a Conclusion Follows from the Information Given

Quantity A	Quantity B	
3. $950^{2,000}$	$10^{6,000}$	Ⓐ Ⓑ Ⓒ Ⓓ

Explanation

In this question, you are asked to compare the quantity $950^{2,000}$ with the quantity $10^{6,000}$. Note that both quantities are written in the form "base to a power." If the bases were equal, you would be able to compare the quantities by comparing the powers. Because powers of 10 are easier to work with than powers of 950, it is reasonable to try to compare the quantities by rewriting the quantity $950^{2,000}$ as a power of 10. Unfortunately, there is no obvious way to do that. However, if you can approximate 950 by a power of 10, you may then be able to use the approximation to compare the quantity $950^{2,000}$ with the quantity $10^{6,000}$.

Note that 950 is close to, but a little less than, 1,000, or 10^3. Raising both sides of the inequality $950 < 10^3$ to the power 2,000 gives the inequality $950^{2,000} < (10^3)^{2,000}$. Since $(10^3)^{2,000} = 10^{6,000}$, you can conclude that $950^{2,000} < 10^{6,000}$. Thus, Quantity A is less than Quantity B, and the correct answer is **Choice B**.

This explanation uses the following strategies.
Strategy 5: Simplify an Arithmetic or Algebraic Representation
Strategy 9: Estimate

Set A consists of 40 integers, and set B consists of 150 integers. The number of integers that are in both set A and set B is 20.

Quantity A	Quantity B	
4. The total number of integers that are in set A or set B, or both	170	Ⓐ Ⓑ Ⓒ Ⓓ

Explanation

In this question, you are given that the number of integers in set A is 40, the number of integers in set B is 150, and the number of integers that are in both A and B is 20. You are asked to compare the total number of integers that are in set A or set B, or both, with 170.

This is the type of question for which a Venn diagram is usually helpful to represent the information given. The following Venn diagram is a representation of the integers in sets A and B.

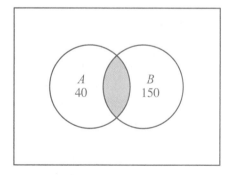

Note that there is no number in the shaded region of the diagram—the region representing the integers in both A and B. In fact, the number of integers in both A and B is included in both the number of integers in A and the number of integers in B. It is a good idea, therefore, to redraw the Venn diagram so that the numbers are separated into three categories: the integers in A only, the integers in B only, and the integers in both A and B. The revised Venn diagram follows.

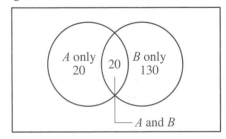

Observe that summing the numbers of integers in set A only, set B only, and both A and B yields the total number of integers that are in set A or set B, or both. Therefore, Quantity A is $20 + 130 + 20$, or 170, and the correct answer is **Choice C**.

Another approach is to realize that if you listed the integers in set A and the integers in set B, you would have listed the integers that are in both A and B twice and all of the other integers once. So the total number of integers in set A or set B, or both, is equal to

(number in set A) + (number in set B) – (number in both sets)

Thus, the number of integers in set A or set B, or both, is $40 + 150 - 20$, or 170, and the correct answer is **Choice C**.

This explanation uses the following strategies.
Strategy 2: Translate from Words to a Figure or Diagram
Strategy 8: Search for a Mathematical Relationship

x is a negative integer.

	Quantity A	Quantity B	
5.	2^x	3^{x+1}	Ⓐ Ⓑ Ⓒ Ⓓ

Explanation

In this question, you are asked to compare 2^x with 3^{x+1}, given that x is a negative integer. One way to approach this problem is to plug a value of x in both expressions and compare the results.

You are given that x is a negative integer, so the greatest integer you can plug in for x is -1.

For $x = -1$, it follows that $2^x = 2^{-1} = \dfrac{1}{2}$ and $3^{x+1} = 3^{-1+1} = 3^0 = 1$.

In this case, 2^x is less than 3^{x+1}. However, to conclude that Quantity B is greater, it is not sufficient for 2^x to be less than 3^{x+1} for one particular value of x; the relationship would need to be true for <u>all</u> negative integer values of x. To analyze this relationship further, plug in another value of x, for example, -2.

For $x = -2$, it follows that $2^x = 2^{-2} = \dfrac{1}{2^2} = \dfrac{1}{4}$ and $3^{x+1} = 3^{-2+1} = 3^{-1} = \dfrac{1}{3}$.

Again, 2^x is less than 3^{x+1}, but note that these values are closer together than the previous values of 2^x and 3^{x+1}. It appears that the relationship between the quantities may differ for smaller values of x, so now try plugging in -3 for x.

For $x = -3$, it follows that $2^x = 2^{-3} = \dfrac{1}{2^3} = \dfrac{1}{8}$ and $3^{x+1} = 3^{-3+1} = 3^{-2} = \dfrac{1}{3^2} = \dfrac{1}{9}$.

In this case, 2^x is greater than 3^{x+1}.

Since 2^x is less than 3^{x+1} for $x = -1$ and 2^x is greater than 3^{x+1} for $x = -3$, the relationship between these two quantities cannot be determined from the information given. The correct answer is **Choice D**.

Since both quantities are algebraic expressions, another way to approach the comparison is to set up a placeholder relationship, denoted by $\boxed{?}$, between the two quantities and then to simplify to see what conclusions you can draw. As you simplify and draw conclusions, keep in mind that x is a negative integer.

$$2^x \boxed{?} 3^{x+1}$$
$$2^x \boxed{?} 3(3^x)$$
$$\frac{2^x}{3^x} \boxed{?} 3$$
$$\left(\frac{2}{3}\right)^x \boxed{?} 3$$

For any value of x (including negative integer values of x), the value of 3^x is positive, so dividing by 3^x does not affect any inequality that might be represented by the placeholder. Since each step in this simplification is reversible, the simplification reduces the problem to comparing $\left(\frac{2}{3}\right)^x$ with 3, given that x is a negative integer. Note that $\left(\frac{2}{3}\right)^x = \left(\frac{3}{2}\right)^n$, where $n = -x$; so the problem can be reduced further to comparing $\left(\frac{3}{2}\right)^n$ with 3, given that n is a positive integer.

Because $\frac{3}{2}$ is greater than 1, the value of $\left(\frac{3}{2}\right)^n$ becomes greater as n becomes larger. For small values of n, $\left(\frac{3}{2}\right)^n$ is less than 3, but for large values of n, $\left(\frac{3}{2}\right)^n$ is greater than 3. Therefore, the relationship between Quantity A and Quantity B cannot be determined from the given information, and the correct answer is **Choice D**.

This explanation uses the following strategies.
Strategy 10: Trial and Error
Strategy 13: Determine Whether a Conclusion Follows from the Information Given

$$(x + 3)(y - 4) = 0$$

	Quantity A	Quantity B	
6.	xy	-12	Ⓐ Ⓑ Ⓒ Ⓓ

Explanation

In this question, you are given that $(x + 3)(y - 4) = 0$, and you are asked to compare the product xy with -12. Since $(x + 3)(y - 4) = 0$ and the product of two numbers can equal 0 only if at least one of the numbers in the product equals 0, you can conclude that $x = -3$ or $y = 4$, or both.

Consider the case $x = -3$. When $x = -3$, you can choose any number as the value of y and the equation $(x + 3)(y - 4) = 0$ will be satisfied. Depending on the particular value of y you choose, the product xy may be greater than, less than, or equal to -12. For example, if $y = 1$, then $xy = -3$ is greater than -12; and if $y = 10$, then $xy = -30$ is less than -12.

Since different examples for the value of y yield different relationships between Quantities A and B, the relationship cannot be determined from the information given. The correct answer is **Choice D**.

This explanation uses the following strategies.

Strategy 5: Simplify an Arithmetic or Algebraic Representation
Strategy 10: Trial and Error
Strategy 13: Determine Whether a Conclusion Follows from the Information Given

> Geoff used $630 to buy a new guitar. This amount was 15 percent of his earnings last summer.

Quantity A	Quantity B	
7. The amount of Geoff's earnings last summer <u>not</u> used to buy the new guitar	$3,570	Ⓐ Ⓑ Ⓒ Ⓓ

Explanation

In this question, you are asked to compare the amount of Geoff's earnings last summer <u>not</u> used to buy a new guitar with the amount $3,570. You are given that Geoff used 15% of his earnings last summer, or $630, to buy the new guitar. So the relationship between Geoff's earnings last summer and the amount he spent to buy the guitar can be expressed by the equation

$$(0.15) \times (\text{Geoff's earnings last summer}) = \$630$$

Therefore, you can conclude that Geoff's earnings last summer totaled $\frac{\$630}{0.15}$, or $4,200. Since Geoff earned $4,200 last summer and spent $630 of his earnings to buy the guitar, the amount he did <u>not</u> spend to buy the guitar was $4,200 − $630, or $3,570. Therefore, Quantity A is equal to Quantity B, and the correct answer is **Choice C**.

This explanation uses the following strategy.

Strategy 1: Translate from Words to an Arithmetic or Algebraic Representation

> Set S consists of 5 objects.

Quantity A	Quantity B	
8. The number of subsets of set S that consist of 1 object	The number of subsets of set S that consist of 4 objects	Ⓐ Ⓑ Ⓒ Ⓓ

Explanation

In this question, you are given that set S consists of 5 objects and are asked to compare the number of subsets of set S that consist of 1 object with the number of subsets of set S that consist of 4 objects. Recall that a set R is a subset of set S if all of the members of R are also members of S.

Note that if you select 1 object from set S, there are 4 objects in S that you have not selected; that is to say, each subset of S with 1 object corresponds to a subset of S with 4 objects. Therefore, the number of subsets of S with 1 object is equal to the number of subsets of S with 4 objects. Since Quantity A is equal to Quantity B, the correct answer is **Choice C**.

Another approach to solving this problem is to consider a particular set of 5 objects and determine all of the subsets consisting of 1 object and all of the subsets consisting of 4 objects. For example, let $S = \{a, b, c, d, e\}$. There are 5 subsets of S consisting of 1 object: $\{a\}$, $\{b\}$, $\{c\}$, $\{d\}$, and $\{e\}$; there are 5 subsets of S consisting of 4 objects: $\{a, b, c, d\}$, $\{a, b, c, e\}$, $\{a, b, d, e\}$, $\{a, c, d, e\}$, and $\{b, c, d, e\}$. Clearly, the particular 5 objects in S do not change the fact that the number of subsets of S consisting of 1 object is equal to the number of subsets of S consisting of 4 objects. The correct answer is **Choice C**.

This explanation uses the following strategy.

Strategy 8: Search for a Mathematical Relationship

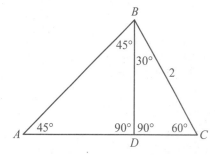

Quantity A	Quantity B

9. The length of line segment AC 3   Ⓐ   Ⓑ   Ⓒ   Ⓓ

Explanation

In this question, you are asked to compare the length of line segment AC with 3.

Note that in the figure, the vertical line segment divides triangle ABC into two right triangles. Based on the fact that the sum of the measures of the angles in a triangle is 180°, you can conclude that the triangle to the left of the vertical line is a 45°-45°-90° right triangle and the triangle to the right of the vertical line is a 30°-60°-90° right triangle. The following figure shows all of these angle measures, along with a new label D at the vertex of the right angles.

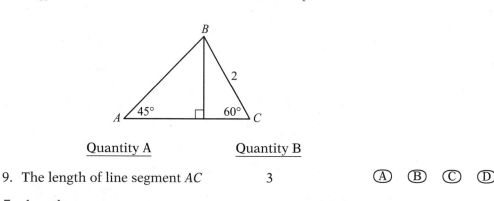

Note that the length of AC is equal to the length of AD plus the length of DC. Also note that AD is a leg of the 45°-45°-90° triangle and DC is a leg of the 30°-60°-90° triangle.

In the figure, you are given that the length of BC, the hypotenuse of the 30°-60°-90° triangle, is 2. No other lengths are given. Recall that if the length of the hypotenuse of a 30°-60°-90° triangle is 2, then the length of the side opposite the 30° angle is 1, and the length of the side opposite the 60° angle is $\sqrt{3}$. So, in the 30°-60°-90° triangle BDC, the length of DC (the side opposite the 30° angle) is 1, and the length of BD (the side opposite the 60° angle) is $\sqrt{3}$.

Now consider the 45°-45°-90° triangle ABD. Since this is an isosceles right triangle, its legs, AD and BD, have equal length. Since the length of BD is $\sqrt{3}$, the length of AD is also $\sqrt{3}$.

As noted above, the length of AC is equal to the length of AD plus the length of DC. Since the length of AD is $\sqrt{3}$ and the length of DC is 1, it follows that the length of AC is equal to $\sqrt{3} + 1$.

Recall that in the question you were asked to compare the length of AC with 3. Because $\sqrt{3}$ is less than 2, it follows that the length of AC, which is equal to $\sqrt{3} + 1$, is less than $2 + 1$, or 3. Hence, Quantity B is greater than Quantity A, and the correct answer is **Choice B**.

This explanation uses the following strategies.
Strategy 6: Add to a Geometric Figure
Strategy 8: Search for a Mathematical Relationship

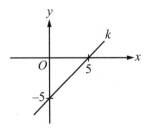

10. What is the slope of line k in the xy-plane above?

  (A) −5   (D) 1

  (B) −1   (E) 5

  (C) 0

Explanation

Recall that if a line passes through the points with coordinates (x_1, y_1) and (x_2, y_2), where $x_1 \neq x_2$, then the slope of the line is

$$\frac{y_2 - y_1}{x_2 - x_1}$$

From the graph of line k in the xy-plane, you can conclude that the x-intercept of line k has coordinates $(5, 0)$ and the y-intercept of line k has coordinates $(0, -5)$. Thus, the slope of line k is

$$\frac{-5 - 0}{0 - 5} = \frac{-5}{-5} = 1$$

The correct answer is **Choice D**.

This explanation uses the following strategy.
Strategy 4: Translate from a Figure to an Arithmetic or Algebraic Representation

$$b - 3, \, b - 1, \, b + 2, \, b + 3, \, b + 4$$

11. The median of the five terms listed above is 5, where b is a constant. What is the average (arithmetic mean) of the five terms?

  (A) 3   (D) 6

  (B) 4   (E) 7

  (C) 5

Explanation

To calculate the average of the five terms, you first need to use the information given in the question to determine the value of b.

You are given that 5 is the median of the five terms $b - 3$, $b - 1$, $b + 2$, $b + 3$, and $b + 4$, where b is a constant. The median of five terms is the middle, or third, term when the terms are listed in increasing order. Observe that the five terms are already given in increasing order. Since $b + 2$ is the third term, you can conclude that $b + 2 = 5$ and thus $b = 3$.

Since $b = 3$, it follows that the values of the five terms are 0, 2, 5, 6, and 7, and the average of the five terms is $\dfrac{0+2+5+6+7}{5} = \dfrac{20}{5} = 4$. The correct answer is **Choice B**.

This explanation uses the following strategy.

Strategy 1: Translate from Words to an Arithmetic or Algebraic Representation

For the following question, enter your answer in the box.

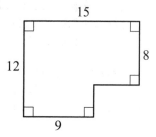

12. What is the area of the region shown above?

Explanation

In this question, you are asked to determine the area of the given region. One approach to solving this problem is to split the region into two rectangles, rectangle R and rectangle S, as follows.

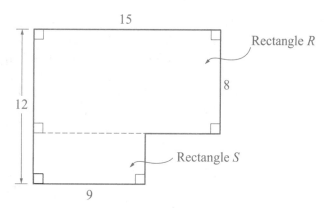

The area of the region is the sum of the areas of the two rectangles. The area of rectangle R is $(15)(8)$, or 120. Since the width of rectangle S is $12 - 8$, or 4, the area of rectangle S is $(9)(4)$, or 36. Thus, the area of the region is $120 + 36$, or 156. The correct answer is **156**.

Another approach to solving this problem is to form the region by removing a small rectangle from a rectangle with length 15 and width 12, as follows.

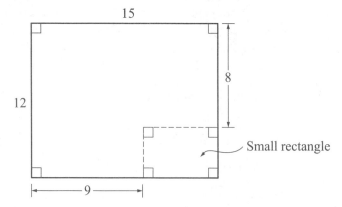

The area of the region is the area of the rectangle with length 15 and width 12 minus the area of the small rectangle. The area of the rectangle with length 15 and width 12 is (15)(12), or 180. Since the length of the small rectangle is 15 – 9, or 6, and the width of the small rectangle is 12 – 8, or 4, the area of the small rectangle is (6)(4), or 24. Thus, the area of the region is 180 – 24, or 156. The correct answer is **156**.

This explanation uses the following strategies.
Strategy 6: Add to a Geometric Figure
Strategy 8: Search for a Mathematical Relationship

13.　During a one-year study, biologists observed the number of fish in a certain pond as well as the percent of the fish that were catfish. At the beginning of the year, there were 300 fish in the pond, of which 15 percent were catfish; and at the end of the year, there were 400 fish in the pond, of which 10 percent were catfish. From the beginning of the year to the end of the year, the number of catfish in the pond

　(A)　decreased by more than 5%　　(D)　increased by 5%
　(B)　decreased by 5%　　　　　　　(E)　increased by more than 5%
　(C)　did not change

Explanation

The answer choices indicate that the question is asking about the percent change in the number of catfish. The number of catfish in the pond at the beginning of the year was 15% of 300, or (0.15)(300), which is 45. The number of catfish in the pond at the end of the year was 10% of 400, or (0.10)(400), which is 40. Thus, the number of catfish decreased by 5.

　　The percent by which the number of catfish decreased from the beginning of the year to the end of the year is

$$\frac{\text{the decrease in the number of catfish over the year}}{\text{the number of catfish at the beginning of the year}} \times (100\%) = \left(\frac{5}{45}\right)(100\%) \approx 11\%$$

Thus, the number of catfish decreased by about 11%. This is a decrease of more than 5%, so the correct answer is **Choice A**.

This explanation uses the following strategy.
Strategy 1: Translate from Words to an Arithmetic or Algebraic Representation

For the following question, enter your answer in the box.

14. On a radio tower, a red light flashes every 6 seconds and a blue light flashes every 10 seconds. If both lights flash together at a certain time, how many seconds later will both lights flash together the next time?

 seconds

Explanation

One way to approach this question is to look at the "flash times" for both lights to see what times they have in common. The following lists show the flash times for both lights as the numbers of seconds after the time at which both lights flashed together.

Red light: 6, 12, 18, 24, 30, 36, 42, 48, 54, 60, . . .
Blue light: 10, 20, 30, 40, 50, 60, 70, 80, 90, . . .

Note that 30 is the first number that is common to both lists. Therefore, if both lights flash together, they will flash together again 30 seconds later. The correct answer is **30**.

Alternatively, you may realize that if the lights flash together, the number of seconds that will elapse before they flash together the next time is the least common multiple of 6 and 10. To find the least common multiple of 6 and 10, begin by writing each integer as the product of its prime factors.

$$6 = (2)(3)$$
$$10 = (2)(5)$$

Since 2 is a factor in both products, but 3 and 5 are factors of only one of the products, the least common multiple of 6 and 10 is (2)(3)(5), or 30. Therefore, if both lights flash together, the next time they will flash together is 30 seconds later. The correct answer is **30**.

This explanation uses the following strategies.

Strategy 1: Translate from Words to an Arithmetic or Algebraic Representation
Strategy 7: Find a Pattern

For the following question, select all the answer choices that apply.

15. If $a < b < 0$, which of the following numbers must be positive?

Indicate <u>all</u> such numbers.

A $a - b$
B $a^2 - b^2$
C ab
D a^2b
E $a^2b + ab^2$

Explanation

In this question, you are given that $a < b < 0$ and are asked to determine which of the answer choices must be positive. Note that the condition $a < b < 0$ means that a and b are negative and that $a < b$.

Choice A: $a - b$. In the question, it is given that $a < b$. Subtracting b from both sides of the inequality $a < b$ gives the inequality $a - b < 0$. Therefore, $a - b$ must be negative.

2

2

Choice B: $a^2 - b^2$. Since a and b are negative, you can square both sides of the inequality $a < b$ to get the inequality $a^2 > b^2$. Then you can subtract b^2 from both sides of the inequality $a^2 > b^2$ to conclude that $a^2 - b^2 > 0$. So $a^2 - b^2$ must be positive. Alternatively, note that $a^2 - b^2$ can be factored as $(a - b)(a + b)$. The factor $a - b$ is Choice A, which must be negative, and the factor $a + b$ is the sum of two negative numbers, which also must be negative. Thus, $a^2 - b^2$ is the product of two negative numbers, so it must be positive.

Choice C: ab. Because a and b are negative, you can conclude that their product ab must be positive.

Choice D: a^2b. Because a^2b can be written as $(a)(a)(b)$, which is the product of three negative numbers, you can conclude that a^2b must be negative.

Choice E: $a^2b + ab^2$. By the reasoning in the explanation of Choice D, Choice E is the sum of two negative numbers. Therefore, you can conclude that $a^2b + ab^2$ must be negative.

Choices B and C must be positive, and Choices A, D, and E must be negative. The correct answer consists of **Choices B and C**.

This explanation uses the following strategies.

Strategy 5: Simplify an Arithmetic or Algebraic Representation
Strategy 13: Determine Whether a Conclusion Follows from the Information Given

16. A flat rectangular picture, represented by the unshaded region in the figure above, is mounted in a flat rectangular frame, represented by the shaded region. The frame is 1 inch wide on all sides. For what value of x, in inches, is the area of the frame equal to the area of the picture?

(A) 4
(B) 5
(C) 6
(D) 7
(E) 8

Explanation

In this question, you are asked to determine the value of x for which the area of the frame is equal to the area of the picture. To do this, you need to express both the area of the frame and the area of the picture in terms of x and then find the value of x for which the two expressions are equal.

The area of the picture is the area of the inner rectangle, and the area of the frame is the area of the outer rectangle minus the area of the inner rectangle. Since the area of a rectangle is the length times the width, you need to know the length and width of the inner and outer rectangles.

In the figure, you are given that the length of the inner rectangle is x inches, but the width is not given. However, since you know that the width of the frame is 1 inch, it follows that the width of the inner rectangle is equal to the width of the outer rectangle minus 2 inches, or $x - 2$ inches. Thus, the area of the inner rectangle is $x(x - 2)$ square inches.

In the figure, you are given that the width of the outer rectangle is x inches, but the length is not given. However, since you know that the width of the frame is 1 inch, it follows that the length of the outer rectangle is equal to the length of the inner rectangle plus 2 inches, or $x + 2$ inches. Thus, the area of the outer rectangle is $x(x + 2)$ square inches.

Since the area of the frame is the area of the outer rectangle minus the area of the inner rectangle, the area of the frame is
$x(x + 2) - x(x - 2) = x^2 + 2x - x^2 + 2x = 4x$ square inches.

Now you are ready to set up the equation. Set the expression for the area of the picture equal to the expression for the area of the frame and solve the resulting equation for x, as follows.

$$x(x - 2) = 4x$$
$$x^2 - 2x = 4x$$
$$x^2 - 6x = 0$$
$$x(x - 6) = 0$$

There are two solutions to the equation, $x = 0$ and $x = 6$. Since x represents the length of a picture, in inches, the solution $x = 0$ does not make sense in this context. Therefore, when $x = 6$, the area of the picture equals the area of the frame. The correct answer is **Choice C**.

This explanation uses the following strategies.

Strategy 4: Translate from a Figure to an Arithmetic or Algebraic Representation
Strategy 5: Simplify an Arithmetic or Algebraic Representation

Questions 17 to 20 are based on the following data.

PERCENT OF THE 300 PEOPLE IN GROUP 1 AND THE 400 PEOPLE
IN GROUP 2 WHO HAVE SELECTED AILMENTS

Respiratory Ailment	Percent of People in Group 1 Who Have Ailment	Percent of People in Group 2 Who Have Ailment
Allergic sensitivity to endotoxins	14%	21%
Asthma (allergic)	3%	4%
Asthma (nonallergic)	2%	3%
Hay fever	4%	10%
Sneezing and itchy eyes	8%	11%
Wheezing (allergic)	5%	6%
Wheezing (nonallergic)	2%	5%

17. The number of people in group 2 who have hay fever is how much greater than the number of people in group 1 who have hay fever?

    (A) 37
    (B) 35
    (C) 32
    (D) 28
    (E) 24

Explanation

In group 1, there are 300 people, 4% of whom have hay fever. Therefore, in group 1, there are (0.04)(300) people, or 12 people, who have hay fever. In group 2, there are 400 people, 10% of whom have hay fever. Therefore, in group 2, there are (0.10)(400) people, or 40 people, who have hay fever. Since 40 − 12 = 28, it follows that there are 28 more people in group 2 who have hay fever than there are in group 1. The correct answer is **Choice D**.

This explanation uses the following strategy.

Strategy 4: Translate from a Figure to an Arithmetic or Algebraic Representation

18. For the seven ailments, what is the median of the numbers of people in group 2 who have the ailments?

    (A) 20
    (B) 22
    (C) 24
    (D) 26
    (E) 28

Explanation

The median of the seven numbers of people in group 2 is the middle number when the numbers are listed in increasing order. To find the middle number easily, first order from least to greatest the percents of people in group 2 who have the seven ailments, then find the median of the percents, and finally calculate the number of people corresponding to that percent.

The following table shows the percents of people in group 2 who have the seven ailments, ordered from least to greatest.

Respiratory Ailment	Percent of People in Group 2 Who Have Ailment
Asthma (nonallergic)	3%
Asthma (allergic)	4%
Wheezing (nonallergic)	5%
Wheezing (allergic)	6%
Hay fever	10%
Sneezing and itchy eyes	11%
Allergic sensitivity to endotoxins	21%

The median percent, which is the fourth number in the list, is 6%. Thus, the median number of people in group 2 who have the ailments is (0.06)(400), or 24, and the correct answer is **Choice C**.

This explanation uses the following strategies.
Strategy 4: Translate from a Figure to an Arithmetic or Algebraic Representation
Strategy 8: Search for a Mathematical Relationship

19. The number of people in group 1 who have the ailment wheezing (allergic) is what percent greater than the number of people in group 1 who have the ailment wheezing (nonallergic)?

  (A) 50%   (D) 200%
  (B) 75%   (E) 300%
  (C) 150%

Explanation

In group 1, there are 300 people, 5% of whom have allergic wheezing and 2% of whom have nonallergic wheezing. That is, (0.05)(300) people, or 15 people, have allergic wheezing and (0.02)(300) people, or 6 people, have nonallergic wheezing. Therefore, in group 1, the number of people who have allergic wheezing exceeds the number who have nonallergic wheezing by 9, which is $\left(\frac{9}{6}\right)$(100%) greater than 6, or 150% greater than 6. The correct answer is **Choice C**.

This explanation uses the following strategy.
Strategy 4: Translate from a Figure to an Arithmetic or Algebraic Representation

For the following question, enter your answer in the boxes.

20. What is the ratio of the number of people in group 2 with the ailment sneezing and itchy eyes to the total number of people in both groups with the ailment sneezing and itchy eyes?
  Give your answer as a fraction.

Explanation

In group 2, there are 400 people, 11% of whom have sneezing and itchy eyes. Therefore, in group 2, there are (0.11)(400) people, or 44 people, who have sneezing and itchy eyes. In group 1, there are 300 people, 8% of whom have sneezing and itchy eyes. Therefore, in group 1, there are (0.08)(300) people, or 24 people, who have sneezing and itchy eyes. So the total number of people in both groups who have sneezing and itchy eyes is 24 + 44, or 68. Thus, the ratio of the number of people in group 2 who have sneezing and itchy eyes to the total number of people in both groups who have sneezing and itchy eyes is $\frac{44}{68}$. The correct answer is $\frac{44}{68}$ (or any equivalent fraction).

This explanation uses the following strategies.
Strategy 4: Translate from a Figure to an Arithmetic or Algebraic Representation
Strategy 5: Simplify an Arithmetic or Algebraic Representation

21. Of the people in a certain survey, 58 percent were at most 40 years old and 70 percent were at most 60 years old. If 252 of the people in the survey were more than 40 years old and at most 60 years old, what was the total number of people in the survey?

 Ⓐ 1,900
 Ⓑ 2,100
 Ⓒ 2,400
 Ⓓ 2,700
 Ⓔ 3,000

Explanation

In this question, it is given that of the people surveyed, 58% were at most 40 years old and 70% were at most 60 years old. Therefore, 70% − 58%, or 12%, of the people surveyed were more than 40 years old and at most 60 years old, and you are given that 252 people are in this group. Let x be the total number of people in the survey. Then 12% of x is 252, that is, $0.12x = 252$, and so $x = \dfrac{252}{0.12} = 2{,}100$. Therefore, the total number of people in the survey was 2,100, and the correct answer is **Choice B**.

This explanation uses the following strategies.
Strategy 1: Translate from Words to an Arithmetic or Algebraic Representation
Strategy 8: Search for a Mathematical Relationship

22. If $x > 0$, which of the following is equal to 1.25 percent of x ?

 Ⓐ $\dfrac{x}{80}$

 Ⓑ $\dfrac{x}{8}$

 Ⓒ $\dfrac{x}{4}$

 Ⓓ $\dfrac{5x}{8}$

 Ⓔ $\dfrac{3x}{4}$

Explanation

Since the answer choices are fractional expressions, to answer the question you need to convert 1.25% of x to a fractional expression. Note that 1.25% is equivalent to the decimal 0.0125. Converting the decimal 0.0125 to a fraction and simplifying gives $0.0125 = \dfrac{125}{10{,}000} = \dfrac{1}{80}$. Thus, 1.25% of x is equal to $\dfrac{1}{80}$ of x, or $\dfrac{x}{80}$, and the correct answer is **Choice A**.

This explanation uses the following strategy.
Strategy 5: Simplify an Arithmetic or Algebraic Representation

23. Alice earns *d* dollars and has *t* percent of what she earns deducted for taxes. How much of what she earns does Alice have left after taxes?

   (A) $d(1 - 100t)$ dollars

   (B) $d(1 - 10t)$ dollars

   (C) $d(1 - t)$ dollars

   (D) $d(1 - 0.1t)$ dollars

   (E) $d(1 - 0.01t)$ dollars

Explanation

Recall that *t* percent can be expressed as $\frac{t}{100}$, or $0.01t$. Therefore, the amount that Alice has deducted for taxes, which is *t* percent of *d* dollars, can be expressed as $0.01td$ dollars. The amount that Alice has left after taxes is the amount that she earns minus the amount that she has deducted for taxes, or $d - 0.01td$ dollars. Note that $d - 0.01td$ is an algebraic expression with two terms, each containing *d* as a factor. Factoring out *d* from each term results in the algebraic expression $d(1 - 0.01t)$. The correct answer is **Choice E**.

This explanation uses the following strategy.

Strategy 1: Translate from Words to an Arithmetic or Algebraic Representation

For the following question, select all the answer choices that apply.

24. A student made a conjecture that for any integer *n*, the integer $4n + 3$ is a prime number. Which of the following values of *n* could be used to disprove the student's conjecture?

   Indicate <u>all</u> such values.

   [A] 1

   [B] 3

   [C] 4

   [D] 6

   [E] 7

Explanation

Recall that a prime number is an integer greater than 1 that has no positive divisors other than 1 and itself.

The answer choices for this question are integer values of *n*. Any of the answer choices for which the integer $4n + 3$ is <u>not</u> a prime number could be used to disprove the conjecture that for any integer *n*, the integer $4n + 3$ is a prime number.

To answer this question, you must determine for each of the answer choices whether the integer $4n + 3$ is a prime number. The evaluations are as follows:

Choice A: For $n = 1$, the integer $4n + 3$ is $4(1) + 3$, or 7, which is a prime number.

Choice B: For $n = 3$, the integer $4n + 3$ is $4(3) + 3$, or 15, which is not a prime number.

Choice C: For $n = 4$, the integer $4n + 3$ is $4(4) + 3$, or 19, which is a prime number.

Choice D: For $n = 6$, the integer $4n + 3$ is $4(6) + 3$, or 27, which is not a prime number.

Choice E: For $n = 7$, the integer $4n + 3$ is $4(7) + 3$, or 31, which is a prime number.

Therefore, of the answer choices, only Choices B and D, that is, $n = 3$ and $n = 6$, result in integers $4n + 3$ that are not prime numbers. Thus, the correct answer consists of **Choices B and D**.

This explanation uses the following strategies.

Strategy 10: Trial and Error

Strategy 13: Determine Whether a Conclusion Follows from the Information Given

25. Eight points are equally spaced on a circle. If 4 of the 8 points are to be chosen at random, what is the probability that a quadrilateral having the 4 points chosen as vertices will be a square?

Ⓐ $\frac{1}{70}$

Ⓑ $\frac{1}{35}$

Ⓒ $\frac{1}{7}$

Ⓓ $\frac{1}{4}$

Ⓔ $\frac{1}{2}$

Explanation

For questions involving geometry, it is often helpful to draw a figure representing the information in the question as accurately as possible. The figure below shows a circle with 8 equally spaced points, labeled *A* through *H*, and quadrilateral *BCDH*, which is one of the many quadrilaterals that have 4 of the 8 equally spaced points as vertices.

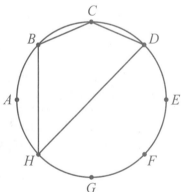

The probability that a quadrilateral having the 4 points chosen as vertices will be a square is equal to the following fraction.

$$\frac{\text{the number of squares that can be drawn using 4 of the 8 points as vertices}}{\text{the number of quadrilaterals that can be drawn using 4 of the 8 points as vertices}}$$

To calculate the desired probability, you need to determine the number of squares and the number of quadrilaterals that can be drawn using 4 of the 8 points as vertices.

To determine the number of quadrilaterals, first note that since the 8 points lie on a circle, every subset of 4 of the 8 points determines a unique quadrilateral. Therefore, the number of quadrilaterals that can be drawn using 4 of the 8 points as vertices is equal to the number of ways of choosing 4 points from the 8 points shown. The number of ways of choosing 4 points from the 8 points shown (also called the number of combinations of 8 objects taken 4 at a time) is equal to $\dfrac{8!}{4!(8-4)!}$. You can calculate the value of this expression as follows.

$$\frac{8!}{4!(8-4)!} = \frac{(8)(7)(6)(5)(4!)}{(4)(3)(2)(1)(4!)}$$

$$= \frac{(8)(7)(6)(5)}{(4)(3)(2)}$$

$$= 70$$

Thus, there are 70 quadrilaterals that can be drawn using 4 of the 8 points as vertices.

Because the points are equally spaced around the circle, there are only 2 squares that can be drawn using 4 of the 8 points as vertices, namely *ACEG* and *BDFH*, as shown in the following figures.

 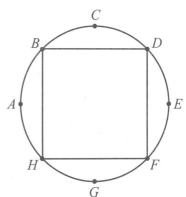

Therefore, the probability that the quadrilateral will be a square is $\dfrac{2}{70}$, or $\dfrac{1}{35}$, and the correct answer is **Choice B**.

This explanation uses the following strategies.
Strategy 2: Translate from Words to a Figure or Diagram
Strategy 8: Search for a Mathematical Relationship